REALISM

REALISM

A CRITIQUE
OF
BRENTANO
AND
MEINONG

by

Gustav Bergmann

THE UNIVERSITY OF WISCONSIN PRESS
Madison, Milwaukee, and London, 1967

Published by the
University of Wisconsin Press
Madison, Milwaukee, and London
U.S.A.: Box 1379, Madison, Wisconsin 53701
U.K.: 26–28 Hallam Street, London, W. 1
Copyright © 1967 by the Regents of the University of Wisconsin
Printed in the United States of America by the George Banta Company, Inc.,
Menasha, Wisconsin
Library of Congress Catalog Card Number 67-12003

TO THE GLORIOUS MEMORY

OF

ALEXIUS MEINONG

Preface

FREUD said of *The Interpretation of Dreams* that it was the sort of
book a man writes only once in his life. This book is of that sort. It
is also very long. Such a book ought to speak for itself. So I send it
into the world without any introduction except for one remark about
the way it is written.

There are two kinds of philosophical criticism, and, perhaps, only
two kinds of writing in philosophy. The inductive critics try at the
same time to make the cross and nail their intended victim onto it.
Those who write deductively first make the cross and, while making it,
affect, except for an occasional glance, an almost studied unconcern for
the victim. I am virtually incapable of writing inductively. The best I
can do, therefore, is to do without disguise, pretext, or apology, the one
thing which I may hope not to do too badly. This book has four parts.
The first is a short treatise on general ontology. The second expounds
the dialectics of representationalism. The third deals critically with
Brentano; the fourth, with Meinong. The criticism in the last two parts
requires a minimum of exposition. But both criticism and exposition
are highly selective.

I have continued to learn much from Edwin B. Allaire and Reinhardt Grossmann. With the former, who is my colleague, I have
naturally talked more. In my memory an intensive exchange about

Descartes during the summer of 1964 stands out. Grossmann's concern with Brentano and Meinong preceded and stimulated mine. Since then he has had his say about both in a book of his own (*The Structure of Mind*, University of Wisconsin Press, 1965). Allaire has stated some of his ideas on Descartes in a study about to appear in *Dialogue*.

In the spring of 1963 my friends at Indiana University invited me to give the Mahlon Powell Lectures. The five lectures I delivered in April 1964 are the seed of this book.

The University of Iowa awarded me one of its temporary research professorships for the first semester of 1964/65.

May Brodbeck painstakingly constructed an index which should be very helpful.

My wife skillfully and faithfully read the proof.

Mrs. Gertrude Corless typed the difficult manuscript with unflagging zeal and remarkable accuracy.

A bibliographical note will be found at the end of the volume.

G. B.

Iowa City, Iowa
February, 1966

Contents

BOOK TWO: BRENTANO AND MEINONG

Part III: Brentano

Part IV: Meinong

BOOK ONE
FACTS, THINGS, IDEAS

How I wish I could keep up with the leaders of modern thought as they pass by into oblivion.

MAX BEERBOHM

Part I
General Ontology

SECTION ONE

FACTS AND THINGS

TO *exist*, to be an *entity*, to have *ontological status* are the same. One who uses these words differently I cannot even hope to understand unless I assume he is using them more narrowly than I do, so that what exists in his sense also exists in mine though not always conversely. Nor do I understand any but the most strictly univocal use of 'exist'. There are several kinds of existent different from each other, not just as cats differ from dogs, but so radically that the differences fall into the province of ontology. What one completely fails to understand, he cannot profitably discuss. So I shall take it for granted that the words and phrases which stand for the most fundamental notion of ontology are univocal.

The second most fundamental notion is that of a *constituent*. Some entities are said to be constituents of others. For one entity to be "in" another and for the former to be a constituent of the latter is the same.

This use of 'in' will always be marked by double quotes. Roughly speaking, an entity is *simple* if and only if it has no constituents; or, to speak with the mathematicians, if it has no other constituent than itself. Otherwise it is *complex* or, synonymously, a complex. The qualification, roughly speaking, covers a certain feature of my own ontology. (In my world the subsistent I call existence is "in" all entities; the one I call particularity is "in" all particulars; and so on.) But this feature makes for the most part no difference for what I am about in this book. So I shall for the most part ignore it.

In some contexts 'constituent', 'component', and 'part' are interchangeable. In ontology, as I shall speak, they are not. The three words will be employed to express three different meanings. Thereby hangs one of the main themes of this book. To unfold it completely, or even to introduce it carefully, will take much time and great effort. Yet I wish to strike it, however lightly, at once. This requires that in the next few paragraphs I use without explanation some words whose use in ontology will only afterwards be accurately explained.

Many philosophers divide the entities they recognize into two kinds. One kind is simple; the other, complex. Yet they do not have a clear notion of a complex. From this lack of clarity spring many woes. Their dialectic is the theme I want to strike.

Let us glance at my own ontology which, inevitably, will have to serve as a foil throughout, particularly when it comes to evaluating others. It will indeed save words if I call it the *foil*. Having recently expounded it, I shall either assume it to be familiar, or, at most, recall this or that part of it very rapidly. I shall not, however, abstain from either discussing it wherever that will help, or, as at this very point, from improving it wherever I can.

In the foil, all complexes are "facts" and all "facts" are complexes; all simples are "things" and all "things" are simple. "Things," though, are not the only constituents of "facts." Each "fact" has at least one constituent of the ontological kind I call "nexus," which in turn is a subkind of the ontological kind I call "subsistents."

The words which in the last paragraph appear between double quotes are among those which will afterwards not be used without previous explanation. Each stands for an ontological kind. Such a kind is also called a *category*. I, too, shall use this word. So I shall take a moment to free it from a superficial ambiguity.

To distinguish clearly between "things" and "facts" and to have a clear notion of complex is, as we shall see, virtually one and the same. "Things" are constituents of "facts." As to 'category', now, some use it so that "things" and "facts" are two fundamental categories of all ontologies which clearly distinguish between the two. Upon another use of the word, it makes no sense to say of the entities of one category that they are "in" those of another. I find the first use both safe and convenient. So I shall say, for instance, that the three fundamental categories of the foil are those of "things," "facts," and "subsistents."

The lack of clarity of which I accused some philosophers in the distinction between "things" and "facts" is, *as we shall see*, intimately connected with an unnoticed ambiguity of 'complex'. Take a world, such as mine, in which there are "universals." The latter, we shall also see, are "things" and not "facts." Yet many philosophers, including until now myself, have divided "universals" into those which are simple and those which are "complex." These double quotes, around 'complex', mark not just an anticipatory use but, rather, the unnoticed ambiguity. *As I shall presently show*, a "universal," since it is a "thing," cannot, even though it may in some other sense be "complex," be a complex in exactly the same sense in which a "fact" is one.

In the foil, for example, green, square, and being both green and square are three "universals." The first two are simple. Or, at least, we may safely assume that they are. The third is of the kind which I, too, have called "complex." Now I see that green cannot be a "constituent" of being both green and square in exactly the same sense in which it is a constituent of some "facts," such as, say, a spot's being green.

Even after one has seen the ambiguity, one understands the temptation. Clearly, (being) green and being both green and square have something to do with each other and this something is such that as long as ontologists will be as inaccurate as they have been for so long, they will be tempted to speak and think of the former (green) as a constituent, or part, or component, of the latter (being both green and square). Nor is it easy to be completely accurate in these matters. To judge from the record and, in spite of all efforts, my own fumblings, it is indeed as difficult as anything. Nor can one do without an elaborate terminology to safeguard the distinctions he has made. We shall of course soon choose another word to stand for the "complexity" of "things."

I have struck the theme. To pursue it further right now would serve no purpose. Let us pretend, then, that we are innocent of all ontological uses of all the words which in the preceding paragraphs appeared between double quotes, and begin at the beginning, as it were, except for using 'constituent', 'simple', and 'complex' as they were first introduced without, of course, the ambiguity.

There are minds and there are bodies. Minds know bodies as well as minds, including themselves. Bodies do not know anything. The dis-

tinction cuts deeply. Whether it makes minds and bodies two ontological kinds depends on how one uses 'ontological'. Upon one use it
doesn't. Thereby hangs a point.

Each ontology has a ground plan. What that means will presently
show itself. In any ontology articulate and worth while, bodies and
minds are constructed upon the same ground plan. Call a world without minds but otherwise like ours *truncated*. Minds being the only
knowers, our world will, and the truncated world will not, contain the
ontological ground of knowing. Otherwise, minds are things among
things. That is why much will be gained and nothing lost if for quite
some time we shall limit ourselves to the truncated world. In this world
there are trees, stones, tables, color patches, and so on. As we ordinarily
speak, we call these entities things. I shall here call them *ordinary objects* or *ordinary things*, reserve 'object' and 'thing' without the qualify-
ing adjective for a more technical use.

What are the constituents of an ordinary thing? Let us simplify still
further by considering a momentary cross section of a truncated world
in which there are two kinds of color patches and nothing else. One
kind is red and round; the other, green and square. Red, round, green,
and square are *properties* of ordinary objects. The properties of an
ordinary object are among its constituents. As you know and as I shall
presently remind you, even in a world as poor as this one, the properties
of an ordinary thing do not exhaust its constituents.

There may be properties such that each of them is had by only one
ordinary object. Yet, several ordinary objects may have *exactly the
same* property. I, for one, do not understand any other use of 'property'.
According to some philosophers no two objects have exactly the same
property. What they mean is best understood by considering how in the
case of colors we use 'shade'. According to those philosophers, two
ordinary things, even though they may be of the same color, are never
of the same shade. This gambit I dismiss out of hand.

An ordinary thing having a certain property must have an ontological ground which, as one says, accounts for it. In other words, there
must be "in" the thing, or, synonymously, there must be among its
constituents at least one entity such that if it were not among the
thing's constituents, the latter would not have the property. A *character* or *universal* is a single entity that accounts for a property. Thus, in a
world in which there are universals two ordinary things have exactly
the same property if and only if *literally the same* universal is "in" both.
Notice that, as I speak, 'universal' and 'literally the same' are words of
the ontological vocabulary while 'property' and 'exactly the same' are
not. In my world there are universals. But it would defeat my purposes

if I considered only such worlds. All I take for granted is, first, that several things may have exactly the same property, and, second, that a thing's having a property must have an ontological ground. This ground, *whatever it may be,* I shall call a *quality.* That is of course a very special use for which I enlist a very common word. It will permit us to speak clearly and yet concisely about some important distinctions.

Consider now a momentary world of several spots such that each of them has two and only two properties, namely, a shape and a color. No two spots have exactly the same shape and the same color. There is at least one color and one shape, say, blue and oval, such that there is no spot that has them both. In this world the class of all properties of an ordinary object is a pair class.

Assume that there is in this world a spot, α, which is both red and round. Keep in mind that there is none both oval and blue. Consider two pairs of qualities; one, call it the first, consists of red and round; the other, call it the second, of oval and blue. The spot and the four qualities are five entities. One may of course deny that. Brentano, as we shall see, does deny it. The result, as we shall also see, is disaster. So, for the time being, I dismiss this gambit.

The members of the first pair make a spot; those of the second pair don't. What is the ontological ground of the difference? One who denies that this question must be asked and answered does not know what ontology is about. The best I could do for him is to try to enlighten him in metaphilosophical discourse. So I turn to the question.

There are two styles of answering the question. One may hold that α is a complex among whose constituents are the members of the first pair. As you now see, I took this style for granted when asking, a while ago: What are the constituents of an ordinary thing? This is the complex style. In *complex ontologies,* as I shall call them, some entities are constituents of others. Accordingly, some are simple, some are complex. The former are "in" the latter; or, ignoring for the moment some of the distinctions to come, the former are parts or components of the latter. The characteristic notion of an ontology in this style may be very blurred. Yet it remains clearly distinguished from that of the function style. In *function ontologies,* as I shall call them, some entities are, as one says, "coordinated" to some others, without any connotation whatsoever of the one being "in" the other, being either a constituent or a part or a component of it. A function is such a coordination. Or, as one says, very misleadingly and at the same time very revealingly, in view of the anthropomorphic suggestion of 'rule', a function is a coordination rule.

There are functions. Of course there are. A complex ontologist need not deny that. All he must claim is that *each* function has an ontological ground which is not itself a function. Russell made this claim and through his so-called theory of descriptions proved it. Or, at least, this is the philosophical import of his analysis according to which every sentence containing such phrases as 'the father of', which stand for functions, can be expanded into another containing instead only such expressions as 'father', which stand for the appropriate relations.

A function ontologist is one who claims that *some* functions are their own ontological ground; and, if he has the sense of his style, that all properties and relations can and must be grounded in functions, just as an equally sophisticated complex ontologist will claim that at least *some* of the latter are their own ontological ground.

I have already tipped my hand more than once; for the first time at the very beginning, when I called the notion of constituent rather than that of function the second most important notion of ontology; the last time in the last paragraph, when asserting that Russell has proved the one claim every complex ontologist must make. Mine is a complex ontology. Yet my choice, if it be one, does not depend on the adequacy of Russell's or any other proof. What compels me, in a manner that leaves me no real choice, lies deeper than argument can reach. I simply do not understand how any coordination among entities can be its own ontological ground. Who or what does the coordinating? I cannot silence the question. That is why I prefer 'coordination' to Frege's 'function'. The mathematical respectability of the latter may drown what I cannot silence. We have come to the end of direct argument. Or, if you please, we have reached one of the "premisses" on which my own ontology rests. To say that is one thing. To dismiss the function style out of hand is another thing. No ontologist can afford to do that. Nor shall we be able to ignore it in this book.

Frege's is a function ontology. It also is so articulate and elaborate a piece of dialectic that it must be dialectically probed even if one rejects prior to all dialectic its distinctive "premiss," namely, that some functions are their own ontological ground. Frege's challenge I have tried to meet elsewhere. This book is not about him. Even so, we shall not be able to ignore the functional style. More or less explicitly, it will be with us throughout. It is indeed our *antifoil*. Why that is so will be seen presently.

Return to where I broke off in order to say what had to be said about the two styles. We were in a world of spots, each with only two properties, one a shape, one a color. No two have exactly the same shape and color. (That is how we avoid being interfered with by the problem of individuation.) The spot is red and round. None is oval and blue, though there are some which are oval and some which are blue. There was also a question which we had just decided must be answered. Then we broke off.

The first pair, red and round, unlike the second, oval and blue, "makes" a spot. What is the ontological ground of this difference? You see now that I used 'make' because it is neutral with respect to the two styles. But I shall continue in the complex style. The other, after all, is merely our antifoil, to which I shall turn only when it will be needed to make as clear as I can what I judge to be irremediably confused.

In my style, then, the question has only one answer. *An ordinary thing is a complex; its qualities are among its constituents; but they do not exhaust them.* In the paradigm, α, in addition to the qualities which ground red and round, respectively, must have at least one further constituent "connecting" them, as blue and oval are not connected. This third constituent I call a *nexus*.

Is the nexus in two spots literally the same? Meinong, we shall see, would hold that it isn't. But it will not prejudge anything I shall be concerned with for quite some time if we assume that it is. I shall express this by saying that in several spots literally the same nexus occurs several times.

Qualities, then, need nexus to connect or tie them into ordinary things. A nexus does not need a further entity to tie it to what it ties, otherwise we would have entered upon an infinite regress. That is Bradley's famous argument, which I take to be familiar. This difference between qualities and nexus is so profound that it concerns the ontologist. It is, as one says, categorial. Qualities are *things* among things; nexus, *subsistents* among subsistents. With respect to the Bradleyan feature, all things are like qualities; all subsistents, like nexus. Or, rather, this is the way I use 'thing' and 'subsistent' in ontology.

In our world of spots, there are thus at least two categories—qualities and nexus. How about the spots themselves? Are they, too, things? Or is the difference between an ordinary thing—say, an apple and one of its colors—categorial? The difference is categorial. But I cannot state the reasons for this answer as accurately as the fundamental nature of the question requires without first at least stating another "premiss" not just of mine, but of all ontologies, in either style, which are sufficiently articulate to be of interest. Instead of a "premiss" one could thus speak of a "principle of general ontology."

A collection of entities is as such not itself an entity. This is the "premiss." The crucial notion in it is that of a *collection*. We considered what I called two pairs of qualities. Each pair, together with the nexus of this world, forms a triple. Presently we shall consider these triples.

These two pairs and these two triples are four collections. A collection, as I shall use the word, is not a class. In the foil, for instance, there are classes, or, what amounts to the same, classes are entities. A collection is, rather, what is meant by the extension of a class. More precisely, a collection is the extension of a class if and only if, as in the case of our pairs though not in that of our triples, the entities in it are all of the same (Russellian) type. At this point you may wonder how I use 'class' and 'extension of a class'. Nor, even if you don't, will these few words suffice. The claim that my "principle of general ontology" really is one, will have to be justified. But it will be safe to postpone what has to be said until the matter at hand is disposed of.

Assume for the sake of the argument that the qualities and the nexus "in" a spot are all its constituents. Call the nexus ν. Consider two triples; one, call it the first, consisting of ν and the two qualities in α; the other, call it the second, of the two qualities grounding blue and oval, respectively, and again, ν. The first triple exhausts the constituents of α. As to the second, while there could be a spot whose constituents it exhausts, there is in fact none. What is the ground of this difference?

In the complex style, there is only one answer. In the first triple, though not in the second, the nexus actually connects the two qualities into a *complex*. This complex or fact and the circumstance that one of the three entities which are its constituents actually connects the other two is one and the same. In the case of the first triple, there is thus a complex whose constituents it exhausts. In the case of the second, there is no such complex.[1] That is the difference.

The spot α is an entity. The first triple is not. It follows from our "premiss" that α cannot be the triple. What, then, is it? Abstractly, there are two possibilities. Let us list all the entities in the case. There are the four qualities; there is ν; there is one complex (fact). That makes six. One of the two abstract possibilities is so to assay α that it is the complex. That is done in the foil. Upon this alternative, there is a categorial difference between things and ordinary things. The latter are facts (complexes), not things. In the foil, for instance, as in ontology I use 'thing'; apples are not things but facts. In the paradigm, there are upon this alternative all together six entities.

The second abstract possibility is to assay α as a further thing, so that in this case there are all together seven entities in the paradigm.

---

[1] More accurately, as we shall see much later, there is in the foil in this case a potential complex, potentiality being one of the two modes, with an ontological status all of its own, which is the lowest of all. The other mode is actuality, of course.

The issue really before us in exploring the alternative is that of things versus facts. When it was first mentioned, there was no argument. I merely struck a theme. Now I am ready to support the dichotomy by an argument that roots it as deeply as it can be rooted.

If α is to be a further thing then it can, in the complex style, only be a "complex" thing whose three constituents are the two qualities and the binary nexus, ν, which ties them into a fact. If α is to be a thing, then it cannot also be this fact. Otherwise we are back to the first alternative. Moreover, what would in this case become of the difference between facts and things? Thus, since the triple itself is not an entity, there must be a further (ternary) nexus, call it μ, which ties two qualities and ν into a "complex" thing *if and only if* ν ties the two qualities into a fact. This, however, violates the very notion of nexus; for a nexus needs no tie to tie it to what it ties. Specifically, if two qualities are already tied by a binary nexus (ν), what does it mean to tie the pair of them and this nexus once more by a ternary nexus (μ)? What is being tied into what? The only apparent way out is to make μ into a binary nexus which does not connect some of the triples each of which consists of two qualities and ν, but, rather, some pairs of qualities. In other words, μ would connect two qualities into a thing *if and only if* ν connects them into a fact. Such an ontology is clearly redundant. Nor will μ alone do. For there remains, irreducibly, the "circumstance" that some pairs, such as red and round, but not some others, such as blue and oval, are connected by μ. And a circumstance is a fact, not a thing. That shows the apparent way out to be a dead end. The second alternative is not viable. Nor of course does the argument just hold for the paradigm. We have established what before has been merely asserted: In the complex style, *there are no things which are complexes in exactly the same sense in which facts are.* That puts ordinary things and their qualities into different categories. Presently we shall see that if one insists on putting them into a single one, the best he can do is to adopt the style of the function ontologists.

The argument just concluded will not convince anyone not already convinced that there are nexus. Nor is that surprising if, as we now do, one grasps completely the dialectical connections among the four propositions which are gathered in the next paragraph. Making all these connections explicit is, I believe, as far as one can push the argument; or, what amounts to the same, we have bared the deepest root of the dichotomy among facts and things.

(1) *One who does not recognize the ontological status of nexus cannot have a clear notion of complex.* (2) *To have such a notion and to distinguish clearly between things and facts is virtually the same.* (3) *Ordinary things*

are not things but facts (complexes). (4) *There are no things which are complexes in exactly the same sense in which facts are.*

Jointly, the four propositions immediately yield a fifth. One who does not understand the need for nexus is in danger of either blurring or completely missing the distinction between simple and complex. What will the ontology of such a one be like? In the extreme case it will have the following three features. As long as we ignore subcategories, limit ourselves to categories as fundamental as are in the foil those of things, subsistents, and facts, all its entities will belong to a single category. Are these entities things or are they facts? Literally, the question makes no sense. The two categories stand or fall together. Yet I shall venture to say right now what happened in the tradition. In a manner of speaking—that manner, alas, which one cannot do without when trying to understand what is inherently confused—the entities of this single category are more nearly like things. Why this happened will become ever more clear as we proceed. Being more nearly like things, are the entities of the single category more nearly like simple things or like complex ones? The answer is what one would expect. They are more nearly like simple things.

These features, we see, are structurally so connected that an ontology is likely to possess either none of them or all three. *There are no nexus. All existents are things,* at least after a fashion. *All things are simple,* at least after a fashion. These are the three features. They are also the three major facets of the doctrine I call (extreme) *reism,* just as I call reistic in tendency any ontology which more or less markedly has at least one of the three. Virtually all ontologies on record are more or less reistic. Brentano was an extreme reist. Meinong came very close to breaking these shackles. I, of course, reject reism. For me, therefore, that is one of his glories.

A reist who holds that both the spots and their qualities exist has only one way of grounding the difference between the two pairs of qualities considered, the one which "makes" a spot and the one which doesn't. He must construe the spot as a function of the pair of qualities which, as I hold, are "in" it. (And he must so specify this function that for the other pair its value is "zero." Remember the sweeping use Frege makes throughout of the "null-thing.") Perhaps this is plausible already. I shall of course return to it. But it will pay if we first turn to what has to be said about collections.

Consider the property of being both green and square. In the foil it is a thing. More precisely, it belongs to a subcategory of things which has an ontological status all its own, much lower or weaker than that of a simple thing such as green. *Why* this is so is a story which will not be told until much later, in Section Five. *That* it is so, however, I shall until then take for granted. This will prove to be good strategy and do no harm.

Green and square we take to be simple things. Being green and square is one of those one is naturally tempted to call "complex," with green and square among its "constituents." We know by now that this is a blur. So we need a new set of words to be used in these cases and no others. Let us agree to call the subcategory to which being both green and square belongs *derived things*. ('Defined', which, as we shall see, suggests itself instead of 'derived', I avoid because of its linguistic flavor.) Literally, derived things have no constituents. We shall say that they have *quasiconstituents*. Green and square, for instance, are two quasiconstituents of being both green and square. The third, represented by 'and', requires a word of introduction.

In the foil, 'this is green', 'that is red', 'this is green and that is red' stand for three facts, the first and the second being constituents of the third. That makes 'and' stand for a nexus, provided only one takes for granted that, facts being even more "independent" of each other than things are from things, two facts do not "make" a third unless they are tied by a nexus. That gives and ontological status. As for conjunction, so for all connectives. (With this, by the way, Frege agrees. For he makes them functions and insists that functions are objective, which is his way of saying that they have ontological status.) *That* this is so I shall in this book take for granted. *Why* it is so I have argued elsewhere and do not intend to repeat an argument which, weak as it seems to some of my keenest critics, I can as yet not improve. Notice, though, how it all fits with the two major "premisses" that facts are entities and that a mere collection of entities (facts) is not itself an entity (fact).

We have come upon a distinction which our natural languages miss. Green, square, being both green and square, are three things. The first two are simple, the third is derived. It follows that in the two expressions 'this is green *and* that is red' and 'being both green *and* square' the particle does not stand for the same entity. In the former it stands for a nexus; in the latter, merely for a potentiality, which is not a category but the mode whose ontological status is the lowest of all.[2] Of all this, much later. For the moment, let us agree on a word. 'And', in such expressions as 'being both green and square', stands for a *quasinexus*. Again, as for conjunction, so for all connectives. In the language we speak, 'and', 'or', 'if-then', and so on, sometimes stand for connectives (subsistents), sometimes for quasinexus (quasisubsistents). Most of the

---

[2] The other mode is actuality. See n. 1, above.

time the ambiguity does no harm. Occasionally, when it might, quasinexus will be marked by boldface, as in 'being both green **and** square'.

I am ready to explain my use of 'class', 'extension of a class', and 'collection', which is not of course limited to the foil. Otherwise it could hardly be a principle of general ontology that a collection, since it is not a class but merely (in some cases) the extension of one, is not an entity. But the use is best explained by means of a specific ontology. So I turn to the foil.

The things of the foil are either characters (universals) or particulars. The latter are all simple. A character is either simple or derived. Being both green and square, for instance, which we already know to be a derived thing, is a derived character. *The classes of the foil are a kind of derived character.*

In the foil, Tom, Dick, and Harry are very complex facts. But it will make things less stuffy and do no harm if we borrow their names and make them stand for three things, either particulars or characters. You may, for instance, think of them as alternative names of the qualities which ground three colors. (Remember the neutral use of 'quality' on which for the time being we agreed. In an ontology with universals, such as the foil, qualities are of course characters.)

Take now the property of being either identical with Tom or identical with Dick or identical with Harry. The foil assays this property as a derived character of the sort I call a *class*. Disjunction, of any number of terms, is a nexus; being-identical-with is another kind of subsistent. (Some call this kind a logical relation, of which much later.) The expression standing for the class is '**being either identical with Tom or identical with Dick or identical with Harry**'. The boldface calls attention to a distinction already made. The quasiconstituents of our example are three things and two quasisubsistents, one of the latter occurring thrice.

What sort of derived character is a class? Before answering, I must remind you of a feature which, as far as I know, is at least implicit in many ontologies in which there are classes. The things of these worlds fall into subcategories more or less like the Russellian types; and the things which are quasiconstituents of a class all belong to the same type, one step below that of the class itself. E.g., if Tom, Dick, and Harry are all of type zero (particulars), then our example is a character of the first type.

A class is a derived character such that its quasiconstituents which are things are all of the same type; and it stands to these things as our example stands to Tom, Dick, and Harry. In other words, a class, with one exception, is always a being either identical with . . . or identical with . . . and so on. Its only quasiconstituents which are not things are therefore **identity** and **disjunction**. The exception is the so-called null-classes (being and not being identical with . . .).

The *extension* of the class which serves us as an example is three things: Tom, Dick, Harry. The extension of a class is a *collection*. The only reason why not every collection is the extension of a class is that the entities of a collection need not all be things, just as its things, if any, need not all be of the same type. The pairs of qualities we considered are the extensions of classes; the triples we also considered are not. I shall occasionally employ brackets '[· · ·]' to mark classes; braces '{ · · · }' to mark collections.

I have shown, not only how I use 'class', 'extension of a class', and 'collection', but also that I can consistently hold classes though not collections to exist. But I also undertook to convince you, or try to convince you, that a certain proposition which I need not repeat is a "premiss" not just of my own ontology but of all.[3] Presently I shall try. First for three comments.

First. Some may suspect that the distinction between classes and collections is one too many. I shall dispel the suspicion by baring its structural root. Nominalism, as I shall sometimes use the term, very broadly, is the doctrine that there is only one type (subcategory) of things. (That makes for an affinity—or should one say continuity?—between nominalism and that facet of reism according to which all existents are things.) The distinction between classes and collections on the other hand, or, more precisely, between classes and those collections which are their extensions, presupposes the recognition of at least two types, one of the class itself, the other of the things in its extension. A nominalist thus cannot have both classes and collections. Under such pressure he opts for the lower type. That is but a facet of his nominalism. Hence, if he uses them at all, he will tend to use the three expressions ('class', 'collection', 'extension of a class') synonymously for what I call collections; and he will add, quite consistently from where he stands, that classes do not exist. The structural root of the suspicion is nominalism.

Second. Eventually, I promised, I would give *a* reason why the ontological status of *all* derived things is low. In the case of classes there is an *additional* reason, which I shall give right now, that makes their ontological status even lower. Let me first remind you of a special use of possible.

---

[3] More accurately, of all ontologies sufficiently articulate to be of interest. I shall not always repeat this obvious qualification.

'Possible' has several philosophical uses which require explication. One use, which is ordinary or commonsensical and therefore requires no explication whatsoever, is the rather special one I have in mind. If one says, for instance, that in a collection of four things there are six "possible" ones of two things each, he uses 'possible' in this way. I call this the combinatorial use of 'possible'.

A world is finite if and only if all its classes are finite. In a finite world there is not only for each class exactly one collection which is its extension but also, conversely, for every *possible* collection of things of the same type exactly one class whose extension it is. Call this the one-one correspondence of classes and collections, without repeating each time the obvious condition the collection must fulfill. The italicized use of 'possible' is combinatorial. That makes the one-one correspondence a truth of common sense. In a finite world there is for every possible collection, which itself is not an existent, a class, which exists, and, in one-one correspondence, conversely. This is the additional and, I submit, very obvious reason for the ontological status of classes being very low indeed.

Third. Since there are no expressions of infinite length, we cannot for an infinite collection write down the expression which, if we could, would stand for the corresponding class. In an infinite world, therefore, one must not take for granted that there is a class for every possible collection. If one did, the sense he would have to appeal to would be arithmetical rather than common. But a *mot* is not enough. One who extends the one-one correspondence to all worlds must be prepared to argue his case. I believe that the argument can be made. These problems have something to do with the so-called axiom of choice. They have long fascinated me; I hope there will still be time to express my present thoughts on them. In this book they have no place. We may safely limit ourselves to finite collections. Or, if you please, we may safely assume that there is a class for every collection.

A collection of entities is not itself an entity. I shall now try to show that this proposition is a "principle of general ontology" in the only way in which one can show this sort of thing, which is by a striking example. It is striking because, while denying that there are classes, it yet distinguishes, *within the limits of its articulation*, between collections of things on the one hand and those things, *which it alleges to exist*, that do in it the job which classes do in others. I am speaking of the ontology of Nelson Goodman,[4] which, even though I reject it as inadequate on

---

[4] The comments on Goodman, here and elsewhere in this book, are limited to what serves its purpose. Thus they not only ignore many details but are very selective. For these details as well as for much else, I refer once and for all to

several scores, I yet judge to be more articulate and profound than any that has recently been proposed. Nor is it just the striking example we need. It will also serve by directing our attention to the antifoil, which will always be in the background, even though, once it has been set up, it will for very long stretches not even be mentioned.

Goodman's talk is not always as explicitly ontological as mine. Yet he is as committed an ontologist as any. And the ideal-language method he uses often makes up for the lack of explicitness. Two examples will show why this is so. The entities he explicitly recognizes are all either ordinary things or qualities. His use of 'quality', as it happens, unlike the one on which we have agreed for the time being, is not neutral. His qualities, we shall see, are my simple universals. Right now, that makes no difference. What matters is, rather, that the expressions which in his calculus stand for qualities and ordinary things, respectively, are of the same syntactical kind. For it is of the essence of the method that entities represented by expressions of the same syntactical kind belong to the same ontological kind (category), provided only that their ontological status is recognized at all. That shows how Goodman's method supports my diagnosis that the entities he explicitly recognizes are all things, which in one respect makes him a reist. The other example is what he calls the overlapping, the being-together, and the matching of things. One thing's overlapping another is in his calculus expressed by a sentence. Sentences stand for facts. That leaves no doubt that overlapping is what I shall presently call a "connection." As for overlapping, so for being-together and matching. These are some reasons for my diagnosis that these three are the fundamental nexus of that world. (There are other reasons, of which more later. A connection, we shall see, is not necessarily a nexus.) Nor am I disturbed by Goodman's failure to recognize their ontological status, which makes him a reist in a second respect. Rather, I am encouraged by the example thus provided for the claim that the several features of reism tend to go together. For the moment that will do. In the next paragraph I repeat what is now needed in the form in which it will be used.

If one makes this ontology as articulate as it can be made, overlapping becomes a nexus. Hence, whatever is derived from overlapping also acquires ontological status, though of course not necessarily that of a nexus.

In what follows I do not proceed as Goodman does. He derives from overlapping by means of a definite description and some "axioms" a

---

Alan M. Hausman's "The Ontology of Nelson Goodman" (Ph.D. diss., Univ. of Iowa, 1966). I am very grateful to Hausman for what I have learned from the inspired stubbornness with which he often more than held his own in many discussions.

certain function. I take this function to be primitive. My only purpose is to show that if the ontology is made as articulate as possible, this function acquires ontological status. For this purpose the difference between Goodman's and my ways makes no difference. That follows from what has just been said and repeated. The reasons for my taking this way rather than his are that it is shorter and, even more importantly, that it affords a more uncluttered view of what I take to be the essential structure. It also limits us to finite classes and collections. This, though, is a price we have already paid. So I shall not, when speaking of collections, always add the qualification that they are finite.

Goodman's is a binary function coordinating to any two things a and b one and *only* one third, $\sigma(a, b)$. Of this function several propositions which he calls "axioms" are true. E.g.,

(1) $$(x = u) \cdot (y = v) \supset \sigma(x, y) = \sigma(u, v)$$

(2) $$\sigma(x, y) = \sigma(y, x)$$

(3) $$\sigma(\sigma(x, y), z) = \sigma(x, \sigma(y, z))$$

(4) $$\sigma(x, \sigma(x, y)) = \sigma(x, y).$$

(1) secures the italicized 'only'. By (2) the function is symmetrical. By (1), (2), (3) one can from σ for each n derive an n-ary function $\sigma_n(a_1, a_2, \cdots, a_n)$. And so on. We need not worry about a complete set of "axioms." The above suffice to make the following propositions plausible.

(a) One may safely suppress the subscript in 'σ_n'. (b) For every collection there is one and only one thing which is the σ of all its things (but not conversely). (c) In this world, in which there are no classes, the σ of all the things of a collection is, with three exceptions, in all respects like, and does all the jobs of, the class which in my world corresponds to the collection.

Goodman calls his function *sum*, represents it by '$+$'. I adopt his word, but stay with 'σ'. The three exceptions are as follows.

(e1) While there are (in my world) the null-classes of the several types, there is (in his) no null-thing. (e2) The converse of (b) does not hold, not because there are things which are not sums but, rather, because for some things there is more than one collection whose sum they are. This follows immediately from (c). Think of the many ways in which a class can be decomposed into subclasses jointly exhausting them. (e3) The things of a collection and the thing which is its sum are of the same type.

(e1) is rather a technicality. (e2), which is crucial in Goodman's strategy, plays no role in mine. The heart of the matter is (e3).

If I asked Goodman to direct my attention to three colors, he could satisfy the demand. If I asked him to do the same for the alleged thing which is their "sum," or, for that matter, for the "sum" of a color and a pitch, he could not. That leaves me no choice. I cannot but reject his ontology, or, as I like to say, his world, for reasons no argument can reach. For an ontologist's creation, which is *a* world, is of course meant to fit *the* world. And I simply cannot fit his world to the one in which I find myself. (Some worlds, I insisted earlier, deserve the dialectical attention even of those who cannot but reject them. If I did not believe this, I would not write this book.)

We are finally ready to conclude a line of thought that has been pending. Each of the three fundamental nexus of Goodman's world does a crucial job. Being-together ties qualities into ordinary things. This will be seen at the end of Section Two, where the remainder of the antifoil will be set up. Matching grounds all relations. Of this there will be only a single fleeting hint in Section Six. From overlapping the sum-function is derived. That is the only purpose it serves. Assume now that one makes the ontology as articulate as possible. Then both overlapping and σ acquire ontological status. That shows that this world, in many respects so strikingly different, is yet in one respect like mine. In it, too, a collection is not an entity; not trivially, as one might think as long as thought remains blurred, because collections are classes and there are no classes in it, but, rather, as one sees if thinking accurately, because its creator goes to the extraordinary length of introducing a fundamental nexus (whose ontological status he does not recognize) for the sole purpose of coordinating to the things of each collection a further thing, which he calls its sum (to which he cannot direct my attention), to take the place and do the job of the class which in my world corresponds to the collection. That concludes the argument. *In Goodman's world, in which there are no classes, sums do and collections do not exist.* That is the striking example. I take it, then, that what I claimed to be a "general principle of ontology" really is one, and conclude with two comments. (The two parenthetical clauses above mark the limits which in the comparative study of ontologies one cannot reasonably and safely expect to exceed.)

First. The dichotomy analytic-synthetic, although not among the concerns of this book, is yet so fundamental that inevitably it will play a role at several places. It is indeed the reason for the double quotes I put around 'axiom'. One may of course use his words as he chooses. Some uses, though, are more confusing than others. Certain synthetic

sentences of scientific theories are called axioms. The use of the same
word for sentences which are analytic has been the source of more confusions than any other. Are Goodman's "axioms" synthetic or analytic?
Let us look at our sample of four.

A true sentence is analytic if and only if all descriptive signs in it
occur vacuously, i.e., if and only if it remains true under all possible
substitutions for them by others of the same types.[5] What according to
Goodman is true of overlapping is not true of, say, being-louder-than.
One who, misled by the notation, mistakes 'σ' for a descriptive relational predicate of the first type, will conclude that (1)–(4) are synthetic. However, σ is a nexus, which makes 'σ' a logical sign, corresponding to 'ϵ' in 'xef' rather than to 'r' in '$r(x, y)$'. Hence, if there were
such an entity as σ and if (1)–(4) were true of it, these four sentences
would be analytic. Goodman uses 'axiom' in the way I find so confusing.
Nor is that surprising, since he also rejects the analytic-synthetic distinction, which is one of the reasons why I cannot accept his ontology.

Second. There is no such function as σ in our world. That is why, in
the argument just concluded, I did not scruple to make it primitive.
But assume now, for the sake of another argument, that there is such
an entity and that Goodman's "axioms" are true of it. Let the latter
again be represented by (1)–(4). In this case, not being a function
ontologist, I could not take σ to be primitive. What, then, would I do?

I would claim, *first*, that there is in this world a ternary fundamental
nexus, τ, such that it actually connects three things a, b, c into the fact
$\tau(a, b, c)$, or, equivalently, that '$\tau(a, b, c)$' is true, if and only if c is the
sum of a and b. I would claim, *second*, that of τ certain propositions are
true, such as, e.g.,

(1') $$\tau(x, y, z) \cdot \tau(x, y, u) \supset z = u$$

and

(2') $$\tau(x, y, z) = \tau(y, x, z),$$

which correspond to (1) and (2), respectively. And I would, *third*, write

---

[5] Strictly speaking, this is a necessary condition for (only-if) rather than an explication of (if-and-only-if) analyticity. The missing clause requires that there be a
set-theoretical interpretation of the functional primitive or primitives upon
which all substitution instances become set-theoretical truths. If one holds, as I
do, that the adequate explication of analyticity must be purely syntactical, this
clause must be made explicit. The reason it is usually suppressed is that the interpretation of 'ϵ' as class-membership is taken for granted. Goodman's sums are
merely idiosyncratically disguised classes. Thus the required interpretation for
'σ' and 'τ' is available, and the "axioms" for them satisfy the missing clause. See,
however, n. 8 of Section Two.

'$\sigma(x, y)$' for '$(\imath z)\tau(x, y, z)$', thus introducing the abbreviation which reflects how the binary function is derived from the ternary nexus. Goodman, you remember, succeeds in deriving the binary function from the binary nexus he calls overlapping and which serves no other purpose. This is a technicality which rather obfuscates what I want to bring out, namely, that an n-ary function can always be derived from an appropriate $(n+1)$-ary nexus. Hence, even if there were some very strange functions in the world, we would yet not be forced to adopt the function style.

TWO FUNDAMENTAL TIES

I N the world of the preceding section all ordinary things are spots; each spot has two properties; no two spots have exactly the same properties. The last of these restrictions permitted us to ignore a problem which, though in our world as fundamental as any, is yet less so than those we considered in Section One. Now we are about to drop the restriction. First, though, for some distinctions.

A complex is not in all cases uniquely determined by the collection of its constituents. In some cases there is more than one way in which the subsistents among the latter may connect, group, or bracket those which are things. What I call the *assay* of a complex includes this additional specification. In the ideal-language method, it is provided by the sentence that stands for the complex. There will thus be occasion to speak of the *assay* of a complex; of the *collection* of its constituents; and, with respect to the latter, of the one (or several) *classes* of things (of one or several types) in it. For the spot α of the world we are about to leave, for instance, the sentence 'ν (red, round)' is the assay; {red, round, ν}, the collection of its constituents; [red, round], the single class of things. "Two" entities yielding literally the same assay are literally, or, as one says, numerically, one and not two. That is another "general principle of ontology." For this principle one need not argue. It is the very idea of ontology. So I shall sometimes call it *the fundamental principle*.

'Realism' has two main uses. Realism₁ is the doctrine that there are universals. Its opposite is *nominalism*. Realism₂ holds that some things are not mental. The problem to which we turn when removing the restriction involves the dichotomy realism₁-nominalism.

Let α and β be two spots of exactly the same shape and exactly the same color; [a_1, a_2] and [b_1, b_2], the two classes (pairs) of qualities "in" them. Call the nexus again ν. Assume again that each spot has exactly three constituents. Then the assay of α yields a_1 and a_2 connected by ν

and nothing else; that of β, b_1 and b_2 connected by ν and nothing else. That presents us with the following alternative.

(1) If we choose realism$_1$, then the qualities in the case are universals. Hence, the properties being exactly the same, a_1 is literally the same as b_1; a_2, literally the same as b_2. Hence, by the fundamental principle, if each spot had only three constituents, α and β would be one and not two. Each spot, therefore, must have at least one further constituent, and these further constituents must not be literally the same. (2) If we choose nominalism, then a_1 and b_1, though perhaps exactly alike, whatever that may mean, are not literally the same. Similarly for a_2 and b_2. In strict logic a nominalist is therefore at this point not forced to search for further constituents. Yet many of them do introduce further constituents whose sole function—or, at least, whose main function—is exactly that of the further constituents which at this point only realists are forced to introduce. That raises a structural question which will be answered in the next section.

The problem to which we have turned is *individuation*. In a world in which no two ordinary objects have exactly the same properties it doesn't arise. Or, if you please, its solution is obvious. In such a world an ordinary thing is "individuated" by the class of its properties, or, as I shall henceforth say in this context, by the class of its ordinary properties. Our world is not of this kind. What then makes two things which agree exactly in all ordinary properties two and not one? The answer is familiar. The *principium individuationis* of our world is space and time; in a temporal cross section it is space alone. The two spots, being two, are at different places. That makes in our world the problem of individuation part and parcel of the ontology of space and time. But, then, 'place', as I just used it, or, for that matter, 'space' and 'time', are as ontologically noncommittal as 'property'. What, then, are the ontological alternatives for the further constituent—I assume for the moment that it is just one—which both realists$_1$ and nominalists introduce at this point?

This further constituent, though not of course an ordinary property, has yet been claimed to be a property. Which use of the word makes sense, although perhaps not truth, out of the claim? The relevant notion has two parts. One part is that properties (as well as the qualities which ground them) are or have natures in the sense that two different properties are intrinsically and not merely numerically different. The other part I cannot state without recalling a distinction among the uses of 'possible'.

It is possible$_1$ for several ordinary things to have exactly the same property. In a language perspicuously reflecting an ontology, an ill-formed expression marks what in its world is impossible$_1$. In our world, for anything both to have and not to have a property, though possible$_1$, is impossible$_2$ (analytically false or contradictory). For something to be all over both red and green, while possible$_1$ and possible$_2$, is impossible$_3$ (false a priori).

It is possible$_1$ for several ordinary things to have exactly the same property. That is the second part of the relevant notion. This is one thing. There may be properties such that it is impossible$_3$ for more than one ordinary thing to have any of them. This is another thing. Those claiming that the further constituent is a property take advantage of the distinction, make that constituent one of a whole class of properties such that it is impossible$_3$ for more than one ordinary thing to have any one of them. Such properties I call coordinate properties; the qualities grounding them, *coordinate qualities*.

There are two ways of solving the problem of individuation. One way, we now see, adds to the things "in" an ordinary thing either one coordinate quality, e.g., a *place* in a momentary cross section of our world, or a class of such, e.g., a place and a *moment*. Upon this gambit, all the things "in" an ordinary thing are qualities, belong to the same subcategory (type). Or, as for brevity's sake I shall say whenever there is no danger of confusion, *they belong all to the same category*. Presently that will become very important.

Places and shapes are not unconnected. Assume, for instance, that space is atomic, i.e., that, in some sense of 'sum', each place is a sum of space atoms, such an atom being a place which has no other place in it, in the sense in which the area of the smaller of two concentric circles is in that of the larger. In such a world, a shape is but an arrangement of places. This is indeed Goodman's assay of space, place, and shape. It is not mine. But it will help if for a while we ignore this connection between place and shape and, at the same time, proceed as if space were atomic. More specifically, I shall for a while proceed as if ordinary things were indivisible.

The second way of solving the problem of individuation is to make the further constituent a *bare particular*. This notion, too, has two parts. Bare particulars neither are nor have natures. Any two of them, therefore, are not intrinsically but only numerically different. That is their bareness. It is impossible$_1$ for a bare particular to be "in" more than one ordinary thing. That is their particularity. For a coordinate quality, we remember, it is merely impossible$_3$ to be "in" more than one ordinary thing. That is a rather striking difference between the two solutions. The second grounds individuality more deeply (a priori false versus ill-formed). Upon this alternative, the things "in" an ordinary thing *do not all belong to the same category*. One is a bare particular; all the others are qualities. Again, that will become important.

There is a very widespread and very deep-seated resistance against things which are bare. Some philosophers have argued that the very notion is absurd. None of their arguments is good. So I shall not in this section examine any of them, and shall leave what will have to be said about Brentano's until later.

A quality is either a universal or a perfect particular. The perfect particulars grounding one property in two ordinary things are two. That is their particularity. Yet they are not bare. That, I presume, is their perfection. Being two, they could, as was pointed out, be used to solve the problem of individuation. The structural reason why many nominalists nevertheless introduced perfect coordinate particulars will be discussed later. Right now I wish to call attention to the fact that, as far as I know, bare particulars invariably go with universals. Why, one may ask, is this so? Why has no major nominalist, taking advantage of the structural possibility, proposed an ontology of both bare and perfect particulars? I can think of two reasons.

A bare particular is a mere individuator. Structurally that is its only job. It does nothing else. In this respect it is like Aristotle's matter, or, perhaps more closely, like Thomas' *materia signata*. Only, it is a thing. More precisely, it is no more nor less "independent" than a quality, be the latter a perfect particular or a universal; the common limits of this independence being set by the principle of exemplification which, on the side of quality, keeps universals from being "separate" or Platonic universals just as, on the side of "matter," it satisfies without excess that "materialistic" urge which, I believe, has driven many to nominalism, simply because they did not know how to satisfy it without excess. As for the question in hand, it seems plausible that with a thing doing the individuating and nothing else, particularity is, as it were, completely drained out of the qualities. Thus they become universals. This is one plausible reason for there being no nominalistic ontologies with both bare and perfect particulars. The other is the very deep-seated resistance against bareness. In trying to understand why, even though in strict logic they wouldn't have to, nominalists often do introduce perfect coordinate particulars, we shall (in Section Three) also come to understand this resistance.

An ordinary object need not, like the spots of the paradigm, have just two (simple) ordinary properties. Nor is there any reason why different kinds of such objects should not differ in the number of properties they have. Nothing will be lost, though, and words will be saved by assuming that this number is *n* for all of them. In a world with bare particulars, call it I, that makes for $n+1$ things "in" an ordinary thing. In a world without bare particulars, call it II, the number depends on the number of (simple) coordinate qualities required for individuation. In a temporal cross section of our world, a place would suffice. Without that restriction, it takes a place and a moment. That makes the number either $n+1$ or $n+2$. In I, ν connects a class of things all but one of which are of the same category (quality); the remaining one belongs to another (bare particular). In II, the things ν connects are all of the same category. In this sense, *the fundamental nexus of II is homogeneous; that of I, inhomogeneous.* Moreover, just as for the nexus of I it is impossible₁ to connect only things of the same category, so it is impossible₁ for the nexus of II not to do just that. That makes the difference between the two ties ontological. Let them be represented by 'ν_1' and 'ν_2', respectively. The universals of I will be represented by capitals with subscripts; its bare particulars by lower-case letters without subscripts. That makes $\{a, A_1, A_2, \cdots, A_n, \nu_1\}$ the collection of the constituents of α in I. In II, with time, let it be $\{i_1, i_2, a_1, a_2, \cdots, a_n, \nu_2\}$, where i_1 and i_2 stand for a place and a moment, the a_i for ordinary properties. The spot itself is in I the fact $\nu_1(a, A_1, A_2, \cdots, A_n)$, in II, the fact $\nu_2(i_1, i_2, a_1, \cdots, a_n)$. Remember, finally, that the lower-case letters with subscripts stand for qualities, which is but our way of saying that we have not yet decided whether they stand for universals or for perfect particulars. That makes the homogeneity of ν_2 and the inhomogeneity of ν_1 the distinctive difference between I and II.

Looked at as a contrast between two fundamental ties, one homogeneous, one inhomogeneous, the difference between I and II may not seem very exciting. So I shall make it my next task to show that it is massive and well-grounded in the tradition. That requires some preparation.

In Section One a function (σ) was derived from a nexus (τ). As we saw when writing '$\sigma(x, y)$' for '$(\imath z)\tau(x, y, z)$', the derivation is reflected in a definite description. Nexus, too, can be derived from others. In this case the reflection is a definition. We shall next derive two nexus, one from ν_1 in I, one from ν_2 in II.

The nexus derived from ν_1 will be represented by 'ϵ' and called *exemplification*. '$a\epsilon A$' is a well-formed sentence if and only if 'a' and 'A' stand for a bare particular and a universal, respectively; it is true if and only if a is *the* bare particular and A is *one* of the universals "in" an ordinary thing. This is the gist of the first definition. With its formula we need not bother. The words will do very well. $(a\epsilon A)$ is a fact of the sort called atomic. Eventually a few things will have to be said about these facts.

The nexus derived from ν_2 will be represented by ' C ' and called *real component*.[1] The schema '$x \mathsf{C} \nu_2(i_1, \cdots, a_n)$' or, abbreviated, '$x \mathsf{C} \alpha$', is well-formed if and only if 'x' marks the place of the name of a quality; it becomes a true sentence if and only if the variable is replaced by the name (or a description) of one of the $n+2$ qualities, $i_1, \cdots, a_n$, "in" α. This is the gist of the second definition. Again, the words will do very well.

I point at α and say (S) 'This is green'. In I, (S) becomes '$a\epsilon A$', with 'a' and 'A' standing for the bare particular "in" α and for the universal green, respectively. In II, (S) becomes '$a_1 \mathsf{C} \alpha$', with 'a_1' and 'α' standing for that quality in the spot which grounds the color green and for the spot itself, respectively. If you are in doubt, consider that there is in II nothing else it could stand for. In I, the 'this' of (S) thus stands for a bare particular, i.e., for a thing which according to this ontology is "in" the spot, while in II it stands for the spot itself, which is a fact. That should convince anyone that the difference between I and II is both massive and important for the tradition.

I turn next to another major difference between these two ontologies. Suppose for the sake of the argument that there are "complex" things. Many philosophers take that for granted. Or, just to practice our terminology, they are not aware of the crucial difference between the constituents of facts (complexes) and the quasiconstituents of (derived) things. That makes the supposition only too realistic, alas. Let us also agree to call occasionally *categorial entities* those which either are things or are facts "in" which there is at least one thing.[2]

In I, there are three kinds of categorial entities—bare particulars,

---

[1] This, though derived, is a nexus, not a quasinexus. Nor is it a pseudonexus. (The latter notion will be introduced presently.) The boldface is thus really out of place. The reason it is used nevertheless is that ' C ' will occur very rarely, while the pseudonexus in the case, for which I reserve '$\subset$', will occur very frequently. As for the signs, so for the words. 'Real component' is clumsy. But it will occur very rarely and permits us to reserve 'component' for what will have to be mentioned very frequently.

I am trying to build up a terminology and a notation which are sufficiently accurate and yet not too unmanageable. That takes time, patience, and some effort. Those who are impatient or bored or even annoyed should consider that the comparable effort in mathematics is much greater, and remember what Plato said about geometry and the philosophers.

[2] Two plus two being four is a fact "in" which there are no things. A thing's being identical with itself is a fact "in" which there is only one. The subsistents themselves are of course a category with several subcategories of their own, such as the connectives. Yet there will be no awkwardness. All one has to do in order to avoid it is to use occasionally 'ontological kind' or, briefly, 'kind' instead of 'category'.

universals, and facts; in II there are only two—qualities and facts. α is a fact in both I and II. If one ignores facts or has not yet made up his mind about them, he is left with two kinds of categorial entities in I, and with only one in II.

Put yourself now in the place of a I-ontologist who, as yet undecided how to assay α, asks himself whether it would fit in one of the two kinds already available to him. α is not bare. That eliminates one of the two. To fit into the other, α would have to be a universal that has a particular "in" it. Thus it would be "complex." The notion of such a universal is repugnant, irrespective of whether or not one distinguishes between complexity and "complexity." That eliminates the other kind available. Our I-ontologist is virtually forced to decide that α belongs to a third kind.

Not so a II-ontologist. Before he has decided on α, there is only one kind available to him; and the entities he finds in it so far are all simple things (qualities). On the other hand, if *he* does not distinguish between complexity and "complexity," or, what we know virtually amounts to the same, if *he* is not completely clear about the distinction between things and facts, there is in his world nothing which makes it counterstructural, as it is in I, to assay α as a "complex" thing. It should help to bring out the importance of this difference between I and II if it is stated as follows:

To distinguish clearly between facts and things and to be completely untainted by reism is virtually the same. This is part of the fourfold structural connection that was uncovered in Section One (p. 11). Now we have come upon another. Unlike a I-ontologist, a II-ontologist, unless completely free from that taint, will be tempted to assay ordinary things not as facts but as things. Thus he may be put in a way that leads to either overlooking or ignoring the category of fact. Overlooking or ignoring; it seems so incredible that I hardly know how to put it.

One who has yielded to the temptation finds himself in a world of enticing simplicity. Its categorial entities (nonsubsistents) are either simple (qualities) or "complex" (ordinary things); but they are all of the same kind. That makes the temptation so great that I would rather speak of a strong structural suggestion. We of course shall not succumb. Yet we have come to understand why one who does, at least in part because he is not clear about the ontological status of nexus (subsistents), may end up as an extreme reist who holds that all entities, not just all categorial ones, are of the same kind. Notice, finally, that the entities of this single kind are all either qualities or "complexes" of such. That supports the claim made in Section One (p. 12) that the entities which the reist recognizes are "more nearly like things than like facts."

Most ontologies of the tradition share a certain feature. This feature I shall now state. That it is so widely shared I shall not prove. This book as a whole is a part of the proof.

Most ontologists hold more or less explicitly that ordinary things are "things" rather than facts and yet at the same time "complexes" of other "things." This is the feature. The other things may all be universals; or they may all be perfect particulars; or they may be universals and bare particulars. For the point at hand the differences between these three possibilities make no difference. The only difference, as we saw, is that an ontologist in whose world there are both bare particulars and universals is the only one who has the benefit of a very strong structural countersuggestion. Nor would it make any difference if in addition to these three there were still other possibilities, which I have missed, either because I do not know enough, historically, or because my imagination is not keen enough, structurally.

The root of the feature is reism. More or less extreme reism more or less explicitly dominates the tradition. That is why the feature is so widely spread. The most extreme recent exponent of reism is Brentano. The most notable recent exceptions are Frege and two of Brentano's students, Meinong and Husserl. Each of these three, each in his way, explicitly recognizes that at least one nexus exists.

The three facets of reism structurally go together. Yet, if you reflect on the way the argument has been conducted in the last section, you will agree that the refusal to give ontological status to at least one nexus lies perhaps even deeper than the other two. So I shall occasionally call this the *key* facet of reism, or, briefly, its key.

The connection between reism and the feature should by now be clear. But the point is so crucial, also for my over-all strategy, that I shall state it once more, with a twist of the key to bring in the antifoil.

If an apple and the categorial entities which go into its "making" are both "things," then the latter cannot be "in" the former, cannot, as we say, be tied into it by a nexus but, rather, the former can only be a function of the latter. A nexus is one sort of entity, a function is another. That is where in a moment the antifoil will come in. On the other hand, how can we expect an ontologist to be sensitive to the difference between the two sorts, functions and nexus, unless he recognizes that both exist? That shows one reason why the key is the key. (As far as I know, the first ones to recognize the ontological status of functions were Frege and, perhaps, Russell; Frege quite explicitly; Russell much less so, if at all, in his analysis of descriptions.)

I conclude that the ontologies which have the feature, i.e., if I am right, virtually all ontologies of the tradition, are not only mistaken but irremediably blurred. Such an ontology holds that ordinary "things" are "made" out of other "things" without acknowledging the existence of whatever does the "making." This is the mistake. The irremediable blur, *la petite tâche irréparable*, appears only if one tries to make such an ontology as articulate as possible, which requires that whatever "makes" the apple out of the categorial entities which it indubitably involves be itself recognized as an entity. Then one discovers, as we just did, that this should-be entity is neither a function nor a nexus but, if anything, *a function mistaken for a nexus*. I shall speak of a *pseudonexus*.[3] The reasons for diagnosing it as a pseudonexus rather than as a pseudofunction, i.e., a nexus mistaken for a function, are, first, that the classical ontologists did think of the categorial entities which the apple involves as somehow "in" it while, second, they were completely unaware of the finer distinctions by virtue of which, if the apple is to be a "thing," it can only be a function of those other "things."

There are no pseudonexus. Such an entity would be a monstrous hybrid. Monsters do not survive in a world worthy of interest, *after* it has been made as articulate as is possible. I, for one, hold that some classical ontologies are of very great interest. That determines my strategy.

To make the classical ontologies as articulate as possible, one must pay the price of keeping some monsters artificially alive. This is the idea of the antifoil. Let me state it without the image. In the antifoil there are pseudonexus. Hence, since the very notion of such an entity is irremediably blurred, so is the antifoil itself. If, however, the notion were not blurred, the antifoil would not be blurred at all since everything else in it is (I hope) both clear and articulate. That is why it will be indispensable to us. This is one thing. To hold, as of course I don't, for otherwise I would hardly make it the antifoil, that this ontology is also adequate, is quite another thing.

Now for four brief points. Then the pseudonexus which will be with us through the rest of the book will be introduced.

First. The world of the antifoil is not II. It is, rather, the one in which a II-ontologist finds himself after having succumbed to the temptation against which, as we saw, a I-ontologist is structurally protected.

---

[3] As to terminology, notice the distinction between 'quasi' and 'pseudo'. There is nothing wrong with a quasi-something, after it has been recognized for what it is and the distinctions required have been made. A pseudo-something, on the other hand, is a monster. E.g., there is nothing wrong with calling one entity a quasiconstituent of another as long as one is aware of the difference between constituents (of facts) and quasiconstituents (of derived things). But the pseudoconstituents upon which we shall come in a moment are derived monsters.

Second. The antifoil is not clearly and explicitly a world in the function style. It, is, rather, *a function world mistaken for one of complexes,* just as a pseudonexus is a function mistaken for a nexus. That makes it less than accurate to say, as I did, that the antifoil to be designed would be a function ontology. But there was no way of avoiding the inaccuracy before we had reached the point at which we now are.

Third. At the end of the chapter we shall discard the designations I and II. In the foil, which is a I-ontology, ϵ, we shall presently see, can serve as the fundamental nexus. Any world with this fundamental nexus will henceforth be called an ϵ-*ontology.* In the antifoil, which is not a II-ontology, the fundamental pseudonexus will be represented be 'γ'. Any ontology with this fundamental pseudonexus will henceforth be called a γ-*ontology.* Much of this book explores the dialectic generated by the contrast between these two types of ontology, or, more concisely, between ϵ and γ. Yet it would be merely tedious to repeat over and over again that γ is really a monster. Recall what has been said earlier: Even though the function style will always be in the background, it will for long stretches not even be mentioned. Thereby hangs the next point.

Fourth. The ordinary things of the antifoil will henceforth be represented by lower-case letters without subscripts, 'a', 'b', and so on, even though in the foil the same letters stand for particulars, which makes my use of them as ambiguous as that of 'this' in 'this is green' with respect to I and II. Yet I shall (I hope) manage to avoid confusion. As for signs, so for words. The cautionary double quotes around 'thing' which appeared each time I spoke about the categorial entities of a γ-world will henceforth be omitted. Nor will γ always be called a pseudonexus; not that I shall ever call it a nexus, for that would be confusing; I shall simply use the Greek letter. This is one example of how I propose to manage. As to the ordinary objects of a γ-world, since I do not want to call them "things" and dislike speaking of them too often as things, let us agree to call them *clusters.* That permits us to state the contrast between the two worlds in a new way. *In an ϵ-world ordinary things are facts; in a γ-world they are clusters.* This is another example of how I propose to manage. We shall (I hope) soon have acquired a terminology and a notation which are sufficiently accurate without being unnecessarily cumbersome.

Suppose that in the antifoil the categorial entities involved in the spot a are again the $n+2$ qualities[4] i_1 to a_n. That makes

$$(4) \qquad\qquad a = \gamma(i_1, i_2, \cdots, a_n)$$

[4] Strictly speaking, since qualities are a kind of things, this occurrence of 'quality' ought to be surrounded by double quotes. But remember the new dispensation.

the controlling formula. As long as one firmly grasps that while (4) is a sentence, '$\gamma(i_1, \cdots, a_n)$' is a definite description, one is neither in II nor in the antifoil but, rather, in a function world with the fundamental subsistent γ. The definite description itself either succeeds or fails, depending on whether or not there is a spot involving the $n+2$ qualities mentioned in it, but it is not, like a sentence, either true or false, such as for instance the sentence '$v_2(i_1, \cdots, a_n)$', which is true or false depending on whether or not there is the spot which (assuming it to be there) I called a. And, of course, if in (4) 'a' is replaced by the name of another spot, then the description succeeds and (4) is false.

One leaves this world and enters the γ-world which will be our antifoil as soon as, either losing or lacking a firm grasp of all this, one begins to think of the $n+2$ qualities as "in" the spot. For then, whether one knows it or not, γ has become a pseudonexus and the $n+2$ qualities are not really constituents but, rather, *pseudoconstituents* of a. (In the world one has left there might be good reasons for calling them, without confusion, quasiconstituents of a!)

If γ were a nexus, one could from it by means of a definition derive another. This nexus, which is binary and asymmetrical, ties one thing to another if and only if the latter is an ordinary object, e.g., a, and the former one of the qualities involved in it, e.g., either i_1 or $\cdots$ or a_n. We shall represent this connection by '$\subset$', call it *component*, and say, e.g., that a_1 is a component of a ($a_1 \subset a$). Since γ is a pseudonexus, the notion of a component, too, is irremediably blurred. *To be a component is to be a pseudoconstituent.* 'Component' will be used in no other way. This is still another of the expedients by which I hope to avoid confusion without splattering every page with words that begin with 'pseudo'. I shall simply use 'γ', '$\subset$', and 'component' instead.[5] Notice, finally, that while γ and $\subset$ are both irremediably blurred, no blur or taint of any kind attaches to the derivation of the one from the other. That illustrates what was claimed earlier: The rest of the antifoil is both clear and articulate.

To examine all abstract possibilities at crucial points strengthens one's grasp as well as conviction. Since we are at such a point, let us listen to a questioner who is concerned with such a possibility. "I grant that there are facts as well as things and that there is a certain spot if and only if a certain fact obtains (is actual). *It does not follow* that, as in an ϵ-world, the spot and the fact are one and not two. There remains the possibility that the spot is a thing that is there if and only if the fact obtains. Redundant as at first sight such a world may seem,

---

[5] The reasons for my choice of some other words and symbols must now also be clear. See n. 1, above.

how can you be certain that it is not the one in which we live?" I shall quiet the doubt by showing that the alternative is trivial, or, perhaps better, that it is *merely redundant*.

Take Goodman's world, made more transparent by deriving its sum-function (σ) from a ternary nexus (τ). Its spots, alas, are things; and there are three qualities in each spot (a); one a place (a_1), one a moment (a_2), one a color (a_3). Yet this is not a γ-world, at least not without a major qualification. For its spot a is there if and only if the fact $\nu^3(a_1, a_2, a_3)$ obtains, where ν^3 is a ternary nexus.[6] That makes it more accurate to say that, *after a fashion*, Goodman's world realizes the possibility which preoccupies the questioner. If it were completely articulated, its spots would therefore be ternary functions of qualities, e.g.,

$$(5) \qquad a = \gamma^3(a_1, a_2, a_3).$$

Nothing can force us to adopt the function style (p. 21). We derive γ^3 from a quaternary nexus (κ) such that '$\kappa(a_1, a_2, a_3, a)$' is true if and only if (5) is true. For κ to do this job it is sufficient that it fulfill the following conditions of the sort Goodman calls "axioms."

$$(6) \qquad (\exists u)\kappa(x, y, z, u) \equiv \nu^3(x, y, z)$$

$$(7) \qquad \kappa(x, y, z, u) \cdot \kappa(x, y, z, v) \supset u = v$$

$$(8) \qquad \kappa(x, y, z, t) \cdot \kappa(u, v, w, t) \supset C_1 \vee C_2 \vee \cdots \vee C_6.$$

(6) merely states the basic idea. (7) and (8) guarantee that there is at most one spot for a triple and exactly one triple for each spot. The six 'C' stand for the sentences obtained by the permutations of 'u', 'v', 'w' in '$(x=u) \vee (y=v) \vee (z=w)$'.

A little reflection shows that in any world with the two nexus σ and ν^3, the derived quaternary nexus defined by

$$\text{'}\kappa(x, y, z, u)\text{'} \quad \text{for} \quad \text{'}[u = \sigma(x, y, z)] \cdot \nu^3(x, y, z)\text{'}$$

fulfills (6), (7), (8). Hence, a spot of any such world may be "assayed," not as the fact that its qualities are connected by a certain nexus, which fact must be there if the thing is to be there, but, rather, as the sum of its qualities. Still differently, every spot is the sum of a triple, but $\sigma(a_1, a_2, a_3)$ is a spot if and only if $\nu^3(a_1, a_2, a_3)$. Now you only have to remember, first, that every collection (supposedly) has a sum, and, second, that sums are but this world's idiosyncratic substitutes for classes, and you will see why the alternative the questioner wanted us

---

[6] ν^3 is of course closely related to, though not the same as, Goodman's being-together, which he represents by 'W'.

to consider is at best *merely redundant*. At worst, it is *very misleading*, since the alleged "assay" does not include the ground of the sum's "being" a thing.

Goodman, probably because his world is not as articulate as it could be, is misled very badly at least once, when he fails to distinguish between the thing $\sigma(a_1, a_2, a_3)$, which is always there, and the thing $\gamma^3(a_1, a_2, a_3)$ which is there if and only if the definite description '$\gamma^3(a_1, a_2, a_3)$' is successful, or, equivalently, if and only if the fact $\nu^3(a_1, a_2, a_3)$ obtains.[7] Fatal as the slip is, it does not surprise me, since the creator of this world fails to recognize the existence of either function(γ^3) or nexus (ν^3). That is why I said that his world realizes the abstract possibility only "after a fashion."[8]

The first four of the five comments which follow do not introduce any new major idea, merely unpack and apply those we have already acquired. Thus they may seem pedestrian rather than exciting. Yet they will help by preparing some tools as well as providing some check of, and insights into, how things hang together. The last comment is of a different sort. It concludes the section by directing attention to a new major theme.

First. There is a point, as obvious as it is important, that can be ignored no longer. *In a temporal world bare particulars are momentary entities.* In temporal worlds of type I, including the foil, a bare particular is therefore the single individuator, not of an ordinary thing but, rather, of a momentary cross section of one. As for I, so for II, and, derivatively, for all γ-worlds, including the antifoil. The only difference is that in a temporal world of type II or γ a momentary cross section is individuated, not by a single thing but, rather, by two—a place and a moment. In the next comment we shall look into what this difference entails. Right now I want to make an agreement about words. Unless something to the contrary will be said, what I shall call

---

[7] This slip was discovered by Hausman.

[8] If you recall what was said in n. 5 of Section One, you will see that there is an impasse with respect to analyticity. 'ν^3' and 'κ', unlike 'σ' and 'τ', do not have a set-theoretical interpretation of the sort required. That makes (6)–(8) not just "axioms" but axioms, i.e., synthetic truths into which certain statements enter by virtue of their syntactical form alone. This is against the very idea of a nexus and, in the linguistic reflection, against that of syntactical form. From where I stand, this feature alone makes the whole development unacceptable. Yet it is not surprising. It merely shows that the distinction between the analytic and the synthetic stands or falls with that between the logical and the descriptive, among connections and, in the linguistic reflection, among signs. But, then, again, why should one care if, like Goodman, he rejects the ontological status of either connection?

an ordinary thing is merely a momentary cross section of one. This way of speaking is not as arbitrary as at first it may seem. For most problems, *though of course not for all,* the differences between an ordinary thing and one of its cross sections make no difference. Or, what amounts to the same, very much of ontology, *though of course not all,* can be done in a temporal cross section. This is a very deep-lying feature of time. To explore it is not the business of this book. At some places the differences obtrude. At these places we shall of course distinguish between ordinary things and their momentary cross sections. At all other places the agreement will do no harm and save words.

The fundamental nexus of I and II are ν_1 and ν_2, respectively. The assertion, a while ago, that ϵ can serve as the fundamental nexus of I is as yet without support. This support I am now ready to provide. That requires a few words about the notion of *symmetry*.

ν_1 is $(n+1)$-ary; ν_2, $(n+2)$-ary. Are they symmetrical in the familiar sense that the order of the arguments in the parentheses after, say, ν_2, makes no difference? In other words, is '$\nu_2(i_1, i_2, a_1, \cdots, a_n)$' true if and only if '$\nu_2(c_1, c_2, \cdots, c_{n+2})$' is true, where the '$c$' stand for an arbitrary permutation of the original arguments?

ν_2 is homogeneous, ν_1 is not; that is why I shall make these remarks about ν_2, add what needs to be added about ν_1 afterwards. The categorial things "in" an ordinary thing of a world of type II or γ, although they are all qualities, which is why ν_2 is homogeneous, are yet not interchangeable in all respects. In Goodman's world, for instance, one must be a place, one a moment, one a color. Two colors and a place won't do; nor of course will three moments. Thus, if he wished, an ontologist could make 'ν_2' formally asymmetrical by an agreement to write first the name of the place, then that of the moment, then that of the color. Yet, this would be a mistake, since it makes the notation less perspicuous than it can be and thereby, more likely than not, betrays either a blur or at least a blank in ontological thought. The truth that (in Goodman's world) a place goes with a moment and a color rather than with two other places, as well as many similar truths (in his world or in any other), such as that a pitch always goes with a loudness, that nothing has both a pitch and a color, and so on, and so on, are from where I stand all a priori. The a priori lies deep; it is necessary$_3$; its negation, impossible$_3$. But the categorial lies even deeper; a categorial truth, accordingly, is necessary$_1$; its negation, impossible$_1$. ν_1 and ν_2 being nexus, it follows that the "asymmetries," dependencies, and exclusions to be taken into account when deciding whether or not these nexus are symmetrical, ought to be of a categorial nature. Since they are all at most a priori, I suppose that '$\nu_2(i_1, \cdots, a_n)$' is symmetrical in all its

arguments. Turning to '$\nu_1(a, A_1, \cdots, A_n)$', we notice immediately
that the difference between the bare particular a and the n universals
A_i is categorial. So we decide to put 'a' in the first place, then suppose
again that ν_1 is symmetrical with respect to its remaining n arguments.
I used 'suppose'. Yet the supposition proves extraordinarily successful.
That shows how two features of the foil, the symmetry of the fundamental nexus, with the obvious qualification for a, on the one hand,
and, on the other, the distinctions among the several kinds of necessity, possibility, and impossibility, hang together. γ-ontologists, on the
other hand, not by chance, as we shall come to understand, do not distinguish the three kinds of impossibility and necessity, categorial,
analytic, and a priori. Rather, they lump them all together under the
common label of a priori.[9]

Let once more $\{a, A_1, \cdots, A_n\}$ be the collection of categorial entities in a spot of the foil. Our world is such that for each a there is one
and only one class $[A_1, A_2, \cdots, A_n]$, though not of course conversely,
otherwise there would be no need for particulars. Hence, since ν_1 is symmetrical in the A_i there is a one–one correspondence between

(9) $\nu_1(a, A_1, A_2, \cdots, A_n)$

and

(10) $(a \epsilon A_1)$ and $(a \epsilon A_2)$ and $\cdots$ and $(a \epsilon A_n)$,

such that (9) and (10) are either both true or both false. That shows
that ν_1 can be replaced by ϵ, or, more accurately, that it can be replaced
by ϵ and conjunction. The role of the latter provides an opportunity for
checking, by means of three remarks, how in the foil things hang together.

Notice, *first*, that each of the n parentheses in (1) stands for an atomic
fact; that the spot itself is also a fact, call it the $(n+1)$st; but that by
the general principle a mere collection of n facts (complexes) does not
make a further one. Yet everything is in good order. A glance at (10)
shows that it stands not for a mere collection but, rather, for a complex, namely, a fact in which n atomic facts are tied together by conjunction, which in the foil is a nexus.

At this point a critic might wish to raise an objection. So I shall *next*
explain how he (and I) use some words I shall put in his mouth.

A nexus may or may not connect any two (or more) of the categorial
entities—things or facts, as the case may be—for which it is categorially
possible (possible₁) to be so connected. A nexus is the weaker the more

---

[9] This structural connection will become clear in Section Ten.

of those entities it could connect actually are connected by it. Or, at least, this is a very reasonable use of 'weak' in ontology. Take the 'and' of the foil; in Goodman's world, take σ, or, more precisely, τ. In his world, any two things have a sum; in mine, any two facts are connected by and. That makes σ in his world and and in mine two nexus as weak as a nexus can be.

We are at last ready for the critic. He observes that the n atomic facts "in" the spot are "connected" by the circumstance that the same particular occurs in all of them and that therefore conjunction, whose ontologization makes him uneasy anyway, need not be appealed to. I insist that strictly speaking the circumstance, though very special, cannot replace a nexus. Or would anyone be willing to say that two spots are one entity *merely* because they are of exactly the same color? For the rest I agree. For one bare particular to occur in two facts is one thing; for one character so to occur is another thing; the difference is part and parcel of that between the two kinds. In this respect, the circumstance is special indeed.

The critic now changes his attack. He observes that while conjunction is a nexus as weak as any, the ontological status of the spot is the highest of all. Or, what he takes to be the same, he insists that the "connections" among any two of the categorial entities in the spot are very "close." I quite agree. But I add, first, that a "connection," as he just used the word, very broadly, is not necessarily grounded in a nexus; I add, second, that the "closeness" of this particular one is in the foil adequately and accurately reflected by two other features. One is the circumstance just called special; the other, some of the a priori truths that had to be mentioned a short while ago. We have no reason to be discouraged. So far the foil seems to be reasonably articulate.

Second. In a world otherwise of type II or γ but with a single individuator the situation is the same as in I. ν_2 can be replaced by a single binary nexus and conjunction. The only difference is that while ϵ, like ν_1, is inhomogeneous as well as asymmetrical with respect to a, this nexus, like ν_2, is homogeneous and symmetrical. In a spatiotemporal world of type II or γ individuation requires two things; we called them i_1 and i_2. This produces some differences.

Let $\{i_1, i_2, a_1, a_2, \cdots, a_n\}$ be the collection of the categorial entities in the spot. Our world is such that for each collection $\{i_1, i_2\}$ there is *at most* one class $[a_1, a_2, \cdots, a_n]$, though of course again not conversely. The root of the differences is that, unlike the single individuator of I, the collection $\{i_1, i_2\}$ is not as such an entity and can therefore not be connected by a binary nexus with each of the a_i. There are two ways out.

One may, *first*, derive from ν_2 a ternary nexus, call it ω, such that there is a one–one correspondence between

(11) $$\nu_2(i_1,\ i_2,\ a_1,\ a_2,\ \cdots,\ a_n)$$

and

(12) $\omega(i_1,\ i_2,\ a_1)$ and $\omega(i_1,\ i_2,\ a_2)$ and $\cdots$ and $\omega(i_1,\ i_2,\ a_n)$,

(11) and (12) being either both true or both false. That shows that ν_2 can be replaced by the ternary ω and conjunction. There is no need for going into the details once more. But it may help if I point out that ω is the ontological ground of what some philosophers speak of as an ordinary quality's "occupying" a space-time cell.

The *second* way has two variants. The idea common to both is to tie first i_1 and i_2 into an entity by one binary nexus and then, by another, this entity to each of the a_i. Casting about for the entity required, one comes upon two possibilities. One is (a) the class $[i_1,\ i_2]$; the other, at least for one who holds that there are such entities, (b) the sum $\sigma(i_1,\ i_2)$. *Ad* (a). Upon this variant a "class" would be "in" an "ordinary thing." That is counterstructural for both II and γ. For γ there is the additional circumstance that in worlds with only one kind of categorial entity classes as such are counterstructural. That is after all why Goodman invented his sums. *Ad* (b). Upon this variant, ν_2 can be replaced by a single binary nexus in combination with τ and conjunction.

Third. Consider an ϵ-world. Let A and B be two of its classes such that every member of A is a member of B (but not conversely). A is a (proper) subclass of B; or, as I shall say, A *is contained in* B; in symbols: $A < B$. The connection represented by '$<$' is a derived nexus, transitive and of the sort often called a logical relation.

In a γ-world with sums to do the jobs of classes one can define a derived pseudonexus such that $\sigma_1 \nleqslant \sigma_2$ if and only if every pseudoconstituent of σ_1 is a pseudoconstituent of σ_2. As you see, I represent this pseudonexus by '$\nleqslant$', but shall not bother to give it a name; if necessary, we can always say that one sum is pseudocontained in another; for the most part, though, I shall simply say σ_1 is contained in σ_2. $\nleqslant$, too, is transitive and, in general, corresponds to $<$ as sums correspond to classes. Yet $<$ and $\nleqslant$ are two and not one. The former is a nexus in I; the latter, a pseudonexus in γ.

Fourth. Consider a γ-world. Replace the letters 'i_1' to 'a_n' by the more convenient 'c_1' to 'c_k'. That makes $\gamma(c_1,\ \cdots,\ c_k)$ an ordinary thing (cluster). If γ were a nexus, $k-2$ others, $\gamma^2, \gamma^3, \cdots, \gamma^{k-1}$, could be derived from it as follows. '$\gamma^i(d_1,\ \cdots,\ d_i)$' is true if and only if there is a cluster (ordinary thing) such that the d_i are all among its qualities.

Since γ is merely a pseudonexus, the several γ^i are all pseudonexus. Similarly, if a cluster were a complex, $\gamma^2(c_1, c_2)$, $\gamma^3(c_1, c_2, c_3)$, and so on, would all be complexes. Since a cluster is a "thing," so are all these entities, which may conveniently be called *subclusters*. The double quotes around 'thing' recall the irremediable blur. (I promised not to recall it too often. But this is a strategic passage. So I want to be especially cautious.)

The c_i, $\gamma^2(c_1, c_2)$, $\gamma^3(c_1, c_2, c_3)$, and so on, up to the full cluster, are all things of the one kind or type that exists in this world. Accordingly, a single quality, say, c_1, is "in" a cluster in exactly the same sense in which it is "in" some subclusters and in which some subclusters are "in" some others as well as "in" some (full) clusters. These are all pseudonexus. Or perhaps they are a single pseudonexus. As far as I can see, the difference makes no difference. It will be safe to represent them all (in case they are counted as more than one) by '$\subset$', which, as originally introduced, stood only for the pseudonexus between a single quality and a (full) cluster; just as it will be safe to omit the superscripts after 'γ'. Thus we shall write, not only, as before, $c_1 \subset \gamma(c_1, \cdots, c_k)$, but also $c_1 \subset \gamma(c_1, c_2)$, $\gamma(c_1, c_2) \subset \gamma(c_1, c_2, c_3)$, and so on; and shall say that in all these cases the entity mentioned at the left of '$\subset$' is a *component* of that mentioned at the right.

$\subset$ and $\not\subset$ are both transitive; they are both pseudonexus in a γ-world with sums; and they are, alas, only too easily confused with each other.[10] Yet they are two and not one. There are two ways of convincing one's self that this is so. One is very simple; the other, more methodical. The simple way is to consider some sum for which there is no "corresponding" cluster. In this case some entity will be contained ($\not\subset$) in some other without there even being any "corresponding" third entity of which the first could be a component ($\subset$). Taking the other way, one will point out that $\not\subset$ and $\subset$ are "derived" from two different nexus; the former, from τ; the latter, from ν_2. This, though, is a very special use of 'derive'. It would be better to say that starting from

---

[10] The following is not only a structural explanation of how easily one might "slip" in Goodman's world; it also brings out the blur in his peculiar "identification" of the sum with the ordinary thing, in all those cases in which the latter exists, by making clear that even though the sum always exists, it would, without the "identification," not even be "in" the ordinary thing in those cases in which the latter exists.

My reason for calling Goodman's spots ordinary things rather than clusters is that at least implicitly he recognizes the ontological status of $\nu^3(a_1, a_2, a_3)$. Structurally his reism is thus not extreme. Rather, as I shall presently put it, his world hovers uneasily between II and γ. Yet he denies explicitly that anything but things exists. Thus everything becomes blurred. *Hinc illae lacrimae.*

either τ or ν_2, one arrives at either $\lessdot$ or $\subset$, respectively, if one has made the fatal mistake that leaves the irremediable blur.

Goodman's paradigmatic triples will do as well as our k-tuples for a last point. In his world a certain color and a certain place may be "in" many spots, yet there may be no spot in which this color and this place are combined with a certain moment. This shows that while in a (full) cluster γ is as strong as a "nexus"[11] can be, *the strength of the γ in a subcluster is rather weak;* the weaker, the smaller the number of the qualities it ties together.

Right now all this sounds like the clanking of empty machinery. Later on the machine will do some work for us. There will be a great deal of talk about clusters, subclusters, components; about one class being contained in another; about the strong and the weak γ; and in all this talk the distinctions we have just made will be of the essence.

Fifth. The *nominalism-realism* issue has several strands. To master its dialectic, one must first separate them, then explore all their connections.

Many a nominalist, if only he were not a reist who shuns all nexus, would insist that he finds the notion of an inhomogeneous fundamental nexus incomprehensible. Goodman, even though a reist, tells us that he could not but reject this notion for reasons which he believes no argument can reach.[12] One need not share his belief in order to appreciate an insight which isolates the strand which structurally (though not, alas, historically) is the most important of all, since, as I shall try to show, it lies deeper than all others.

Let me for the moment use the traditional word to refer to this single strand. Then *a world is "nominalistic" if and only if its fundamental nexus is homogeneous.* A world of type II or γ is thus "nominalistic." So is Goodman's world, which hovers uneasily between II and γ, even though, irrespective of what he himself may say, its qualities are universals. (My desire to isolate this strand of "nominalism" in nominalism in order to determine on what it depends as well as what depends on it alone is the major reason for temporarily using 'quality' so that a quality may be either a universal or a perfect particular.)

[11] Since these are notions which will be with us throughout, I once more prefer tediousness to lack of caution and recall that the γ^i are all pseudonexus and that therefore whatever strength any one of them may have is irremediably blurred.

[12] I use the same phrase as on an earlier occasion in order to indicate how deep the point lies. Remember that I, for instance, rejected the idea of a fundamental function, or, as it was put, of any function's being its own ontological ground, for reasons which (I believe) "no argument can reach."

Presently we shall come upon two direct structural connections; one, between the rejection of inhomogeneous ties and a deep-seated aversion against bare entities; the other, between this aversion and reism. Jointly, these two connections establish one between nominalism, "nominalistic" or otherwise, on the one hand, and reism on the other. In view of the latter connection, one understands why the fundamental nexus of a nominalistic world is always implicit and, therefore, must be uncovered by making the world as articulate as possible. All this complicates the dialectic to which we now turn.

SECTION THREE

CONNECTIONS

A CONNECTION'S obtaining among two or more entities is a fact. The ontological ground in addition to the entities connected, which by our general principle this fact must have, is a connector entity, or, briefly, a *connector*. All the connectors (and pseudoconnectors) we have so far encountered are a few nexus (and pseudonexus). Are there others? If there are, are they all nexus?

One color's being brighter than another is a fact. A fact is a single entity; the two colors are two. Clearly, the colors are "in" the fact. Equally clearly, they are not its only constituents. There must be a further one, which is a connector, or further ones, at least one of which is a connector. In the sentence 'This is brighter than that' these further constituents are represented by 'is brighter than'. Ordinarily we call being brighter a relation. I avoid the word in order to reserve it for a narrower use. That is also why I am using 'nexus' as I do. Most of the few philosophers who recognize that nexus exist, call them relations.

This color's being brighter than that is one fact. The book's lying on the table is another. Colors are simple; books and tables are not. In an ε-world that makes for a difference between the two examples. In the first, the entities connected are both things; in the second, they are both facts. The connector could in either case be a nexus. In a γ-world, books and tables are things, or rather clusters. The two connectors themselves could again be nexus. As to what they actually are I shall at the moment say nothing except that, since all γ-ontologies are more or less explicitly reistic, we must be prepared to find either that the ontological status of all their connectors is explicitly denied, or, at best, that its recognition is merely implicit.

The two examples drive home the point that there are numerous connectors. That provides an immediate answer to the first question. *There are many more connectors than the few nexus we have so far encountered. Are all these further connectors nexus?* The answer is not im-

42

mediate. But it is worth working for. We shall get at the root of some major structural differences between ϵ and γ.

What are the possible answers? A connector cannot be a fact. That leaves three possibilities. It is either a nexus or a thing or it belongs to a category of its own. Meinong, except in one case, opted for the third possibility. Even so, until we come to him, we may safely ignore it. That leaves two possibilities and transforms the question as follows. Are all connectors nexus or are some of them things? In the foil, if a connector is a thing then it is a universal; in a γ-ontology, it is a quality, i.e., either a universal or a perfect particular. *I propose to display fully the dialectic of the connections issue independently of the choice between perfect particulars and universals, just as eventually I shall show that the dialectic of this very choice depends partly on that issue.* If that can be done, then the connections issue, or, as one usually says, the relations issue, lies deep indeed.

Facts are *independent* in a sense in which things are not. This is but another way of stating the Principle of Exemplification. Nor is this categorial independence of facts from each other affected by some of them being otherwise "dependent" on some others, either analytically or a priori.[1] Something's being colored and its being extended, for instance, are two facts which "depend" on each other. This "dependence," though, is merely a priori and not, like the one which concerns us, categorial. Some others are merely analytic. Presently the threefold distinction between the categorial, the analytic, and the a priori will become very important.

Things, though categorially dependent on each other in a sense in which even atomic facts are not, are yet categorially independent of each other in a sense in which subsistents in general and nexus in particular depend on things.[2] The essence of the dependence of things is the Principle of Exemplification; that of their independence, the need for nexus to tie them into facts. *Facts, we shall say, are independent$_2$; things are dependent$_2$ and independent$_1$; subsistents are dependent$_1$.* We cannot go on without first recalling one feature of dependence$_1$ and looking into two others.

Bradley's regress must be stopped; otherwise one either is driven to

---

[1] Causal dependence (necessity$_4$, possibility$_4$, impossibility$_4$) hardly deserves mention in ontological discourse. A philosopher too concerned with what causally depends on what rather than being content with assaying the causal connection is as likely as not on his way either to cosmology mistaken for metaphysics or to Hegelianism or, perhaps, to both.

[2] This is not completely accurate, as may be seen from such facts in the world's form as (p) $(p \lor \sim p)$. But, then, these are facts of a very special kind and the inaccuracy will do no harm.

idealism or finds one's self in a world of items completely disjoined. The first aspect responds to this dialectical necessity. A subsistent, nexus or otherwise, does not need a further subsistent to tie it to what it ties or to what it is attached to otherwise. This aspect, call it the *first*, is the most fundamental. Since it is also familiar, it will suffice to recall it. In examining the other two it will be safe to stay with the foil.

Take the fact represented by 'Either this is red and round or that is green and square'. The things among its constituents are two particulars and four universals, say, a, b, A_1, A_2, A_3, A_4. If told that these are all the things "in" a fact, you can infer something else, namely, that this fact has two more constituents; one a connective; the other, exemplification. If, on the other hand, you were told some of the things "in" this fact, you could not, on categorial grounds alone, make any inference as to what the rest of them are. Call this the *second* aspect of the difference between things and subsistents with respect to dependence₁.

If also told that the connective in the fact is disjunction ($\vee$), you will know that $\{a, b, A_1, A_2, A_3, A_4, \epsilon, \vee\}$ is the collection of its constituents. But you still will not know the fact itself, or, what amounts to the same, its assay; if only because the fact represented by 'Either this is red and square or that is green and round', which is indubitably different from it, yields the same collection. Nor would it help to list ϵ as often as it actually occurs. Since each of the universals must be exemplified, we do know without any such listing and on categorial grounds alone that ϵ occurs at least four and at most eight times, the latter in the case that each of the two particulars exemplifies each of the four universals. In this example we also know, on a priori grounds, that ϵ occurs exactly four times. Nor finally would it help if, in those cases in which one cannot on any ground infer the exact number of occurrences of ϵ, we were provided with this number (or, as I put it, if ϵ were listed as often as it actually occurs). It would still remain open what in these occurrences is tied to what. This is the *third* aspect in which things and subsistents differ with respect to dependence₁. Notice, though, that in this respect the foil's universals resemble ϵ. To see that, recall what has just been pointed out. As long as we limit ourselves to categorial grounds, we cannot exclude that one, some, or even all of the universals in the collection are exemplified by each of the particulars in it. Nor would a listing of how often each is in fact exemplified provide all the additional information an assay requires.

The first aspect has an immediate consequence. A connector cannot be a thing and nothing else. But there remains the possibility that the ground of a connection is a thing together with a ternary connector which ties it to the two entities connected. Such things (and connectors) I call *relations*. But I shall not, in this section at least, call the ternary nexus relational, since that might prove confusing. We are ready for a last transformation of the original question: *Are all connectors nexus or are some of them relations?*

If one wants to answer this question the thing to do is first to ask another. The first aspect lies so deep that the very distinction between things and subsistents stands or falls with it. The second and the third are but two sides of one coin. Since the third is a bit more elaborate, no harm will be done if we make it stand for both. Thus we arrive at the question which must be asked first. *Do all connections have the third aspect of all nexus?*

The answer one gives depends on whether he is an ϵ- or a γ-ontologist. The differences which make the difference are two. In an ϵ-world there are bare entities; in a γ-world there are none. ϵ-ontologists distinguish between the categorial, the analytic, and the a priori; γ-ontologists lump all three into one, label it the a priori. These, though, are but two poor hints. The total dialectic is very complex. The thing to do is to unpack it step by step, establishing the structural connections as the several distinctions and propositions become available.

As a *first step* I shall by means of an example establish the following proposition. *In an ϵ-world the spatial connections cannot but have the third aspect of all nexus.* As for space, so for time. But a spatial example from the foil will do.

Take three ordinary things, α_1, α_2, α_3, which disagree in color but agree exactly in all other properties and are at distances δ_{12}, δ_{13}, δ_{23} from each other; no two of these distances being equal; δ_{12} being that between α_1 and α_2, and so on; A^1, A^2, A^3, being the three colors. If, given the ontological assays of α_1, α_2, and α_3, we are provided with information from which to infer which of the three distances connects which of the three pairs of ordinary things, then the connection does not have the third aspect characteristic of all nexus. Otherwise it does, since, given the difference in color, the possible alternatives indubitably yield different facts. That is why I introduced the colors. On the other hand, we may take it for granted that the color universals provide no cues as to the distances.

The assays of the three ordinary things are

(1) $\qquad\qquad (a_1\epsilon A^1)$ and $(a_1\epsilon A_2)$ and $\cdots$ and $(a_1\epsilon A_n)$,

(2) $\qquad\qquad (a_2\epsilon A^2)$ and $(a_2\epsilon A_2)$ and $\cdots$ and $(a_2\epsilon A_n)$,

(3) $\qquad\qquad (a_3\epsilon A^3)$ and $(a_3\epsilon A_2)$ and $\cdots$ and $(a_3\epsilon A_n)$,

respectively. Disregarding the colors, (1), (2), and (3) disagree only in the particulars. That leaves two possibilities. Either (a) the connections are so assayed that the connectors connect a_1, a_2, a_3, respectively, or, (b) they are taken to connect any two of the three facts (1), (2), (3). (a) Particulars, being mere individuators, provide no cue whatsoever as to the distances in which the ordinary things "in" which they are may be from each other. (b) The situation is essentially the same. Disregarding the color universals which provide no cues, (1), (2), and (3) are three and not one only because the particulars in them are three and not one; and the particulars provide no cues. It follows that in an ϵ-ontology distance cannot but have the third aspect of all nexus. In the foil, we know, the information or cues would have to be categorial. But there are, as we saw, no cues of any sort. So there was no need to stress this condition.

The crucial premiss of the above argument is the bareness of the particular. Particulars, being individuators and nothing else, have no "natures." The difference between any two of them is merely numerical. Any two universals, being or having natures, differ intrinsically, or, as one says, qualitatively. The difference between things bare and natured is so profound that it is categorial. They belong, as one says, to different (ontological) types. That makes ϵ inhomogeneous. There is thus a structural connection between the proposition established and the inhomogeneity of ϵ. It is strengthened by the circumstance that, as we shall see, in γ-ontologies, whose nexus is homogeneous, the proposition does not hold. (Nor does it hold in the worlds we discarded, of the type we called II.)

In an ϵ-world all spatial and temporal connections have the third aspect of all nexus. This is the result of the first step. It yields two structural suggestions; one, very strong; the other, not very weak. By the one which is stronger, one may expect that an ϵ-ontologist will assay all spatial and temporal connections as nexus. By the one which is weaker, one may expect him to go further, assay all connections as nexus. Yet he is the only one who assays not only the spatial and temporal connections but also numerous others as relations, which are things, rather than as nexus, which are merely subsistents. In the next two steps we shall uncover the overriding structural countersuggestion that accounts for this contretemps.

A particular, though bare, is yet a thing. So is the universal it exemplifies, or, perhaps better, which it happens to exemplify. The two face each other as equals, as it were; equally independent$_1$ of, and equally dependent$_2$ on, each other. Also, being bare, a particular provides no cue whatsoever as to which universal or universals it may or may not exemplify. That is why I just said: happens to exemplify. Let me express this state of affairs by saying that a particular and a universal it exemplifies are *wholly external* to each other. The notion of an "individual" which as such provides cues concerning its "properties" is one of the murkier ingredients of the notion of substance. Nor is it just murky. I judge it to be so hopeless that though I shall have to say quite a bit about the substance notion, I shall in this book say virtually nothing about that murky and hopeless part of it.

An ontologist whose "individuals" and "properties" are wholly external to each other is virtually forced to recognize the ontological status of the fundamental nexus between them, which in turn will make it easier for him to recognize that every connection must have an ontological ground. We have arrived at a basic structural insight. *The claim that there are bare particulars and the recognition of the ontological status of all connections entail each other.* Put differently, reism and bare particulars clash. Still differently, a world with bare entities not completely disjoined from everything else must contain at least one connection that is wholly external. Let these insights count as our *second step.* These particular connections, with the obvious silent premises added, are deductive. But I shall also speak of structural entailment in the case of suggestions which are very strong even though not necessarily deductive.

(1) This is green. (2) This is to the left of that. Assume that both these facts are atomic. An ε-ontologist assays (1) as a bare particular tied by an inhomogeneous fundamental nexus which is binary to a universal which is a character. His assay of (2) yields two bare particulars tied to a universal which is a relation (relational thing) by an inhomogeneous fundamental nexus which is ternary. As it happens this particular ternary nexus is also asymmetrical in the particulars. This, though, is beside the point. The point is, rather, that one who does not strain at the nexus in (1) has no reason for straining at that in (2). *The two claims that there are nexus and that there are relations go together.* The former entails the latter. This insight we count as our *third step.*

Combining the second and the third step, one arrives at a further proposition. *The recognition of bare particulars entails that of relations.* This is the overriding suggestion we were looking for after completing the first step. Since ε-ontologists recognize bare particulars, they are not likely to assay either spatial or temporal or any other relations as mere nexus. (I risk and shall continue to risk the inaccuracy which lies in speaking of a relation by itself rather than together with the appropriate nexus. Similarly, I shall sometimes say that a philosopher recognizes the ontological status of a connec*tion* rather than, more accurately, that there is in his world a connec*tor* which is its ontological ground.)

Let us review and restate what has been gained in the first three steps. *First:* The fundamental tie of a world with bare particulars is inhomogeneous. That of a world without bare particulars may be, and in fact is, homogeneous if and only if it is either nominalistic or, at least, "nominalistic." This is one reason why I have come to believe that a very deep-seated aversion against bare entities is at the very root of the classical dialectic. *Second:* Reism and bare particulars clash. Virtually the whole tradition is reistic. This is another reason why I have come to believe that the resistance against bare entities is at the very root of things. But it might be better to say that the dialectic with which we are here concerned flows from two resistances or aversions, one against bare entities, the other against subsistents, which mutually entail and thus reinforce each other. *Third:* The resistance against relations has been as great as the other two. Russell was really the first to grasp clearly *what* they are and to insist *that* they are (exist). We just saw the close connection. That makes for *three fundamental aversions, against bare entities, against subsistents, and against relations,* which mutually reinforce each other.

Nexus are wholly external to the entities they connect. So of course are relations. In this respect there is no difference between the two. That leaves only one way out for those who because of their fundamental aversions reject external connections. They must adopt the *doctrine of internal connections.* (Usually it is called the doctrine of internal relations. For reists the label will do; we of course must avoid it; in the relevant sense nexus and relations are equally external.)

In the fourth step I shall introduce this doctrine; eventually, in the last, I shall refute it. But I shall first give it a run for its money by showing that in some cases its appeal to untutored common sense is so great that one is justified in adding the *aversion against external connections* as a fourth to the other three fundamental aversions.

It will pay if we take the time for an interlude. I shall first remind you of the so-called *principle of localization,* then present you with a paragraph that contains a certain piece of dialectic, or, as I shall say, briefly, a certain argument. After a comment on this argument we shall be ready for the next step.

An ordinary thing is at each moment at one and only one place. Synonymously, *an ordinary thing is localized.* The proposition is a truism. Replace in it 'ordinary thing' by 'thing' and you obtain a second proposition. *Every thing is localized.* This is the so-called principle of localization. A thing is not an ordinary thing (nor, in an ε-world, conversely). Hence the second proposition does not follow from the first. In a world of universals it is false. I of course judge it to be false. Nor do I know of any argument in support of it that does not take advantage of the transition from 'ordinary thing' to 'thing' by means of which I just transformed a truism into a falsehood. That is why I judge the principle to be not only false but also shallow. The only reason I dignify this falsehood by calling it a principle is the very great impact it has made historically. (Those who identify the fundamental dialectic with its history will exclaim that I am contradicting myself. I am not at all alarmed, merely ask whether anyone else really believes that the historical importance of an idea is a measure of its profundity.)

"Nominalists hold that there are no universals. The premiss from which they argue is the principle of localization. Connectors are either nexus or relations. (Meinong, we shall see much later, makes one of them into a perfect particular. This oddity we may at this point safely ignore.) Relations are universals. A nominalist is thus forced to assay as nexus rather than as relations all the connections, if any, whose ontological status he is prepared to recognize. But this alternative, too, is counterstructural for the following reason. There is a strong suggestion to extend the localization principle from every thing to everything: *Every existent is localized.* Nexus, supposing it makes sense to speak of a nexus as either localized or not localized, are of course not localized. That is why we shall not expect to come in a nominalistic world upon any connector, either relation or nexus, whose ontological status is recognized."

This is the argument. As far as it goes, there is nothing wrong with it. The trouble is, rather, that it does not go far enough and thereby creates an impression which misleads. I shall next state this impression then explain why it misleads.

"A structurally consistent nominalist must also be a reist. A realist, on the other hand, may have connections which exist, nexus and perhaps even relations." This is the gist of the argument. The essential piece of machinery in it is the principle of localization, which, if I may so express myself, first makes all connections into universals and then rejects them on this ground. That creates the impression of a connection between nominalism and reism in which the former is the structural premiss; the latter, the structural conclusion. Or, with a twist, the impression created is that the dialectic of the reism issue, or, synonymously, of the connections issue, depends on whether or not one accepts the principle of localization and on nothing else.

The root of the reism issue is not the localization principle but, rather, the aversion against bareness, or, what amounts to the same, although only a nonreist would put it this way, the aversion against an inhomogeneous nexus. This root is as deep as the principle of localization is shallow. That is why the impression the argument creates is so misleading. This is not to deny that the connections between nominalism, reism, and the localization principle on which it insists are there. But they are only a small and relatively shallow part of the total dialectic. Once the latter is completely unraveled, *the rejection of bareness is seen to be the common premiss of which both reism and nominalism are the structural consequences*, independently of the principle of localization. Two comments to aid memory will help.

1. Remember from Section Two that "nominalism" is not nominalism but, rather, the doctrine that all nexus (if any) are homogeneous; which makes nominalism one of two possible variants of "nominalism." In this section we have seen that "nominalism" and the rejection of bareness entail each other. That permits one to replace the sentence just italicized by another: "Nominalism" is the common premiss; nominalism and reism are the two structural consequences.

2. Remember the ambiguous use of 'quality' on which we agreed. The qualities of a γ-world are either all perfect particulars or they are all universals. Hence, while all γ-worlds are "nominalistic," only some of them are also nominalistic. As we continue on our way, we shall have to consider γ-worlds. Our next example will already be such a world. That shows how the agreement helps me to do what I promised (p. 43), namely, to display fully the dialectic of the connections issue as such, independently of the choice between perfect particulars and universals.

We are about to take the *fourth step*. Three introductory comments will help us to find our bearings.

1. The example in the first step was the three distances among three spots. The second example, in the step we are now taking, concerns three musical intervals. In an ϵ-world, they are the connections between each of the three pairs from among three universals which are pitches. In a γ-world they connect three pairs of qualities which are either universals or perfect particulars. At first, the difference between ϵ and γ will make no difference. Nor will that between the two variants of γ. For our immediate purpose, therefore, we could assay the example in either ϵ or γ. But it will be better to assay it in γ, since that will not only help us to exploit the example now but also permit us to use it later, in the fifth step, when the differences between ϵ and γ and between the two variants of the latter will be of the essence.

2. ϵ-ontologists may, and the foil does, distinguish between the categorial, the analytic, and the a priori. The γ-ontologists with which I am concerned lump these three kinds of truth into a single one, of which they speak as the a priori; or, at best, they do not fully appreciate the importance of whatever distinctions they make. I shall save words by saying that they embrace *the doctrine of the undifferentiated a priori*. What keeps them from differentiating is their representationalism, a doctrine which will be introduced and examined in Part II. Then we shall understand why the undifferentiated a priori of these philosophers is the (structural) conclusion of which their representationalism is the (structural) premiss. But there is nothing to prevent us from using now without further analysis as a premiss what, as the dialectic unfolds, will itself become a conclusion.

3. In the ϵ-world of the first example the spots yielded no clues of any kind, either categorial or analytic or a priori, concerning the distances. Its ontologist was thus compelled to recognize that *at least all spatial and temporal connections are external*. Nor is there any structural feature to keep him from recognizing that they as well as many others, including the intervals of the second example, are not just nexus but relations. More accurately as well as more strongly, not only is there nothing to keep him from, but there are several features which propel him into, taking this path. The root of it all is, as we know, his recognition of bareness. The γ-ontologist travels in the opposite direction. The qualities of the second example, which we may suppose to be the paradigm from which he starts, are not only natured but of such a nature as to make the assay of *at least all musical intervals as internal connections* very attractive to anyone who holds the doctrine of the undifferentiated a priori. That makes in this example the difference between the differentiated and the undifferentiated a priori the one and only difference between γ and ϵ that matters. The other, between the homogeneous and the inhomogeneous nexus, enters only when one tries to extend the gambit of internal connections. The γ-ontologist, in whose world all things are natured, can extend it, from the paradigm to all connections, including the spatial and temporal ones. The ϵ-ontologist, on the other hand, in whose world some things are bare, even if in his assay of the second example he agreed with the γ-ontologist, as in fact he doesn't, from reasons we have come to understand, would yet not be able so to extend the gambit to all connections.

Tones are ordinary things of short duration. For two ordinary things to differ in color and for their colors to differ is one and the same. As for colors, so for pitches. Take then, in a γ-ontology, three qualities, a_1, a_2, a_3; let them be middle c, middle e, middle g, respectively. They make three pairs, (a_1, a_2), (a_2, a_3), (a_1, a_3). The members of each pair are connected. That makes for three facts: a_1 is higher-by-a-third than a_2; a_2 is higher-by-a-third than a_3; a_1 is higher-by-a-fifth than a_3. The fact I shall consider, call it τ, is the conjunction of these three. If you are a musician you will have noticed that I simplify by ignoring the difference between an augmented and a diminished third. Let us also simplify our language by writing 'higher³' and 'higher⁵' for the two hyphenated phrases and 'δ_1', 'δ_2', respectively, for the ontological grounds of the connections they stand for. That makes $\{a_1, a_2, a_3, \delta_1, \delta_2, \&\}$ the collection of the constituents of τ. If we want to ascertain the ontological status of the δ, the thing to do is to start the routine, established in the first example, which begins with a question: *Do δ_1 and δ_2 have the third aspect of all nexus?*

The three truths just mentioned, a_1 being higher³ than a_2, and so on, are a priori but neither analytic nor categorial. Also, they are the only cues the collection yields. That determines the answer of an ϵ-ontologist with a differentiated a priori.[3] Since he insists that the cues he takes from the collection be categorial, he will decide that the δ have the third aspect of all nexus. Hence, once more, as in the case of the spatial distances, he would at least not be prevented from assaying the intervals as nexus, even though, in view of the overriding countersuggestion, as I then called it, he will in fact assay them as relations; which shows in turn how the differentiated a priori and the recognition of bare entities structurally support each other.

The γ-ontologist, who feels free to use the three cues, finds himself in a very different position. He, when presented with the collection, can tell that δ_1, occurring twice, connects the members of the pairs a_1, a_2 and a_2, a_3, while δ_2, occurring once, connects a_1 and a_3. In his world, therefore, the δ do not have the third aspect which I insist all nexus must have (thereby importing into general ontology a distinction which the foil enables me to make). The absence of this aspect makes the connection, in γ, between, say, a_1 and a_2 even closer than that, in ϵ, of two things tied together by a nexus. If you inquire into this use of 'close', I shall tell you that the closer the connection between two entities is, the lower is the ontological status of the connector.[4] If you reply

---

[3] If you think it wrong to confront an ϵ-ontologist with the a_i, you merely have to consider that the only thing needed to make it right is to opt for that variant of γ which is "nominalistic" without being nominalistic.

[4] Some time ago we came upon another symptom of the strength of ontological status (p. 37). The higher the proportion of actual ones among all categorially possible connections, the weaker or lower is the ontological character of the connector. The two symptoms are not incompatible.

that although I have given you an inkling of what is on my mind, you would prefer a definition to this sort of answer, I shall retort that for some philosophical uses definitions are wholly out of place.[5]

δ_1 *and* δ_2, *then, connect in* γ *more closely than* ϵ *does in its worlds. Even so, the* γ-*ontologist is not thereby alone structurally forced to deny the ontological status of all connections.* There remains the structural possibility that in his world all connections are nexus, some or perhaps even all of which tie more closely than, in its worlds, the fundamental nexus ϵ. In the next section we shall exploit this structural possibility which shows that a γ-ontologist, even though he cannot escape the irremediable blur, may yet stop short of reism.

In the foil, where all connections are external, there is none closer than the fundamental nexus. That marks the point at which we are. Whether or not we shall eventually yield to its temptation, we must now face the doctrine of internal connections. I have promised that, before refuting this doctrine, I would present it in as favorable a light as I can. Let me now fulfill this promise by trying to show you how very close, in γ, the connection between, say, a_1 and a_2 really is. The example I shall use will be as simple as I can make it. For, of course, the simpler the example is, the greater is the force it has.

Remember the very special world of my fancy which served us as an example in Section One. Its ordinary things are all spots with three constituents; one a shape, one a color, the third a nexus we called ν. Suppose oval to be one of its shapes; blue, one of its colors. One may know that; or, synonymously, one may be presented with {oval, blue} as a collection from its entities. From this information one can infer that there are some spots which are blue and some which are oval. But one cannot infer from it that there is a spot both blue and oval; or synonymously, one cannot infer that, if the nexus is added to the collection one was presented with, the resulting collection {oval, blue, ν},

---

[5] An ordinary-language philosopher might wish to call to your attention that at this point I am using the method of implicit definitions even though I reject it on other occasions such as, say, in what he, though not I, calls the "grammar of color." I cheerfully admit that I do, then go on to call his attention to the difference which makes the difference. In the case of *philosophical uses*, I start out without knowing what any of the words means and determine in the course of my investigation what they might mean, or what I shall make them mean, by establishing, *among other things*, how they hang together (in so-called implicit definitions). In the case of the *nonphilosophical or ordinary uses* of the most common words, of which the literal use of the color words is as good an example as any, I know at the very start what they mean; or, if I don't, certain nominalistic and psychologistic prejudices to the contrary notwithstanding, I can be taught what they mean, singly and, as one says, by pointing.

is that of all constituents "in" a fact. This inference requires the *additional information* that there is such a collection, i.e., of all the constituents "in" a fact, such that both oval and blue are included in it. A moment's reflection shows that this is but the simplest possible example of the second aspect of all nexus. For the latter requires that if one is presented with a collection of things, together with the additional information that they are all the things in a fact, one be able to infer (some of) the nexus in this fact.

Ask the next man you encounter *whether* there is a fact into which middle *c* and middle *e* enter, and, *if* there is one, *what* it is. The answer, either immediate or after but a moment's hesitation, will be that the latter is higher[3] than the former. The "additional information" of the second aspect is not required. One may express that by saying that this makes the connection between *c* and *e* still closer. From the viewpoint of the foil the expression is no doubt very misleading, since this special closeness depends on using noncategorial cues. But my purpose right now is not to judge; I merely try to make the best possible case for what I reject. As to that moment of hesitation, if there was one and you inquire into its cause, you will very probably be told that the man was puzzled by your speaking of a fact into which the two things enter when all that is involved in this "fact" is their natures. Their natures and nothing else. This is our cue.

The ontological ground of an internal connection lies wholly "in" the two or more entities it connects. More precisely, it lies in their natures. The notion is so crucial that I reword it. *The ontological ground of an internal connection is the natures of the entities it connects and nothing else.* Still differently, an internal connection has no ontological ground of its own, or no additional one, i.e., none in addition to the entities it connects.

The notion is crucial. So I am doing as well by it as I can. Nor am I done. Presently I shall make a further effort to show how tempting it is. Yet, from where I stand, *not just with respect to the foil but in general ontology*, it remains problematic. So we must examine it and explore its structural connections. But it will be convenient to postpone the examination until we have pursued to its end the line of thought we have so far followed in this section.

All γ-ontologists more or less implicitly assay the intervals of the example as internal connections. Nor is that surprising; since, on the one hand, this assay caters to the reistic tendency which we know to be inseparable from the irremediable blur around γ, while, on the other hand, there is in their world no structural countersuggestion. As for pitches, so for loudnesses, colors, brightnesses, and so on. As far as such natured things are concerned, an ϵ-ontologist, we saw, could do the same, even though, as we also saw, in view of the overriding countersuggestion he doesn't.

I interrupt for *three agreements about words* which will save us many.

The connections to which we have so far attended in this section are either spatial-temporal or they are among ordinary qualities such as pitches, colors, and so on; a quality being called ordinary unless it is one of the so-called coordinate qualities, i.e., either a place or a moment, which were first mentioned in Section Two and are to be found only in worlds of type γ (or II). In the foil the connections among ordinary qualities are all assayed as relations. So are the spatial-temporal connections. Yet there is a difference. The latter connect bare particulars; the former, universals which are (have) natures. Since the difference enters into the dialectic, let us agree, *first*, to divide the connections which *in the foil* are assayed as relations into two kinds, calling them *spatial-temporal relations* and *ordinary relations*, respectively. Let us agree, *second*, whenever there is no danger of either ambiguity or misunderstanding and of course without prejudice, to *call in any world* a connection either a spatial-temporal or an ordinary relation if and only if in the foil it actually *is* either the one or the other. Thus, we shall say, for instance, that all γ-ontologists assay all ordinary relations as internal connections. You see how these two agreements save words. Without them we would have to say that γ-ontologists assay as internal connections all those which in the foil are assayed as ordinary relations.

All γ-ontologists assay *some* connections as internal. This is the lesson we just learned. What about the structural pushes and pulls that keep them from, or drive them to, extending this assay to *all* connections? To this question we now turn. Before answering it, let us by means of the foil take stock of all possible connections in all possible worlds.

In the foil all connections appear to be either nexus or relations. I say appear because among those I can think of there are two which as yet have not even been mentioned. One is the connection between premiss and conclusion; the other, that between cause and effect. In a reasonable sense, their examination bears out the appearance. In the foil, all possible connections, or, if you insist, all those I can think of, are either nexus or relations; and, to repeat, if they are relations, then they are either spatial-temporal or ordinary. That suggests a last agreement. Let us agree, *third*, whenever there is no danger of ambiguity or misunderstanding and of course without prejudice, to *call in any world* a connection a nexus if and only if in the foil it actually *is* one. These agreements put us into possession of a handy formula:

Every connection, in any world (even though in this world it may not be assayed as such), *is* (in the foil) *either an ordinary relation or a spatial-temporal relation or a nexus.*

Remember the question before us: How about the pushes and pulls that keep the γ-ontologists from, or drive them to, extending their assay as internal from some connections to all? The formula suggests that we divide it into two. The connections which the γ-ontologists do so assay, only too plausibly, alas, and from which therefore we may assume them to start, are the (simple)[6] ordinary relations. The first partial question inquires into the *extension to spatial-temporal relations;* the second concerns itself with the extension to nexus. The first we shall answer now. The answer to the second had better wait until after we have tackled the dialectic of internal connections as such.

Coordinate qualities are, or are meant to be, qualities among qualities. The places and moments of a γ-world thus are not bare but natured. Dialectically or structurally, therefore, it is possible for a γ-ontologist to assay the spatial (temporal) distance between two places (moments) as an internal connection between them. As for distances, so for all other spatial and temporal relations. That is why I said places and moments are "meant to be" qualities among qualities. Dialectically, that is all that matters, of course.

The dialectic is one thing. Phenomenology is quite another. I have never encountered a coordinate quality. Nor, from what they tell us, have many others.[7] We have once more reached a point at which direct argument ends. I say direct because at some such points, and this is one of them, a question *about*, rather than *of*, ontology may usefully be raised and because one of the possible answers "saves" the proponents of coordinate qualities from the phenomenological cross they would otherwise have to bear. Of this presently.

[6] In the foil, we shall see, derived relations, like all derived things, are in a class all of its own, set apart from "simple" things in a way which makes the qualification in the parenthesis superfluous. But, then, there are derived connections commonly called relations for which the claim of internality would seem far-fetched to anybody. So I try to forestall puzzlement by mentioning for once simplicity.

[7] The doctrine that there are such entities is often called the "absolutist" view of space and time. I do not need the word and shall not use it, partly because there are several variants of such "absolutism." The γ-ontologists with whom I am concerned in this book all recognize coordinate qualities. This is not to say that their "absolutism" springs directly and solely from the overemphasis on things at the expense of facts which they have all inherited from Aristotle. On the other hand, though, it does become the only way they have of solving, at least after a fashion, the problem of individuation, as soon as that overemphasis is combined with the representationalism which they all share. Of all this later, in Part II.

We are ready to answer the first partial question. *All γ-ontologists take advantage of the structural possibility, assay all spatial-temporal relations as internal connections.* Accordingly, they all insist that there are coordinate qualities. This is a very high price to pay. Once paid, though, it enables one, not only to make all relations and (as we shall see) all nexus internal, but also to get rid of all bare entities. The resistance against the latter is, we know, as strong as any. This should increase the willingness to pay the price, particularly if one does not see the structural possibility of a world without bare particulars and with *some* external connections. The example I shall introduce in a moment demonstrates this structural possibility. This will be our *fifth step*. First, though, for a word of warning.

Remember the argument that makes nominalism the structural premiss of reism. The connections it claims do obtain and are, therefore, a part of the dialectic. Yet I warned you against it because, once the *whole* of the dialectic is unpacked, both nominalism and reism reveal themselves as direct structural consequences of the aversion against bareness, independently of the localization principle without which the argument cannot do. What we must beware of now is the opposite danger. In this section, I display the γ-ontologist's aversion against all external connections and argue that it is very strong, or, what amounts to the same, that it is the root of the connections issue as such. But the root is not the whole. In the next section, I shall show that there are other pushes and pulls, less deep yet anything but shallow, which by themselves suffice to account for the γ-ontologist's treating all connections equally, as it were, either assaying them *all as internal*, as in fact he does, or assaying them *all as nexus*, which (we shall see) is a structural possibility his tendency toward reism causes him to ignore.[8]

The third example is a modified nominalistic variant of γ. Its simple things are all qualities. Its qualities are all perfect particulars. Its ordinary things are all clusters of qualities. That makes it a nominalistic variant of γ. Its qualities are all ordinary; none is either a place or a moment. This is the negative half of the modification. Something is taken away; the phenomenological cross is lifted off the shoulders of anyone who propounds this ontology. That alone will not do, though. We must also enable him, by adding to his basic inventory, to provide

[8] Notice the contrast between the *all* at the end of this paragraph and the *some* at the end of the last. In the world described in the next paragraph only some connections, namely, the spatial-temporal relations, are external. In the world that will be considered in the next section all connections are external and, in particular, nexus.

the spatial-temporal relations with a ground. Let us see how that can be done.

Take in this world two ordinary things, α^1 and α^2, which agree exactly in all properties. E.g., they are both red; the ground of their sharing this property being two perfect particulars, say, a_1^1 "in" α^1; a_1^2 "in" α^2. That makes α^1 and α^2 the clusters $\gamma\,(a_1^1, \cdots, a_n^1)$ and $\gamma(a_1^2, \cdots, a_n^2)$, respectively. On the one hand, a_i^1 and a_i^2 being two, the clusters themselves are two and not one. On the other hand, there is no cue whatsoever, neither in the a_i nor therefore in the α themselves, concerning the distance. Hence we are in this world with respect to distance in the same situation in which, as we saw (p. 46), ϵ-ontologists find themselves in theirs, except that we have only one possibility where they still have two. They may assay distance as an external connection either between α^1 and α^2 or between the bare particulars which in their world are "in" them. In the world we are now exploring there are no bare particulars; hence we must assay the distance in question as an external connection between α^1 and α^2. This, however, we may consistently do in either of two ways.

First Alternative. All distances are assayed as nexus. That requires an infinite, or as I would rather say, an indefinite number of nexus, one for each distance. In this world there are *no universals*. A connection in it is either internal or external. All its external connections are nexus. The latter are *all homogeneous*.

Second Alternative. All distances are assayed as relations, i.e., as relational things, one for each distance, together with a *single* ternary nexus which is *inhomogeneous*. In this world there are relational *universals*. Connections are either internal or external. The latter are all relations.

Of the following three comments, the *first* shows that a certain difference between the two alternatives is not a good reason for preferring the second to the first; the *second*, that certain other differences provide γ-ontologists with a good reason for preferring the first to the second; the *third* spells out a lesson to be learned from both.

1. In the foil, or, for that matter, in any world with both nexus and relations, the (fundamental) nexus are few, the (simple) relations are many. This, to be sure, is not a matter of strict logic; yet it is, as surely, a matter of style.[9] Relations, being things, belong to the world's con-

---

[9] Goodman "derives" all relations, spatial-temporal as well as ordinary, from the single nexus he calls matching. Thus he adopts in this respect the ϵ-style. The "derivation" stands or falls with his phenomenalism. So it falls. For details, see Hausman. Let me add, though, since this is the last occasion for mentioning Goodman in this book, that to the extent his formalism recognizes at least im-

tent; nexus, being subsistents, to its form. And, though again as a matter of style rather than of strict logic, it is part of the form-content notion that the world's content is of a multiplicity, and of the variety that goes with it, which would ill suit its form. In the first alternative, there are many fundamental nexus; in the second, there is only one. Thus, if one applies the stylistic requirement, the second appears to be preferable to the first. The appearance deceives; for it makes no sense to apply the requirement since, for one, in the first alternative there are no relations at all but only nexus, and, for another, the latter structurally are but spatial-temporal relations which have been downgraded in ontological status. That leads to the next comment.

2. The nexus of the first alternative do the jobs of spatial-temporal relations. Yet they have the third aspect of all nexus. (This we remember from the first example.) That is why I just called them downgraded universals. One who extends the localization principle to everything (p. 49) will nevertheless reject them, claiming that (as we would put it) even though they are not as "independent" as things, they are yet "universals." This, however, is only one side of the story. To see the other, consider that one whose nominalistic tendencies, while strong enough to exclude universals, are yet not strong enough to exclude "universals," will, if faced with the choice between the two alternatives, have a good reason for preferring the first. Nor is this the only such reason. The other is that in the first alternative, but not in the second, all nexus are homogeneous. This leads to the last comment.

3. There is no bare particular in either alternative. This is our cue for some distinctions. The existence of a single bare particular (which is not completely disjoined from everything else) implies deductively that there is at least one external connection which is a nexus. The inference in the opposite direction is invalid. More precisely, the

---

plicitly the three fundamental nexus of his world, he is the only major γ-ontologist who does not share that deep-seated aversion against all external connections. Not that his explicit reism does not interfere. We have seen at some crucial points that and how it does. But if it didn't, he could explicitly and consistently hold what, things being as they are, he holds only implicitly and inconsistently, namely, that nexus exist and that all connections are nexus. Nor, as we know, does he shrink away from either universals or classes since, whatever he himself may say, structurally his qualities are universals and his sums are (that special kind of universals which are) classes. That is why I am prepared to maintain that structurally his ontology has grown from a single root, his aversion to inhomogeneous nexus. Thus he is right in proclaiming so emphatically his nominalism. All I would add is a pair of double quotes, calling him the most articulate and therefore most interesting and profound "nominalist" on record. See also nn. 10 and 12 of Section Two.

absence of bare particulars does not deductively imply that no connection is external. That is shown by both alternatives. One may attempt to save the equivalence by narrowing its scope. The existence of a single bare particular not completely disjoined implies deductively that there is at least one external connection which is an inhomogeneous nexus. But the absence of bare particulars does not deductively imply that there is no external connection which is inhomogeneous. That is shown by the second alternative. Thus the attempt fails.

The last comment is but the first of two lessons to be learned from the example. The second builds on the first. But it is so important and starts from an observation so striking that it deserves better than to be put at the end of a string of comments.

The history of philosophy is a graveyard of ontologies. Many are so sketchy that one doesn't know how to articulate them. Most of the rest turn out to be so patently inadequate that they hardly deserve to be called possibilities. Our example, in either variant, is at least as sturdy a possibility as any of the γ-ontologies of the tradition. Yet it has never been proposed. That is the observation I find striking. Or, if you please, the omission is glaring. Such an omission is a likely lead to some wrinkle of the dialectic. Let us follow this particular one.

A world's being without external connections deductively implies its being without bare particulars.[10] The inference in the opposite direction is invalid. In other words, the two claims, that there are no bare particulars and no external connections, are not deductively equivalent. Structurally, the mutual suggestion is no doubt strong, so strong that, as we use the word, one may speak of mutual entailment. The fact remains that the dialectic of the connections issue as such has two roots; one, call it the first, the aversion against bare entities; the other, call it the second, the aversion against external connections. This is the second lesson.

The total dialectic of an issue may be very intricate; yet it is always lucid and perspicuous; or so at least I firmly believe. The first root of the connections issue lying as deep as any, its dialectic would be neither lucid nor perspicuous unless the second lies as deep as the first. The price one is prepared to pay for avoiding something is a fair measure of how deep his aversion against it is. The coordinate qualities which all γ-ontologists introduce into their worlds are the price they

---

[10] Or, if you insist on complete accuracy, the bare particulars of a world in which there are no external connections, either because the whole issue has been ignored or because all connections have been assayed as internal, are completely disjoined from everything else. Such a world is not worth considering, not even, on second thought, by a serious theologian.

pay for avoiding external connections.[11] This price, I have claimed but not yet conclusively shown, is as high as any. If the claim is justified, then the two roots lie equally deep and as deep as any. So I shall try to establish the claim conclusively. But it will be better to postpone the job until after having taken the next step.

We are ready to examine the doctrine of internal connections as such. In the *sixth step* we shall probe it dialectically. In the seventh and last I shall present a direct refutation.

a_2 being higher[3] than a_1 is a fact.[12] By the doctrine of internal connections this fact is the collection $\{a_1, a_2\}$ and nothing else. From where I stand, not just in the foil but in general ontology, the doctrine thus violates at least one of two "premisses," namely, first, that *facts are entities*, and, second, that *a collection of two* (n) *entities is not as such a third* ((n+1)*st*). I, of course, accept both premisses. This, though, is now beside the point. The point is, rather, that while neither of the two is deductively implied by any others which lie deeper, structurally they have a common root. If we shall first unearth this root, we shall then be in a better position to counter dialectically what the proponents of the doctrine assert in the teeth of the two "premisses."

Some time ago I asserted that all γ-ontologists *blur the distinction between things and facts.* Probably this made sense to you, since, probably, you took it to be a reference to the impasse, accurately mapped in Section One, into which one gets by assaying both things and ordinary things as "things." But I also expressed myself more strongly, asserted that the γ-ontologists by first blurring the distinction eventually all arrive at *either overlooking or outright ignoring the category of fact.* This you probably took to be a rhetorical exaggeration since, very probably, you asked yourself how any ontologist could possibly either overlook or outright ignore all facts. Yet I meant what I said. So I must answer the question I suppose you asked yourself. First, though, let me state what is gained already.

An ontologist who distinguishes between (simple) things and complexes (facts) will tend to take the two "premisses" for granted even if he does not explicitly acknowledge that nexus exist. With this acknowledgement, the two "premisses" follow from the distinction. If, on the

---

[11] So far this has been shown only for the two kinds of relation. Presently I shall say what is here needed about nexus. The rest may safely be left until later.

[12] What is expressed by a (true or false) *sentence* (of an ideal language) is an (actual or potential) *fact*. Not that this formula proves or otherwise adds anything. It is merely the linguistic reflection of the basic notion of fact. But, then, these reflections have their use. In some contexts they help materially. And they are indispensable methodologically if, as is now so often the case, one has to defend the very possibility of metaphysics (ontology).

other hand, he finds himself in a world where all categorial entities are "things," then the assay of *at least some facts* (as I would call them) as mere collections of internally connected things becomes *at least less absurd.* Thus one may with *at least some initial plausibility* reject the two "premises." The common structural root of the latter is thus what I claim to be the irreducible difference between things and facts.[13]

Some surprises of the dialectic are but the shock of the familiar seen in a new light. The triple caution of the three clauses starting with 'at least' is really quite unnecessary. They merely announce a surprise of this sort.

Let us save words by using in this context 'fact' without prejudice for what in the foil is a fact. Then the question I must answer, put as strongly as possible, becomes: *How can any ontologist overlook or ignore any fact or mistake it for anything else?* The right answer begins with a distinction: *That depends on what kind of fact it is.*

(1) This is either red or not red. (2) a_2 is higher[3] than a_1. (3) This is green. Suppose that in the foil 'this' in (1) and (3) stands for the bare particular in a green spot. Then we know that in γ it stands for a cluster of which the quality that grounds green is a component while the one grounding red is not (p. 27). In the foil, (1), (2), and (3) are three facts. In the foil, (1) is a *formal* fact, or, as I have also called it, a fact in the world's form; (2) is an *a priori* truth; (3) is what is called *contingent*. Let us try to answer the question for each of these three kinds of fact in this order.

How can any ontologist fail to recognize the facts in the world's form for what they are? The answer is immediate. Virtually all philosophers have failed at this point and their failure is part and parcel of their reism. In this century, more than a generation ago, the error was proclaimed more emphatically than ever. That *the world's form is literally nothing* is the master thought of the first Wittgenstein. His only merit, from where I stand, is that he asked the question of the existence of the world's form, i.e., of the subsistents and of the analytic, more clearly and more urgently than any of his predecessors. His answer undid him. For, having once lost the world's form, he was, alas, profound enough eventually to lose its content. Thus everything was lost. The second Wittgenstein talks about language.

Historically, there is hardly a difference between (1) and (2). As the classical philosophers used the word and as it is still being used by almost everyone, to be a "fact" and to be contingent is one and the

---

[13] I say irreducible because at this point we have once more reached the end of argument except, of course, for the indirect support of my gambit by the bit of dialectic that follows in the text.

same. Structurally, there is a difference. At first blush, one might be tempted to say that the ontological status of (1) is even weaker than that of (2), which in turn is weaker than that of (3). Upon reflection, one sees that this makes no sense at all. Every (actual) fact, being independent₂, has the ontological status which in a very obvious sense is the highest of all. To insist on that, as I do, is not to deny, as I don't, that (1), (2), and (3) differ in a very important respect. The foil reflects their differences adequately and perspicuously in the trichotomy *formal-a priori-contingent*. That makes it redundant and therefore anything but perspicuous to reflect it once more by assigning different ontological status to (1), (2), and (3), respectively.

The heart of the matter is (3). How can any ontologist miss the contingent? Presently I shall propose an answer. First for two comments. One says nothing new. What is new in the other is merely anticipatory. Yet they should both help by showing that and how, so far at least, things hang together.

First. For one who holds the doctrine of the undifferentiated a priori, there is no difference between (1) and (2). Or, with a twist, for those holding this doctrine the temptation of overlooking, or ignoring, or mistaking, is as great in the case of the a priori as in that of the analytic (formal). The γ-ontologists with whom I am concerned all hold the doctrine. Eventually, I said, we would come to understand that as a structural consequence of their representationalism. Now I add that, as we shall also see, their representationalism virtually forces them to identify the factual with the contingent.[14]

Second. The connection, in γ, between *c* and *e* is very close; even closer than, in the foil, that established by ε. The closer the connection, the lower the ontological status of the connector (p. 52). One may be tempted to continue: the lower the status of the connector, the lower that of the facts it establishes. This, we just saw, makes no sense. But it seems to make very good sense to suggest instead that the weaker the connector in a fact is, the more easily the latter will be overlooked or ignored. To check whether the suggestion fits, consider the case of conjunction. In the foil 'and' does stand for a nexus. Yet this nexus is as weak as any. Thus one would expect it to be easily overlooked or ignored that, say, (*P* and *Q*) is just as much of a fact as either *P* or *Q*. The expectation is borne out. Otherwise the appeal of the odd doctrine that only atomic facts exist wouldn't be as great as it is.

---

[14] As for them, so for Wittgenstein. His failure to find a way out of the predicament of representationalism is the premiss. His eventual identification of the analytic and the a priori with the conventional is the conclusion. Nor is this connection just structural. It can be proved from the texts.

How could an ontologist possibly miss the contingent? How could he possibly either overlook or ignore the fact, (3), that *this is green* or mistake it for anything else? In ϵ he can't. That is part of the strength of this gambit. In γ the feat can be achieved. Provided one overlooks a certain premiss and fails to make certain distinctions, (3) is in γ only too easily mistaken for what it is not, namely, a formal truth. One who tends toward reism is only too likely to miss that premiss and those distinctions. All γ-ontologists tend toward reism. And we just saw how they manage either to overlook or ignore all formal truths or to mistake them for literally "nothing." That is how the feat is achieved. Now for the detail.

(a) Let 'c_1' and 'b' stand for the quality and the spot as assayed in γ. (3) becomes: c_1 *is a component of* b; in symbols: (4) $c_1 \subset b$. c_1 and b are both things. The former is simple; the latter, a cluster. At first blush one might therefore think of both 'c_1' and 'b' as names. As long as one does, I do not see how he could possibly overlook (4) or mistake it for anything but a fact. (b) 'b' is not really a name but, rather, an abbreviation for a successful definite description, namely (5) '$\gamma(c_1, c_2, \cdots, c_n)$'. *In a γ-world the kernel of fact in (3) is that (5) is successful.* There is no need for writing down the existential formula that stands for this kernel. But keep in mind that it states what I just called the premiss. (c) The premiss deductively implies (6) $c_1 \subset \gamma(c_1, \cdots, c_n)$. One who overlooks the premiss will hold that (4) and (6) are deductively equivalent and that, therefore, (6) by itself is the assay of (3). (d) Consider, in γ, (7) $c_1 \not\subset \sigma(c_1, \cdots, c_n)$; or, for that matter, in ϵ, (8) $c_1 < [c_1, \cdots, c_n]$. Since we are moving in γ, sums and (7) are more appropriate than classes and (8); but the difference makes no real difference for the three points which conclude the analysis. (e_1) Unlike (6), (7) and (8) are formal facts (analytic). (e_2) Failure to hold fast to the premiss on the one hand and failure to distinguish nicely among clusters (γ), sums (σ), and classes on the other are but two aspects of the same tendency toward reism which infects all γ-ontologists. Also, alas, they all ignore γ in favor of $\subset$, which apparently is even more easily confused with $<$, which in turn makes the distinctions even more difficult. (e_3) One cannot miss these distinctions without also missing that between (6) on the one hand and either (7) or (8) on the other. It follows that one who misses the premiss and the distinctions will, on the one hand, *mistake (6) for (3)* and, on the other, *confuse (6) with either (7) or (8)*. That concludes the structural[15] analysis of how the feat is achieved. Let me try

---

[15] While what I am *doing* in a large part of this book is *structural history*, I do not intend to *reargue* the case for this kind of enterprise. But the occasion is important. That is why for once I emphasize 'structural' in order to remind you that while a structural analysis illuminates both the dialectic and the tradition,

to state its gist in an image. The fact (3) is like a grain. As assayed in γ, its kernel is the premiss; its husk is (6). The γ-ontologists' reistic insensitivities cause them first to throw away the kernel and then to mistake the husk for what they mistake for literally "nothing." As you see, I did not indulge in rhetoric when saying that, incredible as it may seem, eventually they find themselves in a world without facts.

A major piece of dialectic has not only a root or roots from which it springs but also one or several centers around which it revolves. The structural analysis we just concluded illuminates one of the major centers of the dialectic and of the tradition which are, inseparably, the concern of this book. So I shall help you to remember it by giving it a name; call it *the story of the lost facts*. We have had a first intimation of it some time ago (p. 39). Now we have heard it in full; yet we have not exhausted it. Its ramifications are many; so we shall have to return to it. But I hope that enough has been said to make you feel some of the exhilaration that rises in me when an argument in hand suddenly both deepens and widens beyond expectation.

Return to the main line of thought. Two threads were left pending. These I shall now tie up. Then we shall take the seventh and last step, a direct refutation of the doctrine of internal connections.

Remember the second half of a certain question which still waits for an answer (p. 56). Can a γ-ontologist consistently extend his assay as internal from all relations to all nexus? Now I am ready to answer. That will tie up one thread (A). Remember next the claim I have made but as yet not conclusively argued (p. 61). The price the γ-ontologists pay by introducing coordinate qualities in order to be able to avoid all external connections is as high as any. Now I am ready to conclude this argument. That will tie up the other thread (B).

Ad A. Limit yourself to the fundamental nexus, then restate the question. Can γ itself in its own worlds consistently be assayed as an internal connection? Philosophers' arguments and answers all lie between two extremes. One is the butcher's axe; the other, the surgeon's scalpel. If you are satisfied with an axe-reply, you can have it immediately and without effort. All γ-ontologists are more or less explicit reists. Extreme reism denies that any nexus exists. To assert of a nexus that it is internal is merely a more decorous and perhaps more sophisticated way of denying that it exists. Here is your axe-reply. But I think we can do better. I shall wield the scalpel twice.

---

it is not a biographical (historical in the narrower sense) guess as to why this or that philosopher made this or that mistake. In general I couldn't care less; and even in the case of Brentano and Meinong I shall limit such guesses to the decent minimum which in a more detailed structural study is a useful and lively tool rather than an end in itself.

Not all γ-ontologists are extreme reists. Yet hardly any of them thought explicitly in terms of either γ or $\subset$. (This is not an unfair off-hand attack on γ. Remember that virtually every one was and is a reist.) Implicitly, as I just remarked, they all thought in terms of $\subset$. The only exception is Meinong, who, in his later life quite explicitly, thought in terms of γ. Eventually we shall come to appreciate that very much. Right now I shall follow the majority.

Take a γ-world so simple that there are only two categorial entities in each of its spots. One is a place, e.g., c_1; the other, a color quality, e.g., c_2. Suppose that there is a spot $\gamma(c_1, c_2)$. The question is, of course, whether the connection ($\subset$) in (9) $c_1 \subset \gamma(c_1, c_2)$ is internal.

All γ-ontologists mistake (9) for an a priori truth. To the two sources of this mistake we shall attend in a moment. Let me first show you how it yields a structural suggestion which is virtually irresistible. e being higher[3] than c is an a priori truth. Higher[3] is assayed as internal. As for higher[3], so for higher; as for higher, so for louder, brighter, and so on. If the connection is internal, then the fact in the case (or, more accurately, what the foil insists is the fact in the case) is a priori. The converse does not follow deductively. It does not follow, that is, that if a fact is a priori then the connection in it is internal. Structurally, however, the suggestion is virtually irresistible. A γ-ontologist who mistakes (9) for an a priori truth cannot but assay $\subset$ as internal. This was the first cut of the scalpel.

The two sources of the mistake are two blurs. One is the blur between γ and σ. Its cause and consequences are part and parcel of the story of the lost facts. The other is the blur most characteristic of nominalism. To clear it up we must first for a moment turn to the foil.

In the foil, the *colors*, green, red, and so on, are first-type characters. Each of them exemplifies the second-type character *Color* and is itself exemplified by some *particulars*. That makes for three levels, if I may so express myself. Whatever has Color also has Shape (and conversely). This is an a priori truth about Shape and Color. But it is simply false and therefore certainly not an a priori truth that whatever is red also is square (and conversely). Or, to say the same thing in a way better suited to our purpose, there certainly is no a priori connection between *this color*, e.g., red, and *this shape*, e.g., square. Nor, if *per absurdum* there were perfect particulars in the foil, would there be such a connection between *"this red"* and *"this square"* of a spot which in fact is both red and square.[16] In a nominalistic world there are perfect particulars

---

[16] The double quotes are to warn you against these phrases. Only a nominalist can use them safely in this context. I, as you must have noticed, avoid them consistently, use subscripts instead. E.g., I let 'red$_1$', 'red$_2$', and so on, stand for the perfect particulars which in a nominalistic world "fall under" red.

but neither colors nor Color, neither shapes, nor Shape, and so on. A nominalist, therefore, almost inevitably, will blur the three levels into one. That is the characteristic blur.

Assume now for the sake of the argument that there is Place and that there are places.[17] In this case there is an a priori connection (α) between Place and Color but not (β) between c_1 and (this cluster whose categorial constituents are c_1 and)[18] c_2. Nor will we be tempted to "infer" from α being a priori that β is. Not so the γ-ontologists who, since they are all nominalists, blur α and β into each other. How, then, can they resist the spurious "inference"? One merely has to ask the question in order to see the source and the strength of the second structural motive that drives them to assaying $\subset$ as internal. This was the other cut of the scalpel.

Ad B. I have never been presented with a coordinate quality. That is why I claimed that the price the proponents of the doctrine of internal relations pay for avoiding all external ones is as high as any. The claim is not conclusively established until two objections clever defenders of the doctrine might raise have been met. One, phenomenological, starts from the data of ontology; the other, methodological, or, as I would rather say, metaphilosophical, from a point on how to do ontology.

An objector states the first point as follows: Since you have not, as you say, ever encountered a coordinate quality in your own experience, you believe that I have tortured mine until it yielded the illusion of such encounter. For the sake of the argument, I grant your point. To use your image, the phenomenological cross I bear is heavy. My defense is that you are bearing one at least as heavy. The only difference is that you haven't yet noticed yours. Once, though, when you tried to present the case for my side, the scandal was almost out in the open. You had just suggested that someone be asked whether there was

---

[17] If *per absurdum* there were Place in the foil, each place would be exemplified by exactly one particular. In Part II this peculiarity will become very important. Now my sole purpose in calling attention to it is to forestall puzzlement. But there is also a reason why I deliberately use place and color, in spite of the peculiarity. Structurally, shape and color or pitch and loudness would have done as well. Psychologically, there is a difference. Since places are merely bare particulars in idiosyncratic disguise, the absurdity of an alleged internal connection between a place and a quality is more easily noticed. Meinong, who did notice it, made much of it! Of all this later, with due care and in considerable detail. The main purpose of the concise hints about Meinong and Brentano which I am beginning to scatter about is to arouse your curiosity.

[18] For this argument the difference between γ and $\subset$ makes no difference (except that if one operates with γ, as Meinong did, one is more likely to be struck by the absurdity mentioned in n. 17). At this point, as you see, arguing in terms of γ would have saved us the words in the parenthesis. But I preferred sticking to my guns.

a "fact" into which e and c entered, and, if there was one, what it was. Then you fairly admitted that the man asked would be puzzled by this use of 'fact' (p. 54). There, though, you stopped. So I put it to you now. It is phenomenologically absurd, as absurd as anything could be, to maintain that, the two things e and c being what they are, the former would not be higher[3] than the latter unless there were also, in addition to these two, a third thing, of the kind you call relational, and still another entity, of the kind you call nexus, and unless this fourth entity tied the other three, which you hold to be "completely external" to each other, into a "fact."

I reply as follows: I distinguish sharply between the phenomenological and the dialectical context. Sometimes, when simultaneously presented with the two pitches, I am also, strikingly, lucidly, and without any torture, presented with the interval as well as with the fact that it connects (obtains between) the pitches. To insist on that, as I do, is not to deny, as I don't, that the several entities presented on an occasion of this sort differ in "feel." Borrowing a kinesthetic image from the classical psychologists, one might wish to say, for instance, that while a pitch is more "palpable" than an interval, the latter is in turn more "palpable" than exemplification; just as Peter, the chair he now sits in, and his sitting in it are "adventitious" to each other in a way in which e, c, and higher[3] are not, which is but a way of calling attention to the difference in "feel" between Peter's sitting in his chair on the one hand and e being higher[3] than c on the other. All this is phenomenology without torture. Dialectically, my assay reflects the phenomenological differences between the several single entities by assigning them to several categories which differ in ontological status; the difference in "feel" between the two facts is reflected in the one being contingent, while the other is a priori. These ontological, or, if you please, dialectical distinctions must and (I submit) do reflect those of "feel." But *the former need not and cannot themselves have the "feel" of the former.* This, I suspect, is a distinction you fail to make. That is why mistakenly you see me carrying a cross which is not there. If my suspicion is justified then your mistake has two sources, one specific, one general. Specifically, you do not recognize that, for all the differences in "feel" and, accordingly, in assay, e being higher[3] than c is just as much a fact as is Peter's sitting in his chair. Generally, you probably do not distinguish the two contexts as sharply as one must and as I do. Notice, for instance, that I just resorted to the bookish 'adventitious' in order to avoid using 'contingent' in both contexts, thus leaving no doubt that the striking nonadventitiousness of certain facts and their a priori nature are two things and not one, which permits me to ground the former in the latter without asserting or even seeming to assert what would indeed be absurd, namely, that they are one and not two.

Here another defender of the coordinate qualities breaks in and asks leave to state the second objection: You assert that no one has ever encountered a coordinate quality. I agree. You believe, not only that the phenomenological and the dialectical context must be cleanly separated, but also that an accurate grasp of their interplay is indispensable for doing ontology. I agree. But I wonder whether your own grasp of that interplay is as accurate as it ought to be. For, if it were, since the task of ontology is to ground what is presented to us, why should you hesitate to "postulate" the coordinate qualities, even though they themselves are not presented, *provided only that they are a dialectical necessity*, i.e., that we cannot without "postulating" them account for what in fact is presented to us. I add, somewhat *ad hominem* and at any rate anticipatorily, that you are particularly ill advised in rejecting the coordinate qualities out of hand without considering the possibility of "postulating" them, since your own distinction between the two modes of actuality and potentiality, without which your own ontology cannot do and which, I gather, will eventually have its part in the enterprise upon which you are here engaged, is not, as you yourself introduced it, grounded in anything presented to us.

I answer as follows: "Postulation" is a method characteristic of science. In ontology it remains a possibility. As a matter of style, though, it should not be resorted to unless there is no other way out. Concerning the first part of your remarks, therefore, I rest my case on the clause italicized in the record I made of them. For it is of course the tenor of my argument as a whole that we are not dialectically forced to "postulate" coordinate qualities. Concerning the second part, I now merely wish to enter two claims whose defense I should like to postpone. I claim, first, that in the case of the two modes there is no other way out. I claim, second, that there is a significant difference between postulating (simple) qualities never encountered and the way I introduce the two modes.

My friend is willing to postpone these arguments. So we are ready for the direct refutation of the doctrine of internal connections which is our *seventh and last step*.

According to many philosophers, things are either "simple" or "complex." We do not apply 'complex' to things, speak instead of derived things, keep in mind that the (simple) things from which a further thing is derived are not literally "in" the latter. Thus we can also do without 'simple'. There are things and there are derived things. The only entities literally "in" a thing are itself and two subsistents.

One of these is existence; the other, either particularity or non-relational or relational universality. (I ignore for the time being the higher types and all but binary relations.) In what follows the two constituents of each thing which are subsistents will be ignored. A moment's reflection after you have read through the brief argument will convince you that considering them would make no difference.

(1) e is higher[3] than c. (2) f is higher[3] than d. We may safely take it for granted that the four qualities grounding the four pitches are things. Qualities are either perfect particulars or universals. If you take them to be the former, let (1) and (2) be about the four tones I just struck; if you take them to be universals, let (1) and (2) be about the four pitch universals in the case. Stopping for another moment's reflection after having read to the end, you will see that once more the difference between perfect particulars and universals makes no difference.

The two circumstances (1) and (2) share a feature, the interval. This feature must have a ground "in" each circumstance and this ground (or grounds) must manifest being the ground (or grounds) of the same feature. According to the doctrine of internal connections the ground of the feature "in" (1) lies wholly "in" e and c; its ground "in" (2), wholly in f and d. But there is nothing (no thing) "in" c but c itself, nothing "in" d but d itself, and so on. Thus the feature has no ground and the doctrine of internal connections stands (in this case) refuted.

A last-ditch defender of the doctrine who does not accept our general principle now tells us that the two grounds are the two collections $\{c, e\}$ and $\{d, f\}$. Another, who accepts the general principle, points at the two classes $[c, e]$ and $[d, f]$ as the two grounds. We first remind the second that in the γ-world he so stubbornly defends there are no classes. This point, though, important as it is, is relatively minor. So we brush it aside and ask both what there is "in" each of the two classes, or in each of the two collections, that manifests their being the grounds of the same feature. They have no answer. All they could do is deny that everything presented to us must have a ground, which is not just a general principle but the very idea of ontology. At this point we break off.

PARTS

U P to now we have assumed that space and time are atomic. That kept out certain issues. Now we drop the assumption. That forces us to face the group of issues which arise when one considers two spots such that one is a "part" of the other. To this group I refer here as the *new theme*.

In this section, I propose to uncover a certain structural tendency within γ. More precisely, I shall show that *the new theme, together with the failure to make a certain fourfold distinction, is the structural source of that tendency*. The demonstration will not require that we consider time. So we shall stay within a (temporal) cross section.

As we agreed to speak, without prejudice, connections are either nexus or spatial-temporal or ordinary relations. Nothing will be lost by limiting the first of these three kinds to the fundamental nexus. In the foil it is, quite explicitly, ϵ. In γ-worlds it is, implicitly, γ; hence their name; or, rather, as we saw (p. 64), it is $\subset$.[1] *The tendency I propose to demonstrate is to put all connections into the same ontological boat, as it were, by assaying them all as nexus.*

Extreme reists deny explicitly that any connection exists. Thus they put them all into the same ontological boat. If that were all I had in mind, it would be trivial. Nor of course is it. The limiting case merely determines my strategy. I shall consider a very special ontologist who explicitly recognizes the ontological status of γ and show how, under the pressures from the new theme and because of the blur which in his thought takes the place where the fourfold distinction ought to be, he is led to assaying both kinds of relations as nexus. In other words, I

---

[1] In this section it will not always be possible to avoid referring to $\subset$ and γ as nexus. So I remind you, once and for all, that they are merely pseudonexus as well as, once more, of the reasons for "countenancing" the irremediable blur. What follows is not only indispensable for a complete grasp of the tradition but also for the most part quite unaffected by the blur and therefore of intrinsic dialectical interest.

shall show how this ontologist, starting from γ, comes to hold that (1) all the connections which ϵ-ontologists insist are grounded in some entity or entities "outside" of the two they connect are indeed so grounded, but that (2) the grounds of all connections are dependent$_1$ entities of the kind which in the foil are called nexus. (1) states the extent to which this very special γ-ontologist agrees with those whose fundamental choice is ϵ. (2) circumscribes their disagreement. He assays both kinds of relations as nexus. Thus he finds himself in a world with, if I may so express myself, just as many connections as there are in an ϵ-world but which, unlike those of an ϵ-world, are all of the same category.

There never was an ontologist who held this view. That is why I call him and his world very special. Yet it is at least as sturdy a possibility as any of the γ-worlds which have been proposed. We have come upon another glaring omission. Such omissions, we know, provide leads to structural connections. This particular one leads to the structural connections among the new theme, the failure to make the fourfold distinction, and the tendency I promised to demonstrate. One reason this special ontology is as sturdy a possibility as any that has actually been proposed is that while, on the one hand, it takes one step in the direction of reism by depressing the ontological status of both kinds of relations, it is, once its viability has been noticed (and as long as the fundamental blur is countenanced), a position sufficiently articulate and perspicuous to resist, from it, any further step in that fateful direction. But there is also a reason why the characteristic feature of this in-between world might have the opposite effect, hastening the rush toward reism. To discover this reason, consider that while virtually everyone ignored the fundamental nexus, the two kinds of relation are much harder to overlook. That shows how this in-between position, even if only implicitly held, may make it easier to ignore all three; putting into the same boat, ontologically, what is less easily overlooked with what is almost universally ignored and thus easing one into reism, which is of course the position that ignores all three. But we have clearly reached the point where the causal way of talking about structural features becomes a game no longer worth the candle. What makes this special γ-world so sturdy a possibility is, above all, that it is as consistent as, and considerably more articulate than, any of those that have been proposed.

I am about to introduce the fourfold distinction. Then we shall be ready to follow the argument in detail. First, though, let me make a point you are probably able to anticipate. Extreme reism trivially obliterates the fourfold distinction. But, again, this is not all I have in mind. The point is, rather, that, even though eventually reism is at the root of it all, the distinctions are subtle and only too easily missed and that, therefore, the failure to make them and the tendency toward reism powerfully support each other.[2]

(1) Something may be a *component* of something; $a \subset b$. This is a (pseudo-)nexus among things. In γ-ontologies it is implicitly fundamental. (2) Something may be *contained* in something. In ϵ-ontologies this is a derived nexus between classes; $A < B$, or, expanded: $(x)(A(x) \supset B(x))$. In γ-ontologies, where sums (σ) do the jobs of classes, there is a corresponding nexus between a sum and what, as we once put it, is pseudocontained (p. 38) in it: $a \not< b$. (3) An entity may be a *constituent* of another. This is the basic ontological notion. In an improved language about the foil, or, for that matter, about any ontology with a completely articulated notion of complex, something's being a constituent of something else is not stated but shows itself; or, what amounts to the same, it is stated by speaking about the language; as, e.g., when pointing out that a being a constituent of $A_1(a)$ shows itself in 'a' occurring in '$A_1(a)$'.[3] That shows how, in this case at least, failure to completely articulate the notion of complex and the familiar error familiarly referred to as the confusion between speaking and speaking about speaking mutually support each other. The classical philosophers were, alas, not forewarned against this confusion. That is why the notion of being-a-constituent belongs in this list. (4) Something may be a *part* of something else. This is a connection I have so far deliberately ignored. The foil assays it as a relation between bare particulars. For this relation I saved the word 'part'. This is a very special and very narrow use of a very common word which is being used very broadly. As long as one so uses it, 'to be a part of something', 'to be a component of something', 'to be contained in something', and 'to be a constituent of something' are more often than not synonymous. Or, perhaps, being a part of something is the generic notion, of which the other three are species. Harmless as the broad use no doubt is in many contexts, it makes it harder to grasp the fourfold distinction. In philosophy, therefore, where the distinction proves crucial, the broad use has been disastrous. Except where the word is unmistakably part of an idiom— as in 'part of an idiom'—I shall always use it with the very special and very narrow meaning for which I saved it. When the broad use will have to be mentioned, it will be marked by double quotes.

---

[2] Remember what was said earlier (p. 57) about the intermediate level between roots and center.

[3] In writing '$A_1(a)$' instead of '$a\epsilon A_1$', I avail myself, as I often shall, of the *Principia Mathematica* notation.

Much of what will have to be said about parts I have only recently expounded in considerable detail.[4] So I shall avoid repetition by being at certain places very concise. Also, I shall limit myself to two examples. One, call it the first, is two concentric circles. The other, call it the second, is a square with one of its diagonals, say, that from the upper left to the lower right. Or, to be for once as explicit as one need not always be, I shall work with temporal cross sections of these two figures.

Take either example; ignore the inner circle or the diagonal, as the case may be. The area or extension of the figure is a bare particular. Its shape, circular in the one case, square in the other, is one of the characters (universals) exemplified by it. A single color spread over the whole area is another character it exemplifies. Put the diagonal back into the square. Paint one triangle red; the other, green. Take the diagonal out again (presently you will see why I say that). In this case the square particular is neither red nor green nor, of course, red and green. Rather, it exemplifies no color; only its "parts" do. The most obvious objections against assaying "areas" or "extensions" as bare start from the spatial connotations of 'area' and 'extension'. My answers to these objections belong to what I shall not repeat.

The connection I call *being part of* is exemplified by the areas of the inner and the outer circle. The former is part of the latter. (Again, if the lines bother you, as perhaps they should before certain things will have been said, paint the area of the inner circle one color, enough of the outside of the outer circle another, then "remove" the lines.) This connection, call it (a) for the moment, I assay to be a relation, i.e., an entity of the same category as (b) being-higher[3]-than, which connects e and c and the relation of (c) being-rounder-than between shapes. In the first example, for instance, the shape of the inner circle is *rounder* than that of the outer one. Yet there is a difference between (a) on the one hand and (b) on the other. (a), being exemplified by particulars, is of the first Russellian type, (b) and (c) are of the second. Thus they belong to different subcategories. Both (a) and (c) are spatial; (b) is not. In the second example, each of the two triangular particulars is a part of the square one. Also, the latter is the "Sum" of the two former. Of that presently.

We shall have to stay with the foil a bit longer. Thus it should help to give you a sense of direction if we cast a quick glance at what goes on in the other camp. What I assay as a particular, which is bare, a γ-ontologist assays as a place, which is a quality. He does use the word I use when saying of one area that it is "part" of another. If, however, he

<hr>

[4] See the essay "Synthetic *a priori*" in *Logic and Reality* (University of Wisconsin Press, 1964).

were familiar with my use of 'constituent', he would insist that to be a constituent and to be a "part" is one and the same. Thus, though we use the same word, we do not mean the same thing. In the foil, one particular's being part of another implies no more the former's being a constituent of or "in" the latter than e being higher than c implies that e is a constituent of c. That shows the impact of assaying being-part-of as a relation. I suppose you are puzzled.

Turn back to the passage, in the paragraph next to the last, where I called one circular shape *rounder* than the other. That, too, may have puzzled you. Quite possibly, you did at first not even understand, then decided that, willfully and artificially, I call a "curve" (at one point) rounder than another (at another point) if and only if the "radius of curvature" of the one (at that point) is smaller than that of the other (at that other point). I spoke deliberately, of course, though not I think either willfully or artificially. What is artificial, even though customary, is to speak about space in terms of the axiomatic system or calculus known as geometry, Euclidean or otherwise. The cause of its being customary is of course the notorious success of interpreting the geometrical calculus into space.

Space is perceptual, or, if you prefer the word, phenomenological. That is one thing. The "space" of Euclidean or any other geometry is another thing. The "space" of that partially interpreted axiomatic system which physicists speak and think of as "physical reality" is still another.[5] What I mean by 'space' are not those "spaces" but space. The way I used 'rounder' draws attention to that. That makes the way I spoke the only proper one. In ontology, the geometrical way is not only artificial but also confusing. "Extensionless points," for instance, are the simples, or among the simples, of many geometries. In space, on the other hand, or so at least I shall argue, there are no extensionless points. Again, unless one distinguishes between space and "spaces," it will seem to him that "indivisible areas" and "extensionless points" being contradictories, he has no other choice than one of these alternatives, either of which is disastrous. Nor does this particular disaster depend on whether areas are assayed as bare particulars or as qualities. Of all this presently.

The square particular (c), I said, is the "Sum" of the two triangular ones (a, b). You surely noticed the capital letter and the quotation marks. I shall drop the latter but keep the former, in order to distinguish between the two meanings or uses of 'sum', represented by 'σ' and 'S', in γ and ϵ, respectively. In the case of σ, you will remember, I limited myself to finite sums. In the case of S, I shall go even further,

---

[5] See the essay "Physics and Ontology" in *Logic and Reality*.

stay with pairs, brush aside everything that is either mere routine or the business of the mathematicians.

The γ-meaning. σ is the familiar pseudonexus, a function (definite description) mistaken for a nexus that ties "things" into "complexes" which are themselves "things." Its only peculiarity, which enables sums to do the jobs of classes, is that it actually connects any two things. In other words, all substitution instances of '$σ(x, y)$', "name" something. (For γ this is of course not so. '$γ(a, b)$', for instance, is a "complex name" that fails.)

The ε-meaning. Let '$(Pt(x, y)$' stand for the fact that x is part of y and consider the following proposition: *For any two areas,* a, b, *there is one and only one other,* c, *such that (1)* Pt(a, c) *and* Pt(b, c) *and (2), if* Pt(d, c), *then, for each* x *such that* Pt(x, d), *either there is a* y *such that* Pt(y, x) *and* Pt(y, a), *or there is a* z *such that* Pt(z, x) *and* Pt(z, b), *or both.* In the foil this proposition is an a priori truth about space. If it is true, then the definite description starting with 'the area such that', which is based on it, will be successful for any two areas a, b. '$S(a, b)$' is an abbreviation of this description. What it describes, reflection on the proposition will tell you, is c, or, if you please, the total area of a and b. (You realize no doubt why I avoid 'sum', resort to 'total area'.)

I repeat. Completely articulated, σ and S are both functions. The major difference in this respect is that while S is in ε recognized for what it is, σ is in the γ-manner mistaken for a nexus. They also agree in both being universally successful. But there is again a major difference. *The universal success of σ is but the idiosyncratic expression of the nature of all classes, whatever their members may be; that of* S *is, quite uniquely, a consequence of the most fundamental of all a priori truths about bare particulars, or what amounts to the same, about space and time.*

Let me add two comments. They shouldn't be necessary; yet they might help, and I want to be as clear as I possibly can. One. The success of '$S(a, b)$' does not depend on a and b being contiguous, as in the example. Any two areas will do. In this respect, too, Sums (S) and sums (σ) are alike. Two. Since S neither is a nexus nor is being mistaken for one, $S(a, b)$ is not and need not be a complex (or "complex") whose constituents (or pseudoconstituents) are a and b, just as the son of Peter and Mary, assuming that they have one, does not have either Peter or Mary among his constituents, or, if you please, is not made out of them, except in a sense that is clearly irrelevant.[6]

Perhaps you are no longer as puzzled as I supposed you were when first told that in the foil areas are assayed as bare particulars although

---

[6] All I am doing, as I trust you see, is elaborating the dichotomy function-complex.

they have parts and may even be disconnected. This assay, however, has a consequence which, if it has occurred to you since, may have puzzled you even more, although for no better reason. This consequence I shall discuss next. But it will pay if we first take a closer look at the bareness of the bare particular.

Every complex, even if as elementary as this-being-green, has a structure, and conversely. Every derived thing, even if as elementary as being-both-green-and-square, has a structure, and conversely. If you disagree, you will have to tell me what you mean by 'structure'. Pitches and colors have (are) *natures*. But, being neither complexes nor derived things, they have no structure. *To be bare is to have neither nature nor structure.* The particulars of the foil, being mere individuators and nothing else, are bare. To insist on that is merely to take the crystal of Aristotelian prime matter and break it into a myriad splinters, as it were. More literally, the bare particulars of the foil are not derived things. The point is so important that I shall support it by three comments. The third merely proposes a phrase which will help us to keep it before our minds.

(1) The linguistic vehicle of derivation is definition. That much we know already. Eventually we shall see that all derived things are represented by defined predicates. An expression representing a bare particular is either a name or a definite description. This shows, in the linguistic reflection, that a bare particular could not possibly be a derived thing. (2) In the foil, there are things and derived things. In γ-worlds, "things" are either "simple" or "complex." Hence, if *per absurdum* there were bare particulars in a γ-world, they would have to be "simple." (3) *Bare particulars could not possibly be either complex or "complex" or derived.* In other words, they have *neither constituents nor pseudoconstituents nor quasiconstituents* (p. 13). Since we do not need 'simple' to qualify 'thing', let us use it to express this idea. *All bare particulars are simple.*[7]

Remember now what we were about before I took time out for this brief digression on natures, structures, bareness, and simplicity. I promised to discuss a consequence of the proposition that bare particulars (areas) are simple.

[7] How about a disconnected area, e.g., the total area of a triangle, a square, and a circle outside of each other? Some may balk at the idea that even in this case "there is no structure." There is structure indeed; only it is not "in" the four areas as such but, rather, in the facts that no two of the three partial ones overlap, that the total one is their Sum, that each of the three partial ones has the shape it has. The total one, by the way, could consistently be considered as having literally no shape at all, just as an area which is not monochromatic literally has no color.

Turn to the second example, the triangular particulars a and b and their Sum, $S(a, b)$ or c, which is square (A_1). c being A_1 is a fact. Call it α. For what follows it makes no difference whether or not A_1 is a derived thing. So I assume that it is not. Hence, *if* c *is simple*, α is atomic and its assay is $A_1(c)$.

The Sum of a and b being square is a fact. Call it β. Its assay is $A_1(S(a, b))$. That shows that the three things A_1, a, b are among the constituents of β. So is Pt; for '$S(a, b)$' is merely an abbreviation such that in the expansion of '$A_1(S(a, b))$' the name 'Pt' occurs. But there will be no need for mentioning this fourth thing "in" β. So I shall ignore it.

α and β either are or are not *the same fact*. If they are, then they have, necessarily though not sufficiently, the same constituents. This is not possible unless 'c' is merely an abbreviation for an expression representing a complex, among the constituents of which are a and b. If so, then c is not simple. We have arrived at a remarkable conclusion. *One who holds that* c *is simple must also hold that* α *and* β *are not the "same" fact.*

In the foil, α and β are indeed two and not one. Nor is the distinction *ad hoc*. The context or contexts which helped me to recognize it are quite different. Nor of course do I reject, whatever that may mean, all uses of 'same'. I merely call attention to a threefold distinction I have made among them.[8]

(1) Upon the first use, which is the loosest, 'P' and 'Q' represent the $same_1$ fact if and only if one can be obtained from the other by replacing names with proper descriptions. This is the case of α and β. They are the $same_1$ fact. So are Caesar's having been murdered and Calpurnia's husband having been murdered. (2) Upon the second use, which is stricter than the first but looser than the third, the facts represented by 'P' and 'Q', respectively are the $same_2$ if and only if 'P if and only if Q', is analytic. Since the proposition which makes all substitution instances of '$S(x, y)$' successful descriptions, though synthetic a priori, is not analytic, this is not the case of α and β. They are not the $same_2$. (3) Upon the third use, which is the strictest, "two" facts are one and the $same_3$ if and only if they yield the same assay. α and β, we saw, are not the $same_3$. In ontology, the relevant use is the third. Otherwise, it would not be ontology. Except for unmistakably idiomatic contexts, I have not in this book used 'same' in any other sense. Nor shall I. One who remains unaware of this threefold distinction cannot do justice to the ontological status of the connectives nor master the dialectic of intentionality. Not surprisingly, these are the two contexts in which I

---

[8] See, for instance, pp. 95–97 of *Logic and Reality*.

first made use of it. The simplicity of bare particulars I now add, not *ad hoc*, as a third.

Our friend, the special γ-ontologist, has been waiting in the wings for quite some time even though we have as yet not gathered more than a part of what it takes, by way of contrast and background, to understand completely what he does and why he does it. But I am ready to have a first go at it provided you permit me to assume that there is something he takes for granted. Why he, and not just he alone, does that we shall understand presently, after having attended to the rest of the background.

Suppose that the spot α is white. In the foil that makes c, A_1 (square) and A_2 (white) the things "in" it. a and b, though parts of c, are not "in" α. Our friend assays the entities I assay as a, b, c, A_1, A_2 as five qualities, a_1, a_2, a_3, a_4, a_5, respectively. Whether these qualities are universals or perfect particulars is still left open. Nor does it matter. α itself is assayed as the cluster of a_3, a_4, a_5.

a_1, a_2, a_3 are coordinate qualities of the kind called places. About the connections among them our friend speaks as I do, says that a_1 and a_2 are "parts" of a_3. Yet he does not mean what I mean. For *he takes it for granted that places are not simple.* How, then, will he assay the connection between, say, a_1 and a_3? The answer is not difficult.

His ordinary things are clusters. A constituent in his world is therefore either a quality or $\subset$. (I assume that even though he recognizes that $\subset$ exists, he is like all other γ-ontologists in ignoring γ.) Thus, if he were the reist which by special dispensation he is not, he would use 'component' and 'constituent' synonymously and hold that the only constituents of an ordinary thing are the qualities which are "in" it. Add now the supposition, which is only too realistic, that he does not distinguish between 'component' and 'constituent' on the one hand and 'part' on the other; remember that he takes for granted that a_1 and a_2 are "parts" of a_3; and you will see how he is driven to conclude that a_1 and a_2 are two "constituents" or "components" of a_3. Nor does our special friend's recognition of $\subset$ save him from this drift. The only difference is that when he asserts a_1 and a_2 to be two components of a_3, he will recognize the ontological status of the (pseudo-)nexus represented by '$\subset$' in '$a_1 \subset a_3$' and '$a_2 \subset a_3$'. (If he recognized γ and σ, he might add either, consistently, that a_3 is $\gamma(a_1, a_2)$ or, inconsistently, that it is $\sigma(a_1, a_2)$.)

A useful bit of pedantry will provide a breather. Since our friend holds both $a_1 \subset a_3$ and $a_3 \subset \alpha$, and since $\subset$ is transitive, he will also hold that $a_1 \subset \alpha$. That makes every part of the area of the spot a "part" or "component" or "constituent" of the spot itself. In the foil both being a part and being a constituent are transitive. But they are two and not one. In the foil, therefore, even though *a* is a part of *c* and *c* is a constituent of α, it does not follow that *a* is either a part or a constituent of α. If you now remember what has been said about α and β not being the same$_3$, you will once more see that and how things hang together.

Let us take stock. I promised to show how the pressures of the new theme may lead an ontologist who starts from the recognition of $\subset$ to assaying both kinds of relation as nexus. What I have just shown is how he will be led to assay *one spatial relation*, namely, *Pt*, not just as a nexus but outright as $\subset$. In this demonstration the pressures of the new theme were represented by the premiss[9] that places are not simple; the role of the fourfold distinction, or, rather, of the failure to make it, by the tendency not to distinguish between "parts" on the one hand and "components" or "constituents" on the other. Thus I have already fulfilled part of my promise. To fulfill the rest, I must do two more things. I must show how the structural suggestion plausibly spreads from *Pt*, first to all other spatial and temporal relations, then to all ordinary ones. And I must trace the premiss to its sources. It will be best if we attend first to the premiss. That requires that we bring in the rest of what the new theme provides by way of background and contrast.

Remember the distinction between space and "space," between the ontology (phenomenology) of the former and the geometry of the latter. Euclidean "space," or, rather, any of those axiomatizations of it which have affected philosophers more deeply than others, is an uninterpreted calculus whose "lines" and "areas" are "classes" of "points"; the "points" themselves are "extensionless" or "indivisible," also "simple" in the sense of themselves not being classes of anything. As far as I can see, that is all 'extensionless point' means in this context. Nor do I know what it could possibly mean in any other. Be that as it may, the geometricians think of areas as "classes" of "extensionless points." That is a very major feature of their schema. This feature is the source of a fallacious way of thought common to that vast majority of philosophers who, because of the schema's success, more or less crudely confuse it with space. These philosophers all think of areas as classes of points. Call this the *basic fallacy* (about space). To see that it is one, one merely has to consider that an area cannot be just a class of extensionless points, or, to borrow from the geometricians another word with overtly ontological overtones, that it cannot just "consist" of such points, but that there must also be those connections among the

---

[9] It will save words without doing any harm if I call premiss what I suppose our friend takes for granted.

latter by virtue of which one area is connected, another disjoined, one square, one round, and so on. But, then, once a philosopher has fallen under the spell of the mathematicians, he is only too likely to miss the obvious.

A victim of the basic fallacy has no choice. He cannot but take for granted that no area is simple. It has not taken us long to discover within the new theme the source of the pressure that pushes our special friend, and not just him alone, toward the premiss. Two brief comments will establish the point beyond doubt. A third, which will take a bit longer, rounds it out by using the crucial distinction between the space of our world and the "space" of the mathematicians for the purpose of completely unraveling the dialectic of divisibility, an issue very prominent in the tradition which, as we shall see, Brentano worried all through his career.

First. Suppose that the areas a and b are two classes of extensionless points, A and B.[10] Then a will be a part of b ($Pt(a, b)$ in the foil, or, in the special γ-world, $a \subset b$) if and only if A is contained in B ($A < B$). If you now remember the broad use of 'part' which makes not only a "part" of b but also A "part" of B, you will see how the basic fallacy and the failure to make the required distinctions structurally support each other. (This time, we utilized the shift from 'being a part' to 'being contained'; last time, that from 'being a part' to either 'being a component' or 'being a constituent'. Having thus connected all the four terms of the distinction, we shall not need to return to it.)

Second. The basic fallacy, I said, consists in assaying areas as classes (of extensionless points). Perhaps you noticed that it would have been more consistent to say that committing the fallacy consists in assaying areas as collections. But, then, we know that classes and collections are only too easily confused; either trivially, if one is an explicit reist, or more subtly, if finding one's self in a context which carries a strong reistic suggestion. That is why I saved this comment until now and why I now take the opportunity to point out that, however vague or naive the geometricians' ontology and, accordingly, their notion of class may be, the basic fallacy carries a strong reistic suggestion. Areas, if I may so express myself, are so palpably there and so manifestly do so very well in holding their "points" together, apparently without any

---

[10] If you are sensitive to this sort of thing, you will notice that I have run out of letters for a notation which is completely consistent without being too clumsy. Notice, too, that since I am analyzing the effect which the basic fallacy has in γ, I should speak of sums rather than of classes and of $\lessdot$ rather than of $<$. But this difference, we know, is merely idiosyncratic. Besides, the basic fallacy is not by any means limited to γ.

glue. Apparently without any glue! That is the temptation, of course. I venture the opinion that reism in general has drawn strength from its specious plausibility in this particular case.

Third. Take a sheet of paper. Paint part of it one color, the rest another. Or cut it into several pieces without dislocating any of the pieces. In either case you will have "divided" a particular into several parts. More precisely, after you have done what I asked you to do, there will exist what wouldn't have existed if you hadn't done it, namely, several particulars such that, first, each of them is a part of the one which is in the original sheet and, second, the latter is their Sum. (The illustration overflows the temporal cross section; what is being illustrated does not.)

Having divided the sheet, you may divide its parts. Can the procedure be iterated indefinitely? The answer is No. Eventually the area will be so small that no brush or knife will be fine enough to divide it. Hence, some may wish to argue, there are atoms of space, indivisible extensions. Or, at least, an atomist could not do better than to adduce this fact in support of his claim. To my mind, the support is not strong enough. The "last" area, i.e., the one to which we can no longer successfully apply either brush or knife is still something which if we could apply them, would have parts. In other words, the particular exemplifying a shape, which is the thing I see as long as I see anything at all, is the sort of thing that is divisible. Still differently, I have not the slightest idea what one who speaks about space (not "space"!) could possibly refer to when speaking about indivisible areas. *The "last" area is neither "indivisible" nor, whatever that might mean, an "extensionless point."* There is neither paradox nor any other difficulty in this proposition. The contrary impression, which unhappily dominates the tradition, has two sources. (1) In "space" there are only two alternatives. Either there are extensionless points or there are areas which are indivisible.[11] *Tertium non datur.* We escape between the horns of the specious dilemma by distinguishing between space and "space." (2) Interpreting the Euclidean calculus into space requires counterfactual assumptions of the kind called idealizations. One of these is that the division of areas can be iterated indefinitely. That permits, with notorious success, the interpretation of "extensionless points" into certain infinite series of areas. This is but the beginning of a long story, of course. But the story is familiar. Nor do the details matter. What matters is, rather, that those philosophers who, because of the spectacular success

[11] The mathematical qualifications which that requires, concerning point sets which are not areas, are quite unimportant.

of this interpretation, failed to distinguish between "space" and space, threw away the key to the dialectic of "divisibility."

(One who holds that there are no "extensionless points" in space, must consistently also hold, as I do, that there are neither "lines" without breadth nor "surfaces" without width.—We may safely stay within two dimensions.—One who uses either 'point' or 'line' when speaking about space speaks therefore merely of areas of very special kinds and shapes. What I am really presented with when presented with the diagram one associates with the first example, for instance, are four areas. I need not, I think, continue. You understand now why at the beginning of this section I suggested twice that in case they bother you, you remove the lines, use the paint brush instead.)

There is only one task left. We must show how the suggestion to assay all connections as nexus plausibly spreads, first from Pt to all other spatial-temporal relations, then to all ordinary ones.

Our friend assays the connection between a_1 and a_3 as an occurrence of the fundamental nexus of his world ($a_1 \subset a_3$). A perfectly natural way of referring to this connection is to say that one area lies *inside* of another. (You will appreciate my using 'inside of' instead of 'in' if you remember that I use the latter to express one entity's being a constituent of another, in which case, however, I surround it by double quotes.) Take now two areas which are *outside* of each other; two others which are *contiguous*, like the two triangular areas in the second example. Clearly, to be inside, to be outside, to be contiguous are so very much alike, so very much the same sort of thing, that no ontologist will assign them to different categories. I, of course, assay them all as relations, which are things. Our friend, having identified one of them as an occurrence of his fundamental nexus, will assay all three of them as nexus. To say that he has a structural reason for doing that is an understatement. What else could he reasonably do?

Having shown how the plausibility spreads from the one crucial spatial relation (Pt, inside) to two others (outside, contiguous), I shall not, I trust, jump too big a gap by taking it for granted that it spreads in the same way to all others. That leaves the ordinary relations. We must convince ourselves that our friend has good structural reasons for and no such reasons against putting, say, the distance between two areas and the interval between two pitches into a single category. But, then, that is virtually obvious. In his ontology an area is a place and places and pitches are both qualities. Next to the fact that their fundamental nexus is homogeneous this is indeed the most salient feature of all γ-ontologies. Pitches and places are thus in the same category. Could there be a better structural reason for also putting both sorts of connections, those between places and those between pitches, into a single category? Nor is there in our friend's world any reason or suggestion that would keep him from doing just that.

We have come to the end of a long line of thought. Unless I am mistaken, I have proved the proposition I set out to prove: *In a γ-ontology which recognizes the need for a fundamental nexus there is a structural suggestion to assay all connections as nexus.* As we know, no γ-ontologist has clearly recognized the fundamental nexus. Like virtually everyone else, they are all more or less explicitly reistic. How, then, one may ask, does the proposition help us to understand the positions they actually held? I have answered this question at the beginning. But it may help if I conclude by repeating the answer. The insight we gained leads us to expect and, should the expectation be justified, to understand a certain feature of the γ-ontologies which have actually been proposed. *γ-ontologists treat all connections equally badly or equally well, putting them into the same ontological boat, as it were.* Brentano, we shall see, treats them all very badly. For he is an extreme reist, although he is aware of the difference between a sum and a cluster and tries to account for it in his way. Meinong, on the other hand, in his heroic though futile struggle against reism, tries to do *equal* justice to all connections by the *same* means. This is indeed, as we shall see, part of the job his "ideal objects" are supposed to do.[12]

---

[12] In Part IV we shall see that his distinction between *real* and *ideal* relations makes the generalization a bit too sweeping. Here, though, it helps and will do no harm.

PERFECT PARTICULARS AND UNIVERSALS

CONSIDER two or more spots of *exactly the same* shade. In other words, the several spots have exactly the same color property. I continue the practice, which will do no harm, of using the color words as if each of them were the name of a single shade rather than, ambiguously, of each of a whole class of such. The gambit that there are no two spots of exactly the same shade I dismissed at the very beginning (p. 6). The intellectual motive behind it is obvious. If there were no two ordinary things having exactly the same property, universals would have no job to do. To take for granted, as I do, that there are such ordinary objects is one thing. To take for granted, as I don't, that there are universals is quite a different thing. The difference reappears in two phrases. The property, I said, is exactly the same, not *literally the same*. 'Exactly the same', as I use it, carries no ontological commitment.[1] It merely refers to a situation which presents a certain ontological problem. 'Literally the same' I use only in ontological discourse such that 'to be literally the same', 'to be one and not two', and 'to be the same₃' are synonymous.

The problem presented by the situations whose existence I take for granted is familiar. What is the ontological ground of the two spots' having exactly the same color? Either the ground is a single thing which is "in" both spots. Such things are called *universals*. Or the ground is two things, one "in" each spot. Such things are called *perfect particulars*. Except where the context leaves no doubt a word representing a universal will be capitalized; lower-case initials and subscripts will be employed in referring to perfect particulars. E.g., one of the two articulate solutions of the problem holds that the ground of the two spots' having exactly the same color is Red; the other, that it is red₁ and red₂. That merely formalizes conventions we observed on earlier occasions.

---

[1] Nor of course does 'property'.

*Realists*₁ hold that there are bare particulars and universals but no perfect particulars.[2] Articulate *nominalists* hold that there are perfect particulars but neither bare particulars nor universals. *Virtually all γ-ontologists are more or less explicit nominalists.* The most noteworthy recent exceptions are the early Husserl, and Goodman. At Goodman's world we glanced. The realism₁ of the early Husserl is Platonistic.

Even though virtually all γ-ontologists are nominalists, I have so far refrained from committing them (if I may so express myself). Verbally that was achieved by putting a very common word to a very special use. A quality, as we agreed to use the word, is either a universal or a perfect particular. The agreement had two purposes, one general, one specific. Its general purpose was to bring together, and thus get a clear view of, all the distinctions between ε and γ which do not depend on the universals issue;[3] or, just to rehearse the agreed-upon use, which do not depend on whether the "qualities" of a γ-world are perfect particulars or universals. This general purpose has been fulfilled. The specific purpose is comparable to that which an anatomist pursues when he provides a clear view of, say, a nerve by ablating some of the tissues which surround it. Specifically, my purpose is to provide a clear view of the structural connection between the doctrine of internal connections and nominalism—or, if you please, between the connections issue on the one hand and the nominalism-realism issue on the other—by "ablating" all other issues which impinge upon or interact with the latter. Thus to disencumber this connection is the first task I have set myself in this section. Canceling right away the agreement about 'quality' will not make it more difficult. But we cannot afford to waste a good word. Since the "simple" things of the ontologies we shall have to consider are all perfect particulars, we shall save ink and breath by agreeing to use henceforth 'quality' so that *a quality is a perfect particular.*

The problems or intellectual motives dialectically connected with the nominalism issue are of two kinds. Some are rather shallow. Some lie very deep; or, at least, they lie deeper than the issue itself.

Among the shallow motives which caused and still cause philosophers to embrace nominalism two stand out. One is the localization

[2] For the distinction between realism₁ and realism₂ see p. 22. I shall have to say a good deal about both; hence the subscripts. Yet there are many contexts such as, e.g., the whole of this section, in which there is no doubt which of the two is meant. In such contexts I shall often suppress the subscript.

[3] The "universals issue," the "realism-nominalism issue," or, briefly, the "nominalism issue" are one and the same. I am sure that there is no doubt about that in your mind. But I prefer wasting a footnote to causing you even a moment's hesitation on anything so fundamental.

principle. The other is exaggerated anti-Platonism, which is a fallacy connected with the rejection of Platonic universals. The arguments they inspired are numerous. Each has several variants. Each variant has been repeated over and over. Neither variation nor repetition has improved them. Nor are these arguments just shallow; they are also very familiar. Those connected with the localization principle we disposed of in Section Three. To those connected with exaggerated anti-Platonism we shall presently devote a few paragraphs. First for a comment to show how and why at this point our strategy pays off.

In the preceding four sections the nominalism issue has been mentioned again and again. A few times a putative connection was disclaimed. On most of these occasions, however, attention was called to some structural connection between the nominalism issue on the one hand and one of those which at the time occupied us at the other. That these latter issues are all independent of, or, synonymously,[4] that they lie deeper than the nominalism issue, we know from the way we proceeded. That is where the strategy pays off. There is now no further need for either reviewing or disentangling these connections, all of which are either partial or indirect[5] or both. All that remains to be done is to call attention to the one connection which is neither partial nor indirect. *The "existence" of at least one internal connection is the structural premiss; nominalism, the structural conclusion.* This is the connection I have in mind. To demonstrate it is the *first task* of this section. Let me begin with a reflection about what is deep and what is shallow; then I shall say what has to be said about exaggerated anti-Platonism; after that we shall be ready for the task.

The issue of internal connections lies as deep as any. That makes its direct connection with the nominalism issue a matter of great *structural import*. The localization and exaggerated anti-Platonism issues are both shallow. Of the former I have shown that already; of the latter I shall show it in the next few paragraphs. First, though, I want to make another attempt to forestall misunderstanding by repeating for both what has been said already about the former (p. 49). Shallowness is one thing; effectiveness, or, on a larger scale, *historical import*, is another. Let no one believe that because I do not admire certain arguments, I underestimate the weight which they have carried through the centuries and, alas, still carry. It can hardly be overestimated. But, then,

---

[4] I say synonymously because to be thus independent is the very meaning of 'lying deeper', as I use the phrase in ontological contexts.

[5] Let A and B be the joined structural premisses; C, the structural conclusion. In this case I say that either A alone or B alone *partially* implies C. Let A structurally imply B; B, structurally imply C. In this case I say that A *indirectly* implies C.

to repeat that, too, making this weight the measure of one's admiration is historicism at its worst.

A Platonic universal is a universal that is *separable*. The two halves into which you divide a square piece of paper by cutting it along one of its diagonals are separable from each other. Each of the two halves *can* exist or *could* exist "by itself" even if the other would not exist, had never existed, or would cease to exist. That is what in ontology it means to be "separable," except that the 'can' and the 'could' require specification. So far we have encountered three degrees of impossibility and necessity. Here we have come upon the fourth. What is impossible₄ is what contradicts a synthetic a posteriori generality of the kind called a law of nature. To be possible₄ is to entail no such contradiction. This is the weakest degree of impossibility. It lacks virtually all ontological interest. Such lack does not bode well for the career of a would-be ontological notion of which it is an ingredient. But we must take the tradition as we find it. The notion has played a very great role indeed, not least, as we shall see, with Brentano. Upon the explication I just proposed it has two versions. In the broader one, 'can' and 'could' represent possibility₄. In the narrower version, they exclude the three stronger degrees of impossibility without, however, excluding impossibility₄. A perfect color particular, for instance, "could" not, upon either version, be separated from a shape particular as long as it is considered as the relevant a priori truth[6] that everything which is colored has a shape (and conversely). Which of the two versions an ontologist has in mind is not always clear, particularly if he does not clearly distinguish among the several kinds of impossibility. Brentano, we shall see, in his own way and for reasons of his own, is very subtle at this point.

Platonic universals, I repeat, are separable universals. Or so at least I shall use the phrase. In some ontologies in which they occur they may or may not also have other features; e.g., their ontological status may be higher than that of anything from which they can be separated. Our concern is with one thing only. *A universal need not be separable.* In the foil, the Principle of Exemplification makes particulars and universals equally inseparable from each other. Nor is this impossibility just a matter of natural law but, rather, the strongest of all, impossibility₁.

You may have wondered whether to be separable from each other is

---

[6] I put it this way because of the threefold distinction we made in Section Three (p. 66). The connection between Shape and Color is a priori; that between *red* and *square* is not; nor, assuming that there are perfect particulars, is that between *this red* (e.g., red₃) and *this square* (e.g., square₇) in the spot before me. But we also remember that the γ-ontologists' nominalism makes them insensitive to this distinction. Thus they might hold red₃ to be inseparable from square₇.

the same as to be independent$_2$ (p. 43). The two notions are close but not identical. Consider the fact which in the foil is assayed as $(A_1(a) \cdot A_2(a))$, with 'A_1', 'A_2', and 'a' standing for Square, White, and a particular, respectively. The universal and the particular in each of the two atomic facts $A_1(a)$ and $A_2(a)$ depend$_2$ on each other. Each of the two atomic facts is independent$_2$. Yet, in view of an a priori truth which has just been mentioned, they are not separable from each other.

The resistance against Platonic universals has always been very deep. So it may be prudent to repeat once more what should be obvious. A universal need not be Platonic. I, for one, am prepared to die in the last ditch for both beliefs; that there are universals; and that they are not Platonic. Nor, on the other hand, do I hold that the Principle of Exemplification, of which the rejection of Platonism (separable universals) is but an immediate consequence, is shallow. The exaggerated anti-Platonism which I insist is shallow, is, rather, the fallacious inference from the true premiss that there are no separable universals to the nominalistic conclusion that there are none.

I am ready to tackle the first task.

The "existence" of at least one internal connection is the structural premiss; nominalism, the structural conclusion. Establishing this connection is the task. Transposing the formula will fit it more closely to the argument I shall present: One cannot make an articulate case for nominalism without acknowledging at least one internal connection. One more transformation makes the formula completely accurate and specific: *Provided one rejects the Platonic alternative (separable universals), one cannot make an articulate case for perfect particulars without introducing an alleged internal relation of equality, or, as it is also called, exact similarity.* I reject separable universals out of hand. So I shall henceforth ignore the alternative they provide.

Perfect particulars are "simples."[7] Historically, that is beyond doubt part of the notion; nor would anything be gained structurally by abandoning it. Particularity and existence, the two subsistents which according to the foil would have to be "in" each particular, do not affect

---

[7] The double quotes around 'simple' in this context indicate, as always, that I use the word (for dialectical purposes of my own) as it is used by those philosophers who divide "things" into "simple" and "complex." That makes a simple thing one "in" which there is no other but itself. We, realizing that no complex can be a thing, can do without this use of 'simple'. (I realize as well as I hope you do that I am hammering the same point again and again. But I have myself missed it long enough to be profoundly convinced of its elusiveness and, therefore, of the need for such insistence. Behind it all is of course that most fundamental of all dichotomies, between function and complex, which occupied us in Section One.)

the arguments; so we may ignore them. Perfect particulars are not bare, of course. On the other hand, there is nothing "in," say, either red_1 or red_2 to ground either the place or the moment at which it is. This, we know, is the job γ-ontologists assign to that special kind of perfect particulars I call coordinate qualities, which in turn ground nothing else but places and moments. So we may stay with those perfect particulars which ground ordinary properties. Red_1 and red_2 will do very nicely. Each of them supposedly grounds the color and, as we just saw, nothing else.

Red_1 and red_2 are "associated" with each other in a sense in which each of them is associated with every other perfect particular that grounds exactly the same color and with nothing else. Or, if you like the phrase better, in this sense they "belong together." If you dislike both phrases and search for another, you will discover how difficult it is to find one free from ontological connotations. "Sharing something," for instance, suggests the idea of a common constituent. So let us resign ourselves to 'association'.

The association must have an ontological ground. There are two possibilities. The ground either is a connection between red_1 and red_2 or it is two entities, one "in" red_1, one "in" red_2. (1) If the ground is a connection, it is either a relation or a nexus. γ-ontologists, we know, if they considered this possibility, would assay the ground as a nexus rather than as a relation. But, then, *nexus and relations are equally external to what they connect.* Hence, upon either alternative, there would be nothing "in" either red_1 or red_2 that grounds the color. Since they ground nothing else, they would therefore be bare. (2) Red_1 and red_2 are simple. Hence the two entities which upon this alternative ground the association are red_1 and red_2 themselves. What, then, associates these two? We stand at the beginning of an infinite regress. The only way to avoid it is to make the "two" entities one, namely, the universal Red. I conclude that the doctrine of perfect particulars is not tenable. "Perfect particulars" are either (1) bare or (2) universals.

Those unwilling to accept the conclusion can do no better than insist that it rests on a premiss which they are prepared to reject, namely, that there are no internal connections. If there are some, then the alternatives (1) and (2) above are no longer exhaustive. There is the possibility that (3) red_1 and red_2 are two simples associated by the *internal connection of equality.* That creates the following situation.

One who is committed to nominalism may or may not see that when the argument has reached this point he must embrace (3). If he doesn't, his nominalism is hardly articulate. If he does and if he is prepared to enter upon the dialectic of internal connections, making as good a case for them as can be made (and as I have tried to make in Section Three), I shall of course still think him wrong and refute him (as I have tried to do in Section Three). Yet I shall be the first to insist that his position is sufficiently articulate to deserve respect, to require attention, and to be relevant to much that is good in the tradition.

We have come to the end of the argument except that, since it is so crucial, I shall take the time to defend it against an objection which is not very profound. The objector I have in mind argues as follows. "You have not exhausted the alternative you call (2). Upon this alternative red_1 and red_2 are both natured entities. Hence, you argue, since they have exactly the same nature (and, not grounding anything else, are this nature[8]), they are literally one. That overlooks the possibility that red_1 and red_2, though being their own natures, are exactly the same without being literally the same." Here is what I would answer: The notion of exact sameness (as I use the word, commonsensically) has no place in ontological discourse. To believe that it does is to confuse the ground with what it is supposed to ground. In other words, when saying that these two spots have exactly the same properties, I use 'exactly the same' and 'property' commonsensically and, therefore, without ontological commitment. In ontology we ask: What is the ground of exact sameness? You, speaking ontologically and therefore using 'exactly the same' and 'nature' with ontological commitment, tell me that the ground of the feature, i.e., of this case of exact sameness, is the two natures' being exactly the same. Hence, either the ontological question (What is the ground of exact sameness?) is not a good question[9]—that is, there was no question to begin with—or you have merely taken the first step of an infinite regress. But permit me to make your mistake the occasion for a comment on words. In the tradition the supposed internal connection of equality is, as I remarked (p. 89), also spoken of as "exact similarity." Standing where I stand and speaking as I do, I must of course not use the phrase in this context. So I shall avoid it whenever I can, and, when I can't, surround it by double quotes. Notice finally that, once the ambiguity of 'exact similarity' is out in the open, the gist of my reply to you can be stated in a single

---

[8] This presupposes that a thing's nature is "in" it. This is of course so; but it is not always clearly seen. The reasons why it isn't involve the activity component of the substance notion on the one hand and the a priori on the other. But I shall not explore them either here or elsewhere in this book. There is a need for selection as well as a point of diminishing return even in the sort of enterprise I have embarked on.

[9] This is the position now taken at Oxford. According to these philosophers, one who asks for the (ontological) ground of this or that (commonsensical) feature merely misuses language without noticing it.

sentence: The alleged internal connection of "exact similarity" is nothing but exact similarity in ontological disguise. Still differently, with a causal twist, we are so familiar with exact similarity, take it so much for granted, that some have smuggled it into ontology without noticing that there it will do them no good unless they have first made it an entity of some sort or other.

The problem whose solution I made my first task is part of a larger dialectic. We have solved the problem; but we have not yet unpacked the dialectic. To complete this larger job one must face three more tasks. To these I now turn.

Sometimes, when presented with two spots, I am also presented with their being exactly the same in color. Or, not to put too fine a point on it at this stage of the game, I am sometimes presented with exact sameness. Hence exact sameness must have an ontological ground. That is not just a principle of general ontology but its very idea. Here we once again touch rock bottom.

Some of the most articulate γ-ontologists assay exact sameness so that its ground is the internal connection of equality. Call this the γ-assay. I believe to have established conclusively that there are no internal connections. Hence, if I am right, the γ-assay stands refuted. This, though, is not enough. Upon my conception of the philosophical enterprise there are three more things to be done. I must, first, produce my own assay of exact similarity. I must, second, single out all the problems affected by the difference between the two assays. I must, third, establish all the structural connections between the differences among the solutions which have been proposed for these problems on the one hand and the differences between the two assays on the other. (The second and the third of these three steps belong to the dialectical justification of the first. That illustrates the role of the dialectic in the enterprise.)

The foil assays exact similarity as a derived subsistent. We cannot present this assay nor explore its implications effectively without first doing a job that has been postponed too long already. We must *clarify the ontological status of derived entities*. This is the *second task* I have set myself in this section.

The ontological status of all derived entities is peculiar; the peculiarity is such that even the status of derived things is very weak. This is what I have claimed several times. But I never stopped to justify the claim. This is what I must now do. It will be best if we begin with derived things, then proceed to the class of derived subsistents I shall call pseudocharacters and pseudorelations.

A thing (of the foil) is either a bare particular or a character (relation or otherwise). Bare particulars are simple, in the sense in which we decided to retain this word (p. 77). That is, they have neither constituents nor pseudoconstituents nor, like all derived things, quasiconstituents. It follows that all derived things are characters. The example we used in Section One and which will continue to serve us well was the character of being-red-**and**-square. Its quasiconstituents are red, square, and the quasinexus **and**. The reason for calling **and** a quasinexus without going to the length of calling red and square quasicharacters has something to do with the burden of Section One. Neither red nor square nor **and** is literally "in" the derived thing. In this respect they are all alike, just as this feature is adequately expressed by calling them all quasiconstituents. The extra emphasis provided by 'quasinexus' calls attention to the fact that, whatever it may or may not be "in," **and** is not literally a nexus.

The linguistic reflection of derivation is definition. The best way of clarifying the ontological status of the derived entities is to attend to their linguistic reflections, i.e., to the definitions of the expressions representing them. Consider, then, a language in which 'R' and 'S', both of type 'f', represent Red and Square, respectively, but which has no expression that can stand in place of the predicate variable 'f' and represent being-red-and-square. Into such a language such an expression can, as one says, be introduced by the definitional schema

(D) '$(R \& S)(x)$' for '$R(x) \cdot S(x)$'.

Nor is there anything wrong with saying this sort of thing as long as one does not forget two points, one merely technical, the other of considerable philosophical import. One must not forget, first, that in spite of its graphic complexity, which is to remind us of how it has been introduced and what it represents, '$(R \& S)$' is a single predicate. One must not forget, second, and this is the philosophical point, that a language which perspicuously represents an ontology (or, as one says, an ideal language) does not contain any definitions at all. As long as these two points are kept in mind, the claim is easily justified in four short steps.

First. Strictly speaking, (D) is a definitional schema rather than a definition. Such a schema becomes a definition by substitution for the free variables in it. E.g., substitution of 'a' for 'x' yields the definition

(D_a) '$(R \& S)(a)$' for '$R(a) \cdot S(a)$'.

As you see, each constituent of the right side, except a, of course, corresponds to a quasiconstituent of the derived character. What makes our example so handy (I avoid 'simple'!) is its having only three quasiconstituents: two things and (one occurrence of) one quasinexus. The more quasiconstituents a derived thing has, the more complicated (I avoid 'complex'!) it is. At least one of its quasiconstituents must be a thing, otherwise it itself would not be one. The others will be either quasinexus or they will, in the quasi-way, correspond to generality and existence.[10]

Second. The ontological status, such as it is, of $(R \& S)$ does not of course depend on anyone actually proposing the definition (D), which would be absurd, but, rather, on the form of the facts which are its substitution instances being such that this definition is syntactically possible. What the form of a fact is I shall not explain once more but merely remind you that although, like everything else, it is reflected in language, it is not itself anything linguistic, just as what is conveniently expressed by saying that the defined term in (D) is a predicate is not a matter of language but the ontological ground of $(R \& S)$ being a character.

Third. If it helps you, assume for this step that '$R(a) \cdot S(a)$' is true, or, what amounts to the same, that $R(a) \cdot S(a)$ is an actual and not merely a potential fact. Definitions are abbreviatory stipulations and nothing else. Thus the "two" facts represented by the two sides of (D_a) are one and not two. In this sense, the left side mentions no entity which is not also mentioned on the right. That drives home the point once more. The only reason for calling $(R \& S)$ an entity, or, what amounts to the same, the ground of $(R \& S)$ is that formal feature of the fact $R(a) \cdot S(a)$ whose linguistic reflection is the syntactical possibility of introducing (D). This, I submit, amply justifies the claim that the ontological status of derived things is both peculiar and very weak.

Fourth. Centaur is a derived character; so is dog. The only difference of ontological interest is that while the latter is exemplified, the former is not. Or, to say the same thing differently, while the right sides of the substitution instances of the definitional schema for 'centaur' are all merely potential facts, at least one of those of the 'dog' schema is actual. One may express this by saying that while dog is an actual derived character, centaur is merely a potential one. Notice that this makes all the empty classes (of the different types) merely potential characters.[11] Even so, nothing untoward will happen as long as one

[10] Generality and existence are the two subsistents represented by the universal and the existential operator, respectively. See the essay on "Generality and Existence" in *Logic and Reality.*

[11] Classes, we remember, are a special kind of derived character. A derived character is a class if and only if the right side of the corresponding definitional schema is an enumeration. Since they are derived characters, the ontological status of classes is weak. The additional reason which makes it even weaker than that of

remembers that this is merely a transferred, or, as one might say, merely a secondary use of 'actual' and 'potential'. Upon the primary use, what is actual or potential is a complex (fact) and nothing else. The definitional schemata reflecting derived characters make it possible to transfer this use to the latter. But it makes absolutely no sense to say of a (simple) thing that it exists in the mode of potentiality. If one forgets that, he will be in trouble.

That much for derived things. What needs to be said about other derived entities is merely a variation of the same idea. So it will not take long.

Consider the schema

$$(D') \qquad \qquad \text{`}Eq(x, y)\text{'} \quad \text{for} \quad \text{`}(\exists f)(f(x) \cdot f(y))\text{'}.$$

Unlike the right side of (D), that of (D') contains no expression representing a thing. This linguistic difference between (D) and (D') represents an ontological one between the entities represented by the expressions they "introduce." (R & S) is a derived thing; Eq is a *derived subsistent*. The two expressions, (R & S) and 'Eq' are alike in being both predicates. As it happens, they are also of the same type; the only difference is that 'Eq' is, as one says, relational. Because of this similarity, the entities represented by such expressions have been called "logical characters" and "logical relations," also "structural properties" and "structural relations." Since characters and relations are things, these expressions are misleading. I shall avoid them and, for want of better words, speak of *pseudocharacters* and *pseudorelations* instead.[12] These labels have at least the virtue of reminding us that what they label are not really characters and relations. The integers and transitivity, for instance, are pseudocharacters of at least the second type. As to ontological status, pseudocharacters and pseudorelations, being derived subsistents, stand to the fundamental ones among the latter as derived characters and relations stand to those which so many call "simple." Thus their ontological status is very low indeed. That of transitivity, for instance, is even lower than that of exemplification or conjunction. Thus one who tends toward reism is even less

---

other derived characters is that there is a class for each (combinatorially) possible collection. All this we know already. But rehearsing it might help you to check, as one should from time to time, that and how things hang together.

[12] Notice the different use of 'pseudo' in, say, 'pseudonexus' and 'pseudorelation'. In the former it marks an irremediable blur. Or, as I put it, a pseudonexus is a monster I keep artificially alive. The latter merely marks my belief that it is not safe to apply indiscriminately the same label, 'relation', to the members of a collection of both things and subsistents. The only excuse I can offer for this ambiguous use of 'pseudo' is that I am running out of words.

likely to recognize the existence of such entities than he is to recognize the existence of the fundamental nexus which, at least implicitly, must hold his world together—if it is to be a world and not merely *membra disjecta*.

'*Eq*' stands of course for 'being equal in some respect'. 'Being equal' means either just that or strictly nothing. 5 and $2+3$, for instance, are equal in numerosity. The assay of this special use of 'equal' does not concern us here. When axiomatists speak of equality *tout court*, they speak, without specifying it, of some entity which has the "structural" features (i.e., pseudocharacters and pseudorelations, such as, e.g., transitivity) of all equalities-in-some-respect.

As for equality, so for sameness. A while ago I said that I did not then want to put too fine a point on the matter. Now is the time to insist. 'Being exactly the same' means either 'being exactly the same in some respect' or strictly nothing. The two spots of the example, for instance, are exactly the same in color and what I am sometimes presented with when presented with two such spots is exact sameness with respect to color. The supplementary assay that requires is represented by

(D″)   '$Eqcol(x, y)$'   for   '$(\exists f)Col^2(f)\cdot f(x)\cdot f(y)$',

where 'Col^2' represents color, which is a character of the second type. About such characters I shall have more to say presently. In the meantime, notice that, since Col^2 is a thing, so is $Eqcol$. It is a derived relation, not a pseudorelation. Yet it is peculiar in that the only thing in it is of the second type and that, *loosely speaking*, it is one of the "specifications" of the pseudorelation Eq. That makes it "look like" a pseudorelation, gives it the "feel" of one, if I may so express myself.

Let us take stock. The derived entities which concern us here are of two kinds.[13] Either they are derived things, characters or relations; or they are pseudocharacters or pseudorelations. We have clarified the ontological status of either kind. In the course of these clarifications we saw that the foil assays as a pseudorelation (*Eq* and, loosely speaking, its "specifications," such as *Eqcol*) what the more articulate γ-ontologists assay as the "internal relation"[14] of equality. Thus we hit two

---

[13] The only other kind I can think of are those I find it more natural to call derived nexus rather than pseudorelations. But the difference, if any, is one of taste and style only.

[14] No harm will be done if henceforth I refer to this alleged connection as the *internal relation of equality*. The tradition, as you know, only too characteristically, has virtually ignored the distinction, on which I insist, that makes relations a species of the genus connection.

birds with one stone. We completed the second task, which was to clarify the status of derived entities, and we took the first of the three steps we planned, which was to confront the two assays, in the foil and in γ, of exact similarity. The remaining two steps were to trace and unravel the differences between ε and γ which depend on the difference between the two assays. This will be the fourth and last task of this section. It will expedite it if I first do something else. I shall next explore the use to which, *structurally speaking and at least after a fashion,* the γ-ontologists have put the internal relation of equality. This is the *third task* of this section.

I almost always speak structurally. Why then emphasize it now? Why add "after a fashion"? You may suspect that I am up to something special. The suspicion is justified. I am about to introduce an expository device of a very special sort. This will be the second such device. In Part II there will be a third. The pseudonexus γ and ⊂ are the first. Pseudonexus, you remember, are monsters. Now I am about to introduce some wraiths. A monster is not a wraith and a wraith is not a monster. Monsters are, or spawn, irremediable blurs or confusions. Wraiths are unjustifiable illusions. But we can safely leave these distinctions until after having been a bit more literal for a while.

Let us first make an agreement about a word. For those preoccupied with phenomenology exact similarity may be, and probably is, of considerable interest. Not being so preoccupied myself, I am not particularly interested in it beyond making sure of the foil's adequacy by making sure that it, too, has a ground. This ground we found in the subsistent I called equality. Once this has been done, there is in the foil no great need for either the word or the thing. So I shall put the word to another use. Henceforth, unless something to the contrary will be said, the word, *equality*, will have one meaning only. It will stand for that alleged "internal relation of equality" which γ-ontologists must introduce if they want to make the best possible case for their nominalism.

No ontologist can say anything worth while unless he either recognizes that there are universals or is able to entertain with some plausibility the mistaken belief that there are in his world substitutes for them which (he thinks) can do what (as we know) only universals can do. (This I believe to have shown; otherwise I would not propound the foil.) In the first case, his is an ε-world; in the second, he is a γ-ontologist with something worth while to say. (That there are such γ-ontologists I take for granted; otherwise I would not write this book.) The second case gives rise to a question. How can an ontologist maintain this illusion? Or, as I put it on a similar occasion, before telling the story of the lost facts, how can the feat be achieved? The question is very important; so I shall answer it very carefully, in three steps.[15]

First. Equality is but exact similarity transplanted from the world of common sense, where it is so familiar that it is taken for granted, to ontology, where it does not belong; without it being noticed, just because it is so familiar and because, alas, the very idea of ontology is not always as firmly grasped as one might wish, that in ontology exact similarity is of no use unless first made into an existent of some sort or other. That is how I just put it (p. 92). It is but another way of saying the same thing, looking at the other side of the medal, as it were, if one adds that this is why some very good philosophers were able to maintain the illusion that somehow equality is there without really being there. In other words, the peculiarity of equality, together with some shortcomings of their own, enabled them to hold simultaneously two views which, after they have been made fully explicit, are seen to contradict each other, namely, first, that equality is an internal relation, i.e., *does not exist as such*, and, second, that it is somehow there, i.e., that it *does exist*. If you need further convincing as to how easily and plausibly one may be deceived, remember that what these philosophers are speaking about is (in the foil) merely a derived subsistent, i.e., an entity of very weak ontological status, such as, say, transitivity, which because of this weakness is very easily overlooked, or, what amounts to the same, of which it is taken for granted that somehow it is there (exists) without being there (existing). If you still hesitate, ponder the following question. Did not and does not virtually everyone take it for granted that the transitivity of, say, being longer or being higher-in-pitch is there (exists), without transitivity as such being there (existing)? If an ontologist has become the victim of such an illusion, I shall say that there is in his world a *wraith* or spook. *The fundamental illusion of γ is the wraith of equality.* I call it fundamental because, though merely a wraith, it yet spawns others.

Second. Let 'Eq' stand for 'equality'. Let a_1 be a perfect particular, say, one of those grounding the color green. Consider the definition

$$(\text{D}''') \qquad\qquad \text{`}\widetilde{Gr}(x)\text{'} \quad \text{for} \quad \text{`}\widetilde{Eq}(x, a)\text{'},$$

and you will see that, after a fashion, it introduces a predicate representing a derived character, $\widetilde{Gr}$, which is coextensive with the "class" of

---

[15] What follows is a structural analysis in exactly the same sense in which the story of the lost facts in Section Three is such an analysis. See also n. 15 of Section Three.

all perfect particulars that ground the color green. I say after a fashion because, equality being what it is, $\widetilde{Gr}$ itself is merely a wraith. *Ex nihilo nihil fit.* Yet, as you see, one wraith has most plausibly spawned another; for there is no flaw in the process of derivation (definition) as such. The double quotes around 'class' are to remind you that, as a γ-ontologist assays his world, there are no classes in it. As for $\widetilde{Green}$, so for $\widetilde{Yellow}$, $\widetilde{Red}$, and so on. They all are merely wraiths; they are all best thought of as "classes." As we shall try to acquire a closer understanding of γ, these peculiar "classes" will have to be mentioned very often. Yet I do not want to wear out the metaphor by calling them wraiths or spooks again and again. Nor do I want to put 'class' between quotation marks every time. So I shall employ a typographical device, speak of these "classes" which are mere wraiths as Classes, just as for any particular one of them I shall continue to use the name of the corresponding character with the tilde.

Nothing worth while can be said about a world without either universals or at least some more or less plausible substitutes to do their jobs for them. This we took for granted. What we discovered is that in a γ-world the substitutes are the wraiths we just decided to call Classes. This, I submit, is the major use to which, "structurally speaking and at least after a fashion," the γ-ontologists have put equality. If this diagnosis is correct, then it is very important. So I shall support it by a third comment.

Third. In the foil, classes exist. There they are simply a special kind of derived character of specially weak ontological status which it is therefore especially easy to overlook. In a γ-world there are no classes. If its ontologist is as clever as Goodman, he will see to it that their jobs are done by sums, of which he could at least consistently assert that they exist. Otherwise, we know, there are in such a world only collections which, as we also know, do not exist, e.g., the collection (not class or Class!) of all perfect particulars grounding the color green. But, then, alas, collections, classes, and Classes will only too easily be confused with each other by anyone who, like virtually all γ-ontologists, is under the double pressure of reism and nominalism. In other words, a γ-ontologist is a likely victim of the illusion that collections can do all the jobs of classes (or Classes). Clearly, this particular illusion and that other one, which I called fundamental, to the effect that equality somehow both is and is not there, will mutually support each other in strengthening a third, namely, that those additional wraiths, $\widetilde{Green}$, $\widetilde{Yellow}$, and so on, which have been spawned by $\widetilde{Eq}$, can do the jobs of universals, provided only one also believes that classes can always stand in for other characters. But, then, this latter belief has been held more or less explicitly by virtually all nominalists; more explicitly by the more "moderate" ones.[16]

What is the ground of both spots' being green? The ε-ontologist answers that it is the thing Green, which is a universal, or, more accurately, a nonrelational, nonderived character of the first type. The γ-ontologist finds this ground in two perfect particulars, partly, perhaps, because he suffers from the illusion that the Class Green can do the job of the universal. These are the two articulate positions on the universals problem in the narrower sense. In the broader sense, it is a group of related issues, of which the narrower problem is the nucleus. The issues in this group are those the answers to which are most immediately influenced by the stand one has taken on the narrower problem. To unpack the dialectic of this influence or connection is the *fourth and last task* to which I now turn. Among this group of issues there are two such that the solution of all others depends on how they are solved.[17] I shall treat these two problems separately, first state each

[16] The support this third step of my structural analysis receives from the historical record is as striking as it is familiar. There has been more than one recent nominalist who rejects universals because, as he tells us, classes can do their jobs! Others tell us that if they were forced to choose between universals and classes, they would prefer the latter, since they are the lesser evil! *Nomina sunt odiosa.* But perhaps we should on this occasion discuss a certain ambiguity of 'class' which hasn't been exactly helpful.

A world is extensional if and only if any two coextensive predicates of it are in all contexts mutually substitutable *salva veritate*. Such predicates as well as the characters they represent are often called *identical*. Our own world, if truncated (p. 6), is extensional.

Upon the narrow use of 'class', a class is a derived character introduced by (finite or infinite) enumeration. Upon the broad use, every character of an extensional world is a class. It follows that in an extensional ε-world the universal (class in the broad sense) Green and the class (narrow sense) of all bare particulars exemplifying Green are identical. Similarly, if there were classes in an extensional γ-world, the Class Green and the class (narrow sense) of all perfect particulars grounding this color would be identical. Yet there is no difficulty in keeping the two uses apart; i.e., there is nothing which is literally a class in both senses. For, to be identical is one thing; to be the same$_3$ is another thing. Identity, so understood, is, if anything, a fourth kind of sameness (same$_4$), not literally the same, yet as weak as sameness$_1$.

Added to proof: I believe now that this assay of classes, as well as some other formulations in this chapter, is mistaken. Fortunately the mistakes do not affect the developments in this book. Yet there is much to be said. I still hope to say it. (*January 1967*)

[17] This I shall not prove. After having read to the end, you will see that it is obvious.

of them together with the solution of the foil, then examine the "solutions" available in γ.

The first problem in the foil. Green is a color. *e* is a pitch. Square is a shape. What is the right assay of these three facts? Or, what amounts virtually to the same, what is the correct assay of the entities represented by 'color', 'pitch', and 'shape'? The foil's answer is familiar. 'Color' represents the thing Color (Col^2), which is a universal, or, more accurately, a nonrelational, nonderived character of the second type. That makes green being a color an atomic fact with three constituents. Two are characters, of the first and of the second type, respectively; the third is exemplification. As for Color, so for Pitch, Shape, and so on. The first problem is, not surprisingly, that of the characters of the higher types, or, more precisely, it is the problem which in the foil is solved by the claim that some things are nonrelational characters of a higher type. The second problem, no more surprisingly, is that of the higher-type relations.[18]

The foil, then, recognizes that some nonderived higher-type characters exist. Our nominalistic critics find this answer distressingly *ad hoc.* Thus they merely smile when we point out to them that once the higher characters are correctly assayed, some "problems" which have long worried philosophers are no longer problems. Such success, which they judge to be spurious, merely increases their distaste. How can one defend one's self against the charge of doing too well? I shall present two arguments. Both are dialectical.

1. Universality is a category. The several types are several subcategories. One way of expressing the critics' uneasiness is to say that they wonder how all these subdivisions could be of ontological import. One part of the answer, which I need not repeat, has been given by Russell, when he gave reasons why expressions violating the type rule should be considered as ill-formed. The other part goes more directly to the heart of the matter. The main category here, if I may so express myself, is thinghood. Dividing this category into two, bare particulars and universals, the ϵ-ontologist implicitly accepts the type distinction. For he accepts quite explicitly that certain "complexes," e.g., two bare particulars connected by ϵ, are impossible$_1$; or, to say the same thing differently, he accepts explicitly, first, that ϵ is inhomogeneous, and second, that all connections are external. And what is this if not the

---

[18] There is of course the question whether these characters and relations can be introduced as higher-type derived things, and whether, if this can be done, it must be done. For my answer, see the essay "Synthetic *a priori*" in *Logic and Reality.*

first step on the road on which the distinction between the first and the second type is the second, and so on? You see why this defense is dialectical. I contend that the charge of *ad hoc* is very superficial. Structurally, once an inhomogeneous fundamental nexus has been accepted and, not of course independently[19] thereof, the externality of all connections has been recognized, the door is open to the higher types, so widely open indeed that not introducing them when they are needed to do a job would be counterstructural.

2. The uses of such second-type words as 'color' are essentially of two kinds. (1) 'green is a color' is an instance of the one; (2) 'the color of my wife's hair is beautiful', an instance of the other. In communication and, psychologically, in thought, the convenience of the definite description in (2) is probably indispensable. Ontologically, it is irrelevant. So I brush it aside. That leaves (1). This sentence states an a priori truth (fact). So do all others of its kind. The existence (ontological status) of such facts is only too easily overlooked and has in fact been overlooked by all γ-ontologists. This we remember from an earlier occasion (p. 63). Now I merely add that one who thus slights the whole fact is more than likely also to slight at least some of its constituents. Some time ago I made this argument for the pseudonexus in $a \subset \alpha$ (p. 67). Now I apply it to the second-type character represented in (1). What makes this defense dialectical is the claim that our critics do not see what is there to be seen, namely, some characters of the second type, because they are blinded by mistakes which they make in other contexts.

The first problem in γ. Green is a color. What is this proposition about? Consider a γ-ontologist sufficiently profound to understand that the question requires an ontologically articulate answer. If he is as profound as I suppose, such Classes as Green, Red, Yellow, one for each color, are available to him. If he were to proceed as ϵ-ontologists do, he would therefore assay color as a Class of Classes, a "class" of the second type, as it were, whose members are Green, Red, Yellow, and so on. This however, is not what he does. Nor is the structural reason for his not doing it as well as for his doing what in fact he does hard to discover. The ontological ground of the Class Green he conceives, however implicitly or confusedly, to be any of its members, say green$_7$, together with equality; that of the Class Yellow, any of its members, say yellow$_{29}$, and, again, equality. Nor does he have any other idea, however implicit and however confused, of the ontological ground of any Class. That leaves him only one way. He conceives of color as a

---

[19] Establishing this connection was part of the burden of Section Two.

Class whose ontological ground is any of its member qualities, red_8, yellow_{29}, green_{17}, or what have you, and, again, an internal connection. Only, this time the connection is not equality but, rather, an alleged internal connection of "similarity." Red_8 and yellow_{29}, for instance, are "similar" in that each of them grounds a color, while neither of them is in this respect "similar" to a quality that grounds either a pitch o͠r a place. Color thus becomes, not the Class of all color Classes, $\widetilde{\text{Green}}$, $\widetilde{\text{Red}}$, $\widetilde{\text{Yellow}}$, and so on, but, rather, their set-theoretical su͠m. *Green and Yellow are contained in Color:* $\widetilde{Green} < \widetilde{Color}$; $\widetilde{Yellow} < \widetilde{Color}$. The matter is so important that it warrants two comments.

1. In γ-ontologies there are no universals and therefore, of course, no classes. But we saw how one may become deluded into thinking that there are in such worlds at least Classes, i.e., those wraithlike "classes" of qualities. Now we also see where and why the illusion stops. There couldn't possibly be Classes of Classes; there could not even be the wraith of any character of a higher type. The more fully one realizes how deeply ingrained this way of thinking was and, alas, still is, the more he will admire the contribution of Russell.

2. We have come upon a structural connection of the kind I had in mind when setting myself the last task. *Those who solve the narrower universals problem by means of an internal relation of equality, which as we remember they also speak of as "exact similarity," are structurally forced to solve the broader problem by means of an alleged internal relation of "similarity,"* or, perhaps, by a whole class of such relations. Of this presently. Notice first how certain verbal habits facilitate certain transitions of thought which are merely "verbal," in the pejorative sense of the word with which we are all familiar. You know of course the transition I have in mind. It leads from "exact similarity" to "similarity." (The quotation marks are to remind you that, so used, 'similarity', like 'equality', stands for a wraith.)

The second problem in the foil. The problem, we know, is that of the higher relations. Relations either are spatial-temporal such as, e.g., simultaneous and part (Pt); or they are ordinary such as higher and brighter.[20] ϵ-ontologists are structurally propelled toward assaying some relations of either kind as (underived) things, together with a fundamental nexus which is in all respects like ϵ, except for being ternary (if the relation is binary). This we saw in Section Two. The foil is an ϵ-world. Accordingly, some of its relations of either kind are (underived) things: some others, derived (relational) characters. Yet there

[20] It will help if at this point you recall the way of speaking on which we have agreed. A connection is *without prejudice* called a relation if and only if the foil assays it as a relational thing (either underived or derived).

is in the foil also a difference between the two kinds, spatial-temporal and ordinary. Some spatial and temporal relations are the only relational things of the first type. Higher[3], for instance, being a connection among pitches, is already of the second type. This difference is closely connected[21] with the correct assay of space and time, with bareness, and with the a priori. Thus it cuts very deeply. Yet it makes no difference for what we are about.[22] The only reason for mentioning it is that, since we shall stay with higher-in-pitch, which is an ordinary relation, some of the higher-type things we shall have to consider are of the third type.

The example we most frequently used is higher[3]. In exploring the narrower problem of universals it has served us well. For the broader problem it will no longer do by itself. Now we must remember that higher[3] is but one member of the higher[i]-*series* (higher[2], higher[3], higher[4], and so on) as well as that there is also *higher*, without superscript, if I may so express myself. What is the ontological ground of this whole *structure?* This is, in an example, the problem of the higher-type relations. I shall not and need not solve it completely. But the last of the following five comments will contain as much of the solution as our purpose requires.

I. The key words in the last paragraph are, indispensably, *higher* and *series*, and, as a matter of convenience, *structure*. Nor will it be inconvenient to proceed as if my purpose were to explain this use of 'structure' which, though convenient indeed and therefore quite common, is yet neither indispensable nor very precise.

II. (1) For every i, one of two things is higher[i] than the other only if it is also higher. (2) The higher[i] are not just a class but a series. (2a) For every higher[i] and for every higher[j] that precedes it in the series, if of three things the first is higher[i] than the second, while the third is higher[j] than the second, then the third is *between-in-pitch* the first and the second. A moment's reflection will show you that (2a) is a truism. There are other such truisms. We could list them as (3), (4), and so on. But it will be safe to break off.

III. Remember the question. What is the ground of this whole structure? To answer it is the same as to answer the following two. (a) What is the correct assay of the entities represented by 'higher', 'series', and 'between-in-pitch' and such cognates of them as we may come upon when examining the members of the class of truisms just mentioned? (b) What is the nature of these truisms, i.e., are they analytic, merely a

---

[21] For an analysis of these connections, see the essay "Synthetic *a priori*" in *Logic and Reality*.

[22] See, however, the next to the last paragraph of this section. And there is of course also the familiar theorem by Wiener and Kuratowski.

priori, or perhaps even contingent, and what, if any, are the connections among them? It will be economical to postpone answering until after a comment which will presently help us to understand what goes on in the other camp.

IV. (a) Remember what was said about *Eq* (not $\widetilde{Eq}$!) and *Eqcol*. The former is a derived subsistent of the kind called a pseudorelation and therefore of an ontological status so low that it is only too easily overlooked (or taken for granted, which, as we know, spawns a wraith). '*Eqcol*', in whose definition the thing *Col²* is mentioned, stands for a derived thing that is peculiar in a way that causes it to be easily mistaken for a "specification" of *Eq*, which in turn causes its existence to be as easily overlooked as that of any other derived subsistent. All this, I trust, you remember (p. 96). Remember, too, what was said about the mathematicians' (axiomatists') equality *tout court*. It is not really an entity but, rather, their way of speaking about any entity, either *Eq*, or *Eqcol*, or equality in some other respect, which exemplifies certain pseudocharacters (transitivity, symmetry, and so on).

(b) As for equal, so for between. Notice that I wrote 'between-in-pitch' rather than 'between', thus putting the entity in the category of *Eqcol* rather than in that of *Eq*. But there is of course again the between *tout court* of the axiomatists, only too easily confused with any of its "specifications" such as between-in-pitch, between-in-brightness, between-on-a-line, and so on, which again causes the existence of all the latter to be as easily overlooked (or taken for granted) as that of all derived subsistents.

(c) Sometimes we say, commonsensically, that of three things one is *more similar* or *closer-in-pitch* to the other than is the third. I call the expressions commonsensical because such similarities and their degrees are no doubt sometimes presented to us. I italicize the words in order to call attention to the entities which therefore they represent. I abstain from putting double quotes around the words because, unlike equality ("exact similarity") and the alleged internal relation of "similarity," *similarity-in-pitch* and its *degrees* are not wraiths. To see that, one merely has to realize that they are easily derived from between-in-pitch and therefore, alas, as easily or even more easily overlooked or taken for granted. If, for instance, the second of three pitches is between the first and the third, then the latter will be less similar to the first than is the second. This, to be sure, is merely a hint. But it will suffice. The details are the business of the phenomenologists and of the axiomatizers.

V. If you now return to the two questions of III you will see that the ε-ontologist encounters no difficulty whatsoever in grounding the whole structure. With respect to the first question, III(a), the heart of the matter is that he is prepared to recognize the existence of some underived higher-type things. In connection with I(1), for instance, he may introduce an underived third-type character, *Higher*, exemplified by each member of the higher-series and by nothing else. He may introduce an underived ternary relation of the second type, *Betwpitch*, in which he grounds betweenness among pitches. He may introduce both *Higher* and *Betwpitch*. Or he may introduce only the latter and try to derive from it a character coextensive with the former. I am sure that there are alternatives. I am equally sure that dialectically they make no difference. So we may safely leave them to those whose business they are. With respect to the second question, III(b), it is clear that while (in the foil) all members of the class of truisms in II are a priori truths, none of them is either analytic or merely contingent. The connections among them will depend on which entities, if any, are introduced as derived. If, for instance, a (character coextensive with) *Higher* is derived from *Betwpitch*, then, if I am not mistaken, II(1) in conjunction with some of the between-axioms deductively implies that II(2) and II(2a) so imply each other.[23]

We have pursued the solution of the higher-type relations problem as far as our purpose requires. The choice among the alternatives and the details of each we may safely leave to others. What matters dialectically is one thing only. An ε-ontologist prepared to recognize that some underived higher-type things exist will have no difficulty in solving the problem. Not so the γ-ontologist to whom I now turn.

The second problem in γ. Let us stay with the example and the old phrases. How do γ-ontologists ground the whole structure? Their plight is so great and so manifest that it will not take us long to understand it completely. The best they can do is what in fact the best among them have done. They introduced a whole *class* of internal relations of different *degrees* of "similarity." As usual, the quotation marks are to remind you that the members of this class are all wraiths. You will no doubt also recall the disastrous facilitating effect of thinking and speaking of equality, which is at least a more plausible wraith than all these "similarities," as "exact similarity." But I must direct your attention to something else. 'Degree', which I just used, implies that there is a single series; 'class', which I also used, suggests that there is none, but "merely" a class. The clash spots a fatal weakness.

The commonsensical use of 'more (or less) similar' I understand. Nor, as we saw, do I have any difficulty grounding it in the foil. ('More

---

[23] That is why I labeled them (2) and (2a) rather than (2) and (3).

or less' is the mark of a *single* series, of course.) That is why I can also understand what γ-ontologists have in mind when calling one pitch more similar to another than to a third, even though, unfortunately, they ground the difference in two internal relations, and, in particular, in two "similarities" of different "degrees." Similarly, if for the sake of the argument you grant that places are qualities, you will understand why they tell us that of two places at different distances from a third, the one closer to the latter is more similar to it than the one farther away.[24] But we are also told two more things.

We are told, first, that any two pitches[25] are more similar to each other than either of them is to either a color or a shape. This I can still understand provided I may take it to mean that there are *several* mutually exclusive series of similarities of different degrees (without at the moment worrying how the whole structure is grounded) and that, while any two tones belong to the same series, a pitch and a shape or a pitch and a color do not.

We are told, second, at least by implication, that, say, a pitch is more similar to a color than to a taste in exactly the same sense in which, say, middle *e* is more similar to middle *c* than is middle *g*. Of what this could possibly mean I have not the slightest notion. Nor of course do you. So you may be incredulous and ask me where to look for the implication. The implication, if that be not too weak a word, lies of course in the thesis that the problem of the higher-type relations can be completely solved by means of a class of "similarities" of different "degree." This is the thesis which the best among the γ-ontologists propose. If you want a formula, *they solve the problem of the higher-type characters by means of "similarity," that of the higher-type relations by means of a class of "similarities" of different "degree."*

The inadequacy of this attempt at a solution is perhaps even more striking in the case of the second problem. The criticism I just made of it, in connection with class and degree, suffices by itself to show that it must fail. Four more comments, three structural, one phenomenological, will drive home how feeble and foredoomed it really is. Then I shall be done.

Structurally, since what even the best could do is so little, you may

---

[24] Dialectically the example is very smooth as well as instructive. Phenomenologically it drives home the shocking absurdity of coordinate qualities. That is why I chose it, of course.

[25] The tradition, being nominalistic, speaks in these contexts of tones, which are conceived as perfect particulars, rather than of pitches. I have, whenever I could, avoided this roughness by speaking of one "thing" being higher in pitch than another, and so on.

wonder what has been done by those less excellent. The answer is, very simply as long as I am permitted to put it my way, that some were content with a single internal relation of "similarity," thus showing themselves lacking in that finer sensitivity for the ontological need which finds its expression, however inadequate, in the explicit postulation of a huge class of "similarities" of different "degrees." But, then, even with the best and even in the case of a single series of "degrees," what is the ground of its being a series rather than merely a class of "similarities"? Somewhere there lurks, unnoticed, the absurd idea of an internal relation of the second type.

Again structurally, the members of this huge class are of course merely the doubly idiosyncratic substitutes of the several higher-type things which the foil recognizes. I call them doubly idiosyncratic because they cater to two aversions, one general, one special, as it were. All these many "similarities" are internal relations. Thus, being merely wraiths, they all cater to the general aversion against external connections. Each of these "similarities," if it really existed, would be a relation of the first type. Thus they all cater to the nominalists' special, or, as I am almost tempted to say, additional aversion against universals of the higher types.

Still structurally, one may wonder how, once this huge class of different "similarities" has been admitted, the ontological status of all its members could have been ignored. At this point I am torn between the desire not to be too concise and the fear of becoming tedious. We have seen again and again that, how, and why, the ontological status of certain entities is easily overlooked. We know that and why certain kinds of facts are not recognized as such. We also know how these two shortcomings reinforce each other. I have, I think, reached the point at which the danger of becoming tedious is the one to be shunned most.

Phenomenologically, one wonders how a "solution" so patently inadequate also in this respect could have appeared to be acceptable for so long. A partial explanation lies in the unseemly haste and brevity with which the whole problem of relations has always been dispatched.[26] No one, for instance, at least not as far as I know, has ever said as brutally as I just did that the "solution" does not even make prima facie sense unless it makes sense to assert such absurdities as

---

[26] The second of Meinong's *Hume Studien*, "Zur Relationstheorie," is an intelligent as well as, as early as 1882, intelligently critical account of the modern history of the relations issue. Thus it also contains the evidence that the views I attribute to them have actually been held by the γ-ontologists with whom I am concerned.

that, say, pitches are more similar to shapes than to smells. The source
of this striking weakness of the tradition is, I believe, the Aristotelian
view of relations. In Brentano, exacerbated by his extreme reism and
nominalism, this view reached its extreme. That makes it advisable to
postpone the consideration of certain matters concerning relations
until we shall get to Brentano.

I am ready for three concluding remarks.

Let us give a moment's attention to our special friend from Section
Four, the one whose world has so far not been proposed by anyone.
How would he fare on the universals issue? Remember the two "premisses" from which he starts and the "conclusion" at which he arrives.
The "simple" things of his world are all perfect particulars, which
makes him a γ-ontologist. He explicitly recognizes that $\subset$ exists, which
is what makes him so special. These are his premises. He concludes
that there is a large class of external connections, as many as there are
in the foil, but that, unlike those of the foil, they are all nexus rather
than (relational) things. What, then will he be able to do, first about
the narrower universals problem, then about the higher-type characters and the higher-type relations? If you suppose him to be structurally consistent, his answers to these three questions are rather
obvious. He will start by introducing, not an internal relation but,
rather, a nexus of equality (exact similarity). From where he stands,
that solves the narrower problem quite satisfactorily. In answering the
second question, he will introduce a single nexus, without degrees, of
similarity, such that any two (perfect particulars grounding) pitches
(or shapes, or colors, and so on) are similar to each other but not to
anything which is not a pitch (or a shape, or a color, and so on). If he
then uses this nexus to derive from it a certain kind of classes,[27] he will
have provided himself with entities which can do at least some of the
jobs of Pitch, Shape, Color, and so on. In answering the third question,
finally, he will be able to get by, at least after a fashion, by introducing
some further nexus such as, e.g., a ternary betweenness *tout court*,
which he could then use, in conjunction with other entities, to ground
the several series. E.g., he could ground the pitch series in this nexus
of betweenness in conjunction with the entity, derived in the second
step, that does in his world the job of Pitch. All together, you see,

---

[27] By means of such definitions as, e.g., '$\overline{Col}(x)$' for '$sim(x, a)$', where a is a
particular grounding some color. If there were classes in a γ-world, $\overline{Col}$ would be
of the first type. In this respect it is like $\tilde{Col}$. On the other hand, though, since *sim*
is an acknowledged existent, it would at least not be a wraith. That is why I did
not identify $\overline{Col}$ with $\tilde{Col}$ and, also, why I did not put double quotes around
'class' in this context.

while he does not of course, from where I stand, do too well, neither does he do too badly.

The nominalists' special aversion against the higher-type universals is without ground. These universals are supposed to be even more "abstract" than those of the first type. If one inquires what that means, one discovers that it could not possibly mean anything except, perhaps, that they are of a higher type, which makes the proposition a tautology. In other words, the first-type universals are neither "more localized" (whatever that may mean) than the higher-type ones; nor is the nexus between, say, Color and Green either more or less inhomogeneous than that between Green and the particulars which exemplify it. Yet I have no doubt that this prejudice has played a role in the traditional dialectic. For this I can think of two structural reasons. One such reason, or source, we came upon when we discovered that and why, as I then put it, the illusion stops at the first level, i.e., why there couldn't possibly be Classes of Classes (p. 103). The other likely source is exaggerated anti-Platonism. But, then, a universal of a higher type need no more be Platonic than one of the first. In the foil, for instance, the principle of exemplification holds for all types. Just as colors are inseparable from the particulars they exemplify, so Color is inseparable from colors. Thus it remains safely anchored to bare particulars, those splinters of Aristotelian matter which satisfy all reasonable "materialistic" urges.

The γ-ontologists' way of grounding, or, rather, alas, of not grounding, what the foil grounds in the higher-type universals, together with the pseudocharacters and the pseudorelations they exemplify, is glaringly inadequate. I have made a point of emphasizing both the structural and the phenomenological aspects of this inadequacy. When we shall come to Brentano, I shall return to the attack. So it may not be amiss to conclude by balancing this emphasis with another. I am not at all concerned with asserting again, with or without repeating the arguments, what I have asserted and argued before. My aim is, rather, to understand as accurately as I can the structural reasons and intellectual motives which caused certain philosophers to make what I am convinced are very bad mistakes. For I am also convinced that some of these philosophers also said many things which are both true and very important, and that, therefore, understanding the structural connections between the true and the false in what they said cannot but greatly increase our own grasp.

SUBSTANCES

T HE dialectic of substance does not center on a single problem. Rather, it revolves around a cluster of such. That makes the notion very complex. Yet one among these problems stands out. If you ask any philosopher what job substances are supposed to do, he will tell you, irrespective of whether or not he himself admits them into his world, that *"substances" account for the identity of ordinary objects through time and change*. Then he may or may not add that since this job is as important as it is, substances, not surprisingly, also do some others. In other words, he will tell you that, having introduced substances for this particular purpose, one will soon discover that they also serve some others. Presently, I shall isolate and distinguish by subscripts several substance notions, or, if you please, several ingredients of the traditional notion, one for each of the jobs or problems in the cluster. For the moment, though, when speaking of "substances" as the entities supposed to do the one job that stands out, I rather use double quotes.

Let us look at the italicized formula, make first some agreements about words, then get out of the way what is obvious. The use of 'accounting' is ontological; so I would rather speak of grounding. Until now we have used 'object' and 'thing' synonymously; called apples, stones, trees, and so on, ordinary objects. 'Thing' I shall use as before, reserving it for my own ontological talk (except in contexts which unmistakably are merely idiomatic). E.g., I shall continue to speak of the perfect particulars of a γ-world on the one hand and of its clusters and their subclusters on the other as its "simple" and "complex" things, respectively.[1] But we shall save breath and ink without incurring any

---

[1] Eventually we shall have to introduce further ties which, stronger than the weak γ (p. 40), connect some qualities, not just into subclusters but, rather, into *complex particulars*. This, though, is in the future (Section Eight). And, of course, complex particulars, too, are a kind of "things" of γ. The double quotes around

inconvenience by agreeing henceforth to use 'object' instead of 'ordinary object'. That makes apples, stones, trees, and so on, *objects* (though of course in the foil not things). So used, 'object' corresponds to the German *'Ding'*, as Brentano uses it, also to the way in which he, but not Meinong, uses *'Gegenstand'*. The last agreement is about 'identity through change and time'. The way change and time go together makes the phrase redundant. One might as well use either 'identity through change' or 'identity through time', depending on which is better suited to the context. As to 'identity', the philosophers who, unlike myself, do not distinguish among the several kinds of sameness, more often than not use 'same' and 'identical' synonymously. I, as you must have noticed, use only the former as, after a fashion, they use both.[2] That frees the latter for something else. Henceforth I shall use *'identity'* so that it stands for what is here meant by 'identity through time and change' and for nothing else. These agreements permit us to shorten the original formula. *"Substances" ground the identity of objects.*

I am sure you know what the formula means. Yet I would at this point rather be tedious than too concise. Objects begin and cease to exist. While existing they may and in fact do change. Generation and corruption, however, present no problem that interests me in addition to those of change. Nothing will therefore be lost if we consider only the changes objects undergo while existing. An object, while undergoing change, remains yet "identical" with itself, or, as one says, though I shall not say it, it remains the "same" object. Hence a "substance" cannot do the job it is supposed to do unless it is literally the same (same$_3$) at two points in time and throughout the interval between them. The distinction between identity and (the four kinds of) sameness permits us to state the issue of "substance" very succinctly. "Substantialists" solve the ontological problem presented by the identity of objects by means of an entity which is literally the same at two points in time and in the interval between them. Antisubstantialists, like myself, must think of other solutions.

The "substances" (and the substances) of the tradition are all things and are all "in time." Nor would anything be gained dialectically by ignoring these two ingredients of the notion. What, then, does it mean

---

'simple', 'complex', and 'thing' continue to serve the same purpose, calling attention to the irremediable blur produced by the failure to distinguish accurately between things and facts, functions and complexes (Section One).

[2] I say after a fashion because unless one makes these distinctions, he cannot but sometimes speak inaccurately. For another use of 'identical' and 'identity', connected with extensionality, which I would rather call sameness$_4$, see n. 16 of Section Five.

for a thing to be "in time"? The only entities of the foil which are "in time" are its bare particulars, i.e., those and only those things which exemplify the temporal relations of being earlier, later, and simultaneous. In γ this explication does not work, of course. Yet the idea is easily transferred. In γ-worlds, *as far as we have come to know them up to this point*, the only things "in time" are their perfect particulars and those clusters (with their subclusters) which are temporal cross sections of objects.[3] Or, at least, this is the primary meaning of 'being in time'. Derivatively, in the foil as well as in γ, one may, and I shall, say that objects are in time. Hence, all "substances" are things in time which are the same$_3$ at two time points and throughout the interval between them. Such things are called *continuants*. "Substances," whatever else they may be, are continuants.

I interrupt for a useful bit of pedantry. The Euclidean schema of Section Four is but a part of the Newtonian schema; and, just as the "space" points of the former are extensionless, so the "time" points of the latter are without extension in "time," or, as I shall rather say, they are *instants*. There are of course no instants in time (not: "time"), just as there are no extensionless points in space (not: "space").[4] Yet, alas, as with space, so with time. The success, and therefore the impact, of the Newtonian schema has been so great that the very phrase, 'time point', suggests the notion of an instant. The reason why, in spite of this awkward suggestion, I just used and shall continue to use the phrase, is that I have no choice. The only alternative I can think of is 'moment', which is already pre-empted. Moments, as we speak, are the temporal coordinate qualities of γ. Notice, finally, that if the distinction between the world in which we live and the schemata of science is as sharp as I make it, then no moment is "instantaneous."

In the first five sections everything has been done in the temporal cross section. It is indeed my contention that a very large part of ontology, though of course not all of it, can be so done. The dialectic of change or "substance" obviously does not belong to that part. This dialectic, however, though no doubt it stands out in the cluster, is not the whole of it. Three other problems arise already in the cross section. More accurately, each of these three has a core which arises already in the cross section. The reason for speaking in each case of the limited

---

[3] There is in each such cross section a moment (as well as, in the objects of the truncated world, a place). The notion of a temporal cross section is already familiar. But it will be taken up again in a moment. Notice, too, that, having explicated the notion, I am dropping the double quotes around 'in time'. The distinction between the primary and the derivative use, though important in some contexts, is of no great consequence to us.

[4] The double quotes are here operated as in Section Four. See p. 75.

problem (in a world without time) as the core of the larger one (in a temporal world) is that what a philosopher will do about the latter depends on what he has done about the former, in conjunction with what he does about the problem of change. That determines my strategy. *I shall first discuss the three limited notions; then introduce that of "substance," which I shall call substance₄ and still another one, to be called substance₅.* The entities which do the three limited jobs I call *momentary substances.* The extension of the dialectic from them to a world with change will (as I just said) be obvious. (For "substances" the very phrase, momentary substance, is a contradiction in terms. I use it in order to call attention to the nontemporal problems in the cluster, hoping that it will give you pause without jarring you too much.)

The two structural reasons for this strategy are obvious. For one, it supports the contention that a very large part of ontology can be done in the cross section. For another, it separates what can be separated and therefore, quite irrespective of this contention, must be separated. But there are also other reasons, in the tradition in general and the work of Brentano and Meinong in particular, which recommend the strategy. So I interrupt once more, this time for some comments in structural history, which should increase your understanding, not only of why in this section I proceed as I do, but also of my over-all plan and what I try to achieve in this book.

The notion of substance which dominates the tradition is Aristotle's. Its explication is inseparable from the dialectic of three issues. One is that of agents and activities. Aristotle's substances are not only "substances," i.e., substances₄, but also agents engaging in activities (substance₅). The other two issues were joined around two familiar dichotomies. One is the *form-matter* dichotomy; the other, that of *attributes versus accidents.* Aristotle invented them both.[5] I shall save words by speaking of these three issues as *agency* and the two dichotomies.

Aristotle's substance notion, then, which dominates the tradition, is inseparable from agency and the two dichotomies. Yet there is a difference between the former and the latter. The *two dichotomies* have not, I think, repaid the huge efforts so many have expended for so long on clarifying them. That puts them, in my considered judgment, among the heaviest dead weights that have burdened the tradition. So I shall in this section say as little about them as I can and outside of it, except

---

[5] Quite possibly, unless I am mistaken in what I glean from the scholars, with the intention not only of avoiding Platonic universals, but also of mitigating Plato's anthropomorphism which, still half-clouded by myth, was even cruder than his own.

at a very few places, nothing at all. The notion of *agency* is not unique, alas, in being irremediably blurred. But it is unique in its crude and ineradicable anthropomorphism which makes it not only the greatest single liability of the traditional dialectic but also, far beyond that, the heaviest "philosophical" drag on the intellectual development of man. Were I free to choose I would therefore ignore it completely. But its impact on a very large number of problems, including some of those which concern me in this book, is so great that I have no choice. In this section, I shall say as little about it as I can. But we shall have to return to it and pay a good deal of attention to it at several crucial points.

Brentano and Meinong both stand in the Aristotelian tradition. Thus you may wonder whether one who holds the views which, quite deliberately of course, I just stated so harshly, should undertake the task of examining the ontologies of these two thinkers. Will he not fail in his grasp? Or, even if he doesn't, will he not lack that measure of sympathy, or at least empathy, without which one cannot in philosophy completely unpack what one rejects? The prospect is not as dim as you may fear.

Brentano also had a keen historical interest in Aristotle and, unlike Meinong, professed himself to be his disciple again and again. As a historian he attended to all aspects of the classical substance dialectic. But there is in this respect a clean break and a sharp contrast between Brentano the scholar and Brentano the thinker. And what goes for Brentano, in this respect also goes for Meinong. My concern is, selectively, with the thinker. The scholar I shall completely ignore.

With respect to the three issues, there is again a difference between the two classical dichotomies (form-matter, attribute-accident) on the one hand and agency on the other. The *two dichotomies* both Brentano and Meinong brush aside without ceremony. Nor are they in fact influenced by them except at one point, where Brentano's thought shows the impact[6] of the attribute-accident pattern. To this point, when we

---

[6] As usual, this is a structural comment, not a biographical guess. For the rest, I prefer anticipating in a footnote to not satisfying those who can get something out of the briefest of hints. As everyone knows and as I shall presently recall, "substances" are hidden. The color and shape of an apple, for instance, are presented to us in a sense in which its "substance" is not. This distinction is inextricably connected with the attribute-accident pattern. The continuant perfect particulars as which Brentano assays our minds are hidden in this sense. This, I believe, is the point where the pattern impinges. But, then, at the end of his life, he also came to hold the view that the cluster of coordinate qualities which according to him is a body's momentary substance, is hidden from us. Nor do the bodies of his world have any nonmomentary substance. (See also what is said above toward the end of the paragraph.)

shall come to it, attention will of course be called. The case of *agency* is different. Large parts of the work of both men are completely free from it. That is one reason why I admire them. But there are other parts, perhaps as large and more central, which are under its influence. That is why we shall have to return to it and pay a good deal of attention to it at several crucial points. Yet its influence on these men is curiously diluted. To put it in a nutshell, their Selves are not only continuants but also agents engaging in activities (substances$_5$). With respect to bodies, however, they are both radical "antisubstantialists." This difference is indeed one of the features on which I shall base my diagnosis that Brentano, for all the fervor of his realism$_2$, is structurally an idealist. Meinong, we shall see, at the very end of his career, in a last frantic effort to reach the realism to which he came so tragically close, changed his mind.

This diagnosis fits well with something else. Both Brentano and Meinong, although the former even more than the latter, were throughout their philosophical careers preoccupied with the limited problems (cores, as I called them) which are solved by introducing the *three notions of momentary substance*. The one I shall list third would in fact not even have occurred to me, nor would I have emphasized it as much as I shall, were it not for the importance it has in the thought of Brentano.

I do hope that these comments will have increased your understanding, not only of why I shall now proceed as proposed, but of my over-all plan. I also hope that you have acquired some inkling why the fivefold distinction within substance, which at first seems so pedantic, so "ahistorical," so "biased" against Aristotle, serves some purpose in a book which is also about the last two great Aristotelians.

The examination of the three momentary notions is best prefaced by a remark that applies to all three. There are two ways of proceeding. One may consider a world literally without time. Such a world contains no temporal entity. That makes it less than completely accurate to call it a temporal cross section of anything. If, for instance, it is a γ-world, then its clusters (objects), which inaccurately we call cross sections (of objects of our world) do not (like the latter) each have a moment among their constituents. This is one way. The other way is not to stay within a single cross section (of our world) but to consider instead the class of all temporal cross sections of all (its) objects (without, however, paying any attention to these objects themselves). The second way is a short-cut to the eventual extension from the cores to the problems of our world. This is therefore the way we shall take. So I shall use 'cross section' and 'momentary object' synonymously. (Later on, when again dealing over long stretches with what can be done in the cross section, I shall suppress 'momentary', refer to the clusters which are the momentary objects of γ as objects.)

I. *Substances as individuators.* Substances₁ are individuators. With the problem of individuation we are already familiar; so I shall be very brief. A *momentary substance₁* is *the* thing "in" a momentary object which individuates it. As you see, it is part of the notion that it be a single entity, a thing, and "in" the object it individuates. In the foil every momentary substance₁ is a bare particular; and conversely; for it is part of the notion of a bare particular to be momentary and "in" in an object. In γ-worlds, loosely speaking, a momentary object is individuated by a place and a moment, say, p_1 and t_1. I say loosely speaking because it is also part of the notion that a substance is not a class. Accurately speaking, therefore, the momentary object which serves us as an example is individuated neither by $\{p_1, t_1\}$ nor by $[p_1, t_1]$ but, rather, by $\gamma(p_1, t_1)$. Is $\gamma(p_1, t_1)$ a cluster or a subcluster? Or, equivalently, is the γ "in" it strong or weak? The answer depends on how the ontologist who propounds this particular world assays space and time. Upon the so-called container view, $\gamma(p_1, t_1)$ is by itself an object (cluster). Upon all other assays of space and time it is merely a subcluster.

II. *Substances as supports of their qualities.* In substance talk the individuator "in" an object is often said to "support" its ordinary qualities just because it is what it is, namely, an individuator. As for individuators, so for minimal objects and for agents. This use of 'support' is expendable. There is, however, a specific meaning that can be given to this word in these contexts which I think worth identifying and calling attention to.

No γ-ontologist (except Goodman, if one decides to include him) countenances either space or time atoms. That makes place and time the two dimensions none of whose qualities are simples. With the use of 'part' which is so unhappily frequent among γ-ontologists, nor just among them, a pitch has no "parts"; a hue has no "parts"; the very idea is absurd. But each place and each moment has "parts"; or, as I would say if I were a γ-ontologist, each place and each moment has components.

Take a red spot or a middle c. We say that the quality, red, is spread over, extends all through, or that it fills, the place (area). We do not say that the place is spread or extends all over, or that it fills the quality. We say, or at least we might say, that the pitch fills, or extends through, the moment, but not that the moment fills, or extends through, the pitch; and so on. The ontological ground of this phenomenological asymmetry is not hard to find. If the quality red "fills" a place, it also

fills all its "parts." The converse, on the other hand, since color qualities have no "parts," does not even make sense.

In the temporal cross section $\gamma(p_1, t_1, a_1, \cdots, a_n)$, $\gamma(p_1, t_1)$ *supports*
$a_1, a_2, \cdots, a_n$. This is how I express the asymmetry just pointed out.
Call an entity "in" an object which in this sense supports some of its
qualities a substance$_2$. That makes $\gamma(p_1, t_1)$ a *momentary substance$_2$* of γ.
The momentary substances$_2$ of the foil are, as a moment's reflection
will show you, its bare particulars. For, in the foil there is the relation
being-part-of and there are the a priori truths about it, such as that
each bare particular, though simple, has parts. It follows that in γ as
well as in the foil the two notions are coextensive. *Their momentary
substances$_1$ are also their momentary substances$_2$ and conversely.*[7]

I take the ease with which the notion of a substance$_2$ can be accounted for in both ϵ and γ to bode well for its significance. If it still
seems a bit far-fetched to you, think of Descartes, whose substance
notion was sufficiently non-Aristotelian to make him think and talk of
substance as merely an attribute among attributes, or, in γ-language,
as a quality among qualities, and in particular, for bodies, as "extension"! To be sure this attribute supposedly stands out somehow, somehow is characteristic. But, then, what does that mean? Perhaps that it
supports the others?

III. *Substances as minimal objects.* The *substance$_3$* or *the* minimal object in an object α is an object β such that (1) α is "in" β, and (2) no
entity "in" β, except β itself, is an object. The definite article in 'the
minimal object' takes for granted that there is one and only one sub-
stance$_3$ in each object. Yet, unless space and time are atomic, there
obviously are none. So we add the clause that (3) β must not be produced by "dividing" α either spatially or temporally. Stated in ϵ-
language, (3) requires that the particular (or particulars) in α and β are
the same in each temporal cross section; stated in γ-language, it requires that α and β occupy at each moment the same place. Even with
(3) added, there remains the abstract possibility of more than one
minimal object in α. This, though, is the sort of generality which is

[7] Brentano, we shall see, held the container view, or something more or less like
it, for a very long time, abandoned it only shortly before he died. Also, while the
role in his ontology of the ideas connected with the notion of substance is very
great, there are no nonmomentary substances of any kind "in" the bodies of his
world. His minds, on the other hand, are individuated by continuants (sub-
stances$_4$) which are also agents (substances$_5$). These are some of the reasons why
his use of 'substance' shifts with the context and the time of the utterance and
why all merely scholarly attempts, which do not go to the dialectical heart of the
matter, of making it consistent, are doomed to failure. Again, you see why I insist on the fivefold distinction.

merely tedious. So I disregard it. If there are no others, every object is trivially its own minimal object. So I exclude this triviality. Now we are ready for the question. *Are there minimal objects?* The notion seems strange. Perhaps you will remember that, as I just remarked, my only reason for introducing it is the large role it plays in Brentano's thought. Because of this role we shall have to return to it. But a few comments about *momentary substances₃* will not be out of order now.

1. Let us start in γ. Suppose for the sake of the argument that a place (p_1), a moment (t_1), a shape (a_1), and a color (a_2) are all the perfect particulars in a momentary spot, α. ($\alpha = \gamma(p_1, t_1, a_1, a_2)$.) To say that $\gamma(p_1, t_1)$ is the momentary substance₃ in α is to propose the container assay of space and time. It follows that, if this assay is adopted, the three momentary substance notions become coextensive. The momentary substances₃ of such worlds are also their momentary substances₁ and their momentary substances₂, and conversely with respect to both of the latter.

2. The substance₃ "in" an object is *separable* (p. 88) from the rest of it. But the rest of the object, or, more precisely, in γ-ontologies, every quality "in" the object but not "in" its substance₃ and every cluster of such, "depends" on its substance₃ in the very strong sense that, unless there are qualities not "in" objects, which Platonistic belief is of course not held by any γ-ontologist, it could not exist without its substance₃, which is separable from it but from which it is not separable.

3. The last idea is generalizable. Include for the moment the brightness (a_3) and the saturation (a_4) of the color among the things in α. One may reasonably hold that a_3 and a_4 depend on a_2 in exactly the same sense in which a_1 and a_2 depend on $\gamma(p_1, t_1)$, and that therefore, relatively to a_3 and a_4, a_2 is a *secondary* substance₃. *Objects peel like onions;* that is the idea. If you look for better examples, you will have to wait until we come to Brentano's assay of minds. These examples you will, I think, find impressive. Or you will at least be impressed with the large role the notion plays in his thought.

4. One who is under the impact of these ideas may use them to arrive at a gradation among a priori truths. In the foil there is no such gradation. If, for instance, I were to apply my notion of such truths to a γ-world, I would call it an a priori truth that a cluster, to be a cross section of an object, must contain a place and a moment, just as I would call it another such truth that a cluster which is such a cross section cannot contain a color quality without also containing one which is a shape, and conversely. But I am sure you see how under the influence of our notion one may come to believe that the "dependence" of either a_1 or a_2 on $\gamma(p_1, t_1)$ is "greater" than the mutual "dependence" of a_1 and

a_2 on each other; or, what amounts virtually to the same, how he may come to believe that the first of the two a priori truths I mentioned lies "deeper" than the other.

5. Not by chance, I have stayed with γ. I do not know how the notion of a substance$_3$ could be adapted to a world with bare particulars. In such a world, as you may infer from the preceding comment, it all comes down to the several truths within an ungraded a priori.

IV. *Extension of the first three notions to a world with change.* Let the subscript i run over 1, 2, 3. What is a (nonmomentary) substance$_i$? The answer is obvious. A substance$_i$ is a continuant "in" an object such that, for every time point at which the object exists, it is the momentary substance$_i$ "in" the cross section of the object at this time point. Are there substances$_i$? The answer, again rather obviously, is No, for both ϵ and γ, *at least as far as we have come to know the entities of γ-worlds up to this point.* But we need not hurry too much. I shall first make a *distinction*, then look at an *example*, conclude with a *comment*.

The *distinction* is between bare and perfect particulars. Bare particulars are momentary. As I just reminded you, this is part of the notion. *A perfect particular (quality) may be a continuant.* If, for instance, a tone continues for an hour at the same pitch, the perfect particular which in a γ-assay grounds this pitch is a continuant which spans an hour.

The *example* is a truncated world that differs from ours in two respects. For one, there is no spatial change whatsoever. Thus there is no locomotion. Nor do objects change in either size or shape. Yet they do undergo changes, e.g., in color. For another, there is no generation or corruption. To see why I introduce the second feature, consider that in our world it could happen that the sole reason for a person who will sit a hundred years hence in the chair in which I now sit not being I is the difference in time. By virtue of the second feature there is thus, in this world of my fancy, a one-one correspondence between objects and places. By virtue of the first, "an object's place" is a continuant. In a γ-survey of this world, an object's place (i.e., the place which is "in" it at all time points) is not only its substance$_i$, but also, since the place is the same$_3$ at all time points, its substance$_4$. Of this, more presently.[8]

The *comment* animadverts once more on the usefulness of the fivefold distinction within substance. In our world, there are no substances$_i$. In the foil, there are instead temporal series of bare particulars, held together in the familiar fashion by the laws connecting the cross sections of objects. The first to propose a solution in this style of the ontological problem presented by the identity of objects was Berkeley. That is

[8] More precisely, places would be substances$_1$ and substances$_2$; they would be substances$_3$ only on the supposition that a place by itself is a minimal object. But, then, in a world of this sort the supposition seems very natural.

why, ignoring all details and refinements, I shall sometimes speak of
the Berkeley solution. As for ϵ, so for γ-worlds without substances$_4$,
such as the truncated world of Brentano.

In these worlds, therefore, there are no (nonmomentary) substances$_i$
but merely, as in ϵ, temporal series of momentary substances$_i$, held together in the Berkeleyan manner. But there are also γ-worlds with
substances$_4$ (which are also substances$_5$), such as the complete (i.e.,
nontruncated, so that it includes minds) world of Brentano. What these
"substances" are supposed to be we do as yet not know. But we know
already that their temporal cross sections are not and could not possibly be those $\gamma(p_k, t_k)$ which are in fact the momentary substances$_i$ of
these worlds. Thus we have spotted the source of a likely blur in the
undifferentiated notion of substance.

V. *Substances as continuants.* I know of no major ontology in the
tradition, nor, for that matter, of any one which, without having exerted
a major influence, is of structural interest, whose substances$_4$ are not
also substances$_5$. Structurally, you will see, the distinction is helpful
nevertheless. A substance$_4$ is, quite simply, a continuant "in" the
object, which, being a continuant, establishes its identity by being the
same$_3$ at all time points in the object's span of existence. In the γ-world
I just designed, for instance, an object's place is its substance$_4$. This is
one reason why I took the trouble of designing the example. But it also
helps by providing a way of speaking and thinking about the traditional notion of "substance," that helps one to understand the intellectual motive behind it as well as its fatal weakness. Or, at least, it helps
me. In our world there is of course no property of an object, or, at
least, there need not be any, which does not either begin or cease to
exist, either once or several times, during the object's span of existence.
Still more cautiously, there is no such property as long as a "property"
is something that is or could be presented to us in the sense in which,
say, a disposition[9] is not and cannot. Yet dispositions are, and in some
contexts are therefore quite properly spoken of as, properties. This is
the cue. Trying to understand the traditional notion of "substance,"
the best I can do is to think of it in analogy to the places of that world
of my fancy, i.e., as one or several[10] "hidden" properties, or, in ontological γ-language, as either a single perfect particular or a subcluster of
such "in" the object. Except for two very special features a substance$_4$

[9] I use 'disposition' rather than 'dispositional property' quite deliberately. See
my essay "Dispositional Properties and Dispositions" in *Philosophical Studies*, 6,
1955, 77–80.
[10] Behind the alternative *one versus several* lurks the classical issue of the simplicity of substantial natures, or, what amounts virtually to the same, of the so-
called multiplicity of forms.

is thus a perfect particular, either simple or complex.[11] The first special feature is that it is a continuant whose span of existence coincides with that of the object; the second, that it is "hidden behind" rather than "one among" the particulars "in" any of the cross-sectional clusters of the object.

Notice, finally, the historical connection of this notion with the two classical dichotomies. For one, the attribute-accident contrast, though probably not exhausted by, is yet inextricably connected with, that between "hidden" and "presented." For another, the connection between "substances" and "natures" is historically as close as it can be. Yet, natures were thought of as generic, substances as specific or "individuals." Hence the familiar pattern. A substance (undifferentiated use) is thought of as a compound of form (i.e., a nature) and matter. The latter supposedly does the individuating. The trials and tribulations of this dead end (a few pages back I spoke of dead weights) are familiar. Yet I want you to notice how the blur I just spoke about appears on this occasion. The temporal cross sections of a substance$_4$ are not and could not possibly be what we know they would have to be, namely, the $\gamma(p_i, t_i)$ which are in fact the momentary substances$_i$ of this world.[12]

VI. *Substances as agents.* Although, as I just remarked, there are in the tradition no substances$_4$ which are not also substances$_5$, agency has a dialectic all of its own, which makes the distinction structurally useful. To this dialectic I now turn.

The piece of wax first had a certain shape. After I squeezed it, it had another shape. I was the agent. The change in the piece of wax was wrought by my activity. While engaging in it, I was active; the piece of wax, passive. Commonsensically there is no problem.

Ontologically, an *agent* is a source of *activity.* 'Agent' and 'activity' are not synonyms. I, for one, would not know what it could possibly mean for anything to be its own source. *An agent is a thing* such that, if there were no agents, objects would not undergo changes. This, though, is merely one half of the notion. The other half is that for a change actually to occur, an appropriate agent must at the appropriate time engage in an appropriate activity. *An activity* is not a thing. *In fact, it belongs in no ontological category whatsoever.* Agents are at least things. So there is a category for them. *Activity is a pseudo-ontological category.*

---

[11] A "complex particular" would be a subcluster if the tie among its simples were not stronger than the corresponding weak γ. The notion will be introduced in Part II.

[12] See also n. 7, above, and what was said there about Brentano's shifting use of 'substance'.

This is not to say that there are agents. In the foil there are none, just as (if you like formulations with a paradoxical flavor) there is no change in it. I am merely explicating some notions.

A substance₅ is the agent in an object. Its activities produce changes in the object "in" which it is as well as in others. In the latter case it, or perhaps the object "in" which it is, is *active*. The object in which the change is produced, or perhaps the agent "in" it, is *passive*. That shows how 'active' and 'passive' are used in this sort of pseudo-ontological talk.

In strict logic an agent (substance₅) would *perhaps* not need to be a continuant (substance₄). However, nothing would be gained structurally by considering this possibility, *if it is one*, while historically a good deal would be lost. Agents act *purposively* and *freely*. Whether or not such purposiveness and freedom are made part of the notion, they certainly have been and still are the dominant motive of those who insist on there being agents. Structurally, it may well be that the notion of a momentary entity acting purposively and freely does not even make sense. That is why I said "perhaps" and "if it is one." But we need not pursue. Nor shall I in this book more than mention what I have dealt with elsewhere.[13] There has been and there still is the unfortunate belief that the purposiveness and freedom of agents are incompatible with the thesis of scientific determinism. This belief is not just false; it has long been intellectually disreputable; it has been and still is that worst of all "philosophical" drags on the intellectual development of man. As you gather, I am prepared to die in the last ditch for two propositions. First, that unfortunate belief is false. Second, there are in fact no agents.

There is one more point. The connection between substances₄ and substances₅ is, I said, constant throughout the tradition. There ought to be some structural reasons for that. Two stand out. Remember, first, the "dispositions" which are the only properties one could reasonably hold to be continuants "in" the objects of our world. The anthropomorphic suggestions that connect "disposition" and "agency" are obvious. Remember, second, the group of laws in which the anti-substantialists ground the several series by means of which they solve

---

[13] For an analysis of the notion and thesis of scientific determinism, see my *Philosophy of Science* (University of Wisconsin Press, 1957). But I hurry to add, lest you think either that things are simpler than they are or that I believe my task to be easier than it is, that Brentano, from whom one can learn so much, not only included minds which are agents into his world but also called himself a determinist. If that inclines you to dismiss Brentano as not really worth while, think of Leibniz. (Incidentally, Brentano was an ardent admirer of Leibniz. That shows once again that and how things hang together.)

the problem of identity. The "nature" of the agent "in" an object "disposes" it to "produce" the properties which by these laws it has.[14] In other words, it is the "nature" of the "hidden" agent to produce those (nondispositional) properties which by its "nature" the object has. In this proposition the two occurrences of 'nature' stand either for one entity or for two. In the first case, the proposition is a tautology. In the second, it is the first step in an infinite regress. That is another fatal weakness of the tradition. Molière's sneer at the *vis dormitiva* is fully justified.

VII. *A genetic fallacy.* Agency is not only the source of an intellectual scandal which goes far beyond the traditional dialectic; it is also within the latter the source of a fallacy whose impact on ontology has been as great as it is deplorable. I conclude with an analysis of this fallacy.

Consider two qualities, a, b; let c be either a quality or a cluster of such. Make three assumptions. At a certain moment a and b are, while c is not, among the components of (the temporal cross section of) an object α; at a certain later moment c is, but a and b are not, among its components; this change has been produced by an activity of the substance in α. In such situations a substance-ontologist says such things as that *c is made out of a and b*, or that *c is a "complex" whose "constituents" are a and b*, and so on.[15] What leads the rest of us occasionally to say the same things in some such situations is the belief that the change occurring in them is an instance of a causal connection of the kind also called genetic. The obtaining of such a connection is a fact; call it F. (Upon the Humean type of assay of causal connections which the foil adopts, F is very complex.) Using 'complex' and 'constituent' ontologically, c is either simple (G_1) or a complex. If it is a complex there are four possibilities. (G_2) Neither a nor b is among its components. (G_3) Either a or b but not both are among its components. (G_4) Both a and b are components of c; but c has still other components which are things. (G_5) a and b are the only components of c which are things. *F not only does not entail any of the five mutually exclusive alternatives G, but is compatible with the negation of any of them.* This is the point. Those who miss it are in danger of mistaking a genetic diagnosis for an ontological assay. That is the deplorable mistake. It has been made again and again. Examples will not be lacking in what follows. But you see already the propriety of calling activity a pseudo-ontological category.

---

[14] In many of the classical ontologies such "production" is outright "creation" under God. Notice, too, that I ignore the problem of so-called transeunt causation for which substantialism has no adequate solution.

[15] More accurately, these "components" of "complexes" are but pseudocomponents of clusters. But the difference makes no difference; so I let it go.

Part II
Representationalism

INTRODUCTORY REFLECTIONS

I SEE the paper in front of me. I remember that I took it out of the drawer. I think of what I want to write on it. I wonder whether I shall ever cover it. As I use 'know', generically, these are four *knowing situations*. It would seem more natural to speak of four cases of awareness; but I need 'awareness' for another job. In the foil there are reasons why the generic use of 'knowing' is not as strange as at first it may seem. In the γ-ontologies we shall mostly talk about, we shall soon come upon a word suitable for generic use. In these worlds every knowing situation is a *conceiving situation*. Not that 'conceiving' represents what the generic use of 'knowing' represents. Yet the γ-ontologists' use of their word will permit us to get along without overstraining the generic use of mine. So I ask you to put up with it for a while.

Every knowing situation involves three entities: one which knows,

125

another which is known, and a connection between the one and the other. What knows is a mind, or, more precisely, a constituent of a mind, of the sort called an experience or an *act*. Many philosophers, including Brentano, Meinong, and myself, prefer 'act'. The notions of a mind and of an experience or act are commonsensical and, within common sense, completely unproblematic. The problem is how to assay minds and acts. What is known in a knowing situation is called the *intention* of the act "in" it. When I perceive that the sheet of paper is white, its being white is the intention of this act of perceiving. When I think about Jupiter's carryings-on with mortal women, these carryings-on are the intention of this act of mine. To say of anything that it is an intention is to say merely that it is the intention of an act. That makes the notion of intention commonsensical and, within common sense, completely unproblematic. The problem is how to assay certain intentions.

Perceiving, believing, remembering, thinking of, imagining, and so on, are different species of the genus knowing. In ontology that raises the question how to ground, or, with a topographical metaphor, where to locate the differences between the several species. Shall we so assay the act that the ground, whatever it may turn out to be, of these differences is entirely "in" it, with the assay of the connection itself, whatever it may turn out to be, remaining unaffected by them? Or shall we ground the differences in the connection? The task I set myself would be even more difficult than it is, nor probably would it have attracted me, if I did not agree with the ontologists whose work I want to examine on this most fundamental issue. We all ground the species not in the connection but in the act. That enables me to propose an agreement which will save words. An act, or perhaps some constituent of it, depending on how one assays it, *intends* its intention. Let us agree to use 'intend' and 'intending' so that they stand for the connection in all knowing situations.

What is a mind? As the question is meant, ontologically, the proper answer is an assay. The foil proposes one. Different γ-ontologists propose different others. But, again, there is between the foil and the γ-ontologies I shall examine a measure of agreement which permits me to take certain things for granted. I take for granted that there are simple things which are mental. I take for granted that minds are mental complexes and that all the simple things "in" them are mental.[1] I take

---

[1] As you see, we have reached a stage where I think it safe to speak of the "things," the "simples," and the "complexes" of γ-worlds without adding double quotes. Nor do I have any desire to worry the same point over and over, no matter how fundamental it may be. Yet I also want to be clear. So I remind you once more of what I trust has by now become so ingrained that I shall not with-

it for granted that acts are "in" minds, more precisely, "in" temporal cross sections of minds; or that, perhaps, they are such cross sections. Being able to take that much for granted, I shall also be able to proceed for quite some time without any detailed reference to the foil's assay of minds, acts, and the knowing situation, provided only you will permit me now five brief remarks in order to make clear immediately, or at least to single out for future clarification, what cannot safely be ignored.

1. In the foil, among simple things, mental-nonmental is a dichotomy among universals. Particulars, being bare, are literally neither mental nor nonmental. That is why the distinction between minds and bodies is (in the foil) not categorial (ontological). It also makes literally false what I just asserted, namely that the things "in" a mind are all mental. But the falsehood will save us words without doing any harm in the contexts in which I shall "take it for granted."

2. In the foil, to be nonmental, to be physical, to be perceptual, are three and not one. The distinctions are needed for the solutions I proposed for the problems in the realism-idealism cluster, including those of perception.[2] The problems themselves are crucial for what I am here about. These distinctions of mine, however, are not; or, rather, they are so only at a much later stage, after much of what our interest here centers on has been taken care of. So I shall put my own distinctions aside and, except for some special contexts much later, speak of trees, stones, chairs, and so on, as physical objects or bodies. That will permit me to talk more nearly like the philosophers in the tradition I am examining, which always helps to make things easier.

3. The subsistents of the foil are neither mental nor physical. The γ-ontologists, we know, are all more or less explicitly reistic. Thus they are hardly aware of the subsistents. But it is only fair to say that to whatever extent they would be aware of their ontological status, they would agree that those entities which ϵ-ontologists assay as subsistents are neither physical nor mental. (I express myself as circumstantially as I do, speaking of those entities which ϵ-ontologists assay as subsistents, because one who assays all relations as nexus and, therefore, as subsistents, like my very special friend whom I hope you have not forgotten, would consistently have to hold that some subsistents such as, say, the spatial relations, are physical.)

4. *In the foil, the connection intending is assayed as a fundamental*

---

out special occasion remind you of it again. A cluster, for instance, is not really a complex (fact) but, rather, a pseudocomplex; or, with the category of fact completely ignored or overlooked, a "thing" of the kind called "complex."

[2] For these solutions see the "Realistic Postscript" in *Logic and Reality* (University of Wisconsin Press, 1964).

nexus (M). How the γ-ontologists assay it is a very major question which we must not prejudge. But again, there is a helpful measure of agreement. No γ-ontologist ever assayed intending either as a thing, either simple or complex, or as a fact. So I shall take for granted that it is neither the one nor the other.

5. Bodies are objects, and, in the truncated world, objects are bodies. Since we have now begun to consider the world as a whole we must agree how we are henceforth going to use 'object'. Are minds "objects"? Bodies and minds are both complexes. That we may again safely take for granted. But to say that minds are objects would not only not serve any purpose but almost certainly become a source of confusion unless there is something in the "structure" of both which, in spite of the very different "natures" of the (simple) things "in" them, provides a ground for applying the same label. Once more my task is simplified by a measure of agreement. In the foil as well as in the tradition I under- took to examine, bodies and minds are so assayed that it not only makes sense but is helpful to call them two kinds of objects. What differences there are, in addition to those entailed by that between facts and pseudocomplexes, come out in the two assays of the act. But it will be safe to ignore them in this section provided you will permit me in the next few pages to speak as if the knower "in" a knowledge situa- tion were not the act "in" it but, rather, the mind "in" which this act is.

In the foil all objects are facts but not all facts are objects. Some things are "in" objects; if they are characters they may be "in" more than one; if they are relations they may be "in" none. In γ-ontologies objects are things and all things are "in" objects. Facts, we know, are under a shadow. Radical as these differences are, for the introductory reflections I am about to present they make no difference. So I shall sweep them aside by constructing a sort of topographical schema or map of the world which is so gross and so incomplete that these radical differences either will not appear in it at all or, if they do, will not de- tract from its usefulness for those reflections.

Some complexes are mixed, i.e., some of the simple things among their constituents are physical, some are mental. A person is such a complex. So certainly is every knowing situation which is a case of veridical perception. Our use of 'object' is not yet fully established. So it could conceivably commit us to count some mixed complexes as ob- jects. The map I am about to construct ignores such "objects." Thus, should there be any, this is one respect in which the map will be incom- plete.

Divide a sheet of paper in two equal halves by drawing a line down its middle from top to bottom. Make for each simple thing[3] in the world a mark on the paper which is to serve as its picture. (I use 'picture' because for obvious reasons I want to avoid 'represent'.) Put the mark in the left half if the thing is mental, in the right half if it is physical. Draw a closed curve around each class of marks depicting all the simple things "in" a single object; let the curve serve as the picture of this object. What the map you will thus obtain will look like depends on whether you embrace ϵ or γ. In either case, though, each simple thing and each object will have a picture; each picture will be in one of the two halves; none will straddle the dividing line. For, of course, every simple thing and every object (unless there are mixed ones which, should there be any, we don't depict) is either physical or mental. (Notice, too, that I have quietly returned to operating within the usual cross section.)

Looking at this crude map, I cannot resist the metaphor of two realms. All mental things and objects belong to the first realm, or, briefly, to the First; all physical ones belong to the Second; and there are of course no others. Thus all simple things and all objects are depicted on the sheet; its left half is a map of the First; its right half is a map of the Second. Let us check how much of a case of veridical perception comes through on this crude map. I perceive a chair. My mind and the chair appear as two closed curves in the left and right halves, respectively. The connection between the two, intending not being either a simple or a complex, has no picture.

Everything that has been said so far is merely preparation. Now I am ready to start.

Some particles, the physicists tell us, are so unstable that their life span is but a few millionths of a second. They nevertheless value the discovery of a new particle of this sort very highly. To understand that, one must consider how such discoveries are made. The impulse always comes from theory. In the first stage, somewhere in the computations something does not come out as according to the accepted theory it should. In the second stage, some theorists figure out that if there were an unstable particle of a certain kind, everything would come out as it should, on paper as well as in the laboratory. In the third stage, theorists and experimentalists consult on how to demonstrate that the particle which ought to be there actually is there. Then the trap in the laboratory is set. If the intended game obliges, everything is well. To

---

[3] I of course would simply use 'thing' rather than 'simple thing', or, should the emphasis be required, speak of a nonderived thing. See n. 1. But perhaps you have already noticed the convenience of using in these contexts 'simple' and 'complex' as the other side does.

the theorist, in particular, the discovery of the new particle is like having found a key to a door which he had not been able to unlock.

I propose to construct an ontology which is so extremely unstable that quite possibly no philosopher has ever entertained it except for a brief moment.[4] My purpose is similar to the physicists'. I expect to use this unstable ontology as a key, to enhance by means of it my structural understanding of some others which at first sight seem more stable and actually have been proposed. Perhaps you will think that I did this sort of thing once before, in the case of the γ-ontology I called very special. There is a similarity; but there is also a striking and important difference. My very special friend, who assayed all connections as subsistents, does not only not exist but, if he did, would be very lonely. He is an explicit nonreist in a world of reists. That puts a limit on the implicit influence of what he saw on those who hardly surmised that there was anything to be seen. Nor is his ontology particularly unstable, even though, being a γ-ontology, it cannot, if I am right, stand up indefinitely under the proper dialectical probing. But there is still another similarity that might have struck you. What I am about to do now, for the third and last time, is like what I have done twice before in this book. I resort once more to something which, unless I am completely mistaken, is not only an expository device but also a sharp tool of structural analysis. The first of these devices were the pseudo-entities I called monsters; the second, the illusions I called wraiths. Now I am introducing an ontology so unstable that it is properly compared with the most unstable particles of modern physics. First monsters; then wraiths; now worlds less stable than a flicker. Perhaps you find my machinery a bit cumbersome. If you merely wonder whether it is really needed, I beg you to suspend judgment. If you are one of those who believe that all good philosophy can and must be done without all machinery, symbolic or otherwise, then this book has not been written for you.

The unstable ontology I am about to construct is the very heart or core, the structural core, if you please, of representationalism. Thus, had anyone actually held it, during the last three hundred years or so,

---

[4] If asked to guess which philosopher whom I have not read might have propounded an ontology more or less like my most unstable prototype I would name Bolzano. I hope that I shall still have time to read Bolzano and do something about him. Certainly my appetite has been whetted by the four striking pages Reinhardt Grossmann devotes to him in his essay on "Frege's Ontology" (*Philosophical Review*, 70, 1961, 23–40). If Grossmann is right, then Bolzano may well be a major ontologist to be rescued from the captivity in which he is still being held by a motley of logicians, positivists, and mere scholars.

he would have found himself a representationalist in a world of representationalists. For, alas, ever since Descartes virtually everyone either was or still is a representationalist, or, what is perhaps even more unfortunate, either accepted or still accepts enough of representationalism's basic gambit to foredoom his own struggles against it. (Brentano and even Meinong, we shall see, are two cases in point.) The only reason therefore, if I may so express myself, for the prototype's not having been widely held is that it is so patently and so dramatically unstable. But, then, representationalism itself is inherently unstable, leading to either idealism or phenomenalism; and that is of course why the unstable prototype will prove to be a powerful key to its dialectic.

Representationalism is a doctrine concerning the assay of all knowing situations. I perceive a chair. The chair is the intention of my act. According to the doctrine, what is before my mind is not the chair itself but something else which "represents" it. The representative is called an *idea*, in this case, the idea of the chair. This is so, irrespective of whether or not the perception is veridical. Nor is the doctrine limited to perception. As for perceiving, so for all other species. Whatever is "before my mind" when it intends something is an idea, or perhaps ideas.

The doctrine is strange. A host of questions and a number of objections immediately come to mind. If all we are ever presented with are representatives, how do we know that they represent anything, and, in case only some of them do, how do we know which do and which don't? The question is obvious. There is hardly a clever beginner to whom it has not occurred. So I shall call it the sophomore's question or objection. Obviously it has no satisfactory answer. That is why asking it is one way of challenging the very idea of representationalism, or, as I shall say, since it will be better to avoid the casual uses of the key word, of challenging its basic gambit.

If one accepts this basic gambit, another host of difficulties crowds in. How about our knowledge of ideas? Do we know them, too, only through their representatives? How about self-knowledge? How about the representation of the intentions of beliefs such as, say, that all dogs are mammals? Is the representative in this case one idea or is it two, that of a dog and that of a mammal? If it is two, how are they connected so that we may ground in what is presented to us the difference between the two beliefs; that all dogs are mammals, on the one hand; and that none are, on the other? And so on, and so on. These are just three among the many problems one has to face if he accepts the basic gambit. These problems and the solutions that have been proposed for them are part and parcel of the dialectic of representationalism, which will occupy us through the rest of this book. Right now I want to reflect on the basic gambit.

Stay with the paradigm and turn to the map. My mind is in the First. Or, if you will permit me to say so, it is a first. The chair is a second. *The idea is a third!* If representationalism is right, or, rather, if the unstable prototype of it which I am about to construct is right, then the map we made is incomplete, not just in the way in which we have always known it to be so, but in a new and more radical way. The cause of this more radical incompleteness is that in the prototype there are three realms and not just two. Thus, if the prototype is right and we want to make a map of the world as complete as the old one is in case it is wrong, we must start anew.

We divide the sheet by two vertical lines into three strips. The leftmost strip is a map of the First; the rightmost, one of the Second. The strip between them is the map of the Third. Every mark in it depicts an idea; every idea is depicted by such a mark. Pick now three marks on a horizontal line, one in each strip; let them be the pictures of my mind, of the idea of the chair, and of the chair itself respectively. Looking toward the chair, I find the idea of it "before" my mind. Thus it is indeed a *Vorstellung*. The map brings that out. Standing between the mind and its intention, the idea also stands "in front of" the latter. The map again brings that out. In the German prefix '*vor*' this particular use of 'in front of' reverberates, too!

Push now the mark in the middle a bit toward the top so that we can conveniently draw with three dotted lines the triangle determined by the three marks. The long base line, from the first to the second, from the picture of my mind to that of the chair, may be taken to stand for the intending in the case. Our first map did not have a picture of this connection; that is why I asked you merely to dot the lines. The short line to the right, between the third and the second, represents the connection between the representative and what it represents. That there must be such a connection follows from the very idea of ontology. If there were none, what could be the ground of the one "representing" the other? This connection has been spoken of as a "falling under." The phrase is pretty and handy. So I shall borrow it from the tradition. *The chair falls under the idea which represents it.*

Turn to the third line, the short one to the left, from my mind to the idea of the chair. What could it possibly stand for? A moment ago we took it for granted that the long base line stood for the intending in the case. Now we wonder. Was that just a thoughtless carry-over from the first map we made? Should not, if the prototype is right, this short line to the left be taken to stand for the intending in the case? But, then, is

not admitting that it does tantamount to admitting that the sophomore's objection cannot be met? If you don't see that immediately, ask
yourself what in this case the long base line would be standing for.

Obvious and destructive as it is, the sophomore's objection is merely
epistemological (How do we know?). Thus it is not structurally quite as
fundamental as another one which, in addition to being just as obvious
and just as destructive, is ontological (What is there?). *There is no
Third.* This is the most fundamental objection. It is just common sense.
Every simple thing and every object is either physical or mental (or,
possibly, mixed). There is nothing which is a third. Every idea, therefore, finds itself in a precarious equilibrium, as it were. Sooner or later,
and for the most part sooner rather than later, it is bound to topple and
fall, either into the First or into the Second. That shows in an image
why the prototype is so unstable. This image of an impossible balancing
act with a foregone unhappy ending is the modest but I think worth-
while gain for the sake of which I have wasted your time and mine on
drawing more or less silly maps.

If it falls to the left, into the First, an idea becomes a mental thing.
The sense data of the phenomenalist and, very probably, Hume's ele-
ments are ideas which have fallen to the left. Senses, as Frege uses the
word, are ideas which have fallen to the right, into the Second. So, as
some British philosophers have used the word, are propositions. If,
finally, one accepts the theological premiss, then the balance can be
maintained. The third is "in" God. This is the way out of Malebranche.
(So far I have hardly mentioned any name except, occasionally,
Meinong's and Brentano's; nor do I plan to mention many others in the
rest of this book. But there are a few places where a few names should
help; and this, I think, is one of them.)

I have shown, on the level of generality appropriate to these introductory reflections, that the "prototype" is unstable, just as I have
made clear, I trust, that the idea of a representative as such does not
imply anything about its being either mental or physical or a third. I
have not yet shown or even made plausible, however, that the unstable
tripartite ontology I am constructing actually is the prototype of all
representationalist ontologies. Or, to put it as once before, I have not
yet shown that if it were not for its patent instability or even absurdity,
many or perhaps all representationalists might have proposed it. The
point is crucial. So I shall make it in three ways. If I am right, the basic
gambit, however implicit, of representationalism is that there is a
Third. So we must ask ourselves, if there were a Third, what major
problems which otherwise may seem insoluble could be solved? Or,
considering the formidable difficulties one still confronts after having

accepted the basic gambit, which problems could at least be swept under the carpet? This is a question in structural history. The answer is that *there were three such major problems or predicaments, one skeptical, one nominalistic, one scientific.* I shall conclude these introductory reflections by describing them briefly.

Representationalism rose, rather abruptly, at the time of Galileo and Descartes, in response not to a single intellectual challenge but to the combined pressures of three. Two of these predicaments were old; one, new. One may reasonably surmise that the supervening of the one which was new triggered the abrupt innovation. Nor have the historians been idle. There is, I take it, plenty of evidence, of the sort they can marshall, to support the surmise.

The *skeptical predicament* is as old as the Skeptics' puzzlings about perception. What is it I see when seeing what is not real, as in a case of perceptual error? Nor is it just a matter of perception. What and where are the colors, shapes, and sounds which we sometimes so vividly imagine? Nor is it just a matter of the "images" that go with imagining, remembering, and believing. What is the intention of a false belief or a false memory which I hold without there being any "images" before my mind? Ideas clearly provide an answer to all these questions. They are always there. Only, in those cases where questions of the sort I just asked spot a problem, they do not represent anything. Thus the problem is solved. Or, rather, it is swept under the rug unless one recognizes the formidable new question to which the representationalist "solution" gives rise. What is the *criterion* by which to decide whether or not an idea represents something? Everyone knows Descartes' answer. The idea must be clear and distinct. Eventually, we shall very thoroughly discuss Brentano's and Meinong's answers. The foil not only rejects representationalism but so radically eradicates throughout the whole of the dialectic the last traces of the very idea of a criterion that the price it pays, the recognition of potentiality as a mode of existence, may seem prohibitive to some. Of all this later. Now I merely want to point out that even though it was well known to the later Greeks, nor possibly wholly forgotten in the middle period, the skeptical predicament did not by itself suffice to make the way of ideas the high road of all philosophy.

The *nominalistic predicament* is as old as, or even older than, the skeptical one. Probably a case can be made that Aristotle either was the first nominalist or at least took the first steps toward the nominalists' ontological desert. But we would not need to make this case even if instead of being merely structural analysts we were as historians concerned with the actual history of the decisive decades. However things might have stood earlier, there is no doubt that ever since the late Middle Ages nominalism was dominant. What made it dominant, at the expense of realism₁, was very probably a widely shared aversion to Platonic universals in conjunction with Occam's vigorous advocacy of the localization principle. But, again, whether or not these were in fact the major motives or causes does not at all matter for my purpose. What matters is, rather, that, first, the intellectual ambience was in fact nominalistic, from whatever causes or motives; and that, second, nominalism will not do, is dialectically untenable. There simply is no articulate ontology without either universals, in which case it could be fully articulate, or with at least a simulacrum or an illusion of universals, in which case it may be able to stay in business for some time and make some contributions to the dialectic. All but the most shallow, therefore, will try to preserve such a simulacrum. Or, with a change of image, if the universals are being driven out of their rightful homes, all but the most shallow will try to find a place of refuge for them. That is indeed what happened. The Third is the ontological Cloud-Cuckoo-Land where the universals took refuge. *Ideas are universals in exile from reality.* Structurally, therefore, all ideas are—or, as I should say, perhaps, if only from consideration for the sad fate that soon overtook those that fell to the left, into the mind—all ideas, including those of particulars, *were* originally universals, just as a one-class is still a class. As we proceed I shall make very much of this point; now I merely want to introduce it. But I shall not, for once, abstain from supporting it by a text.

I must here in the entrance beg pardon of my reader for the frequent use of the word *idea*, which he will find in the following treatise. Its being that term which, I think, serves best to stand for whatsoever is the *object* of the understanding when a man thinks, I have used it to express whatever is meant by *phantasm, notion, species,* or *whatever it is which the mind can be employed about in thinking;* and I could not avoid frequently using it.

The passage is from the end of Locke's Introduction to his *Essay*. Just look at the words. Phantasm! Notion! Species! Specially, species! How impressively they confirm the diagnosis, document the overarching structural continuity. How minor, compared with it, seems the famous disagreement between Locke and Descartes about the "origin" of our ideas, or, as Locke himself put it, in the last sentence of the Introduction, only one short passage away from the one I just cited, "how they come into the mind." *One short paragraph only from the mind's being employed about something to this something coming into it!* How hard it is for an idea not to topple and fall! As to Locke's list of words, we shall soon add 'concept' to it. For a concept is what a mind is about or "conceives," whatever, as I would say, the species of the act may be. In German, a concept is a *Begriff*. *'Concept'* and *'Begriff'*, *'idea'* and *'Vorstellung'*—you see why I shall use them all synonymously. But we must go on. Notice first, though, that the nominalistic predicament, painful as it must have been to all but the most shallow, did not suffice to trigger the basic gambit of representationalism, neither by itself nor in conjunction with the supporting pressure that might possibly have come from the background to which the skeptical argument found itself relegated until, after the eruption of representationalism, the score was more than evened by its occupying for so long so much more of the front of the stage than it deserves.

We must not get lost in scraps of history. Whatever did or did not happen from whatever cause, the structural connection between the nominalistic predicament and the rise (if I am right) of the tripartite prototype is again clear. If there were a Third, then, since its denizens structurally are universals, the problems which cannot be solved without universals *might seem* solvable. I say *might* and I say *seem* because even if there were a Third, ideas dwelling in it would be separate or Platonic universals. Or, what amounts to the same, one who adopts the prototype because he thinks, as in the first flush he well might, that the ideas in it permit him to answer the questions no nominalist can answer, will eventually have to face another unanswerable question: What does it mean for a thing to "fall under" an idea?

The third problem or group of such, the new ones which precipitated the development, is that of the *scientific predicament*. This is a double pattern; so I shall discuss it in two steps.

First. The name as indissolubly connected with the scientific predicament as Descartes' is with the rise of representationalism itself, is Galileo's. The trouble is that, whether or not the perception is veridical, if the new science is right, then a part of what is presented to us is never real. I need not, I trust, more than mention the Galilean distinction between primary and secondary qualities, in order to bring it vividly before your mind, together with all the dialectical consequences it has had. Nor is there any need for pointing out how smugly *ad hoc* Descartes' famous criterion really was. Clear and distinct among our ideas (which are not innate) are, as he claims, exactly those which represent the things which according to the new science are real, or, as I shall say, for the sake of bringing out the connection, the things which are in the Second. Perhaps it will make the connection even clearer if I use the same image as before. Some ideas such as, say, the idea of something blue, are refugees not only from the nominalistic desert but also from the new science. This is a third very good reason why the unstable tripartite ontology I am about to construct may be a prototype and master key to the dialectic of representationalism.

In Brentano and particularly in Meinong, we shall see, this implicit structural motive of all representationalism, the urge to find a Third where colors, pitches, and so on, may dwell in safety, becomes quite explicit.

Second. This is one occasion on which the form-matter doctrine has to be mentioned. The point is simple enough and, once more, the paradigm of veridical perception will serve. As long as all the qualities which are presented are deemed to be in the chair, the Aristotelian-Thomistic assay of perception will do, or, at least, it might do, provided the details can all be worked out, which is always difficult. What happens upon this schema is, all details apart, that a single substantial form informs both the mind and the chair. Perhaps you wonder whether I realize that such a single form is a universal and that, therefore, what I just said contradicts what I said a while ago, namely, that the ambience was dominated by post-Occamist nominalism. I am fully aware of, and completely unimpressed by, the formal contradiction. Who ever thought that no two of the several ideas influential at any given time contradicted each other? Also, the staying power, or, if I may so put it, the unchecked credit enjoyed by a doctrine as venerable and as ingrained as the Aristotelian-Thomistic account of perception remains very great long after it has ceased to agree with all the rising patterns. Eventually of course something will snap, specially under a shock. In this case the shock was provided by the scientific predicament. As long as the "qualities in the mind" (I speak for once and for obvious reasons as Locke sometimes does) and those "in the chair" are the "same," the notion of a single substantial form informing both the mind and the chair may at least seem to make sense and, because of its realistic$_2$ implication, remain attractive. As soon as some of these qualities are no longer in both mind and chair, it no longer even seems to make sense and loses all attraction. Thus the realistic$_2$ tie snaps and the trend toward idealism sets in.[5]

---

[5] This aspect of the total dialectic I illuminated in *Logic and Reality*. That is why I am here so brief. If you do not know or do not remember how the foil resolves the scientific predicament, there is ample time. What may need to be recalled on this score can safely wait until much later.

CORES AND FRINGES

THE job I undertook of constructing an ontology has barely been begun. The only thing we accomplished is to establish one feature. The ontology to be constructed must be tripartite in the sense explained. This is so because, if I am right, this feature will make it a key to the dialectic of representationalism, or, what amounts to the same, a prototype, in some respects, of all representationalist ontologies. We also know what in such contexts it means to be right. I shall be proved right if and only if the ontology I shall construct will pass certain tests. It must itself have, and contribute to the structural understanding of, certain salient features of all representationalist ontologies. Only after having passed these tests will it deserve to be called their prototype. But you will not, I think, object if, in order to save breath and ink, I anticipate the outcome of the tests by henceforth simply speaking of *the prototype* instead of, more accurately but very tediously, of the ontology which I am constructing and which, if I am right, and so on and so on.

At the heart of the matter are the tests. These cannot be made before the prototype has been specified, not necessarily in every detail, yet far, far beyond the single feature we have established. Thus we are forced to make certain choices.

Descartes is a representationalist; so is Locke; so are Brentano and Meinong. Yet their ontologies differ. Some of the differences between any two among them are very major. Naturally, since they are all representationalists, they also agree in some respects. Nor is that all. Fortunately, though not surprisingly, the tradition in general and representationalism in particular being what they are, the major representationalist ontologies share not only certain features but also a style. More or less explicitly, they are all γ-ontologies. *The prototype therefore, will be a γ-ontology.* That, though, is merely a first choice, narrowing the range within which we shall have to make others before

138

we can actually begin the construction. In considering these further choices, I shall limit myself to considering four philosophers—Descartes, Locke, Brentano, and Meinong. The limitation, I think, is historically justifiable, but I shall not even try to justify it.

To say of Descartes and Locke that they are γ-ontologists is one thing; to say it of the younger pair is another. The ontologies of the latter fit the description more neatly and the information conveyed by so describing them is more specific than in the case of the older pair. This is not to say that the description fits the older pair but poorly and conveys no valuable information about it. I merely wish to be properly careful by pointing out that there is a difference. For the rest, I shall make no attempt whatsoever to prove that Descartes and Locke both fit the description, even though in this Part there will be a comment or two about each. If that seems improper to you, let me avoid quarrels which make no sense by rewording what I just said. At a few places in Part II, I shall comment on problems which in the form in which I shall state them undoubtedly occupied Descartes and Locke. That much for the first qualification.

The second concerns the younger pair. That they are both γ-ontologists will be shown beyond doubt in Parts III and IV of this book. But, then, there are γ-ontologies and γ-ontologies. Not surprisingly, therefore, there are differences between these two. Brentano is an extreme reist and an extreme nominalist. Moreover, his commitment to the basic gambit of representationalism is so strong, his grasp of its dialectic so profound and so accurate that, in spite of his undoubted and indubitable devotion to the ideals of realism$_2$, he ends up a structural idealist. Or so at least I shall argue. Meinong on the other hand, if I am right, is among all thinkers in this tradition the one who comes closest to throwing off the shackles of representationalism. That is why I have become so devoted to his memory, and also, alas, since in spite of his long and heroic efforts he failed, why he became the most valiant knight errant of this great cause. Since he struggled so hard and never quite got there, his thought was always in flux. A historian would not speak of *the* ontology he proposed. Even the structural historian will occasionally have to speak of two, the one with which he started and the one over which he died. Except for one important difference the early one is the same as Brentano's. Or at least it is reasonably close to it. Brentano, after all, was his teacher. The one over which he died is all his own.

That makes for five ontologies, even with the limitation I introduced without justifying it; Descartes', Locke's, Brentano's, and the two of Meinong. Which shall be our inspiration in constructing the prototype?

A prototype need not, nor perhaps should it, copy any single one of the things it purports to be the prototype of. Nor am I trying to produce either a copy or, perhaps even worse, a composite, in the sense in which the pictures of fugitives that artists employed by the police draw from several descriptions are called composites. My choice is entirely determined by the dialectic. As it happens, though, not too surprisingly perhaps, even after the little that has been said, the prototype I am about to construct is reasonably close to what I take to be Meinong's first ontology.

An ontology is not sufficiently articulate to deserve being taken seriously unless it satisfies two conditions. *It must have a ground plan and must apply this plan consistently throughout.* To discover its ground plan, if any, I look for its assay, if any, of the truncated world, and, in particular, of its objects, such as stones, trees, chairs, and so on. Examining this assay I discover what its categories are. Then I can form an opinion as to whether it addresses itself to the great problems and how by means of its categories it proposes to solve them. If under informed dialectical probing its solutions do not stand up long enough to make the game worth the candle then the ontology is inadequate, does not deserve serious attention. Lest you mistake the negative way in which I express myself for high-handedness, let me also express a belief I hold very firmly. I believe the great problems to be so difficult that no one has and quite possibly no one ever will propose solutions for all of them which are all completely adequate. If you ask me to name the great problems, I shall merely say that the section headings of Part I are a good sample.

The second condition, I said, is that the ground plan must be applied consistently throughout. What I meant was that it must be applied to minds. But I did not want to tip my hand before I was ready to explain. Now I am; nor will it be difficult provided you permit me for once to use 'thing' as broadly as we all use it outside of ontological discourse.

Minds are in the world; minds are merely "things" among "things." Let me unpack the formula by stating what it does and what it does not mean. It *does not mean* that minds are in all respects like trees or chairs. There is indeed one respect, their intentional feature, in which minds are unlike all other "things" in the world. The formula *does mean* that a certain expectation ought to be borne out. I say expectation, or presumption, rather than, more strongly, requirement, only because I do not want to weaken the point by even the slightest overstatement. The expectation, then, is that no categories need be added when from the truncated world one turns to minds. The categories needed to assay the former ought to suffice for assaying the latter. Two reminders will convince you how reasonable the expectation is. Remember, first, how fundamental categories are. The foil's ground plan, for instance, is laid out by the three major categories of *things* (without double quotes), *subsistents*, and *facts*, with things divided into the two highest subcategories of *bare particulars* and *universals*. Remember, second, that in the foil there is indeed an entity to be found only in worlds in which there are minds and thus adequately grounding their uniqueness, namely, the intentional tie (M). But, then, this entity is a subsistent among subsistents and, in particular, a nexus among nexus. Thus it fits into the ground plan. If, on the other hand, an ontology cannot assay minds without adding to the categories which suffice for its truncated world, then it assigns to minds a position so extraordinary that, stylistically even though admittedly not in strict logic, it is on the way to idealism.

It will pay later if I now try to illuminate the point further. I shall describe, in a general way, two violations of the presumption which actually have occurred in the representationalist tradition, and I shall try to make plausible, in a general way, why each may become the source of difficulties.

The first violation. If the truncated world is a γ-world without universals then there should not be universals "in" minds either. Otherwise the presumption is violated. Structurally, ideas are universals. Hence, if the ideas of a γ-world have fallen into its minds—and we know that inevitably they will fall either to the right or to the left—there is the clear and imminent danger that in some confused and confusing way there both will and will not be universals "in" minds. (This, I believe, is the case of Locke's general ideas; see p. 166.)

The second violation involves time. Thus it is not literally categorial. But the role of time is unique. Speaking without ontological commitment, minds and trees are both continuants. Ontologically, the problems of time and change are not only unique but of extraordinary depth and difficulty. *Yet they are exactly the same for trees and for minds! This is crucial.* Anyone who violates this symmetry, or indifference, by making time a "category" in the First only is therefore an idealist, literally and not just stylistically. This is the case of the later Husserl, in whose world Time and Self "constitute each other." Yet his was merely the last step on a road on which, as we shall see, his teacher Brentano took the first when he made Selves the only simple things which are literally continuants.

We are ready to start the construction.

All simple things of the truncated prototype are qualities (perfect particulars). Its objects are series of their temporal cross sections. Each such cross section is a cluster, e.g. $\gamma(p_1, t_1, a_1, b_1, \cdots, n_1)$, individuated by $\gamma(p_1, t_1)$. Being a γ-ontology, the prototype suffers from the irremediable blur. Its clusters are not really things[1] but merely "things"; γ and $\subset$, even if explicitly recognized, are not really nexus but merely pseudonexus; and so on. If within these limits the prototype were fully articulated, γ and $\subset$ would be its main subsistents,[2] the former fundamental, the latter derived. Meinong's second was the γ-ontology which most articulately strained away from reism. Brentano, though an extreme reist and unusually outspoken about it, was also sufficiently profound to introduce a feature which he meant to do the jobs of γ and $\subset$. This is our cue. *The prototype explicitly recognizes γ and $\subset$.*

The philosophers whose ontologies we want to examine are all nominalists. There are thus no universals in either the First or the Second of their worlds. But none of them was shallow. Thus they often thought and sometimes spoke as if there were those wraiths we called Classes (p. 99). The thing to do, therefore, if the prototype is to serve, is to pretend that in it, too, there are Classes. Take green. Let a_1, a_2, a_3, $\cdots$ be the simple qualities which in the truncated prototype ground this color. We shall pretend that it contains also the Class $\tilde{A}$ of all a_i. $\tilde{A}$ is one thing; the idea or concept of green—I shall call it $\overline{A}$—is another. $\tilde{A}$ is a wraith in the Second; $\overline{A}$, a dweller in the Third. The a_i, or, if you please, the extension of $\tilde{A}$, are the things which fall under $\overline{A}$. And, to take up an earlier metaphor, $\overline{A}$ is what $\tilde{A}$ has become after it took refuge in the Third. These are the very distinctions and connections on which my analysis will be built. But I must not run ahead of it. Classes correspond most directly to characters. How about relations? We shall not need to commit ourselves until we come to Brentano and Meinong.

In the prototype a mind is the series of its cross sections. Each member of the series is a cluster of qualities (perfect particulars). Among the latter there is a moment but no place. Minds, as one says, are in time but not in space. Every moment is a component of all cross sections "in" which it is. Thus it does not *by itself* individuate any of them. What, then, does individuate minds? Eventually the question must be faced; so we take notice. But nothing in this part will depend on the answer. So we need not commit the prototype on this most important point.[3]

---

[1] I.e., they are not things as I use 'thing' in ontological discourse.

[2] In calling these two the "main" subsistents of the prototype, I ignore among others the connectives and existence itself, thus taking cognizance of the fact, however deplorable, that with the exception of Frege and Husserl no one recognized clearly the ontological status of any of them.

[3] Though we need not "commit the prototype," you will no doubt remember

The minds of the prototype clearly are objects. Its objects thus are either bodies or minds. Minds are like bodies in that much of their ontology, though of course again not all of it, can be done in the cross section. As for minds, so for the complete (i.e., nontruncated) world. Thus I shall persist in my ways; use 'object', when dealing with what can be dealt with in the cross section, to refer not to "the whole object," but rather, to a cross section of either a mind or a body; make the required distinctions between whole objects and a cross section of it only if the problem under discussion spills over the latter. There are of course such problems. An example will help.

Take perceiving. With the *usual meaning*, what one perceives is the whole object. Yet there is also a *special meaning* or use, such that what is perceived is a cross section simultaneous with the act whose intention it is. Some will disagree. Nor is there much point to the special use unless my analysis of perception is adequate. This analysis[4] I shall not present and defend once more, either here or elsewhere in this book, even though some things which will have to be said later do in fact contribute to the task of that presentation and that defense. But the matter had to be brought up now in order to avoid puzzlement. For I shall henceforth use 'perceiving' in both ways. Thus we must make a choice. Either we employ subscripts, distinguish the special and the usual case as, say, perceiving$_1$ and perceiving$_2$, respectively. Or we agree that unless something to the contrary will be said, 'perceiving' will stand for one of the two, say, for perceiving$_1$. Since much can be done in the cross section, the second alternative is the more economical. So I choose it. Keep in mind, then, that if nothing to the contrary is being said, the intention of an act of perceiving is a cross section simultaneous with it. That leads to the next point.

The knower in a knowing situation is the act "in" it, not the mind "in" which the act is. *An act is a momentary entity and it is complex.* Everyone who concerns us agrees. So does the foil. So therefore does the prototype. There, though, the agreement ends. Nor can we continue to ignore the disagreements, as we did in Section Seven. *In the*

---

what was said in the section on substance about Brentano's Selves. According to his latest views, they are like coordinate qualities in two respects. They individuate and they are hidden. But they are also the only continuants (substances$_4$) of his world! So you see already how in this ontology the problem is solved.

[4] For its main outlines, see the "Realistic Postcript" in *Logic and Reality*. The context of that essay requires a threefold distinction, marked by subscripts, with perceiving$_1$ and perceiving$_2$ corresponding to the special and the usual case, as above. The intention of a perceiving$_1$ is characteristically narrower than that of a perceiving$_2$. A perceiving$_3$, on the other hand, is but the last in a series of perceivings$_2$.

foil, an act is a fact. In the prototype it is a thing of the kind called a complex particular.

The notion of a *complex particular* is new. So it must be properly presented. First, though, for a preparatory comment.

Complex particulars are also thought of as *complex qualities*. By each word in these two labels there hangs a point. Being entities of γ, complex particulars are not really complexes but merely "complex," not really things but merely "things." In the words of the old metaphor, the irremediable blur makes them monsters. In this respect they are exactly *like clusters*. This, though, is merely one half of the story, the half that hangs by 'complex'. The other half is that the proponents of complex particulars think of them as unitary (I avoid simple) constituents of clusters. In this respect they are, or at least they are thought to be, *like perfect particulars* (simple qualities). This point hangs by 'particular' and by 'quality'. In the prototype, we shall see, it is represented by the circumstance that the nexus "in" a complex particular is different from, and, in a sense, stronger than, that "in" a cluster.

We are ready for an orderly presentation of the new notion. That will be the first of *three steps*. In the second, attention will be called to a certain feature of all acts as well as to some differences between the assays of the act in the prototype and the foil, or, if you please, in γ and ϵ. In the third step I shall show how a certain problem which because of the feature arises in γ, though not in ϵ, can be solved by assaying the acts of γ as complex particulars (complex qualities).

First step. Having just noticed that, like all "complexes" of γ, complex particulars suffer from the irremediable blur, we may safely continue to ignore it.[5] The categorial constituents of a complex particular are some, though not all, of the perfect particulars (simple qualities) in a cross section of an object. In this respect, there is no difference between a complex particular and a subcluster. In another respect they differ. The tie in a subcluster is one of the weak γ (p. 40). The tie in a complex particular is a new fundamental nexus. I shall call it *joining*, in symbols: ι. Complex particulars will accordingly sometimes be called *joints*. If, e.g., a and b are the simple qualities in one that is complex, '$\iota\,(a, b)$' is a successful description of the latter. Let $[a_1, a_2, \cdots, a_n]$ be the class of all (simple) qualities in (a cross section of) an object; $a_{i_1}, a_{i_2}, \cdots, a_{i_k}$, an arbitrary (proper) subclass of it. The subcluster $\gamma(a_{i_1}, a_{i_2}, \cdots, a_{i_k})$ exists. That is indeed the way the "weak" γ "in" it

---

[5] I.e., whenever it proves convenient, I shall in speaking about complex particulars continue to use 'thing', 'simple', and 'complex' in the way they are used in γ for clusters and as until recently I have used them myself.

is derived from the "strong" one "in" the cluster $\gamma(a_1, a_2, \cdots, a_n)$. If you don't remember, turn back to page 39. It does not follow that every subclass is the class of categorial entities "in" a complex particular. If it were, there would be no point to the new notion. This we shall see presently. But you see already that, as we use 'stronger' in this context, *each ι is a stronger tie than the weak γ which corresponds to it.*[6] (Notice, too, that I use 'ι', like 'γ', for any number of arguments. That is why I speak of *each ι* and of *the γ* that corresponds to it.

ι is introduced because without it a certain problem cannot be solved. Yet the appearance of a new fundamental tie is a very major event. That raises two questions. Did Brentano and Meinong themselves see the problem? If they saw it, did they solve it in this way? The answer to the first question is an unqualified Yes. In replying to the second, I first remind you that Brentano was an extreme reist. So he did of course not solve either this or any other problem by means of a subsistent. But then I hurry to add that what he actually did is (as we shall see) best articulated by what I am doing now. Meinong's case, we shall see, is very special.

Let a, b, and c be the complex particular $\iota(a_1, a_2)$, the cluster $\gamma(a_1, a_2, \cdots, a_n)$ and the subcluster $\gamma(a_1, a_2)$ of the latter, respectively.[7] *c is literally "in" b.* In symbols: $c \subset b$. This is as it ought to be since the only ground for c's being an entity is a_1's and a_2's being "in" b, which in turn makes the nexus "in" c derivable from as well as weaker than that "in" b. *a, on the other hand, is not literally "in" b.* To grasp that firmly, you merely have to reflect for a moment on what has been said already. What, finally, is the nexus between, say, a_1, and a? Clearly, it can be derived from ι in exactly the same way in which $\subset$ is derived from γ. Equally clearly, it is not literally $\subset$. So we shall represent it by '$\subset_\iota$'. Thus we have: $a_1 \subset_\iota a$; $a_2 \subset_\iota a$.

Is a in b? I have no doubt that all γ-ontologists would answer in the affirmative. Literally, we know, they are wrong. At best, what they say is blurred. Notice, first, that while italicizing 'in', I avoided the double quotes which mark our own ontological use. Notice, second, that, since they are all more or less explicit reists, the γ-ontologists are most unlikely to make a distinction that rests wholly on the difference in strength between two nexus. Small wonder, therefore, that a's being *in* b is for them a part of the very notion of a complex particular. When-

[6] This states accurately what in the preparatory comment I expressed by saying that the nexus "in" complex particulars is *in a sense stronger* than that "in" clusters.

[7] As you see, I am limiting myself to a "binary" example. Nothing will be lost.

ever it matters, we shall have to pay attention to this belief of theirs. But we shall at least keep our own powder dry by italicizing 'in' in such cases rather than surrounding it by double quotes.

Second step. Acts vary in two respects. I may remember something, perceive it, think of it, and so on. In the foil this respect is grounded in the species. Also, everyone who concerns us agrees that this respect is grounded in the act itself, not in the intending (p. 126). The intentions of acts vary, of course. It does not follow that there is a respect in which two acts themselves differ if and only if their intentions differ. But again, everyone who concerns us agrees, and so does the foil, that there is such a respect. In the foil the two respects are grounded in the species and the thought, which are universals. In the prototype they are grounded in two qualities, each of which is a constituent of the act. That makes the act itself a complex thing. The constituent which varies with the intention I shall call the *core;* the one which varies with the species, the *fringe.* Not that these two words have much to recommend themselves; but they will do and I cannot think of any which will do better without borrowing from some specific ontology, which understandably I do not want to do.

In the foil, each core is a character of the kind I call *thought;* each fringe, one of the kind I call *species.* A thought and its intention are two and not one. In this respect, the prototype is like the foil.[8] A core of the prototype and its intention are two and not one. Nor could that be otherwise, since collapsing the two commits one most explicitly to idealism, and the γ-ontologists we consider all wanted to be realists. In other respects, there are significant differences between the foil's and the prototype's assays of the act.

In the foil all intentions are facts (complexes). In a formula: *all awareness is propositional.* Yet the foil's cores (thoughts) are all simple; more precisely, they are underived characters of the first type. This contrast between the complexity of all its intentions and the simplicity of all its cores is indeed one of the most distinctive features of my world.[9] In γ-ontologies, at least some intentions are things.

---

[8] For Brentano at least this is not true in the case of self-knowledge. But the exception makes no difference for the point at hand.

[9] I do not intend to propound once more the foil's assay of the act and of the knowing situation. But it may help you to recall it if I remind you of its reflection in an improved language. Intentions, being facts, are represented by sentences, 'P', 'Q', 'R', and so on. Thoughts, being underived characters, are represented by such expressions as '$\lceil P \rceil$', '$\lceil Q \rceil$', '$\lceil R \rceil$', and so on, which have all the syntactical properties of undefined predicates. The intentional nexus is represented by 'M'. $\lceil P \rceil MP$, $\lceil Q \rceil MQ$, $\lceil R \rceil MR$, and so on, are facts in the world's form (analytic).

(Whether or not all are depends at least in part on how well the ontology "succeeds" in overlooking or outright ignoring all facts.) The core of an act intending a thing is in these ontologies simple if and only if the thing intended is simple. If the latter is complex, so is the core of the act intending it. The prototype follows suit, makes some of its cores simple, some complex.

Since in the prototype some cores are complex while in the foil they are all simple, one may reasonably surmise that there are certain problems which arise in the prototype but not in the foil. The surmise is borne out. Nor is it unreasonable to anticipate that these problems can be solved, at least after a fashion and up to a point, by assaying complex cores as complex particulars. With these matters we shall deal in the next section.

As for cores, so for fringes. In the foil all fringes (species) are simple; more precisely, they are underived characters of the first type. The prototype, following the γ-ontologies which concern us, assays one kind of fringe as simple, all other kinds as complex. Again, one may reasonably anticipate that some problems which arise only in worlds some of whose fringes are complex, can be solved by assaying the latter as complex particulars.

We are finally ready for the problem I mentioned when outlining the three steps.

Consider a mind, or, more precisely for once, consider a cross section of a mind "in" which there are several acts. There is nothing either in the foil or in any of the ontologies which concern us to exclude the occurrence of such cross sections. Suppose that there are exactly two acts "in" the one we consider. Suppose also that neither the two cores nor the two fringes are the same$_3$. That makes for two cores and two fringes among the constituents of the cross section. Which core "goes with" which fringe? Or, in more formal ontological language, which constituents of the assay of the cross section do the job of "pairing off" the cores and the fringes "in" it?

This is the problem. Its solution in the prototype is the third step, which is still ahead of us. Probably you can anticipate it by now. Nor will it take long. First, though, for two comments. They will not only provide some structural insights but also show why I proceeded the way I did.

1. In the foil the solution of the pairing-off problem is immediate. Or, if you please, it is built into the assay of the act. The acts of my world are facts. This is another of its distinctive features. Specifically, an act is a bare particular exemplifying two (simple) characters, one a thought, the other a species. Such bare particulars I have called

awarenesses.[10] Among the constituents of the cross section in our example there are thus not only two thoughts (cores) and two species (fringes) but also two bare particulars (awarenesses) which do the pairing-off. For a species and a thought "go together" if and only if they are exemplified by the same awareness.

2. The foil's cores and fringes are all simple. In the prototype, as in the γ-ontologies which in this respect it follows, some cores and some fringes are complex. Some problems which arise in the γ- but not in the ϵ-assay of acts are due to this difference. Or, to say the same thing differently, they would not arise if the prototype's cores and fringes, like those of the foil, were all simple. These problems, though, are one thing; our pairing-off problem is another. Just as the latter problem arises in the foil, where all cores and fringes are simple, so it would also arise in the prototype, even if the latter's cores and fringes were all simple. In the foil, we just saw, its solution is built in. In the prototype, as we shall see in a moment and as I am sure you can by now anticipate, it is solved by introducing complex particulars, or, what amounts to the same, by introducing the new fundamental tie, joining (ι). Thus we have come upon three structural insights of importance. (1) On the one hand, the need of γ-ontologies for complex particulars does not depend on some of their cores and fringes being complex. (2) On the other hand, if this need is satisfied by the introduction of complex particulars, then the structural suggestion of solving by means of the new fundamental tie thus introduced also those problems which arise in γ-ontologies only because some of their cores and fringes are complex, becomes as strong as it could possibly be. (3) The need, or the job to be done, is that of pairing-off, or, more generally, in the problems to be taken up in the next section, of grouping natured entities (simple qualities) "in" a cross section. In ϵ this job, or, if you insist on being completely accurate, the corresponding job is done by bare particulars exemplifying pairs or groups of characters. In the clusters of γ I see no other way of doing it than by a plurality of fundamental ties of different strengths.

Third step. I hear your voice while I think of what I shall say after it will have ceased. There are two acts (g_1, g_2) "in" my mind; two cores (v^*, s^*), corresponding to the voice and what I shall speak about respectively;[11] and two fringes, a hearing (h) and a thinking (t). We know

---

[10] Convenient as this appellation is, one must not forget that it is purely contextual. Being bare, awarenesses have no natures in general and, in particular, are neither physical nor mental.

[11] v^* and s^* are cores; v and s, their respective intentions. Since this argument involves only cores, we could have done without the asterisks. But I did not want to deviate from a notation which from the next section on will be indispensable.

from what has been said that nothing will be lost by assuming the two cores and the two fringes to be simple (in γ); the two acts are complex, of course (in γ as well as in ϵ). Assume also that (in γ) the core and the fringe "in" each of the two acts are the only two things "in" it.

In the prototype, as in the γ-ontologies which in this respect it follows, the two cores and the two fringes are assayed as perfect particulars (simple qualities); g_1 and g_2, as the two complex particulars $\iota(v^*, h)$ and $\iota(s^*, t)$, respectively. This, as I have said twice already, must by now be obvious. But I want to make sure, and that is why I built the whole argument toward this point and made it a step by itself, that you grasp clearly and firmly why there is no other way out.

v^*, s^*, h, t are four simple qualities among the constituents of the cluster which is the cross section of my mind. Hence, every pair and triple among them determines in the familiar fashion a subcluster, as does the quadruple itself. (1) $\gamma(v^*, h)$, (2) $\gamma(s^*, t)$, (3) $\gamma(v^*, t)$, (4) $\gamma(s^*, h)$ are four among them. It follows that g_1 cannot be (1); g_2 cannot be (2); since, if they were, I would also be thinking the voice and hearing what I shall speak about (not: my future speaking), as is shown by (3) and (4) respectively. The only way out is to introduce a nexus connecting (simple) qualities into things which are not just subclusters. This is the point.

We have come to the end of a line of thought. The thing to do next is to examine carefully and in detail the cores and fringes of γ. This is a major job. So I shall leave it for the next section, and conclude this one with some reflections on the structural connection between representationalism on the one hand and the complexity of all but one of the fringes in γ on the other.

In the foil each species is a simple universal. In the prototype all fringes but one are complex particulars. Nor is there any choice. The prototype merely accepts what all representationalists agree upon. The contrast thus has two halves; universal versus particular is one; simple versus complex, the other. The first is accounted for by the differences between the two ground plans. Thus one would not expect it to be connected with a difference both specific and important between the ways in which the prototype and the foil assay either the act or the knowing situation. Nor is it in fact so connected. The simple-versus-complex half is.

Let us look at some of the things assayed as species and fringes, respectively. Perceiving is one; believing is another; remembering is a third; and so on. The crucial one, on which the difference hangs, the representationalists call *conceiving* (*vorstellen*). The one which in the foil *in one respect* corresponds most nearly to conceiving is *entertaining*.

I say "most nearly" and not "accurately" because, while one can conceive a thing, e.g., a sheet, or perhaps even only a thing, the intention of an entertaining can only be either a fact, e.g., that the sheet is white, or a potential fact, e.g., that it is purple. *Loosely speaking*, the one respect in which conceiving and entertaining very nearly correspond to each other is that they both involve a suspension of belief. Notice, though, that this use of 'belief' involves no ontological commitment as to the assay of believing. That is why I warned you that I was speaking loosely and, also, that the "correspondence" is not accurate. 'Conceiving' and 'entertaining' thus remain the accurate and proper γ and ϵ words respectively. As long as we speak loosely, though, there is an expression equally acceptable to both sides. They are both willing to say that while either conceiving or entertaining something, they are *thinking of* it. Occasionally I shall take advantage of this verbal agreement. (Meinong eventually said that one makes an *Annahme*.)

In a second respect, conceiving and entertaining differ radically. This difference, which is the heart of the matter, can be spotted by the phrase 'being presented with'. Linguistically, 'being presented with' and 'presentation' are the best translations of *'etwas vorstellen'* and *'Vorstellung'*, respectively. In the foil one is always presented with the intention itself (which always exists, either as an actual or as a potential fact, wherefore we know a price has to be paid). That makes in the foil "grasping" the intention a one-step operation, as it were. Linguistically, consider the connections between *concipere, capere, grasp, grip, greifen, begreifen;* and remember that an idea is not only a *Vorstellung* but also a *Begriff* and a *concept*, i.e., what one grasps (*begreift, concipit*).

In a representationalist world, except perhaps in the case of self-knowledge, which we leave to one side until later, an intention cannot be grasped, if it can be grasped at all, except "through" its representative. Or should I perhaps say that in such a world one grasps the intention "by" grasping the representative? I hope you will appreciate why I avoid saying that at this point. For one, since I want to give the representationalist a run for his money, I do not wish to embarrass him unnecessarily by expressing myself in a way which cannot but bring to mind the sophomore's objection and the need for a criterion on an occasion where we deal with neither of these two points but with some other aspects of the total dialectic. For another, I do not wish to prejudge the question whether there are acts by means of which ideas themselves are grasped in exactly the same sense in which, by means of other acts, which no doubt are much more common, we grasp the intentions of the ideas these latter acts involve. Nor need we weaken our case by either unnecessarily embarrassing the representationalist or prejudging anything. What matters now is clear already.

In a representationalist world every act which is not merely a conceiving is, as it were, a two-step operation. I believe that there is a tree. I can believe that whether or not there is one. But I could not believe it unless, while believing it, I thought of the tree. For I cannot, in any act, whatever its species may be, grasp anything without grasping it "through" its idea. That is the point. The rest is easy. To perceive one's friend is "more" than just to think of him. Thus, if one holds that one cannot do the latter without doing the former, he is virtually forced to assay fringes as follows: *Conceivings are simple qualities. All other fringes are complex particulars. One constituent of each such complex particular is a conceiving.* More or less explicitly this assay has in fact been proposed by all representationalists. The prototype cannot but follow suit.

The other constituent (or constituents) of a fringe, which we are not yet quite ready to examine, I shall for the moment call the specific constituent. The very notion suffices to dispel whatever blur may still surround the metaphor of the two steps. Take a believing. Conceiving "through" its idea the intention it involves is the first step. "Adding" the specific constituent is the second. Nor could there be a second step without there being a first, just as there can be no conceiving, which is a fringe, without a core while, on the other hand, there can be a first step without there being a second. That not only unpacks the metaphor but also spots the only respect in which it lets us down. Both steps may be taken simultaneously.

For the time being that concludes our analysis of the representationalists' fringes. If you have a sense of structure you probably noticed a weak spot in it. The weakness is not that anything which is there is wrong, but, rather, that there is something which in strict logic would not need to be there. The point is very instructive. So I shall discuss it.

Let the intention of an act which is not merely a conceiving be a. Let the core of the act be a^*; its fringe, (c, x), where c is a conceiving, x a specific constituent.[12] (I suppress, a bit inconsistently, the subscripts

---

[12] As you see, I assume without further ado that what holds the simple constituents of a complex fringe together is ι. There is of course the abstract possibility of a whole series of fundamental ties of graded strengths. But there is no point in such overelaboration of a speculative prototype. Later on we shall see that Brentano, in his own reistic way, i.e., without acknowledging a single subsistent, realizes this conception. Remember what has been said when we discussed substances$_3$. His objects peel like onions (p. 119).

usually attached to the names of particulars.) That makes the act itself
$\iota(a^*, \iota(c, x))$.[13] But, then, if you try for a moment to think algebraically, you will see that this formula reveals the structure of all acts. The
differences between them depend wholly on what 'a^*' and 'x' stand for.
'c', on the other hand, always stands for a conceiving, i.e., for one of
those simple qualities which ground conceiving; i.e., it stands, as closely
as in a γ-world that is possible, always for the same thing. If this is so,
what job does it do? Structurally or algebraically at least, would not
$\iota(a^*, x)$ do as well? Or, less algebraically, is there a structural reason—*I
deliberately ignore phenomenological ones*—why conceiving should not
be "absorbed" into the core?

I can think of two answers. One belongs to structural history. So I
shall leave it to the end. The other I cannot explain without a certain
distinction among the proponents of the doctrine of internal connections. Since in Parts III and IV this distinction will become very important, I might as well make use of this occasion to introduce it.

The proponents of the doctrine of internal connections are either
moderates or extremists. Middle e has a nature; so does middle g. The
extremists hold that the ground of g being higher[3] than e lies "in" g
alone, or, if you please, in its nature, and in nothing else. Or, speaking
for once traditionally, they hold that the ground of a relation may
wholly lie "in" one of its terms. Brentano, who takes this position, calls
such terms *relativlich*. Eventually, for want of a better word, I shall
borrow his. The notion it stands for is irremediably confused. Trying to
grasp it firmly is to see that it is also absurd. As you read on you will
notice, if you haven't noticed it already, that the rejection of this confused and absurd notion is one of my deepest commitments.[14] The
moderates hold that the ground of the connection in question does not
lie in one of the two pitches alone but in both, or, if you please, in their
natures, and in nothing else. According to this view, then, an "internal
connection" is one whose ground lies wholly "in" *both* the entities it
connects. From where I stand, there is, as you know, no connection at
all. Hence, for once, the double quotes. Yet this view is obviously less

---

[13] Notice that if one wants to make do with a single ι, this nexus cannot be
associative. E.g., $\iota(a^*, \iota(c, x))$ and, say, $\iota(c, \iota(a^*, x))$ are two and not one. But,
then, the latter is impossible on a priori grounds. As you see, the idea of the notion of the natural groupings of the skins of the onion reappears.

[14] I.e., as I have been told by one of my keenest critics, E. B. Allaire, it is one of
the distinctive features of my world that it carries Russell's "discovery" of "relations" to its structural extreme. He is right, of course. Why otherwise the ontologization of M and of potentiality, not to mention exemplification and the
connectives? Of all this later.

extreme and, after a fashion at least, more reasonable than the other. Meinong, we shall see, was a moderate.

Return to the question. Is there a structural reason why conceiving should not be "absorbed" into the core? We are ready for the first answer.

The source of the extremists' view is Aristotle's assay of the act. This we shall see in Part III. But we may safely take for granted that the tradition which concerns us is dominated by Aristotle. Thus it makes sense to look for an answer to the Aristotelian-extremist assay of the act. Acts, we know, must be connected with the ideas they conceive. If ideas were intentions, these connections would be intendings. This, though, is beside the point right now. The point is, rather, that according to the extremists the ground of the connection of an act, *either with the intention or with the idea*, lies, just as in the case of the pitch particular, in the *relativliche* nature of the act itself. About this, we shall see, they are quite explicit. So they should be prepared to answer another question. Where in the act does its *Relativlichkeit* sit? Or, a bit more formally, which constituent has the job of grounding it? The answer is clear. Implicitly at least, this is the job done by the conceiving. That is why it is always there. Or, to say the same thing differently, with a structural blur which, however, historically strengthens the point, *the structurally "expendable" constituent of all fringes is nothing but the connection called intending withdrawn into the act itself.* (The blur lies in the ambiguous use of 'intending', which stands once for something that actually connects, once for what is merely *relativlich*.)

I turn in conclusion to the second answer, which is a point in structural history: An act is not an activity and an activity is not an act. In the later phases of representationalism that gradually became clear, I think. To Meinong and Brentano it is crystal clear. That is not to say that in this type of ontology acts and activities must never have anything to do with each other. An act may (however redundantly) be the product of an activity of the mind "in" which it is. But, then, even if there is or if there were such a "genetic" connection (p. 124), according to the *new style* the representationalists created and which becomes so crystal clear in Brentano and Meinong, the act and the activity still are or still would be two and not one. In the Aristotelian-Thomistic account, unless I am wholly mistaken, that is not so. In the *old style*, that is, an act of perceiving is the "abstracting" of a substantial form; and an "abstracting" is an activity. Thus, if conceiving is thought of as a minimal act in the old style, then the expendable constituent in it may be thought of as "corresponding" to the minimal activity of which in this style even a minimal act consists. Yet there has been a sea change. The "activity" of the mind, having risen, as it were, from underneath or behind its qualities (p. 122), is no longer "hidden" but floats on its surface. Before it rose, it was an activity, hence not a thing; after it has risen, it is a simple quality, hence a thing and not "hidden." You are aware, no doubt, that I am not only speaking very concisely but also piling metaphor upon metaphor. Yet I shall not stop to unpack anything. The point should be clear as it stands. The "expendable constituent" of the fringe is a kind of survival or structural fossil, reminding us that at least some features of the assays in the new style cannot be completely understood without also considering those in the old style.

Perhaps you have noticed what I shall express by a pun. The '*c*' in '$\iota(a^*, \iota(c, x))$' may be taken to stand for the initial not of 'conceiving' but of 'consciousness'.[15] Yet I shall not pursue. *Est modus in rebus.*

---

[15] The foil's account of "consciousness" is radically different. There each "conscious state" is one by virtue of being the intention of an act of direct awareness, which latter, though "in" the cross section, is not "in" the conscious state. See the essay on "Acts" in *Logic and Reality.*

THREE SCHEMATA

THE assay of the act in the prototype is anything but complete. For the features I shall fill in next veridical perception will do as a paradigm. Or, rather, it will do very well for the second and the third of the three schemata which I shall present in this section; for the first it is much too complicated. So I shall "pare down perception" until what is left contains neither more nor less than what is needed to grasp the point I want to make first. That is why the first paradigm will seem quite artificial. The advantage gained will be worth the price. For it seems quite difficult to grasp the point unless it has first been isolated. Yet it is crucial; unless it is grasped firmly and clearly, the increasing complexities of the second and the third schema and, eventually, of perception of the whole object cannot be mastered. The artificiality, or seeming artificiality, of the first paradigm is thus a matter of strategy. About the connections between strategy and dialectics no more need be said. I merely promise that I shall not at any time take unfair advantage of the artificiality.

Veridical perceptions are caused by objects. An object, even within a cross section, never is a single quality; always is a cluster. It does not follow that when perceiving an object or a cluster we perceive all the qualities "in" it. To me it is evident that we don't. About this there has been much confusion. Since this confusion is one of the fatal weaknesses of representationalism, we shall have to examine it. That will be done, by means of the third schema, in Section Ten. In the meantime you can help me to keep out the confusion by accepting as the paradigm of the first schema a situation whose intention is a single simple quality *and nothing else*. Perhaps you are worried because you think that the paradigm is not just artificial but also, in some strong sense of the term, impossible. If so, a distinction will help. For a quality not to be "in" a cluster surely is impossible. This, though, is one thing. Whether a single quality, whatever company it may or may not keep, can be the

155

whole intention of an act is quite another thing. So you need not worry.

The intentions of the second schema will be less rudimentary than those of the first; those of the third, even less limited than those of the second. Yet none will exceed what is simultaneous with the awareness "in" the act. Perception thus will remain "pared down" throughout this section. Or, to recall a distinction made in the last section (p. 143), even in the third schema 'perceiving' will be used with its special meaning. The usual meaning, or case, in which what I "perceive" when perceiving a chair or a table is the "whole object," will have to wait until the next section. Even there, though, we shall attend only to some aspects of it.

Suppose that the intention of the first paradigm is a_1; the core of the act in it, a_1^*. Let a_1 be green$_1$, one of the qualities which ground green. a_1 is a particular, of course. So is a_1^*. What else could it possibly be in a γ-world whose ground plan is consistently applied throughout? Is a_1^* simple (i.e., a perfect particular) or is it complex? A major part of the dialectic of representationalism turns on the question whether the core which goes with a complex intention is itself complex. Of this we have already had an intimation in the last section. But no twist will be lost if we assume, as I shall, that the cores of acts intending simple qualities are themselves simple. That makes a_1^* simple. *Both* a_1 *and* a_1^* *are simple qualities (perfect particulars).*

The representative in the paradigm is $\overline{A}$. Is it, too, a particular? If I am right, the answer is No. The particulars of the prototype are all either in the First or in the Second. Nor of course is $\overline{A}$ a universal. There are no universals anywhere in this world. Being an idea, or, as I put it, a third, $\overline{A}$ is *sui generis*. Yet, I also claimed that structurally $\overline{A}$ is a universal. The claim went with a metaphor. Ideas are universals in exile. But ontological discourse is literal. Metaphors, however attractive they may be and however poignantly they may illuminate a passage in structural history, have no place in it. What, then, does it literally mean to be structurally, though not literally, a universal? *It means that universals and ideas are alike in two respects.*

An idea is something under which several things fall. In the paradigm, the idea of green ($\overline{A}$) is something under which perfect particulars fall, just as in an ϵ-world the universal green (A) is something which several bare particulars exemplify. Call this for the moment the one-several feature. Universals and ideas both have the *one-several* feature. That is the *first respect* in which they are alike. If you object that this does not amount to anything, or that it does not even mean anything, as long as we don't know what it means for one entity to fall under another, you confuse two things. Falling-under remains forever unclear. Nor can it do the job which exemplifying does. No doubt you remember that I stressed that myself. This is one thing. That falling-under, whatever it may mean, on the one hand, and exemplifying, on the other, share the one-several feature is quite another thing and anything but unclear, just as it is very clear that, however vainly, the representationalists all expected the former to do the job of the latter.

Having accepted the paradigm, you cannot reasonably object to my making copies of it. Consider, then, an indefinite number of rudimentary perceptual situations. The intention and the core of the first are a_1 and a_1^*; those of the second, a_2 and a_2^*; those of the third a_3 and a_3^*; and so on. The a_i are all perfect particulars grounding the property green; or, if you please, they are all members of the Class $\bar{A}$; or, even, if you are willing to make enough copies, they are all the members of $\bar{A}$. As for the a_i, so for the a_i^*. They are all perfect particulars; the property each of them grounds being the one a mind possesses if and only if the core of an act intending a member of A is "in" it. Accordingly, the a_i^* are all members of a Class $\bar{A}^*$, and, again, if you are willing to make enough copies, they are all the members of it. For there is of course no difficulty whatsoever about Classes whose members are mental. The ground plan, you remember, must be applied consistently throughout.

As you see, quite a few entities, or would-be entities, are involved. There is the idea, $\bar{A}$, which is in the Third. There are the a_i and the a_i^*, which are in the Second and the First, respectively. There are the two Classes, $\bar{A}$ and $\bar{A}^*$, the former in the Second, the latter in the First. There is, finally, though of course only in ε-worlds, the universal A. Let us make a list: (1) $\bar{A}$, (2) a_i, (3) a_i^*, (4) $\bar{A}$, (5) $\bar{A}^*$, (6) A. It is obvious in itself, though also a corollary of the crucial point I am about to make, that confusing any two of these six leads to disaster.

The idea presented in all copies, if I may so express myself, is $\bar{A}$, *i.e., literally one entity.* This is the point I wanted to make first and in isolation, as it were, because I believe it to be so crucial that, having called the prototype the key to the dialectic of representationalism, I am tempted to call it the key to the key. Perhaps it will help if I again call attention to the difference between two things. $\bar{A}$ is a single entity which is "in" all copies. This is one thing; and it is perfectly clear. That $\bar{A}$ is a dweller in the Third and that therefore it is not at all clear what sort of entity it is, or, for that matter, whether there are such entities at all, is quite another thing.

Which is the *second respect* in which ideas and universals are alike? The answer is but another corollary to the crucial point. In an ε-world, the universal in several green objects is the same$_3$. Hence, what I intend, or, which in these worlds amounts to the same, what I am presented with when perceiving on different occasions different green objects is, as far as the color is concerned, the same₃. As a γ-ontology assays what on these several different occasions I intend, a_1 on the first, a_2 on the second, and so on, it is of course not literally the same. But the idea, $\overline{A}$, with which I am presented (i.e., which I conceive) on all these occasions is the same₃. If you wish, you may express that by saying that, as far as presentation is concerned, ideas and universals share the *literal-sameness feature*. This is the second respect in which they are alike. That establishes the literal ontological meaning I shall continue to express concisely by saying that structurally ideas are universals.

These are the bare bones of the first schema. The schema itself, if you insist on being literal about it, is the pared-down-perception paradigm together with its copies. The feature it illuminates is present in all knowing situations of the prototype. Am I right? Or, what amounts to the same, does this feature of the "prototype" really help to make it one, in the sense claimed and explained? You will not and you must not expect to find a "proof" in the next five, ten, or even twenty pages. As always, the proof of the pudding is in the eating; and the pudding, as always, is this book as a whole. But, then, in philosophy there is much to be gained by putting some flesh on the bare bones. So I shall add *three comments*. Each will be a small step toward the "proof." Or, in the words of the other metaphor, each will put a bit of flesh on the bones.

First. The feature agrees with the way 'idea', 'concept', '*Begriff*', and '*Vorstellung*' are used, by the representationalists when speaking philosophically, as well as, more often than not, by all of us, in all sorts of contexts. We speak of *the* idea or *the* concept of green, not of concepts or ideas of (this shade of) green. To be sure, there are contexts in which the plural is used. We speak of different ideas or concepts of the state. That, though, corresponds to speaking of the several ideas of several colors.

There is also some support in the way we speak, the representationalists philosophically, all of us more often than not in all sorts of contexts, for that feature of the feature which corresponds to the common-names doctrine. The idea of green is also the idea of something green (*etwas gruenes*), just as what we conceive, according to Brentano and Meinong, is *etwas gruenes*. *Something green* is not *a green*! '*A* green', or '*this* green', would be, and in English philosophical discourse is, a suitable appellation for one of the a_i. 'Something green (*etwas gruenes*)', on the other hand, is as close as one can come with an English (German) phrase to the notion of a common name which, as one says, names *indifferently* or ambiguously. Or, to say the same thing differently, *if ideas were what of course they are not, namely, words, they would be common names.*

Notice that the 'something' in the phrase 'something green' makes it ambiguous in still another sense. The entities falling under the "idea of something green" may be the a_i; or they may be all the clusters (objects) of which an a_i is a component. Once the Class in the case is $\tilde{A}$; once it is the Class of all green objects ("things"). In the latter case, 'something green' thus stands for 'some thing (object) which is green'. This ambiguity has been a source of troubles. We shall encounter them presently.

Second. An objector argues as follows: Every idea, you hold, represents indifferently any one of the several things that fall under it. Or, as you put it, if an idea were a word, it would be a common name. This, I take it, is why you stressed 'indifferently'; common names, as we all know, having been said to name indifferently any one of several things. Probably you are now ready to add that just as upon your view there are no ideas, so there are no common names. Nor, alas, will you fail to point out that, as this shows, your several beliefs hang together. I grant that they do. It does not follow that any single one of them is true, or plausible, or even credible. Or is it credible that, however implicitly (to speak as you do), the representationalists held a view upon which we are never presented with anything but (structural) universals? Are we not again and again presented with objects which, even if I don't use the word as pedantically as you do, are yet, in a sense which is sufficiently clear, "particulars" and therefore not universals? Are you then really prepared to commit the representationalists to the absurd view that we are never presented with "objects"?

In a sense I am; in a sense I am not. The sense in which I am is the sense in which a one-class is still a class and not literally its single member. The sense in which I am not is best understood by considering how very well one-classes can quite often stand in for their single members, or, as one might put it, how very well they can in many contexts do many of their jobs; *as long as one does not mind a certain blur and the constant danger of confusion.* Nor therefore is the view to which I am "committing" the representationalists as patently absurd as the objector wants to make it seem. As you may gather, we are about to put quite a bit of flesh on a rather large bone.

Take a place. In a γ-world it is a quality (p_1). The idea of it, the idea-of-this-place, ($\overline{P}$), is therefore a (structural) universal. Yet $\tilde{P}$ is a one-Class, p_1 being the only perfect particular that falls under $\overline{P}$. As for $\overline{P}$, so for any idea which manages to "contain" that of a place. The notion of one idea "containing" another is problematic indeed. Its examination, or, rather, the examination of a part of it by means of the other two schemata, is our next task. But we need not wait until it will have been performed. We are already in a position to take stock of a most important structural connection, provided only we are prepared to accept provisionally the notion that every idea which somehow manages to "contain" the idea of a place represents a single object, in the sense that the single object any one of them represents is the one and only thing which falls under it.

Upon the basic representationalist gambit, if all ideas are structural universals, then, if there were no spatial (and temporal) qualities, there would be no way, not even by "representation,' of conceiving objects or any other "particular." The structural connection, you see, is between representationalism on the one hand and the γ-assay, if I may so express myself, of space (and time) on the other. More specifically, we have come upon a structural reason why *a representationalist must be a γ-ontologist!* Since these philosophers in fact all are γ-ontologists, the growing number of our diagnoses continues mutually to support each other. This particular one is so important that I shall take the time to put it in its proper setting by a quick glance at the foil and an even quicker one at the way things were done in the "old style."

The problem is individuation and, if I may so express myself, its reflection in the act. In the foil, what is presented to me when perceiving the tree is the fact, (*F*), of this particular (*a*) being a tree. *a* individuates the tree itself. In the thought, a reflection of this individuation is preserved, in spite of the thought's ($\ulcorner F \urcorner$) being simple. Or, rather, it is preserved because the thought is simple, since this very simplicity provides the structural possibility for that uniquely strict correspondence between *F* and $\ulcorner F \urcorner$ by virtue of which everything in *F* is reflected in $\ulcorner F \urcorner$.

Upon the account in the old style, there is in the tree a substantial form, which is a universal, and something else, which individuates it. I have never accurately understood how that works, or, even, how it could possibly work. But we may take for granted that this is the schema; just as we may take for granted that what goes for the tree also goes for me. In me, too, there is a substantial form and there is an individuator. When perceiving the tree, I "abstract" from it its substantial form, which latter, being a (structural) universal, yet also safely remains in the tree itself and there, within the Second, is safely individuated by its own individuator. On the side of the act, though, in the First, it would remain unindividuated unless "I" myself lent it the support of my own individuator. Upon the old account, all details apart, that is exactly what "I" do. If only after a fashion and in a certain sense, while perceiving the tree, "I" (or should I say my individuator?) become the tree. The details of this schema cannot, I am convinced, be worked out. But, again, we may take for granted that this is how things are supposed to work out. If they do, then, we see, individuation is taken care of.

On the side of the tree, if I may so express myself, the representationalists, who invented the "new style," do what we just saw they are forced to do. They provide for individuation by coordinate qualities. On the side of the act, a core is not a substantial form, to be individuated by what (if anything) individuates "you" or "me," but, rather, a quality among qualities in the cluster which is my mind. On the one hand, therefore, the core itself needs no further entity to individuate it. On the other hand, it must reflect what individuates the intention. That leaves two alternatives. Either one does what is being done in the foil, of which no one ever seems to have thought; or one does what in fact all representationalists did, making the core a complex particular which "contains" the reflection (p_i^*) of what individuates the tree itself (p_1). (Notice that I call p_i^* a reflection, not a "representation." The "representing" in the case is done by $\overline{P}$. To confuse the two is to confuse cores and ideas. This brings us to the last of these comments.)

Third. What becomes of an idea after it has fallen into the mind? By now the answer should be obvious. Having fallen to the left, into the First, an idea becomes *the* core which goes with it. But, then, 'the' is without ground. $\overline{A}$ may and will become any or all of the a_i^*. All cores are particulars. All ideas are (structural) universals. Thus, when a philosopher tells us that all ideas are particulars, we know immediately that in his world they have fallen into the mind.

All ideas are particulars. That is exactly what Locke tells us. That, though, is merely the beginning of his woes. Ideas, according to him, are either "particular ideas" or "general ideas." All ideas being particulars is one thing; some ideas being "particular ideas" is another thing, of course. "General ideas" are "particular ideas" (i.e., in reality, a_i^*'s) which the psychologists in some miraculous way have trained to do the job of ideas ($\overline{A}$). Nor, alas, poor Locke, is that the full measure of his troubles. That miraculous training is one story. The activity of the mind called abstraction is another. Locke fuses and confuses the two stories, even though they have nothing to do with each other. To understand exactly what happened we must first examine the notion of abstraction. This is one of the things we shall do next, by means of the second schema. So I shall say no more about Locke at the moment, return to him later, after that examination will have been concluded.

We are ready for the second schema.

The schema adds to the rudimentary intention. Use 'a_1', 'a_1^*', '$\bar{A}$', and so on, as before; let b_1 be one of the (simple) qualities grounding the property square; use 'b_1^*', '$\bar{B}$', and so on, analogously. The intention of the second schema is $\gamma(a_1, b_1)$. Thus it is complex. Naturally there is also an idea and a core "in" the situation. If we make copies, there is still only one idea—this we have learned and take over from the first schema—but there are several intentions and several cores. (Two situations may have the same₃ intention, but they cannot have the same₃ core.) Let the subscripts 'i' and 'j' run over all the members of $\bar{A}$ and $\bar{B}$, respectively; 'k' and 'l' over those subsets of these sets whose members are constituents of the intention of a copy. That makes '$\gamma(a_k, b_l)$' an expression which will serve us as 'a_i' has and 'b_j' might have served us in the first schema.

$\gamma(a_1, b_1)$ is complex. How about the other entities in the situation? In the prototype these are two questions, one about the idea, one about the core. In the foil, there being no ideas, there is only one question, which corresponds, although not accurately, to that about the core. The correspondence is not accurate because, while in the foil all intentions are complex, none of them is a thing: they are all facts. All thoughts, on the other hand, which in the foil are the things that correspond to the cores, are simple. That provides a helpful contrast. In the prototype, if the intention is complex, so is the core. (Of this we had a first glimpse in the last section and another right now, when considering the reflection of individuation.) This contrast gives rise to further questions. But we are not yet quite ready for them.

What is the proper way of referring to the idea and the core, in words and in symbols? Unless we are cautious, we may prejudge some of the questions that arise by the very way in which we express ourselves. At this point our little symbolism repays the small effort we made in developing it by forcing us to be cautious. A moment's reflection will show you that the only safe way, safe because not prejudging anything, of referring to the idea and the core is by (1) '$\bar{I}(\gamma(a_1, b_1))$' and (2) '$[\gamma(a_1, b_1)]^*$', respectively. The bar in (1) and the bracket in (2) are for extra safety. The former is to remind us that the expression stands for an idea; the latter, that the core corresponds to the cluster as a whole. If, say, $\gamma(a_7, b_9)$ is the intention "in" a copy, $[\gamma(a_1, b_1)]^*$ and $[\gamma(a_7, b_9)]^*$ are of course two and not one. (1) standing for an idea, on the other hand, (1) and '$\bar{I}(\gamma(a_7, b_9))$' stand for the same₃. Thus it might be even safer to write '$\bar{I}(\gamma(a_k, b_l))$' instead of (1). But I don't think that this extra caution will ever be necessary. The corresponding Class, finally, should extra caution be indicated, will best be represented by '$Cl(\gamma(a_k, b_l))$'.

With our sensibility thus sharpened by the symbolism let us turn to the words. The first thing to note is that we must not expect to find a safe way of speaking with that majority of representationalists who, like Locke, confuse cores and ideas, or, if you would rather have it this way, who identify ideas with cores. As to the ideas, all representationalists speak of *the idea of something both green and square.* Since the grammar of this phrase has affected their thought, since I cannot think of one more accurate which is not terribly clumsy, and since if necessary the artificial notation will keep us straight, I shall follow suit. Notice, though, that this way of speaking increases the ambiguity of 'something' in certain phrases. Take 'the idea (of something) green', 'the idea of something both green and square', 'the idea of some thing (i.e., object) which is green'. The entities falling under the three ideas so referred to are simple qualities, binary clusters (if I may so express myself), and objects, respectively. Whenever necessary, one could, and I shall, call attention to this ambiguity and its dangers by writing 'the idea of something¹ green', 'the idea of something² green and square', 'the idea of something° green', respectively. (The last superscript is the initial of 'object'.)

"The intention of the second schema is complex; so therefore are its idea and its core. The *parts* of the intention being a_1 and b_1, those of the idea must be $\overline{A}$ and $\overline{B}$; those of the core, a_1^* and b_1^*." There is no doubt that more or less explicitly the representationalists all reasoned in this way, from the complexity and the *parts* of the intention to the complexity and the *parts* of the idea and the core. That the inferences are invalid we understand already. It does not follow that the conclusions invalidly arrived at are false. From where I stand, they are false; for one, because there are no ideas; for another, because all thoughts are simple. But there is no point in reasserting or even rearguing my own beliefs. The task is to unravel the dialectic of those held by the representationalists.

If you remember how hard I tried in Section Four to discourage the broad use of 'part', you may wonder why I resuscitate it at this most delicate point. My purpose is to call attention to the obliteration, in which I am convinced this very use has had its share, of a very radical difference between intentions and cores on the one hand and ideas on the other. But we need not throw caution to the winds. I shall continue to mark the broad use of 'part' in this context by italicizing the word; now as well as, whenever prudence requires it, later on.

In the case of intentions and cores, there is no doubt that *parts* are "constituents which are things." The only comment one might wish to add is that the more explicit the reism of the ontology under consideration happens to be, the more vacuous becomes the qualification "which are things." The *intention* of our schema is a cluster. That makes its (categorial) *parts* its components. $a_1 \subset \gamma(a_1, b_1)$; $b_1 \subset \gamma(a_1, b_1)$. Nor does any new question about the intentions themselves arise in this context. About *cores* there are *two*. Why did the representationalists assay $[\gamma(a_1, b_1)]^*$ as a complex whose only *parts* (constituents which are things) are a_1^* and b_1^*? Which nexus connects a_1^* and b_1^* into $[\gamma(a_1, b_1)]^*$?

The case of the *idea* is more difficult; or, rather, the ontological status of ideas is so problematic that I, for one, cannot but insist on being told what, if anything, it could possibly mean to say of the two ideas of something green and of something square that they are the two *parts* of the idea of something both green and square. That raises a *third* question. What, if anything, does it mean for one idea to be a *part* of another?

The task ahead will take some time. So I shall restate it. We must answer *three* questions. *Why did the representationalists assay* $[\gamma(a_1, b_1)]^*$ *as a complex whose parts are* a_1^* *and* b_1^*? *What is the nexus in this complex? What, if anything, does it mean for one idea to be a part of another?* I shall present my answers, in this order, in three steps. Then we shall be ready for the third schema.

First step. The representationalists' argument for assaying $[\gamma(a_1, b_1)]^*$ as a complex with the two constituents a_1^* and b_1^* has two premisses. One is their empiricism, a familiar thesis I shall state in three parts. The other, if this sort of thing can be called a premiss, is the genetic fallacy, which was discussed in Section Six (p. 124). Descartes, of course, did not share the empiricist thesis for all ideas. Yet I take him to have shared it for some, just as I believe that the reservations he certainly would have made for some others do not affect what I am about.

Assume that all the intentions a certain mind has perceived until now are clusters of two qualities, one a shape, one a color. Whenever he perceived such a cluster, it was the latter which was active, its activity "impressing" the core on the mind, which to this extent was passive. This is the first part of the empiricist thesis. On it all representationalists agree. The act as a whole, as always, is a complex of two constituents; one is a core; the other is a fringe, in these cases a perceiving. Has the act as a whole been "impressed"? On this the representationalists disagree among themselves. But, again, the disagreement makes no difference for what I am about.

Add to the assumption by supposing that up to now the mind in question has perceived only two kinds of binary clusters, one of green and square, the other of red and round. This mind is yet capable of engaging in two kinds of activities. He can conceive the four simple ideas of something green, of something red, of something square, and of something round. This is the activity called *abstracting*. Without ever having perceived anything both red and square or anything both green and round, he can also conceive two other ideas, namely, first that of something red and square, and, second, that of something green and round. This is the activity called *combining*. Minds can abstract and combine simple ideas. This is the second part of the thesis of empiricism.[1] If, finally, the mind in question has never perceived (either the simple idea of green according to the first schema or) a cluster of which a quality grounding green is a component, he would not have been able to conceive either this simple idea by itself or any other idea of which it is a *part*. This is the third and last part of the empiricist thesis.

The activities of abstracting and combining establish between the cores upon which they operate, on the one hand, and the cores which are their products, on the other, connections of the kind we called genetic. The genetic fallacy, we know, consists of mistaking such connections for ontological assays. In other words, the "materials" upon which the activity is exercised are uncritically mistaken for the assay of its "product." No more needs to be said. You understand already how one who accepts the empiricist thesis and commits the genetic fallacy cannot but conclude that, say, a_1^* and b_1^* are the two constituents of $[\gamma(a_1, b_1)]^*$. That completes the first of the three steps. Two comments will add savor.

1. The talk in the argument I just presented, in part also on behalf of the representationalists, is all about intentions and about cores. Ideas, not by chance, come in only as afterthoughts. First, there is the cluster; then, "impressed" by it upon the mind, there is the core. As far as the ideas are concerned, all that needs to be said is that for a certain act to be "in" a mind and for this mind to conceive the idea which goes with the core "in" the act are, as it were, two aspects of one situation. Not that they are literally one. That is why I say: as it were. Yet, in some sense, they may seem to be one. This sense, to be sure, is irremediably blurred, just as the ontological status of ideas is incurably precarious. The blur and the precariousness are but the two sides of one coin.

[1] Some uses of 'activity' and 'active' are commonsensical and therefore harmless. Some others are neither the one nor the other. That was indeed the burden of the discussion of substances₃ at the end of Part I. Are the activities of abstracting and combining to which our philosophers appeal activities in that categorial sense which, if I am right, is anything but harmless and makes no sense at all? The answer is complicated. Nor does what I am here about depend on it. So I shall postpone consideration of these matters. Yet the question will even at this point occur to many readers. So I mention it lest my silence cause them to be puzzled.

Brentano was accurate enough to know that there was trouble. But his accuracy merely drove him to absurdity. Of this later. Right now I merely want you to notice that the very way the talk naturally runs is a symptom of the ontological frailty of ideas, or, if you please, of the instability of the Third.

2. Remember Locke who, mistaking cores (a_1^*) for ideas $(\overline{A})$, not only made all ideas particulars in the mind but divided them into "particular ideas" and "general ideas," the latter being the result of "abstraction," which is a miraculous I-know-not-what, enabling one among these particulars, say, a^*, to function as if it were a structural universal of sorts, "representing" indifferently the several a_i, each of which is also "represented" singly by its "particular idea," a_1 by a_1^*, a_2 by a_2^*, and so on. This is the Lockean notion of "abstraction," confused in itself beyond repair. That we saw earlier. Now we see that Lockean "abstraction" has nothing whatsoever to do with abstraction, the notion just expounded by means of the second schema. Thus we can appreciate how disastrously Locke compounded his confusion by talking about both "abstraction" and abstraction without distinguishing between the two. The mess is so bad that the best one can do is speculate how it came about.

According to Locke, there are not only the a_i^*, say, n of them, but also, set apart from them by its function, a $(n+1)$st, a^*. That reminds me of the medieval doctrine of exaggerated realism, according to which, if there are n objects each of which is a man, there is also a $(n+1)$st, namely, mankind. The latter, though a universal, upon this clumsy doctrine is yet also an object, just as Locke's a^*, though adapted to a special function, is yet also a particular. And it is of course this special function of a^* which, making it a structural universal of sorts, also makes it, *if only by verbal association*, something which is "abstracted," either from the a_i, or perhaps even from the a_i^*, just as upon the old-style account a universal (substantial form) is "abstracted" in perception. Abstraction proper, on the other hand, the notion I explicated, *in another verbal association*, also "abstracts" something, in the sense of detaching it from something else, as a single grape is detached by plucking it from a cluster, or, again, as, after a fashion at least, upon the old-style account of perception a substantial form (universal) is detached from its individuator by the perceiving mind. One may speculate that these two verbal associations are in part responsible for the mess.

Second step. Write 'c_1^*' for '$[\gamma(a_1, b_1)]^*$'. *What is the nexus in c_1^*?* With the exception of Meinong, of whom presently, the representationalists were all more or less explicit reists. Trying to answer, we cannot therefore expect much help from them; must decide for ourselves, on purely structural grounds, for the sake of making the prototype as articulate and thereby as useful as, by our own standards, it can be. The prototype assays c_1^* as the complex particular $\iota(a_1^*, b_1^*)$. Or, in literal answer to the question, the nexus in complex cores is joining (ι). This will not come as a surprise. I merely yield to the second of the structural suggestions, uncovered in the last section, which I listed (p. 148) before demonstrating that, even if its core and fringe are simple, an act cannot in γ consistently be assayed as a subcluster of the mind "in" which it is. I shall next present a similar demonstration, to the effect that c_1^* cannot be $\gamma(a_1^*, b_1^*)$; then add four comments. But I shall be very succinct throughout: in the demonstration because we are on familiar ground, in the comments because they are meant to provide perspective by raising some questions which we shall return to later rather than answer exhaustively the first time.

Make two assumptions. Assume, first, for the sake of the argument, that $\gamma(a_1, b_1)$, a_2, b_2 are three objects. Assume, second, that we can in a single act of perceiving intend two objects, say, something[1] green (a_2) "and" something[1] square (b_2). The first assumption, though counterfactual, is completely harmless; nothing will be lost; no distortion has been introduced. The second assumption seems to produce a difficulty, even if one takes for granted, as in discussing γ-ontologies one must, that a *single* object rather than, as in the foil, only a fact, can be an intention. The difficulty is that an intention of *several* objects, say, a_2 "and" b_2, cannot literally be the collection $\{a_2, b_2\}$, since, from where I stand, an intention must exist,[2] and since, as we know from Part I, collections literally do not exist, not even, provided only it is fully articulated, in a γ-ontology. Happily,[3] though, Part I also provides the way out of the apparent difficulty by providing the "single" object $\sigma(a_2, b_2)$ as an acceptable assay of the intention of the single act of perceiving.

Consider two acts of perceiving. The first intends $\gamma(a_1, b_1)$, i.e., something[2] green and square; the second, something[1] green (a_2) "and" something[1] square (b_2).[4] It follows that a_1^* and b_1^* are among the con-

---

[2] Either actually or potentially.

[3] We have come upon another point that affords a check of the sort one ought to make from time to time. As you see, things keep hanging together.

[4] That the two intentions differ, not only numerically but also in kind, I take for granted. This is one of the phenomenological data philosophy is about, in the sense that they give rise to the dialectical problems. But they are not themselves anything to be argued about. If your world is different, then I cannot talk with you. If at certain crucial points you are phenomenologically either blind or careless then you cannot be a philosopher, even though philosophy is not just phenomenology.

stituents of the core (c_1^*) of the first act; a_2^* and b_2^* among those of the core of the second. If so, then $\gamma(a_1^*, b_1^*)$ and $\gamma(a_2^*, b_2^*)$ are also "in" the cores of the first and of the second act, respectively. Hence, if c_1^* were $\gamma(a_1^*, b_1^*)$, then $\gamma(a_2^*, b_2^*)$ would be c_2^*, i.e., the intention of the second act would not be something[1] green and something[1] square but, rather, something[2] green and square. Thus the two intentions would not differ in kind. It follows that c_1^* cannot be $\gamma(a_1^*, b_1^*)$. That concludes the demonstration. Now for the comments.

1. Let us check whether the second assumption is necessary. The possibility it excludes is that perceiving simultaneously two (or more) objects is to have a subcluster of two (or more) acts of perceiving a single object "in" one's mind. Let then w_1, w_2, w_3 be three fringes of the kind called perceivings; and consider the single act (1) $\iota(w_1, \gamma(a_1^*, b_1^*))$ on the one hand and the binary subcluster of acts (2) $\gamma(\iota(w_2, a_2^*),$ $\iota(w_3, b_2^*))$ on the other. A moment's reflection will show you that, prima facie at least, (1) and (2) could serve as assays of the two acts. That is why, prima facie at least, the second assumption is necessary.[5]

2. To demonstrate that the complex core c_1^* cannot be the subcluster $\gamma(a_1^*, b_1^*)$ is one thing. To show that it must be the joint $\iota(a_1^*, b_1^*)$ is quite another thing. The first we just did. The second no one can do. There remains the abstract possibility of an additional fundamental tie,[6] or even of a whole series of such, of graded strengths, "in" cores and "in" fringes. But there is no point in overelaborating a speculative prototype. That is why I proceed as I do.[7]

[5] The possibility thus excluded is also excluded by a premiss or principle of representationalism which in Brentano and Meinong has become crystal clear. (In Locke it is not, otherwise he could not have propounded his "subjectivistic" assay of relations. See on this point the essay on "The Problem of Relations in Classical Psychology" in my first book, *The Metaphysics of Logical Positivism* [New York, 1954; new ed., University of Wisconsin Press, 1967].) By this principle different intentions would correspond to different acts even if there were no fringes, or, equivalently, if an act's core were its whole. Since I myself accept this premiss I should like to make three points concerning what it does and doesn't mean and what it does and doesn't entail. (1) It doesn't deny that, given a physical object, it still depends on several other factors, including the state of mind of the perceiver, what, if anything, he perceives. (2) It insists on a strict one-one correspondence between the intention of what, if anything, is actually perceived on the one hand and the core of the act, if any, of perceiving it, on the other. (3) Rejection of this principle does not deductively imply minds which are "active" in the categorial sense I reject. Nor, therefore, does this rejection entail idealism. But the stylistic affinity is undeniable and the temptation is great, to say the least. See also the fourth comment above.

[6] Or, rather, just to remind you for once, since we move in γ, pseudo-tie.

[7] See n. 12 of Section Eight. Look also at the following n. 13 and convince yourself once more that a single ι cannot be associative.

3. In Meinong's second ontology, there are connections and there are facts. Or, rather, they are there after a fashion. That his moves are all in the right direction is beyond doubt. That does not mean that they are all right nor that, right or wrong, they are always clear. Some of his insights, though, shine through the mists. One of these precious flashes illuminates what we are here about. So I shall present it; not in his way, which would require many preparations; yet without, I believe, either distorting it or giving him more credit than he deserves.[8]

Start once more from $\gamma(a_1, b_1)$ and c_i^*; remember that γ is an entity and assume, first, that c_i^* has a simple constituent, γ^*, which is a thing and stands to γ as a_i^* and b_i^* stand to a_1 and b_1, respectively. Assume, second, that one can in a single act intend the three entities a_1, b_1, γ; just as, in another single act, one can intend the single entity $\gamma(a_1, b_1)$. Strange as in my context it may sound, though not, as eventually we shall see, in Meinong's, there is nothing absurd about the first assumption. The second produces a difficulty. There is the collection $\{a_1, b_1, \gamma\}$. But since γ, unlike γ^*, is not a thing, there is not, as in the demonstration above, a "sum"[9] to serve as the intention of a single act intending a_1 "and" b_1 "and" γ. But, then, again, in Meinong's world the difficulty does not appear.[10] So I shall ignore it in the prototype. That permits us to repeat the pattern of the demonstration we just went through and arrive at the conclusion that c_i^* cannot be $\gamma(a_1, b_1, \gamma^*)$. This adds an important corollary to some structural insights we already possess. We know already that the complex cores of γ-ontologies require a "new" or "additional" fundamental tie, which makes them into complex particulars, i.e., into things which, though *in* clusters, are not just subclusters but "half way" between simple qualities (perfect particulars) and clusters. The corollary we have now come upon is that this requirement is not due to the more or less explicit reism of γ. In the modified Meinong example, we just saw, both γ and γ^* are recognized. Yet an adequate assay of c_i^* requires an additional fundamental nexus, such as, say, ι in $\iota(a_i^*, b_i^*, \gamma^*)$. That leads to the fourth and last comment.

4. In the truncated world of the prototype one can, unless I am mistaken, get along[11] with γ alone. The need for at least one additional

[8] The main reference is §42 of *Ann*.

[9] $\sigma(a_1, b_1, \gamma)$ is ill-formed!

[10] More precisely, it is shrouded in the mists that hover over his world. But there is no point in anticipating what, while fascinating when systematically and thoroughly explained in detail, remains obscure until such explanation comes forth.

[11] I.e., one can get along for quite a while. Eventually, unless I am wrong, all γ-ontologies break down under expert dialectical pressure.

fundamental nexus arises only in the assay of minds (cores and fringes). Nor would it make any difference for the question I want to raise if the truncated prototype contained n fundamental nexus, either in fact or from dialectical necessity. For in this case, we just learned from Meinong, the assay of minds would require a $(n+1)$st. Since the difference thus makes no difference, let us stay with $n=1$, i.e., with γ alone in the truncated world, γ and ι in the assay of minds.

Is the ι in $\iota(a_1{}^*, b_1{}^*)$ *impressed upon*, or is it a *contribution of*, the mind? This is the question I wanted to raise. Answering it and clarifying the two key phrases in it are virtually the same. (a) If not being impressed means that there is in the fact $\gamma(a_1, b_1)$ nothing, *except this fact itself*, which stands to ι as $a_1{}^*$, $b_1{}^*$, γ^* stand to a_1, b_1, γ, respectively, then ι *is not impressed*. (b) The fact itself, which is of course "more" than the collection $\{a_1, b_1, \gamma\}$ does so stand to ι.[12] In this sense, ι *is impressed*. (c) If to be contributed by the mind means not to be impressed in sense (a), then ι *is contributed by the mind*. (d) If to be so contributed means to be the product of a mental activity, in the categorial sense connected with substances₅ which I reject, then *one can consistently hold that ι is not contributed by the mind*. This follows from (b), for the prototype as well as for the modified Meinong example.

The distinctions required show how easy it is to slip. Neither Brentano nor, alas, even Meinong held clearly and consistently what we just saw to be compatible with the need for the "new" or "additional" nexus. The third and the fourth comment thus serve as an advance notice. We have, as it were, discovered the back door through which "active" minds (substances₅) enter the worlds of these two thinkers.[13] Notice finally how the notion of the mind's, *on its own, as it were*, "combining" what it has first "abstracted" adds to the temptation.

Third step. What does it mean for an idea $\overline{N}$ to be a *part* of another, $\overline{M}$? When we tried to answer the second question, about the nexus in complex cores, we had to shift for ourselves. Since the representationalists were all more or less explicit reists, they hardly saw that there was a question. But we had enough of a ground plan to go by. So we managed without their guidance. With respect to the third question the situation is quite different. The ontological status of ideas is precarious, to say

---

[12] More precisely, the fact corresponds to $\iota(a_1{}^*, b_1{}^*)$ or $\iota(a_1{}^*, b_1{}^*, \gamma^*)$, in the prototype or the modified Meinong example, respectively.

[13] The discovery should, and I hope will, increase your insight into the structural significance of that most distinctive feature according to which the cores (thoughts) of the foil are simple. Of all this much more in Parts III and IV. But the matter surely is important enough to justify an advance notice that fits so well with the point at hand.

the least. More bluntly, there is no Third. Thus no ground plan can help. That keeps me, for one, from having any clear notion of what it might mean for one idea to be a *part* of another. The representationalists, on the other hand, whether or not their notions were clear, all had a good deal to say on this point. Under the circumstances, we cannot but look to them for guidance. Nor, having received it, shall we have much choice. The best we can do is to ascertain on what they all agree, then articulate it as best we can and incorporate it into the prototype.

As the representationalists speak, for the idea $\overline{N}$ to be *contained* in the idea $\overline{M}$ is the same as for the former to be a *part* of the latter. 'Part' has been used so broadly that it does not provide much of a cue. 'Contains' does. As we have used it, it stands for the derivative nexus between a class and any of its subclasses. If X and Y are two classes, the former is contained in the latter $(X < Y)$ if and only if every member of X is a member of Y. Call this the old use of 'contains'. *Saying of one idea that it is "contained" in another is a new use.* The double quotes mark the distinction. Things will not get too involved, though. The new use, we shall see in a moment, is derived from the old one in a manner which will permit us to drop the double quotes without danger of confusion.

All representationalists *meant* to use 'contain' so that one idea "contains" another if and only if two conditions are fulfilled. I say that they meant to use the word in this way rather than that they did so use it because in certain cases the conditions, *as I shall state them*, are not fulfilled. This, though, it will turn out, is more a nuisance than a real difficulty. I shall therefore first expound what I have no doubt was really meant and attend to the nuisance later.

Let $\tilde{M}$ and $\tilde{N}$ be the two Classes of things which fall under the ideas $\overline{M}$ and $\overline{N}$, respectively. If examples help, think of $\overline{M}$ and $\overline{N}$ as the ideas of (something[1]) green and of (something[1]) colored, respectively. That makes $\tilde{M}$ the Class of all perfect particulars grounding green (a_i); $\tilde{N}$, that of all those grounding colored. *The idea $\overline{M}$ "contains" the idea $\overline{N}$ if and only if (1) $\tilde{M}$ is contained in (not: contains!) $\tilde{N}$, and (2) $\tilde{M}$ being contained in $\tilde{N}$ is either an a priori or an analytic truth.* These are the two conditions. In terms of the example, the idea of colored is contained in that of green because it is an a priori truth that the Class of all particulars grounding a color contains that of all those grounding green. Now for five comments.

1. (2) is stronger than (1). Less formally, (2) is (1) plus something else. There was thus no need for mentioning (1) at all. Or, if you please, there is only one condition and not two. My reason for setting (1) apart is purely expository. In the total dialectic of the representationalism

issue the "something else" is of the greatest importance, demands and deserves the most careful and most detailed attention. Such attention it will receive in Section Eleven. For the limited purpose of this section, with one exception in the concluding comment, (1) will do. So I put into (1) what I now need, make (2) a signpost for things to come.

2. The foil distinguishes between truths which are analytic (necessary$_2$) and those which are "merely" a priori (necessary$_3$). Some representationalists don't. Or, if they do, the analytic is for them merely a kind of the a priori. Soon we shall understand why this is so. For the moment just note that the phrasing in (2) is mine and not theirs.

3. The new use of 'contains' being in this way derived from the old, there will be no danger of confusion if henceforth we drop the double quotes and even use the same symbol ('$<$'). I restate the two conditions in this notation: $\overline{N}$ is contained in $\overline{M}$ ($\overline{N} < \overline{M}$) if and only if (1) $\tilde{M}$ is contained in $\tilde{N}$ ($\tilde{M} < \tilde{N}$), and (2) ($\tilde{M} < \tilde{N}$) is either an analytic or an a priori truth. The characteristic reversal in the positions of 'M' and 'N' is but a thinly disguised bit of familiar machinery. Use 'A' and 'B' as both predicate and class signs, write '$>$' for the horseshoe, and you obtain: $A < B$ if and only if $(x)[A(x) > B(x)]$.

4. One point not needed for the limited purpose of the moment is yet so obvious and at the same time so crucial that I shall not refrain from calling attention to it. Containing is the obvious candidate for a fundamental nexus between ideas. So we had to find out what it means for one idea to be contained in another. We did find out, but not, as one would expect, by examining ideas. Rather, we attended to the Classes of things which fall under the ideas and to the familiar connections among these Classes. Isn't that in itself impressive evidence that there is no Third, that there are no ideas?

5. We are ready to dispose of the nuisance. The representationalists all hold that the idea of (something^1) colored is contained in that of (something^1) green. Since the Class of all particulars grounding green is contained in that of all those grounding a color, everything is well. The representationalists hold that the idea of something^o green is contained in that of something^o both green and square. Since the Class of all green and square objects is contained in that of all green objects, everything is again well. But the representationalists also said that the idea of (*something*) green is contained in that of (*something*) green and square without always realizing that the corresponding connection between the corresponding Classes obtains only if the two italicized occurrences of 'something', which this time I deliberately left without a superscript, both stand for 'something^o'. To spot the nuisance, one merely has to assume what seems very natural indeed once one has accepted the way

of ideas, namely, that the first and the second of these two occurrences of 'something' stand for 'something^1' and 'something^2', respectively. That makes one of the two corresponding Classes a Class of perfect particulars (a_i); the other, one of certain binary clusters $(Cl(\gamma(a_k, b_l)))$. And the latter is of course not a subclass of the former. Thus, if we wanted to speak as the representationalists did, some tedious rewording of the conditions would be required. I do not think we need to bother. It will be more profitable to glance quickly at a plausible reason why the inaccuracy has not been noticed. If, like Locke and so many after him, one collapses cores and ideas, then a_1^* and $\iota(a_1^*, b_1^*)$ become two "particular ideas"[14] of, say, something^1 green and something^2 green and square, respectively. Also, we have $a_1^* \subset_\iota \iota(a_1^*, b_1^*)$ and $b_1^* \subset_\iota \iota(a_1^*, b_1^*)$.[15] Nor does it require any special argument to show how easily an ι-component may become a *part*. Just remember Section Four. The reason is so plausible indeed that one may turn around, as it were, and cite it in evidence for the almost irresistible temptation to collapse cores and ideas.

We are ready to turn to the third schema.

(1) The chair on which I now sit is an object; the one at the side of my desk is another. (2) Chair is a kind of object. (3) The idea of a chair is the idea of a kind of object. The sentence (1) is neutral. (2), however informally, is ϵ-talk. 'Idea', if taken seriously, belongs to γ-talk. The transition from (2) to (3) seems most natural. Yet, taken with the literalness required of all ontological discourse, (3) is a mere jumble of words. In a γ-world, there are no kinds. Or, if you please, its "kinds" are its Classes; only we must not forget that, for purposes of our own, we merely pretend that there are Classes. This is one half of what is wrong with (3). The other half is that, with a blur which easily misleads and has in fact misled many, every idea $(\overline{X})$, including those of places and moments, is the idea of a "kind," the latter being the Class $(\check{X})$ of all things which fall under it. That makes even such phrases as 'the idea of *a* chair' not as safe as one might wish. 'The idea of something^o (some object) which is a chair', which corresponds accurately to 'the idea of something^1 (which is) green' seems safer. But we shall be safe enough if, dropping the indefinite article, we use *'the idea of chair (Ch)'*.

Let us test the distinctions on 'the idea of object $(\overline{O})$'. $\check{O}$ is the Class of all objects. $\overline{O} < \overline{Ch}$, or equivalently, as long as we ignore condition (2), $\widetilde{Ch} < \check{O}$. Generally, $\overline{X}$ is an idea such that $\check{X}$ is a Class of objects if and only if $\check{X} < \check{O}$, or, equivalently, $\overline{O} < \overline{X}$. Our strategy, we see, has not provided us with an equivalent both short and safe for 'an idea such

---

[14] This is of course Locke's use of 'particular idea'. See p. 161.
[15] If you have forgotten what '$\subset_\iota$' stands for, turn to p. 145.

that the Class of all things falling under it is a Class of objects'. 'Idea of object' obviously won't do; 'idea of some object' is unsafe, to say the least. I shall remedy this embarrassment by using 'idea°' as a synonym for the phrase which is safe, but, alas, not short. Thus we shall be able to say such things as that the idea of chair is an idea°.[16]

The third schema is a classification of all ideas°, which takes its cue from Meinong's discovery, in his first major contribution (*HumeSt.* I), as early as 1877, of the proper way to distinguish in γ between the two dichotomies *particular-universal* and *concrete-abstract*. In γ-ontologies this distinction is crucial. That is why Meinong's contribution is so brilliant. ε-ontologists ground the first dichotomy differently, of course; and it is part of their strength that they can do without the second. Be that as it may, we cannot introduce the classification without some preparations which will take longer than what they prepare for. Common as that is in philosophy, it may yet help if I first tell in a brief paragraph and almost with a pun what these preparations are about and why they are needed.

On the one hand, the third schema is a classification of all ideas° which will help us to understand what (in γ) could reasonably be meant by 'abstract'. On the other hand, the idea of object, which of course is inextricably involved with that of an idea°, is itself very "abstract." That makes it necessary that we first attend to the idea of object and the classical worries about its "abstractness." This is what will be done in the preparations, to which I now turn.

'Abstract' and 'concrete' have been used philosophically. In philosophical talk about the foil they need not occur. Their proper explication in γ we shall presently learn from Meinong. Until then, therefore, I shall feel free to use the two words without any explication whatsoever, although for safety's sake between double quotes, simply appealing to the familiar way, capable of degrees, in which some ideas are said to be more "abstract" than some others. The idea of color, for instance, is said to be more "abstract" than that of red; the idea of object, more abstract than that of chair. For some representationalists the word marks a source of concern. The cause of the concern is their empiricism. According to this thesis, we have "come by" all our ideas through "experience," which means that (the cores "of") all ideas we conceive either have been "impressed" upon our minds, in either sensation or reflection, as Locke would have it, or have been produced from (the cores "of") such ideas by abstracting, combining, and perhaps a few

---

[16] I trust that by now you appreciate how very difficult it is to talk fairly and accurately about an ontology not one's own. If you do, then you will not mind putting up with such "words" as 'idea°' and 'something¹'.

other such activities. The point is that the more "abstract" an idea is, the harder it is actually to provide it with such a pedigree and the more reason there is for worrying whether that can be done at all. As you know, this is the point where the Lockeans and the Cartesians clash. The former must work and worry, because they insist that all our ideas are "come by" in this fashion. The latter hold that at least some "abstract" ideas, being "innate," as they put it, need no such pedigree. Thus they can relax. Brentano in this respect went all the way with Locke, or, as one says, with the empiricists, against the rationalists. My own stake, or even interest, if any, in these stale old issues is very small. Yet their impact has been very great. Thus we shall not be able to ignore them completely. What little will have to be said about them belongs in the next section, in the context of perception, in connection with still another dichotomy, that of *distinct-indistinct*.[17] Yet, little as it is, it will suffice to show how the foil manages to bypass these issues.

Since we cannot start on the job of classifying ideas° without a clear notion of the idea of object and since this idea is more than sufficiently "abstract" to worry the "empiricists," I shall next, without worrying *in abstracto* about its "abstractness," introduce it in a way that should satisfy every "empiricist." Or rather, I shall introduce one not quite so "abstract" yet "abstract" enough to do the job.

Objects, as we speak, are either "whole objects" or, more often, cross sections of such. Also, objects are either minds or bodies. (Flashes or sounds are like cross sections of the latter.) Nothing will be lost, all jobs will be done, and no distortion will be introduced if through the rest of this section we assume that all objects are momentary spots and that each such spot is a ternary cluster of a place, a shape, and a color.

There are no places (place qualities); they are merely the brain children of the representationalists. Even Brentano eventually admitted that they are not presented to us. Yet he insisted that they are there (exist). So did Meinong. The disagreement is so radical, or, to be blunt, from where I stand the error is so monstrous that one may well on this ground alone dismiss these ontologies. If one does not want to do that, since so much in them is very fine, even though it does not stand up eventually, one cannot in discussing them ignore the coordinate qualities. Thus we must design a way of speaking about them, which though it cannot be smooth, the error is too monstrous for that, is at least intelligible.

[17] Probably you sense here the requirement which determines the strategy of the exposition. The dialectic of perception requires an accurate grasp of all three distinctions, *concrete-abstract*, *particular-general*, *distinct-indistinct*, and of their interplay in the tradition.

So far we have made do with 'p_1' and '$\overline{P}$'; the former standing for a certain place, assayed as a quality; the latter, for the idea of it. Naturally there is no p_2, p_3, and so on. $\overline{P}$ is a one-Class; p_1, its only member. Why then, one may ask, keep the subscript in 'p_1'? I kept it in order to be reminded that $\overline{P}$ and the one-Class $[p_1]$ correspond accurately to the idea of green ($\overline{A}$) and the Class $[a_1, a_2, \cdots]$ of all particulars grounding green. Now we must modify the notation so as to accommodate the multiplicity of places. Superscripts will do the job. Let p_1^1, p_1^2, and so on, be places; $\overline{P}^1$, $\overline{P}^2$ and $\overline{P}^1$, $\overline{P}^2$ the corresponding one-Classes and ideas, respectively.

Use for the moment '$\widetilde{Pl}$' to refer to the Class of all places, p_1^1, p_1^2, $\cdots$. Which (if any) is "the idea ($\overline{Pl}$) such that $\widetilde{Pl}$ is the Class of all things falling under it"? Notice, first, that 'the idea of something[1] *colored*' and 'the idea of something[1] *shaped*' refer to the two ideas which correspond to $\overline{Pl}$ in the dimensions of color and shape, respectively. Notice, second, that, in spite of the accurate verbal analogy, 'the idea of something[1] *placed*' will not do; if used to refer to $\overline{Pl}$, it is grossly misleading. There is in fact no phrase less unwieldy than the one I just put between double quotes by which to refer accurately and safely to $\overline{Pl}$. Nor is that surprising. Since there are no places, why should there be such a phrase? For our special purposes the lack of one is nevertheless an inconvenience. I shall fill the need as best I can by using 'something[1] which is a place' like 'something[1] which is green' and, accordingly, 'the idea of something[1] which is a place' for $\overline{Pl}$.

Let $\widetilde{Sh}$ and $\widetilde{Col}$ be the Classes of all perfect particulars grounding shapes and colors respectively. $\widetilde{Sh}$ has many sub-Classes which are not one-Classes; e.g., those of all particulars which ground triangular, quadrilateral, angular, round, oblong, and so on; and between these Classes there obtain the usual connections of inclusion, exclusion, and overlap. As for $\widetilde{Sh}$, so for $\widetilde{Col}$. If one uses some color words for shades rather than for classes of such, the number of sub-Classes of $\widetilde{Col}$ which are not one-Classes becomes rather large. If for the sake of the argument we add Bright, Dark, and so on, their number becomes even larger and the network of connections among them grows. E.g., the Class of all particulars grounding both bright and pink will be a sub-Class of that of all those grounding both bright and red, which in turn will be a sub-Class of the Class of all those grounding red.

Each p_1^i determines a one-Class which is a sub-Class of $\widetilde{Pl}$. But since in fact there are no places, we are hard pressed to name a sub-Class of $\widetilde{Pl}$ which is not a one-Class. For our special purposes this is again an inconvenience. I again fill this need as best I can; take my cue from the four quadrants of the visual field; assume that $\widetilde{Left}$, $\widetilde{Right}$, $\widetilde{Upper}$, and $\widetilde{Lower}$ are four subclasses of $\widetilde{Pl}$ which are not one-Classes.

If you now stop to reflect for a moment, you will see that we are already in a position to introduce the two notions of *object* and of *idea of object* in a manner that cannot but satisfy every "empiricist" representationalist who is prepared to grant, as in fact they all are, that the mind is capable of "abstracting" the three ideas $\widetilde{Pl}$, $\widetilde{Sh}$, $\widetilde{Col}$. The desired substitute of 'object' is *'something³ which is a place and shaped and colored'*. The substitute for the 'idea of object' is *'the idea of something³ which is a place and shaped and colored'*. This must by now be obvious. So I hurry on to the third schema, which, as you remember, is a classification of all ideas° that takes its cue from Meinong's γ-way of explicating the two dichotomies particular-universal and concrete-abstract.

Take 'the idea of something³ which is . . . and . . . and . . . '; for the first, second, and third blank put expressions corresponding to sub-Classes of $\widetilde{Pl}$, $\widetilde{Sh}$, $\widetilde{Col}$, respectively. 'The idea of something³ left and triangular and pink' is an example; 'the idea of something³ (right and upper) and angular and dark' is another. *Each such substitution yields (the name of) an idea° and (the name of) each idea° can be produced by such a substitution.*

Now for Meinong's explications. An idea° is *"particular"* if and only if the Class of all objects falling under it is a one-Class. Otherwise it is *"general."* The distinction between "abstract" and "concrete" is one of degree and is a bit more complicated. In explaining it I shall permit myself a few verbal short-cuts; after all the pains I have taken these should cause no trouble.

Each of the three blanks must be filled to obtain the name of an idea°. If you put in the first blank 'a place', the resulting idea° will be of *maximal abstractness* in the first respect, irrespective of how you fill the second and the third blank. If you put in the second blank 'shaped', the resulting idea will be of maximal abstractness in the second respect, irrespective of how you fill the first and the second blank. Similarly for the third blank. The most abstract idea°, being of maximal abstractness in all (three) respects, is the idea of object itself. At the other extreme, each object has a completely determinate place, shape, and color. If you put the names of three such completely determinate qualities in the respective blanks, the resulting idea° will be of *maximal concreteness* in all respects. Between these two extremes lie many degrees. But I do not think I need to continue, except for pointing out one important feature.

Particularity and maximal concreteness do not coincide.[18] Every idea° of maximal concreteness has only one object falling under it, but

---

[18] This formula is one of the main keys to the understanding of what the representationalists have to say on perception. See Section Ten.

not conversely. Take "the idea of something[3] which is P^1 and shaped and colored." It is in two respects of maximal abstractness. Yet, being completely determinate in respect to place, it is, like all other such ideas, a particular idea, irrespective of how the other two blanks are filled. "The idea of something[3] which is P^2 and oblong and dark" is another example, less abstract than the first, yet not maximally concrete. Again, I need not continue.[19]

That much for the third schema. I shall now use it to illuminate an old formula. Then I shall be done.

Ordo et connectio rerum est ordo et connectio idearum. The words are Spinoza's. Their sense, as it must be, is shared by all representationalists. We are now in a position to recover it completely. In doing that I shall use 'particular' and 'general' as Meinong does. No idea[o] corresponds accurately to an object (*res*). Those which come closest are particular ideas, i.e., those which have exactly one object falling under them. Keep this in mind, use ' $<$ ' so that it stands for the connection between a class and any of its proper subclasses, and distinguish two cases.

(a) $\overline{X}$ is a general idea[o]; $\overline{Y}$, one which is either general or particular. In this case, *if $\overline{X} < \overline{Y}$, then $\tilde{Y} < \tilde{X}$.* To settle the question of whether the converse holds, one must remember the second condition: $\overline{X} < \overline{Y}$ if and only if ($\tilde{Y} < \tilde{X}$) is either a priori or analytic.[20] Assume, then, that the relevant a priori truths about objects (spots) are *all those and only those* which hold by virtue of some such truths in one of the (three) relevant respects. E.g., since it is an a priori truth that the Class of all particulars grounding pink is a proper sub-Class of that of all those grounding red, just as it is such a truth that the Class of all particulars grounding triangular is a proper sub-Class of that of all those grounding angular,

---

[19] Perhaps you want to insist that the idea of something[1] colored is even more "abstract" than that of an object and that, therefore, Meinong's explication falls short of what it ought to be. Since I do not believe that 'abstract' has a useful place in ontological discourse, I am not very interested either in this gap or in the proper way of filling it. This, though, is beside the point. The point is, rather, that one who senses this "difficulty" has caught the very spirit of the representationalists. Brentano, for instance, resolves the "difficulty" by claiming that, ideas of something[1] . . . (as I would have put it) being unthinkable, whenever we think of "something green" what we really conceive is the idea of a green object, i.e. (as I would put it), of something[3] which is a place and shaped and green.

Structurally, P^1, P^2, . . . correspond to Green, Red, ... The difference is, alas, that (in the foil) there are no place-universals, either uniquely exemplified or otherwise. So you are warned not to become a victim of the notation. But one cannot, I think, understand what is going on without in a sense playing the game of the other side, even in the notation.

[20] This is the only use made in this section of condition (2). See p. 171.

it is a relevant a priori truth that the Class of all pink triangular objects is a proper sub-Class of that of all red and angular ones. Hence, by our explication of containing among ideas, the idea^o of something^3 red and angular is contained in that of something^3 pink and triangular. As in this example, so in all others. If you make the assumption, then the converse holds: If $\tilde{Y} < \tilde{X}$, then $\overline{X} < \overline{Y}$.

(b) $\overline{X}$ and $\overline{Y}$ are both particular ideas^o. In this case, if $\overline{X} < \overline{Y}$ then $\tilde{X} = \tilde{Y}$. Hence the second condition is fulfilled in the direction from left to right, if, as usual, ' $<$ ' is taken to stand for ' $\leq$ '. Checking on the converse, one comes upon a revealing "flaw." All representationalists rightly hold it to be an a priori truth that there cannot be more than one object at one place. If this is so, then, by the second condition, of the two ideas, of something^3 P^1 and green, and of something^3 P^1 and square, one would have to be contained in the other. Yet no representationalist would be willing to say that. Thus some tedious rewording of the second condition in order to accommodate the case of two particular ideas is required. I shall not bother. We have reached the point of diminishing returns. What is revealing about the flaw is merely the place at which it occurs. Ideas are (structural) universals. From where I stand, they are all artifacts. Yet there is a difference among them which one might express by saying that even if there were general ideas, particular ideas would be mere artifacts, invented for the sole purpose of doing the job only particulars can do. Small wonder, therefore, that when it comes to particular ideas, "flaws" appear. Or, less metaphorically, what goes for general ideas, may and often does require adaptation before it fits particular ones. (Notice that the a priori truth concerning the number of objects at a place is not among those covered by the assumption in (a).)

Return now for a moment to that famous formula of Spinoza's. As far as I can see, (a) completely exhausts its sense; (b), if anything, qualifies it. I must say that I find that rather disappointing. The words have such a pretty ring.

PERCEPTION

To intend something is to be presented with something else, which is its representative. This is the basic gambit of representationalism. Are the representative and the represented really always two and not one? The question becomes pressing in two cases. One is that of our knowledge, if any, of ideas as such; the other, that of knowledge of Self. Brentano, following Aristotle, holds that every act, whatever else it intends, also, on the side or incidentally,[1] as it were, intends itself. The dialectic of these two cases reveals two of the three major predicaments of representationalism. In the next section we shall examine them. Or, at least, we shall face them. This section deals only with the perception of bodies.[2] Thus we may assume that intention and representative are two; the former is in the truncated world (i.e., in the Second); the latter is an idea or ideas (i.e., in the Third).

The representative is *an idea or ideas*. The disjunction spots an issue. Is the representative always a single idea? Is it always several? Or is it sometimes a single idea, sometimes several, depending on what the intention happens to be? Each question corresponds to one of the three possible solutions. At first sight the last alternative seems the most plausible. Suppose I am now wondering whether all dogs are mammals. Upon the last alternative there are in this case the two ideas of dog and of mammal before my mind. Suppose I now perceive my dog Fido. In this case I am presented with the single (though quite possibly very complex) idea of Fido. You see why, prima facie at least, this alternative is the most plausible. Let us agree to call it so. Then we can say that there are three alternatives, or answers, or solutions to the *general issue* I raised; one *plausible* (sometimes one, sometimes several), two

---

[1] The Greek phrase is ἐν παρέργῳ. Brentano repeats it several times.

[2] I add for once "of bodies," because some also speak of knowledge of Self as perception, or inner perception. But I shall not follow this use. Perception *tout court* thus means always perception of bodies.

180

implausible. Upon one of the latter, the representative is always a single idea; upon the other, it is always several. Call the former and the latter the *monistic* and the *pluralistic* solution, respectively.

Brentano propounds the monistic solution. If one were asked to select a single feature by which to distinguish his brand of representationalism from all others, this particular one would serve as well as any. Not that it is the only good answer. Other features of his world are equally distinctive. But they all structurally entail each other. That is why the answer is as good as any.

We shall not in this section examine Brentano's monistic gambit. This will be done in Part III. Then we shall see, not only that it reflects (in the Third) his extreme reism (in the First and the Second), but also that, even on his own terms, or, as one says, intrinsically, it fails. He cannot consistently so assay all intentions and all acts that all representatives are single ideas. Nor of course, extreme reism being as starkly inadequate as it is, will his failure surprise us, valiant and often ingenious as his struggles were and rewarding as therefore their examination will turn out to be. All this, though, belongs in Part III. Why, then, you may ask, vouchsafe this bit of information about Brentano just at this point. I prefer being obvious or even tedious to being obscure. So I shall answer.

In this section we shall examine a cluster of *special issues* concerning the kind of act the representationalists call *perceptual judgment* (*Wahrnehmungsurteil*). One of these issues is at the heart of the cluster. I shall state it by means of a paradigm.

Sometimes, on coming upon a certain spot, one perceives it to be white. Or, staying as close as possible to the way the representationalists speak, one makes the perceptual judgment that it is white. 'This spot is white' stands for the intention of the act. The ideas presented to it upon the plausible solution are two; that of this spot and that of white. These are the perceptual situation and the perceptual judgment which will serve as paradigm throughout. Let us agree to save words by referring to them as *the situation* and *the judgment*.

How many ideas are in fact presented in the situation; two, as the plausible solution has it, or only one? This is the special issue at the heart of the cluster. You see why I called it special. It is a special case (perceptual judgments) of the general issue (all acts) with which I started but which we shall not in its generality examine in this section.

The general issue, we know, has three possible solutions. One I called plausible; the other two, implausible. Yet a thinker as profound as Brentano defended with every fiber of his strength, unwaveringly, throughout his career, one of the two implausible ones. That not only shows that the dialectic of representationalism forces its proponents through strange paces; it also should go a long way toward convincing you that the special questions I am about to examine lie very deep. That is why I vouchsafed this bit of information about Brentano at this point. Presently I shall turn to perception. First for a remark that will place the issue in a larger setting.

How many ideas are presented, one or several?[3] The question is about representatives, not about the intentions they represent. Yet there is a connection. If the intention "involves"[4] two Classes, say, Dog and Mammal, one inclines to the belief that the ideas represented are two, Dog and Mammal. If the intention "involves" only the one-Class Fido, one tends to hold that Fido is the one and only idea represented. That is, as we saw, what makes the monistic and the pluralistic solution implausible. Following this line of thought, one arrives at two suggestions which, attractive as they may seem at first sight, are yet shallow.

I of course hold that all intentions are facts.[5] Common sense, either because untutored or from a doctrinaire commitment to ordinary language, protests. Sometimes, it points out, the object clause of an act verb stands for an object ('I perceive the spot'); sometimes it stands for a fact ('I wonder whether all dogs are mammals').[6] Common sense, or at least ordinary language, thus yields two suggestions. It suggests, first, that intentions are either things or facts. It suggests, second, that the representative is either a single idea or more than one depending on whether the intention represented is a thing or a fact. Three observations will show that these suggestions are shallow.

(1) The spot, my dog Fido, and all other objects are in the foil not things but facts (complexes). And this, in the foil, is a matter of the ontology of the truncated world which has nothing whatsoever to do

---

[3] *What difference does this difference make for the assay of the act in the knowing situation?* For the time being I ignore this question. In Part III it will come to the fore. Notice that I replace 'several' by 'two'. That fits the case of the judgment. Nor will anything that now matters be lost.

[4] The studied evasiveness of 'involves' is meant to spare the nominalistic sensibilities of the representationalist. Nor of course must one ever forget that Classes are wraiths.

[5] It is merely to repeat what has been pointed out before if I call your attention to the fact that this distinctive feature of the foil is dialectically balanced by another, at least as distinctive, namely, the simplicity of all its cores (thoughts). In the foil there are of course no ideas. But if, *à la* Locke, thoughts were ideas, then the solution of the general issue which, since they are not, does not even arise in the foil, would be monistic. That, too, shows the force lines in the dialectic.

[6] I avoid, deliberately of course, 'I perceive that this spot is white'. See the first of the three observations above.

with intentions, acts, and, should there be any, ideas. (2) This is a good place to remember that the clusters of γ are not really things but merely "things (pseudocomplexes)"; even though there is really no point in trying to say anything about γ without making allowance for the irremediable blur. (3) One may think that a representationalist will accept the two suggestions, or that he will at least opt for the plausible solution, if he distinguishes clearly between things and facts. This is too simple. To distinguish clearly between facts and things is one thing. To have a clear notion of fact (complex) is quite another thing. Meinong, for instance, emphatically insists on the distinction. That is part of his glory. But his notion of fact is anything but clear. That is one of the causes of his failure. Structurally, we shall see in Part IV, his "facts" are but a strange and precarious kind of "things."[7] Structurally, therefore, a representative could in his world always be the single idea, however complex, of one of these strange and precarious "things." Is that what he himself taught? Eventually we shall find out. Right now I merely want to convince you that it takes more than a bit of "common sense" or "ordinary language" to justify dialectically the solution which I called the only plausible one.

We do not yet see the details. But we sense already that, as the dialectic unfolds, either of the two implausible solutions may have much to recommend itself. Thus one may reasonably expect the representationalists to disagree among themselves as to which of the three possible solutions is the right one. With respect to the general question they do. Some hold, with Brentano, that what one is presented with in any knowing situation is a single idea. Others hold that in some knowing situations we are presented with more than one idea. This (I believe) is the case of Descartes and Locke. Meinong's, as I just remarked, is very peculiar. Yet, in spite of these disagreements with respect to the general question (all acts), unless I am badly mistaken, the representationalists who concern us all agree with respect to the special question (perceptual judgments).[8]

(One of the points just made could be expressed by saying that dialectically either of the two "implausible" solutions may be as plausible, or perhaps even more so, than the "plausible" one. Things having turned out this way, you may think that my choice of 'plausible-im-

---

[7] Specifically, they are a kind of *ideale Gegenstaende*. The phrase is very familiar; the notion, we shall see, is very difficult.

[8] This agreement of theirs, supposing I am right that they all agree in their assay of the perceptual situation, supports my claim that the questions set aside for examination in this section lie very deep and therefore deserve this special attention.

plausible' is awkward. I admit that it is not smooth. But the only two alternatives I could think of seemed even rougher. One was to add and repeat each time 'prima facie'; the other, to use the pair 'natural-non-natural (artificial)'. That is why I chose as I did, hoping that no harm would be done, particularly since we shall not need to use the two words in this way many more times.)

The representationalists with whom we are concerned all agree that *a perceptual judgment is an existential judgment plus something else.* Call this "something else" the *excess.* What is the representationalists' notion of existential judgment? What is the excess? The complete answer to the first question is very long; the part of it we now need, very short; particularly if you will permit me to state it in mixed language, taking one word from Meinong, one from the foil.[9] *An existential judgment is an act whose species is perceiving and in which one is presented with a single "particular" idea.* The intention of the existential judgment in the paradigm is expressed by 'There is this spot'. Its species, or, rather, the "judging" which corresponds to it in the representationalists' worlds, raises many problems.[10] For a first quick glance, though, this will do. Let us cast another such glance at the second question.

What is the excess? I have long been puzzled, even though I have long been sure that the representationalists' answer was not what it would have to be if either confusion or absurdity are to be avoided. Eventually the puzzlement became a gnawing irritation. This irritation, together with a few closely related ones, rather than curiosity about this or that philosopher, no matter how much I have come to admire him in the meantime, goaded me into undertaking the present study. The admiration, rewarding as it may be, is merely a by-product. The main result is that I am now even more firmly convinced that what these important philosophers said was either confused or absurd. For only now (I believe) I understand accurately not only what they said but also why they said it and why it is either simply false, or con-

---

[9] The responsibility that no harm will come from the mixture is mine, of course. If you don't trust me, watch me closely. The double quotes around 'particular', 'general', and, should prudence require it, 'concrete' and 'abstract', here and through the rest of the section, indicate that the words are used in Meinong's sense, as explained in the third schema of the last section. His word thus is 'particular'; mine is 'species'.

[10] Let a be the spot; $Thsp$, the one-Class of which it is the only member. The intention of the existential judgment is '$(\exists x)\ Thsp(x)$'. The "particular" idea presented in this act is $Thsp$; the perceiving, which according to the mixed formula is "in" it is really a judging that $Thsp$ represents. Of the difficulties to which all this leads and of the confusions to which it only too easily gives rise much will have to be said in the rest of this book.

fused, or even absurd. In the case at hand, (I believe) I know now accurately, not only what they thought the excess was, but also why they thought it and what is wrong with it. This belief determines my strategy. I shall proceed in two steps.

The first step expounds what I take to be the structurally consistent γ-assay of what is presented in a perceptual judgment. Or, if you wish to go on speaking in a certain way, the first step expounds the assay of the situation in the prototype, which is of course not the one the representationalists proposed. In the second step I shall say what needs to be said about the one they did propose.

First step. Remember the two meanings of 'perceive' (p. 143). With the usual meaning, the intention of an act of perceiving is a whole object; with the special meaning, it lies in a cross section. We agreed to use the word with its special meaning. I stay with the agreement, but supplement it with another. The usual meaning will in this section be marked by double quotes. Thus, *we perceive cross sections, "perceive" whole objects.* At the end of the first step and throughout the second we shall have to talk about both kinds of act. That is why the supplementary agreement is needed.

Call the object in the situation α. Notice that I call it the object in the situation, not the intention of the act. Nothing will be lost if we make two assumptions. Assume, first, that (in γ) all (momentary) objects are ternary clusters such that the perfect particulars in them ground a place, a shape, and a color, respectively; or, equivalently, assume that a something^o is a something^3 which is a place and shaped and colored. In other words, we stay with the simplification (schematization) of the last section. Assume, second, that the situation is a case of veridical perception; or, what amounts to the same, assume that one of the particulars in α, call it a_2, is among those grounding the color white. Suppose now that α is square and that the place and shape particulars "in" it are p_1^1 and a_1, respectively. That makes a_1 one of the simple qualities grounding square and $\alpha = \gamma(p_1^1, a_1, a_2)$. Let us also agree to save words by using 'representative' so that, unless something to the contrary is said, *the representative in the situation is all and not just part*[11] of what is presented to the judgment.

I am ready to state my claim. Upon every structurally consistent γ-assay, or, if you still wish to speak this way, upon the assay of the prototype, *the representative in a perceptual situation is always two ideas. More precisely, it is one idea being a posteriori contained in another.* An idea being contained in another is a "fact" of the Third. How the gambit of such "facts" works in the long run is a further question. Closely

[11] Broad use of 'part'! 'Representative' has already been so used. Now, though, we must make sure.

connected, as we shall see, with one of the three major predicaments, it eventually leads to catastrophe. This, though (if I am right), is the ultimate fate of all γ-ontologies. There is yet much to be learned by distinguishing in and among them what is structurally consistent from what is not and what works for a while from what collapses immediately.

I made a claim; I must support it by argument. The claim contains a new notion; I must first of all explain this notion. The argument I shall conduct by making and supporting four smaller claims. Then the support of the larger claim, the one I just made, will take no more than a moment.

An idea, as no doubt you remember, is *contained* in another, $\overline{X} < \overline{Y}$, if and only if (1) $\tilde{Y} < \tilde{X}$ and (2) the proposition ($\tilde{Y} < \tilde{X}$) is an a priori truth. Henceforth we shall say that $\overline{X}$ is a posteriori *contained* in $\overline{Y}$ if and only if (1) is true and (2) is false. Under the circumstances you might think it advisable to replace 'contained' by 'a priori contained' and '$<$' by two symbols, one for each kind of containment. As it happens, since in most cases the context leaves no doubt, we shall get along quite well with 'contains' and '$<$'.[12]

The intention of the judgment is one thing; the representative before it is another. Yet it stands to reason that if there are two ideas in the representative, then there must be two Classes involved[13] in the intention such that each of the two ideas corresponds to a Class as, say, $\overline{\text{Dog}}$ corresponds to $\overset{\sim}{\text{Dog}}$. Notice that, even though this proposition "stands to reason," it does not entail its converse. There remains always the possibility that the representative is a single complex idea which the mind "makes" out of the two.[14] Be that as it may, since the proposition, as it stands, stands to reason, the thing to do next is to find the two Classes involved with the intention of the judgment.

Consider (1) 'This spot is white', (2) 'This object is white', (3) 'This is white'. (1) stands for the intention of the judgment. My *first small claim* is that (1), (2), (3) stand for one and the same. With respect to (1) and (2), this is but a restatement of our simplifying assumption that

[12] These distinctions are connected with one of the three major predicaments. This is why, as we shall soon see, if 'contain' were to be replaced, the most suitable candidate would be 'conceptually contained'. Notice in the meantime that in this paragraph 'a priori' stands for the undifferentiated notion which makes the analytic a part of the a priori.

[13] I use 'involved' for the same reason as before, but omit the double quotes. See n. 4, above.

[14] As we shall see and as by now you may have guessed, this is Brentano's choice, which in the case of perception seems to support his monistic gambit yet eventually fails because one cannot consistently extend it to all intentions (of all acts).

all objects are spots. With respect to either (1) or (2) on the one hand and (3) on the other, what could 'this' possibly stand for if not, by Meinong's schema, for "something° which is P^1 and shaped and colored"? Perhaps you will object because, accurately, the clause between double quotes does not refer to α but, rather, to the one-Class of which it is the only member. I reply that, as was pointed out with great care at the very beginning, without the occasional substitution of things and one-Classes for each other, nothing worth while can be said about representationalism. However, since we are on this subject, let me ask you to note for later reference that, since "something° which is P^1 and shaped and colored", or, idiomatically, "this" is a one-Class, "the idea of something° which is P^1 and shaped and colored," or, idiomatically, "the idea of this" is "particular."

Call A and B the two Classes determined by "something° which is P^1 and shaped and colored" and "something° which is a place and a shape and white," respectively. A is the one-Class whose only member is "this"; B, the Class of all white objects. My *second small claim* is that (4) '$\bar{A} < \bar{B}$' is a fourth expression for the intention of the judgment. This claim I defend by meeting three objections. (a) The first objector asserts that (5) '$a_2 \subset \gamma(p_1^1, a_1, a_2)$' stands for the intention.[15] I refute him by pointing out that perceiving "this object" to be white and perceiving "this square white object" to be white (if one can be said to perceive this sort of thing) are two and not, as his assertion implies, one. (b) The second objector balks at the occurrence of Classes rather than things in the intention. I answer, as before, that without this substitution nothing worth while can be said about representationalism, if only (supposing I am right) because all ideas are structurally classes (universals) in exile. (c) The third objector wants to replace $\bar{B}$ in (4) by $\bar{W}$, which is the Class of all white particulars. (His objection is quite possibly an echo of (5).) Him I merely remind of the feature which in the last section (p. 172) I called a nuisance. Thereupon he withdraws the objection but remarks that in view of this nuisance (2) 'This object is a white object' is the most accurate idiomatic expression of the intention. I agree.

Consider another perceptual situation, different from the paradigm, whose intention is idiomatically expressed by 'This square is white'. My *third small claim* is that in all respects but one the intention of this situation is like that of the paradigm. They differ in that the idea (concept) corresponding to "this square" is less "abstract" than that corre-

---

[15] This *seems* to agree with my first comments on the γ-assay of this being white in Section Two (p. 27). Notice, though, that there I wrote $a_1 \subset \alpha$! (5), or its equivalent, which we shall soon meet again, occurs for the first time in the story of the lost facts in Section Three (p. 64).

sponding to "this." Yet they are both "particular"! This claim needs no further defense. Just reflect on it for a moment.

My *fourth small claim* is that (in the prototype) the intentions of all perceptual situations expressed by such sentences as 'This is white' or 'This square is white' consist of a Class, $\bar{X}$, being contained in another, $\bar{Y}$; where the former is a one-Class; the latter, the Class of a certain kind of object. This claim follows immediately from the preceding three.

Turn now to the *original larger claim* that in every structurally consistent γ-assay of the situation the representative consists of one idea being a posteriori contained in another and you will see that one more step will provide us with a very strong argument in support of it. Just combine the fourth small claim with the explanation of what it means for one idea to be a posteriori contained in another! In the paradigm, for instance, the representative consists of the idea of (a) *white* (object) being so contained in that of *this object:* $\bar{B} < \bar{A}$.

I take it, then, that these five claims, the four small ones as well as the original larger one, need no further support. Yet it is worth pointing out how well they agree with the logical schema of Aristotle. Since there is no doubt about the very large influence this schema has had on everybody,[16] the agreement supports not just these claims but the proposed analysis of representationalism as a whole.

In the Aristotelian schema "All A are B," or, as it is only too often written, "A is B," is supposed to schematize not only 'All dogs are mammals' but also 'Socrates is a man'. Surely you know not only how much embarrassment that has caused but also that the solution which has been proposed "replaces" Socrates by the class of which he is the only member. Or should I perhaps write 'Class' instead of 'class'? The agreement is striking indeed; nor of course by coincidence. Just as there are no proper names[17] in the schema, so there are no bare particulars in the worlds of Aristotle and of the representationalists.

"Perceiving," like perceiving and all other acts, is momentary. The difference between perceiving and "perceiving" lies in their intentions. In "perceiving," as in many other kinds of act, the intention overflows the cross section, extends over an interval of time. Every adequate assay must ground this difference. In the foil, the intention of a "per-

---

[16] And on Brentano and Meinong in particular! Both, very annoyingly and at first confusingly for anyone with modern logical sensibilities, always write "A is B," meaning once "*All A are B*," once "*The A is B*."

[17] Or, as I would rather say, since I am not a nominalist, zero-type names. For in the foil the marks which in improved languages stand for bare particulars are not the only names. 'Green', 'blue', and so on, are others. A "proper name" is just a name; otherwise I wouldn't know what the phrase stands for. Nor of course are there "common names." That is the other side of the antinominalistic coin.

ceiving" contains something else, in addition to the cross section of the corresponding perceiving, if I may so express myself. The details don't matter.[18] Brentano adds to the act of perceiving further (simultaneous) acts, each either intending an earlier or anticipating a later cross section of the whole object "perceived." Again, the details don't matter; at least not right now. Meinong does not at this point add anything significantly new.

Second step. The representationalists assay the judgment as an existential judgment plus something else, which I called the excess. In the paradigm, the intention of the existential judgment is expressed by 'There is this (object)'. The representative before it is the single "particular" idea of this object. In other situations, such as the one of the third small claim ('This square is white', 'There is this square') the single "particular" idea in the representative before the existential judgment is more "concrete." Otherwise there is no difference. *The excess, according to the representationalists, is an analysis of the single idea presented to the existential judgment.* Three preliminary remarks will help us to understand and to judge what that means. The first calls attention to still another use of 'perceiving'; the second establishes the relevant meaning of 'analysis'; the third will remind you of the story of the lost facts.

1. "I perceived something to the left. My perception was from the very beginning sufficiently *distinct* for me to judge that what I perceived was a square spot. Yet it was at first so *indistinct* that I did not perceive its color. Then, when I attended to what I saw, my perception became sufficiently *distinct* for me to judge that the spot was white." Such occurrences are most frequent. Common sense calls them perceivings. We must be more discerning. As we have spoken and as I shall continue to speak, the occurrence is neither a perceiving nor a single "perceiving" but, rather, a series of "perceivings." Call such an occurrence a *perceiving*.[19] As to "distinct" and "indistinct," we see now that what common sense so qualifies is not one intention, or one species, or one act, but, rather, two different intentions of two acts, one earlier, one later. The earlier contains fewer features than the latter. That is why the latter is called (relatively) distinct; the former, (relatively) indistinct. What remains one and presumably unchanged throughout the occurrence is the spot itself, or, as I put it before, the single object in the several situations.

We have come upon an important distinction. Of two ("particular")

---

[18] See "The Revolt Against Logical Atomism" in *Meaning and Existence* (University of Wisconsin Press, 1960) and the "Realistic Postscript" in *Logic and Reality*.

[19] There is thus perceiving, "perceiving," and *perceiving*.

ideas of one object, one may be more "concrete" or less "abstract" than the other. If one wishes to use 'distinct-indistinct' as a synonym for this use of 'concrete-abstract', he may of course do so. If, however, the two words are used as I just used them in describing the occurrence, then it makes simply no sense to say of an idea that it is either distinct or indistinct. Still differently, distinctness and indistinctness (unless they are the same as concreteness and abstractness) are always something about an idea in relation to an object, never anything about an idea as such.

2. Take an object that does not (noticeably) change during an hour, or a day, or some other suitable interval, say, a chair, or a painting, or a rock. Make yourself or ask someone else to make during this interval a series of increasingly detailed and accurate descriptions of the object. An *"analysis"* of the object is either the doing of this sort of thing, which is an activity; or it is its result, i.e., either the whole series, or, more frequently, its last member. These are two clear meanings of that very ambiguous, much overworked and much abused word, 'analysis'. Double quotes will indicate that I use it with this meaning, or, rather, with one of these two closely related meanings. Notice that throughout an "analysis" its object remains unchanged. Notice, too, that if we used 'distinct-indistinct' for descriptions as for ideas, we could say that the first description in the series (of the same unchanging object) is the most indistinct; the last, the most distinct.

3. Turn now to page 64; replace '$\gamma(c_1, c_2, \cdots, c_n)$' by '$\gamma(p_1^1, a_1, a_2)$'; consider again the sentence (5) '$a_2 \subset \gamma(p_1^1, a_1, a_2)$'; remember the way in which at the end of the story of the lost facts I presented its gist. The kernel of the fact whose γ-assay is expressed by (5) is that the definite description in it succeeds, i.e., that there is a cluster such that the class of its categorial constituents is $[p_1^1, a_1, a_2]$. (5) itself states merely its husk. Also, for reasons we need not rehearse, the husk is only too easily mistaken for an analytic truth (fact), i.e., for something which in turn is only too easily mistaken for "nothing." Or should I perhaps say: mistaken for a mere "analysis"? Presently I shall say it. Now I merely call your attention to the verbal bridge which leads from 'analytic' in 'analytic truth' to "analysis."

Remember what I claimed.[20] According to the representationalists, the excess is always an analysis of the single idea presented in an existential judgment. Now I specify this claim as follows. (a) The paradigm

[20] The claim is so crucial that you will expect some textual evidence, at least for Brentano and Meinong. You will find it throughout their work. But see in particular Brentano, *Psych.* III, 22–32; Meinong, *Erfahrungsgl.*, §4, esp. p. 21, also *Stellung*, p. 58.

that guides the representationalists is neither perceiving, nor "perceiving," but *perceiving.* (b) The existential judgment ('There is this (object)') is the first in the series of "perceivings" in the *perceiving;* the perceptual judgment itself ('This (object) is white') is the last. (c) What "occurs" in between is an "analysis" of the intention of the existential judgment.

I shall now do three things. I shall unpack (c); I shall show that the representationalists' account is mistaken and untenable; I shall identify its structural root and drift. Then, after a last comment, I shall be done.

"The intention and, accordingly, the representative, remain one and the same throughout the series. The former is expressed by 'There is something^o which is P^1 and square and white'; the latter, accordingly, is the idea of something^o which is P^1 and square and white. The *mind* at first *sees* the representative only *indistinctly,* as the idea of something^o which is P^1 and shaped and colored. Then the mind *attends* to this idea, bending over it and analyzing it, as it were. As a result of the *analysis,* the idea becomes more *distinct,* is *seen* to contain that of white." That unpacks (c).

The tell-tale words I italicized show that this account is irremediably anthropomorphic and therefore irremediably confused. Three remarks will put that beyond doubt. (1) The "analysis" is not of an object but, rather, of an idea which presumably remains "unchanged," i.e., which is presumably presented throughout the series. (2) Applying 'distinct-indistinct' consistently, one would have to say, not that this one and presumably unchanging *idea* is at first indistinct, then becomes distinct, but, rather, that the several *ideas of this idea,* which are successively presented to the mind, become more distinct. This bares the logical heart of the anthropomorphism. We stand at the beginning of an infinite regress. Hartley, in an unforgettable metaphor, spoke of the eye within the eye. (3) The "analysis" is an activity rather than its result. Or perhaps it is both. In either case, the suggestion of "active" minds (substances$_5$) is overwhelmingly strong. That is why I italicized 'mind' and 'analysis'. I conclude that the representationalists' account of perception is mistaken and untenable.

The structural root of the mistake is a truism with which they supported their nominalism. According to this truism, there are no *indeterminate* objects. A triangle is either equilateral, or isosceles, or rectangular, and so on. There is none which is not either the one or the other, just as there is no spot which is colored without being (a completely determinate shade of) either red, or blue, or green, and so on. This specious argument for nominalism swayed many, Brentano and Meinong among them. Speaking of abstract objects, they all insist that there are none and that, therefore, nominalism is true. I, as you noticed, used 'indeterminate', reserving 'concrete-abstract' for ideas. Yet there is a connection. Even the most "concrete" idea of an indeterminate object (if there were any) would still be "abstract" (though it may, as we know, be "particular").

'Objects' here means neither things, either underived or derived, nor entities, but what in earlier sections we called ordinary things or objects, chairs, trees, rocks, and so on. All objects are completely determinate. In asserting their premiss the nominalists are thus right. Of course they are. But they are disastrously wrong in deducing from this truism under the influence of their more or less explicit reism what it does not imply, namely, that there are no derived characters (things), having some ontological status, such that the definitions reflecting their derivation either (a) completely omit or (b) only generically describe some of the properties which all objects exemplifying them possess. Any definition of 'triangle' not mentioning angles is an instance of (a). 'Colored' ('$^\wedge[(\exists f)\ Col^2(f)\cdot f(x)]$') provides an example of (b).[21] That derived characters have ontological status, though of course not that of objects, I need not and shall not argue again, just as I shall take for granted that, if a is a bare particular that exemplifies green, *a being colored* is an (actual) fact (and thus may serve as the intention of a true thought), although it is not the same₃ fact as *a being green*.[22] You see now why I said the foil bypasses certain stale old issues (p. 175).

In order to see how the representationalists' "rejection of abstract objects" leads to their mistaken account of perception, you must combine it with their empiricism and still another mistake, at which we caught them earlier.

Their empiricism causes them to believe that all the ideas presented to the mind in a *perceiving* are impressed upon it by the object. Hence, they infer, "the" idea impressed must be completely determinate from the very beginning. If you accept this fallacious inference, then you have no choice but to accept their account of perception. Putting myself in their shoes, I would accept their empiricism, i.e., I would agree that when the mind is presented with something in *perceiving*, its being

[21] If your memory needs refreshing, turn to the discussion of derived entities and their ontological status in Section Five.

[22] In symbols, the two facts are represented by '*green (a)*' and '$(\exists f)[Col^2(f)\cdot f(a)]$', respectively. Since this paragraph moves in the foil, and since in the foil there are no coordinate universals, the illustration employs 'Col^2' rather than what would correspond to 'Place'. The application to 'this (object)' is obvious, I trust.

presented is (roughly speaking) caused by *the* object in the situation(s). The inference is nevertheless fallacious because, first, it makes the mistake, at which we have caught these philosophers already, of confusing the single object of the *perceiving* with the several different intentions of the different "perceivings" in it; and because, second, the one-one correspondence is between intentions and ideas (supposing that there are any), not between the object on the one hand and either intention or idea (or, for that matter, core) on the other.

This, then, is the root of the mistake. The drift of it is not hard to discover. A realist, if he chose to speak this way, could consistently say that the several "perceivings" in the *perceiving* of, say, a chair, are an "analysis" of this chair. According to the representationalists, this *perceiving* is an existential judgment plus an "analysis" of the idea of the chair. As far as the excess is concerned, *they thus replace the chair, which is in the Second, by its idea, which is a third, destined sooner or later to fall into the First.* That leaves no doubt. The drift is toward idealism. For perception, the existential judgment is the only connection with the Second that is left. Brentano, we shall see, severs it by collapsing the existential judgment with the existence of what it intends.

Let us check one more point.

What is the "intention" of the excess? The question is fuzzy; hence the double quotes. For the excess is either wholly or at least in part an activity. Yet there is no doubt as to which answer would be most nearly right, or, if you please, which answer the representationalists would be most likely to give. The "intention" is $a_2 \subset \gamma(p_1^1, a_1, a_2)$. This fact, we know, they tend to mistake for an analytic truth and, therefore, for "nothing." The "representative," accordingly, is the idea of (a) white (object) being contained in that of this square white object.[23] "Inten-

---

[23] Perhaps you waver at this point, think for a moment that this "fact" in the Third as well as the two corresponding ones, the intention in the Second and the one involving cores in the First, really is analytic. In this case I suggest that you reread what has been said in the story of the lost facts about the role played by the success of a certain definite description. If then you come back and ask what becomes of this whole analysis of mine in case "the" description fails, or, what amounts to the same, in case the perceptual judgment is not veridical, I shall urge you to distinguish among three things, namely, the description of an object, which is what the story of the lost facts is about; the description of a core; and the question whether or not a "representative" represents. If you do that, you will see that the judgment's not being veridical does not at all affect my analysis except that in this case some facts are potential rather than actual. As you also see, I achieve conciseness at the price of "mixing" languages. Do not forget, though, that if the mode of potentiality were added to a γ-world which consisted only of the First and the Second of the prototype, one could without structural loss omit its Third. You have nevertheless touched a sensitive point, or, more pre-

tion" and "representative" are in one-one correspondence. If the former will be mistaken for analytic, so will the latter. At this point you see how the verbal bridge that leads from 'analytic' in 'analytic truth' to "analysis" may add specious plausibility to the untenable assay of perception. Crossing it, one starts, at one end, by mistaking "representation" and "intention" (of the excess) for analytic, arrives at the other believing that a perceptual judgment is an existential judgment plus a fuzzy something which is "merely an analysis" and therefore really "nothing."

---

cisely, a connection with another weakness of the representationalists. This weakness we have not yet pinned down. So we are not ready to appreciate the connection. But I shall call it to your attention in good time.

THREE PREDICAMENTS

IN the tripartite world there are bodies, ideas, and minds. Thus the representationalists must be prepared to answer three questions. How do we know bodies? How do we know ideas? How do we know minds? Trying to do that, they run into three different though related groups of problems which are all insoluble. That is why, tipping my hand, I speak of three predicaments. In this section we shall attend to this central part of the dialectic. In other words, a bit more dramatically, we shall make the representationalists face their predicaments. But it may seem that by the way I approach them I am getting myself into some troubles of my own, one major, one minor.

The heart of the philosophical enterprise is ontology. I have repeated the formula tirelessly, again and again. Yet, when it comes to probing the sick center of representationalism, I propose to do that by examining the dialectic of three questions which sound epistemological. How does one *know* bodies, ideas, and minds? That is why it may seem that I, or at least the formula of which I have made so much for so long, am in major trouble.

In the last section, I spoke several times of *the* three major predicaments. That seems to imply that there are exactly three. The very title of this section, without saying it outright, yet suggests it. You, however, remember a predicament which, when it was first mentioned in the introductory section of Part II, seemed to you as formidable as any. If we know something only through a representative, how can we know that there is something the latter represents? This is the question, I called it the sophomore's objection, that leads to the predicament you remember. So I shall, conveniently though a bit unfairly, call it the sophomore's predicament. Considering it, you cannot but wonder. Is the sophomore's predicament one of the three above or is it a fourth? If it is a fourth, then I have got myself into at least some minor trouble by bandying the numeral three about as I did. Nor is it lost on you that, whether it be one of the three questions or a fourth, the sophomore's objection, too, sounds epistemological.

A friend tries to help me out of the minor trouble by suggesting that the sophomore's objection is the first question. How do we know bodies? I reject the suggestion but welcome the cues it provides for an answer that will clear me on both counts.

The formula which seems to get me into major trouble does not stand alone. Epistemology, according to its first corollary, is but the ontology of the knowing situation. In this context, you remember, 'knowing' is used generically, for any situation in which an act intends something, whatever its species may be.

The sophomore's question not only seems but is epistemological. The first question, as I meant it, is not. Presently I shall make sure that they really are two. Then we shall also be able to reword one of them in a way which precludes their being mistaken for one. But it will help if I first suggest a plausible reason why my friend, in his desire to help me, did make this mistake.

How do we know bodies? The representationalists, being good "empiricists," all start the same way. The primary source of such knowledge is perception.[1] But that merely transforms the question; or, rather, it limits it to its core. For now we ask for an (ontological) assay of the perceiving situation. Notice, first, that if you accept this transformation, you agree that, as I meant it, the first of the three questions is ontological. Notice, second, that the representationalists do answer it. Some of the details such as, for instance, whether the representative is one or several, were the burden of the last section. But we must recall the broad outlines.

"A *veridical* perceiving situation contains an object (body), an intention, a representative, and an act of perceiving. The intention is but an aspect of the body. If we are careful where it matters, as, e.g., in the last section, no harm will be done by saying that the act intends the body. What is presented to the act, though, is not the body (nor one of its aspects) but, rather, the representative (which stands in one-one correspondence to the intention). In the case of a *nonveridical* perceiving the situation is the same except, of course, that there is no object (and no intention). Yet there is the act and there is the representative before it." This in broad outlines is the assay we are offered. You rush in with

---

[1] As far as I can see, this is the only clear and important meaning of 'empiricism' which has survived the indiscriminate and partisan use of the word and its derivatives. In this sense, Aquinas was an empiricist and so was Descartes, even though the latter insisted that some of the ideas which enter into the perceiving situation are "innate," or, as I would rather say, ideas of reason. *Ideas of reason*, we shall soon see, are one thing; *truths of reason* are another.

a question. Are the act and the representative in the two cases really exactly the same? The question is shrewd. But I refuse to be rushed, introduce first a pair of words which will save us many.

To intend something "through" a representative, or, as I shall also say, "by" being presented with the latter, is to know[2] it *indirectly*. To know something without there being a "third" to mediate between the knower and the known is to know it *directly*. I shall not in this section use 'direct-indirect' in any other way. In terms of structural possibilities, we shall presently see, there are two ways of knowing something directly. But we need not thus elaborate the useful dichotomy in order to find the answer to the preliminary questions I raised for the sake of easing our way into the issues.

How do we know bodies? How do we know that an idea with which we are presented represents something? These are the two questions of which I want to make sure that they are two and not one. My friend, I submit, collapses them into one for one of two bad reasons. Either he takes it for granted that we know ideas and minds directly and that therefore representationalism qua representationalism (if I may so express myself) need not worry about them. Or he believes that even though we may know them (or some of them) only indirectly, the main difficulty of representationalism qua representationalism lies nevertheless in finding a satisfactory answer to a single question about bodies. He is wrong in either case.

How do we know ideas? How do we know minds? Directly or indirectly? It will turn out that either answer leads in either case to difficulties which are insuperable and, if anything, even more formidable, just as dialectically they cut even more deeply, than those encountered by worrying epistemologically the representationalists' answer to the first question: How do we know bodies? That is why my friend's reasons are bad reasons. Historically, though, there is a point. To collapse the two questions for one of these reasons is to share the preoccupation of the early representationalists who, under the triple goad of the nominalistic, the skeptical, and the scientific predicament (Section Seven) were so worried by the first of the three questions, about bodies, that they gravely underestimated the difficulties of the second and the third, about ideas and about minds.

Suppose someone challenges my claim that the second and the third questions are more formidable than the first. I answer as follows: On the one hand, as I have just reminded you, the representationalists[3] do

---

[2] Generic use of 'know'!

[3] Or, rather, in view of the deadly flaw revealed in the last section, the prototype! Nor need I remind you of the ultimate fate which awaits all γ-ontologies if Part I stands up.

provide an articulate and at least prima facie adequate assay of the
perceiving situation, while, on the other hand, as I promised to show,
they cannot furnish such an account of our knowledge of either ideas or
minds. Thereupon you agree, if only for the sake of the argument, that
the representationalists' (or, rather, the prototype's) assay of the perceiving situation is the one I attributed to them, but insist that, since it
fails to "distinguish" between the veridical and the nonveridical case,
it is not even prima facie either adequate or articulate. At this point,
having become a victim of the epistemologism that still oppresses us,
you fail to distinguish between ontology and epistemology. The double
quotes around 'distinguish' mark the blur. In other words, what you are
looking for is not, ontologically, an *assay of the perceiving situation* but,
rather, epistemologically, a *criterion of veridical perception*, or, with the
revealing twist which (if I am right) can be given to all "merely"
epistemological questions, you are looking for the ontological ground of
a criterion. Clearly, I must next answer the question which, equally
clearly, you will ask next. How do I in this context use 'criterion'?

There is of course a difference (as I shall briefly call it) between the
veridical and the nonveridical case. For this difference every adequate
ontology must account. The representationalist assay accounts for it in
the most simple and straightforward fashion, which I believe is also the
only one that works dialectically. In the veridical case, the object is
there. In the nonveridical case there is no object. (Or, as the foil has it,
in the former the complex intended exists in the mode of actuality; in
the latter, in that of potentiality.) Otherwise there is no difference. The
answer to the shrewd question is Yes. Act and representative (if any)
are exactly alike. *A criterion is a difference in the act or in the representative*, i.e., something which is or is not there, either in the one or in the
other or in both, depending on whether the object is or is not there.
(You see now why I insisted on the ontological twist.)

Let us survey the structural possibilities. The difference lies either
only in the object, or only in the representative (if any), or only in the
act, or in any two of them, or in all three. Or, as one might want to say,
since representatives and cores are in one-one correspondence, if one
believes, as I do,[4] that there are no ideas, the difference lies either in the
object, or in the core, or in the fringe, or, and so on. Descartes puts it in
the representative. The ideas must be clear and distinct. Brentano, we
shall see, puts it in the fringe.[5]

[4] So, we shall see, does Brentano.

[5] This is another of those distinctive features of his world any two of which entail each other (p. 181). It is also, as I hope you sense already, the structural root
of his idealism. Meinong's "solution," as so often, is too complicated and too
quixotic to be illuminated by so simple a schema.

The foil rejects the very idea of a criterion and pays the price of recognizing the ontological status of the mode of potentiality, of which more anon. It deplores the dominance of the compulsive search for a criterion of veridical perception as one of the most crippling features of epistemologism and offers an explanation, psychological, structural, and historical, of why and how the compulsion gained its grip.

Psychologically, not much needs to be said. To search for a criterion is but one way of searching for certainty; and the search for certainty, from all indications, is a very major, if not the major, intellectual expression of the restless anxiety in our hearts. Representationalism withholds the object; offers the representative instead. That increases the anxiety. *Structurally*, if the difference is to lie in the representative, the very notion of a criterion requires that the world be tripartite. Even if the difference is to lie in the act, the notion fits much better in a world where the object itself is withheld. The compulsion is a symptom of the increased anxiety. *Historically*, therefore, not much need be said either. *Representationalism and the compulsive search for a criterion go together.*

If you now stop to reflect for a moment, you will see that the preliminary questions have all been answered and that I really never was in any trouble, either major or minor. But let us check.

The sophomore's question ought to be unpacked as follows: Is there a criterion by which one can tell whether an idea—not necessarily of a body but also, if there be such, of either another idea, or a mind—represents? The answer is No. The representationalist makes two mistakes. In his preoccupation with knowing bodies he mistakes this question for the first of the three with which I started. In his fixation on a criterion he mistakes the failure to find one for a predicament. Thus we arrive at the following conclusion. How do we know bodies? What, if any, is the criterion? These really are two questions. The first is ontological; the second, epistemological. The three questions which get the representationalists into trouble are: How do we know ideas? How do we know minds? What is the criterion? The first two of these predicaments they gravely underestimate. The third becomes one only because they take it for granted that there must be a criterion.

About criteria I have nothing more to say. Thus I shall proceed as follows: I shall examine the dialectic, first of knowing ideas, then of knowing minds. Next I shall apply the results of this examination to a pattern about which Brentano had much to say and which, since it is more or less closely related to what Descartes so conspicuously worried about, I shall call the *Cogito*. Then I shall conclude this section and this Part with some comments on the foil's notion of potentiality.

Suppose that there are ideas and that we know some of them, either directly or indirectly. If we knew indirectly *all* those which we do in fact know, we would be faced with an infinite regress. *Some,* therefore, we must know directly. In the gap between this 'some' and this 'all' nothing dialectically worth while is lost. Suppose, then, that we know all ideas directly.

Structurally, in terms of possibilities, there are two kinds of direct knowledge.[6] Knower and known are either two or they are one. If they are two, then they face each other directly, without an intermediary third. Or, as I have said and shall continue to say, the known is presented to the knower. Being presented is a connection. Thus it must (if I am right) be grounded in something which is neither "in" the former nor "in" the latter. If knower and known are one, the former is said to know itself. One also speaks of self-knowledge or knowledge that is *reflexive.* Is there such knowledge? Brentano takes the affirmative; the foil, the negative. In the dialectic of knowing minds the disagreement is crucial; in that of knowing ideas it makes no difference. I know of no worth-while ontology that ascribes knowledge to anything but minds or things mental.[7] Nor would anything be gained dialectically by trying this gambit. Thus I shall suppose that, as long as ideas have not fallen into minds, the latter (sometimes) know (some of) the former. Or, equivalently, we may safely suppose that ideas, to be known, must be presented to minds.

I am ready to do two things. I shall make it my *first* business to show that *the notion of an idea presented to a mind is hopelessly elusive.* Part of the nuance I try to catch by using 'hopelessly elusive' rather than 'irremediably confused' is that there are no ideas. My *second* business will be to discover and dissect a powerful structural motive for clinging to the assumption that ideas are known. In other words, I shall show why *representationalists take it for granted that ideas (if there are any)[8] are known.* But it will help you to appreciate these two results if, anticipating them, I first do something else.

The prototype, I claimed, was most unstable. Ideas immediately lose their balance. Suppose they fall into the mind. Now we can make a slow-motion picture of this sudden accident. I select three slides.

(a) The issue of self-knowledge arises only if the phrase is taken with

---

[6] Or so at least I shall suppose for the time being. One may reasonably question whether reflexive knowledge is even structurally possible. The question is subtle; the answer takes time; nor do we need it in this section. So I shall not examine this issue until in Part III we encounter Brentano's claim that every act knows itself.

[7] Structurally and by his intention, though not, alas, by common sense, this covers Leibniz.

[8] I add the qualification because, as we shall see, Brentano escapes between the horns of *this* dilemma by denying that there are ideas.

the literalness proper to ontological discourse, as, for instance, in considering the question whether, when one knows that he is perceiving something, the ground of his knowing it is the reflexive knowledge of the act of perceiving. As long as we speak commonsensically, we all agree that minds do know themselves. Common sense thus tempts us to take for granted that reflexive knowledge, which is one of the two structurally possible kinds of direct knowledge, exists. Suppose, then, that this is taken for granted.

(b) Knowledge of ideas, if any, is direct. The only alternative is an infinite regress. That there is such knowledge is taken for granted. That is one of the two results we anticipate. The other is that the notion of an idea presented to a mind, or before a mind, remains hopelessly elusive. Since there are only two possible kinds of direct knowledge, that leaves only one alternative. A mind knows the idea "before" it as it knows itself or whatever is "in" it. That makes the temptation to change 'before' to 'in' almost irresistible. If one yields to it, the idea has fallen into the mind.

The temptation draws further strength from two sources. If one is overly concerned with the dialectic of knowing bodies, one will tend to put ideas and minds into the same boat[9] (and take too lightly all questions about knowing either). This source is historical, as it were, and by now, I trust, rather obvious. So I turn to the other source or motive, which is structural and more interesting, even though I don't think it ever reached consciousness.

(c) Between a mind and an idea presented to it there is a connection. The only connection which the philosophers who concern us really understood, or, rather, the only connection they were accustomed to and took for granted, is that between an Aristotelian substance and its attributes; or, as I would rather say, in order to distinguish between what does and what does not depend on what, the only connection they took for granted, was that between a cluster and the particulars that are "in" it. Ask yourself how such a philosopher would assay minds "in" which he believes there are ideas, and you will see how easily, not to say almost inevitably, the latter, once they have lost their balance, turn into cores.[10]

[9] Or, to say the same thing differently, one will not see that to be "in" the mind and to be the sort of thing that can be directly known are neither the same₃ nor necessarily coextensive. For a modern offspring of this distinction, with a different though not unrelated meaning of 'direct', see the "Realistic Postscript" in *Logic and Reality*.

[10] This is what happened, not only (if I am right) confusedly and confusingly in the case of Locke (p. 161), but also, as we shall see, with admirable clarity, in Brentano's.

We are ready for the two tasks I set myself.

To *know* an idea is to be *presented* with it. This, I take it, is a premiss we have acquired and may trust, provided only we do not forget three further propositions. (1) 'knowing' stands in this context for a genus whose species are perceiving, believing, remembering, doubting, and so on. *Entertaining* (*thinking of*) is among these species. (2) Knowing and *intending* are two and not one. Yet every knowing involves an intending. In the prototype as in the foil, an act's core intends its intention; its fringe determines the species to which it belongs. (3) Upon the representationalist gambit, one knows some things "through" their ideas or "by" being presented with the latter.[11] From these three propositions follow three others. (4) It follows from (3) that when knowing something indirectly, e.g., when perceiving a chair or believing that iron is hard, one does not, in the one case, know the idea of the chair, nor, in the other, the idea (or ideas) of iron being hard. (5) It follows from (2) that knowing an idea and intending it are two and not one. (6) It follows from (1) and (2) that *to think of something* (*conceive or entertain it*) *and to know its idea are two and not one. This phenomenological truth is not only a cornerstone of the whole dialectic; it is also the truism which, being such a cornerstone, it ought to be.* Or is it not a truism that when thinking of horses, what I think of are horses, which are objects in the Second, not the idea of horse, or, for that matter, the several ideas of several horses, which are all alleged dwellers in the Third? (Yet it was not the least of Brentano's merits that he firmly grasped and steadily held on to this truism.)

A quick glance at the six propositions will show you that knowing an idea, in any species, would have to be something radically different from knowing anything else. That is why, whenever it will help or be prudent, I shall henceforth say that to know an idea involves *attending* to it.[12] This will keep our words straight. How about the things? Holding the six propositions together and looking at them more closely, you will see that *the notion of attending to an idea* (*or ideas*) *is hopelessly elusive.*

The intellectual motive, which the representationalists had and to which I now turn, for first taking it for granted, then clinging to the assumption, until Brentano finally shattered the illusion, that we can attend to ideas, is inextricably intertwined with a supposed dichotomy

---

[11] In the tripartite map of Section Seven intending is the long base of the dotted triangle; being presented, the short side at the left.

[12] You see what suggested the choice of the word. *At*tending to an idea, if there were such a thing, would stand to knowing it as *in*tending stands to knowing in the case of something which is not an idea.

in knowledge, which is a very major theme of the tradition and in turn inseparable from an even larger one, namely, the nature of knowledge in general.

Knowing is either a priori or a posteriori. This is the dichotomy. As it stands, the formula is ambiguous. From where I stand, the question that spots the ambiguity immediately imposes itself. Is the dichotomy one among *knowings* or one among *knowns?* In the great tradition it is held that there are two dichotomies, one among knowings, one among knowns, so corresponding to each other that the one kind of knowings grasps[13] the one kind of knowns, while the other grasps the other. Brentano and the foil agree that there is only one dichotomy, disagree on where it is. Brentano puts it into the fringes, which, as we shall see, is the gist of his doctrine of evidence and, also, the root of his idealism. The foil puts the dichotomy in the intentions, which fits with its realism, then divides the a priori half of it in the by now familiar tripartite manner (necessary$_1$, necessary$_2$, necessary$_3$).

The dichotomy has found several expressions. The metaphor of the two eyes, of reason and of sense, is the most poetical. The one which contains the cue we need calls the two kinds of knowledge conceptual and empirical, respectively; or, as I shall say, with a contraction that goes to the heart of the matter without either losing or prejudging anything, *conceptual* and *perceptual*.

Concepts are ideas, and conversely. This is the cue to the two dichotomies. On the side of the knowns, the split is between *"ideas"* and the particular things that "fall under" them; on the side of the knowings, between attending to *ideas* and, in perception, intending particular things. *A priori or conceptual knowledge is of ideas; a posteriori or perceptual knowledge, of particular things.* This is the pattern which the representationalists inherited from their predecessors and kept alive for another three hundred years.

The last paragraph is but a string of rough-and-ready formulae. Thus, like a mountain rising above a plain, it will help you to find your way. Yet it is still shrouded by clouds. I shall next try to make two rents in this shroud.

Consider the first two occurrences of 'ideas'. The one between double quotes refers to universals in the known. Originally, universals were Platonic. 'Fall under' thus stands for what originally was Platonic par-

---

[13] In the foil the "knowings" are species, of course; the "knowns," facts which are intentions. As it will turn out and as probably you sense already, the two kinds of "grasping" are attending and intending. But the view here taken is so large that for once I cannot bring myself to speak as circumstantially, not to say pedantically, as for the most part one must.

ticipation; hence the double quotes. Nor is the reference to Plato far-fetched or out of place. The mistaken belief that universals must be Platonic was, as we know, one of the major causes of the great persecution that drove them all into exile, transforming them into those dwellers in a shadowy Third to which the second occurrence refers. Yet, "ideas" and ideas are two and not one. That is one respect in which these formulae are but rough and ready. The very roughness helps to bring out a continuity, or connection, between representationalism and its predecessors. This connection, though, we have understood already.[14] Another roughness provides a cue to the connection which we are trying to understand now.

Whether in perceiving we are, according to the foil, presented with a fact in the Second, or, perhaps, according to the tripartite prototype, with a "fact" in the Third, rather than, as the representationalists claim, with a single idea, however complex, may be, and in fact is, controversial. That makes it also controversial whether, as the foil claims, all awareness is propositional, i.e., whether the intentions of all acts are facts, or, equivalently, whether every intention is expressed by a sentence. But it is not at all controversial that what the tradition calls "knowledge" in general, and, even more evidently, if that be possible, what it calls a priori knowledge in particular, is propositional. If you hesitate to assent, think of the four sentential patterns, "All A are B," "Some A are B," and so on, into one of which according to the Aristotelian schema every "unit" bit of knowledge can be cast.[15] That spots the other respect in which the formulae of that guidepost paragraph are but rough and ready. They ignore, or slur over, the crucial feature that

---

[14] I do not really believe that it needs to be spelled out for anyone who has read up to this point. However, I prefer once more being cautious and tedious to being reckless and not understood. A priori knowledge, which according to the representationalists is of ideas, is also, according to them, the "better" knowledge. According to Plato, the "best" knowledge we can have is of "ideas." The new double quotes, around 'better' and 'best', mark a new ambiguity. Plato's scale of 'good' and 'better' in this context was probably not primarily and certainly not exclusively epistemological. The representationalists' was. But the ambiguity does not at all weaken the connection. We are here touching the same anthropological rock bottom which we touched when talking about the "compulsion" in the search for a criterion. This rock bottom *of* philosophy is there and the student of the dialectic cannot but touch it every now and then, even though it is not itself *in* philosophy. Nor, of course, in spite of what some lost souls now want us to believe, does it contain everything that can be said *about* philosophy.

[15] If you wonder about perceptual knowledge, return to n. 16 of Section Ten. If after that you still fear that I shall force perceptual into the mold of conceptual knowledge, you will be relieved of part of this fear almost immediately and of the rest very soon.

every bit of a priori knowledge involves not just a single idea but always a connection of at least two.[16] A comparison which uses a certain common way of speaking, even though this way has been the source of a fatal confusion, will yet help. Treating for a moment ideas as if they were things and using 'see', 'know', and 'about' as the man in the street does, a bit of a priori knowledge is not like what *seeing a chair* would be like, if Aristotle and the representationalists were right in holding that a chair is a single thing and not a fact, but, rather, like *knowing something "about" the chair*, e.g., the fact that it is brown. The fatal confusion lurks behind 'about'. No harm will be done by relegating a few words about it to a footnote.[17] We have already come upon the intellectual motive we were looking for.

On the one hand, still speaking with the man in the street, a priori knowledge is "about" ideas; or, as I would rather say, returning to my customary way of speaking, it is knowing a "fact" in the Third, or, equivalently, a "connection" of some sort or other between two (or more) ideas.[18] On the other hand, it is against the grain of both ordinary language and common sense to say or believe that one can know anything "about" something to which one cannot attend. That spots

[16] 'Involves' indicates, as usually, that my tongue is still in my cheek. But it will not stay there much longer. According to the Aristotelian schema, the ideas connected are always exactly two. That alone is a cue to the troubles, coming to a head with Brentano, which the representationalists had with the "existential judgment."

[17] From where I stand, 'about' here merely indicates that, like all others, the intention of this seeing is a fact and that of this fact the particular is one constituent; the color, another. (I treat the chair as if it were a particular. Nothing that matters here will thereby be lost.) Historically, this 'about' has been appealed to and is still being appealed to by those nominalists who, not wanting to allow anything but particulars into the Second, try to convince us that 'This chair is brown' is "about" one thing and one thing only, namely, the particular. Meinong, to his glory, in the first part of *Annahmen*, saw through this grammatical sleight of hand. That didn't stop it, though. (Apparently nothing ever stops anything in philosophy.) At Oxford it is now perpetrated under the cover of distinguishing between two kinds of expression. The ones are said to designate (pick out); the others, to describe. In 'This chair is brown', 'This chair' designates, 'brown' describes; the whole sentence is "about" the particular *and nothing else*. Nor is there any doubt about the connection between this "linguistic" sleight of hand (arguing more or less explicitly from the ordinary use of 'about') and the representationalists' account of perception. The existential judgment picks out (designates) what the alleged "analysis" describes. I prefer my Aristotle straight.

[18] Double quotes, around 'fact', 'connection', 'constituent', and so on, here and elsewhere, in discourse about "entities" of the Third, mark, wherever I think it may be needed or at least helpful, my irreducible resistance to the Third. But, then, we cannot give it a run for its money without talking about it articulately; which means, from where I stand, without talking about it "ontologically."

both motive and connection. The representationalists take it for granted that there is a priori knowledge. That is the motive. The bit of common sense whose rejection is against the grain provides the connection.

The structural insight is so crucial that it bears repetition. We now see clearly the motive and what it is the motive of. *The representationalists hold, or take it for granted, that there is a priori or conceptual knowledge and that to have such knowledge is to know some connections among ideas. Hence, they must also hold, or take it for granted, that we can attend to ideas.*[19] *The ideas of their worlds, or, as I put it, the Third, thus does four jobs rather than three. The Third not only relieves, or, rather, seems to relieve, the three predicaments of Section Seven; it also provides, or, rather, seems to provide, a new ontological ground for maintaining in the old way the distinction between the two kinds of knowledge.*

The notion of knowing ideas is hopelessly elusive. Yet the representationalists have a powerful structural motive for holding that ideas can be attended to. Having made good these two claims, as I believe I have, I accomplished the two tasks I had set myself. Yet there is more to be said about the dialectic of knowing ideas. So I start on a string of *six* comments. Then we shall be ready for the dialectic of knowing minds.

First. A critic tells me that I overstress the representationalists' need for grounding conceptual knowledge. I meet the attack with a counterattack, point out to him that their concern with such knowledge has distorted their conception of *all* knowledge. Just remember the trumpet call at the beginning of Book Four of Locke's *Essay:*

Knowledge then seems to me to be nothing but *the perception of the connection of and agreement, or disagreement and repugnancy of any of our ideas.*

This is an opening statement, about knowledge *tout court,* not just either conceptual or perceptual knowledge, about both of which much is said in the sequel! The criticism is no doubt justified. Only, the critic addressed it to the wrong party. It is not I but the representationalists who make too much of conceptual knowledge. With a slight overstatement, to bring out the stresses and strains in the dialectic, they make conceptual knowledge the paradigm of all knowledge. When it comes to perceptual knowledge, they pay the price. This we shall see in the fifth comment.

---

[19] Unless they take the way out which, as we shall see in Part III, led Brentano to his implicit idealism. The way out now fashionable and, alas, structurally just as idealistic, is recommended by those who follow the second Wittgenstein in making all "conceptual truths" a matter of language, or of convention, or a way of life, or what have you. Of these two evils, Brentano's is no doubt the lesser. But we need not choose between them.

Second. What are those "connections," of agreement or disagreement, among ideas, which presumably we discover by attending to them? I can think of two, inclusion (containment) and exclusion. $\overline{A}$ being included in $\overline{B}$ is what so far we have called $\overline{A}$ being contained in $\overline{B}$; in symbols: $\overline{A} < \overline{B}$. The idea of colored is included in that of red. The ideas of red and green, or, more accurately, as we know, of something° red and of something° green, exclude each other. (We shall not need a symbol for exclusion.)

Third. Assume for the sake of the argument that the ideas of a satyr and of a sylvan deity are connected like those of red and colored and, also, that we may know the "fact" of which they are two "constituents," and of which being contained is the third. Yet there are no satyrs and no sylvan deities. That spots a dichotomy which, not surprisingly, is one of the centers around which the dialectic of representationalism revolves. To know connections among ideas is one thing; to know that an idea represents is quite another thing. The latter kind of knowledge is called *existential;* the former I shall call *hypothetical.*[20] According to the representationalists, every unit bit of knowledge is either the one or the other. If you remember what has been said in Section Nine about Locke's confusions, you will see that; even though he limits what he says to the ideas he calls once abstract, once general; even though he calls once universal, once general what I call hypothetical and calls experience what I call perception; he yet confirms this diagnosis by what he tells us at the end of the third chapter of Book Four:

If the ideas are abstract, whose agreement we perceive, our knowledge is universal. *For what is known of such general ideas, will be true of every particular thing in whom that essence, i.e., that abstract idea, is to be found:* and what is once known of such ideas, will be perpetually and forever true. So that as to all general knowledge we must search it and find it only in our minds. Truths belonging to essences of things (that is, to abstract ideas) are eternal; and are to be found out by contemplation only of those essences: as the existence of things is to be known only from experience.

What impressive confirmation and at the same time, alas, what almost incredible confusion! The sentence which begins with 'For' leads to the next comment. That is why I added the italics.

Fourth. Nothing will be lost if we stay with inclusion. One who holds that he can know the "fact" $\overline{A} < \overline{B}$, must consistently also hold that the

---

[20] 'Hypothetical' not only suggests this important dichotomy but also permits us to avoid 'universal' and 'general'. 'Universal' I want to avoid for the obvious reason that we must also talk about universals; 'general', because it is one of the four words I occasionally want to use, between double quotes, as Meinong used them (the other three are 'particular', 'concrete', 'abstract'). See also n. 23, below.

two ideas $(\overline{A}, \overline{B})$ and the "connection $(<)$" between them are "presented"[21] to him in exactly the same way. That puts the former two and the latter together, in a boat which is fated to founder. Just as I cannot, merely by attending to two ideas, know whether and, if anything, what they represent, so I cannot, merely by attending to the "fact" of the "connection" between them $(\overline{A}<\overline{B})$, know that the latter represents the fact of another connection $(\tilde{B}<\tilde{A})$ between two Classes, of qualities or objects; and this would be so even if I knew what in fact I don't know, namely, that $\overline{A}$ and $\overline{B}$ represent indifferently any of the members of the Classes $\tilde{A}$ and $\tilde{B}$, respectively.[22]

At this point you remind me of how I "explained" inclusion: $(\overline{A}<\overline{B})$ means, either wholly or in part, $(\tilde{B}<\tilde{A})$. I reply by reminding you first that when offering this "explanation" I pointed out how grave a doubt it cast on the ontological status of ideas (p. 172). Then I add that in offering this "explanation" I set a trap which, as you see, has now sprung shut. For there is not the slightest doubt that the representationalists take for granted what the "explanation" states. Thus they are faced with the following dilemma. Either $\overline{A}<\overline{B}$ and $\tilde{B}<\tilde{A}$ are, as one says, the same by definition. In this case talking about ideas is but a confusing way of talking about Classes. Or one can know the "fact" $\overline{A}<\overline{B}$. In this case one cannot bridge the gap, has no reason whatsoever to believe that $\overline{A}<\overline{B}$ represents the fact $\tilde{B}<\tilde{A}$.

Poor representationalism! Like Sebastian it already bleeds from so many wounds. Yet we add this most cruel one. The gap is ghastly indeed. The representationalists do not even notice it, take for granted what the "explanation" states! I can think of no better explanation of their blindness than what is one of the pillars on which the whole argument of this book rests: Structurally ideas are universals; or, as Locke has it, they are the essences of things. This explanation, too, is impressively supported by the passage from Locke I just quoted.

Fifth. Now for perception. Whatever disagreements there are about it, and we know that they are many and important, the representationalists all agree, and the prototype agrees with them, about three things. Everyone agrees, first, that some such bits of knowledge as the one whose intention is expressed by 'This spot is white' are come by in acts of perceiving and cannot be come by in any other way. Everyone agrees, second, that the ideas of this spot and of white are two and not

---

[21] Perhaps I should rather say that one can attend to all three in exactly the same way; hence the double quotes. Somewhere some roughness is unavoidable, whatever words are chosen. The confusions causing it are not of my making.

[22] Nothing would be gained if I expressed all this more circumstantially by mentioning the null-Class.

one, as well as, third, that this bit of knowledge involves a connection between them.[23] These three features produce a situation which is very awkward, to say the least.

Some connections among ideas we can grasp by attending to the "facts" whose "constituents" they are; some others, only by intending facts in perception. The eye of reason, or at least of our reason, is, as it were, not keen enough to see all connections among ideas. That this is awkward or at least very peculiar *on the side of ideas* I take to be obvious, even though a Lockean might insist that it is neither the one nor the other since, not by chance, the eye of reason fails us only in those cases when one of the ideas is what he calls particular. But that merely spots the confusion, which I need not retail once more, behind the way *he* uses 'particular'. *On the side of things*, the situation is very awkward indeed because it intermingles three or four things in a way in which they cannot be intermingled without inviting almost certain disaster, namely, (1) the fringe (species) in perceiving; (2) the question whether certain ideas represent or (2a) certain acts of perceiving are veridical; and (3) the question whether (and how) certain ideas are connected. If you reflect for a moment you will also see why this unhappy mixture cannot but increase the craving for a criterion.[24]

Sixth. The idea of colored is contained in that of red; the idea of something° white in that of something° white and square. The representationalists, very plausibly from where they stand, hold that both these connections can be grasped by attending to ideas; or, equivalently, as we put it before (p. 186), they hold that the containment is in both cases not merely a posteriori.[25] Yet there is a difference. It is best brought out by shifting from ideas to Classes. The Class of all particulars grounding red being contained in that of all those grounding colored is a truth which, although a priori, is synthetic. That the class of

---

[23] One of these two ideas happens to be "particular," in Meinong's clear, though not of course in Locke's hopelessly confused, sense. Brentano, in spite of the apparent contradiction to what was said earlier, can be brought under this schema, provided only one replaces ideas, which he does not believe exist, by the cores corresponding to them which in his world, without Lockean confusion, do the jobs of ideas. 'Involves', used noncommittally as usual, covers his case.

[24] In n. 23 of Section Ten, I promised to remind you of it when we came to a certain point that would enable you to appreciate it more fully. This is the point.

[25] You see now why I said earlier that if 'contained' were to be qualified every time, the dichotomy 'conceptual-empirical (perceptual)' would be preferable to 'a priori–a posteriori'. In representationalist ontologies the latter is explicated in terms of the former. More precisely, if for brevity's sake I may use 'because', a piece of knowledge is a priori *because* it involves a connection that can be grasped by attending to concepts (ideas). The second Wittgenstein repeats this pattern. Only, in his case the shared feature is that these truths are merely "linguistic."

all white and square objects is contained in that of all white objects is analytic.

The doctrine of the undifferentiated a priori ignores the distinction between what is "merely" synthetic a priori and the analytic. The representationalists either ignore the distinction, or, if they acknowledge it, do not make much of it. Or so at least I have claimed repeatedly. Now we finally understand why this is so. What moves them above all is whether or not a bit of knowledge is conceptual, i.e., whether or not it can be known by attending to ideas. The analytic and the synthetic a priori, very plausibly from where they stand, are both on the same side of this fence. This shared feature overshadows for them any difference they may or may not acknowledge.

I turn to the dialectic of knowing minds, or, rather, as one says, not necessarily with ontological literalness, of a mind knowing itself. The dialectic of one mind knowing another will not be discussed at all in this book; just as, ignoring whatever knowledge a mind may have of itself in memory, imagination, and so on, I limit myself to what some call self-perception. The older representationalists and Brentano do not even consider the possibility that such knowledge might be indirect.[26] This is but one side of a coin that has passed through our hands already. Its other side we saw when in the case of ideas we encountered and accounted for the propensity of taking for granted that being mental and being the sort of thing that can be known directly are coextensive (with the usual allowance for the hiddenness of substances, if any). That leaves two alternatives. A mind knows itself either directly or reflexively. The question which is the most fundamental as well as the most difficult in this part of the dialectic asks whether reflexive knowledge is even a structural possibility (possible₁). This question we shall ignore until later. The rest will not take long.

So far we have spoken of a "mind" knowing itself. So far this has done no harm. Now we must be more accurate. Literally, a knower is an act. The question thus is whether an act, either directly or "reflexively," knows either itself or the cluster "in" which it is or the substance,[27] if any, behind the cluster. The double quotes indicate that,

---

[26] Meinong once more defies classification. In the foil, we know, all knowings are direct, none is either indirect or reflexive.

[27] These are of course either substances₄ or substances₅. For the argument the difference makes no difference. But there is the traditional "hiddenness" of substances to contend with. The *Cogito* pattern, we shall see in a moment, reaches them by inference; Brentano, as we shall see much later, by a move characteristically his own. Notice, too, that I have taken to using 'directly' where, more accurately, as the words have been introduced, I should use 'directly but not reflexively'. But no harm will be done.

except in the case of an act literally knowing itself rather than, say, the cluster "in" which it is, we have used 'reflexive' more broadly than before. Let us stay with the act and the cluster, leave what little will have to be said about substances until we come to the *Cogito*.

There is of course also the distinction between a "whole mind" and a cross section. In the total dialectic of self-knowledge (in the relevant sense) it looms very large. For the one issue I wish to discuss it makes no difference whatsoever. Or, perhaps better, it can be bracketed out. This will become clear in a moment. So we shall stay in a cross section.

Suppose first that one holds all acts to be reflexive. (The alternative that only some are, while some others are not, does not yield anything dialectically very interesting.) This gambit raises no *immediate dialectical* question. The only two questions are whether it is *phenomenologically adequate* and whether it works *dialectically in the long run*.

Suppose next that while no act knows itself reflexively, some are known directly. Let a_1 be an act so known. That requires that there be another a_2, which knows the former directly. a_2 may in turn be known directly by a third act, a_3, and so on. Schematically at least, the series need not break off. Perhaps an image will help. Picture the mind as a sphere;[28] each member of the sequence a_1, a_2, a_3, and so on, as a small lighted area of its surface. That does raise an immediate dialectical question. But this question remains the same if one assumes that the little areas are all lighted at the same moment. That is why we can safely stay within a cross section. Assume, then, that a_1, a_2, a_3, and so on, are all complex particulars in a single cluster.

a_2 knows a_1 directly; a_3 so knows a_2; and so on. That raises no immediate problem. (Nor does the variant that a_3 knows a_1 and a_2 directly produce anything interesting.) *The one problem is whether* a_2 *knows that itself and* a_1 *belong to the same cluster.* For a_2 to know this it is a necessary condition that it know the cluster (or subcluster) which I shall write $\gamma(a_1, a_2)$. A bit unsystematic as it is, the notation does not, I trust, require explanation. But you will do well to remember the confusing way in which the representationalists use 'distinct' and 'indistinct'. For that will help you to see that for a_2 to know $\gamma(a_1, a_2)$ in the relevant sense it does not suffice for it to know this cluster "indistinctly," but that it must be "presented" with a_1, with a_2, and with the nexus between them. Hence it would have to know itself reflexively, which is excluded by assumption. I conclude that *none of the acts in the series can know that*

---

[28] Hollow or otherwise, depending on whether or not you believe that there are substances. I take this image from the essay on "The Ontology of Edmund Husserl" in *Logic and Reality*, where it has been elaborated and, I believe, served quite well.

itself and any of the others are "in" the same cluster. Call this the *roughness* in direct (but not reflexive) self-knowledge. That will save words in the discussion of the *Cogito* to which I now turn.

What I call the *Cogito*[29] is a pattern for an argument. It purports to provide a *single existential premiss* and a set of *conceptual premisses*, concerning which certain assumptions are made, such that I, or, for that matter, anyone else, can deduce from them (1) that I exist, and (2) that some of my ideas represent.

The pattern ignores two questions closely related to (2), namely, first, how I can know what the entities falling under the ideas which represent are like; and, second, how that ghastly gap between $\overline{A} < \overline{B}$ and $\tilde{B} < \tilde{A}$ can be bridged. The explanation I would suggest for a representationalist's not finding the first of these two questions as pressing as it really is, is the same I offered for the gap's not being noticed. One who, however implicitly, thinks of an idea, say, that of green, as a universal, will take it for granted that what falls under it is green. With respect to the second question, a warning ought to be issued against what formally seems to be an answer. This apparent answer makes containing (between ideas) itself an idea that represents inclusion (among Classes). The trouble is that, structurally, it thus makes a nexus into a universal, which cannot but lead to disaster.

Let us make sure that we know how certain words and phrases are used in this context. An "existential premiss" is either a sentence which states that a certain thing—i.e., in γ, an object or a quality—but not an idea, exists. Or it is a sentence from which such a sentence can be deduced. A "conceptual premiss" is a statement about ideas which, if true, is an a priori truth. One sees immediately that from a set of conceptual premisses no statement which, if it were used as a premiss, would be called an existential premiss, can be deduced. (1) is such a statement. That is why the pattern needs at least one existential premiss. The "I" or "Self" of the pattern is a nonmomentary substance.

The assumptions fall into two groups. According to the first, we have some innate ideas, or, as I would rather say, ideas of reason, i.e., ideas we have not come by in perception (including self-perception, or, as Locke has it, reflection). Some of these ideas are ontological, such as, e.g., those of substance and of attribute. Some are theological. Ac-

---

[29] I say "what I call the *Cogito*" because I want to make is as clear as I can that I do not ascribe it to Descartes, even though I am reasonably certain, and therefore usefully call it by this name, that it is *more or less closely related* to a *part* of what he worried about. Thus you must not mistake this analysis of a certain type of argument for a discussion of the Cartesian texts. Scholars who find this sort of thing distasteful ought not to read philosophical books.

cording to the second group of assumptions, we can by attending to ideas of reason come to know some conceptual truths about them (i.e., some "facts" whose "constituents" these ideas are). Some of these truths are ontological; some, theological. Each conceptual premiss expresses such a truth and is, therefore, with one possible exception, a bit of hypothetical knowledge, not asserting the existence of any thing (quality or object). The possible exception is some conceptual premisses of the theological kind. They make no difference for what concerns us. The following are three conceptual premisses of the ontological kind: (3) Every attribute inheres[30] in exactly one substance. (4) An act is an attribute. (5) A substance in which at least one act inheres is a Self.

Brush aside what does not matter in the context by taking for granted that a sentence stating that a thing is either directly or reflexively known deductively implies another which states that this thing exists. That directs us to the existential premiss of the pattern: (6) *A certain act is known, either* (a) *reflexively or* (b) *directly.* From (6a) in conjunction with (3), (4), (5) it follows deductively that the act mentioned in (6) inheres in a Self, which, assuming that the act is one of "mine," is "I." Thus (1) is reached. If the existential premiss is (6b), we find ourselves faced with a roughness exactly like the one we encountered when we proved that an act which knows another directly cannot know that itself and that act are "in" the same cluster. Go back to that proof, replace 'cluster' and 'in' by 'substance' and 'inhere', and you will see that the proof still holds. It follows that the sentence deducible from (6b) in conjunction with (3), (4), (5) is not (1) but in a certain respect weaker than (1). Notice this roughness, then waive it, suppose that (1) has been reached.

In the second step the pattern deduces from (1) in conjunction with a number of conceptual premisses of the theological kind the sentence (2), or, more precisely, the sentence which states that those of my ideas which are *clear and distinct* represent. For, if they didn't, then the creator, who by some of the theological premisses must exist if I am to exist, would be a deceiver, which contradicts some other of those premisses. Clearness and distinctness seem[31] to be features of ideas, or,

---

[30] I waive the question what connection among ideas this supposed connection among things involves.

[31] I say seems because, to venture one comment about Descartes, he also tells us that *as such* the idea of, say, green, even though it does not represent (or, at least, does not represent anything like itself) is yet clear and distinct. Is this so because, being "in" the mind, it can be known directly? Or is this so because, being an idea, it can be attended to? The texts are very difficult. Even so, it is

at any rate, something in the Third. (2) *thus provides a criterion.*
Within the dialectic of representationalism, that makes the second step
the decisive one. If you accept its conceptual premisses, you will (I
suppose) also have to accept its conclusion.

This is the *Cogito* pattern. If you now take a good look at it, you will
see that it does not achieve much and even that only after a fashion.
For one, the conceptual premisses of the ontological kind are so strong
that they make the first step, from (6) to (1), rather trivial. For
another, the conceptual premisses of the second step, which as we just
saw is for the representationalists the decisive one, are all of the theological kind, which under the circumstances is rather unfortunate.

Now for a few concluding comments on the foil.

A knowing, whatever its species, involves an intending. The act's
core—in the foil, the thought "in" it—intends the intention. Intending
is a connection. Thus there are three alternatives. (a) Intending has an
ontological ground which is neither "in" the core nor "in" the intention. (b) The ground is the core and the intention and nothing else. (c)
The ground is the core alone.

(a) is the only alternative open to those who reject the doctrine of
internal relations; (b) is available to the *moderates* among the proponents of that doctrine; (c) to the *extremists*. According to the latter, the
ground of an intending lies wholly in the *relativliche*[32] nature of the
core. Or, perhaps, it lies wholly within the act of which it is the core;
the difference makes no difference for what I am about.[33]

Those opting for either (a) or (b) must face a classical difficulty. We
sometimes perceive objects which are not there; we imagine centaurs;
we often believe what is false; we remember, with or without imagining
them, events which never took place; and so on. In all these cases the
intentions do not, as one says, "exist." That leaves only two alternatives. Either one opts for (c) or one gives those intentions which, as one
says, do not "exist," some ontological status.

I, as you know, reject the doctrine of internal relations for reasons no
argument can reach. (c), if that be possible, I find even more absurd
than (b). So I must choose (a). In the foil, the ground of intending is
the subsistent M. The intentions which do not, as one says, "exist,"
exist in the *mode of potentiality*. Equivalently, in the foil every well-

---

clear that if God can "deceive" us about the conceptual premisses, then what I
here call the *Cogito* collapses completely, not to say trivially. Descartes seemed
to believe that God could so deceive us. Leibniz and Brentano disagreed.

[32] If you don't remember these uses of 'moderate' and 'extremist' or have forgotten what '*relativlich*' means, turn to the end of Section Eight.

[33] See the last two paragraphs of Section Eight.

formed sentence of an improved language stands for a fact either *actual* or *potential,* depending on whether the sentence is either true or false. There is a price to be paid for all this. It is not what some may believe it to be. Yet it is high. Presently I shall give this issue the attention it requires. Let me first spend on another the few words which are all it deserves.

My willingness to pay the price is even greater because of what I just called the even greater absurdity of (c). Many will disagree, pointing out that whatever the problems of other "connections" or "relations" may be, it is sheer common sense that there can be thought of what there is not. As it happens, this is what Aristotle said, and, following him, Brentano. But the majority of those who are now taking this view did not, I think, learn it from either. Rather, they are misled by science. That is why they might ask me the following question: Is it not obvious that certain circumstances inside my organism, if triggered by certain stimuli impinging on it from the outside, may cause my brain to be in exactly the same state in which it would be if I saw a tree even though there is no tree to be seen? I would answer that this is obvious indeed; then add that the brain state is not the act, that science is not philosophy, and that therefore all their question reveals is their implicit materialism.[34]

Another critic, more worthy of attention, who believes that if there were no minds, there would be no need to ontologize potentiality, concludes that this is a prohibitive price to pay for the accommodation of minds. In other words, he believes that if the foil limited itself to the truncated world, it would not be dialectically forced to give ontological status to potential facts. If his belief were true, the price would be prohibitive. So I shall next show why it is false.

The way I use 'exist' in ontology, all it takes to be an entity is to have *some* ontological ground. *The ground of potentiality is the world's form.*[35] Nor can any ontology, of any world, truncated or including minds, be adequate unless its form is given ontological status. The philosophical problems of the truncated world, for instance, cannot all be solved without recognizing that its form exists. Hence, potentiality is not the

[34] Within science, where it belongs, I am as good a "materialist" as any. If you look for reassurance, you will find it, together with a more detailed criticism of ontological materialism, in the "Realistic Postscript" of *Logic and Reality.*

[35] What that means and why it is true I cannot and need not expound once more. But even the merest hint may prompt your memory. The linguistic reflection of the world's form is, roughly speaking, what makes a string of an improved language well-formed or ill-formed, respectively. And this difference in the reflection surely must have a ground in what it reflects.

price, *if any*, which has to be paid for what the critic calls accommodating minds. I say "if any," because, *broadly speaking*, there is no price at all. I say "broadly speaking," because it is true, of course, that in the truncated world there is no *M*. But, then, *M* is merely a subsistent among subsistents. Thus it fits into the ground plan (p. 141). Also, there are good reasons which make introducing it the just price for the introduction of minds.[36]

The attention of another critic, who is very sympathetic to what I am trying to do, has been caught by a phrase: *the way I use 'exist' in ontology*. He suggests, quite reasonably, that I could make things easier for myself by not speaking the way I do. For then I wouldn't offend deeply ingrained verbal habits by insisting that what in a familiar sense does not "exist" at all yet exists in another sense which is anything but familiar. I answer as follows. There are the things and there are the words. *As to the things*, the differences between the two modes are huge indeed and the foil recognizes them all. Yet there is one feature they share. Deep as it lies and hard to grasp as it is, one cannot without grasping it resolve the whole dialectic. *As to the words*, we should not be their slaves, must try to become their masters. It will help us to master them if we recognize that, *given the task, the tradition, and the verbal habits of ontology and ontologists, the proper word for the one feature shared is 'existence'.*

Remember what has been said: The price for ontologizing potentiality is not what some may believe it to be; yet it is high. We know now what it is not. What, then, is it and why is it high? This is where the notion of a criterion comes in, and that is of course why I conclude this section and this Part with these comments.

A fact of the foil is either actual or potential. This, its mode, is an ontological feature of it, just as its category, particularity, is such a feature of a particular. (A mode is of course not a category. I use 'feature' because it is the most noncommittal and nontechnical word I can think of for that purpose.) Yet the foil radically rejects the notion of a criterion. Thus it must consistently also hold, as it does, that when one is presented with a fact, or, synonymously, when a fact becomes the

---

[36] Or, rather, of thoughts. For the distinctive feature of *M* reflects accurately and perspicuously the distinctive feature of thoughts. The former is that $\ulcorner P \urcorner \, MQ$ is analytic or contradictory depending on whether or not *Q* is the same₃ as *P*. The latter consists in that one-one correspondence between thoughts and their intentions by virtue of which "two" thoughts are one if and only if their intentions are the same₃, thus making thoughts (or, if you please, minds) unique in that they alone among things reflect (though not, of course, create) the world's form. See also the conclusion of the essay on "Ontological Alternatives" in *Logic and Reality*.

intention of a thought, one is not presented with its mode. The only "criterion" for mode is contextual, or, as one says, coherence.

(I am sure you realize why I used 'criterion' and, also, why I put it between double quotes. I used it because it is the traditional word; put it between double quotes because, having used it the way I did, I must not also without this precaution use it in the traditional way. If I did, how could I say without confusion that since the foil rejects the very notion of a criterion, its "criterion" is coherence? A "criterion" is more usually called a *criterion of truth*. So it may help if I add that while the foil's *criterion of truth* is coherence, its *theory of truth*, as it is often called, is like that of all realistic ontologies one of correspondence; i.e., it holds that what makes a thought—and therefore, derivatively, a belief, an assertion, and a sentence—true is its intention being actual and not merely potential.)

The two modes are the only ontological features not presented to us. The inclusion of two such features is the price to be paid for the ontologization of potentiality. To see how high it is, remember the discussion I staged in Section Three between myself and a clever opponent (p. 69). Recalling the image we used should help you to recapture the spirit. I put it to him that by insisting that there are coordinate qualities with which we are not presented, he takes a heavy phenomenological cross upon his shoulders. He had many answers. One was that, supposing there are in fact no such qualities presented to us, I was particularly ill-advised in trying to keep him from "postulating" them, provided only they were a dialectical necessity, since I myself did exactly the same thing by introducing the two modes. At this point I asked permission merely to enter two claims which I promised to defend later. Now, as you see, the time when I must defend them has come.

One claim was that there is a significant difference between what is being done in the one case and in the other. Coordinate qualities are simple things. Facts are neither simple nor things but complexes. That makes the distinction between those among them which are actual and those which are merely potential (possible₁) *sui generis* and, even though we are not presented with it, entirely different from the introduction of simple things with which we are not presented. That is why with good conscience I join those who hold that it makes absolutely no sense to introduce potential (simple) things, be they the perfect particulars of γ or the bare particulars and (nonderived) characters of ε. And I conclude this particular argument by pointing out that one cannot really appreciate it unless one grasps clearly the distinction between things and facts. Nor is this surprising, since both the distinction and the argument lie on that level of the dialectic which is the deepest of all. A sort of closure has thus been achieved. The first, systematic half of this book began with the distinction and ends with the argument.

The other claim was that while in the philosophy of space I can make shift without the coordinate qualities, the introduction of the two modes and thereby the acceptance of one ontological dichotomy not presented to us is a dialectical necessity. The first half of this claim, concerning the philosophy of space, I have already supported as well as I can. Nor is it here relevant. The other half is hardly a claim but, rather, a confession. Nor do I have any defense beyond that to which every philosopher is reduced when the chips are down. The price is high, and I am far from certain that even if one is willing to pay it the ever-receding goal of mastering the whole of the dialectic can be reached. But I know of no other way in which the job could possibly be done and I am reasonably certain that all other attempts, including those of the two great thinkers to whom I now turn, have failed.

BOOK TWO
BRENTANO AND MEINONG

Denn die einen sind im Dunkeln
Und die andern sind im Licht
Und man siehet die im Lichte
Die im Dunkeln sieht man nicht.

BERTOLT BRECHT

Part III
Brentano

SECTION TWELVE

INTRODUCTION

IN Brentano's world there are only objects, either minds or bodies. In his truncated world there are thus only bodies; stones, trees, chairs, and so on. Nothing else exists. There are neither universals nor particulars, either bare or perfect or complex. There are no connections, either subsistents or relations. Such a world cannot be structurally consistent unless there are no facts in it and its objects are all simple. Brentano's world, incredible as it may seem, is consistent in this monstrous respect. Examined closely and described accurately, it is seen to be but a desert of simple objects totally disjoined from each other. Its ontology is yet very elaborate. But, then, is it not also incredible that an ontology so patently inadequate should repay the considerable effort which, since it is also elaborate, one must make in examining and describing it closely and accurately?

221

There is no point to introductions whose sole purpose it is to convince the reader that what the author is about to do is worth doing. But there are introductions and introductions. On the one hand, Brentano's ontology is not easy to understand; nor therefore is it easy to describe accurately. That makes it difficult to achieve that alternation of exposition and criticism, both fluent and lucid, or at least not too crabbed and not obscure, which one ought to aim at when undertaking a task of this sort. On the other hand, Parts I and II have put us into possession of a considerable apparatus, developed at least in part with a view toward this task. In this situation an introductory section, consisting wholly of reflections designed to provide some preliminary orientation about matters both strange and difficult, should do some good. I shall present these reflections as a numbered string of comments or remarks. The last is about Brentano's metaphilosophy. The one preceding it indicates how the issues I take up are distributed over the several sections. If at that point you will have a first glimpse of the reasons that led me to select just these issues and to discuss them in just this order, the Introduction will have served its purpose. But I do not feel like starting without first making explicit what I just implied. Both exposition and criticism are selective. For I am not, as a historian of the sort I am not, concerned with Brentano's views on all issues nor with how they developed in the course of his career, but, rather, as a philosopher of the sort I am, with what is interesting about them.

First. What is an object? The examples leave no doubt; nor does our earlier use; yet I want to make sure that there is no misunderstanding. The objects of Brentano's truncated world are the entities which in earlier sections we called ordinary objects but which he himself, whenever he wants to distinguish them from minds, calls *physical objects.* That makes the apple I perceive a physical object. I would rather call it a "perceptual object," reserving 'physical object' for the swarm of molecules, or what have you, by which science replaces[1] the apple. Ordinarily, 'object' will do. Sometimes, though, apples and stones have to be set apart from minds. On these occasions I shall continue to speak as I have for some time and call them physical rather than perceptual objects, thus following Brentano rather than my own preference. For I do not wish to deprive myself of the convenience that lies in borrowing from the author one examines as many expressions as is possible without danger of confusion. But one cannot without incurring grave danger of this sort use one expression for the two kinds of entities

---

[1] For this use of 'replace' and a discussion of the issues involved see "Physics and Ontology" and the "Realistic Postscript" in *Logic and Reality* (University of Wisconsin Press, 1964).

just mentioned, those we perceive on the one hand and those by which science replaces what we perceive on the other. Since we follow Brentano in spending 'physical object' on the former, we must choose another expression for the latter. I shall use 'scientific object'. That makes the swarm of molecules, or what have you, by which science replaces the apple we perceive, a *scientific object*.

Minds, whenever they have to be set apart from physical objects, I shall continue to call *mental objects*. Brentano uses 'psychic' instead of 'mental'. 'Object', as he speaks, has two German equivalents. One is *'Ding'*; the other, *'Gegenstand'*. The latter, though, is ambiguous; also stands for 'intention'. (So, incidentally, does the German *'Object'*.) *'Ding'* is univocal. To be a *Ding*, either *physisch* or *psychisch*, and to be an object, either physical or mental, is one and the same.

Philologically, 'Ding' and 'thing' go together. Notice, therefore, the radical difference between our uses of 'thing' and *'Ding'*, respectively. As I speak, (simple) universals as well as particulars (either bare or perfect) are (simple) things. In his world there are no such entities. Thus, when he must mention them in discussing the views of philosophers with whom he disagrees, he insists that they are not, and does not call them, *Dinge*.

Second. Recall the notion of the ground-plan test. Applying this test to an ontology, one first examines its assay of the truncated world, tries to discover its categories. The latter determine the ground plan. Then one turns to the ontology's assay of minds and the knowing situation. If these further assays require no additional categories, we say that they fit the ground plan. If they do, the ontology has passed the test. If it fails, it is either overtly idealist or at least structurally on the way toward idealism. That is why I speak of a test and of either passing or failing.

Brentano's ontology passes with flying colors. Its minds and its bodies are but subkinds of a single ontological kind. The former and their knowings involve no category not already involved in the assay of the latter. By this test, therefore, Brentano is a realist$_2$. Yet there is a twist so peculiar that attention ought to be called to it without delay. More strongly, a hoax is being perpetrated against which you ought to be warned right away; if only because what in spite of it remains the best order of exposition, which therefore I shall follow, cannot but produce certain impressions; and because eventually these impressions will have to be undone, which would be even more difficult than it is unless the warning has been issued in advance. The hoax is enormous. The distinction between physical and scientific objects is plain. Yet the latter will allow us to pinpoint the former.

An entity of this world of objects and nothing but objects is either a mind or a body. From this formula I started. The distinction we made allows us to probe it with a question. Is a body a physical or a scientific object? The right answer is that it is a scientific object. In Brentano's world, or as I would rather say, more cautiously, *in what he thinks of as his world*, an existent is either a mind or a scientific object. The reasons for the caution will soon transpire. It will be better to attend first to two questions which at this point impose themselves with great urgency. The first asks why the answer I gave is the right one. The second, assuming that it is, inquires into the ontological status in this world of the physical objects about which its author has so much to say, although not, characteristically as we shall see, quite as much as about minds, while about scientific objects we hear virtually nothing.

"What is really there we do not perceive; what we perceive is not really there." The words are mine rather than his.[2] Yet they express accurately what he believed. The colors and sounds we perceive are not anything outside of our minds; to hold that they are involves one in contradiction. Of this he was always firmly convinced. Equally firm and unshakable was his belief that our perceptions are caused by existents outside of our minds and not themselves mental. *Thus he remained all through his life in the throes of the scientific predicament.*[3] *That is one of the things one must never forget when dealing with Brentano.* For the moment, that will do for the first question.

What, then, is in this world the ontological status of the "physical" objects which we perceive (and which therefore I would rather call "perceptual")? If, knowing as yet nothing about Brentano, you permit yourself to be guided by the suggestion implicit in the very plan as well as in the first half of this book, you may venture a guess. You may guess that this world's physical objects are its Third, or, more cautiously, since they seem more like objects than universals in exile, that they play a role and have a status structurally very similar to those of the ideas which are the Third of the prototype. The guess is wrong. There is no doubt about Brentano's *eventual answer*. His physical objects are neither "in" minds nor elsewhere. They are *literally nothing and nowhere*. ("In" minds, we shall see, there are, roughly speaking, only the

---

[2] More precisely, they are a free translation of the last two sentences of the long paragraph on p. 28 of *Psych.* I. Notice that 'perceiving' is here used as I use it and shall continue to use it, for Brentano's *auessere Wahrnehmung*. His *innere Wahrnehmung*, which I shall call knowledge of self, grasps what is really there.

[3] If you have forgotten what is meant by 'scientific predicament', turn back to where it first appears, in Section Seven.

cores of acts intending physical objects.) For the moment that will do for the second question. Where and what is the hoax?

An ontologist in whose world there are minds and bodies is on the face of it a realist₂. In describing his world, the thing to do, or, as I just put it when claiming that there was a hoax, the best order of exposition is to begin with a description of its trunk. What then should I do? Should I begin by describing the realm of physical objects, whose "ontology" is expounded with great detail but which do not really exist? Or should I begin by describing the world of scientific objects, of which we are told nothing, even though outside of minds they are all that exists?

The questions are rhetorical. If one insists on this order of exposition because one believes, as I do, that even under these extraordinary circumstances it is the best, one must begin with describing and examining the ontology[4] of physical objects. To this task I shall put my hand in the next section. Nor do I have any choice in the later sections of Part III, until we shall come to the final reckoning in the last, but to proceed as if this world's physical objects were its Second, even though in fact they are neither its Second nor its Third but literally nothing. That shows what I meant when speaking of a hoax and of certain impressions produced by the order of exposition which eventually must be undone.

As no doubt you begin to sense, the situation is extraordinary indeed. So I shall venture two statements, both very general and most concise. Yet they will (I hope) throw some light on what I have come to think of as the two halves of the Brentano story.

In his world there is no Third. On the face of it he is thus not a representationalist. Yet we shall see that one cannot understand what he says nor why he says it unless one looks at him as one who, while vigorously rejecting some of the worst nonsense in representationalism, could yet not free himself from the fundamental patterns of this nonsensical doctrine and therefore failed in the long run. Or, to say the same thing differently, *even though on the face of it he is not, yet structurally he remains a representationalist.* This is the first remark, or, if you please, the first half of the story.

In his world there are minds and there are bodies. Nor does the assay of the former and of the knowing situations in which they enter involve any category not already involved in that of the former. *On the face of it, he is thus a realist₂. Structurally he is an idealist.* This we shall see in

---

[4] I shall henceforth omit the double quotes. Once the point has been made, they are merely tedious.

the next to the last section of Part III and, in what I just called the final reckoning, in the last. *Eventually he was driven to almost explicit idealism*, or, to say the least, to the most patent structural idealism; not surprisingly and almost inevitably, I would say, since representationalism has no other possible issue. The more profound and vigorous a thinker is, unless he can free himself completely from the fundamental patterns of representationalism, the more likely it therefore is that he will eventually be driven to idealism. This is the second remark, or, if you please, the other half of the story. (It is of course also the reason for the caution I displayed when I said that there are bodies as well as minds "in what he thinks of as his world.") The two halves of the story are each other's converse, as it were. Nor of course are they otherwise unconnected. The hoax, as one would expect, has its part in the plot. But we shall see that it is far from being all of it.

Third. About Brentano's *eventual* answer there was, I said, no doubt. His physical objects are literally nothing and nowhere. *Eventually*, I also said, his structural idealism prevails. Or at least it obtrudes. Both remarks were meant to suggest change. Brentano did not hold the same views on all issues throughout his philosophical career. Change, though, may be either vacillation, or continuous development, or a sudden break. There was occasional vacillation; there was some development; but there never was a break. Seen from within the system, the changes were all corrections and other improvements rather than additions or new starts. Nor need one hesitate to call them improvements even when looking at the system from without, just as one may admire the intellectual courage and the untiring zeal with which they were made. For they are indeed improvements in the very important sense in which a philosopher improves what he has to say by unpacking it even if, as in this case, he thereby merely articulates his failure.

Developments of this sort concern the historian proper more than the analyst. The former may (and in this case I hope will) find them an absorbing subject. I propose to describe and examine the eventual ontology.[5] Yet there is no point in being rigid. Some of the developments one might expect to be cues to either trouble spots or otherwise important joints of the dialectic. If they are and if mentioning them suits my nonhistorical purpose, I shall not hesitate to mention them. Occasionally I shall even add some historical information in a footnote.[6]

---

[5] The earlier contrast (p. 139) between Brentano's single ontology and Meinong's two was thus a slight oversimplification. But you see now why it serves my purpose and does no harm.

[6] The most strategic "improvements," in the order in which we shall encounter

Fourth. In the world we are now entering there are, I claimed, no facts, and all its objects are simple. Can that be literally true? Or, if it is, are there not in it at least some wraiths of fact, or, as I would rather say, not to wear out the image, are there not at least some *near-facts*, just as in the prototype, though there are no classes in it, there are at least Classes. The answer is a narrowly circumscribed Yes. For some facts (I use the word commonsensically), though by no means for all, there are in this world the corresponding near-facts (i.e., something which has a wraithlike ontological status). That makes it advisable that we provide ourselves with a division of all facts.[7] It will prove helpful throughout the rest of the book.

At first sight the division will seem not only quaint, particularly to anyone not wholly unfamiliar with modern logic, but also confused. The confusion is apparent. The quaintness is real. Nor is it just logical

---

them, concern the so-called double judgments, the *entia rationis*, and the perception (not: the ontology!) of space and time.

In the texts, these and some other changes stand out very clearly and, for two reasons, even dramatically. The major reason is that the bulk of the texts consists of short essays and fragments, some of the latter from letters to those who were closest, Kastil, Kraus, and Marty, which were selected, arranged, posthumously edited, and provided with copious notes and introductions, always scholarly, often helpful, sometimes penetrating, by Kastil and Kraus. A minor reason is that while some of these changes were made under the pressure of criticism, largely from these correspondents, some others were resisted by the latter for quite some time. The two editors eventually came to agree with their master. Yet the struggle cannot but show in their work. Personally of equal devotion but intellectually much more independent, Marty held out, never accepted what he thought, correctly, to be incompatible with the realism to which he stubbornly clung.

Alfred Kastil and Oskar Kraus came to Brentano through Marty, whose students they were at Prague. (That is why Brentano sometimes calls them *Enkelschueler*. Meinong and Husserl were his own students in Vienna.) Marty, Swiss by origin, died in 1914, three years before Brentano. He was, like the latter, an ordained priest and one of Brentano's two earliest philosophical friends. Stumpf, who was the other, left the seminary just in time before ordination. Bolzano, too, was a priest. That is what it took to break the Kantian grip on German philosophy.

Anton Marty was the outstanding semanticist in the group, philosophically as well as otherwise. From the glimpses I have had, I am as impressed with his profundity and thoroughness as, alas, with his inability to cut through and conclude. Yet he deserves better than the oblivion which has been his lot. Some information about his work and life is to be found in the two introductions to the two volumes of his *Gesammelte Schriften* (Halle: Niemayer, 1916 and 1918) by Kraus and by Kastil, respectively.

[7] Or, more precisely, from where I stand, of all actual facts. But there is no need for insisting on that at this point.

but also, at least from where I stand, ontological. I shall therefore proceed in three steps. The first merely presents the division. The second dispels the appearance of confusion. In the third I shall explain why the division will be useful to us, not in spite of its quaintness but, rather, because of it.

I*a*. To this kind belong all facts represented by the substitution instances of the schema Brentano writes '*A is B*'. Examples: Peter is blond; this square is red. These are the *positive nonrelational atomic* facts.

I*b*. To this kind belong all facts represented by the substitution instances of the schema he writes '*A is not B*'. Examples: Paul is not blond; this square is not blue. These are the *negative nonrelational atomic* facts.

II*a*. These are the *positive relational atomic* facts. Examples: Peter loves Mary; this tone is louder than that. Upon Brentano's assay of relations they are, as we shall see, instances of I*a*. Thus they have no schema of their own.

II*b*. These are the *negative relational atomic* facts. Examples: Paul does not love Joan; this spot is not brighter than that. Like those of II*a*, and for the same reason, these facts have no schema of their own.

III*a* and III*b*. These are the *positive* and the *negative existential* facts. Examples: (a) There is a dog; (b) there is no centaur. The schemata associated with them by Brentano are '*A is*' and '*A is not*', or, synonymously, '*A exists*' and '*A does not exist*'.

IV. These are the *categorical* facts. They are the substitution instances of the four schemata '*All A are B*', '*Some A are B*', '*No A are B*', '*Some A are not B*', or, in the familiar notation, **a, i, e, o**. We may safely skip the examples.

V. All other facts.

Now for three clarifications. The third deals with an important point. The first two are merely about words. I have borrowed two terms, one from the old logic, one from the new, and used them differently from the way they are used in their original contexts. Once pointed out, these differences need not cause confusion. (The choice of terms is only too often one of the least evil. If you quarrel with mine, I invite you to do better.)

1. The old logic uses 'categorical' more broadly, so that all schemata containing two terms are categorical. Upon this use, which I do not follow, not only the facts of IV but also those of the first four kinds, from I*a* to II*b*, are categorical.

2. In the new logic 'atomic' is used more narrowly. I borrowed the word because I wanted to avoid both 'particular' and 'individual'. No

one would nowadays call a substitution instance of either '$\sim f(x)$' or '$\sim r(x, y)$' atomic, since 'not' is now counted as the monadic "connective," just as in the foil negation is a subsistent. Yet I called the facts in I*b* and II*b* atomic.

3. In the four schemata of IV and therefore, presumably, in all others, '*A*' and '*B*' mark the places of predicates. That makes sheer nonsense out of '*A is B*' and '*A is not B*', the schemata of I*a*, and I*b*, respectively. There are two ways out. One is to replace '*A*' by '*The A*', which changes the schemata into '*The A is B*' and '*The A is not B*'. This works only if the definite description succeeds. The other way is to replace '*A*' by '*Someone A*', which turns the schemata into '*Someone A is B*' and '*Someone A is not B*'. This is what Brentano has in mind, even though, however deplorably,[8] he writes '*A is (not) B*', as, for the sake of the familiar convenience following him, I did.

'*Someone A is B*', though intelligible, is not good English. '*Irgendein A ist B*' is very good German. That, though, is beside the point. The English formula is (I believe) the most accurate and least confusing way to indicate that in the schemata of I*a* and I*b* the nominalist Brentano uses '*A*' as a common name, i.e., as the supposed name of a *single but not further specified* object of the kind *A*.[9]

Notice the difference between 'someone' in the amended versions of the schemata for I*a* and I*b* and 'some' in two of the schemata of IV. In '*Some A are B*', for instance, 'some' stands for 'at least one (either one or several)', while 'someone' stands for '(exactly) one (of a kind), no matter which (if there are several)'.

Having become aware of the distinction between 'some' and 'someone', or, what amounts to the same, between taking '*A*' in these schemata to mark the place of either a predicate or a common name (whatever that may be), one cannot but wonder about the proper reading of '*A is*', the schema of III*a*. Let us for the time being agree on the "modern" reading, which makes '*A is (exists)*' synonymous with '*There are some A*'. Is that what Brentano had in mind? The question could not be more to the point. Yet I cannot even begin to answer it in this Introduction. Notice in the meantime that of the two possible wordings

[8] For evidence, see *Psych.* II, 166. For a first hint of this trouble, see n. 16 of Section Ten.

[9] '*An A is B*' might also do, although I think less well. The equivalents of *irgendein(er)* are *aliqui(s)* in Latin, *quelqu'un* in French, *un certo* and *un determinato* in Italian.

I know of course that according to the nominalists a predicate is but a "common name," but that makes no sense and is a major source of trouble, including the need for this preliminary clarification, in which, as you see, I stick as closely to the words and keep as far away from the things as is possible.

of the example, 'there are (some) dogs' and 'there is *a* dog', the former corresponds to the "modern" reading; the latter is the one I chose.

That should suffice to stave off confusion.

Among the quaint features of the division one stands out. The disproportion between the residual class, V, and any one of the others, or even all others taken together, is striking. The former contains at least[10] the substitution instances of all the schemata of the lower functional calculus, which are infinite in number and include all those of the sentential calculus, with the sole exception of the few in I*a* to IV. This disproportion has two reasons. One is external; the other, internal.

The logic of Brentano, of his circle, and of virtually all his contemporaries was the old logic, Aristotelian or very nearly so. Thus they thought that the variety of sentential form was exhausted by the seven classes I*a* to IV, together with a very minute segment of the residual class, generated by some sentential connections (conjunctive, disjunctive, hypothetical), which the old logic knew under the name of "relation."[11] Naturally, not to say inevitably, these logical blinders also restricted their ontological vision. Thus their ontological assay of facts, such as it was, was circumscribed by the division. This is the external, or, if you please, the historical reason for that (to us) striking disproportion. That shows why the division is useful, or, rather, why it is convenient. The internal, or, if you please, the structural reason why we shall find it not just convenient but also very helpful, lies deeper.

Literally, I claimed, Brentano's world is without facts. Nor, I added, even if one includes its near-facts, as of course we shall, since without them it would be without interest, are there enough near-facts to correspond to all facts. Now I specify. *The near-facts available all correspond to the positive nonrelational atomic facts of I*a*.*

This world thus remains a desert or near-desert, even if for the sake of the interest one colonizes it with near-facts. My world, by contrast, is a jungle. Nor, perhaps, some may insist, just by contrast. If you agree with them, you may suspect me of being unfair to Brentano, making his desert appear even emptier than it is in order to gain favor for my jungle. I shall try to allay this suspicion.

In my world, the foil, there are not only positive atomic facts, negative facts, existential and general facts, but also, most scandalously, potential facts. But you must not allow this great scandal to detract

[10] I say at least because, if you accept the foil, then the residual class contains, in addition, the substitution instances of all schemata of the higher functional calculus, including those with sentential variables, as well as of all M-patterns.

[11] Just remember, from the old logic texts, the triad of quantity, quality, and relation.

your attention from the smaller ones. Speaking commonsensically and without ontological commitment, one says readily enough that Peter's not being blond is a fact. But who is prepared, as I am, to grant ontological status to negative facts? Even nowadays many call it a matter of fact that a certain (nonanalytical) generality is true.[12] But who will insist, as I do, that in spite of all differences between them, such generalities share with positive atomic facts the one and indivisible ontological status of fact?

Even the majority of the distinguished minority who explicitly recognize the ontological status of some facts agree with the Wittgenstein of the *Tractatus* in denying such recognition to all but the positive atomic ones. Dropping[13] the 'near' in 'near-fact' (and ignoring his peculiarly inadequate assay of relations) makes Brentano a member of this majority among the minority. Not dropping it leaves him a member of the Aristotelian crowd. That alone should convince you, not only that I am not likely to be unfair to him by making his desert appear emptier than it is, but also that his ontology repays the effort its study requires, if only because he walked to its lonely end the path whose earlier and easier stretches have always teemed with the many. The villain in the piece is I.

We have already come upon the structural reason why the eightfold division will be useful to us. Some have acknowledged the ontological status of positive atomic facts (I*a* and II*a*). Even in Brentano's reistic universe there are near-facts corresponding to the nonrelational ones (I*a*) among them. The moment one goes further, the resistance sets in. Historically as well as structurally, the main battlegrounds have been three. There is the issue of *negative facts* and that of those facts which the new logic represents by statements containing *quantifiers*. There are the issues connected with an adequate assay of *relations*. In our division the respective kinds are I*b* and II*b*; III and IV; and II*a*. Brentano, who wrestled with all of them, did not even achieve the status of near-facts for any of them, nor, for that matter, for that minute segment of the residual class which he considered. Had he succeeded, we would have had to inquire whether what he did also worked for the remaining bulk

---

[12] I say even nowadays because if they hail from Oxford they consistently couldn't and therefore shouldn't. For there they believe that some nonanalytical generalities, such as everything colored being extended, are linguistic conventions. Thus, since they have no way of drawing a line between these generalities and all others, they cannot consistently say anything else about the latter. See "The Revolt Against Logical Atomism" in *Meaning and Existence* and "Strawson's Ontology" in *Logic and Reality*.

[13] In the next section, after having said what is necessary about these "entities," I shall drop it myself.

of this class. Since he failed we need not bother. That is why the division will be so useful and why, in particular, the inflation of the residual class need not concern us.

Fifth. The eight kinds of *fact* in our classification are one thing; the eight kinds of *judgment*[14] are another. Whether Peter's not being blond and all dogs' being mammals are two entities may be controversial. My judging that Peter is not blond indubitably is one; so is your judging that all dogs are mammals. That is why every serious ontologist, even though he may deny ontological status to all or some of the eight kinds of fact, must yet accept the task of providing adequate assays for the eight kinds of judgment.

A judgment is an act. In Brentano's world, we shall see, an act's being "in" a mind is a near-fact. So is its "consisting" of a core and a fringe. Thus he can, and of course does, accept the task; presents us with assays of the eight kinds of judgment. To the details of how that is done we shall attend later. No details are needed to understand the following remarks. Yet they should help you to find your way through the apparent meander of the exposition.

Realism₂ has a common-sense core. Unpacked, it is known as the correspondence theory of the nature of truth. I shall save words by calling it the *correspondence view.* This bit of common sense is in effect a necessary condition every realistic ontology must fulfill. Every act, or at least every judgment, must have two constituents which are *objective* and *subjective,* respectively, in the following sense. The objective constituent, which I call the core, corresponds to the act's intention. If what the core of a judgment intends is there (in the foil: actually exists), then the judgment itself is true or false depending on whether the subjective constituent, which I call the fringe, is a believing or a disbelieving. If what the core intends is not there (in the foil: exists merely potentially), then the order is reversed, the judgment being either true or false depending on whether the fringe is a disbelieving or a believing.

Brentano's intended paradigm of all judgment is the existential kind

---

[14] I would rather speak of *belief* and *disbelief.* But once more I shall follow Brentano and, whenever possible, use his word, which is also the traditional one (judgment, *Urteil, iudicium*). Descartes, in a passage of the third meditation of which Brentano and his annotators make much, when proposing a trichotomy among acts (*cogitationes*) which, to say the least, is very close to Brentano's *vorstellen, urteilen, lieben-hassen,* speaks of *ideae, iudicia, voluntates sive affectus.* See, e.g. *Ursp.,* p. 45.

Notice that, phenomenologically at least, believing-that-P and disbelieving-that-not-P are two and not one. See E. B. Allaire, "Negative Facts and Belief," *Philosophical Studies,* 11, 1960, 1–3.

(IIIa and IIIb).[15] His assay of it fulfills the necessary condition. So does that of the judgments corresponding to *positive nonrelational atomic facts* (Ia), although eventually, overimpressed with some phenomenological distinctions, he himself came to believe that it didn't. Not so for the remaining six kinds. His assay makes them what he called double judgments. These, we shall see, do not fulfill the necessary condition. The *doctrine of double judgments* is thus an *implicit repudiation of the correspondence view*. Yet his intention always remained realistic₂. That makes this doctrine the *first major breakdown* of his ontology. Or, rather, it is the first we shall encounter in this exposition.

Sixth. In the first of the following five sections of Part III, I shall describe and examine the truncated world of Brentano. More precisely, if you will only recall the hoax, I shall describe and examine the realm of his physical objects. In the second of these sections I shall attend to his assay of minds, excluding the doctrine of double judgments, which will be taken up in the third.

Brentano, like all structural representationalists, insisted on a criterion.[16] Having located it in the subjective constituent of the judgment, which is the gist of his *doctrine of evidence,* he is eventually driven to an *explicit repudiation of the correspondence view*. This is (in the order of my exposition) the *second major breakdown*.

In the next to the last section of Part III, the tangle around the doctrine of evidence will be unraveled. In the sixth and last I shall first examine the assays of space, time, and selves; then proceed to what I called the final reckoning, in which it will be shown how Brentano's explication of 'exists' in '*A exists*', which has its two roots in his reism and in his intended paradigm of all judgments and which in turn is one of the roots of the tangle around evidence, leads to a *third major breakdown* by preventing him from consistently asserting that the scientific objects, which he believes to be the only ones outside of minds, exist independently of the latter.

Seventh. Philosophy today is beset by two great evils. One is the overconcern with metaphilosophy; the other, the mistaking for philosophy of all sorts of talk, psychological, grammatical, and otherwise, about language, or, as I would rather say, with a word that leaves no doubt where such talk belongs, about communication. The two evils are intimately connected. But it is not my intention to explain once more

[15] Where there is no danger of confusion the roman numerals are used for both classifications, of judgment and of fact.

[16] If you have forgotten the difference between a *criterion of truth* on the one hand and a theory concerning the *nature of truth* on the other, turn back to the last pages of Section Eleven.

either why these are evils, or why and how they are connected. Nor do
I wish to dwell at length on Brentano's metaphilosophy. As it happens,
though, the day's evils add to its interest, making it so interesting indeed that it would not be right for me to ignore it completely. But I
shall be very brief and shall not return to the subject, even though, in
his own writings and in those of some of his students, the place it occupies and the attention it receives are considerable.

For Brentano the heart of the philosophical enterprise is ontology.
Yet he was aware and took full advantage of a distinction that makes
him, in the only good and important sense of the phrase, *the first linguistic philosopher*. It will save time if in supporting this claim I lend
my own words to a thought that was lucidly his. The distinction is
between *ordinary language*, i.e., the language we all speak, also when
philosophizing, on the one hand, and a schema of the sort called an
ideal or *improved language*, on the other. Such a schema, which, even if
it were possible, it would be most cumbersome to use for either thought
or communication, perspicuously reflects an ontology. Ordinary language does not. One who understands and appreciates the distinction,
as he did, will also understand and appreciate, as he also did, the two
tools an ontologist can fashion for himself if he attends in the proper
way to language.

One of these tools is the *philosophical critique of ordinary language*. It
helps the philosopher in search of an ontology by examining those features of ordinary language which prevent it from perspicuously reflecting any. The other tool is *reconstruction*. To reconstruct an ordinary-language statement is to transcribe it into an improved language. A
philosopher who proposes an assay may attempt to reconstruct some
representative statements about what he has assayed. These attempts
will serve two purposes. They will reveal whatever lack of coherence or
consistency there is in the assays already proposed; and they will provide cues for others still to be undertaken.[17]

Brentano not only skillfully and quite systematically used both tools,
he was also fully aware of, and most articulate about them; certainly,
as far as I know, much more articulate than anyone before him. That is
why I claimed that, in the only good and important sense of the phrase,
he was the first linguistic philosopher.[18] A few pointers as to what he

[17] These cues will in the nature of things be more specific than those provided
by the first tool.

[18] To recognize this is one thing. That his improved language perspicuously reflects an extreme and utterly inadequate ontology is something else. One may
reasonably suppose that the extremism and inadequacy of the philosophy have
kept the metaphilosophy from receiving the attention and recognition it deserves.

actually did will flesh out the generalities. Then I shall be done with this Introduction.

All existents are objects. That is the reism. It makes the words which stand for objects the very bones of Brentano's improved language. These words are all names, either common or proper. That is the nominalism. A name is associated with a concept (*Begriff*). Concepts, we know, are really ideas. That is where the structural representationalism shows. A name is common or proper depending on whether the associated concept is particular or general,[19] i.e., whether the objects falling under it are one or several.[20] 'Julius Caesar' and 'Jupiter' are proper names. 'Green', which is short for 'something° green', or, more accurately, for 'someone green object', is a common name. Names are in this improved language the only expressions that signify independently. Or, as he says, they are *autosemantic*. That is why I called them the bones of the language. All other words are merely *synsemantic*. This dichotomy[21] is the fundamental idea of his reconstruction.

Homonymy, in the sense of meaning varying with context, and the multiplicity of grammatical form among words (or expressions) standing for entities of a single (ontological) category are part of the price ordinary language pays for flexibility. These are but two elementary insights of its philosophical criticism. Let us see how Brentano applies them to the German '*Object*', translated by 'object', which is one of his key words. Consider the following two sentences of ordinary language: (1) *Jupiter is an object.* (2) *Jupiter is the object of Smith's thought.* In (1), quite reasonably in this reistic universe, 'object (*Ding*)' is taken to be synonymous with 'existent (*Seiendes*)'. So used, autosemantically, it is a common name associated with the most general concept. Yet there is still an alternative. (a) If 'object' stands not only for what is there but also for what it is categorially[22] possible to be there, then (1) is true.

[19] When speaking about *particular concepts* and *general concepts*, I mean, here and always, what Meinong meant. See Section Nine. I say that names are *associated* with concepts, even though earlier in this Introduction I asserted bluntly that there is no Third in Brentano's world, because in this more sensitive context I do not wish to prejudge certain issues. Eventually, we shall see, he came to believe that all our *distinct* concepts are general.

[20] This is not accurate. 'Jupiter' is in this language a proper name, if only because there is a perfectly good particular concept associated with it, even though no objects fall under the latter. 'Round square', on the other hand, is a common name, even though it is an a priori truth that there are no round squares. What makes the difference is *categorial* in the sense of depending on what in this word individuates. There will be much about all this later. In the meantime the inaccuracy will do no harm.

[21] It brings to mind the terminists' dichotomy *categorematic-syncategorematic*.

[22] See n. 20, above, and the first of the two concluding comments.

(b) If 'object' stands only for what is there, or, in his words, for what is *real* (real) or *wirklich* (actual), then (1) is false.[23] In (2), 'object' serves as a synonym of 'intention', synsemantically, and is not, even though like all nouns and adjectives it may seem to be, associated with a concept. Accordingly, it disappears from the transcription, which reads (2') '*Smith is a Jupiter-conceiver*', where 'Jupiter-conceiver' is a common name.

This should give the flavor. Since I shall not burden my exposition with his improved language, the flavor is all we want. I conclude with two comments; the first to impress you with the cleverness of the metaphilosophy; the second to shock you with the absurdity of the philosophy.

First. A linguistic philosopher who tells us that there are no facts, must be prepared to answer the question how he knows what 'fact' means. If he knows his business he will answer as follows: " 'Fact' may of course occur synsemantically, just as one may, and as I do, talk about the word. The issue is whether it has an autosemantic use, i.e., whether some substitution instances of, say, '*A is*' are *names*. One who holds that they are proposes a schematism which does not perspicuously reflect the world's structure. Or, to say the same thing differently, he asserts what, transcribed into the right schematism (i.e., the improved language I propose), becomes ill-formed and is thereby shown to be categorially impossible (impossible₁). As you see, I can say all this without myself using 'fact' autosemantically. Thus, a lover of paradoxically sounding formulations may indeed say that I do not know what 'fact' means." Two remarks will complete the point.

1. Brentano was *literally* asked this question[24] and *very nearly* gave the answer I attributed to the linguistic philosopher. The only reason I say very nearly is that he would not and could not have used 'ill-formed' or 'categorially impossible (impossible₁)', since, as a structural representationalist, he was not in explicit command of the distinction between the several kinds of possibility, impossibility, and necessity. Yet I have no doubt that on some occasions, as, for instance, when answering this question, he did want to set aside categorial impossibility. So I shall not hesitate to do it for him whenever I believe that I express what he himself sensed but could not articulate.

2. Notice the malignant tenacity of the reistic assumption as it appears in the italicized use of 'name' in the next to the last paragraph. It is assumed, or, rather, it is taken for granted that an expression cannot

---

[23] The point does not depend on the circumstance that, if Jupiter existed and we perceived him, what we would perceive when looking at him is not *real* or *wirklich* because it is not a scientific object. (That shows how advisable it is to play along with the hoax.)

[24] By Oskar Kraus. See *WuEv.*, pp. 98 and 202n26.

stand for anything without "naming" it. The foil insists, with the first Wittgenstein, that the radical difference between the two ways of standing for something, of a (true[25]) sentence and of a name, respectively, is one of the pivots of all "linguistic philosophy." That places the assumption. On the one hand, it is but the linguistic reflection of the failure to distinguish clearly between facts (complexes) and (simple) things; on the other hand, it speciously supports reism by a *petitio elenchi*.

Second. What makes a judgment, and, derivatively, the sentence expressing it either true or false? No linguistic philosopher can escape the question. Perhaps you think that while (if I am right) there is no hope for seven of the eight kinds, Brentano may yet be able to answer it for the sentences expressing judgments about near-facts (I*a*). You may think, for example, that (2′) is so assayed that to assert it is to assert that 'Smith' and 'Jupiter-conceiver' are two names of a single object, which circumstance, if it obtains, is, roughly speaking, the near-fact grounding the truth of (2′).

Things are even worse than you think. One must not forget that the intended paradigm of all judgments is existential (III) and that there are in this world no existential facts, neither "near" nor otherwise. Thus, while the judgments I*a* are, as mentioned, the only ones that can be fitted into the paradigm, the way you so reasonably suggested of grounding their truth or falsehood in agreement with the correspondence view is in fact not open to Brentano. We have penetrated to the brink of that void which makes it possible for him, although, alas, not plausible, to construe the *sentence* 'A *is* (*not*)' as synonymous with '*believer-that-*A-*is-*(*not*)', which is a common *name* of the improved language.[26] This is a pellucid linguistic expression of the structural idealism. It also shows how the reism comes in. Just ask yourself what, *if anything*, in this world of objects and (as we shall see) near-objects (accidents) and of nothing else, a sentence could possibly "name" except a judgment, which is an accident of a mind; or what its truth could possibly be grounded in (very circuitously, as we shall see) except the alleged accident of such accidents which Brentano calls evidence.

---

[25] I add 'true' to make clear that my view on potentiality does not enter the argument.

[26] In taking this fatal step he was, as he tells us, guided by a passage in Aristotle (*Met.* 1017a,33), which he cites again and again. This is the passage in which Aristotle most impressively reveals his basic reism by insisting that in '(That) *A is, is* (true)' the second occurrence of 'is' does not signify being-proper but merely being-as-to-truth (ὄν 'ως ἀληθές, *ens tamquam verum*) and therefore nothing outside of minds.

THE TRUNCATED WORLD

EVERY ontologist is a dialectician. Dialecticians argue. Arguments have premisses. Every ontology, therefore, has some *ultimate premisses*. These are of two kinds. Those of one kind, I shall call it the first, are in one respect like the axioms of a scientific theory. Just as a scientist must deduce (prove) all his theorems from his axioms but need not "prove" the latter, so the ontologist need not "prove" an ultimate premiss of this kind. But there are also two differences. One is that ultimate premisses of this kind are acceptable only if they state *obvious phenomenological truths;* the other, that the ontologist's task is not to deduce anything from them, but, rather, to show that the assays they permit are adequate. This task has a positive and a negative side. The former is descriptive; the latter, dialectical. Into the latter, argument enters. An ultimate premiss of the second kind is acceptable only if it is what in Part I was called an *ontological principle;* a proposition being such a principle if and only if it is so fundamental that, on the one hand, it cannot be argued for directly while, on the other, to disagree on it is to disagree on the very nature of the ontological enterprise.

I am sure you know what I mean by 'acceptable'. But it will be better to take no chances. Unless all its ultimate premisses are acceptable, an ontology either is irremediably inadequate, or, at best, it has not been made as explicit as one can, and therefore must, make it.

Two examples will help. (F₁) *When presented with something, I am also presented with its existence.*[1] Otherwise I would not know what it meant for anything to exist. (F₂) *There is a one-one correspondence between entities and their assays.* (F₁) and (F₂) are two ultimate premisses, of the first and of the second kind, respectively, of the foil.

Brentano was a dialectician more formidable than most. Yet he made mistakes, in his ultimate premisses as well as in what he did with

---

[1] Including presentation in imagination and, even, disbelief. This is one of the advantages of admitting potentiality as a mode of existing.

them. These mistakes not only make some of his arguments fallacious, they also hide the true structure. I shall meet the challenge by trying to do three things concurrently. I shall in this section describe the ontology of his truncated world,[2] reveal its true structure, and expose the fallacies.

This ontology has two ultimate premisses, one of each kind. Call the one that belongs to the first kind the first; the other, the second. The first is false. The second is an unrecognized fusion of two propositions. One is a true ontological principle; the other, an obvious falsehood.

(B₁) *Objects are the only existents.* This is the first premiss.[3] It establishes the extreme reism. Thus it is patently false. Yet it will pay to show how its being false follows from two of the foil's premisses. One of the latter is (F₁). According to the other, which is of the second kind, the phenomenological or hard-core use of the ontological key words, such as 'exist', is in ontology the only proper one.[4] It follows that, when presented with an object of a certain shape and color, I am presented with the existence of not only the object but also the shape and the color. That much is immediate. It suffices to falsify (B₁). Whether the shape and the color are grounded in universals or in perfect particulars or, perhaps, in something else, is a further question.

An ontologist's use of 'exist' is either hard-core or special. If the latter, it is a key to everything he does. Brentano's use or meaning, we just saw, is special. To exist, for him, is to *exist separately*.[5]

α is *separate* from β if and only if, with a certain proviso, it is neither categorially nor logically nor a priori impossible that α exists and β doesn't. Or, rather, this is the way I put it, with the narrow use of 'a priori'. Brentano, using the phrase broadly, would simply say that α is separate from β if and only if it is not a priori impossible that α exists and β doesn't. For, as with all structural representationalists, his is the doctrine of the undifferentiated a priori, in spite of some intimations to the contrary, particularly, as we saw at the end of the last section, in connection with his metaphilosophy. The proviso merely forestalls a

---

[2] The richest single textual source for the material in this section is the *Kategorienlehre*. Kastil's notes to it, covering ninety pages of small print, are very useful.

[3] I suppress here and in the sequel the adjective whenever there is no doubt that what is meant is an ultimate premiss.

[4] See *Logic and Reality*, p. 303.

[5] I use 'separately' rather than 'independently' for two reasons; one negative, one positive. Negatively, we have already found a use for 'independent'. In the foil, as you surely remember, all (simple) things are independent₁; all facts, independent₂. Positively, 'separate' goes well with 'separable', which will have to be introduced presently as the best translation of Brentano's *abtrennbar*.

possible blur or unnecessary worry. α may be separate from β even though causally depending on it, whatever the assay of the causal connection in this world may turn out to be. *To exist separately is to be separate from everything else.* Objects exist separately.

The second premiss he calls the principle of the *identity of indiscernibles.* Of the two propositions which it fuses without distinguishing between them, one is ontological, the other epistemological. Call them (oB_2) and (eB_2), respectively. (oB_2) is (F_2). Spelled out, it thus reads as follows: "Two" entities yielding the same assay are literally one (same$_3$) and not two; conversely, if an alleged "assay" fits two (or more) entities, it does not exhaust, and thus is not an assay of, either. (oB_2) is a true principle. (eB_2) is the following obvious falsehood: Two entities such that, if we *were* presented with each by itself, we could not tell which is which, or, what as long as they are so presented amounts to the same, of which we could not tell whether they are one or two, are literally one (same$_3$). I say *were* presented rather than *are* presented because the proposition is also applied to what cannot be presented by itself. One way of calling attention to the absurdity of (eB_2) is to point out that it collapses *exactly the same* and *literally the same.*

The second premiss is about assays. Or so at least I claim. Yet I also make the extreme claim that in this world all entities are objects and all objects are simple. What, then, you probably are asking yourself, is the relevance of assays in a world of this sort?

Its objects are not, like Aristotle's, compounded of form and matter, nor, like Thomas', of essence and existence. Brentano's background being what it is, that lends some initial plausibility to the extreme claim. Literally, I hope you will soon be convinced, it is true. Yet it is also true, as it must be if his world is of any interest, that there are near-facts in it and, corresponding to them, near-things. The best way of getting at these and the "assays" they require is to start from the prototype, surprising as at first that may seem in view of the background, rather than from either Aristotle or Thomas.[6] This I shall now do in four steps. But let me first say that except for an occasional comment we shall through all these steps[7] be able to stay in a cross section. Thus I shall suppose whatever seems more convenient at the time,

---

[6] In the second half of this section, which deals with Brentano's assay of relations, Aristotle will come in with a vengeance. For an explicit rejection of his form-matter doctrine, see *Psych.* II, 243; for an equally vigorous repudiation of Thomas' "*verfehlte Lehre von der Zusammensetzung aller Dinge aus Essenz und Existenz,*" *WuEv.*, p. 129. *Zusammensetzung* is a particularly good word. What is *zusammengesetzt* has constituents and therefore is not simple.

[7] And through all but the last section of this Part.

either that the clusters which in a cross section stand for physical objects are individuated by a place alone or that they are individuated by a place and a moment.

The *first step* can be made in a ternary world *à la* Goodman. Suppose, then, that each object cluster has three categorial constituents, a place, a moment, and a color. Let $\gamma(p_1, t_1, a_1)$ be such a cluster, or, as I shall again say, let it be a *spot* of this world. Call $\gamma(p_1, t_1)$ the space-time *cell* in it. Remember that the latter, since it individuates the spot, is the (momentary) substance$_1$ "in" it. Notice that, since we are going to stay in a cross section, we could have omitted the moment, thus making the cluster binary and p_1 alone the substance$_1$ "in" it.

Brentano propounded through almost the whole of his career an absolute view of space and time. At the very end, not long before he died, he changed his mind. The impact of the change, though considerable, is yet limited. There is much it does not affect at all. That is one of the several reasons why it is convenient to proceed as I shall; attributing to him the absolute view, not only here but wherever it suits my purpose, except for the last section of this Part, where his assay of space and time as well as the late change[8] and its impact will be discussed in detail.

In the prototype and upon the absolute view, the cell $\gamma(p_1, t_1)$ will still be there and itself an object after the spot has been so moved that it "becomes" $\gamma(p_2, t_2, a_1)$. This is the very gist of the absolute view. The way I put it formally overflows the cross section; yet it is as transparent as it is harmless. Still in the prototype and upon the absolute view, the spot and the cell are two objects; the latter, rather obviously, is the substance$_3$ as well as the substance$_1$ "in" the former.[9] In Brentano's world the cell, though not separate from the spot, is yet *separable* from it. But, then, is in this world an "object" thus separable though

[8] The change in the *ontology* of space and time is one thing. Another change, also very late in his life, in their *epistemology*, is quite another thing. Structurally we shall see, the two changes are independent of each other.

For another use of 'absolute' in the ontology of space and time, which I have deliberately avoided, see n. 7 of Section Three.

In the eventual ontology there are still coordinate qualities. That is why the impact of the change is limited. The important difference is that in the eventual assay, unless $\gamma(p_1, t_1, a_1)$ is there, the space-time cell "in" it is not there either. This eventual "relativism" is in some respects like my own, as expounded in the essay on the "Synthetic *a priori*" in *Logic and Reality*. The important difference is that I replace the coordinate qualities by bare particulars exemplifying shapes, durations, and, jointly, the only simple relations of the first type. Of all this much more later, in Section Seventeen.

[9] At this point you may find it helpful or perhaps even necessary to reread all or some of Section Six.

not in fact separate from another really an object? Would it not perhaps be better to speak of it as a near-object, or, more fittingly, as a potential object,[10] since by moving the spot and thereby actually separating what is separable, we may make it one?

I postpone the answer in favor of a comment on "substance," to be followed by a good look at what Brentano has to say about the color in the spot and, in connection with that, about particulars, either bare or perfect, and universals, either simple or derived. Then I shall turn to the question.

The notion of substance$_3$, or, more precisely, momentary substance$_3$, just put us on the track of Brentano's near-objects. The latter in turn will put us on to his near-facts. Thus you may surmise that the "substances$_3$" of his world play a crucial role in it. The surmise is correct. The double quotes indicate that eventually I shall relegate them to the status of near-objects. Structurally that makes little difference. Perhaps you also surmise that his world is like the prototype except that, however strangely, certain subclusters are merely near-objects, i.e., as one might very fittingly say, although we decided not to say it, they exist only potentially, while certain others, even more strangely although in view of his special use of 'exist' intelligibly, are held not to exist at all. We shall see that this surmise, too, is correct. It follows that there are no substances$_4$ and hence, of course, no substances$_5$ in his truncated world. *In this important Aristotelian sense he is not a substantialist. The physical substances about which he tells us so much are all either (momentary) substances$_3$ or the (momentary) substances$_1$ which coincide with them.* As long as that is not clearly seen, it is virtually impossible to understand what he says.

How about the color in the spot? We know of two ways of grounding it, either in a simple universal or in a perfect particular. Brentano rejects both; holds that a ground for the color as such does not exist. He even calls either kind of entity *unthinkable.* The expression suggests that he holds it to be categorially impossible for either simple universals or perfect particulars to exist.[11] Let us see how his two ultimate premisses led him to this strange conclusion.

Consider two spots of exactly the same color. Suppose that in the

[10] My only reason for not using 'potential object' and 'potential fact' instead of 'near-object' and 'near-fact' is that 'potential' stands for one of the fundamental notions of the foil.

[11] Consistently I should therefore, when speaking for him, put double quotes around 'particular' and 'universal'. As to 'unthinkable', consider that the unthinkable is the kind of nonsense which in an improved language becomes ill-formed.

prototype they assay as $\gamma(p_1, t_1, a_1)$ and $\gamma(p_2, t_2, a_2)$, respectively.[12] In the prototype the color is grounded in the perfect particulars a_1 and a_2, respectively, which, though connected by the (alleged) internal relation of equality (exact similarity), are yet two and not one. Brentano argues from his second ultimate premiss, or, more precisely, from the false-hood (eB$_2$), that since a_1 and a_2 are exactly similar, they are literally one. From this he infers that (1) colors are either universals or have as such no ontological ground at all. Hence, if he can also convince himself that (2) there are no universals, he will have arrived at the strange conclusion that (3) colors as such have no ontological ground at all.

(2) he infers from (B$_1$). All existents are objects. All objects are localized. Universals are not localized. Hence there are no universals. The second and the third of the three premisses of this argument are true. The argument itself, we know, is nothing to be proud of. This, though, cannot be helped. It did at least not take us long to discover, in the case of colors, a very major pivot of this ontology: *An object's color has as such no ontological ground whatsoever.* As for colors, so for all other ordinary properties.

Presently we shall explore the implications of this strange proposition. It will pay to take time out for three comments. The first makes a connection with the assay of relations which will be discussed in the second half of the section. The other two dispose of some items which are most conveniently disposed of at this point.

First. The argument for (1) implicitly rejects the notion of an internal relation of "equality." This notion, we know, is problematic indeed, even more so than that of an internal relation in general, of which it is a very special case. An internal relation, we remember,[13] is grounded in the natures of the (several) entities it connects. We also remember that the doctrine of internal relations has two variants. I just stated the moderate version. According to the extremists, the ontological ground of every "relation" lies in a single one of the entities it "connects." Brentano, we shall see, is an extremist. That fits well with his rejecting that internal relation (in the moderate's sense) of "equality" among "discernibles," which is, as we saw in Section Five, the *sine qua non* of an articulate doctrine of perfect particulars.

Second. The argument against perfect particulars applies equally to those which are bare. Brentano is well aware of that. Thus he tells us,

[12] Even though of a single cross section, t_1 and t_2, if in Brentano's world each existed separately and not merely as one of a pair of "substantial determinations," would there be only "equal" yet not literally the same.

[13] If your memory of some of the notions and arguments mentioned in this paragraph needs refreshing, turn to Sections Five and Eight.

not only that *there are no bare particulars*, but also that, like their perfect counterparts, they are *unthinkable*. To this false proposition he
adds the true principle (oB$_2$) and the common-sense truth that there
are, or at least that there could be, objects which agree exactly in all
ordinary properties. From these three premises he then validly draws
the false conclusion that the individuators (substances$_1$) in any two
objects must be (as one says) qualitatively different. In this way he
"dialectically" arrives at a *doctrine of spatial and temporal coordinate
qualities*. (Or, rather, this is for the time being the quickest way of
stating, without doing any harm, the doctrine at which he arrives.[14])
If we are presented with these qualities, or at least with some of them,
everything is well. If, as he eventually came to believe, we are in fact
not presented with any of them, nothing is lost. For in this case we
shall be justified in "postulating" them. This is the import of the
double quotes around 'dialectical'.[15]

Third.[16] The universals of the foil are either *simple* or *derived*. Green
is simple; triangle, derived. The former are (simple) things. The latter,
we called them derived things, have an ontological status all their own
and much weaker than that of things. With this difference goes another.
(Simple) things (particulars and universals) as well as objects are completely determinate; derived things are not, or, at least, they need not
be. E.g., every object exemplifying the universal triangle has three
angles each of which is of a completely determinate size. Yet in the
definition that is associated with the universal angles may not even be
mentioned.

The traditional arguments against universals are two. The first, from
localization, we just rehearsed. Supposedly it disposes of all universals.
The false premiss in it is that all existents are objects. The second argument, from indeterminateness, supposedly adding to the case against

[14] Brentano and his students rather speak of the *species specialissimae* or "last
differences" of space and time. This is not at all unreasonable. Take p_1 and a_1.
Calling them both qualities, though quite proper in the prototype, in their world
obscures the ontological difference between them. To pinpoint the latter, stay in
the cross section, suppress the moment. Then p_1 is by itself a near-object, both
substance$_1$ and substance$_3$, while a_1 by itself is not even thinkable! In traditional
terms, the difference is that p_1 is a *substantial determination*, while a_1, *if there were
in this world such an entity*, would be an *accident*. All this will become clear soon.
As for p_1, so for a space-time cell. But time is in this world even more peculiar
than in others. So we had better stay away from it until Section Seventeen.

[15] The eventual change in the epistemology of space and time here alluded to is
the one mentioned in n. 8, above. The relevant argument about "postulation" is
the one at the end of Section Three.

[16] The distinctions relevant to this comment have been made in the second step
of Section Five.

derived universals, goes as follows: All existents are completely determinate; derived universals are not completely determinate; hence there are no derived universals.[17] The false premiss is that all existents are completely determinate. Brentano not only, as we just saw, made the first argument his own, he also adopted the second (see, e.g., *Psych.* II, 137). Nor is that surprising. He takes (B_1) for granted, combines it with the common-sense truth that all objects are completely determinate, and infers validly that there are no (derived) universals. That does not make his second argument better than his first. But he at least clearly distinguished between the two, which is more than can be said of some.

We are ready for the question I put off. Let α and β be a spot and the space-time cell in it. Or suppress all moments and let β be the place alone. The difference makes no difference. What matters is that, in either case, β is the substance$_3$ (and substance$_1$) of α. In the prototype both α and β are objects and the latter is (with the familiar blur) "in" the former ($\beta \subset \alpha$). The question was whether in Brentano's world β is merely a near-object, i.e., if I may again so express myself, an object that would be there had the spot been moved in time.

The color in α (i.e., in the prototype, a_1) does not as such exist. The cue to the answer lies in this strange proposition we uncovered. To bring it out, ask another question. Are α and β two or one? Brentano is admirably explicit. They are two. Yet there is no existent which is "in" α but not "in" β. From the viewpoint of the prototype, or, much more radically, from that of any complex ontology, this is absurd. The only remedy I can think of is equally radical. This is not, I submit, a complex ontology, not even in the blurred sense in which the prototype is one. That is why I hold that all its objects are simple and reduce its substances$_3$ to the wraithlike status of near-objects. *The ontology is not a complex ontology; its objects are all simple; its substances$_3$ are mere wraiths.* These are but three ways of saying the same thing. We have penetrated to the heart of the matter and laid it bare. The reism is as extreme as it could possibly be.

One may distinguish between α and β, as Brentano does, holding that they are two and not one, or, more accurately, that they would be two

---

[17] The appeal, although not, alas, the quality, of this bit of reasoning is increased by a familiar unexamined use of 'individual'. Those walking this verbal bridge use without noticing it the word in two ways. Once it is used synonymously with 'existent' and hence, in Brentano's case, with 'object'. (Just remember the nominalistic formula: only individuals exist.) Once it is taken to be synonymous with 'completely determinate'. Thus it is either overlooked or explicitly denied that, with the only intelligible meaning of the phrase, a simple universal such as, say, (a definite shade of) green is "completely determinate."

if β were an (actual) object, just as one distinguishes between an "empty" cell and another, "filled with color," both of which in this world are (actual) objects. This is one thing. To ground the distinction adequately is quite another thing. This, we saw, he cannot do. So he hides behind a phrase, tells us that the difference between α and β is merely a *distinctio modalis*.[18] A reist who wants to borrow a pretty phrase from the tradition is never at a loss.

This was the first step. None of the three remaining ones will take us as long, even though for the third and the fourth we shall have to enlarge the universe. The *second step*, on which I now start, can still be made in the ternary world of the first.

If β were an (actual) object, it indubitably would be "in" α, in the sense which 'in' has in all complex ontologies. Equally indubitably, if such an ontology is fully articulated, one of its entities being "in" another is a fact. Since β is merely a near-object, its being the substance$_3$ of[19] α is merely a *near-fact*. That shows how things hang together. *In Brentano's world there are no facts.* This is but a fourth way of saying what has just been said in three others.

Again, in a fully articulated complex ontology two objects do not make a fact unless connected by a further constituent with ontological status. If, for instance, α and β were in the prototype, which we articulated as fully as its irremediable blur permits, β would be a component of $\alpha(\beta \subset \alpha)$. Hence, were it not for the blur, β would be a constituent of α, $\subset$ would be a nexus. Things being what they are, β is merely a pseudoconstituent of α while $\subset$ is merely a pseudonexus.

In Brentano's world there are no connections of any kind, neither relations nor nexus nor pseudonexus. That is but a fifth way of saying the same thing; and it must by now be as obvious as that, from where I stand, at least one connection with ontological status is indispensable. It seems once more as if his ontology could be dismissed out of hand. As it happens, these obvious observations call attention to one of its most intriguing features. After a fashion, there is in it something that takes the place of a fundamental nexus. Only after a fashion, of course, yet in a very articulate and sophisticated way.

β *can* exist without α; α *can't* exist without β. A cell, even if "empty," is an object. Something colored *must* be an object, i.e., a cell "filled with

---

[18] E.g. *Kategl.*, p. 134, with a reference to Suarez' doctrine which makes the *distinctio modalis* different from the *distinctio rationis* on the one hand and the *distinctio realis* on the other, "greater" than the former, "smaller" than the latter. Either that means differences in ontological status among existents, or it means nothing. In Brentano, therefore, it means nothing.

[19] As you see, I avoid 'in', even without double quotes. But we shall soon come upon a suitable label for this "near-connection."

color." What is the nature of these "can," "can't," and "must"? Brentano, holding that by itself or as such, either as a perfect particular or as a universal, a color is *unthinkable*, also *supposes* it to be categorially impossible for α to exist without β existing. β, on the other hand, is separable from α. He expresses this by saying that β is *unilaterally separable*[20] from α. *Unilateral separability is the something which, if anything could, would take the place of a fundamental nexus.* If the diagnosis is correct, then the notion is important. The first of the following four comments will provide us with a convenient phrase; the other three will confirm the diagnosis.

1. Having called β a near-object, and, accordingly, its being the substance$_3$ of α a near-fact, we should consistently call unilateral separability a near-connection. Yet we shall not need to do that. Brentano himself has provided us with a very suitable phrase. He says that (a) β *is modally included in* α.[21]

2. In the prototype (a') $\gamma(p_1, t_1) \subset \gamma(p_1, t_1, a_1)$ corresponds to (a). The reasons why, mistaking it for either a logical (necessary$_2$) or an a priori (necessary$_3$) truth, one may not recognize (a') for what it is, namely, a fact, have been displayed in the story of the lost facts (pp. 63 ff.). All these reasons also operate in the case of (a) with Brentano; only more so; since he supposes (a) to be necessary$_1$. I shall not of course retell the whole story of the lost facts. But it will help if in the remaining two comments we recall the two parts of it which are especially pertinent.

3. Color and place particulars such as, e.g., a_1 and p_1, are one thing; the two universals Color and Place are another. Only nominalists will miss the distinction. If you don't, then you may (and should) recognize that there is a necessary connection (in some sense of 'necessary') between Color and Place while at the same time insisting that there is nothing necessary (in any sense of 'necessary') about *this* color (or, if you believe there are color particulars, any single one grounding it) being at just *this* place rather than at any other. This is a bad gap in Brentano's argument. Since he was a nominalist, he did not notice it. I marked it by italicizing 'supposed' when stating his argument.

4. After a fashion, unilateral inseparability corresponds to $\subset$. But there is in this world nothing[22] that would, in any fashion, correspond to γ. This is pertinent because if, however implicitly, one thinks in terms of $\subset$, he is less likely to notice the gap we just spotted. Or, to say

---

[20] In German: *einseitig abtrennbar.*

[21] In German: *modal befasst.* This is the same use of 'modal' as in 'modal distinction (*distinctio modalis*)'.

[22] Except perhaps the bilateral inseparability of place and moment in the cell. This, though, is clearly beside the point. Nor does Brentano himself pay much attention to it.

the same thing differently, one who, even if only implicitly, thinks in terms of γ, will find it much harder to convince himself of what (I submit) is most implausible indeed, namely, that just *this* color (a_1) necessarily goes with just *this* place (p_1), or, if you please, with just this place and this moment (t_1). This shows in turn how important it is that by itself the color (a_1) of this world, unlike the cell, is not even a near-object. For how could there be a nexus, or a quasinexus such as γ, or even a near-nexus, between what is not even "thinkable" and anything else? Thus if one presents Brentano (justifiably, I believe) as an ontologist who, structurally speaking, thinks in terms of $\subset$, one must also make it crystal clear that he is completely innocent of γ.[23]

The prototype background for the *third step* must be at least quaternary. Suppose, then, that all its objects (clusters in the cross section) contain exactly four perfect particulars such as, e.g., $\gamma(p_1, t_1, a_1, b_1)$, where a_1 and b_1 ground a color and a shape, respectively. As you see, I once more ignore the connection between place and shape in order to provide us with a convenient example. Let us also agree so to use 'α' and 'β' that they stand for '$\gamma(p_1, t_1, a_1, b_1)$' and '$\gamma(p_1, t_1)$', respectively.

In the prototype there are the two subclusters, $\gamma(p_1, t_1, a_1)$ and $\gamma(p_1, t_1, b_1)$. As such they exist. Call them δ_1 and δ_2, respectively. What, if anything, corresponds to them in the world of Brentano? The question is worth asking because (1) β, which in the prototype is the substance₃ of α, is there "in" both δ_1 and δ_2. It must be asked because (2) neither δ_1 nor δ_2 is an object. Moreover, (3) neither δ_1 nor δ_2 is separable from α, since the connection between shape and color is a priori,[24] just as, for the same reason, (4) δ_1 and δ_2 are *bilaterally inseparable* from each other.

Brentano grants δ_1 and δ_2 the status of lesser wraiths. Less fancifully, what he does is best described by saying that he admits not only β but also δ_1 and δ_2 as near-objects, though the latter two with an even more shadowy ontological status than the first. For this (1) to (4) provide two good reasons.

First. Unlike a_1 or b_1 or, for that matter, $\gamma(a_1, b_1)$, δ_1 and δ_2 are not only localized; they are also, by the cell which they modally include, fully individuated; or, rather, they are individuated to Brentano's satisfaction.[25] This, he points out, quite consistently from where he stands, though not making them separable, makes them at least

---

[23] This is one of the pivotal differences between Brentano and Meinong.

[24] Having once pointed out the gap at this point, we may and must whenever it suits us ignore it; otherwise there would be no point in continuing the analysis.

[25] From where I stand, perfect particulars, if there were any, would not only be localized but also individuated "to my satisfaction." The roots of the disagreement, which we have already discovered, are his two ultimate premises.

"thinkable," as, say, a_1 is not. This is one difference to justify the different treatment. On this point he is most explicit, supporting it with a proposition from Leibniz' doctoral dissertation which he either quotes or cites repeatedly.[26]

Second. From where I stand and as I analyze his world, the connection between δ_1 and δ_2 is merely necessary$_3$, i.e., a priori in the narrower sense, as I use the phrase, while that between either δ_1 or δ_2 or α itself on the one hand and β on the other is categorial (necessary$_1$) and therefore "stronger." About this difference he was not quite as explicit as one might wish; nor of course could he be, since he embraced the doctrine of the undifferentiated a priori. Yet I have no doubt that he felt it.

δ_1 and δ_2, I thus submit, while they ought to be counted as near-objects, are yet even more shadowy than the substance$_3$, β. Perhaps you suspect me of making one distinction too many, putting too fine a point of my own on what he does. A look at his words should allay the suspicion.

His use of 'part' is extremely broad, though not therefore necessarily ambiguous; for he is himself aware of some of the differences. For instance, he tells us that though β, δ_1, δ_2 are all "parts" of α, the former, though not an object, is at least a possible object while the latter two, not being separable, are merely "logical parts." His usual term for a logical part is the Aristotelian *'accident'*. But he takes great care to point out the differences between Aristotle's and his own use of the word. Aristotle's accidents, unlike his own, are (I lend his thought my words) more or less like perfect particulars which, not being individuated to his satisfaction, are not even thinkable and therefore not even wraiths or shadows of existents. Also, while Aristotle's accidents are *in* his "substances," in some sense of 'in' which is not at all clear either to Brentano or to myself, each of the latter's accidents, though modally included in an object, includes itself the latter's substance$_3$, which is also its substance$_1$ and, as we know, the only "substance" to be found in the truncated world of this great "Aristotelian."[27] That much for the thing. As to words, it will again be convenient to follow the text. As I shall speak, then, unless something to the contrary will be said, *an accident is a near-object which, being inseparable from and therefore merely a "logical part" of "its" object, is modally included in the latter and*

---

[26] *Omne individuum sua tota entitate individuatur.* See, e.g., *Psych.* II, 203.

[27] The butt of these irony quotes is neither Aristotle nor Brentano but the clichés which as far as I know were spread by virtually everyone outside the latter's circle who wrote about him. One just cannot be a useful "scholar" or "historian" in or of philosophy without grasping the dialectic.

For textual evidence that Brentano's substances are above all substances$_3$, see, e.g., *Kategl.*, p. 128.

itself modally includes the latter's substance₃ which, unlike the accident, is separable.

Before taking the *fourth step* we must once more enlarge the universe. Looking at color more closely, one soon discovers that it is not a single attribute but, rather, three; hue, brightness, and saturation.[28] In the prototype this refinement may be accommodated by putting in place of the single perfect particular a_1 a group of three, say, a_{11}, a_{12}, a_{13}, grounding a hue, a brightness, and a saturation, respectively. But no harm will be done if in order to keep the complication to a minimum we throw saturation out again, thus limiting ourselves to a_{11} and a_{12}.[29]

The connection between hue and brightness is a priori (in the foil: necessary₃). It is also symmetrical; or so at least common sense suggests. Thus one would expect Brentano to make $\gamma(p_1, t_1, a_{11})$ and $\gamma(p_1, t_1, a_{12})$, or, to be for once more accurate than I usually am, one would expect him to make what in his world corresponds to these two subclusters two bilaterally inseparable accidents of α. This is not what he does. According to him, a_{12} is as closely connected with a_{11} as color as a whole is with the cell. As he expresses it, a_{11} and a_{12} are with respect to each other a *secondary substance* and a *secondary accident*, respectively; the former is (relatively) separable from the latter; the latter, not even "thinkable" without the former.[30] Nor is there any reason why there should not be a tertiary accident with respect to which a secondary one is the tertiary substance, and so on; while, on the other hand, $\gamma(p_1, t_1, a_{12})$ is not even "thinkable" and hence not, unlike either $\gamma(p_1, t_1, a_{11})$ or $\gamma(p_1, t_1, a_{11}, a_{12})$, an accident modally included in α. That unpacks completely what was said much earlier (p. 119): *The objects of his world peel like onions.* Two comments will sharpen the point.

First. "Within" the *physical objects* of the prototype there is a single (quasi-)nexus. If, for example, the object (cluster) itself is quaternary, say, $\gamma(c_1, c_2, c_3, c_4)$, then $\gamma(c_1, c_2, c_3)$, $\gamma(c_1, c_2,)$, and so on, are all subclusters and the nexus in all ten of them is the one we called the weak γ. Whatever "grouping" there is "within" the object can be accounted

---

[28] I use 'attribute' as the psychologists use it and 'hue' so that it includes not only what they call chroma but also the white-black series.

[29] In Brentano's physical and psychological color theories hue happens to be more closely associated with saturation than with brightness. But these theories are today completely without interest; and saturation may to anyone not familiar with these matters seem more esoteric than brightness. So I drop the former rather than the latter.

[30] He is very self-conscious about, and not a little proud of, this particular "improvement" as well as the several others by which he modifies the ontology of Aristotle, whom he calls his master. Next to the latter, the philosophers he probably admires most are Descartes and Leibniz. His bête noire is Kant.

for by the a priori (necessity₃). With *mental objects*, we saw, that does not work. The "groupings" required "in" them can only be achieved by further and "stronger" ties which bind more "closely." Or, if one wants to make do with a single additional tie, the one we called ι, one must stipulate that it is not associative.[31] Brentano's distinction among the several orders of substance and accident achieves these "groupings." Thus, *if modal inclusion could really substitute for $\subset$, this distinction of his would do the same for ι.* That is why, even though there is no substitute for the fundamental nexus, what he does instead is so articulate and so sophisticated.

Second. The connection between brightness and hue is patently symmetrical. Thus one is puzzled by his making the former (relatively) unilaterally separable from the latter instead of making them bilaterally inseparable from each other. The puzzlement disappears as soon as one discovers the examples which guided him. These are all mental. We need not anticipate them. It will suffice, first, to mention that all acts will turn out to be accidents of minds; then, to remind you that in the representationalist scheme of things, while conceiving is (relatively) separable from all other fringes, the latter are not even "thinkable" without the former. I say relatively separable because of the core; but conceiving something is of course as complete an act as, say, believing it. Of all this much more later. One thing, though, is clear already. *Brentano models his assay of physical objects after that of minds.* In the charge of structural idealism which I am drawing up against him this is perhaps only a minor count. Yet it adds much to the idealistic flavor.

We have reached the halfway point of this long and important section. So it will be well to take stock. Remember the proposed division of facts, from the positive nonrelational atomic ones (I*a*) to the residual class (V). Of these eight kinds or classes, I*a*, I claimed, is the only one for which Brentano can account, at least after a fashion. A moment's reflection will show you how that is done. Just remember the examples: Peter is blond; this square is red. Peter, or, more accurately in the truncated world, Peter's body, is an object; his blondness, an accident; the fact of his being blond, the near-fact[32] of this accident being

---

[31] See nn. 12 and 13 of Section Eight, also n. 7 of Section Nine.

[32] Having reached this point, I shall henceforth, whenever there is no danger of confusion, drop the 'near' in 'near-fact' and speak of something being modally included in something else as a "fact" or even, occasionally, as a fact. But I shall never call an accident an object; nor shall I so refer to a substance₃, except when discussing the absolutist assay of space and time. Remember, finally, that (if I am right) *Modalbefassung* (modal inclusion) is the only kind of "fact" there is in this world.

modally included in this object. As for Peter and blond, so for this square and red.

Imagine that we could ask Brentano to comment on the division. If he agreed and used 'fact' as we do, here is what he would say: "You made two mistakes. Six of the eight classes you set up are empty. There simply are no facts of these six kinds, although there are of course (as you call them) the corresponding six kinds of judgment. This was your first mistake. All the facts there are, are positive and atomic. Moreover, every relation is grounded in one accident only of only one of the objects related. (I am, as you say, in this respect an extremist.) Hence, since you intended to produce an ontologically perspicuous division that goes as far or cuts as deep as one can, you should have gathered all positive atomic facts into a single class instead of distributing them into two, depending on whether they are, as one says, nonrelational (I*a*) or relational (II*a*). That was your second mistake. This is not to say that, as far as it goes, the dichotomy relational-nonrelational is not legitimate. The point is, rather, that if one cuts as deep as one can it disappears. For, I repeat, details apart,[33] *a relation is merely a special kind of accident.* Hence, if accidents are in my world, which in your niggling way even you grant by calling them near-objects, so are relations. Those critics who insist that there are none are either confused or, at least, confusing. If they were both clear and fair, they would say instead that they judge my assay of relations to be patently inadequate."

Inadequate as it is, Brentano's assay of relations is yet very elaborate, just as its impact, throughout the system, is as great as one would expect it to be if one remembers that the issue is part and parcel of the connections issue[34] and that the latter lies as deep as any. The inadequacy of the assay is patent indeed. Its impact is not; or, at least, it is less so. That makes tracing and uncovering it, accurately and wherever it appears, a major part of unraveling the dialectic. To trace and uncover the impact of something one must know it in some detail. The thing to do next, therefore, is to examine the assay.

Brentano's assay of relations takes off from Aristotle's. So I turn to the latter. First, though, since it is not difficult and may help, let me say in a general way how the two stand to each other. Aristotle, more prudent than courageous, sensed certain difficulties but did not pursue

---

[33] The qualification covers the kinds of relations ordinarily so called which, as we shall presently see, have their ground in "ordinary" accidents rather than in those "special" ones which in this world ground the only "real" relations.

[34] Modal inclusion, which as we just saw takes the place of the fundamental nexus, is accordingly, as we shall presently see, one of the six kinds of relations Brentano distinguishes.

them. Brentano, more courageous than prudent, went to the lonely end
of the road his master had opened. That makes his assay more articulate and therefore more interesting though also more patently, not to
say spectacularly, inadequate.

Aristotle's existents fall into ten kinds, or, as they are called, *categories*. One is that of *primary substances*. These are our objects. They
are the only entities that enjoy full ontological status. Among the other
nine categories is that of accidents. These are Aristotelian[35] accidents,
of course. Structurally, therefore, they either literally are, or, at least,
they are very similar to, perfect particulars; even though the clusters of
such particulars which are the objects of the prototype are structurally
very different from primary substances. For the purpose at hand, this
difference between the two assays, Aristotle's and the prototype's, does
not matter. What matters is, rather, another structural agreement.
More or less clearly, accidents are "in" primary substances in about
the same sense in which the prototype's perfect particulars are "in" its
clusters.[36]

Accident is only one of the "nonsubstantial" categories. Yet they
are, all nine of them, also called the "accidental" categories. For this
there is a good reason. Every existent, to whichever of the nine categories it belongs, is held to be "in" an object in exactly the same sense
in which each accident is "in" one. "Everything except primary substance is either predicable of a primary substance or present in a primary substance."[37]

Relation is one of the accidental categories. The ground of a relation
is thus "present in *a* primary substance." Must it be "in" a single of
the objects related or may it be distributed between them? The answer
is, indubitably, that it must be in a single one. The ground of a relation
is thus an "accident," i.e., something either literally an accident or
structurally very similar to, not to say indistinguishable from, one.[38]

[35] I shall not in these few paragraphs about Aristotle always repeat the adjective, particularly since for the matter at hand the difference between the two
kinds of accident makes no difference.

[36] I say *more or less clearly* and *about the same* because full clarity requires, as
we know, a complete and accurate grasp of the nature of complexes, or, what
amounts to the same, of the distinction between things and facts, that distinction which, as must by now be abundantly clear, is in a sense the main theme of
this book. That is why I struck it in Section One.

[37] *Cat.* 2a,33–35. 'Present in' is a very good expression for "in." What is predicable (e.g., dog) of a primary substance (e.g., Fido) corresponds to the Classes
of the prototype and need not concern us.

[38] Thus I shall not bother to mark this broad use of 'accident' by double quotes.
For support, see *Cat.* 11a,37–40: "Further, if anything should happen to fall
within both the category of quality and that of relation, there would be nothing
extraordinary in classing it under both these heads."

This is the basic premiss of Aristotle's assay of relations. It keeps him from assaying them as connections or, even, as internal relations between accidents, one in each of the objects related, in what I called the moderate version of the doctrine. So I shall call it *the extremist premiss*.

Aristotle, on one occasion (*Top.* 146a,36–146b,5), when trying to clarify the nature of relations, takes the linguistic turn. One object, he points out, stands in a certain relation to another if and only if the former has a property such that the "predicate" naming it contains an expression referring to the latter. E.g., Paul is taller than Peter if and only if there is "in" the former an accident (commonly) named[39] 'taller than Peter', just as, in case he is blond, there is "in" him an accident (commonly) named 'blond'. This is merely another way of stating the extremist premiss. But it is also a very convenient way if one wants to show how, jointly with a second premiss, it leads to a difficulty. From Aristotle to Brentano, this difficulty has been one of the centers, if not perhaps the center, of the dialectic of relations. So we must understand accurately how it arises and what it is.

(a) An object undergoes a change if and only if one of its accidents begins or ceases to exist. (b) An object does not undergo a change merely because it begins or ceases to stand in a certain relation to another. This is the second premiss. Since it has two parts, I shall call it *the bipartite premiss*. It is in the "substantialist" spirit of, and undoubtedly taken for granted within, the Aristotelian ontology.

The difficulty arises as follows. Suppose three things. (1) At a certain moment Paul was taller than Peter. (2) At a later moment Peter has either ceased to exist or so grown in the meantime that Paul has ceased to be taller than he is. (3) Paul has undergone no change whatsoever between these two moments. It follows that the accident (commonly) named 'taller than Peter', which is the only ground of his being taller than Peter is "in" Paul at both moments. Yet he is at the later one not taller than Peter.

This is the difficulty. Presently we shall inquire what Aristotle and Brentano do about it. But it will help if we first illuminate the situation by comparing it with that in the foil. Again, it will pay to say a bit more than is needed immediately. The rest will be needed very soon.

Take two spots, α and β, in a single cross section of the foil. *a* is the

---

[39] Presently we shall see that, *if there were perfect particulars* (*accidents*) it would make sense to say that, if I may so express myself, such a "predicate" is a *common description* of some of them. But the notion of accidents such that it would be a *common name* of them is, *even if there were accidents*, irremediably confused, not to say purely verbal. This way of stating it is therefore also a good way of showing that the extremist premiss itself is irremediably confused. That, though, is right now beside the point.

bare particular in α; b, that in β. l_1 and l_2 are two very narrow rectangular shapes.[40] l_1 is exemplified by a; l_2, by b. l_1 and l_2 are characters of the first type; taller, a relation of the second type between them, or, for that matter, between any two, in the right order, of the series of such shapes. In an improved language, "α is taller than β" must be unpacked as follows: "a and b are the bare particulars in α and β, respectively; they exemplify l_1 and l_2, respectively; l_1 is taller than l_2." Neither shape ceases to exist if the particulars, and thereby the spots, do. The bare particulars of the foil are clearly distinguished from the characters they exemplify. The perfect particulars of the prototype are not so distinguished from the wraiths they "exemplify." These wraiths are Classes of the first type. For either characters or relations of the second type, such as, e.g., taller, there are not even wraiths (p. 103). The roots of this difference are the realism$_2$ of the foil on the one hand and the *nominalism* of the prototype on the other.

The foil explicitly rejects the bipartite premiss, replaces it by (a′) and (b′). According to (a′), objects are series of cross sections. The identity[41] of Paul at the two moments, for instance, is not grounded in the sameness$_3$ of a continuant "in" him. According to (b′), two entities are not even identical, in the familiar Leibnizian sense, and therefore a fortiori not the same$_3$, unless they agree in all properties and all relations they exemplify.

(a′) alone suffices to prevent the difficulty from arising in the foil. The rest will serve very soon.[42]

Aristotle saw and worried the difficulty. Yet he left it in abeyance, partly, or so I suppose, because he was immobilized by two considerations that pulled him into opposite directions while at the same time permitting him the illusion that the problem is soluble, as on his terms it is not.

On the one hand, he held acts to be relational and was well aware that one can intend what does not exist. He concluded that there are at

[40] The letter 'l' is taken from 'length', of course. As to this assay of length, remember what has been said in Section Four about space and "space." It will soon be clear why I avoid 'length', and replace even 'longer' by the awkward 'taller'.

[41] For this use of 'identity', which does not exclude change, see the beginning of Section Six.

[42] It is also needed to distinguish nicely what depends on the nominalism and what on the bipartite premiss. Suppose the identity of Paul to be grounded in a continuant (substance$_4$) "in" him. There would still be no difficulty provided (1) it is recognized that in this case moments must be nonbare entities of some sort; (2) l_1 and l_2 are made universals exemplified by continuants "in" objects; (3) one understands that to say of an object that it exemplifies a universal is in this world merely an ellipsis for saying that it exemplifies the universal at a certain moment (or at certain moments).

least some relations whose terms[43] need not exist. The direction of this pull may be indicated as follows: There is perhaps some sense in which even at the later moment Paul is still taller than Peter.

On the other hand, Aristotle held that relations have the lowest ontological status of all, or, as he himself expressed it (*Met.* 1088a,22): "what is relative is least of all things a kind of entity or substance." The direction of this pull is seen by thinking of it as a tendency toward the moderate doctrine of internal relations: Since these entities have so little "being," their ground is perhaps distributed between both terms so that, after all, Paul will not at the later moment be taller than Peter.

Brentano tackled the difficulty. To understand what he did we must first take a look at another development.

Aristotle himself in his prudent fumblings discovered the notion of the converse relation. Stay with Paul and Peter. By the extremist premiss, the former is taller than the latter by virtue of the accident taller-than-Peter which is "in" him. Hence, by the same premiss, the latter is shorter than the former by virtue of the accident shorter-than-Paul. These two accidents are an example of what Aristotle calls *correlatives* (*Cat.* 6b,26). Let us use the new notion to restate what we know already. Had he been prepared to ground the relation (as well as its converse) in both correlatives, Aristotle could have adopted the moderate version of the doctrine of internal relations, which, inadequate as it is from where we stand, would yet have kept him out of the trouble we are discussing. For the latter arises only if one insists on grounding Paul's being taller than Peter in one of the two correlatives (taller-than-Peter) alone, Peter's being shorter than Paul in the other (shorter-than-Paul) alone, instead of grounding each of them in both.

Paul being what he is, the relation in which he stands to Peter obtains not by virtue of Peter's being John's son, or slender, but, rather, by virtue of his being something°-shorter-than-Paul.[44] If, therefore, one

---

[43] In the traditional terminology, if one object stands in a certain relation to another, the former is called the *foundation* (*fundamentum*) of this relation; the latter, its *term*. The foundation of a relation is thus the term of its converse, and conversely.

[44] Nothing will be lost by omitting the "correlative" argument for the converse. More importantly, one ought to be aware of how improper it is for a defender of the extremist premiss to say, as I just did, that the relation in which Paul stands to Peter does or does not obtain "by virtue" of anything "in" the latter. Apparently this has not been noticed. Nor is that surprising. How could a doctrine so absurd have survived so long and done so much harm without all sorts of oversights, equivocations, and *non sequitur*. Nor of course would I otherwise go to all this trouble.

asserts such propositions as that Paul is taller than John's son, or than something⁰-slender, he refers to the term of the relation by what the medievals called a *determinatio mere extrinseca* (*d.m.e.*), i.e., by an expression mentioning merely what, though "in" the term, is yet irrelevant (extrinsic) to the truth of the proposition.

Brentano almost defiantly proclaims the extremist premiss, which makes the Paul-Peter problem insoluble. He mistakenly believes that he has solved it because, without noticing it, he uses the notion of a *d.m.e.* in a manner that amounts to a *petitio principii*. Understanding accurately what happened requires six steps.

1. As soon as we turn to Brentano, the accidents we are speaking about are no longer perfect particulars but "logical parts" of objects, modally included by the latter and in turn so including their substances₃. Reflection will show you that this difference makes no difference for the argument at hand.

2. Replace the accidents temporarily by universals. In the case of Paul and Peter, for instance, replace the two correlatives by the two characters l_1 and l_2, which I now for the first time openly call two *lengths*, that of Paul (l_1) and that of Peter (l_2). Thus we might as well also replace 'taller' by 'longer'.

3. l_1 is longer than l_2. This relational fact makes 'longer than l_2' an indefinite, or, if you please, a common (see n. 40, above) description of l_1, though not of course a name of it, either common or otherwise.

4. Brentano argues as follows: 'longer than l_2' is a *d.m.e.* of l_1; hence the extremist premiss is true. Thereby he commits a *petitio principii*. If two objects (entities) stand in a certain relation, one may in stating it use a *d.m.e.* for its term by referring to it with an expression which, not mentioning the correlative "in" it, mentions only what is irrelevant for the obtaining of the relation. Hence, to call 'longer-than-l_2' a *d.m.e.* of l_1 is to take for granted what is to be shown, namely, that for l_1's being longer than l_2 everything but l_1 is irrelevant. The next two points suggest two plausible structural reasons or motives for the mistake.

5. This is the place where what has just been said about the foil comes in handy. I suggest, first, that it becomes more plausible, or, at least, that it becomes less absurd to think of 'longer-than-l_2' as a *d.m.e.* of l_1 if, however implicitly, one thinks of the several "lengths" as universals which do not perish with what exemplifies them. I suggest, second, that so thinking of them makes it easier[45] to overlook the

---

[45] I.e., easier than it would be if, as consistently one should, one thought of them as localized and perishable accidents. Brentano, who was an extreme nominalist, was of course not conscious of this motive. But, then, I do not see how any

need for the second-type relation longer. I suggest, third, that the very word 'length' and the imagery that goes with it enhance the illusion of length being a property that is "intrinsically relational." Remember also the resistance against higher-type relations which in Section Five we encountered even in less extremely nominalistic γ-ontologists. These are the reasons why I asked you to replace the accidents temporarily by universals. Now the device has done its job.

6. Concepts differ in generality depending on the number of objects that fall under them. Being-of-length-l_1 is a concept; or, equivalently, 'being-of-length-l_1' is a common name of all objects of length l_1. Brentano argues that what goes for 'being-of-length-l_1' also goes for 'being-longer-than-of-length-l_2'; the only difference being that the concept for which the second expression stands is more general than the first. We of course understand that, even if there were common names, the second expression would not be one, but, rather, a common (indefinite) description of the kind that presupposes a relational fact. Even so, one can see how the way of concepts may become a temptation, strong enough to be called a structural motive, to mistake 'being-shorter-than-l_1' for a common name, which in turn facilitates mistaking it for a *d.m.e.*

An objector interrupts: "The view you attribute to Brentano makes even more manifest the threat Aristotle sensed. One who holds it cannot but insist, not only that Paul is at the later moment actually taller than the man who has outgrown him, but also that he is actually taller than the dwarf I now imagine and shorter than the giants of the old fables, even though neither the one nor the others ever existed or will ever exist. That makes me wonder whether Brentano really held this view."

The objector sees but does not foresee. The threat he sees is real. But he does not foresee the bold maneuver by which Brentano escapes it.

Being taller (longer) is a relation of the kind Brentano calls a *relation of comparison*.[46] The expression is traditional. It implies, by contrast, that there are (in Aristotelian terms) relations without two correlatives. To the extent this is meant or implied, the notion is confused. Yet this is what Brentano meant. Everything I call a relation, with one exception of which presently, is what he calls a relation of comparison.

---

philosopher, even one as strong and determined as he was, could in his implicit thought always avoid the "contamination" of universals. Nominalism is too absurd for that. Of the structural reason in the last comment Brentano was fully aware, used it himself as an argument that *d.m.e.* are "names" of concepts.

[46] In German: *Vergleichsrelation* or *Komparativrelation*.

According to Brentano a relation of comparison so-called is not really a relation. This is the maneuver. More specifically, what one asserts when asserting that Paul is taller than Peter is either that Paul is of a certain length, or, perhaps, that Paul is of this length as well as that Peter is of a certain other. Thus, what seems to be a statement of relation is merely a statement attributing a single "nonrelational" accident to a single object, or, perhaps, it is a conjunction of two such statements.[47] There is nothing "really" relational about either correlative or a relation of comparison. Thus the latter are not "really" relations.

The man has the courage of his convictions. The maneuver proves that once more. It also immediately provokes a question. Are there in his world any "real" relations and what, if there are some, are they like?

The paradigm that shapes his answer is the act. Acts are accidents of minds intending objects which need not exist. Yet intending, according to him, is a "real" relation; an act, an accident which is *intrinsically relational* or *relativlich* (p. 152). This means, if anything, that there is an ontological distinction between the two kinds of accident, e.g., those grounding the color white or being-of-length-l_1 on the one hand and those which ground thinking-of-Caesar on the other. What is this *ontological difference?*

The best answer Brentano can give, or, rather, the best I can give for him, since, though he gives it himself, he is not quite as blunt, is as follows: The color and the length, although not intrinsically relational, also have "relational" names, such as the *d.m.e.* 'brighter-than-black' and 'longer-than-l_2'. They thus have both kinds of name, relational and nonrelational. *An accident that is relativlich has only relational names.* This is the alleged difference.

The answer takes the linguistic turn. Correctly executed, the turn never hurts, sometimes helps very much. In this case it covers a disastrous shift. The answer, we shall eventually see, is epistemological. *Every epistemological answer to an ontological question is a primrose path to idealism.* This particular disaster is the impact which the inadequate relations assay has throughout the system. My strategy in tracing and uncovering this impact is to do everything possible in order to keep

---

[47] In Brentano's improved language the alternatives are expressed by 'Paul is taller than Peter' (one statement) and 'Paul is taller than Peter *is*' (two statements). This we shall understand after having become acquainted in Section Fifteen with his assay of relational judgments, i.e., with his epistemology of relations. For their ontology, see, e.g. *Kategl.*, pp. 120, 166 ff., 237. The last two references, though, like most of the many others one could give, mix the two kinds of assay which it is my strategy to keep apart. On p. 174, for instance, there is the epistemological explanation of the false *Schein der Zweigliedrigkeit aller Relationen.*

ontology and epistemology from being confused. So I shall not pursue; continue later, in Section Fifteen, where I now leave off; turn instead to Brentano's classification of relations; then conclude with a look at one of the classes.

His relations fall into the following six kinds: (a) modal inclusion, (b) relations of comparison, (c) whole-part relations, (d) intentional relations, (e) cause-effect relations, (f) boundary relations.[48]

Notice, *first*, that the class (b) appears in the list even though its members are not "really" relations. The reason for including them is what one would expect. The judgments intending them are of the same structure as those intending the other five classes. Of this, as just announced, later. Notice, *second*, that since in this world the ground of every relation is a single accident in a single object,[49] its relational "facts" are all near-facts. Notice, *third*, the structural difference between (a) and the other five classes. The ground, such as it is, of an accident's being modally included in an object is (roughly) the latter's inseparability from the former. The supposed ground of a certain object's standing in a certain relation is a certain accident's being modally included in it. Brentano must have overlooked this difference; otherwise he would not have included (a) in the list. Nor is one likely to notice it unless he distinguishes between subsistent connections and (those I call) relations. And, again, how can one help overlooking this distinction if he denies ontological status to all connections?

Brentano speaks of cause-effect relations. The foil insists that these connections are not (what I call) relations. His assay of them is one of the weakest parts of the system. Nor is it particularly original. So I

---

[48] I take the list from Alfred Kastil, *Die Philosophie Franz Brentanos* (Bern: Francke, 1951), p. 132. The 320 pages of this extraordinary book are almost completely a patchwork of sentences and paragraphs from Brentano's writings. One who wants to look up something will occasionally find it useful—if he knows and understands the system already. One wonders what sort of man would care to do this sort of pastiche. Yet how can one not be moved by the boundless devotion? Kastil started writing the book when he was in his seventy-fifth year; finished it in little more than a year's time; died before it was published.

[49] Except the apparent and accounted-for exception of 'Paul is taller than Peter *is*'. See n. 47, above.

I use the occasion to add two more comments which may save puzzlement to those who think accurately. (1) An articulate case for the moderate doctrine of internal relations rests, as we know, on "equality." *Kategl.*, pp. 176 ff., consistently assays equality and difference as relations of comparison. (2) As one would expect and as we shall see, the distance between two places is assayed as a relation of comparison. Yet places are not accidents but "in" substances₃. Like those of (c) and (f), these relations are therefore not in this sense accidental. As for space, so (with the usual complications) for time.

shall say no more about it than the minimum we need, where we shall need it, at the beginning of Section Sixteen, as background for his account of the a priori. The connections in (d) are of course those between acts and their intentions. Nothing need be said about them on this occasion. The ones we want to look at are those in (c).

Take several objects; or, since their number makes no difference as long as they are more than one, take two spots in a cross section; call them α and β; suppose that they neither touch nor overlap. *These two objects are assayed as a single third*, call it γ, such that α is a part of γ, as of course is β, thus providing two examples of the whole-part relation. γ is the *whole;* α and β are among its *parts*. Three comments will show how crucial and how striking that is.

1. In this world there are neither sums (σ) nor classes but only single objects.[50] That is why I avoided both 'sum' and 'class'; said instead, a bit awkwardly, that these two objects are assayed as a single third. Yet, obviously, Brentano's wholes, just like Goodman's sums, can do some of the jobs of classes. This is crucial for at least two reasons. For one, arithmetic cannot be grounded adequately without either classes or, at least, some entities which can do some of their jobs. And, as one would expect from a man of his tastes and tradition, the ontology of arithmetic was among Brentano's major concerns. For another, we know already what in the next section will be established accurately, namely, that every act of this world is supposed to intend a single object. Yet we often think of, or otherwise intend, "classes" of objects. E.g., I yesterday perceived a pair of oxen.[51] If there were no wholes, this would lead to a difficulty.

2. Brentano's assay not only disagrees with Aristotle (*Cat.* 3b,16) for whom all objects (primary substances) are "one and single"; it also strikingly agrees with the foil. His wholes structurally correspond to the foil's Sums (S) of bare particulars; hence the similarity between his and the foil's assay of space and time.[52]

3. There is a connection between α and γ; and this connection is of a sort often presented to us. I do not see how anyone could disagree

[50] The epistemological feature that corresponds to this ontological one has already been mentioned in the last section. The intention of an existential judgment is always some*one* object, never *some* (one or several).

[51] This, quaintly, is Brentano's favorite example. The position itself he always held and never abandoned. See, e.g., *Psych.* II, 242–43, in a passage dictated two months before he died, after he had changed his mind on some related questions about space.

[52] For the differences, see n. 8, above, also the fourth comment below. If you have forgotten the foil's assay, you will find what you need in Section Four. When I first proposed it, I was completely unaware of Brentano's.

with either proposition. But one may, and I do, disagree with two others. One may insist, on phenomenological grounds, that what is presented to us on such occasions is (in Aristotelian terms) neither a single accident, "in" either α or γ alone, nor two correlative ones, one "in" α, one "in" γ. One may insist, on dialectical grounds, that even if there were such accidents, presented or not, they could not by themselves ground any connection. We need not rehearse either argument. But we must look more closely at Brentano's assay. The connection, or, as he calls it, the relation, is, he holds, grounded in a single intrinsically relational accident which is "in" the whole, i.e., in the example, "in" γ. The reason given is that while γ could not be what in fact it is unless α were a part of it, so that the former necessarily has the latter as a part, the latter by itself or as such is not necessarily a part of the former.[53] That fits with what we have noticed again and again. The "necessity" or supposed necessity of a fact ($Pt(\alpha, \gamma)$) causes the illusion that the connection in it (Pt) need not be given ontological status.

Two more comments will conclude the line of thought and the section. The first provides one of those checks one ought to make from time to time in order to assure one's self that things keep hanging together. The second is about (f), the last of Brentano's six classes.

4. His wholes, I said, correspond to my sums (S). I did not say that his whole-part "relation" corresponds to my Pt. The reason I didn't is that while his dreamed-up accident "in" the whole is *relativlich*, the relations among the foil's particulars, of which Pt is one, if only these particulars were not bare, would be, from where he stands, relations of comparison. My particulars being in fact bare, they are what I had in mind when pointing out a while ago that, with one exception, everything I call a relation he would insist is a relation of comparison and therefore not "really" a relation.[54]

5. α and β, we supposed, neither touch nor overlap. What happens if they do? Or, to speak with the foil, what happens if the bare particulars "in" them are either contiguous, or overlap, or one is a part (Pt) of the other? If they touch, they raise for him the "problem" of *boundaries*, i.e., of the connection between a boundary and what it bounds. If, say, one of the bare particulars is a part (Pt) of the other, they raise for him the "problem" whether the former is actual or merely potential. A

---

[53] In *Kategl.*, p. xxv, Kastil says the same thing linguistically by pointing out, with commendable accuracy, that while upon this assay 'whole (having-something°-as-a-part)' and 'something°-having-α-as-a-part' are names, 'part' occurs only synsemantically in 'α is a part of γ'.

[54] This exception is, as it were, the converse of his "substantial" relations of comparison, modal inclusion, and whole-part. See n. 49, above.

boundary is for him literally extensionless, either a point without any extension whatsoever, or a line without breadth, or a surface without width, depending on the number of dimensions considered. In this respect he is like those who fail to distinguish between "space" and space. That makes the first of the two "problems" a problem for him. In another respect he does make the distinction, insist as he does that, say, a line is not the "sum" of an infinite number of extensionless points, although partly, alas, for the wrong reason, since he also believes that the very idea of an infinite manifold is absurd.[55] This halfway position is a source of many troubles, which caused him to worry and to write a good deal about the two "problems," and, in connection with them, about (f). The Leibnizian concern with infinity and continuity, the persistent, although inconclusive, attempts to distinguish between "space" and space do him honor. Yet, what he did on either score is completely without interest today. So I shall ignore it completely, except for pointing out that, as we shall see, he holds with his usual consistency that the present is an extensionless "point" in time and therefore not, as so often in the British tradition (as well as in the foil) a specious present so called.

[55] This is not to say that he did not know Bolzano's pioneering attempts to resolve the so-called paradoxes of the infinite. He knew and, alas, rejected them. See his letter cited by Kraus in *Psych.* I, xlvii, also the rather arid *Versuch ueber die Erkenntnis* (ed. Kastil; Leipzig: Meiner, 1925).

MINUDS

IN Brentano's world, there is "in"[1] each cross section of a mind a momentary substance$_3$ which is also its substance$_1$. In this respect minds and bodies are alike. In two others they differ. "In" each momentary substance$_3$ of a body there is a place and a moment; "in" each momentary substance$_3$ of a mind there is a moment but no place. More familiarly, bodies are in space and time; minds, in time only. This is the first, obvious difference. The second is that "in" the several momentary substances$_3$ of a mind there is a single continuant. That makes the latter a substance$_4$ which may reasonably be called a self even though it is not, as we shall see, a substance$_5$. Selves are the only continuants of this world; in its trunk there are none. This striking difference between Brentano's minds and his bodies does not keep his ontology from passing the ground plan test (p. 140). Yet, categorial or not, the role of time is unique; and the difference adds considerably to the idealistic flavor. Nor, perhaps, is 'flavor' strong enough. 'Structure' may not be too strong.

Striking as the difference is, we may safely ignore it as long as we stay in a single cross section, take for granted that (the cross sections of) both minds and bodies have (momentary) substances$_3$, and do not inquire into the differences between the two kinds of the latter. Thus, since it will be possible to stay within a single cross section until we shall come to the last section of Part III, in which I shall gather what

---

[1] Having said what needs to be said about certain matters in the last section, I feel no compulsion to repeat them over and over again and do therefore not hesitate to put the double quotes wherever they might help even though strictly speaking they do not belong. E.g., I write occasionally that the substance$_3$ of an object is "in" it even though it is only modally included in it, just as I write that the place and the moment (or the Self and the moment) of the substance$_3$ of a body (or mind) are "in" the former even though they are (or must consistently be considered as) mutually inseparable.

needs to be said about time and selves, I shall until then treat minds and bodies *as if* they were exactly alike, i.e., as two kinds of (momentary) objects, each of which modally includes a (momentary) substance₃ which in turn is so included in its several accidents.[2] Nor is that all. One may reasonably expect that the minds of the prototype will furnish as useful a background to set Brentano's minds off against as its bodies did for his bodies.

Ignore for a brief moment the distinction between perfect and complex particulars; call them both particulars *tout court*. (Since there is nothing bare either in the prototype or in the worlds of either Aristotle or Brentano, that will for this brief moment be safe.) The acts of the prototype are particulars: Aristotle's are accidents. As before, in the case of bodies, the difference between the particulars of the prototype and (Aristotelian) accidents makes for many purposes no difference. *Brentano's acts are accidents* in his peculiar and unique sense of 'accident'; otherwise there is again no difference. 'Thinking-of-Caesar', for instance, is in his world no more a (common) name than is 'blue'. But just as 'something⁰-blue' is a common name correctly applied to any object which has a "logical part" such that the *differentia modalis* between the latter and the object's substance₃ somehow corresponds[3] to that color, so 'someone-thinking-of-Caesar' is a common name correctly applied to me at any moment at which my substance₃ is modally included in a "logical part" of mine such that the *differentia modalis* between the former and the latter somehow corresponds to that thought; and this "logical part" is of course a Brentano-style accident, presumably grounding that thought.

We see again what we saw in the last section. If one talks accurately about Brentano's accidents, the sentences become rather long. That makes it fortunate that what holds for most arguments of the last section also holds for most others. The difference between the two kinds of accident makes no difference. Wherever it doesn't, I shall, therefore, after the next few paragraphs, either ignore it, or, even, talk about Brentano's act as if it were what would be left of it if one could do what according to him one can't, namely, "subtract" from it "its" substance₃.

The prototype's particulars are either perfect or complex. The former are simple. The perfect particulars "in" the latter are tied by a

---

[2] This is not completely accurate. Toward the end of this section the continuant in the substances₃ of a mind will have to be mentioned. Thus the asymmetry will be acknowledged. But the mention will be passing and no complication will ensue.

[3] I say for once *somehow corresponds* in order to remind you that I reject this "ground" as inadequate. But, again, I shall not compulsively persist.

nexus closer than γ.[4] An act of the prototype is a fringe and a core connected by ι. Thus it is a complex particular. So, unless they are simple, are the core and the fringe. All this we remember from Section Eight; just as we also remember that this complication, i.e., the need for ι, arises only in the case of minds. In the trunk of the prototype, γ alone will do.

In Brentano's world the complication does not arise at all. The problems we solved by introducing at least one further nexus are taken care of by his doctrine of (relative) unilateral separability as applied to substances and accidents of higher order. To see accurately how that works, suppose that I am now thinking of Caesar, then return for a moment to the example we used in the last section, a body of a certain color and brightness (p. 250). Let α, a_1, a_{12} be the substance$_3$, the color particular, and the brightness particular, respectively, yielded by the body's assay in the prototype. In Brentano's world, this body has two accidents or "logical parts," corresponding to $\gamma(\alpha, a_1)$ and $\gamma(\alpha, a_1, a_{12})$, respectively, with the two important provisos that (1) while there is no accident corresponding to $\gamma(\alpha, a_{12})$; (2) $\gamma(\alpha, a_1)$ and $\gamma(\alpha, a_1, a_{12})$ are a secondary substance and "its" secondary accident, respectively, i.e., the former is (relatively) unilaterally separable from the latter.[5] As for this body, so for my mind. In the prototype my thinking of Caesar is an act with a core and a fringe. Call them b_1 and b_{12}, respectively. In Brentano's world, there is literally no core (b_1) as such and no fringe (b_{12}) as such, just as there are no color (a_1) and no brightness (a_{12}) particulars as such. Yet, if β is my substance$_3$ at the moment at which I am thinking that thought, then there are again two "logical parts" or accidents of my mind, corresponding to the prototype's $\gamma(\beta, b_1)$ and $\gamma(\beta, b_1, b_{12})$, respectively, such that what has just been said under (1) and (2) about α, a_1, and a_{12} holds without any change whatsoever for β, b_1, and b_{12}. This is not of course the whole of the dialectic; yet it is one of its pivots.

---

[4] I.e., more accurately, by either a single nonassociative ι or a whole series of ι of varying "strengths." See nn. 12, 13 of Section Eight, also n. 7 of Section Nine and n. 32 of Section Thirteen.

[5] A moment's reflection will show you that for many purposes nothing would have been lost, had I said, as whenever the difference makes no difference henceforth I shall, that, *in the style of either Aristotle or the prototype*, b_1 and b_{12} correspond to what Brentano means by a secondary substance and a secondary accident, respectively. *Psych.* I, 230–31, shows that he understood from the very beginning the strategic importance for his assay of objects in general and of minds in particular, of what I would call the different strengths of several ι (or, equivalently, of a single one which is not associative), which shows in turn that, in spite of his broad use of 'part', he was aware of the differences between the grammar (as one now says) of 'logical part' and of 'geometrical part (Pt)', respectively.

Brentano tried but failed to fit all judgments into the mold of the existential one, either positive (IIIa) or negative (IIIb). This you remember from Section Twelve. Now I specify. Upon his assay every existential judgment has a core and a fringe; the former corresponds to a single idea; the latter is either an *acknowledging* (IIIa) or a *rejecting* (IIIb).[6] Call these the two paradigms, or, more conveniently, whenever the difference between (IIa) and (IIIb) makes no difference, the *paradigm*.

Not all judgments do in fact fit the paradigm. Eventually he himself recognized that; hence the doctrine of double judgments and the first major breakdown of the system (p. 233). Of this we shall hear more in the next section. The point I am about to make now would be important even if the eight kinds of judgment did in fact all fit the paradigm. Or, with a twist, for what I am about the paradigm indubitably provides the key to the system.

Consider the two possible existential judgments about Peter. Or, to put it as I just did, suppose that the core of each corresponds to the single idea of Peter. One of the two, we are told, acknowledges Peter; the other rejects him. What does that mean? A digression will help; then the answer will not take long.

In Brentano's world there is one and only one simple fringe, which he calls *conceiving* (*vorstellen*). This fringe is "in" all others. More accurately, it is unilaterally separable from all others, which makes it their (relative) substance; them, its alternative (relative) accidents. A quick count will show you that the third level has been reached: substance₃, core, conceiving. That makes conceiving a tertiary substance of which all other fringes are alternative tertiary accidents. Or, to say the same thing still differently, what in this world is the *distinctio modalis* between an act which is not just a conceiving, on the one hand, and the conceiving "in" it, on the other, somehow corresponds to what in the prototype is the perfect particular "in" the fringe, which, since it determines the latter's kind, I called its specific constituent.[7] Call this for the moment the conceiving-assay of fringes. To insist that there are

---

[6] In German: *anerkennen* and *verwerfen* (*leugnen*).

[7] See p. 151. If your memory needs refreshing, reread not just this passage but the whole second half of Section Eight. If you do that, you will see that I am now finishing what we then began but were not as yet prepared to pursue. But let me add one comment. I am almost certain that it is unnecessary. Yet, once more, I prefer being tedious to leaving any doubt on a crucial point. My use of 'conceive', here as throughout this book, is technical, as explained in Section Eight. In the foil, there are entertainings but no conceivings. In the prototype, every fringe, unless itself a conceiving, is a complex particular consisting of a conceiving and a specific constituent. The ontologically neutral phrase (in this book) is 'thinking of'.

conceivings and to propose, with either Brentano or the prototype, this way of assaying fringes are virtually the same.

In a world in which there are ideas, there will be conceivings. In a world in which there are conceivings, there might as well be ideas. *Structurally, representationalism and the conceiving-assay of fringes entail each other.* Familiar as it may seem or sound from Section Eight, let us secure this connection.

To conceive something is to think of it without either believing or disbelieving, either explicitly or implicitly, either that it exists or that it does not exist, either now or in the past or in the future.[8] Conceiving something is thus the same as attending to its idea without either believing or disbelieving that the latter either does or does not represent something. We know that and why the very notion of attending to an idea is hopelessly elusive (p. 202). This, though, is here beside the point; for, had it been generally known and understood, the course of the dialectic would not have been what it was. Thus we have already established the connection in the direction from conceiving to ideas. In the other direction it is even more obvious. If there are ideas then one must (as, again, we know) be able to attend to them without any commitment as to whether or not they represent anything. And what, I ask, could it possibly mean to say that one conceives an idea if not that he attends to it in this uncommitted fashion?

The connection is secured. It will help us to keep it before our minds if I state it in three different ways. (1) Ideas and conceivings structurally entail each other. (2) We need no longer clumsily speak of the conceiving-assay. This way of assaying fringes will henceforth safely and more handily be called the representationalist assay. (3) This assay is not just a matter of detail. Anyone who adopts it (without taking Meinong's peculiar way out, of which more in Part IV) is a structural representationalist. I add the reminder that the prototype's is the representationalist assay of fringes. Nor of course is that surprising, since the world which for brevity's sake I so call is (if I am right) the prototype of all representationalist ontologies.

This concludes the digression. I return to the question. According to Brentano, the positive existentialist judgment acknowledges Peter; the negative one rejects him. What does that mean?

Brentano's, we saw, is the representationalist assay of fringes. Structurally, I claimed, that makes him a representationalist. So I shall now try to answer the question by proceeding *as if he were a repre-*

---

[8] As I use 'exist', the last clause ('either now or in the past or in the future') is redundant. But Brentano on time and existence is, as we shall see, most peculiar and peculiarly confusing. So I add the clause for once.

sentationalist, i.e., as if there were ideas in his world and therefore, in particular, the idea of Peter. Should the attempt fail, we can always try something else. If it succeeds, we shall have hit two birds with one stone; having found, not only an answer to the question, but also rather impressive support for the claim that conceivings and ideas structurally entail each other.

To acknowledge (reject) Peter is to conceive the idea of Peter and, in addition, to believe that the latter does (does not) represent something.[9] In other words, the *distinctio modalis* between acknowledging (rejecting) Peter on the one hand and merely conceiving him on the other somehow corresponds to the specific constituent which, from where I stand,[10] is best called *believing-(disbelieving)-that-Peter-exists,* or, equivalently, *believing-(disbelieving)-that-the-idea-of-Peter-represents-something.* This is the answer. Most plausible in itself, and, of course, amply supported by the texts, it is also the only one I can think of. Nor, just as importantly, is there any way of finding it without proceeding *as if Brentano were a representationalist.* Our stone has hit both birds.

Structurally, or, if you please, implicitly, Brentano always was and remained a representationalist. This, though, is only half of the story. Explicitly he eventually[11] rejected representationalism, casting out

---

[9] A glance at n. 14 of Section Twelve will show you that there is also the abstract possibility of so interpreting the negative judgment that it involves belief in a negative fact rather than disbelief in a positive one. This, though, we shall see, is against the spirit of the system. The object of the game, if I may so express myself, is to get negation out of the world and into the mind rather than the other way round.

[10] I say from *where I stand* because there is in this world no kind of fringe which corresponds accurately to believing (disbelieving). There is only acknowledging (rejecting), either "instinctively (blindly)" as supposedly in perception, or "evidently" as supposedly in "real knowledge," or with different degrees of conviction. These, though, are all, if anything, alternative (fourth-order) accidents of acknowledgings (rejectings). Of all this later, in Section Sixteen.

[11] At the beginning he sometimes spoke as if what is presented to me when I am thinking of something, say, a horse, existed, *while it was being thought of,* in a special way or in a special sense, which, with an old phrase, he called *intentional inexistence.* I.e., a thought's "object" supposedly exists *in* it. (Notice the little position game with the prefix 'in'.) I have not the slightest notion what that could possibly mean. Either the "object" is "in" the mind of the thinker, or it is in the Second, or it is a third. The old phrase merely hides an undeclared third. The trouble is that being undeclared does not make it more stable. Another phrase which Brentano also used and which plays exactly the same role is *ens rationis.* Such an entity, too, either is "in" the mind (*ratio*), or it is in the Second, or it is a third.

Propositions, or, as I would rather say, *facts,* were originally also admitted as

even the faintest trace of a Third. To this second half, more extreme as well as more original than the first, I now turn.

Literally, I repeat once more, there are in this world no ideas. For this explicit nonrepresentationalism there are *four reasons*. 'Explicit nonrepresentationalism' is not a very elegant phrase. But it will help us to keep before our minds *the inevitable tension in Brentano's thought between his structural representationalism on the one hand and his explicit nonrepresentationalism on the other.*

Now for the four reasons. The one I shall list first is good and very impressive. Each of the other three is connected with one of the three major intellectual motives for introducing ideas; i.e., to put it as in Section Seven, each is connected with one of the three predicaments representationalism was designed to avoid. None of these three reasons is either good or impressive.

1. Even if there were ideas, what I am thinking of when thinking of a horse is not an idea but something in the Second. When first calling attention to this phenomenological truth (p. 202), I pointed out that it was a cornerstone of the whole dialectic as well as the truism which, being such a cornerstone, it ought to be; then added that to have firmly grasped and steadily held on to it was not the least of Brentano's merits. Now is the time to add to this praise. For by now we completely understand why one who did so grasp and so hold this truth could not but reject representationalism—if only he had the courage which this step then took. Brentano had the courage. This, then, is the first reason. The horse I have in mind is neither an idea nor of course

---

entia rationis. Or, at least, they were sometimes admitted through this back door. Eventually, they were as rigorously kept out as intentionally inexisting *things*. With respect to propositions, Oskar Kraus traced this development, very interestingly and with commendable candor, by the fragments themselves which he selected as well as by his annotations, in *Wahrheit und Evidenz*. E.g., he includes a short fragment, which he dates "not later than 1902," that seems to grant the conceived horse some sort of "existence" *while it is being conceived*. See *WuEv.*, p. 31. There will be some later occasions for a footnote or two on all this. Right now, I merely want you to notice two things.

Notice, first, that I used 'object' within double quotes, rather than 'intention', as you were perhaps led to expect by the adverb in 'intentionally inexisting'. The reason is that what we intend is of course the horse in the Second. (I say *of course* because otherwise I would not have the slightest notion as to what 'intend' could possibly mean.) Brentano, to his honor, always sensed that. See also what will presently be said about the phenomenological root of his antirepresentationalism.

Notice, second, that, *existing only while being thought of*, the inexisting horses of some early passages were never structural universals but, rather, if anything, Lockean "sense data," i.e., particulars which, in an irremediably confused way, were both "in" and "before" minds. That shows the great strength of his nominalism.

"in" my mind but a physical object.[12] As you see, this reason is *phenomenological*.

2. Another reason is connected with the *scientific predicament*. To spot the connection, remember how we decided to use 'physical object' and 'scientific object'; permit me to speak for a moment of the physical and the scientific horse; and imagine a philosopher who behaves as follows. When impressed by the phenomenological reason, he calls a certain entity presented to him a physical horse. When haunted by the scientific predicament, he mistakenly thinks of the same entity as something in addition to and "between" the act and the scientific horse. Structurally, this mistake makes the physical horse into an idea.[13] Thus he will conclude that if there are no physical objects (ideas) but only minds and scientific objects, then the scientific predicament has disappeared. This provides him with a reason for embracing explicit nonrepresentationalism as a way out of the predicament.

Since the connection is structural, I have asked you to imagine a philosopher who behaves in this way. But I have no doubt that the description fits Brentano, if only because he was all through his career haunted by the scientific predicament and did not (if I am right) know how to dissolve it correctly.

3. A third reason is connected with the *skeptical predicament*. As long as ontological status is denied to the mode of potentiality, there are acts without intentions. Just think of perceptual error and false belief. This is the skeptical predicament. Ideas, by serving as the missing intentions, are supposed to provide a way out of it. We know that eventually this gambit fails (and also, very accurately by now, why it fails). This, though, does not matter right now. What matters is, rather, two features of the extremist assay of connections, or, as Brentano would say, of relations. On the one hand, (a) this assay eliminates the skeptical predicament; on the other, (b) it structurally entails explicit nonrepresentationalism.

[12] In the broad sense of 'object', in which both Caesar and Jupiter are objects (p. 235). In the foil this horse is an actual or potential physical *fact*, depending on whether, as he would say, the *Ding* which he takes it to be does or does not exist.

[13] If the words sound forced, consider that at some place such intellectual violence as Brentano's will inevitably break through the verbal surface. My words are consistent; his thoughts are not. I could have made things *seem* smoother by calling the physical horse what he himself often enough calls it, namely, a phenomenal object or *phenomenon*. But, then, somewhere in this book I would have had to pay a very high price for this verbal convenience; and I have enough on my hands as it is. This, therefore, is one word from which, since I could, I did stay away. But take note of the fact that he himself used it quite frequently, particularly in the earlier part of his career.

(a) must by now be obvious. With respect to (b), remember that an act occurs *if and only if* something is "before," or presented to, the mind of its owner. According to the representationalists, this something is an idea (or ideas) "before" the mind (or the act). According to the extremist assay, there is in all cases (i.e., not just in those of perceptual error, false belief, and so on) literally nothing "before" the mind. To say that an idea or, for that matter, anything else, is presented to a mind is merely a figure of speech. The 'if and only if' I just italicized is taken to stand for 'same₃'. There is always only the "presentation," i.e., the act itself; never anything "presented."[14] Hence, ideas are never presented, which with the latter being what they are, is but a way of saying that there are none.

This time the connection is a bit more complex. So I shall restate it in terms of a "reason." Concern with the skeptical predicament provides a reason for accepting the extremist account and, with it, the explicit nonrepresentationalism it entails, because the latter offers a way out of the skeptical predicament.

4. The reason connected with the *nominalistic predicament* is a bit sweeping, of the axe rather than the scalpel variety. Yet one need not, I think, apologize for a rare stroke of the axe if, as I do, he spends most of his time wielding the scalpel, particularly when the purpose is to illuminate a certain broad connection rather than to strengthen, with still another "reason," the case for there being one.

The nominalistic predicament is the impossible task of managing in a world wholly without universals. Ideas being structural universals, one may nurse the illusion that they can do the jobs which (as we know) only real universals can do and that one will therefore, by introducing them, escape the predicament. Brentano was so resourceful and so embattled a nominalist that he believed he could manage in a world wholly without universals. Why, then, should we expect him to countenance ideas?[15] Or, to say the same thing differently, he was so extreme a nominalist that he rejected even the shadowy universals of the

---

[14] The act, or, more precisely, its core is thus not made to coincide with the idea. The complete freedom from this Lockean confusion is one of the great merits of Brentano. Its price, alas, was absurdity. But, then, is not absurdity much better than confusion?

The scientific horse may or may not be there. But it is of course never presented, nor, more importantly, either intended or in any other intelligible way connected with the act. Thus it remains forever beyond reach. Of this later, in Section Seventeen.

[15] See the last remark in n. 11, above. The connection became even more striking when, after having changed his views on (the epistemology of) space and time, he taught that, (making use of the usual figure of speech though of course without ontological commitment) *all our (distinct) ideas are general (universal)*.

Third. Thus, since the Third is essentially a realm of (structural) universals, he got rid of it.

You know that I judge representationalism to be untenable. Yet I also believe (and said) that the last three of the reasons against[16] it which we just canvassed are neither good nor impressive. It may help if I indicate briefly why I hold this belief. The absurdity of nominalism disposes of number 4. About each of the other two I shall say two things. (3a) The extremist assay is untenable and the proper way of dissolving the skeptical predicament is to recognize the ontological status of potentiality. (3b) One who holds that what is presented has no ontological status whatsoever, does not use 'exist' with its hard-core phenomenological meaning. Yet this is, by an ultimate premiss of the foil, the only proper way of using it in ontology (p. 238). (2a) The proper way of dissolving the scientific predicament is to "replace" the physical object by the scientific object.[17] (2b) The alleged way out makes the physical object structurally an idea. Thus it undoes the advance made by insisting on the phenomenological reason, which as I claimed and as we have by now confirmed, is the one good and impressive one among the four. (This "undoing" reveals the tension I just spoke of, between the structural representationalism on the one hand and the explicit nonrepresentationalism on the other.)

I turn to two dialectical aspects of what we have so far learned about Brentano's assay of the act.

First. In the foil the intentionality of the act is ontologically guaranteed; in Brentano's world it isn't. The proposition contains the new notion of an ontological guarantee.[18] I shall explain this notion and, at the same time, demonstrate the proposition. My main purpose is in fact to introduce the notion, which will soon prove useful, not to say indispensable. The proposition merely states in a new way what we know already.

In the foil a fact is an act *if and only if* it is a bare particular exemplifying a species and a thought. A character (F) is a thought *if and only if* there is a fact (P), either actual or potential, such that FMP.[19]

---

[16] Or, equivalently, *for* explicit nonrepresentationalism.

[17] This dissolution had to be mentioned before and will have to be mentioned again. In the meantime, see the references in n. 1 of Section Twelve.

[18] I adopt and adapt this notion from Douglas Lewis' study of Moore in L. Addis and D. Lewis, *G. E. Moore and Gilbert Ryle: Two Ontologists* (Iowa Publications in Philosophy, Vol. 2, Nijhoff, 1965).

[19] I write deliberately 'F' rather than '$\ulcorner P \urcorner$' in order to keep out what does not belong. But I shall return to the point and then send you back to this footnote. The analyticity of 'FMP', though crucial in some contexts, does not belong either. But the categorial force of the two occurrences of 'if and only if' is of the essence. *For only what has such force is guaranteed by the ontological ground plan.* If you ask

The force of the two occurrences of 'if and only if' is categorial. E.g., it is impossible₁ for anything to be a thought without there being an existent (though perhaps only in the mode of potentiality) which it is about as well as another (though only a subsistent) which connects the two.

An objector interrupts and tells me that the mode of potentiality is problematic to say the least and that M is only too patently *ad hoc*. I reply that he has lost sight of what I am about, probably because he finds these two features of my ontology so objectionable. He forgot that I am not now making a case for my ontology. I am merely using it to explain the new notion by pointing out that, objectionable as it may be, it provides, because of the two features which he thinks make it so, an ontological guarantee for the intentionality of the act. Brentano's ontology clearly doesn't. Or doesn't he himself insist that the intention of an act does not need to have any ontological status whatsoever, just as there is in his world never a connection, of either intending or being presented or perhaps attending, between an act and either its intention or the idea, which, as one says, in what he insists is merely a figure of speech, is before the mind of its owner?

Second. Reread the following passage from Section Eleven: The representationalists hold, or take it for granted, that there is a priori or conceptual knowledge and that to have such knowledge is to know some connections among ideas. The ideas of their worlds, or, as I put it, the Third, thus does four jobs rather than three. It not only relieves, or, rather, seems to relieve, the three predicaments of Section Seven; it also provides, or, rather, seems to provide, a new ontological ground for maintaining in *the old way* the distinction between the two kinds of knowledge (p. 206).

Brentano, too, takes it for granted that there is a priori knowledge. Yet there are in his world no ideas. One cannot attend to what is not there. For him, therefore, it is a mere figure of speech to say that a priori knowledge is knowledge of connections among ideas. Thus he has a problem. He must look for *a new way* of grounding the distinction between the two kinds of knowledge. In Section Sixteen we shall examine his way. Right now I merely want to alert you to the connection. If it were not for his explicit nonrepresentationalism, he would not have to face this problem.

---

why they have such force, I shall answer because they could be replaced by 'means', used in a certain way with which we are already familiar. Given this ground plan, that is what it means to be an act; and so on. This is one thing. The impossibility₃ for a bare particular of this world to exemplify a thought without also exemplifying a species, and conversely, is quite another thing. See also n. 5 of Section Three.

We have learned a good deal about the minds of this world by learning everything we shall need about its structural representationalism on the one hand and its explicit nonrepresentationalism on the other. What else ought we to find out about these minds? I propose to do two more things. First I shall take up the issue of self-knowledge. Then I shall show how the judgments intending positive nonrelational atomic facts (I*a*) can be made to fit the paradigm.

Numerous philosophers, throughout the tradition, including recently Brentano and G. E. Moore, have taught that there is one privileged fringe. The Germans speak of *erkennen* and *Erkenntnis*. In English philosophical discourse the use of 'knowing' and 'knowledge' is often limited to these situations. Speaking as we ordinarily do, without ontological commitment, we all use 'knowing' and 'knowledge' very frequently. I, as you know, even use them generically, for all fringes, quite deliberately, of course, as a way of emphasizing that in the foil there is no privileged fringe for which they might reasonably be reserved. Thus I cannot now use these very common words for something which (if I am right) is merely a philosophers' will-o'-the-wisp. My way out is to qualify them by an adjective, calling *infallible* what Brentano and Moore, when speaking philosophically, call *Erkenntnis* and knowledge, respectively. In print a typographical device will often suffice. Whenever there is no danger of confusion, I shall write *knowledge* and *knowing* when what I mean is infallible knowledge and knowing infallibly.

In my world, I repeat, *there is no infallible knowledge.* Yet the impact the notion has had on the tradition could hardly have been greater.[20] The dialectic of self-knowledge in particular, particularly since the rise of representationalism, is virtually dominated by it. So I open the discussion of Brentano's assay of self-knowledge with some remarks on the dialectic of *knowing*.

What does it mean to *know* something? It is easy to state a necessary condition. If I know that *P* then *P* is the case. Or, equivalently, I cannot know that *P* unless '*P*' is true. To see that the condition is not sufficient, one merely has to remember that those who propound the doctrine that there is *knowledge* use 'believing' and 'knowing' so that one may (correctly) believe what is the case without *knowing* it.

I can think of two ways to unpack '*knowing*'. One is to make the sentence (S) 'If I know that *P* then *P*' analytic (necessary₂). This way is hopeless or even worse.[21] There is no viable explication of 'analytic'

---

[20] Anthropologically, it is all part and parcel of the unending quest for certainty, or, rather, for security, to still our unending fears. This, though, is not a treatise in anthropology.

[21] Unhappily, this is what G. E. Moore tried to do. I say *unhappily* and I said

that makes (S) analytic. The other way is to justify the alleged privilege by an ontological guarantee. This is where representationalism and, with it, the notion of a criterion (p. 198) comes in. Brentano took the way of the ontological guarantee.

A glance at the foil will provide us with some notions as to what an ontological guarantee of *knowing* might be like. There, as you know, the fringes and the cores are the simple characters I call species and thoughts, respectively; an act is a bare particular exemplifying both a species and a thought; the latter is by the subsistent *M* connected with the act's intention. Imagine now a world which is in all respects like the foil except that there is no *M* in it and each fringe is a relation connecting a thought with its intention. In this world all fringes would be privileged in exactly the same sense in which some claim *knowing* is. What makes the difference is the difference, in its very ground plan, between relations and subsistents. A relation, unlike a merely subsistent connection, can only connect what is actual. Let me make the point once more, in a slightly more general way. In a world such that by its ontological ground plan a relation can obtain only between what is actual and not merely potential, all fringes assayed as relations enjoy for their "infallibility" an ontological guarantee. As you see, we have merely rehearsed the reasons why in the foil the connection between a thought and its intention is assayed as a subsistent and why I hold that there are no *knowings*. This, though, is incidental to our purpose, which we have also achieved. We now have some notions as to what an ontological guarantee of *knowing* might be like.

In a representationalist world, knowledge (not: *knowledge*) is either indirect, i.e. by means of an idea (or ideas) representing its intention; or it is direct, in the broader sense, i.e., without anything "between" act and intention. Such knowledge is either direct in the narrower sense or reflexive. Representationalism, we also know, sharpens the desire for a criterion, i.e., for something "in" either the objective (core) or the subjective (fringe) constituent of the act which is there if and only if the latter's intention is actual and not merely potential. Being thus located, a criterion could not possibly be an ontological guarantee of "infallibility." That merely confirms what we knew already. The notion of a criterion is epistemological. Many representationalists, including the

---

or worse because these fumblings of his are among the antecedents of the Oxford philosophy. (S) being true is supposedly (part of) what '*knowing*' means; a proposition true by virtue of what the words in it mean is supposedly a "linguistic" truth; such truths supposedly are analytic; and so on. The pattern is only too familiar and I have dealt with it elsewhere more than once. See, however, for this particular "contribution" of Moore, the long footnote on pp. 317–18 of *Logic and Reality*.

structural representationalist Brentano, thought that they had found one.[22] That is why the distinction is of the essence, particularly in the case of Brentano, who does two things which must be distinguished. He insists—successfully within the system, as we shall see in a moment—on an ontological guarantee for *knowing*. This is one thing. His criterion, we shall see in Section Sixteen, is an alleged (higher-order) accident of acknowledging and rejecting; he calls it evidence. He also insists, as consistently he must, that whenever we *know* something we know it evidently. This is another thing. I continue my policy of doing everything possible to keep epistemology and ontology from being confused (p. 259) by ignoring in this section his criterion completely. In Section Sixteen I shall account for its artificiality and general unsoundness by trying to show that it was tailored to fit such *knowledge* as he claimed there was.

Self-knowledge has always been a strong candidate for *knowledge*. For this there is a phenomenological reason which has nothing to do with representationalism. The foil accounts for this reason by making what I call (direct)[23] acquaintance a species by itself, with a unique flavor of its own. I also grant, of course, that, in fact and with some reasonable qualifications, we have so far not needed to "correct" self-knowledge. But if you urge me to acknowledge that such knowledge is "incorrigible" or "infallible," I shall reply that either you mean what I just said, in which case we have no quarrel, or I do not know what you mean.[24]

In the representationalist scheme of things there is a further reason which makes self-knowledge an even stronger candidate for *knowledge*. Indirect knowledge of either bodies or minds can at best be supported by a criterion. Thus, if one insists on an ontological guarantee, the only candidates that remain are either direct[25] knowledge of either self or ideas (or both) or reflexive knowledge of self.

Brentano insists on an ontological guarantee for *knowledge*. Nor are there in his world any ideas. That leaves self-knowledge as the only candidate and only one question. Is it direct or reflexive?

[22] *This is of course another impressive symptom on which to base the diagnosis of structural representationalism.*

[23] The protective parentheses mark a different use of 'direct'. As I use it in this book, all knowledge in the foil is direct, none is reflexive.

[24] Nor would my answer be essentially different if a critic, trying his luck with still another word, wanted to convince me that while I may well doubt whether what I now see is my typewriter, it does not even make sense for me to say that I doubt the bit of self-knowledge that I am now seeing something, and that therefore this bit is "indubitable." But see, for all this, the "Realistic Postscript" in *Logic and Reality.*

[25] I.e., here and in the rest of this argument, direct knowledge in the narrower sense.

The extremist assay determines the answer. If every act is a *relativliches* accident, then there can be no ontological guarantee for knowledge that is direct (whatever that may mean upon this assay) but not reflexive. Brentano, therefore, insisting that there be *knowledge*, holds, as consistently he must, that every act, in addition to whatever else it may know, ἐν παρέργῳ also *knows* itself.[26] Every act thus has two intentions. An act of either conceiving or acknowledging or rejecting a horse, for example, has as its *primary intention* the horse; through its *secondary intention* it reflexively *knows* itself. Nor is there in this world any other kind of *knowledge*.[27]

[26] The textual evidence for all this, including the requirement of an ontological guarantee which must dovetail with the scope of evidence, is so massive and so pervasive that I refer only to what is probably the earliest statement in *Psych.* I, 196–99. For the argument how by this *eigentuemliche Verwebung* an infinite regress is averted, see *Psych.* II, 138. The point is, very simply, that whatever the fringe of the *primaere Bewusstsein* may be, the *sekundaere Bewusstsein* is always a *knowing*, not only of the former but also of itself. Phenomenologically all this makes to me no sense. This, though, is not now my concern. I merely explore the dialectic of his gambit. For the Greek phrase, see n. 1 of Section Ten.

[27] That recalls the problem, mentioned earlier and put aside for later consideration, which he must solve if he wants to claim, as he does, that a priori knowledge is *knowledge*.

Even reflexive knowledge cannot reasonably be claimed to be knowledge without what I just called some reasonable qualifications. Brentano very carefully details them all, mostly under the heading of evidence. We need not join him in the pursuit of matters which, since they do not really affect the dialectical issues, may safely be left to the efforts of the descriptive phenomenologists. But there is a related question which, though not very relevant to what follows, is of considerable dialectical interest. So I shall confine it to the rest of this footnote. (For an anticipatory reference to it, see n. 6 of Section Eleven.)

Reflexive knowledge carries in any world its ontological guarantee. That eliminates the standard argument against assaying the connection between this very special act and its intention as a (simple) relation. In the foil there are no (simple) reflexive relations, either of self-knowledge or of anything else. Nor do I have the slightest notion what such a relation would be like. This is one thing. The related question, whether the very notion of such a relation ought to be rejected on categorial grounds, is another thing. I shall give three reasons why it ought not to be so rejected. (1) *Phenomenologically*, the image that guides us in the ontology of relations, of a line or thread between two points, draws great strength from all the arguments against both versions (moderate and extreme) of the doctrine of internal relations. So I ask, as far as this image is concerned, what is wrong with a "loop" starting from a point and returning to it? (2) Syntactically, the rule by which, if '. . . x . . . y . . .' is well-formed, so is '. . . x . . . x . . .', has stood us in good stead in constructing an improved language for the foil. By this rule, if '$r(x, y)$' is well-formed, so is '$r(x, x)$'. Nor of course is it difficult to find examples if one admits expressions standing for derived things as substitution instances for either 'x' or 'r' or both. (3) Two things may be identical (in the familiar Leibnizian sense) without being the same[1]. Let a and b be two

Every judgment of the class I*a can be made to fit the paradigm.* We are ready to examine this proposition, which is the last task of this section. First, though, I shall make three preparations; first propose an agreement about words; next select an example; then attend to an issue which I raised earlier but did not pursue, partly because we were then not yet fully prepared to do so, partly because we have only now reached the point at which we must face it.

Remember Peter, who furnished us with an example for the paradigm. Its core, I pointed out (p. 184), corresponds to the single idea of Peter. Now that we have convinced ourselves that there are in this world no ideas, we see that it would have been more accurate to say instead that if the example is assayed in the prototype, its core corresponds to that single idea. Brentano himself, however, speaking freely of the ideas presented to us as well as (in his own way) of the one-one correspondence between cores and ideas, does not deprive himself of these figures of speech which he often finds convenient, except of course when he makes it his business to convince us that they are just that and no more, namely figures of speech. Nor need we be more abstemious than he was. Let us agree, then, that whenever it will be convenient we shall in discussing his world speak as if there were ideas. The main reason I find it convenient is that this way of speaking plots his world against the prototype, which in turn makes it easier to apply to the former what we have learned in constructing the latter.

This spot is red. Call this proposition (F); let it be our example. Call the spot α. Nothing will be lost if we take α to be so simple that, assayed in the prototype, it becomes a ternary cluster. Suppose, then, that (in the prototype) $\gamma(p_1, t_1, a_1)$ is the spot; a_1, the color particular in it. In the foil (F) is a single atomic fact. In the prototype, we remember from the story of the lost facts, it splits into two; (F$_1$) E!α, and (F$_2$) $a_1 \subset \alpha$.[28] (F$_1$) is existential; (F$_2$) is really only a pseudofact. Since we are in a representationalist world, there are also the two ideas, of α on the one hand, and of red, or perhaps of something°-red, on the other. Nor is it easy to see how either of these two ideas could fail to be somehow

---

such things of a world in which there is a (simple) relation R. Depending on whether $R(a, b)$ or $\sim R(a, b)$, '$a = b$' will entail either '$R(a, a)$' or '$\sim R(a, a)$'. Thus a well-formed (and true) sentence would entail what is ill-formed. One may express this by saying that in a language in which '$r(x, x)$' is rejected as ill-formed, the distinction between sameness and identity could not be expressed.

The idea of (3) is not mine but wholly E. B. Allaire's.

[28] 'α' and 'E!α' stand for '$\gamma(p_1, t_1, a_1)$' and '$(\exists x)(\exists y)(\exists z)[\gamma(x, y, z) \cdot (x = p_1) \cdot (y = t_1) \cdot (z = a_1)]$', respectively. Remember too, that both (F$_1$) and (F$_2$) are easily overlooked or at least not recognized for what they are; the former, because α is assayed as a "thing"; the latter, because it is easily mistaken for analytic.

involved in what in such a world is presented to the nonperceptual judgment-that-F. But it will pay in the end if for a while we ignore (F_1), consider only the *nonperceptual* judgment-that-F_2.

We know that the representationalists' perceiving involves only a single idea. Is that true of all acts? This issue, between the *pluralists* and the *monists* (p. 181), we must now face. Again, nothing will be lost if for the time being we limit ourselves to the (nonperceptual) judgment-that-F_2. The pluralists hold with Locke that it involves the two ideas of α and of red; the monists agree with Brentano that it involves only one. How shall we settle the dispute? I shall demonstrate the following proposition: A representationalist untainted by Locke's confusion but unaware of a certain possibility either will side with Brentano or cannot avoid an "anthropomorphic" mistake very similar to the one the representationalists make in their assay of perceiving (p. 191).

In the foil the core of each act is a thing which, though simple, corresponds to a fact.[29] Of this possibility no one has been aware. If one isn't, it is impossible to see how either of the two ideas could fail to be *somehow involved* in what is presented to the judgment.

The deliberate vagueness of the phrase I just italicized has something to do with the confusion that caused Locke to collapse core and idea. Without this confusion the issue can be stated as follows: *How many ideas correspond to the core of the judgment-that-F_2?* Unlike the notion expressed by the italicized phrase, that of the one-one correspondence between cores and ideas is clear.[30]

There is also the abstract possibility that the core of the judgment is a fact. Upon this alternative, the pluralist may try to claim that the two ideas correspond to the two categorial entities "in" the fact which is the core. This is, as far as I can see, the only way of giving a clear meaning to the proposition that the core corresponds to two ideas. Some philosophers,[31] probably under the influence of the Lockean tradition, have opted for this alternative. Yet it is dialectically untenable. This I have

[29] This fact is in the Second, of course. Right now, though, that makes no difference. There remains the abstract possibility of simple ideas representing facts. The structural reason no one has availed himself of it is, very simply, that ideas are structural universals and universals are things, either simple or derived, but surely not facts.

[30] As far as this argument is concerned, there is therefore no difference between Brentano, in whose world there are no ideas, and a representationalist who does not collapse them with the cores to which they correspond. Again, we are impressed with the superiority of Brentano's absurdity over Locke's confusion.

[31] E.g., the author of the *Tractatus*. See 5.542 and what is said about it in the essay "Stenius on the *Tractatus*" in *Logic and Reality*.

shown elsewhere. Nor, even if I hadn't, would we need to tarry, since Brentano, the prototype, and the foil all agree that cores are things. Literally, as I use 'things', that is true only of the foil. Brentano assays cores as accidents. But the difference clearly makes no difference. The cores of the prototype, unless simple, are "things." The irremediable blur of this ontology structurally forces its proponents to side with the monists. Their mind is made up for them, as it were, without their having to face the issue. That is why they are in danger of making mistakes when suddenly brought up against it.

Remember that the expansion of (F_2) is $a_1 \subset \gamma(p_1, t_1, a_1)$. Suppose that the cores corresponding to the two ideas are, respectively, a_1^* and $\iota(p_1^*, t_1^*, a_1^*)$. Notice that there is also the pseudofact $(F_2^*)a_1^* \subset_\iota \iota(p_1^*, t_1^*, a_1^*)$.[32] (F_2^*) does not justify the claim that the core of the judgment corresponds to both ideas.[33] This claim is in fact mistaken. Just consider the following argument. (1) The core cannot be a fact, or even a pseudofact recognized as such, but must be a "thing." (2) The only "thing" that could possibly serve as core of the judgment is the complex particular $\iota(p_1^*, t_1^*, a_1^*)$. (3) But $\iota(p_1^*, t_1^*, a_1^*)$ is α^*, which corresponds to the idea of α. (4) Hence, since the correspondence between cores and whatever they correspond to is one-one, α^* cannot also correspond to (F_2). Yet, alas, the mistaken claim is made plausible by the anthropomorphic image in which the mind arrives at the judgment by bending over α^* and examining it, as it were, thus discovering (F_2^*).

The implicit reism finally has caught up with the prototype. It cannot provide an articulate assay of the judgment-that-F_2. Nor of course can Brentano. Yet in the short run he does better than the prototype, being able, at least in this case, to maintain consistently the monistic position, although only at the price, which will prove too dear, of forcing the judgment into the mold of the paradigm. But we will not, I fear, be able to understand what he does in order to provide himself with the single idea that requires unless we first recall a belief he shares with all empiricists.

A mind furnished with several ideas can by "combining" them in several different ways "make" several others. This is the shared belief. Brentano recognizes several such ways.[34] One is conjunction. A mind

---

[32] In case you have forgotten what '$\subset_\iota$' stands for, turn to p. 145.

[33] I.e., to repeat, the idea of α and the idea of green, or, in our original notation, $\overline{A}$.

[34] For a list, see *Kategl.*, pp. 43–44. Speaking now of conjunction and making later on $\overline{A}$ and $\overline{B}$ the ideas of objects in the style of Meinong, I merely brush aside subtleties which either have been discussed already or which do not affect the dialectic and are therefore without contemporary interest.

furnished with the ideas $\overline{A}$ and $\overline{B}$ can conjoin them into the idea-of-something-both-A-and-B. We ask two questions. (a) Under what conditions does all this make sense? (b) In what sense, if any, are the ideas a mind "makes" out of others "complex"? We cannot answer without remembering what has been said at the end of Section Six.

(a) Unless a mind either is a continuant or at least has one "in" itself, there surely is no sense in saying that it now "makes" something out of what has been presented to it at some earlier moment or moments. It is doubtful indeed whether it makes any nonanthropomorphic sense at all. Be that as it may, there is a continuant in each mind of Brentano's world.[35] Nor does he claim that in "making" ideas minds are "active" in a sense not compatible with the thesis of scientific determinism (p. 123). Or, equivalently, his selves are substances$_4$ but not, or at least not in the poignant sense, substances$_5$. Thus, once more, he stands out. (b) To believe that something is (ontologically) complex merely because the mind has "made" it out of two or more other things is to commit a genetic fallacy (p. 124). In Brentano's world, we know, nothing is really complex. Hence, no idea is really complex. More accurately, no core is really complex. Completely accurately, no accident corresponding to a core of the prototype is really complex. Yet, unless the genetic fallacy is explicitly recognized, there remains a haze of ambiguity. Brentano's cores are slightly blurred by this haze. Somehow, in some ontologically relevant sense, some of them seem to be both "simple" and "complex."

Recall now what Brentano is up to. He wants to provide himself with a single idea such that the core corresponding to it can serve as the core of an existential judgment that will do as an assay of the judgment-that-F. Here is what he does. Let $\overline{A}$ and $\overline{B}$ be the ideas of something$^{\circ}$-which-is-P_1-and-T_1-and-colored and of something$^{\circ}$-which-is-a-place-and-a-moment-and-red, respectively. *He assays the judgment-that-F as the existential judgment which acknowledges something$^{\circ}$-both-*A-and-B. (Thus the two ideas $\overline{A}$ and $\overline{B}$ are both "somehow involved" in the judgment.) Notice that I just said (F), not (F$_2$). A moment's reflection will show you that, being a positive existential judgment, the proposed assay accounts *eo ipso* for (F$_1$). That is why I said at the start that it would pay at the end to ignore (F$_1$) for a while.

Two comments will conclude this section and, at the same time, prepare us for the next.

First. Let C be the idea of *something$^{\circ}$-which-is-*P_1-*and-*T_1-*and-red*. What, if any, is the difference between acknowledging something$^{\circ}$-both-

---

[35] This is the one place where the difference between minds and bodies enters the argument of this section. See n. 2, above.

A-and-*B*, or, what upon the proposed assay amounts to the same, judging that *this spot is red*, on the one hand, and, on the other, acknowledging something⁰-which-is-*C*, or, equivalently, judging that *this red spot exists*. The best answer one can give is that of the two single ideas (and, therefore, cores) one is somehow "complex," while the other is not. Once the haze has been blown away, one sees that this answer does not stand up. Yet the difficulty, if any, is merely phenomenological, i.e., the phenomenological difference, such as it is, between the two intentions does not, as far as I can see, cause any dialectical trouble. Brentano, however, became so impressed with it that eventually he gave up the assay. Of this later.

Second. What we have done fits what I believe to be a rule of thumb. In the trunk of this world nothing is literally complex. The only substitute or would-be substitute for real complexity is provided by modal inclusion, which does not go very far.[36] Hence, since the ontology is very elaborate, there must be other substitutes. The place to look for them is its minds. In the case at hand, the specious "complexity" of some cores enables Brentano to give an articulate and, within limits, successful account of the judgments I*a* even though the facts I*a* are in his world merely near-facts. Now to generalize. If a philosopher who repays study moves toward idealism by impoverishing the trunk of his world, you will probably in its minds find some substitute or would-be substitute for every entity he has suppressed in its bodies. This is the rule of thumb. I shall call it the *conversion rule*.

---

[36] I express myself very concisely yet I trust at this stage without danger of confusion.

DOUBLE JUDGMENTS

A TRAVELER setting out on a journey through strange country provides himself with a map which he will then consult from time to time. Our map is the Introduction to this Part. But I shall reword rather than merely restate the passages (p. 233) we ought to consult at this point of our journey through the strange world of Brentano. That will permit us to take advantage of what we have learned in the meantime. Nor will it do any harm if we continue with the familiar example, letting it again stand for the whole class Ia.

"Ordinary" representationalists cannot adequately assay the judgment that this spot is red. Why this is so we just saw. Having assayed the core of *every* act as a "thing," they did not know what core to assign to *any* act that intends a fact. In the case of the example, Brentano avoids this difficulty by assaying it as an existential judgment, i.e., as an act acknowledging something which is both this spot and red. Or, as I would rather say, in order to bring out the structural representationalism, upon his assay the mind, while conceiving the single idea of something which is both this spot and red, also believes that it represents something. That is how for *some* acts[1] he solves—or, rather, that is how he dodges—the problem on which the "ordinary" representationalist founders. Examining this move, first in itself, then for what it suggests, eventually in the light of a further move which would neither be possible nor even seem plausible without it, one discovers three connections which make it the proximate source of the structural idealism. That makes it so "extraordinary" that I shall henceforth call it Brentano's *first move* rather than the solution of anything.

Each member ($c_i{}^*$) of the class of all cores corresponding to a single idea ($\overline{C}$) is a thing (or, in the prototype, a "thing"). In his world the idea ($\overline{C}$) of something which is both this spot and red is, though "com-

---

[1] I.e., for the judgments Ia.

plex,"[2] a single idea. This is one half of the move. The other half turns a judgment of the class Ia into one of the class IIIa which acknowledges $\overline{C}$. This we saw at the end of the last section. We also saw how, on the side of the First, the specious complexity of the c_i^* substitutes, in the sense of the conversion rule, for the genuine one of the fact that this spot is red.[3] Now we must try to understand accurately what the move implies on the side of the Second.

The positive nonrelational atomic facts Ia are beyond doubt the most palpable of all. Yet the judgments Ia upon this assay acknowledge what is represented by a single idea. An entity so represented is in this world neither a fact nor, for that matter, a near-fact, but a single object.[4] Structurally, therefore, to say the least, the intention of a judgment Ia is upon this assay a single object. That is how the reism prevails and one more reason why the near-facts which for the sake of the structural interest I admitted are wraiths indeed. Anyone who thus suppresses the most palpable facts of the Second[5] takes a giant stride toward idealism. This is *one of the three connections* between the move and the structural idealism. Or, if you please, this is the fatal weakness of this move, even if considered in itself. But there is also a strength which if so considered it preserves. Realizing this strength will help us to retrace another of the three connections.

As Brentano assays it, each judgment IIIa consists[6] of a single core and a single fringe, which are its objective and subjective parts, respectively, and of nothing else. Thus it fulfills the necessary condition for every realistic$_2$ ontology which we called the correspondence view (p. 232). This is the strength.

A *second connection* is provided by what the move suggests. If all judgments could be forced into the mold of the paradigm, or, as I shall also say, if they could all be *reduced*, then the core of every judgment would be a single idea. Thus the problem on which the "ordinary"

---

[2] In this section, unless something to the contrary is said, the double quotes around 'complex' always mark the illusion of complexity produced by the genetic fallacy.

[3] I.e., to be for once more accurate than should be necessary, it substitutes for the genuine complexity of the fact or complex which according to the foil the act intends.

[4] I.e., some*one* single object (of the kind C).

[5] Or, for that matter, of the First. This, though, is beside the point. What counts here is the severe impoverishment of the Second, together with the tendency toward substitution in the sense of the conversion rule.

[6] I do not hesitate to use '*consist*' instead of the usual 'in', since the complexity, in any sense, of any entity of this world is dubious indeed. Nor, on the other hand, do I refrain from speaking occasionally of the *constituents* of an act.

representationalist founders, of assigning at least prima facie plausible cores to judgments intending facts, would be solved. Or, rather, as it was put earlier, in the light of the eventual unhappy ending, the problem could be dodged. That spots the suggestion. Having made the move and by means of it reduced the judgments Ia, one will naturally be tempted to reduce the remaining six classes. Brentano succumbed to the temptation and accepted this program of reduction. Trying to carry it out, he proposed assays which, confused as they are and vague as they remain, yet leave no doubt that none of them consists of a single fringe and a single core and nothing else. Thus they do not fulfill the necessary condition.[7] This is the second of the three connections between the move and the structural idealism. Or, as it was put earlier (p. 233), this is the first major breakdown of the system.

The main task of this section is to demonstrate that none of the six assays in question satisfies the necessary condition. The *third connection* will be one of the major topics of the next section. So I shall not now say anything about it.

In the foil an existential judgment such as, e.g., my now believing that there is a[8] red spot, intends a fact of the kind called existential. In his world, a judgment he calls existential either acknowledges or rejects what, being presented by a single idea, cannot be but objects.[9] Nor is this just a feature of existential judgments. Every judgment and, even more generally, every act, including that of conceiving, intends objects. Nor again has this sweeping claim been suggested by the doomed program of reduction. Structurally at least,[10] the connection runs in the opposite direction. *In this world it is categorially impossible for an act to intend anything but objects.* If this claim lies as deep as its sweep-

---

[7] In the rest of Part III, unless something to the contrary is said, the *necessary condition* always is the condition we called the correspondence view, which every realistic$_2$ ontology must fulfill.

[8] Notice that I say neither 'this' nor 'someone' but 'a'. The existential fact of the foil is $(\exists x)C(x)$. That in Brentano's world the corresponding concept $\overline{C}$ is particular, in the Meinongian sense that only one object falls under it, is beside the point. Yet this is a feature which can easily become a source of confusion. Of this more in the next section.

[9] I say *objects* because positive and negative existential judgments are held to be particular and universal, respectively, in the sense that while each of the former acknowledges some*one* object of a certain kind, each of the latter denies that *any* object of the kind exists. This is Brentano's very special use of 'particular' and 'universal' in connection with judgments. See, e.g., *Psych.* II, 166. Remember also the pair of oxen which is a single object. See n. 51 of Section Thirteen.

[10] I say *at least* because I believe that this is also biographically true. This, though, is the sort of point I do not care to argue.

ingness and the impossibility's being categorial leads one to expect, then it provides a powerful further motive for attempting the reduction. So I shall make it my first business, before starting on the main task, to show that it lies very deep indeed.

"Thinking, in the broad sense which comprises all fringes, is a unitary concept.[11] Hence all possible intentions must be of the same ontological kind, which in this world is of course that of object. For, if they were of several kinds, such as, e.g., object and fact, the concept of thought would not be unitary." This is the argument he repeats again and again in support of the claim. As it stands, I either do not understand it at all or I do not see how it proves the alleged conclusion. But I believe that I sense what he tries to express. Acts for him are one kind of *relativliches* accident. There are other such kinds. Also, intending something is part of what it means to be an act. What he craves, I submit, is some sort of categorial guarantee, not to be sure that all intentions exist, but, rather, for that feature which makes each act what it is rather than a member of one of the other kinds of *relativliches* accident. This guarantee he sees in the requirement that an act cannot intend anything for which it is impossible₁ to exist. Or, perhaps better, he sees it in the possibility₁ for anything an act may intend to exist. That is why (if I am right) all intentions must be objects.[12] The argument he propounds is merely the mangled expression of another whose two premises are his extreme reism on the one hand and his craving some sort of categorial guarantee for acts being what they are on the other.

The point will become very important in the next section. It is also of intrinsic interest. So I shall take the time to inquire what has become of it in the *Tractatus* and in the foil. Consider the following three propositions of the former.

3.02: The thought contains the possibility of the state of affairs which it thinks. What is thinkable is also possible.

3.03: We cannot think anything unlogical, for otherwise we should have to think unlogically.

5.5422: The correct explanation of the form of the proposition "*A* judges *p*" must show that it is impossible to judge nonsense. (Russell's theory does not satisfy this condition.)

Read together, they clearly state a requirement for the formation rules of an improved language. The statement which expresses that, *per absurdum*, I think what is expressed by an ill-formed expression,

[11] In German: *einheitlicher Begriff*.

[12] In the by now familiar broad sense in which both Caesar and Jupiter are objects.

is itself ill-formed.[13] Like Russell's, the improved language of the *Tractatus* does not satisfy this requirement. That is indeed one of the major sources of its author's eventual rejection of this book. After a fashion at least,[14] the foil does fulfill the requirement. By its formation rules '⌜ · · · ⌝' becomes well-formed and the name of a thought if and only if one substitutes for ' · · · ' a well-formed sentential expression.[15]

The main task, to which I now turn, requires four steps. In the *first step*, we shall examine Brentano's assay of the judgments II*a*, i.e., those intending positive relational atomic facts. In the *second step*, we shall examine his assay of the judgments I*b*, i.e., those intending negative nonrelational atomic facts. We know already how he reduces the judgments I*a*. His assay of the judgments II*b*, i.e., those intending negative relational atomic facts, merely combines the first two steps. So we need not, and I shall not, tarry. That leaves the four classes III*a*, III*b*, IV, and V. Of these, the first two are the positive and negative existential judgments, with whose assay we are already familiar and to which the six others can presumably be reduced. That leaves IV and V. In the *third step* we shall attend to the judgments IV, i.e., those intending the four kinds of categorical facts. In the *fourth step* I shall say what little needs to be said about the residual class.

First step. Consider the four judgments intending (1) Peter loves Mary, (2) Peter loves Jupiter, (3) Peter hates Mary, (4) Peter hates Jupiter, respectively. (1), (2), (3), (4) are all positive relational atomic facts. Thus the four judgments all belong to the class II*a*. Call them, too, (1), (2), (3), (4), respectively.[16] (1) will be our example. (2), (3), (4)

---

[13] As I speak and think, the categorially impossible and the ill-formed are one and the same. Or, at least, they lie on the same level, which is the deepest of all. That must by now be obvious.

[14] I say *after a fashion* because making expressions as complex as these syntactically simple predicates and names of simple characters is a move that requires dialectical defense. This defense I have made elsewhere.

[15] That for the first Wittgenstein tautologies and contradictions are ill-formed, partly because, as may also be seen from the propositions I quoted, he never fully grasped the distinction between the categorial (necessity₁) and the merely "logical (necessity₂)" is a circumstance which, though crucial in other contexts, does not affect the point at hand. But see n. 19 of Section Fourteen.

[16] As with the roman numerals, there will be no danger of confusion, particularly since, should the need arise, we can always add 'fact' or 'judgment', speaking of, say, either the fact (1) or the judgment (1), as the occasion requires.

Brentano's favorite example is a flower-lover, which (upon his assay) involves a relation whose term is not an object but a kind. My example avoids this unnecessary complication.

Notice, too, that I discuss the judgment (1) rather than that intending (1') There is someone who loves Mary, which I shall in fact not discuss at all, since what I shall discuss will enable you to figure out for yourself how Brentano analyzes the judgment (1').

will have to be brought in at certain points; so we might just as well list and label them right now.

Suppose that loving is a "real" relation. Equivalently as well as from where he stands more accurately, suppose that Mary-loving is intrinsically relational. Still more accurately and as I would rather say, if only in order to make the strange word fit the strangeness of the notion, suppose that someone-who-is-Mary-loving[17] is a *relativliches* accident.

Brentano's assay of (1) takes its cue from an attempted analogy with the judgment that this spot is red.[18] For the sake of this analogy, think of this judgment as occurring in two successive fractions. (a) In the first fraction I conceive the single idea of something which is both this spot and red. Or, as for the sake of convenience I shall henceforth also say, in the first fraction I form the conception-of-this-spot-as-red. (b) In the second fraction I proceed from the conception to the judgment by acknowledging what in the first I merely conceived. (As you see, I saved words by assuming that the mind which makes the judgment is mine. Nothing will be lost and more words will be saved if we stay with the assumption.)

Trying to proceed analogously in the case of (1), one arrives at the following "description." (a) In the first fraction I conceive of Peter as Mary-loving. (b) In the second fraction I proceed from this conception to the judgment.

The "description" is merely a program. To carry it out one must answer two questions. (a) *What exactly* is the assay of an act which may reasonably be called the conception-of-Peter-as-Mary-loving? (b) *How exactly* does one proceed from this conception so assayed to the judgment? To arrive at the description, we saw, was easy. To answer the two questions, we shall see, is impossible. More precisely, they have in this world no answers that do not lead to dialectical catastrophe. More succinctly, the attempted analogy fails. Brentano nevertheless took his cue from it. Accordingly, he proposed answers to both questions. I shall next state his answers, then show that they lead to dialectical catastrophe.

(a) Brentano assays the first fraction as follows. I conceive two objects; these two conceivings are two acts whose fringes, even though they are both conceivings, differ in another respect; one of them is uni-

---

[17] I try to relieve the dreariness by substituting 'someone-who-is-Mary-loving' for the more accurate 'something^o-which-is-Mary-loving'. Notice, though, that without fussing about it, I do not hesitate to use Brentano's improved language wherever that helps.

[18] The textual evidence for everything I am going to say about Brentano's assay of the judgments II*a* is massive. It is also very repetitive and widely scattered. But you will find a particularly helpful statement in *Psych.* II, 148–49.

laterally inseparable from the other. As a formula this will do; but it needs unpacking, first descriptively, then critically.

(a₁) The two objects conceived are Peter and Mary. (a₂) The act which is the relative substance is called a conceiving *modo recto;* the one which is the relative accident, a conceiving *modo obliquo.*[19] (a₃) Peter is conceived directly; Mary, indirectly. Generally, the *fundamentum* of the relation is conceived directly; its term, indirectly.[20] (a₄) Conceiving a single object and nothing else, one can conceive it only *modo recto*, and there is only one such mode. There are very many oblique modes to conceive an object in, but one cannot conceive any object in any of these modes unless the act of so conceiving it is a (relative) accident of another which conceives another object directly. (a₅) The difference between two acts conceiving one object, say, Peter, once directly, once obliquely, lies only in their subjective parts, i.e., in their fringes. The two cores are the "same," or, rather, more accurately, they are two cores (e.g., $a_1{}^*$ and $a_2{}^*$) corresponding to one idea (e.g., $\overline{A}$). In other words, *modus rectus* and *modus obliquus* are two classes of (kinds of) conceiving such that, while the former has only one member, the latter has very many. This will do for description.

(a₆) The conception-of-Peter-as-Mary-loving has turned out to be *not a single act* consisting of one subjective and one objective constituent and nothing else. I shall express this by calling it a *double conception.*[21] (a₇) Consider (1) and (3). Each of the two double conceptions in their respective first fractions is an act of directly conceiving Peter which has an act of obliquely conceiving Mary as (relative) accident. Where, then, is the difference between loving and hating? Brentano answers that it is in the oblique mode. When Mary is conceived obliquely as being loved (if I may so express myself), she is conceived in one oblique mode; when she is conceived obliquely as being hated, she is conceived in another oblique mode; and so on, and so on. You see now why I said that there are very many indirect modes.[22] (a₈) We

---

[19] Brentano and his editors always use the two Latin phrases, either in the nominative or, adverbially, in the ablative. So, when necessary, shall I. Whenever it is neither unsafe nor inconvenient I shall avoid them, translate '*rectus*' by 'direct'.

[20] As you see, I limit myself to binary relations. Nothing will be lost.

[21] Neither Brentano nor anyone else I know of makes this point accurately. The phrase, too, is mine. I chose it of course in deliberate parallelism to 'double judgment'. This parallelism, too, is neglected; i.e., it is either not clearly seen or not clearly said that in both cases one act is a (relative) accident of another.

[22] This particular claim is so outlandish that I mention now, because of the incontrovertible textual evidence available, an example whose details are better left for Section Seventeen. Suppose I have the conception-of-this-at-a-certain-distance-from-that. Since "this" is the *fundamentum* (which means no more than that

have come upon a very impressive confirmation of the conversion rule. In the foil each relation is a relational thing and there are as many different ones of the former as there are of the latter. A relational fact (complex) is a relational thing tied to the *fundamentum* and the term. In this world, the only ground of a relation is a *relativliches* accident "in" the *fundamentum*. Now, though, we have discovered the substitutes (in the First) for the relational things (in the Second). *For each relational thing (of the foil) there is an oblique mode (of this world)!* Moreover, this substitute is the *subjective* constituent of an act! That is why I find this confirmation so impressive.

(b) Brentano proceeds from the concept to the judgment by adding to the act which directly conceives Peter (in general: to the *fundamentum*) the accident which turns it into an acknowledgment of Peter. In other words, he assays (1) as a positive existential judgment (α) and an (obliquely) conceiving (β) such that the latter is a (relative) accident of the former. (b_1) Consider (2) and (4). Peter may either love or hate Jupiter and I may truly judge either that he does the one or that he does the other even though Jupiter does not exist. That is why the "added" acknowledgment is limited to Peter. (b_2) Upon this assay, (1) is not a single existential judgment and nothing else but, rather, an existential judgment (α) in which another complete act (β) inheres (as a relative accident). I conclude that *the attempt at reduction has failed.* (b_3) Since (1) is not one act consisting of one subjective and one objective constituent and nothing else, I conclude further that *the necessary condition*[23] *is not fulfilled.* (b_4) Suppose, contrary to fact, that (1) consists of α and nothing else. The core of α corresponds to the idea of Peter. Yet the intention of (1) varies with β. I conclude that under this supposition the one-one correspondence between core and intention would be destroyed. (b_5) Suppose,[24] contrary to fact, that (1) can intelligibly be thought of as one act with one objective (γ) and one subjective (δ) constituent. Reconsider (a_7) and you will see that γ is in some

---

'this' is the grammatical subject of 'this is at a certain distance from that'), I conceive "this" directly; "that," obliquely. In *Psych.* II, 217–18, we are told that *there is for each distance a different oblique mode of conceiving "that."*

[23] See n. 2, above. The reason I did not make this point in connection with (a_6) is that in the representationalist scheme of things a mere conception and therefore, presumably, also a double conception do not "represent" anything. (The double quotes warn you that I express a very subtle point very succinctly, not to say unsubtly.)

[24] Marty made this supposition (in the case of double judgments, but the difference makes no difference), in order to make sure that the necessary condition remains satisfied, thus trying to safeguard realism$_2$. Kraus, quite correctly within the system, pointed out to him that the supposition was not intelligible. But he did not of course make the argument above.

vague and confused way a fusion of the core of α and the fringe of β. I conclude that under this supposition the distinction between the subjective and the objective constituent would be destroyed.

(b$_4$) and (b$_5$) strengthen and illuminate the crucial conclusion of (b$_3$). What they jointly amount to may be succinctly expressed by saying that (1) is about nothing. Or, with a twist, the facts[25] IIa are in Brentano's world not even near-facts. Nor is that surprising. Just remember the blatant inadequacy of his assay of relations (not: of relational judgments).

There is still another critical conclusion which I deliberately saved for the end, because it is not only very telling but also attaches to both (a) and (b) as well as to the rest of this section. *The notion of one act being a (relative) accident of another is vague, confused, probably purely verbal, and transparently* ad hoc. Or so at least I conclude; then ask one question. Are we to suppose that, just as they can "make" one core (or, if you please, one idea) out of two others, minds also can in this very elaborate way "forge" two of their accidents which are acts into a third?

The ontology of relational judgments and the epistemology of relations are one and the same. We just finished the examination of their epistemology in this world. Their ontology we examined in Section Thirteen. Some of the last comments related the two. Thus we would be done with relations, were it not for one thread that was left dangling, deliberately, as was then (p. 259) pointed out, in order to keep their ontology and their epistemology from being confused.[26] This thread we must now pick up. Then we shall be done.

Turn once more to the relations called of comparison and remember our example. α *is longer than* β. Brentano's assay of it may be summarized as follows. (c$_1$) Being-of-length-l_1 and being-of-length-l_2 are two accidents; the former is "in" α; the latter, "in" β. (c$_2$) Not mentioning the term of any relation of which α is the *fundamentum*, 'being-of-length-l_1' is a nonrelational (common) name of the accident in α. As for 'being-of-length-l_1', so of course for 'being-of-length-l_2'. (c$_3$) 'Being-longer-than-l_2' is merely a relational "name"[27] of the accident in α. As

[25] Not: judgments. Completely accurately, for once: what in the foil is assayed as the positive relational atomic facts IIa.

[26] For a pioneering attempt at clearing it up, see Reinhardt Grossmann's two recent essays in *Analysis*, 21, 1960, 1–5, and 23, 1962, 20–24.

[27] The double quotes are to remind you that they are not really names but descriptions. Remember, too, that since these accidents have also nonrelational names, their relational ones are *denominationes mere extrinsecae*. Notice, finally, that I saved words by speaking of them as if they were Aristotelian rather than in Brentano's style.

for 'being-longer-than-l_2', so of course for 'shorter-than-l_1'. (c_4) An accident is *relativlich* if and only if it has only relational names. (c_5) Hence, to judge that α *is longer than* β is the "same" as to judge that α is of length l_1, which is a judgment not of IIa but of Ia and acknowledges only α but not β; just as one who judges that α *is longer than* β *is* makes two judgments Ia, which acknowledge α and β, respectively.

We criticized (c_4) and asked but did not answer one question. The criticism was that (c_4) grounds an ontological distinction[28] on a criterion either merely verbal or at best epistemological. The question was why, in spite of this assay, Brentano continued to count the so-called relations of comparison as a kind of "relation." Now we are ready for the answer. Not unreasonably within the system, he made two claims. He claimed, first, that when judging that α is longer than β, I form (in the first fraction of the judgment) the conception-of-α-as-longer-than-β. He claimed, second, that this conception is a double conception. The claim thus is that the ontology of the judgment is structurally the same, irrespective of whether the relation it intends is "real" or merely one of comparison. Now, finally, everything hangs together; and we understand accurately why the criterion in (c_4), though not merely verbal, is epistemological indeed.

Second step. How does Brentano assay the judgments Ib, i.e., those intending negative nonrelational atomic facts? Officially, this is the question before us. The issue behind it is the ontological status of negation. The way to bring it to the fore is to first raise and answer another question. What condition must an assay of these judgments fulfill to be acceptable to him? In his world, nor as we know just in his, there are no negative facts. But negative facts, negative characters, and negation stand and fall together. If one of them has ontological status, so do the other two. Of this more presently. If for the moment you take it for granted, you have all but found the answer. An assay of the judgments Ib will not be acceptable to him unless it suppresses negation in the Second.[29] This is one thing. I say *suppress* because in the foil negation has ontological status. This is another thing. Of it, too, more presently. The conversion rule is a third thing. Putting all three together, you should be able to anticipate the salient feature of the assay he proposed. It provides a substitute in the mind for negation. With the troubles into which it runs we are already familiar. Reduction is not

---

[28] This criticism is thus methodological and not, like those concerned with the actual shortcomings of the assay, substantive. That is why it was then and why it is now singled out.

[29] Or, for that matter, in the First, if the negative fact is in the First. This, though, is here clearly beside the point.

really achieved and the necessary condition is not satisfied. This is the gist. Now for the details. It will pay if we start with a quick glance, first at the foil, then at some reasons why negative facts are, if anything, even less acceptable to him than they are to others. First of all, though, let us agree on an example. "This spot is not green" will do nicely.

In the foil the spot's being green is a fact. Negation, being a subsistent, if attached to it, produces another.[30] If the first fact is actual, the second is merely potential; and conversely. Put now the definition

(D′)   '$(\sim gr)(x)$'   for   '$\sim gr(x)$'

beside

(D)   '$(R\ \&\ S)(x)$'   for   '$R(x)\cdot S(x)$',

which in Section Five (p. 93) was used to introduce the notion of a derived thing. Comparing the two, you will see that $(\sim gr)$ is a character derived from a single universal and negation. Generally, (some) *negative characters are the simplest sort of derived thing*, which shows what I just asked you to take for granted, namely, that negative facts, negative characters, and negation itself are ontologically in the same boat. An objector agrees, but sees in it an additional reason for denying ontological status to all three. Let us listen to what he has to say.

"Horse, stone, tree, and so on, are in your world all derived things. Now, quite consistently I admit, you put negative characters into the same category; or, to speak as you do, you put what is most palpable into the same boat with what is so elusive that it is really nothing at all. Does not this alone show how absurd your hypertrophic ontology is?" I agree that in my world all these entities are in the same category, then point at still another member of it, namely, centaur, which I am sure the objector would not wish to call most palpable, since he does not seem to appreciate that the difference between, say, horse and centaur, which he correctly senses yet so misleadingly expresses, lies not in the two characters as such (which are equally palpable or impalpable, whatever that may mean, since they are not particulars) but, rather, in the circumstance that while the former happens to be exemplified, the latter is not. In other words, I need not and do not shrink from recognizing that these entities all exist and belong to the same category

---

[30] I say *attached* even though, taking my cue from the logicians, I think and speak of negation as the one connective which, being monadic, does not connect anything. Phenomenologically, I submit, one must be blind to deny that when looking at, say, a red spot, one is sometimes presented with its being not green without having to infer this from its being red and the a priori *truth* that nothing is (at the same time all over) both red and green.

because, unlike my objector, I realize that their ontological status is peculiar and very low indeed.[31]

Brentano's minds, whenever it suits him, can do many remarkable things. They can in several ways "make" a single idea (core) out of several others. They can even pile Ossa on Pelion by "forging" one act of theirs to another so that the former becomes an accident of the latter. Yet, when it comes to negation, they are strangely impotent. *There are in his world no negative ideas.* For this doctrine he is prepared to die in the last ditch.[32] Whence such determination? Is it merely another conviction as to what minds otherwise so athletic can or can't do? Or is it, as seems more likely, a symptom of a commitment in general ontology that goes much deeper?

The connection with such a commitment is not hard to find. *If there were negative ideas, there would be negative accidents.*[33] As we all often honor the law in the breach, so Brentano at this point implicitly honored the correspondence view which eventually he explicitly disavowed. That leaves us with only one question. Why must he exclude negative accidents? A quick look at two other worlds will make the answer stand out by contrast.

Look first at the foil. This is red if and only if this particular and that universal are combined; this is not green if and only if this particular and that other universal are separated. The (true) positive or negative judgment corresponds to this combination or separation, respectively.[34]

Look next at an Aristotelian world in which a substance and one of its accidents are two and not one; with the latter, as one says, inhering in the former. At first, it seems that what concerns us is as in the foil.

---

[31] For the details of this far-flung argument see Section Three.

[32] So I shall state it in two more ways, first more literally, then more conveniently, using A, $\overline{A}$, and $\bar{A}$ as they have been used in Part II for three of the entities connected with green. (1) There are no cores corresponding to $\overline{(\sim A)}$. (2) A mind possessing the idea $\overline{A}$ is yet utterly incapable of forming that of the complementary Class of $\bar{A}$, even though, compared with all the "making" and "forging" it can do, this is surely a rather modest feat. Though couched in biographical terms, the ontological diagnosis I am about to present of this otherwise wholly arbitrary limitation on the capacities of minds is of course structural.

[33] Or, more accurately and just as unacceptably from where he stands, it would at least not be impossible₁ for such accidents to exist.

[34] 'Combination' and 'separation' I take from the famous passage at the very beginning of *De Interpretatione*, which is one of the historical pillars of the correspondence view. As it happens, not by chance of course, it is this very passage (16a, 11–12) which caused Brentano to question the correspondence view as early as 1889. See *WuEv.*, p. 18. (This adds considerable biographical plausibility to the structural diagnosis. See n. 32, above. But, I repeat, intellectual biography is not the sort of thing that concerns me.)

Yet there is a difference. The universal of the foil is one; the accidents of this world are many, one for each spot that is green; and there certainly is none whose sole job it would be to stay separated from this red spot. Yet the situation is not as grim as that makes it appear. Just remember that everyone but the most extreme nominalist almost always more or less implicitly relies on more or less shadowy Classes, e.g., that of all green accidents, or, perhaps, of all green objects. And between these Classes and the spot one can again, in a more or less shadowy way, speak and think of combination and separation.

Brentano's extreme reism makes the object and its accident one. More accurately, the latter, modally included in the former, includes in turn the former's substance$_3$. For such "accidents" the two notions (or images) of combination and separation make no sense whatsoever.

We already have our answer. *The structural reason for his last-ditch refusal to admit negative ideas is his double commitment to the extremes of nominalism and of reism.* Now we are ready for the details. What exactly is his assay of the judgment (ω) that this spot is not green?

Let $\overline{A}$ and $\overline{C}$ be the ideas of something$^\circ$ which is P_1 and T_1 and colored and of something$^\circ$ which is a place and a moment and green, respectively. Let α be a positive existential judgment whose core (e.g., a_1^*) corresponds to $\overline{A}$; γ, a negative existential judgment whose core (e.g., c_1^*) corresponds to $\overline{C}$. One will expect α and γ to be somehow involved in his assay of ω; and so of course they are. Yet there is a problem. α asserts[35] that there is *someone* object that falls under $\overline{A}$; γ, that there is *none* falling under $\overline{C}$. Hence, while the intention of ω implies that of α, it surely does not imply that of γ. The problem is to limit the rejection in the would-be γ-constituent of ω to what is acknowledged by its would-be α-constituent. Verbally at least, this may[36]

[35] I write 'assert' instead of 'acknowledge' and 'reject' because the latter prove awkward if one wants to speak both clearly and in a manner that leaves no doubt that there is a Second.

[36] I say *may* because this is not literally what Brentano does. Upon his account, I acknowledge A directly and conceive obliquely *another mind* which judges *truly* of something that it is not B. Accurate analysis shows this account to be either circular or merely an unnecessarily confused and confusing way of saying what I said. But I shall not bother to show that, particularly since the awkward expedient of another mind judging something truly, which is as idealistic in its flavor as the doctrine of truth it presupposes is in its substance, will come up in the last two steps. Thus nothing of interest will be lost. But let me stress again that everything Brentano says about double judgments—always more or less in haste and almost reluctantly, for reasons we shall soon come to understand—is so confused that one cannot be quite sure what he meant. Nor is Kraus of any help. Kastil, though, in the succinct yet lucid explanation of the notion on p. x of his Introduction to the second volume of Marty's *Gesammelte Schriften* (Halle: Niemayer, 1918) agrees with me. Or, rather, I agree with him. See also n. 21, above.

be done in two fractions. The first is a "forging"; the second, a very peculiar kind of "making."

In the first fraction γ becomes a (relative) accident of α. This is expressed by calling ω a *double judgment*. In the second fraction, the mind "identifies" the two ideas $\overline{A}$ and $\overline{C}$. So combined, they supposedly can somehow do the job which would be done by the idea-of-something°-which-is-both-A-and-(not-C), which is of course the single idea the mind could by conjunction make out of $\overline{A}$ and (not-$\overline{C}$), if only there were, as in fact there are not, negative ideas in this world.

The assay fails on three scores. Since it makes ω a double judgment, it falls short of reduction and violates the necessary condition. These are the same two criticisms as in (b₂) and (b₃) above. The third relates to (b₅), where it was pointed out that under a certain supposition the distinction between the subjective and the objective constituent of an act would in the case IIa be destroyed. In the case at hand it has been destroyed. To see that, one merely has to consider that the "identification" in the second fraction could not conceivably do what supposedly it does unless α and γ were an acknowledging and a rejecting respectively.

Two comments will complete this step. The point of the first, though important to Brentano and his circle, seems very minor to me. The second, though by now rather obvious, yet illuminates the very center of the dialectic.

1. We are ready to pick up the thread left dangling at the end of the last section. Remember the objection I called phenomenological. In the assay Brentano first proposed but eventually abandoned, the judgment Ia that A is B becomes the judgment IIIa acknowledging something which is both A and B. What irritated him as well as some others may be stated as follows. 'Both A and B' is symmetrical in 'A' and 'B'; 'A is B' is not. As for Ia, so for Ib. Replace 'B' by 'not-B' and you will see that while 'Both A and not-B' is symmetrical in 'A' and 'not-B', 'A is not-B' is not.[37] Yet between the judgments themselves there is a difference. In Ia, as originally assayed, there is no asymmetry. In Ib, as he assays it, there is the built-in asymmetry between the substance α and the accident γ. Thus, if one is willing to pay the (as we know) prohibitive price of double judgments for the sake of suppressing negation, one may just as well enjoy such minor incidental benefits as the possibility of grounding the asymmetry in question by assaying the judgments Ia, too, as double judgments which are in all respects like judgments Ib, except of course that their accident is an acknowledg-

---

[37] This asymmetry, which is really no more than that between grammatical subject and predicate, naturally seems more important to an Aristotelian than (from where I stand) it is.

ment rather than a rejection. Brentano, under critical pressure, got rid of the irritation by availing himself of this possibility. *In his eventual ontology I*a *and I*b *are both double judgments.*[38]

2. The assay of rejecting as a fringe provides in the case III*b* a prima facie rather plausible substitute (in the First, by the conversion rule) for negation. But the suppression of negation as an existent (in the Second) is no doubt one of the major goals of Brentano. Thus we have uncovered an additional powerful motive for two of the most strategic among his moves, namely, first, his representationalist assay of III, and, second, the program of reduction.

Third step. During the first half of his career Brentano made some proposals which he himself thought of, and his students hailed as, a major reform of logic. What he proposed was a new[39] way of arranging the Aristotelian schema of the syllogism, which may or may not be more perspicuous than others. Nowadays surely no one would describe this achievement, such as it was, as a major reform of logic. Whatever interest it still has is in how it jibes with his ontology. But we cannot uncover this connection without at least a quick glance at what he proposed.

He puts for **a, e, o, i** into the four corners of the square of opposites:

$$\text{(a)} \quad \sim(\exists x)[A(x)\cdot\sim B(x)] \qquad \text{(e)} \quad \sim(\exists x)[A(x)\cdot B(x)]$$

$$\text{(o)} \quad (\exists x)[A(x)\cdot\sim B(x)] \qquad \text{(i)} \quad (\exists x)[A(x)\cdot B(x)].$$

Reading the operators as 'some*one*' turns (i) and (o) into I*a* and I*b*, respectively. Brentano so reads them.[40] In this way he gets two of the

---

[38] Brentano accordingly distinguishes between *anerkennen* (III*a*) and *verwerfen* (III*b*) on the one hand and *zuerkennen* (I*a*) and *aberkennen* (I*b*) on the other. A judgment I*a* is a *zuerkennen*, a judgment I*b* an *aberkennen* of a "predicate" to a "subject" which one has already *anerkannt*. As you see, there is a sort of existential import as well as a (psychologistic) trace of the two "fractions."

[39] More accurately, he rediscovered what, as Couturat discovered in 1901, had already been discovered by Leibniz, who also took considerable pride in it. I take this item from Stumpf's memoir, one of the two appendices to Oskar Kraus's biography (*Franz Brentano*, Munich: Beck, 1919). Kraus's contribution is very useful and, as always, defiantly devoted. Stumpf's memoir is so rich and so delightful that Husserl's, the other, shorter one, is but a poor second. Nor is that surprising. Stumpf's is the free-flowing affection of the younger contemporary serenely secure in his own considerable achievement; Husserl's, though neither undignified nor unappreciative, the conflicted tribute of the student bent on proclaiming his own by then overt version of the master's covert idealism.

[40] That does not mean that he cannot express the modern 'some' but merely that the transcription of the latter becomes a bit more complicated. This detail we can safely skip. But see what has been said on p. 261 about his substitute for classes.

four categorical schemata IV for nothing, as it were. **i** is Ia; **o** is Ib. At this point, though, we must be more accurate. When he first proposed his so-called reform, he was still content with the original assay of **i**. Also, he adopted what he called the "logical fiction" of negative concepts such as, say, $\overline{(\sim)B}$. With this fiction the core of each of the four categorical judgments corresponds to a single idea the mind can "make" by conjunction; out of $\overline{A}$ and $\overline{B}$ in the case of **e** and **i**, out of $\overline{A}$ and $\overline{(\sim B)}$ in the case of **a** and **o**.

That jibes with the ontology as follows. *Every judgment* is a judgment III; either, like **i** and **o**, positive; or, like **a** and **e**, negative. The so-called generality of **a** and **e** is merely a linguistic illusion; they are really two negative existential judgments. I said: every judgment. I should of course have said: each of the four categorical schemata. But we know how prone everyone then was to believe that he had mastered all of logical form, or, at least, that he had acquired the key to it, once he had mastered those four. (Brentano has at least the *very great merit* of having seen clearly that the judgments III are not categorical.)

That much for the state of logico-ontological innocence.[41] After the fall the "fiction" which logically is so useful and so harmless had to be abandoned.[42] The double judgments are the ontological fig leaves. And, as fig leaves will, they create problems.

Even after the fall, if double judgments are accepted, **i** and **o** cause no trouble. Not so **a** and **e**. These two can no longer be assayed as rejections ("negations") of single ideas but are, if anything, negations of judgments. But, then, what could it possibly mean in this world to "reject" judgments? All one can reject is ideas!

[41] You will find it all documented in the 1874 edition of *Psych.* I. The notion of double judgment appears for the first time in the notes and appendix to the 1889 edition of *Zum Ursprung sittlicher Erkenntnis*, then in a book by one of his students (*Die neuen Theorien der kategorischen Schluesse*, Vienna: Hoelder, 1891), which is reported to be based on the logic courses he gave in Vienna during the eighties. This book, by Franz Hillebrand, I have not seen. His widow, Franziska Mayer-Hillebrand, recently published under Brentano's name *Die Lehre vom richtigen Urteil* (Bern: Francke, 1956), which purports to be his logic. Her book, if only because readily available, is of some use. Yet one cannot confidently use it, since sometimes one cannot tell whether the words one reads are Brentano's, or her husband's, or her own paraphrases of either the one or the other. Quite a few of the fragments I can identify had been published already. Nor are the notes she has added up to the standard of excellence set by Kastil and Kraus. The one thing certain is her devotion to a group of which she became one of the three last survivors. (The other two are Hugo Bergmann and Georg Katkov.)

[42] Yet Brentano continued to value his so-called reform of logic very highly, which accounts for the haste and reluctance mentioned in n. 36, above. Or so at least I am inclined to believe.

In this predicament Brentano resorts to an awkward expedient. Since one can in his world form the idea of *someone judging truly that* F, he assays **a** as the rejection of anyone judging truly that **o**; **e** as the rejection of anyone judging truly that **i**.

This is how the four schemata IV are "reduced." After what has been said, the "reduction" judges itself. Two comments will complete what needs to be said.

1. The idealistic flavor of the awkward expedient of resorting to another mind judging something truly is obvious. One reason Brentano might have been less reluctant to introduce it at this point[43] is that, as we shall see in the next section, it is both needed for, and congenial to, his overtly idealistic theory of truth. In this respect the situation is similar to the one we encountered during the second step, when I remarked that since double judgments are needed for I*b*, they may just as well be used to get rid of the irritation concerning the original assay of I*a*. Only, the cracks in the wall become more and more ominous.

2. Ignore the awkward expedient, turn to the formulae (a) and (e) which he puts in the two upper corners of the square and you will see that **a** and **e** are left without existential import. This is as it ought to be. For he insists, correctly, that we can form such concepts as that of a round square, and, equally correctly, that all round squares being round is an a priori truth. Of this more in the next section.

Fourth step. Brentano, we know (p. 230), does attend to a few among the schemata in the residual class. Of these assays[44] all we need and all we want is the flavor. One example will do.

Let F_1, F_2, and F_3 be the facts expressed by '*A* is *B*', '*C* is *D*', and '*A* is *B* and *C* is *D*', respectively. Let α, β, and γ be three judgments intending[45] F_1, F_2, and F_3, respectively. α and β are one thing; γ is another. Nor, of course, in view of the obvious symmetry of the latter with respect to the two former, can an assay of the latter be produced by "forging" one of the two former to the other. The only resort left is the awkward expedient. For one can in this world form and acknowledge the idea of someone with two accidents, one the act of judging correctly that F_1, the other that of judging correctly that F_2. As far as I can see, all sentential compounds require this awkward expedient of another mind judging something truly. Multiple quantification, unless

---

[43] Or even earlier, unnecessarily and very confusingly. See n. 36, above.

[44] The most detailed readily available source is *Die Lehre vom richtigen Urteil*. But see n. 41, above.

[45] This is hasty and inaccurate. As we know already, and as will soon be out in the open, the judgments of this world do not literally intend anything.

I am mistaken, cannot be handled at all. But, then, even though he fancied himself one, Brentano was not really a logician. So one should not blame him too much for not having done better than virtually all of his contemporaries who were.

We have traveled a long way in this section. So it will be well to conclude as we began, with a look at the map. Examining the trunk of this world in Section Thirteen, we discovered its extreme reism and nominalism. Examining its minds in Section Fourteen, we became aware of the tension between its structural representationalism on the one hand and its explicit antirepresentationalism on the other. Examining in some detail its assay of the several kinds of judgment in this section, we saw that, on its own terms, it stands or falls with a certain program. It stands if and only if every judgment can be reduced to a single existential one, with the latter being assayed in the representationalist manner. This is so because if this program succeeded, the necessary condition would be satisfied and there would as yet be no conflict, or at least no open conflict, between the extreme reism and the structural representationalism of this world on the one hand and the professed realism$_2$ of its author on the other. But we also saw the program fail. Thus we witnessed the first of three major breakdowns. In the next two sections we shall see that the representationalist assay of existential judgments is also at the root of the other two.

EXISTENCE, TRUTH, EVIDENCE

IT will be worth our while to inquire what the situation would be like if the program of reduction had succeeded. Suppose, then, contrary to fact, that it succeeded. Sweeping as it is, the supposition will neither distort nor ignore anything.[1] Or, rather, it ignores only what after the last section we may safely take for granted, namely, that the program of reduction has in fact failed.

Upon this supposition every judgment is really a single existential judgment, i.e., either an acknowledging or a rejecting of what is represented by a single idea. What is so represented is in this world neither a fact nor a near-fact but an object. That shows what the situation would have been. Brentano would have succeeded in constructing an ontology of judgment that jibes with his reism. Or, if you please, he would have succeeded in carrying out an epistemological maneuver that could with at least some semblance of plausibility be mistaken for a step toward his ontological goal of suppressing all facts.

In the last section we examined a move I then called his first. It consisted in assaying every judgment IIIa as an acknowledging of an object. Our new supposition makes it advisable to think of it as a (successful) assay of every judgment as either an acknowledging or a rejecting of an object. Between this move and the structural idealism there are (I claimed) three connections. Two of these we just reviewed once more. One runs through the reism with which the move, if it succeeded, would jibe. The other is through the violation of the neces-

---

[1] As it happens, the supposition is not without biographical justification. Brentano's original thesis was that all judgments are "really" existential. Nor was this just a thesis or, as he later called it, a fiction in logic. There is no doubt that it was and always remained his major vision or inspiration, both logical and ontological. That the later doctrine of double judgments actually contradicted the thesis he never realized. Rather, he thought of the former as something which by getting rid of some minor blemishes supported the latter. Hence the haste and reluctance that were mentioned twice. See nn. 36 and 42 of Section Fifteen.

sary condition from which in his determination to carry out the program he did not shrink.

In this section we shall examine another move which I shall call his second. Without the first the second would not be possible. (This is the third connection between the first and the structural idealism. See p. 286.) Successively executed, the two moves land him in plain idealism. The first thus merely approaches what is actually reached in the second. The first, we saw, aims at purging his world of all facts. The second, we shall see, purges it of its Second. This is done by claiming that when one asserts or denies that *A* exists what he really asserts is that he acknowledges or rejects *A*. As for *A exists*, so for *A does not exist*. Upon this assay, the fact that *A* does (does not) exist becomes an accident "in" minds. Yet, if *A* is a physical object, then its existence or nonexistence, i.e., the fact that it does or does not exist,[2] is an existential fact of the Second. That shows how this world is purged of its Second. We have come upon another poignant example of the conversion rule. The entities of the Second which the move suppresses are its (positive and negative) existential facts; the substitutes in the First we are offered for them are the (positive and negative) existential judgments. Nor is that all. Presently we shall see that his assay of the existential facts structurally entails a theory of truth which explicitly repudiates the correspondence view.[3] Of this repudiation I spoke in the Introduction as the *second breakdown*.

This is the diagnosis. If it turns out to be right, the idealism is all but manifest. In the meantime, it will be better not to overwork 'idealistic'. Let us agree to speak of this assay of the facts III and of the theory of truth which is its corollary as the *controversial assay* and the *controversial corollary*.

Brentano had some reasons, which he believed to be good reasons, for adopting the controversial assay. Since the latter is absurd, they could not possibly be good reasons. The task is to show that they are nevertheless of structural interest. Three preliminary comments will help. The first two point at two features which, though not themselves among the reasons he gave, yet create an atmosphere of plausibility for

---

[2] The uneasiness you may feel at this point will soon be relieved.

[3] Or, as we usually call it, the *necessary condition* every realistic₂ ontology must fulfill. Implicitly, we know, this condition has been violated when the doctrine of double conceptions and double judgments was introduced during the execution of the first move. Yet there is a difference between consequences one overlooks and what he explicitly repudiates. This is also why I located the second major breakdown of the system in the controversial corollary rather than, which would have been just as plausible, in the controversial assay.

his mistaking those he did give for good ones. The third derives some cues from foil and prototype.

First. What exactly does the controversial assay suppress? All the existential facts of the Second? Or, more radically, all its facts? Or, even more radically, as I have claimed, all of the Second, i.e., not only its facts but also its objects? I shall say three things. (a) The only facts, or, more accurately, near-facts of this world are those of the class Ia; and these are brushed aside by an epistemological maneuver which, making the judgments that would normally intend them into existential ones, replaces them, at least after a fashion, by existential facts. Yet there are in this world no existential facts. The maneuver is as transparent as it is exasperating. (b) By our supposition all judgments are existential judgments. Hence all facts of this world would be existential facts (if there were any). (c) I take it for granted that if an entity is a physical object, then its existence, i.e., the fact that it exists (see n. 2, above) is a fact of the Second. Yet these facts have all been suppressed. Hence there are no physical objects. Taken together, (a), (b), (c) show that the *crescendo* of the questions from which I started is specious.

Second. If you remember the hoax, you will see that the controversial assay does not literally suppress the Second of this world. For its official Second is the realm of scientific objects, while what is being suppressed is the realm of physical objects. On the one hand, this feature (a) adds to the specious plausibility of the controversial assay while, on the other, (b) it is the root of the third major breakdown. *Ad*(a). He firmly grasped and never abandoned the phenomenological insight that physical objects are not mental. Structurally, though, they sometimes occupy the place of ideas. This alone would tempt him to suppress them (p. 271). Nor is there anything in his would-be realism₂ to keep him from doing just that if they are not really his would-be Second. *Ad*(b). In the next section we shall see that the same feature prevents him from consistently and articulately maintaining that entities of his would-be Second exist outside of minds. Thus it becomes the proximate source of his final failure. In the meantime, no harm will be done if we keep playing along with the hoax and continue to speak of the physical objects of his world as if they were its Second.

Third. Upon the transcription into the prototype (p. 267) which enabled us to understand his assay of the judgments III, when I acknowledge something, I conceive its idea and (at the same time) believe that there is something falling under the latter, while when rejecting something, I conceive its idea and (at the same time) believe that there is nothing that falls under it. Consider for the moment only ideas under which something falls. Such an idea is (in Meinong's sense) either particular or general.[4] If the former, there is only one thing (or "thing") falling under it; if the latter, there are several. This brings up some points already familiar from Part II, which, though obvious if once understood, have yet been a major source of confusion.

Every idea ($\overline{A}$), whether particular or general, is a (structural) universal. The entities, if any, that fall under it are not universals but either particulars (a) or "things (α)." No idea literally represents the things (if any) that fall under it. Every idea ($\overline{A}$) literally represents a Class ($\overline{A}$) which has either several members or is a one-Class or is empty, depending on whether the idea is general or particular or such that nothing falls under it, respectively.

Let us now try to choose an example. Nothing will be lost and much will be gained if we so choose it that the idea in it is particular. The idea of Peter is particular. But it is also tremendously complicated. So let us instead pick a spot, say, $\gamma(p_1, t_1, a_1)$; call it α; and see whether it will serve. In the prototype, α is a "thing." Thus there is, as we know (p. 279), the existential statement '$E!\alpha$' connected with it. That is why the example, being still too complicated, keeps us from coming to grips with the confusion. So we must try again.

Brentano's objects, the perfect particulars of the prototype and the bare ones of the foil are all three among the simple categorial entities of their respective worlds. Hence, if a is a bare particular of the foil, there is in its improved language no transcription of 'a exists'.[5] As for the foil, so for Brentano. To see that, one merely has to observe that, with the linguistic turn, his controversial assay amounts to introducing 'a exists' into his improved language as a rather puzzling abbreviation for 'acknowledging-a', which is a (common) name of accidents "in" minds.[6] The confusion I want to track down consists in the mistaken

---

[4] One may wonder whether this is quite accurate. Or, perhaps better, one may wonder whether Meinong would not call particular an idea under which in fact nothing falls provided only it is an a priori truth that only one thing could fall under it. If $\gamma(p_1, t_1, a_1)$ is a spot and a_1 and a_2 are two perfect particulars grounding two colors, then the idea of $\gamma(p_1, t_1, a_2)$ is of this sort.

[5] This is of course the source of the uneasiness you may have felt at two earlier occasions. See nn. 2 and 4. But see also *Logic and Reality*, pp. 77–78, for the possibility of introducing into the improved language of the foil, in addition to the indispensable existential operator, a predicate '*exist*' which, while doing no harm and making 'a *exists*' well-formed, is yet futile and expendable since it adds nothing to the expressive possibilities of the language.

[6] Or, if you insist on complete accuracy, since Brentano's accidents are merely

belief that the unavailability of an improved-language statement for
'*a* exists' makes the proposed transcription of his existential judgments
unviable. Or, rather, this is one way of stating the confusion. It disappears as soon as one realizes that the statement which stands for the
intention of the existential judgment (as I transcribed it) is not '*a*
exists' nor, in the negative case, '*a* does not exist' but, rather, in the
prototype, either '$(\exists x)\bar{A}(x)$' or '$\sim(\exists x)\bar{A}(x)$', just as in the foil, where
there are universals, it is either '$(\exists x)A(x)$' or '$\sim(\exists x)A(x)$'. Nor does
it make any difference whether, in the positive case, A is general or
particular; or, equivalently, whether $\bar{A}$ is a class with several members
or the one-Class $[a]$. Or, rather, the only difference it makes is that in
the case of the particular concept (idea) one cannot possibly see clearly
unless one distinguishes sharply—as, alas, no nominalist does—between a one-class and its only member. We on the other hand can put
this case to good use, making it the occasion of the following formulation.

*Let $\bar{A}$ be a particular idea; a, the categorial entity that falls under it; A,
the one-Class which in the prototype it represents. According to Brentano,
the positive existential judgment in the case "acknowledges" something. If
that is to mean anything at all, the entity acknowledged is a. In the prototype, however, the judgment's intention is neither a nor a exists but
$(\exists x)\tilde{A}(x)$.*

For the controversial corollary the distinction between the actual
and the potential mode matters; for the controversial assay it doesn't.
So I shall streamline the discussion of the latter by choosing examples
that keep out of the potential. (Peter exists) and (Jupiter does not
exist) will do very well.[7] Call them (1) and (2) respectively. Since Peter
presumably exists while Jupiter doesn't, (1) and (2) are both actual.

Brentano presents *four arguments for the controversial assay.*[8] They

---

near-things, as an abbreviation for the common name 'someone-who-is-an-*a*-
acknowledger'. Perhaps this will help you to realize that, just as in his world
there are no facts but only objects, so there are in his improved language no sentences but only names.

Notice, too, in a very different vein, the agreement with the anti-Thomism,
documented in n. 6 of Section Thirteen, which appears as soon as one thinks of
'*A*' and 'exists' in '*A* exists' as an essence and the Being it informs.

[7] The parentheses are merely a typographical convenience. Sometimes I shall
replace (1) and (2) by (*a* exists) and (*a* does not exist), respectively, without
worrying about the ensuing ambiguity of '*a*', just as, when speaking about the
foil, I shall not hesitate to let '*a*' stand for a bare particular. Brentano himself, in
the classical style that panders to the confusion we just cleared up, *always* uses
capital letters and prefers the copula to 'exist'. Thus he writes for the most part '*A*
is' and '*A* is not'.

[8] Textual evidence for all four has been gathered by Kraus in *WuEv*. But there
is much more. See, e.g., for the first two, *Psych.* II, 49–50.

all share a tripartite pattern. (a) Each takes for granted that Peter himself is not the entity (1) purports to be. (b) Each gives a reason why (1) is not an entity of the Second.[9] (c) Each concludes that there is nothing except (the several acts of) Peter-acknowledging[10] of which 'Peter exists' could possibly be a (common) name. As for Peter and (1), so *mutatis mutandis* for Jupiter and (2). With (a) we need not quarrel. One who grants (b) will accept (c). The heart of the matter is (b). To bare it, I next pin down two agreements and two differences.

The entity either acknowledged or rejected is a categorial simple which either is there or for which it is possible$_1$ to be there. Hence, the fact which according to (b) is not there is either (1) or (2). One of the reasons we shall be given for its not being there is that we have no idea of existing, or, with the linguistic turn, that 'exist' is not a predicate. (As for existing, so a fortiori for the negative non-existing.)

The foil *agrees, first*, that 'exist' is not a predicate, or, equivalently in my world, that existing is not a character either simple or derived. But it *differs* by adding, *first*, that existing (or existence) exists as a subsistent which is in everything presented to us, in the same way in which, say, particularity is in every particular.[11] The foil *agrees, second*, that the existence of a categorial simple, i.e., in my world, of a bare particular or a universal, is not a fact.[12] But it *differs* by adding, *second*, that there are such facts as $(\exists x)A(x)$ and $\sim(\exists x)A(x)$, where 'A' stands for either a universal or a derived character. The latter may in turn be a class with either several members, or one, or none. Unless these agreements and differences are clearly seen, there remains a haze through which Brentano's four arguments, to which I now turn, may look better than they are.

The *first argument* purports to prove that (1) and (2) are nothing by proving that to exist and its negation are not characters.[13] What it actually proves is something very different. Stay with (1) and assume that existing, or to be an existent, is a character. If so, then we have (in this world) an idea of it. Hence we could conceive (1) by conceiving the

---

[9] Or, had I chosen another example, of the First. But the difference makes no difference and the convenience of my choice is obvious.

[10] Or, more accurately, someone-who-is-a-Peter-acknowledger. See n. 6, above.

[11] Otherwise, I add as usual, I would not know what 'exist' meant.

[12] Notice that *existence's* being in something not being itself a fact corresponds very satisfactorily to *exemplification's* being a tie that needs no further tie. Thus it makes good sense to put them both into the same category of *subsistent*. Such correspondences and such sense are part and parcel of the dialectic that supports an ontology.

[13] Unless, as he points out on several occasions, 'existent' is used synonymously with 'object', in the broad sense which makes both Peter and Jupiter objects and both (1) and (2) a priori truths.

"complex" idea of something which is both A and an existent. Yet we could have no reason for acknowledging what is represented by this "complex" idea which would not also be a reason for acknowledging A itself, and conversely. He concludes that we are caught in an infinite regress and rejects the assumption. I, too, reject the assumption. But I conclude, first, that what he has shown is merely that, even if existing were a character, it would not furnish a criterion that distinguishes the acknowledgings of what is there from those which acknowledge what is not there. Of course it wouldn't. Nothing does. I conclude, second, that this extraordinary mistake reveals the strength of this structural representationalist's yearning for a criterion.

The *second argument* purports to present an additional reason in the negative case. Let 'A', 'B', 'C' stand for 'square', 'green', 'horse'; notice that while (α) '$(\exists x)[A(x) \cdot B(x)] \supset (\exists x)A(x)$' is a tautology, ($\beta$) '$\sim(\exists x)[B(x) \cdot C(x)] \supset \sim(\exists x)C(x)$' is not; then consider the four propositions (a) there is something square and green, (b) there is something square, (c) there is no green horse, (d) there is no horse. By (α), (a) entails (b). By (β), (c) does not entail (d). Brentano believes that if (c) and (d) were entities, the former would entail the the latter; hence, he concludes, they are nothing. How did he arrive at this strange belief?

His reism is so deeply rooted that he cannot form a clear and articulate[14] notion of complex, or, for that matter, of any kind of structure, except the wholly specious one of his "complex" ideas on the one hand and, on the other, the most rudimentary one, within objects, provided by his substances$_3$ and accidents. So he cannot but think of (c) and (d) as two objects which, if they existed (and if we had an idea of nonexisting) would fall under the ideas of something-which-is-a-nonexistent-and-green-and-a-horse and of something-which-is-a-nonexistent-and-a horse, respectively. Thus he is led to apply the pattern (α') '$(\exists x)[Nonexistent(x) \cdot B(x) \cdot C(x)] \supset (\exists x)[Nonexistent(x) \cdot C(x)]$'. That accounts for the strange belief.

The third argument hardly deserves to be listed. Yet I would rather be tedious than seem oblivious of a fundamental ontological premiss. There are no facts; hence there are no existential facts. Obvious as this argument is, it yet calls attention to a most striking feature. *In the improved language of a world without facts there can be no sentences.* Hence 'Peter exists' is construed as a puzzling abbreviation of the common name 'someone-who-is-a-Peter-acknowledger'.

In the *fourth argument* we are told that we have no way of finding out

---

[14] I say *clear and articulate* because there is plenty of "structure" in his double conceptions and double judgments. But their "structure" is neither clear nor very articulate.

"directly" whether or not (1) or (2) are there. In a representationalist world that is indeed so. But, then, for the fact to be there is one thing; for ourselves to be able to find out whether or not it is there is quite another thing. Nor is there in this respect any difference between facts and objects. I conclude that the argument, not having the slightest tendency to show what it purports to show, is merely a variant of the sophomore's objection.

The arguments are all very bad. Yet they are all interesting. At least they confirm our several diagnoses. Two of them betray two of their author's preoccupations, with a criterion and with the sophomore's objection, which mark him clearly as a structural representationalist. The other two show him in the prison of his reism.

This will do for the controversial assay. Its controversial corollary repudiates the correspondence theory of truth. This theory we have so far taken for granted; saved words by calling it the correspondence view or also, for reasons I need not restate, the necessary condition. Now we must look more closely at what the one repudiates while the other takes it for granted. For this purpose I turn to the foil.

In the foil every fringe (species) and every core (thought) is a categorial simple. The intention of each core is a fact. Every fact is either actual or potential. Considering acts whose fringe is either believing or disbelieving,[15] this makes for four possibilities. (1) The fringe is believing; the intention, actual. (2) The fringe is disbelieving; the intention, potential. (3) The fringe is believing; the intention, potential. (4) The fringe is disbelieving; the intention, actual. The belief is true in case (1), false in case (3). The disbelief is true in case (2), false in case (4). Call this the fourfold schema. In the foil, roughly speaking, this schema is the correspondence theory. I say roughly speaking because, examining it closely, one soon discovers that it raises certain questions. The following comments digest these questions as well as the foil's answers.[16]

(1) Consider an intention in the Second, say, a particular exemplifying a certain color. If I believe that it exemplifies this color, my belief is true; if I believe that it exemplifies another color, my belief is false. In either case the belief's intention is a fact in the Second, either actual or potential, depending on whether the belief is true or false. (2) In the foil there is no *knowledge*. Hence, there is no criterion by which we

---

[15] I say believing and disbelieving rather than, as in Brentano's world and the prototype, *a* believing of *a* disbelieving, because in the foil cores and fringes are universals while in those other two worlds they are particulars.

[16] For details, see the "Realistic Postcript" in *Logic and Reality*. The critical particulars mentioned below are introduced on p. 321.

know whether or not any fact, of either the First or the Second, is actual or merely potential. The only way in which we come to believe (know) that it is either the one or the other, either immediately or by inference, is through context. Accordingly, actual vs. potential is an ontological dichotomy of the foil which is not presented to us.[17] (3) Thereby hangs the distinction between *existing* and being *real* on the one hand and the denial of categorial status to it on the other. What exists and is not mental is real if and only if it is actual and mind-independent. Whether or not an entity is mind-independent depends on context. What self-knowledge[18] reveals does in fact cohere and is therefore counted as real. (4) In the foil the fourfold schema applies not only to believing and disbelieving but also to perceiving,[19] remembering, and other species. The particulars presented in a case of perceptual error of the kind called existential or in an image connected with a memory, though not mental, are yet not mind-independent and therefore not real. Such particulars I call critical. (5) Though we need not dwell on certain difficulties which have vexed all realists₂ for centuries, we must take note of two points which their resolution by means of the critical particulars illuminates. (a) *A belief is true if and only if its intention is actual and real*, in which case, if it is physical, it is in the Second. (b) Potential facts make sense. Categorial simples supposed to be merely potential are repugnant. In the foil, partly because all its intentions are facts, partly because it recognizes the existence of the critical particulars, there are no such repugnant potentialities.

The old word is not correspondence but adequation; the old formula for the theory: *veritas est adequatio rei et intellectus.*[20] Aristotle stated it in terms of combination and separation.[21] E.g., a judgment I*b*, if true,

---

[17] As you no doubt remember from the discussion at the end of Section Eleven, this is the only ontological distinction of the foil not presented to us. But see also the discussion at the end of this section.

[18] In a properly narrow sense, which includes an awareness of which I am or was aware while having it but excludes it if I merely remember or remembered that I had it. Notice also that I say *in fact*. There is no criterion, even though the species of self-awareness is *sui generis*. Nor, of course, is any of the foil's awarenesses either indirect or reflexive.

[19] The distinction we make when calling a belief either true or false and a perception either veridical or nonveridical, is thus, from where I stand, merely derivative.

[20] Brentano and his circle either use the Latin tag or speak of the *Adaequations-theorie*.

[21] *Met.* 1051b, 3–5: "He who thinks the separated to be separated and the combined to be combined has the truth, while he whose thought is in a state contrary to that of the objects is in error." See also *De Interpret.* 16a, 11–12, which is cited in n. 34 of Section Fifteen.

separates *in intellectu* what is separated *in re*, namely, an object and a quality. This particular formula of his master, Brentano, because of his extreme reism and nominalism, was, as we know (p. 295), reluctant to accept. The reluctance marks the initial state of a long development. In its final state he explicitly repudiated the theory.[22]

Nor, even in the initial state, were the judgments I*b* his only worry. He felt compelled to make sure that the adequation in the case was neither an equality nor a similarity but at most a one-one correspondence. With this we need not quarrel. Then he started to search for the entity which allegedly corresponds to a true negative existential judgment, such as, e.g., that Jupiter does not exist; and decided that there were only three possibilities. Either (a) there is no such entity; or (b) it is Jupiter, assayed as an *ens rationis*, i.e., as something more or less like an idea;[23] or (c) it is the fact that Jupiter does not exist, assayed either as an entity in the Second or, again, as an *ens rationis*. Eventually, we know, he convinced himself that there are neither facts nor *entia rationis*. That leaves only (a). In this case, therefore, there is no corresponding entity. He concluded that to speak of correspondence or adequation was in all cases merely a *façon de parler*. Thus the final stage was reached.

A judgment, *J*, is either true or false. What makes it either the one or the other? Having rejected the old answer, he realized that he had to devise a new one. Or, with the linguistic turn, since he was much too good a philosopher to believe, as some now do, that the entities which '*J*' and '*J* is true (false)' stand for are one and not two, he found himself in a situation in which he had been before. For, as for '*J*', so, with a difference, for '*A*'. Recognizing that the entities which '*A*' and '*A* is (is not)' stand for are two and not one, he had to find something in which to ground the 'is' and the 'is not'.[24] As we know, he found it in acknowledgings and rejectings, i.e., in either case, in something sub-

---

[22] "Ueber den Begriff der Wahrheit," a lecture delivered in Vienna in 1889 but unpublished until Kraus, very properly, made it the opening piece of *WuEv.*, is an impressive and attractive record of the initial state. The final state had been reached in some of the essays, such as, e.g., "Von den wahren und fiktiven Objecten," which were published in the appendix of the 1911 edition of the *Psychologie*. That makes 1911 a *terminus ad quem*. To judge from other material in *WuEv.*, 1905 is a plausible *terminus a quo*.

[23] See n. 11 of Section Fourteen. The alternative of a "potential Jupiter" he always ignored, quite correctly, from where he stood, i.e., in a world in which all intentions are objects and all objects are categorial simples. From where I stand, this shows the crucial importance of the five points in which I digested the foil's correspondence theory a moment ago.

[24] I express myself very concisely.

jective. Now he must do the same job for 'true' and 'false'. You will
expect, and you will of course be right, that he grounded them, too, in
something subjective. But we cannot accurately understand what he
did without first attending to his doctrine of evidence.

In Section Fourteen, when discussing his notion of *knowledge* (p. 277),
I pursued my policy of doing everything possible to keep ontology and
epistemology from being confused by saying as little as I could, which
was virtually nothing, about *evidence*. Now we must bring the two together. What, then, is his notion of evidence? Informally speaking, it is
a quality of judgments, or, if we stick with our supposition, of acknowledgings and rejectings. In the formal language of his ontology, it is a
relative accident[25] whose relative substance is either an acknowledging
or a rejecting. Some acknowledgings or rejectings have this accident.
Some others don't. So we ask next: Which do and which don't?

In his world there is *knowledge*, i.e., infallible knowledge. Evidence is
its criterion. Hence the two notions must be made to jibe. On the one
hand, what cannot be *known*, may not be known with evidence (or, as I
shall also say, evidently). On the other hand, everything known evidently must be *knowable*. This requirement produces problems, some of
a systematic nature, some phenomenological.

The only *knowledge* in this world is that which an act reflexively has
of itself. But evidence is an accident of acts. Hence, evidence may and
does know itself. It shines in its own light, as it were. That sets a phenomenological requirement. There must be something which is presented to us in all acts of self-knowledge and in no others. Or, rather, he
must make and dialectically defend the claim that there is such a
something.

Some truths of this world are held to be a priori. The truths of logic
are of this kind; so are those of geometry; so are some others. One
would suppose that a generality which is a priori is also evident, and
conversely.[26] That raises a question which I asked earlier but did not
answer. How can one who limits evidence to self-knowledge account

[25] Of the fourth order. Just count: (0) substance$_3$, (1) core, (2) conceiving, (3)
believing or rejecting. The argument, or, rather, the phenomenological claim that
this accident, if taken in the Aristotelian style, is simple (*ein einfaches Merkmal*),
opens quite properly the third volume of the *Psychology*. See *Psych*. III, 2.

[26] The limitation to generalities such as, e.g., that all triangles are plane figures
or that nothing is (at the same time, all over) red and blue is necessary because an
act's self-knowledge, though evident, is not considered to be a priori, on the
plausible ground that, at least as far as we know, the act's occurrence itself is contingent. Notice, too, that self-knowledge is the only kind of *knowledge*, or, for that
matter, of knowledge in which an object rather than a universal is presented to us
(or, more accurately, to itself).

for the supposed evidence of the truths of logic, of geometry, and so on? Now we are ready for the answer. But it will be better if we first finish the pending business of truth.

I may judge truly, or, as he often says instead, I may judge correctly[27] what I either do not or cannot judge evidently. E.g., I may judge correctly what only you can now judge evidently, namely, that your mind now has a certain accident. Thus, while evidence remains his criterion, he cannot simply assay the truth of *J* as its evidence, nor, therefore, its falsehood as the evidence of the judgment which acknowledges or rejects what it rejects or acknowledges. But the complication is slight. At this crucial point I shall let Brentano speak for himself.

"What it all really comes down to is that truth pertains to the judgment of one who judges correctly, i.e., to the judgment of one who judges *as one would judge* who judges with evidence."[28]

The passage speaks for itself, except that the phrase I italicized needs unpacking. I judge as someone else does if and only if his judgment and mine agree in fringe and core. (I express myself this way, quite harmlessly, in spite of the mess which the theory of double judgments makes of both fringes and cores, for the sole purpose of avoiding what is merely tedious.) But perhaps you will ask what in this world is the ground of something agreeing with, or being like, something else. I answer, very simply, that what he calls likeness and equality are in his world relations of comparison (see *Kategl.*, pp. 176 ff.). To say of a judgment that it is correct is therefore merely to specify one of its accidents.

That much about the truth and falsehood of judgments, e.g., the judgment *J* that *A is*. How about propositions? More precisely, what does one acknowledge when acknowledging that (*A is*) *is true?* At this point Brentano resorts to the awkward expedient with which we are already familiar from his theory of double judgments. To judge that (*A is*) *is true* is to acknowledge (someone who judges correctly that *A* is). I have spared you the ordeal of forcing the expression in the last pair of parentheses into the standard of his improved language. Nor would there be any point to the exercise. Incredible as the conceit of an improved language without sentences and of names only at first seems and indeed is, once one has seen through how it is done, as by now surely you have, it loses interest.

The idealism of this theory of truth shows itself. That is why I called

---

[27] In German: *richtig*. The preference has something to do with his ethics, on which there will be a brief comment at the very end of the next section.

[28] I quote this extraordinary statement from *WuEv.*, p. 139, which takes it from a fragment written in 1915.

it the *second breakdown*. What needs to be shown is the mistake, or the mistakes, which caused its author to believe that he was nevertheless a realist₂. As far as I can see, he made two such mistakes. Once pointed out, they are equally obvious. Yet there is a difference. One cuts rather deep; the other is shallow and sophistical. The former I leave for the next section; of the other I shall dispose right now.

Truth may be said to be *objective* in two senses; once because of the required adequation or correspondence with "objective" fact; once because two beliefs such that the sentences expressing their intentions contradict each other cannot both be true. Call the second kind of objectivity for the moment nonsubjectivity; remember that idealism has also been called subjectivism; and you will see how he rather sophistically defends himself against the charge of idealism (subjectivism) by taking advantage of this double use. He tells us, first, that if you and I make two judgments one of which acknowledges what the other rejects, then they cannot both be true. If we ask him how he knows this, he tells us, second, that it is itself an evident truth. He concludes, third, that the theory of truth he proposes is nonsubjectivistic and, therefore, not idealistic. The *quaternio terminorum* is manifest.

I turn now to the problems raised by his notion of evidence. It will be best if we begin with the a priori. That requires in turn that we acquaint ourselves with his assay of the causal connection. All we know of it so far is that it is one of his five kinds of "real" relations (p. 260). Thus we also know that the assay cannot but be most inadequate. Since it is also dreary and dull, I have ignored it as long as I could. Nor shall I now say more about it than is absolutely necessary.

As most philosophers speak, including myself, a cause precedes its effect. As Brentano speaks, some causes are simultaneous with their effects. Since this special case contains the gist of his assay, since it will do for my purpose, and since we decided to gather what little I shall say about his assay of time in the last section, we may as well stay with it. The moon and the tide it causes, or, in general, Newtonian attraction would be an example. For a homelier one, take a cube of steel which lies on a sheet of rubber. The cube's weight, i.e., its being heavy, is the cause; its effect is the sheet's being of a certain shape which for brevity's sake I shall call distorted, since it is different from the one the sheet would have if the cube did not rest on it.[29]

---

[29] The foil's assay of the causal nexus is Humean. Hence its causes and effects are facts, since, schematically speaking, they are instantiations (e.g., $F(a)$, $G(a)$) of the antecedent and the consequent of a formal implication (e.g., (x) $[F(x) \supset G(x)]$). In his world, the cause and the effect are not the respective acci-

We know what he is committed to. He must, and does, assay the connection as a single *relativliches* accident of either the cube or the sheet. The two relational properties in the case are expressed by 'causing the distorted shape (of the sheet)' and 'being caused by the weight (of the cube)'. Yet, according to him, their ground is a single accident. Where, then, we must ask, is this accident, in the cube or in the sheet? You will be able to infer his answer if you remember how he arrived at the decision in the case of the whole-part connection (p. 262). The latter's *relativliche* accidents are in their respective wholes, since the latter, unlike the parts, could not be what they are unless the connection obtained. In the case at hand, the cube would be what it is, namely, heavy, even if it did not lie on the sheet, while the latter would not, since, unless there were an alternative cause producing the same effect, it would not be of the distorted shape. He concludes, first, that 'causing the distorted shape (of the sheet)' is a *denominatio mere extrinseca* of the cube, and second, that 'caused by the weight (of the cube)' is a *relativliches* accident of the shape of the sheet. Generally, *the causal accident, if I may so express myself, is always in the effect, never in the cause*.[30] This he gives with one hand. I turn next to what he takes away with the other, quite commonsensically, alas, yet with an ontological recklessness which is as impressive a symptom of his doctrinaire reism as any.[31]

Like Aristotle, he calls the distorted shape an *affection*. An affection is there only while and as long as the causal accident is there. The latter is presumably in the sheet. Yet the affection does not persist unless the cube lies on it. He concludes that while the causal accident is wholly in one object, it yet requires the support of another. We ask of course: How about the relation of support? The inadequacy is glaring; so is the recklessness. No more need be said.

---

dents, being heavy and being of the distorted shape, but, rather, the two objects with the accidents inhering in them. Or, at least, this is closer to what I take to be the spirit of the Aristotelian assay. But I shall say so little that whatever doubt as to this alternative there might be makes no difference for what I shall say.

[30] Notice that the causal accident, e.g., being caused by the weight (of the cube), and the accident caused, e.g., the distorted shape, are two and not one. This will become important when, in the last section, we shall explore the consequences of the former's, unlike the latter's, not being presented to us in most cases.

[31] Aristotle, we saw, kept worrying these difficulties. His assay of the causal connection, though inadequate, is therefore anything but reckless. The textual evidence, in many long passages and whole fragments of the *Kategorienlehre*, for Brentano's most unsatisfactory assay is so clear and so repetitive that there is no point in selecting a few places.

I conceive something both square and round. My conceiving it causes me to reject it. Also, most crucially, the causal accident in the act of rejecting is in the secondary intention of the latter. Thus I may not only know it, but *know* it, i.e., I may know it evidently. This evidence is the ground on which in this world a priori status is claimed for the proposition rejected. As for this particular generality, of type **e**, so for all others, of type **e** and of type **a**. This is the twist which solves the problem of accounting for the a priori of a world in which only reflexive knowledge is *knowledge*. Looked at in one light, it is ingenious; looked at in another, it is merely a trick. The following five comments will show it in both lights. Then I shall be ready to conclude with some reflections on the phenomenological problems involved.

First. The twist is ingenious in that it realizes, as closely as one possibly could in a world without ideas, the representationalists' basic conception, with which we have long been familiar, that what one knows when knowing something a priori is a connection among ideas, irrespective of whether or not they represent anything.

Second. The twist affords an illuminating insight into how deepseated and pervasive the idealism is. (As you see, I no longer say, as I might have if we were not as far as we are, that this account of the a priori is a further step toward idealism. For how can one make a further step toward a goal he has reached already?) From where I stand,[32] what makes a fact (truth) a priori is something "in" it, not anything extraneous to it. From where he stands, what makes a truth a priori is that our conceiving it causes us to acknowledge it.[33] That is how the idealism reveals itself. The something I just spoke about is put into the judgment. Even more poignantly, since evidence is an accident of fringes, it is put into the subjective part of the judgment. Nor does he just put it there, he even prides himself on putting it there. Or, at least, he chides Descartes for being so confused that sometimes it seems as if what distinguishes his clear and distinct ideas were some something peculiar to the ideas themselves rather than to the judgment.[34]

Third. Acknowledging the premises of a valid argument, sometimes[35]

---

[32] And from where any articulate realist₂ ought to stand if he believes that a certain familiar class of synthetic truths can be set aside, on grounds which are ontologically significant, as more "fundamental" than the rest. For detailed argument, see the essay on the "Synthetic *a priori*" in *Logic and Reality*.

[33] The uneasiness this formulation may cause you will be relieved in the fifth comment.

[34] This is a near-literal translation from *Psych.* III, 24. Once again, no more need be said, except, perhaps, that the gods first blind whom they wish to destroy. For an early statement, see *Ursp.*, p. 50.

[35] I.e., depending on causes which need not be, and for the most part are not,

causes me to acknowledge its conclusion. In either case, I *know* the causal accident. There is thus no difference, either in this respect or as far as I can tell in any other, between the logical or analytic (necessary$_2$) on the one hand and the synthetic a priori (necessary$_3$) on the other. That shows why, like all representationalists, this particular structural one has no very cogent motive for distinguishing between these two kinds of necessity. That fits well his vacillating as to whether or not (I express myself as he does) the axioms of geometry follow from the principle of contradiction alone, without these vacillations having any repercussions in the rest of his system.[36]

Fourth. His a priori truths are all generalities of the kind the representationalists call truths of reason. They are also evident. Evidence, I said, shines in its own light. Since he is also a deist, this raises a question. Could God deceive us with respect to these truths? E.g., could he cause us to *know* that $2+1=4$ or that red is a pitch?[37] Brentano, as he consistently must, agrees with Leibniz, against Descartes, that God could not so deceive us. "To deny him this power is not to deny his perfection but his imperfection."

Fifth. When we "acknowledge" a truth as a priori or "necessary," such as, e.g., that all triangles are plane figures, what we actually do, according to Brentano, is to reject something as "impossible," such as, e.g., (the existence of) something which is both a triangle and not a plane figure. We must understand accurately how at this point the ontology is made to fit with the logic and the epistemology, or, more precisely, with the logic and epistemology before the fall, when judgments **a** and **e** were still assayed as rejections of single ideas.[38]

(1) All triangles are plane figures. (2) All dogs are carnivorous. (3) All dogs are geometricians. (1) is an a priori truth. (2) and (3) are a posteriori. The former is a truth; the latter, a falsehood. The entities

presented to me. This is no difficulty. Or does the cube distort the shape of the sheet unless someone puts it there?

[36] The bulk of the texts concerning this sort of thing is in the less attractive books. But see, for a pleasant and instructive statement of the affirmative, Kraus, *Franz Brentano* (Munich: Beck, 1919), pp. 60–61.

[37] I take these examples and the quotation from Stumpf (in Kraus, *Franz Brentano*, p. 101), who seems to have taken them from his notes of the lectures on metaphysics which Brentano held in Würzburg in 1869. See also *WuEv.*, p. 157, in a letter to Husserl from 1905. As to the disastrous consequences which the view commonly attributed to Descartes would have for the pattern which I called the *Cogito*, see n. 31 of Section Eleven.

[38] As you see, I continue to suppose that the program of reduction can be carried out. This not only permits us to avoid the tedium of the double judgments (and double conceptions); it also helps us to see more clearly what would be wrong with this ontology even if the supposition were not contrary to fact.

involved are all in the Second. In my world, where as it happens the
'all' of the improved language carries no existential import, this is so
whether or not for the sake of the argument the existential import is
added. In his world, in which there is "really" no Second, if the import
is added, (1), (2), and (3) become all false, while without it they are
"really" all true, including (3), on the overriding ontological ground
that in a world without a Second there are no triangles, no plane figures, no dogs, no geometricians, and so on. That alone shows that,
ingenious as it may be, the twist depends too much on the hoax to be
more than a trick. What it all amounts to is this. In a world without
colors there is nothing which is both red and green. Some such (ontological) truisms, unlike some others, we know with (epistemological)
evidence. Or so we are told. Should we be impressed?

The last comment leads into the phenomenological reflections to
which in conclusion I now turn.

Brentano's evidence is a peculiar "quality" presented on *all* occasions
of self-knowledge and on *no* others.[39] Is there such a "quality" in the
foil? The answer is Yes. There is in my world the species of (direct)
awareness, as distinct from all other species as each pitch or color from
all other pitches or colors, which is the species of *all* acts whose intentions are something mental and of *no* others. This is a very important
agreement. But there are also two differences. For one, there is no
reflexive knowledge in the foil. Hence, awareness of the peculiar
"quality" requires a further act, intending the one in which it occurs.[40]
For another, there is in the foil neither *knowledge* nor criterion. Hence,
its (direct) awareness does not, like his evidence, serve as a criterion.
The first of these two differences makes in this context no difference;
the second does; to see why and how we turn to perception.

Since in his world, in which there is no Second, what we perceive does
not exist,[41] he is dialectically forced to hold, as he does, that we never
perceive anything with evidence. What then about those cases of perception, occasionally erroneous but much more often (as the rest of us
would say) veridical, in which we are "certain" that what we perceive

[39] This *all* does not conflict with the *some*(-times) commented on above in n. 35,
provided one takes self-knowledge in the properly narrow sense and makes all
those "reasonable qualifications" about which Brentano has so much to say even
though they are dialectically quite irrelevant. See nn. 25 and 27 of Section Fourteen; also n. 23 concerning the protective parentheses around 'direct' in '(direct)
awareness'. The use of 'quality' here is nontechnical; hence the double quotes. In
his world the peculiar "quality" is an accident; in mine, a species.

[40] For this as well as all other details concerning the foil, see my earlier analyses.

[41] I use 'exist' rather than, as in the next sentence, where I speak for myself,
'real', because he does not make the distinction.

is real. All there is, according to him, in all these cases, is the "instinctual urge" to believe what in fact is false and what we could not *know* even if it were true. Or, as he says, *perception is blind.*[42]

(1) "Certainty" is a quality[43] of some species, such as believing, perceiving, and being (directly) aware of, of which I am sometimes (directly) aware. (2) Some perceivings are as "certain" as any direct awareness. (3) We have learned through experience that our perceptions are not always as "trustworthy" as our (direct) awarenesses. (4) This difference in "trustworthiness" is a mere matter of fact. Nor is it grounded in any entity presented to us. (Such an entity would of course provide a criterion.)

These, I submit, are four phenomenological truths. What Brentano says about the evidence of self-knowledge and the blindness of perception runs afoul of all of them. Thus he is in serious phenomenological trouble. Nor do I know how he could get out of it.

Some would claim that I, too, have got myself into such trouble by introducing the two ontological modes, actuality and potentiality, even though the difference between them is not presented to us. I have already made my defense against this charge, partly at least by an answer so meek that I hoped it would turn away wrath.[44] Now, though, I shall try to strengthen my case by comparing his trouble with the one I am supposed to be in.

He claims that there is a certain "quality" he calls evidence with which we are presented in self-knowledge but not in perception and which, as we just saw, is neither of the two I call "certainty" and (direct) awareness, respectively. Not being acquainted with such a "quality," I conclude that he claims us to be presented with something with which we are in fact not presented. What we do, essentially under the same dialectical pressures, from the realism-idealism issue and the problems of perception, is thus very different. He claims something to be phenomenologically presented which isn't. I merely "postulate" something not so presented.

[42] In this conviction, which he always held, he never wavered. Kraus, quite correctly I think, traces it to 1874, the date of publication of the first volume of the *Psychologie.* See his notes 14, 15, 16 in *Psych.* I, 270.

[43] Or, more precisely, a series of such.

[44] See the discussion at the end of Section Eleven.

SECTION SEVENTEEN

PLACES, MOMENTS, SELVES

IN the first part of this section I shall examine the ontology and the epistemology of the spatial and temporal determinations of Brentano's physical objects. While engaged in this task, I shall of course pretend that the physical objects of his world exist. In the second part I shall take a quick look at his selves. Then I shall drop the pretense that what does not really exist is his Second, and, in the third and final part, exhibit the third and final breakdown by showing why the scientific objects which are his would-be Second cannot in his world consistently be said to exist.

Eventually he changed his views on both the ontology and the epistemology of both space and time. I say eventually because there was only one change on each and because they both occurred very late in his life.[1] The earlier views he thus held through most of his career; the later ones, only for a short time, before he died. Let us call them the first and the second views, respectively. There is thus a first ontology, a second ontology, a first epistemology, and a second epistemology. I shall take them up in this order.

Space, being three-dimensional, is very difficult in the sense in which one-dimensional time is very easy. Neither Brentano nor any other philosopher ever attended to all these difficulties.[2] That makes it safe to limit our examination to what in his world corresponds to the

---

[1] Brentano died on March 17, 1917. The only explicit statement of the second ontology is in a fragment dictated on February 23 of the same year and posthumously published by Kraus under the title "Zur Lehre von Raum und Zeit" in *Kantstudien*, 25, 1920, 1–23. The development of the second epistemology can be traced through the five posthumous essays in *Psych.* II, all from 1917, and the fifth chapter of Part One as well as the third and fourth chapters of Part Two of *Psych.* III, none of which antedates 1914.

[2] Nor, from where I stand, is there any reason for not leaving them to the descriptive phenomenologists on the one hand and the mathematicians on the other.

coordinate qualities p_i and t_i of the prototype and to the spatial and temporal distances between them. For the latter I shall write such expressions as '$d(p_1, p_2)$' and '$d(t_1, t_2)$', respectively; and adopt such locutions as 'p_i is at $d(p_i, p_j)$ from p_j' and 't_m is at $d(t_m, t_n)$ from t_n'; which will often allow us to omit 'spatial' and 'temporal'.

The first ontology. The (momentary) substance₁ and the (momentary) substance₃ of a (cross section of a) physical object coincide. The former individuates the object; the latter is the only entity unilaterally separable from it and therefore, though not itself literally an object, at least a near-object. Since the two kinds coincide, I shall suppress the indices and henceforth speak of the (momentary) substance of a cross section. Suppose that, as assayed in the prototype, the latter is $\gamma(p_1, t_1, a_1, b_1)$, with a_1 and b_1 grounding a color and a shape, respectively. That makes $\gamma(p_1, t_1)$ the prototype entity which corresponds to the substance. The correspondence is close; yet there are differences. In the prototype, p_1, t_1, a_1, and b_1 are alike in all being perfect particulars, i.e., simple categorial entities and as such of course "thinkable," even though each of them is on a priori grounds incapable of "existing independently." In the first ontology, if I may express myself paradoxically, they are all alike in that each of them is unthinkable and therefore not as such or by itself an existent. But there is also this difference that while a_1 and b_1 correspond to two Brentano-style accidents, p_1 and t_1, though mutually inseparable and therefore neither existents nor even near-existents by themselves, are yet jointly the object's substance and therefore among its substantial rather than among its accidental determinations. All this we know from Section Thirteen. If you keep it in mind, no harm will be done if we let 'p_i' and 't_i' stand for these two kinds of determinations and occasionally speak of them as if they existed. But I shall pay my respect to the long verbal association between 'accident' and 'quality' by calling them *coordinates*[3] rather than, as in the prototype, coordinate qualities.

All distances are relations of comparison. Turn to the list on page 260 and you will see that this is indeed the only one among the six classes of relations into which they fit. That makes being-at-$d(p_i, p_j)$-from-p_j and being-at-$d(t_m, t_n)$-from-t_n *denominationes mere extrinsecae* (*d.m.e.*) of p_i and t_m, respectively. A coordinate being at some distance from another, e.g., one time coordinate being later than a second and earlier than a third, does thus not require that the latter two exist. To say of two objects that they are at a certain distance from each other is

---

[3] Brentano and his students call them the spatial and temporal *species*. See n. 14 of Section Thirteen.

merely a way of saying that their respective coordinates are at this distance.[4] The time coordinates of any two objects in a single cross section are equal; or, as one says, the objects are simultaneous.

The second ontology. A momentary substance is a space-time cell. An ordinary (momentary) object is a space-time cell with some qualitative determinations. In terms of the example from the prototype which we have used so often, an ordinary object is at least ternary; its substance, i.e., the space-time cell in it, binary. In the first ontology some space-time cells are objects (though of course not ordinary objects). Accordingly, an ordinary object's substance is not only its individuator (substance$_1$) but also unilaterally separable from it, and, therefore, its substance$_3$. This amounts to an absolutist[5] assay of space-time. In the second ontology, the absolutism is abandoned. This is the only change. Clearly, it is very important. So I shall spell it out.

In the second ontology a cell as such is not an existent. Equivalently, there are no cells without some qualitative determination. Or, as one says, Brentano eventually abandoned the container theory, i.e., the belief in an empty space-time. It follows, at least for the Second, that an object's substance, while still its individuator, is no longer a substance$_3$. Had he lived long enough after having changed his mind, he would no doubt himself have drawn this conclusion.

This will do for the two ontologies. The two epistemologies will take longer. Two preliminary comments will expedite matters.

First. Brentano's minds can "make" some ideas out of some others. Those made he sometimes calls *synthetic;* those out of which they are made I shall for the moment call the building material. To the minds of an empiricist's world all their building materials are furnished by what so many have so vaguely called experience. Brentano was an empiricist. What he meant by experience was, not at all vaguely, either self-knowledge or perception.[6]

What are our ideas of space and time? How have we come by them? Applying what has just been said to these two questions, one sees that they are indeed two and not one. Yet for an empiricist they are not unconnected. His answer to the first sets him the task of so answering

---

[4] Or, rather, in this reistic world, the other way round. As to equality, see n. 28 of Section Sixteen.

[5] I say of *space-time* rather than of *space and time* because, as in the first ontology, the two coordinates of a cell are mutually inseparable. For the ambiguity of 'absolute' in this context as well as for the similarities and differences between the second ontology and my own assay of space and time, see n. 8 of Section Thirteen.

[6] I.e., either *innere* or *aeussere Wahrnehmung.*

the second that all the ideas which he claims we possess are accounted for in a manner consistent with his empiricism.

Second. The two epistemologies share a hidden premiss: *Every acknowledging is simultaneous with the object it acknowledges.* As you see, the premiss is itself epistemological, even though, for reasons which will not at all surprise us, it has, as we shall see, in his world an ontological consequence which is monstrous. It also has an important kernel of truth. We shall best find our bearings by first trying to understand accurately this kernel and how the foil manages to account for it without thereby being committed to that consequence.

Every (bare) particular presented is simultaneous with the act "in" whose intention it is.[7] This is how the foil states the truth I just called the kernel. One cannot appreciate the difference between the two formulae without remembering three things. (1) Acknowledging, we know, is a most slippery notion. In the foil, accordingly, there is no acknowledging. Its place is taken by the three fringes of perceiving, remembering, and believing, whose names may be qualified by either 'truly' or 'falsely'. (2) Earlier, later, and simultaneous are three of the foil's relations, in its sense of 'relation', such that exactly one of them obtains between any two of its particulars.[8] Also, all three are presented to us within the limits of the specious present. (3) In the foil there are existential facts. Hence, if *a* is a particular "in" my present intention, the sentential clause '$(\exists x)\ earlier(x, a)$' is available to me for asserting the existence of a past particular. As for the past, so of course for the future. (That I could not now name a particular either past or future is a different point which disturbs nothing and fits well with everything.)

It follows from (1) and (3) that, while by the formula which (if I am right) is Brentano's hidden premiss the minds of his world cannot acknowledge anything not simultaneous with the act of acknowledging it, the foil's formula does not prevent its minds from "acknowledging" now (at *present*) what is in either the *past* or the *future*.

Only the present exists. This is the monstrous consequence. It fol-

---

[7] Thus I must consistently hold, as I do, that even in the case of a true memory the particulars in the image that may or may not accompany it are not real but of the kind I call critical. But see the "Realistic Postscript" in *Logic and Reality* about so-called sense data in general and, in particular, the long footnote beginning on p. 322.

[8] That ignores overlapping. But see the essay on duration in *Logic and Reality;* also, for many other details on time, "Some Reflections on Time" in *Meaning and Existence.*

lows immediately from the hidden premiss in conjunction with the equally monstrous proposition that to exist is to be acknowledged. Thus no more need be said about it, except, perhaps, that it fits only too well with the extremist position that assays all temporal relations as *d.m.e.* whose terms need not exist.

'Present', 'past', and 'future' are the cues to another, more subtle point, which will come in handy very soon. So I shall attend to it now.

The phenomenologists claim, not unreasonably, that presentness is a "quality," or, as one also says, rather deplorably, that it is a "feel" all its own. The ontologists, trying to ground this quality, get themselves into trouble. To see how that happens, consider the case of perception. There are three possibilities. (a) One may ground the quality in some specific entity perceived, i.e., in the Second. (b) One may ground it in some specific entity in the fringe. (c) One may ground it nonspecifically. Since it depends on some sliding connection between the First and the Second, the quality cannot be anything in the latter. That makes the "objective" alternative (a) calamitous. McTaggart's calamities are, thanks to Broad, notorious. Nor does the "subjective" alternative (b) seem to satisfy. The foil's way out is a corollary to its formula for the kernel. All the particulars *presented* to us are in the *present*. Nor is there any moment of my conscious life at which I am not presented with at least one particular. That makes it plausible, to say the least, to ground *presentness* in the feelings that accompany our being presented with particulars. These feelings are of course "subjective"; and they may be quite specific. Yet, as I just used the word, they are nonspecific. The foil's answer thus falls under (c). Brentano's, we shall see, hovers uneasily between (a) and (b).

The first epistemology. We possess the ideas of some p_i and of some t_i. Or, at least, this is the schema. For space it works smoothly. For time it has never been worked out satisfactorily. Attempting to do so naturally leads one into the second epistemology. Again, in discussing the first with respect to space, it is hardly worth while to distinguish between the two questions, as to what ideas we possess and as to how we have come by them. With respect to time, this is not so. But let us first look at space.

In the first epistemology we are in perception presented with some p_i (and some t_i). I, as you know, shall if necessary die in the last ditch for the phenomenological truth that we are not presented with such entities. But my concern right now is dialectical. The phenomenological truth, which as we shall see the second epistemology recovers, I take for granted. Suppose, then, for the sake of the argument, that we are in perception presented with some p_i. That leaves only one question. How does the mind from this building material make all its spatial ideas? We need not, and I shall not, go beyond two observations.

1. Having been presented with at least one instance of each of several colors, our minds are capable of forming the idea of colored (or, equivalently, of color). At least, this is a standard illustration of the capacity for forming abstract ideas with which Brentano endows his minds. If one accepts this "empiricist" pattern, there is no difficulty in supposing that, having been presented with several p_i, the mind is capable of forming the idea of *place*.

2. Being presented in one cross section with p_1 and p_2,[9] the mind is, as Brentano puts it, *in specie* presented with being-at-$d(p_1, p_2)$-from-p_2. Suppose that $d(p_1, p_2)$ is equal to several other distances, $d(p_4, p_5)$, $d(p_7, p_8)$, and so on; call this "distance" d. Again, I see no difficulty in supposing that, having been presented *in specie* with several instances of d, the mind is capable of forming by abstraction the idea of being-at-d-from-a-*place*, as well as, after having formed several such ideas for several "distances," by a further abstraction the even more general (abstract) idea of being-at-*some*-distance-from-a-place.

Turn to time; suppose that t_2 is earlier than t_1. On the one hand, I cannot, in view of the hidden premiss, at t_1 acknowledge Caesar-at-t_2.[10] More idiomatically, I cannot now *acknowledge* that Caesar lived (existed) in the past. On the other hand, the hidden premiss is compatible with my now, at t_1, conceiving t_2, and, therefore, also with my now *conceiving* of Caesar as having lived at t_2. This, though, is not enough. For I do not now just conceive of Caesar as living then; I now *believe,* or, what in this world amounts to the same, I now acknowledge that he then lived. What is Brentano's way out?

Let me first explain what I mean by a primary act. Each of us is at

---

[9] Either *modo recto* with the one, *modo obliquo* with the other; or, perhaps, directly with both, so that we may acknowledge them both, as in the case of the intention expressed by 'This is longer than that *is*' (p. 259). The difference makes no difference. Thus we need not worry about a passage (*Psych.* II, 200), which, under the pressure of the Stumpf-Hering school of "nativism" in psychology, identifies the *hic* of the *hic et nunc* of the *modus rectus* with the center of the visual field. '*Hic et nunc*', as the readers of the *Logische Untersuchungen* know, is Husserl's pet phrase. Brentano uses it once or twice.

[10] Notice that, even though for brevity's sake I shall express myself this way, a t_i is not literally a date but, rather, a member of a huge class of time coordinates equal among themselves but to no others and such that all of them but no others are, as one says, at a certain date. Similarly, 'Caesar-at-t_2' is merely a more idiomatic way of referring to a certain object one of whose cross sections has t_2 as a substantial determination.

each moment of his conscious life presented with at least one particular. Or, equivalently in his world, each of us at each such moment acknowledges at least one object. Still equivalently, since one cannot acknowledge anything without at the same time directly conceiving it, each of us directly conceives and acknowledges something at each moment of his conscious life. Call an act of this sort a *primary act*.

Suppose next that I am now (at t_1) conceiving Caesar (not: Caesar at t_2); put this conceiving into the "appropriate" oblique mode; then "forge" it to any one of my primary acts at t_1. The "appropriate" oblique mode is the one which corresponds to $d(t_1, t_2)$, just as conversely there is one such mode for each temporal distance. The resulting double judgment is Brentano's assay of my now believing that Caesar then lived. That is how he manages to construe beliefs about the past and *mutatis mutandis* about the future as acknowledgings, not of anything either past or future but, rather, of something present as being either later or earlier than something which itself is not acknowledged. He is very proud of this twist. We notice immediately that we have come upon another instance of the conversion rule. The temporal distances have been suppressed. The substitutes we are offered are a series of oblique modes, which he calls the *temporal modes*. Nor is that all. Since the temporal modes account for the distance, there is (if I may so express myself) no need for the conceiving in the case to be a conceiving of Caesar at t_2 rather than, more abstractly,[11] of Caesar without any determinate temporal coordinate. Thus this "solution" may well weaken the resistance against the phenomenological truth that no (temporal) coordinates are ever presented. This is what I had in mind when I said a while ago that if one tried to work out the first epistemology for time, one is naturally led to the second.

The second epistemology. Upon this view neither spatial nor temporal coordinates are ever presented to us. What, then, is the building material for the spatial and temporal ideas which we in fact possess, and how does the mind manage to make the latter out of the former? Brentano did not face these questions until after he had changed his view. Nor are the answers he then proposed adequate; some of them, unlike those by which the first epistemology accounts for the ideas of place and distance, are not adequate even on his own terms. Yet he started quite properly from the proposition that when presented with a physical object, we are presented with a spatial and a temporal feature. *That* there are such features as well as *what* they are is to me a

---

[11] I.e., in Meinong's terms, the idea of Caesar so conceived is general. Brentano, who uses 'universal' and 'general' synonymously, quite consistently insists, in one of the last fragments, that *all our ideas are universal* (*Psych.* II, 199–200).

phenomenological truth. Yet there has been controversy as to *what* they are. I begin again with space.

When perceiving a physical object, one is presented, not with the idea of its spatial coordinate but, rather, with the more abstract one of *place.* This is his basic gambit. If a similar situation prevailed with respect to color, one would on such occasions be presented with the idea of color *in genere*, without ever having been presented with that of a color, red, green, blue, and so on, *in specie.* This shows how odd the gambit is. I add three comments.

1. Remember the covertly anthropomorphic and therefore irremediably confused way in which the representationalists think of a single perception becoming more *distinct* as one makes an effort to perceive a larger number of features of an object (p. 189). By another closely related and equally confused supposition, the perception of an object is the more *indistinct* the greater the generality (abstractness) of the concept by which it "presents itself." This second confusion accounts for the odd gambit.[12] The mind's eye is, as it were, not keen enough to see the coordinate distinctly; all it can see, indistinctly, is place.

2. According to Descartes, the spatial feature presented is not place but "extension." For this Brentano takes him to task.[13] The foil, disagreeing with both, holds that the critical feature is the shape of the particular presented. If this is right, then Descartes, though wrong, is closer to the truth than Brentano.

3. Distances are held to be perceived. This can only mean that we are sometimes *in specie* presented with a completely determinate relation of comparison without ever having been presented with the nonrelational (absolute) determinations between which it obtains. I do not see how an empiricist could possibly account for this state of affairs. The most he could hope for under the circumstances is to account for the much more general (generic, abstract, indeterminate) idea of one-place-being-at-*some*-distance-from-another. And even that is problematic. Brentano himself noticed the difficulty. But he talked himself out of it by an obvious mistake.[14]

---

[12] The diagnosis is confirmed by content and context of the third chapter of Part One of *Psych.* III. See also the reference to it in n. 20 of Section Ten.

[13] *Psych.* II, 267. For the peculiar grammar of 'extended' and 'extension', see the essay on the "Synthetic *a priori*" in *Logic and Reality.*

[14] "It is impossible to conceive a relation of comparison *in specie* without conceiving *in specie* the absolute determinations it relates; nor can a relation of comparison be conceived *in genere* without conceiving *in genere* that between which it obtains" (*Psych.* III, 104). You see now why I used the two tags '*in genere*' and '*in specie*'. Tracing them will help you to expand the argument I state so concisely. The obvious mistake consists in overlooking that, while the ideas of one-

The problems of time are even more intractable. What makes them so is his insistence that the temporal feature presented to us when perceiving a physical or *knowing* a mental object is an instant, i.e., as one says, an extensionless point in time. Since such a point is really nothing, he must somehow convince himself that it can somehow be stretched into a moment. Hence the many, many very tedious pages about boundaries and the continuum which we can safely ignore,[15] except in one context of which shortly.

In the foil the temporal feature with which one is presented when presented with a (bare) particular is a duration.[16] Such "temporal extensions" are moments, which are in time what places are in space. Had he been consistent, he would therefore have held that, just as the spatial idea presented in perception is that of place, so the temporal one presented in either perception or *knowledge* is that of moment. Actually he held that the one temporal idea presented is that of "present." That is why I said that his solution of the problem of presentness hovers uneasily between the subjective and the objective.[17] What saves him from the calamities of the objective alternative is an insight and a confusion. With the latter we are familiar from space. He thinks of the "present" as the several temporal coordinates indistinctly perceived.[18] The insight is that from the single idea of "present" one cannot even form that of moment. So he looks around for additional building material. This is the context in which one must remember that his "present" is instantaneous.

In such a "present" one is not, as in the foil, presented with earlier and later. So he invents a substitute. If, say, we listen through a certain duration to a tone, then, he tells us, we not only ἐν παρέργῳ *know* at each of its instances that we *modo recto* conceive and acknowledge this tone but we also know, in a short-span series of oblique modes, several conceivings of the tone "as more or less immediately past."[19] Materially,

---

place-being-at-*d*-from-another and of one-place-being-at-*some*-distance-from-another are both abstract (generic), the latter is different from and more abstract than the former.

[15] See the conclusion of Section Thirteen.

[16] Every bare particular of the foil exemplifies a duration, the nonmental ones also a shape. See the essay on the "Synthetic *a priori*" in *Logic and Reality*.

[17] (a) and (b) on p. 324. The subjective side of this teetertotter is what he calls the *modus praesens*, which is nothing but the "temporal aspect" of the *modus rectus* of conceiving, corresponding to the *nunc* in *hic et nunc*.

[18] Thus, unlike in space, where we can conceive and even acknowledge two places in one cross section, we are forever presented with *the* one and only "present."

[19] There is another teetertotter here. One cannot be sure that he always thinks of the acts in the present nontemporal series as conceivings, as I charitably assume, rather than as acknowledgings of something "as past." If the latter, then

this substitute amounts to admitting the specious present, to whose characteristically short span that of the series corresponds. Formally, he can and in fact does argue, taking considerable pride in this bit of sophistry, that it is a *nontemporal series of present oblique conceivings of something "as past."* But let that pass. Ask instead how all other temporal ideas and the temporal modes can be made out of that of "present" in conjunction with the oblique modes of the instantaneous substitute.

Kraus, who at this point is at least as articulate as his master, tells us that it can be done by analogy.[20] Since I have not undertaken to work out in detail what Brentano himself did either only sketchily or not at all, so that his whole ontology may be seen to be adequate, but, rather, to show that what he actually did suffices to reject it, I shall conclude this examination of his assay of space and time with two comments which by themselves suffice to reject it.

First. The series just introduced as a substitute is nontemporal. *The* "present" is forever one and the same. How, then, do we come by the idea of a temporal series of moments? By analogy; or so we are told. What justifies the analogy? How does it get started? The only answer we are offered is the strange claim that the "present" being a member of a series (of "presents"?) is an a priori truth.[21] As it happens, not by chance of course, this alleged a priori truth is one of the pillars on which Husserl's later, overtly idealistic assay of time rests.[22] (As a moment's reflection will show you, the device of the nontemporal series is a substitute also in the sense of the conversion rule. The entities of the Second suppressed and substituted for are the temporal distances within the specious present.)

Second. The nontemporal series is one among fringes. Thus its members are subjective. That amounts to the claim that at least some of the building material out of which our temporal ideas are made is subjective. Being epistemological, this claim is perhaps not quite as strong as the ontological one, by the later Husserl, that "Time and Self constitute each other." Yet they are sufficiently close to leave no doubt that *Husserl did not distort his teacher's realism into his own eventual idealism. He merely brought out into the open what was there.*

----

he has for the specious present abandoned the hidden premiss without which the maneuver described in the next paragraph does not even make sense.

[20] *Psych.* III, 185*n39.* Kraus also mentions negation. But virtually every *Begriffsynthese* involves negation.

[21] Or, as he puts it, this truth is "part of the concept of present." See, e.g., *Psych.* II, 257.

[22] See, also for the next comment, my essay on "The Ontology of Edmund Husserl" in *Logic and Reality*, especially p. 220.

Brentano's selves are hidden. In this they are like Aristotelian substances. All I know (*know*) of mine, for instance, are its (present) acts. These are assayed as the accidents of a continuant individuator (substance$_1$). What he calls my self is this substance$_1$; or, perhaps, it is a continuant substantial determination[23] of it; this is a question of words. In either case, its existence is merely inferred from the ultimate premisses (p. 238). One may express this by saying that these selves are *postulated*. Nor, therefore, outside of some theological speculation, does he have much to say about what is thus hidden and therefore merely postulated. Being averse to such speculation, I shall say even less. E.g., I shall not inquire whether these postulated continuant substances$_1$ are unilaterally separable from their accidents and therefore also substances$_3$, which would further increase the contrast between minds and bodies, since the latter have only momentary substances$_1$ and, upon the second ontology of space, not even momentary substances$_3$.

"Two existents (objects) which, if presented singly, could (in principle) not be distinguished from each other, are really one and not two. Two objects can (in principle) agree in all their accidents. No object is individuated by its accidents alone. There are no bare entities to serve as individuators." These are the premisses from which the little that need be said must start.

Stay within a cross section. If the temporal coordinates of the several physical objects in it were "thinkable" by themselves, they would all be one. Their spatial coordinates, equally "unthinkable" as such, yet vary from object to object. Jointly, they are held to be "thinkable." That is why space-time cells can serve as (momentary) individuators of physical objects. Minds are not in space. Yet, if, as in principle they could, your mind and mine now agreed in all accidents, they would still be two and not one. Hence one is justified in postulating a (momentary) substantial determination varying from person to person, which, jointly with the temporal one, individuates a (momentary) mind. This determination is a (momentary) self.[24] This is the gist of his argument.

Leave now the cross section. It does not follow from what has just been said that my several momentary selves are all the same$_3$ continu-

---

[23] In case it is merely one among several determinants of a substance$_1$ and therefore not even "thinkable" without the others, it is not of course in his world an existent or even a near-existent. But we need not bother.

[24] This settles the question of words in agreement with ordinary usage, which speaks of minds as being in time rather than conversely, and also, I believe, in the spirit of Brentano. Husserl, we saw, might disagree.

ant. Equivalently, it does not follow that, as it was put earlier, a self is a substance₄.²⁵ But we know that his minds "make" ideas out of others; which, as we also know (p. 123), is a strong structural reason for his selves being continuants. There are also theological reasons. So you will not be surprised to hear that he declares them to be continuants.

Even though continuants, these selves are not, or at least not in the poignant sense, substances₅, i.e., they are not spontaneous in a sense incompatible with the thesis of scientific determinism. He holds in fact that all our acts, including those of will, are caused; just as he understands very well that this does not preclude either one act of mine being caused by another, as, e.g., in deductive inference, or some others, e.g., those of will, having all sorts of effect.²⁶ Much of what he has to say about selves is thus remarkably sober. Yet only a very small part of it falls within the scope of this book. All our acts, he tells us, are caused. What, then, we may ask, are the causes of our perceivings. He answers that they are caused by the scientific objects. Thus he finally asserts his realism₂. So I shall show that there is in his world no good reason for accepting his answer, and, even worse, that it is not consistent with what he says about existence. Having thus shown that his ontology finally breaks down, I shall conclude with a passing comment on his ethics.

Loving-Mary is a *relativliches* accident of whoever loves her. As for loving-Mary, so for loving-Peter, loving-Valerie, and so on. Having been presented with several of them, the mind forms by abstraction the idea of loving-someone. As for loving-someone, so for being-caused-by-something, except that the latter is presumably a second-order accident.²⁷ An accident caused by a "supporting" object is an "affection" (p. 315). The object "suffering" it is *passive;* the "supporting" one, *active.* Or is it an object's substance rather than the object itself which is active or passive? If the former, are active and passive themselves accidents? Fortunately, we need not look too closely or expatiate once more on the blurs and inadequacies of the substantialist assays of causation. All that concerns us is the doctrine, which Bren-

---

²⁵ As we now see, this is not quite accurate. As we decided the question, the substance₄ is really a series of "self-time cells," with the same₃ self and different t_i. But, again, we need not bother.

²⁶ I.e., scientific determinism and psychophysical interactionism being compatible, his "determinism" does not commit him to psychophysical parallelism. (I always add 'scientific' or, as here, surround the noun by double quotes, because I reserve 'determinism' for the absurd doctrine that we are not free.)

²⁷ E.g., as in our earlier example, of having a distorted shape. 'Causing-something', on the other hand, is merely a synsemantic expression. For the accident that grounds the causal connection is presumably in the effect (p. 315).

tano asserts over and over again,[28] that with the sole exception of the a priori we are never presented with anything being caused by anything else.

Since he holds this doctrine, he has no good reason to believe that any of our acts, except those which we know to be caused by others, are caused by anything, unless he is prepared to argue the proposition that the so-called principle of causality is an a priori truth. According to this principle, everything (except God) is caused by something else. Unhappily, he does argue that proposition.[29] I reject it out of hand. But perhaps you don't. So I shall show that, even if for the sake of the argument one accepts it, he still has no good reason for believing that our perceptions are caused by his would-be Second. What, then, we must ask, are the bad reasons he mistakes for good ones?

He argues that, since they must be caused by something, our perceptions are caused by entities of which we do not know what they are like but of which we can, with a probability amounting to virtual certainty though not of course to evidence, infer that their multiplicities, agreements, and differences are reflected by the physical objects we perceive. These entities are the scientific objects of his would-be Second. The probability amounting to virtual certainty corresponds to the merely inductively established coherence of the foil's real. This, though, is not his trouble. The trouble is, rather, that, particularly since he is a deist, he could account for the coherence just as well, and, upon his own terms, more naturally in the manner of Berkeley.

This, though, is only part of his trouble. The rest, since it involves him in inconsistency, is even worse. If his scientific objects are to establish his realism$_2$, they must exist independently of minds. But how can one who holds that to exist is to be acknowledged by a mind consistently claim, or, for that matter, how can he, when speaking ontologically, consistently say of anything that it exists independently of minds? The obvious answer reveals the final breakdown. Two quick comparisons with the foil will illuminate it even more sharply.

1. Some acts presumably intend the scientific objects. Otherwise I don't see what good the latter do him. Yet there is, for one, the repre-

---

[28] But see, e.g., *Kategl.*, p. 214. As to the exception, e.g., my now *knowing* that my now rejecting round squares is being caused by my now conceiving their idea, see the discussion of the a priori in Section Sixteen.

[29] You will find his argument for this proposition, together with many other equally unattractive ones for many other equally unattractive propositions in *Versuch ueber die Erkenntnis* (ed. Kastil; Leipzig: Meiner, 1925), which is of all his books I have read the most unattractive. (The so-called principle is of course a truth, but of the sort which belong to what I call a frame of reference. For these matters, see my *Philosophy of Science*.)

sentationalist log jam between intending, attending to, and being presented with. There is, for another, the extremist account of all acts as *relativliche* accidents. Between these two, it is hard to see how any of his acts can in any intelligible sense of the word intend anything.[30] The intentions of the foil's acts all exist and there is a subsistent to connect the former with the latter.

2. His physical objects are the foil's perceptual ones. The former do not exist at all. The latter are real; i.e., they exist independently of minds. Or, if you please, we gain from them the notion of mind-independent existence. Thus we can consistently and intelligibly apply this notion to the entities not presented to us—the foil calls them physical rather than scientific—by which scientific explanation replaces the perceptual objects with which we are presented.[31]

Many who know little else about Brentano yet praise him highly for having established, or re-established, an "objective" ethics. What he actually did is this. He claimed, first, most reasonably, that the fringes of some of our acts are moral approvings and disapprovings.[32] He claimed, second, most absurdly, that just as we can acknowledge or reject something either evidently or at least correctly, so we can also morally approve or disapprove of it either evidently or at least correctly. That makes his notion of right and wrong as "subjective" as that of true and false. In the idealistic night all cows are black. That is why I find all the high praise rather ironical.

[30] Thus a theory of the nature of truth that grounds it in evidence will seem plausible. Hence the mistake, mentioned on p. 314, of which it was said that it cuts rather deeply.

[31] This shows the import of *replacing*, on which I have repeatedly insisted. Notice, too, that in the world of science there are only electrons, or whatever the last word of science may be, in either chairs or nervous systems, while in the *Lebensworld* (as it is now called) there are only minds and perceptual chairs. For a pretty exposition of this bit of the dialectic, see May Brodbeck, "Mental and Physical: Identity versus Sameness," in P. K. Feyerabend and G. Maxwell (eds.), *Mind, Method, and Matter* (University of Minnesota Press, 1965).

[32] In German: *lieben* and *hassen*. Concerning the preference for 'richtig', which goes with both '*anerkennen-verwerfen*' and '*lieben-hassen*', see n. 27 of Section Sixteen.

Part IV
Meinong

THE TRUNCATED WORLD

IN Meinong's world, as in Brentano's, there are only things, either physical or mental. Yet they differ as strikingly as two worlds in the same tradition possibly could. Meinong's things are all perfect particulars; Brentano's are all objects. Objects versus perfect particulars. Here is one striking difference. We might as well, and I shall, begin by taking a look at it. But let us first review and renew our agreements about some key words.

'Object' will be used as in Part III; 'thing', except in patently idiomatic contexts, as in the foil and throughout this book. Meinong's perfect particulars are things; as are of course those of the prototype and the bare ones of the foil. When the latter will have to be mentioned occasionally, I shall continue to call them *bare* particulars. Since Meinong's perfect particulars will naturally have to be mentioned very often, I shall save words by suppressing 'perfect' and simply call them *particulars*. The objects of the foil are facts. Those of the prototype are clusters, which, though not literally things, are "things." The quotes around 'thing' mark *la petite tâche irréparable* (p. 30), the blur produced by γ not being a nexus but merely a pseudonexus, i.e., a function mistaken for a nexus. Let me for the moment call this the γ-blur. Brentano's objects, being all simple, are not just "things" but things.

Examining Brentano's world as closely as one must in order to describe it accurately, we soon discovered that—strictly speaking or, as I shall say, literally—its objects, which are its only existents, are simple. If it were not for a saving blur, an ontology so absurdly impoverished could be dismissed out of hand. But there are the near-facts of modal inclusion. Each ordinary object modally includes all its accidents, each of which in turn so includes the substance₃ of the object. The 'near' in 'near-fact' marks the blur.

Being particulars, the existents of Meinong's world are all simples. Or at least they ought to be. Structurally and implicitly, they really aren't. When dealing with this complication later, we shall see that what matters now, namely, that literally and explicitly there are in his world no objects, is not at all affected by it. That makes for one respect in which the two worlds are mirror images of each other. In Brentano's, there are objects but no accidents; in Meinong's, accidents but no objects.[1] An ontology of particulars only, without objects, is as arid as one of objects assayed as simples and nothing else. So we look again for the saving blur, and, of course, we shall find it.

'Blur' has been used so much for so long that it will come as a relief if I now limit its application. Nor, I trust, will you mind if, in order to do that, I work it in the next paragraph very hard once more.

Meinong's ontology suffers from two major blurs. If you remove them, everything falls into shape. If you don't, you remain bewildered. That makes them very major indeed. Yet they differ from all others we have so far encountered in that during the latter part of his career Meinong himself was aware of them, although not of course as clearly and articulately as one might wish. Toward the end, he even removed one of them completely, without, however, either recognizing its intellectual pedigree or fully mastering its dialectic. Of all this later, in due course. Now I merely wish to select a phrase by which to acknowledge Meinong's awareness of these two weak spots. Let us agree to call them the *two major inaccuracies*. Eventually two suggestive labels for

---

[1] I am for once using 'accident' rather broadly in order to avoid calling Brentano-style accidents particulars.

them will become available. But you see already how the agreement limits our use of 'blur' to those weaknesses, of a certain characteristic kind, which we have so far encountered, such as, e.g., the one I just called the γ-blur of the prototype, or, for that matter, the near-fact blur, which is its mirror image in the world of Brentano.

Let α be an object; $\{a_1, \cdots, a_n\}$, the collection of its particulars. Meinong accepts the ultimate premiss that the collection as such does not exist. Thus he knows that unless he does something about it, he will be left without objects. This is his strength. His weakness lies in what he does. Roughly speaking, he adds a $(n+1)$st particular, of a very special status. But he fails to see that, even though the particular he adds exists if and only if α exists, α itself literally still doesn't exist, even if the particular does, and that, therefore, what he does is inadequate. We shall see all this in due course and not at all roughly, when trying to understand in detail what he does. But we have already spotted one of the two major inaccuracies. It corresponds to the γ-blur in the prototype and to the near-fact blur in the world of Brentano.

Literally, if I am right, there are thus in Meinong's world no objects. He merely mistakes certain collections for objects. What he does is nevertheless sufficiently interesting to justify the usual allowances. I shall sometimes treat these collections as if they existed. He himself eventually calls them complexes (*Komplexe*[2]). We, having put the word to another use, must cast about for a substitute. Precedent recommends 'near-object'; for these "near-objects" are the mirror images of Brentano's near-facts. But a hyphen repeated over and over again becomes tedious. A Greek prefix seems the lesser evil. Let us agree to call these crucial collections *cryptoclusters*.[3]

Literally, the cryptoclusters of this world are but collections of particulars. Its author, however, mistakes them for existents and, in particular, for objects. That makes every "existent" of his world either a thing or a "thing," viz., either a particular or a cryptocluster.

[2] See, e.g., the eighth chapter of *Ann*.

[3] I chose 'cluster' over 'object' very reluctantly and only in order to avoid the typographical embarrassment of 'pseudoobject'. For the expression may give the impression that the roughness is what it is not, namely, an additional blur, added to the γ-blur of the prototype, rather than what it is, namely, a structurally quite different alternative.

Notice, too, that choosing 'crypto' rather than 'pseudo' assigns the latter and the former to the prototype and to Meinong's world, respectively. The reason for this assignment is that behind his cryptoclusters and, as one might call them if one wished, behind his cryptoconnections and cryptofacts, lurk, hidden yet very close to the surface, the objects, connections, and facts of an explicit complex ontology.

What we tried has worked. We have gained a rough notion of a fundamental feature of the world we are entering by contrasting it with one of the world we just left. We might as well try again.

Literally, both men are reists. But there is again a striking difference. Brentano's reism is extreme. Meinong's is curiously and characteristically mitigated. Of this we have already had a glimpse. A quick look will help us to gain a rough notion of another fundamental feature.

Leaving modal inclusion to one side, there is in Brentano's world literally nothing, not even in minds, at least not articulately and without absurdity, to take the places and do the jobs of connections and of facts. With respect to connections, this is an obvious consequence of his extremist position on "relations."

In Meinong's world, there is for each connection and for each fact exactly one particular.[4] The latter is supposed to do the job of the former, connection or fact, as the case may be. The particular I just called the $(n+1)$st is of this sort. The job it supposedly does is in the prototype done by (an occurrence of) γ. This is the glimpse we have had.

These "additional" particulars are the most distinctive single feature of his world. Each of them has what I just called a very special status. What this status is we shall see later. What matters now is that these particulars cannot really do the jobs assigned to them. The mitigation does not achieve its purpose. Yet it is not marred by any blur, either noticed or unnoticed. There are some gaps, to be sure, and some slips. As far as it goes, though, everything is rather well thought out; and even though it does not go far enough, it certainly stretches the reism as far as it can be stretched. A particular supposed to do a connecting job, for instance, "ontologizes" what a moderate thinks of as an internal connection. That brings us face to face with another significant contrast. Structurally,[5] both men espouse the doctrine of internal connections. But Brentano stands with the extremists; Meinong, with the moderates.

What succeeded once has succeeded again. We fixed on a difference, developed it into a contrast, and thereby gained an insight into the world through which we must now find our way. Yet we cannot continue in this haphazard fashion. It is time that we give some thought to our itinerary.

---

[4] By the standards of the foil this is not quite accurate. We shall see that there is trouble about the connectives. Right now, though, this is beside the point.

[5] I say *structurally* because Meinong is not just a moderate but, stretching his reism, "ontologizes" the moderates' internal connections. I realize that at first sight it may seem paradoxical or at least useless and very artificial to call anything an internal connection ontologized. But it will not be long before you see that it is neither the one nor the other.

Brentano's ontology was hard to unravel. Meinong's will not be easy. In the case of the former I devoted the whole first section to the design of a road map, leaving the description of his truncated world to the second. This time I have two reasons for believing that both jobs can be done safely and more conveniently in a single longish section. One reason is that the experience we have gained in mastering the ontology of Brentano will stand us in good stead in exploring Meinong's, which, for all the striking differences, is yet in the same tradition. The other reason hangs by still another contrast.

In Meinong's world, as in Brentano's, there is no Third. Literally, therefore, neither is a representationalist. Structurally, though, the latter always remained one. The former did not. How his structural representationalism eventually drove Brentano into a position almost overtly idealistic even though on the face of it and certainly in intent he remained a realist$_2$, we have seen. Nor have we forgotten the role which his extreme view on connections played in this tragedy.

Meinong's world, or, more accurately, his worlds, including the last, suffer from two fundamental inadequacies. One is his nominalism, which is as extreme and as uncompromising as Brentano's, even though it is also as articulate and as respectable as it could possibly be, since he grounds it in that internal relation of equality which goes with the moderate view he takes on connections. The other fundamental inadequacy we shall soon discover. There are also some large gaps, some serious flaws, and at least one curious limitation. Nor would all these defects—inadequacies, gaps, flaws, and limitations—be what they are if it were not for the fact that he never rid himself of some of the basic patterns of the representationalism from which he started; which is of course why he belongs to his tradition and in this book. Of all this later. Now I merely want to erect a signpost.

Eventually, even though only at the prohibitive price of all these defects, Meinong achieved an ontology not only most ingenious and over long stretches most articulate but also, unlike Brentano's, genuinely nonrepresentational and realistic$_2$ in structure.[6] Thus it is at least free from the absurdities of idealism and therefore not quite as difficult to unravel as Brentano's.[7] This is the second reason why you should have no trouble following the exposition without a preview so detailed that it occupies a whole section.

Presently I shall discuss one aspect of my over-all strategy to which

[6] Or, more accurately, in view of the curious limitation I mentioned, its structure is *almost* realistic. I shall refer you back to this footnote when in the next section the limitation will come to the fore.

[7] This is of course also the reason why I speak of inadequacies, gaps, flaws, and so on, rather than, as in Part III, of breakdowns.

attention must be called in advance. First I assemble three points which have already emerged in a manner that should provide a sense of direction.

This book is dedicated to three great causes, three great struggles of liberation still to be won. The three dragons to be slain are nominalism, reism, representationalism. Meinong's *nominalism*, though as refined as it could possibly be, is extreme. In one of the struggles he thus remained in the rear. His *reism*, curiously and characteristically mitigated as it is, stretched to the utmost, as it were, does yet not stretch far enough. He remained a reist of a very special kind. That kept him out of the front ranks of another struggle. In the third, however, against *representationalism*, he led, and, had he also been in the forefront of the other two, might have conquered, might have arrived at an ontology not only realistic₂ and no longer representationalist but also adequate in all other respects. The one at which he did arrive is not. Yet, at the price of much bizarreness, he came agonizingly close. That makes him the most memorable Don Quixote of a great cause.

The first three of the following four comments provide the background for what must be said in advance about my over-all strategy. The fourth says it.

First. When first envisaging from afar the second half of this book, I insisted that while one could speak of *the* ontology of Brentano, even a structural historian would have to consider the one from which Meinong started as well as the one over which he died (p. 139). When approaching Brentano, we saw that this was too simple. There was some vacillation in his thought, and there was development. Yet there were no breaks and no new starts (p. 226). In its way and in its place, therefore, even though in need of refinement, the first half of the simplification made sense. In Meinong's thought, there are breaks and new starts. The second half of the simplification acknowledges that. Thus it, too, made sense. Now, though, we must refine it.

Everything a serious philosopher does is determined by a rather small number of central intellectual motives, a few convictions and insights which act upon him as pushes and as pulls. A realistic[8] conviction, for instance, and the urge to secure it dialectically which it cannot but produce if the man is serious, may push him away from some positions he inherited while at the same time exerting a pull in the direction of some others. As for this particular conviction, so for the insight that whatever is intended exists. Meinong, we shall see, did not start with this

---

[8] In his nominalism Meinong never wavered; in the dialectic of realism₂ he became increasingly absorbed. That is why we shall save ink by henceforth suppressing the index in 'realism₂', keeping it in 'realism₁'.

particular insight. At a certain point, though, he achieved it, and it immediately became one of his central motives. The realistic conviction he had always shared, though at first rather irrelevantly, since it took some time before he felt its pushes and its pulls. Generally, while Brentano's central motives remained unchanged during a long career, Meinong, as his unfolded, acquired more than one that profoundly affected its course. Naturally, they, too, were but few. Yet it will help[9] us to understand his eventual ontology if, in addition to the one from which he started, we consider two intermediate stages, each marked by the emergence of a central motive. This is the refinement now needed.

Second. Brentano's and Meinong's contemporaries thought of them not only as philosophers but also and at least as much as psychologists. The psychology of the day was a mixture of phenomenology, of pedantry *à la* Wundt, and of what one now calls physiological psychology. In the latter neither took much interest. Of the pedantry both were as free as was then possible. They were both skilled and systematic practitioners of phenomenological description. Yet they moved from different points and in opposite directions.

Brentano was by temperament above all an ontologist; began as one and always remained one. Since he was profound enough to understand rather early in his career that ontology starts from phenomenology, he turned to the latter when he felt that it was needed and did what he thought had to be done. Meinong not only began as a phenomenologist but was all through his life preoccupied with the finer points of this skill or art, much more than a philosopher either need be or should be. But he, too, was profound, and his systematic need, though not perhaps his power, was as great as Brentano's. Gradually yet inevitably, he therefore became more and more of an ontologist. Eventually this interest almost absorbed him; almost, but not completely; nor did he ever completely understand what had happened to him.[10] These differences in point of departure and direction are at the root of a very marked difference in style, in the broad as well as in the narrower sense of style.

In Brentano *l'esprit subtil* and *l'esprit géométrique* are admirably balanced. In Meinong subtilty prevails. His tenacity is heroic. But his flair for the right distinction is not always matched by the ability to exploit

---

[9] I mean of course that it will help the exposition of the structure. Historical (biographical) information is in this book never an end in itself.

[10] Hence all those disquisitions, in the worst nineteenth-century German style, filling so many pages of his later writings which I shall completely ignore, in which he worries about the "position" of *Gegenstandstheorie* as a "science" in its own right and its "systematic relations" with metaphysics, epistemology, logic, mathematics, psychology, and what have you. I do not need and shall not use '*Gegenstandstheorie*'. But if I had to, I would translate it by 'phenomenology'.

it dialectically in the right way and in the right context. He is forever
prone to pursue phenomenological butterflies, sometimes under the
goad of a central motive that has recently emerged, more often just for
the pleasures of the chase. One wishes he had instead taken the time
and the trouble to find out whether and how what he says at the moment jibes with what he has said earlier. These are grave faults. Yet
they pale beside the splendor. And the price for them that has been
exacted from him was high.[11] Even now the place accorded to him in
the succession is not as large as he deserves. That makes me unwilling to
blame him for all these faults more than once. Nor shall I even call
them so but speak instead, whenever they will have to be mentioned, of
his *diffuse style*.

An ontology's style affects all its features, some more, some less. The
impact of his diffuse style on two features of his ontology is as great as
their connection with it is obvious. A quick glance at them will flesh out
the generality.

Brentano's lifelong concern with *logic* was very great. Meinong dis-
patches it with unseemly haste. The most charitable thing that can be
said (and will be said in the last section) is that there is a gap. Nor of
course would this gap have been filled if what we are told instead about
the phenomenology of making inferences were less tedious than it is.

Brentano, if I am right, was the first to philosophize self-consciously
by means of an ideal *language*. Meinong on language sounds more like a
precursor of Oxford. His ear for the shades of the idiom is very fine.
Occasionally, undone by his ingenuity, he even claims that there is a
distinction, merely because if there were one it would suit his dialectical
purpose, where in actual use there is none.[12] I shall restore the balance.
Brentano's ideal language, which we did not really need, I underplayed.
In Meinong's case I shall impose discipline by taking some steps
toward a systematic notation.

Third. Meinong's terminology is obscure and eccentric. Nor is it just
idiosyncratic. Much of it must be blamed on his less than complete
grasp of the dialectic. Thus it has the same source as the diffuse style.
The execution falls short of the vision. The flair is incomparable; the
effort, heroic. But the power of first thinking it all through and then

[11] The controversy with the Brentano circle, though never publicly with Brentano himself, was long-standing and often acrimonious. Marty usually led the
hosts.

[12] As, e.g., the distinction between '*Beziehung*' and '*Verhaeltnis*' in *GeghO.*, p.
396, which is made out of whole cloth and purely *ad hoc*, at least as far as I can
tell, even though I was born to the language. His fellow pupil Husserl, whose ear
was just as sharp, falls in this respect between the two extremes.

saying it simply and clearly is not always equal to the task. Be that as it may, his deplorable terminology is not the least of his handicaps. I shall overcome it by employing from the very beginning my own. But the necessary contacts with his terminology will of course be made, as and when it suits the convenience of the exposition.[13]

Fourth. If you consider these three groups of circumstances, the breaks and new starts, the diffuse style, the eccentric terminology, you will (I hope) approve the course I shall take. *In this section and the next I shall in my own terminology examine first the trunk of his world and then its minds as they appear after the two major inaccuracies have been corrected.* This means that I shall say some things which he does not say at all and some others, which he does say, very differently. How, then, even if everything I shall say should be clear, will you be able to tell that what is being clarified is the world of Meinong? As you see, I recognize that one who proceeds in this way must not expect to get by with attaching the name of an important philosopher to a world he describes simply by pleading his structural propensities without furnishing a reasonable measure of documentation.[14]

For some points in the first two sections of Part IV, I shall, as they come up, furnish about as much or as little documentation as in Part III on Brentano. The third section serves a double purpose. It uses the earlier stages for elucidating the structure of the last ontology on the one hand, and for furnishing the rest of the documentation on the other. In other words, I shall not do certain things until we reach a point where two of them can be done at once. This is the aspect of my over-all strategy to which I thought attention ought to be called in advance.

In the rest of this section I shall in two instalments examine the trunk. The first, which is rather long, works with a familiar example that avoids two substantial complications. Yet it will allow us to describe accurately the second major inaccuracy, i.e., the one which I have as yet not even identified, and to expose the core of the dialectic it obscures. The second instalment, which is rather short, introduces the complications, continues the description, and completes the diagnosis of the first major inaccuracy.

The example, once more and for the last time, is two tones, say,

---

[13] As far as translation is concerned, the question, as with Dr. Johnson's dog, is not how well it is done but whether it can be done at all. Findlay under the circumstances did well enough. So I shall make things as simple as possible by following him whenever I can.

[14] Notice, though, how the propensities show in my speaking of a reasonable measure of documentation rather than of what a historian would accept as proof.

middle c and middle e. In the foil there are (1) two bare particulars, each exemplifying one of two pitch universals (C, E); (2) a connection, assayed as a relational universal of the second type (Hg^3) together with an inhomogeneous, ternary, asymmetrical exemplification nexus; and (3) the fact $(Hg^3(C, E))$ into which this nexus ties the three universals. In the prototype there are in the place of (1) two (perfect) particulars, say, c_1 and e_1. What, if anything, takes or could take the place of (2) and (3) we did not inquire. In Meinong's world there are not only these two particulars but also two additional entities, to take the places and do the jobs of (2) and (3), respectively. Each of these two entities is a particular and they share a special status. Or so I claimed and now claim again. What makes them particulars? What is that status? I shall try to answer.[15] First, though, for a word about words.

Meinong calls the entities which take the places of (2) and (3) *Relationen* and *Objective*. I shall call them *connections* and *Objectives*. As you see, I borrow one of his words, including the majuscule which will distinguish it from the homonymous English adjective, but reserve 'relation' for my own use. As for 'relation', so for 'object'. He calls the four particulars in the example *Gegenstaende*. '*Gegenstand*' is best translated by 'object'. But one cannot without confusion use 'object' as he does and also, as I do, for stones, minds, clouds, and so on. It could even be argued that the confusion which this broad use of 'object' engenders was the "linguistic cause" of his failure to realize that the tables, minds, and clouds of his world are not, upon his own terms, particulars but merely cryptoclusters.[16] So I shall always use 'particular' where he uses '*Gegenstand*', except of course when speaking of his cryptoclusters. That much for the words. Let us also take the first step toward a systematic notation by agreeing to write '$(c_1; e_1)$' and '$(c_1; (c_1; e_1); e_1)$' for the connection and the Objective in the example, respectively.

The language of comparative ontology is so delicate that I shall mark the few comparative uses I shall permit myself by double quotes. A "particular" is one by virtue of its "thinghood" and its "particularity." The former involves "independence" and "simplicity." The latter con-

[15] The argument in support of my third claim, that these entities cannot do the jobs assigned to them, consists of course of Part IV as a whole.

[16] There remains of course the alternative of ignoring the typographical inconvenience mentioned in n. 3; using 'cryptoobject' instead of 'cryptocluster', 'object' instead of 'particular'; and recalling, every time the difference makes a difference, that the foil's objects are in his world merely cryptoobjects. But it seems to me that this alternative not only increases the chance of error, as is pointed out above, but that, everything considered, it is also more cumbersome. If the "translation" of '*Gegenstand*' by 'particular' annoys you, consider that it has at least the virtue to remind you of what (if I am right) is one of the main keys.

trasts with "universality." How about $(c_1; e_1)$ in these two respects?[17]

Let c_2 and e_2 be two other particulars grounding the same pitches. $(c_1; e_1)$ and $(c_2; e_2)$ will both have "particularity" if and only if they are two and not one. In this world they are two. Its connections thus have "particularity." The questions that raises will have to wait.

Of "dependence" and "independence" there is more than one kind. Color and Place "depend" on each other in the familiar a priori fashion. The "dependence" of $(c_1; e_1)$ on c_1 and e_1, Meinong points out, is much greater. As a first attempt at directing attention to the difference this may be of some help, even though, as he himself says, it is "clumsy and inadequate." Then he adds that it might be better to look at $(c_1; e_1)$ as "built upon" c_1 and e_1, which thus are its "indispensable basis."[18] Part of what that means, it turns out, is that *unless c_1 and e_1 were there, $(c_1; e_1)$ would not be there, and conversely*. In order to establish the "thing-hood" of $(c_1; e_1)$, we shall have to show that, in spite of this very close "dependence" on c_1 and e_1, it is yet also "independent," though of course in a different sense. It would help if we had two words for these two kinds of dependence or independence. So I shall no longer say that $(c_1; e_1)$ depends on c_1 and e_1 but, rather, that the former is "connected" with the latter, or, synonymously, that there is a "connection" between $(c_1; e_1)$ on the one hand and c_1 and e_1 on the other. The maneuver merely replaces one ambiguity by another. Thus it seems useless. Yet it has the merit of bringing us up against a distinction so fundamental and so urgent that it will be to our advantage if we attend to it first and only then tackle the task, very fundamental and urgent, to be sure, yet not quite as fundamental nor quite as urgent, of establishing the "thing-hood" of $(c_1; e_1)$ by showing that it has "independence" as well as "simplicity."

(1) Consider a fact of the foil, say, $gr(a)$. $gr(a)$, gr, and a are three entities. Obviously, there is a "connection" between $gr(a)$ on the one hand and gr and a on the other, in a sense in which there is none between the former and any other two things of the foil. This "connection" has its ontological ground in exemplification tying gr and a into $gr(a)$. *The ground of this "connection" is thus (an occurrence of) a connection.* (2) In Meinong's world a connection is a particular; in mine, either a relation or a nexus. These are the two ordinary ways in which I use 'connection', without I trust any danger of confusion. The comparative use, marked by double quotes, is quite different. The italicized sentence exhibits the

---

[17] The most massive sources for much of the first instalment are §§2–7 of *GeghO.* for connections and the third chapter of *Ann.* for objectives.

[18] The three German expressions are *unbeholfen und unzureichend, aufbauen, unerlaessliche Voraussetzungen*. See *GeghO.*, p. 386.

difference. (3) $(c_1; e_1)$, c_1, and e_1 are three entities; and again obviously, there is a "connection" between the latter two and the former, in a sense in which the latter two are not "connected" with, say, the musical interval $(d_4; g_4)$, or, for that matter, in which there is no "connection" between the former on the one hand and two place particulars on the other. (4) Upon my conception of ontology, every "connection" requires an ontological ground. What, if any, is the "connection" between $(c_1; e_1)$ on the one hand and c_1 and e_1 on the other? More generally, what is in this world the "connection" between a connection (not: "connection") and the particulars it connects (not: "connects")?

The distinction the terminological maneuver brought us up against, or, rather, the question it forced us to face, is fundamental and urgent indeed. At first blush you may therefore be disappointed that I do not proceed to answer it immediately. But we shall be in a much better position to answer it after having established the "thinghood" of the "particulars" which are connections. This is therefore what I shall do next, in two steps. The first requires in turn some preparation.

Remember the sentence italicized a moment ago: Unless c_1 and e_1 were there *and what they are*, $(c_1; e_1)$ would not be there *nor what it is*, and conversely. The two clauses which I now added and italicized anticipate an important feature. In this world every particular has a nature. Structurally speaking, these natures are themselves "particulars" and "exist," although not in Platonic separation.[19] Also the "connection" among the three particulars $(c_1; e_1)$, c_1, and e_1 is primarily one among their three natures. This is the feature I anticipate because I need it now. Since I shall establish it in due course, you will not, I hope, object to my using it in the first step.

First step. The foil's things are independent; its subsistents, dependent. Things have natures; subsistents in general and nexus in particular don't. $(c_1; e_1)$, we just anticipated, has a nature. Hence it is neither a "nexus" nor any other kind of "subsistent" and therefore not "dependent" in the sense in which the foil's things are "independent." It does not follow that it is a "thing" rather than, say, a "fact." That is why the conclusion at which we just arrived is only the first of two steps. In the second we shall see how Meinong himself argues that $(c_1; e_1)$ is not a "fact."

Second step. $(c_1; e_1)$ is one entity. If it were a "fact" it would "consist" of c_1, e_1, and at least one further entity. Suppose that it "consists"

---

[19] This illuminates in a flash the troubles at the root of the nature-inaccuracy. (This is the label I shall attach to one of the two major inaccuracies.) If the natures of this world exist, then its particulars, not being "simple," are not really "particulars."

of three entities. If so, Meinong asks, what makes a single entity out of these three?[20] We see again that he accepts the ultimate premiss by which a collection is not an entity. We also see that he does not possess an adequate notion of either nexus or fact. We see, third, that he excludes a certain alternative on the ground that it leads to a Bradley-type regress. More succinctly, *in this situation he rejects the Bradley-regress.* Still differently, in this situation he agrees with Bradley himself and many others, including myself.

I conclude, first, that, not being a "fact" nor, as the first step established, a "nexus," $(c_1; e_1)$ has the "independence" of a "thing." Nor do I see how it could be anything but "simple" unless c_1 and e_1 were among the entities of which it consists, which by the last step they are not. I conclude, second, that $(c_1; e_1)$ is "simple."

We have already established that *the connections of this world are particulars.* But there is further evidence so impressive that I shall acknowledge its force by calling it the third step. We shall not, however, be able to add this step without first taking a quick look at Objectives.

The objective $(c_1; (c_1; e_1); e_1)$ is "connected" with the three particulars c_1, $(c_1; e_1)$, e_1 in exactly the same sense in which the connection $(c_1; e_1)$ is "connected" with c_1 and e_1. This is not to say that there are no differences. There are in fact two. The Objective is "built upon" three particulars; the connection in this case[21] on two. This numerical difference makes no ontological difference. The other does; not surprisingly, since it reflects the difference between the jobs the two particulars are supposed to do.[22] Of this later. The point now is that neither difference prevents or in any way affects the application to Objectives of the arguments by which we established that connections are particulars. I take it, then, that, like its connections, *the Objectives of this world are particulars.*

Third step. "If $(c_1; (c_1; e_1); e_1)$ is there, so are two connections. For to be two among the three particulars on which an Objective is built is to

[20] This is part of what remains after one has taken apart the confused and rambling argument in *Ann.*, p. 261. Another part will be used in Section Nineteen.

[21] I say *in this case* because, as far as I know, Meinong was the first philosopher to recognize that the exclusive concern, such as it was, with binary relations, at the expense of *n*-ary ones $(n > 2)$, was completely unjustified. This insight is of course philosophically significant. Meinong himself credits K. Zindler with it. But Zindler was a mathematician! See *GeghO.*, p. 393.

[22] In the foil, where the place of Objectives, though not of course of connections, is taken by facts, this difference is out in the open. In this world it is masked by both entities being particulars of the same very special status. That is probably why, as we shall see in the second instalment, its author "slips" over it.

be connected." This is the gist of Meinong's argument.[23] Call the two "new" connections $(c_1; (c_1; e_1))$ and $(e_1; (c_1; e_1))$, then consider three points.

(1) After a fashion, these connections correspond to the several "weak" γ which make entities out of the subsets of the set of particulars in a cluster of the prototype (p. 38). Yet there is a difference. (2) If there is the "new" connection $(c_1; (c_1; e_1))$, then there is also the "new" Objective $(c_1; (c_1; (c_1; e_1)))$; $(c_1; e_1)$. Hence there are two more "new" connections. As for $(c_1; (c_1; e_1))$, so for $(e_1; (c_1; e_1))$. And so on. We stand at the beginning of an infinite regress. The weak γ don't produce a regress. That is the difference. (3) *In this situation Meinong most explicitly accepts a Bradley-type regress.* Strange as at first that may seem, it really isn't. It merely confirms the diagnosis that all these entities, being particulars, are independent as well as simple. Hence, although if one of them is there so are all others, none needs any others (or anything else) for its "completion." And it is just this need which makes the regress vicious. Contrast this situation, in which the regress is accepted, with that from the second step, where it is rejected, and you will understand why I find the additional evidence so impressive. By this point there hangs another. It could wait. But the opportunity is too good to miss.

If the success a philosopher deserves is commensurate with his grasp, then Meinong did on relations better than he deserved.[24] He did not for instance as much as mention the nonsymmetry of some connections, which leaves no doubt that unlike Russell (and, alas, like everyone else before Russell) he did not understand how crucially this feature affects the assay of connections. Since he did not understand it, he did not see either that his acceptance of the Bradley regress provided him with means for grounding it. E.g., he could have grounded the asymmetry of the musical interval in $(c_1; (c_1; e_1))$ not being "equal" to $(e_1; (c_1; e_1))$. This gives the idea. There is no need to pursue, particularly since, grave as this defect is, we shall for the most part be able to ignore it, provided only you will keep in mind that the order of the terms in such expressions as '$(c_1; e_1)$' does not stand for anything.[25]

---

[23] *GeghO.*, pp. 390–91. Notice that I ignore the third pair in the triple. It will occupy us in Section Twenty.

[24] That this is so, and why, we shall see later, in Section Twenty, as you may surmise from what has been said about the over-all strategy. But let me remind you now of the difference between the *nonsymmetry* of, say, brother, and the *asymmetry* of, say, louder, on the one hand, and the inhomogeneity of, say, the foil's exemplification, on the other. The familiar word in the context is of course 'relation', not 'connection'. Hence the reminder.

[25] As no doubt you now see, I tried to shock you into this awareness by writing

Let us return to some business begun but not yet finished. There are four entries on our agenda, four questions or groups of questions, which I undertook to answer as soon as it would be convenient. I. What is the "connection" between either a connection or an Objective and the particulars it is "built on"? II. What is the status of natures? What jobs do they do? III. What is that special status of particulars "built on" others? IV. What is the answer to the questions raised by the double quotes around 'equal' in the last paragraph? More generally, how about the problems of a nominalism, very articulate (as I claimed) but also very rigid and further aggravated by a reism stretched so far that not only every tone but also every interval between any two tones is a particular?

I. If you keep in mind that every particular is "simple" and "independent" and consider that c_1, e_1, and $(c_1; e_1)$ are three particulars, you should find it easy to assay the "connection" between the first two and the third. If you still hesitate, weigh the expressions Meinong uses. c_1 and e_1 are said to "determine" $(c_1; e_1)$. The latter is also called the *Superius;* the two former, its *Inferiora*.[26] The "connection" is a function. The *Inferiora* are its arguments; the *Superius*, its value. As for connections, so for Objectives. About all this there is no doubt. Meinong's is a function ontology. The only question left is whether it is an explicit or an implicit ontology of this type. Does he or does he not give ontological status to these functions? The answer is that he doesn't. *Meinong's is an implicit function ontology.* Radical as it is, the inadequacy is yet easily remedied. One merely has to add the required number of functions to the basic ontological inventory. Nor is there any blur like the one γ causes in the prototype. All there is, is a void so vast and so deep that, even though easily filled, it is an inadequacy and not just a gap. Of all this I have again no doubt. For there is not a whisper about these functions. And an ontologist as sophisticated as Meinong

---

'$(e_1; (c_1; e_1))$' rather than, as seems more natural, '$((c_1; e_1); e_1)$'. The point is but an adaptation of the by now very familiar one in the Wiener-Kuratowski lemma.

[26] I ignore '*Fundament*' and '*fundierte Gegenstaende*' and do not bring back '*aufbauen*', not because they do not fit with what I am now about but because they will fit even better with the analysis of the special status of all *Gegenstaende hoeherer Ordnung*. If you feel in need of rehearsing the notion of a function ontology, turn to the first two sections.

My notation, as you now see, is analogous to that of arithmetic; with the semi-colon standing for a function as do the cross and the dot in, say, '$(7+3)$' and '$(5 \cdot 2)$', which stand for the sum and the product function, respectively. But the analogy is partial, since I shall use the semicolon indifferently; sometimes for this function, sometimes for that, sometimes as a variable; relying on the context to leave no doubt as to how it is used each time.

eventually became surely would not have failed to list any major category of his basic inventory. Even so, two comments in support of the diagnosis should help. The first is historical; the second, structural. A third will attempt a thumbnail comparison with the only explicit and articulate function ontology on record.

First. (1) Since an internal connection[27] is grounded in (the natures of) the entities it supposedly connects and in nothing else, the connection itself, if I may so express myself, is literally nothing and can therefore not literally be "connected" with anything. (2) Genetically, as we shall see in Section Twenty, *Meinong's connections are internal connections of the Second; imported into the First, where they were given ontological status; then, without losing this status, re-exported into the Second.* (3) Jointly, (1) and (2) support the diagnosis that connections are "unconnected." (4) Perhaps you will wonder whether and how this genetic reflection applies to Objectives. I answer that, as we shall also see, the only original kind of special-status particulars were the connections; that the Objectives, which were more recent creations, in response to newer pushes and pulls, joined them only later; and that Meinong himself never fully understood the difference between the two kinds.

Second. Anticipate once more the two features which we shall establish in the next step. Every particular has a nature. Every *Superius* is primarily a nature "connected" with the natures of the *Inferiora* on which it is built. These features may lend some initial plausibility to the belief that it is in the nature of some natures to determine another and that, therefore, no "connection" between the latter and the former is needed. Reflection quickly discovers three reasons why this initial plausibility is purely verbal. (1) I know what it means for a color or a pitch to have a nature, or, as I would rather say, to be a nature, in the sense in which a bare particular has none. But the iterative phrase, 'nature of a nature' is mere sound without sense. (2) Natures, if there be such, are entities among entities. Hence the basic premiss concerning collections holds for them as well as for all others. (3) Natures, too, being particulars, are simples.[28] Hence the "connection" of a *Superius* with its *Inferiora* cannot have its ground "in" the former.

[27] Since Meinong was a moderate and since, therefore, the extremist position will not have to be mentioned often in Part IV, 'internal connection' will henceforth stand for what the moderates mean by this phrase.

[28] To unpack the sentence: On the one hand, the arguments I presented for the special-status particulars being simple also hold for their natures. On the other hand, the nature-of-nature illusion may well prevent one from seeing that clearly.

Third.[29] In Frege's world there are objects as well as functions. The latter allow him to do remarkably well without either universals or nexus. The former are particulars. Of two further very special kinds of particulars, one "corresponds" to Meinong's natures. The other kind consists of The True and The False, the two entities responsible for most of the absurdity in his world. At first it seems Meinong has the advantage. Looking more closely, we shall see very soon that each of his special-status particulars is "compounded" of a nature and of *either* being *or* nonbeing, which "correspond" to The True and The False. Thus, he, too, paid a high price of absurdity. Whose price was higher? Neither bought adequacy. So we need not decide.

II. How do natures get into this world and what do they do? One cannot answer without attending to two central motives, first identifying them, then trying to understand how natures relieve the dialectical pressure they create. One was a lifelong concern; the other emerged only after some time. In attending to them I adopt the first schema of Section Nine, which makes things simpler without either distorting them or omitting anything that affects the task at hand. Suppose, then, contrary to fact, that we are sometimes presented with one particular and nothing else. Call it a_1; let it be one of those grounding red.[30] Again, for what we are about it does not at all matter whether a_1 is presented in perception, or memory, or imagination, and so on. In the foil one might therefore just as well[31] say that we *intend* the particular; in Brentano's world, that we *conceive* it. In Meinong's it will be best if in this section we employ the word we agreed to use neutrally (p. 150). Suppose, then, that we sometimes *think* of one particular and of nothing else.

The scientific predicament worried both Brentano and Meinong throughout their careers. Brentano's structural idealism made his way out of it a hoax. This we saw in Part III. As a matter of strategy, though, we had no choice but to play along with the hoax until at the very end we were in a position to expose it. Meinong, too, rather late in

[29] For details, see the essay on "Ontological Alternatives" in *Logic and Reality*. The two "correspondences" pointed out above are very close. Yet the language of comparative ontology is always delicate; hence the cautionary double quotes.

[30] Meinong usually writes 'A' and lets the letter stand for an object; not surprisingly, since he fails to appreciate the difference in ontological status between a cryptocluster and any of its particulars. (The major inaccuracy, which we have already spotted but not yet completely analyzed, since its analysis fits best into the second instalment, is just this failure.)

[31] Or, rather, since 'intend' and 'conceive', as we use them, are more specific, it would be better.

his career, thought he had found a way out. In the last section we shall see that his, too, was a dead end. Until then, we shall again have to pretend that his world's Second[32] is the realm of those objects which for uniformity's sake I shall continue to call physical, even though I would rather call them perceptual. Yet there is a difference. At the end of his career Meinong was a realist. Thus the pretense is not a hoax; and his failure on this score will turn out to be a serious flaw rather than, like Brentano's, a major breakdown.

The lifelong concern I spoke of was the search for a way out of the scientific predicament. As long as one has not found it, he will hold, as Meinong did, that a_1 does not exist.[33] The other central motive was the belief that whatever we think of has ontological status (exists).[34] Hence a_1 ought to exist. That identifies the dialectical pressure. Meinong tried to relieve it by distinguishing between a_1 and the *circumstance* that it exists. Call the latter for the moment the existence-of-a_1. Presently I shall introduce a notation.

a_1 and the existence-of-a_1 are both particulars. The former, unlike all special-status particulars, is not a function of others. Such particulars I call for the moment *ordinary*.[35] The existence-of-a_1 Meinong assays as an Objective. (If he is right) this is the second Objective we encounter. The first was $(c_1; (c_1; e_1); e_1)$. He puts the two in the same boat. Yet they differ radically. Comparison with the foil brings out the difference. $(c_1; (c_1; e_1); e_1)$ corresponds to a *fact* of the foil. I express this by saying that, though a particular, it yet grounds in his world (all whose entities if I am right are particulars) a *state of affairs*. The circumstance that a_1 exists does not correspond to a fact of the foil.[36] Does it nevertheless

---

[32] 'Second' does not really fit, since, as we shall see in the next section, he operates with a *different tripartition*, whose domains I shall of course not call the First, the Second, and the Third. But no harm will be done and convenience will be served if in this section I use a few times these labels.

[33] Unless, of course, he makes it a mental entity, thus taking the first fatal step toward the idealistic misery.

[34] I, as you know, share this belief. In the foil every intention is a fact, either actual or potential, and potentiality is—for complexes (facts) but not for things (simples)—a mode of existence.

[35] Upon this provisional terminology, a particular is either *ordinary* or of *special status*. Presently, when discussing "status," I shall introduce and adopt some of Meinong's adjectives. In the meantime I would rather not use them. Notice, too, how on this occasion I manage, rather *ad hoc*, '*fact*', '*circumstance*', and '*state of affairs*'.

[36] To unpack this: In the foil existence is a subsistent which is in every single one of its entities, actual and potential, just as universality is in every universal. Yet this circumstance is not one of the foil's facts. Nor, therefore, is the existence-of-a, *if a exists*, one of the foil's facts. The italicized clause, inaccurate as it is, will

ground a state of affairs? Meinong claims that it does. I shall show that it doesn't.

Suppose for the moment that 'a_1' stands for a particular of which Meinong does not think he must deny that it exists in order to escape the scientific predicament. *Structurally, he assays a_1 and every other ordinary particular as compounded of its nature and of existence.* This is one of the main pivots on which his world turns. How, then, shall we unpack the formula? What does it imply? What does it suggest? How does it relieve the pressure? I shall present my answers in eight steps.

1. A nature is not a thing; nor of course is existence. Reists use 'exist' so that only things exist. Meinong, who was a reist, did not until the very end, when it was too late, if I may so express myself, acknowledge that natures (and existence) might exist, even though implicitly they had long been pivotal members of his basic inventory. Nor did he ever clearly see that if his natures exist then his particulars are not simples. These are but two aspects of his reism. The major inaccuracy, of which I said (p. 336) that he neither recognized its pedigree nor mastered its dialectic when belatedly he corrected it, is nothing but the group of blurs that can be traced to these failures. So I shall henceforth call it the *nature inaccuracy*.

2. Let a_1^n and a_2^n be the natures of a_1 and a_2, respectively. a_1^n and a_2^n are two and not one. Generally, Meinong's natures are "particulars." A particular is existence compounded with a "particularized" nature. This is the cue to the pedigree. One does not need to know much about Thomas[37] in order to know that in his world an object is a "particularized" essence actualized by an act of being. Yet it suffices. Just replace in the last sentence 'object', 'essence', 'actualized by', and 'act of being' by 'particular', 'nature', 'compounded with', and 'existence', respectively. Is there a plausible structural reason[38] that kept Meinong

---

yet serve to remind you that, being simples, the foil's particulars either exist in the mode of actuality or not at all.

[37] Nor, alas, do I know much. Yet I venture three comments for the benefit of others as ignorant as myself. (1) A Thomistic essence is "particularized" by the *materia signata* in it, actualized by an act of being. (2) An Aristotelian object is supposedly "particularized" but of course not actualized by matter. (3) (Aristotelian) matter and *materia signata* are two and not one. Concerning the replacement of 'object' by 'particular' in the sentence above, see n. 30.

[38] A plausible biographical reason is not hard to come by. At Meinong's time and place and in his ambience Thomism was neither widely known nor, if known, readily given its due. Considering Brentano's background, one might at first think that this generality does not apply to his student Meinong. Then one remembers the teacher's vigorous repudiation of Thomas. See n. 6 of Section Thirteen; also the intriguing remark in the autobiography, written in the year of his death, that

from identifying his ontology as the ingeniously modified Thomism which in so many respects it is? I shall answer this question later.

3. Write 'ex' for existence; '$(a_1^n{:}ex)$', for the existence-of-a_1. Distinguish colon and semicolon. The former marks $(a_1^n{:}ex)$ as a particular compounded of, or, as I shall sometimes also say, as a combination of, a_1^n and ex. The latter marks $(c_1; e_1)$ and $(c_1; (c_1; e_1); e_1)$ as particulars determined[39] by two and three other particulars, respectively. $(a_1^n{:} ex)$ is the entity of which he claims and I deny that it grounds a state of affairs.

To the connection $(c_1; e_1)$ corresponds in the foil a relation, which is a thing.[40] The Objective $(c_1; (c_1; e_1); e_1)$, which grounds a state of affairs, corresponds to a fact. That it thus reflects the distinction between thing and fact by one of its own is one of the great merits of this "stretched-to-the-utmost" reism. Two of its particulars may determine a connection. (Presently we shall see that any two of them do in fact determine more than one.) But they do not and *cannot*, without a third which is a connection, determine what corresponds to a fact.

What, then, does '$(a_1^n{:} ex)$' stand for? Positively, a_1, the circumstance that it exists, $(a_1^n{:} ex)$, and the circumstance that a_1^n and ex combine with each other are in this world neither four nor two but one. Negatively, Meinong made a distinction where even upon his own terms (if he had only fully understood them) there is none. a_1 and $(a_1^n{:} ex)$ are one and not two. The structural source of the mistake is the nature inaccuracy. Or, to say the same thing with more words, would one not almost expect that one operating with natures and existence without realizing that they themselves exist and that therefore his particulars are not really simple, succumbs to this temptation of making one dis-

---

the threads connecting *Gegenstandstheorie* with the scholastic philosophy remain to be investigated. See *Die Deutsche Philosophie der Gegenwart in Selbstdarstellungen*, p. 146.

[39] Or, as he also says, they are built upon those other particulars. I would rather say, and whenever we ought to be aware of that vast and deep void shall say, that they are *functions* of them. While the semicolon thus stands for functions, the colon stands for the even more fundamental circumstance of Thomistic combination.

[40] More accurately, a connection of Meinong's corresponds to either a relation, either simple or derived, or a pseudorelation (p. 95), or a nexus of the foil. But the inaccuracy does here no harm. Nor does the number of argument particulars, two in the one case, three in the other, if you will keep in mind that it is not essential. The *cannot* toward the end of the paragraph signifies that if one develops the notation systematically, certain contexts will become ill-formed by substituting in them the name of a connection for that of an Objective, and conversely. Notice, finally, how the dichotomies line up: combination versus determination, (Thomistic) compounding versus function, circumstance versus state of affairs.

tinction too many, particularly if, as will soon transpire, it serves his purpose only too well?

Meinong, very much to his credit, remained uneasy about this duplication of entities. Yet his diffuse style undid him. One of his students provided him with a formula which he repeats over and over. "The object *has* being; the Objective *is* being."[41] Uninterpreted, this is merely an incantation with which he exorcises his disquiet, as some try to master their fears by whistling in the dark. Interpreted, in the only way it makes sense, the formula pinpoints the same mistake in another way, thereby displaying another confusion in the nature-inaccuracy bouquet. What *has* being, in the sense of having it added to itself, is a_1^n. What *is* being, in the sense of including it in itself, is a_1. The first half of the formula wrongly identifies a_1^n with a_1; which is one extreme of confusion likely to be engendered by the nature inaccuracy. At the other extreme one denies that a_1^n exists.

Having made my case, I shall henceforth, whenever the exposition requires it, speak *as if* a_1 and $(a_1^n : ex)$ were two and not one; the former an ordinary particular, the latter an Objective.

4. What purpose is served by the fortuitous duplication? The answer will not come as a surprise. It relieves the dialectical pressure from the color particular that ought both to exist and not to exist. More precisely, it is the first of two steps. The second, which it makes possible, achieves the purpose. One of the two particulars into which the original one is split (if I may so express myself) exists irrespectively of whether the other does or doesn't. This is the gist of the second step. In executing it, Meinong goes beyond Thomas, adds a further entity, *non-being* (*nonex*), and lays down the following schema.

An Objective[42] *is a nature combined with either* ex *or* nonex. *Whatever*

[41] *Das Objekt hat Sein; das Objectiv ist Sein.* The student's name was R. Ameseder. See, e.g., *Stellung*, p. 20 and, for what is above called the other extreme, *Ann.*, p. 61. Meinong was not as fortunate in his students as Brentano. The most important are probably Ernst Mally, his successor in the chair at Graz; Alois Hoefler, who had a high position in the Ministry of Education in Vienna and was *Dozent* at the university there; Vittorio Benussi and Stefan Witasek. The last two were mostly psychologists; and their contributions have earned them a small place in the history of this field. (In 1894, Meinong founded, and until his death in 1920 remained director of, a psychological laboratory, which was the first of its kind in any university of the Habsburg Empire.) Christian Ehrenfels, a student of Brentano who became professor in Prague, also came under the influence of Meinong. He wrote on ethics, supposedly with great merit.

[42] The only reason why I limit myself to Objectives and for the time being ignore connections is that at this point the latter give rise to one of the two complications which are better kept out until we can concentrate on them in the second instalment.

the nature may be, one of these two combinations, though never both, will exist.[43] In the case at hand, a_1^n combines with *ex* into the Objective $(a_1^n: ex)$ if and only if a_1 exists. If there is no a_1, its nature yet may and in fact does combine with *nonex* into the particular $(a_1^n: nonex)$, which exists. As no doubt you sense, we have come upon one of the features which caused me to say that Meinong won his victories only at the high cost of much bizarreness (p. 340).

At this point two structural suggestions become virtually irresistible. One is that what we really think of when thinking of a_1 is always an Objective, either $(a_1^n: ex)$ or $(a_1^n: nonex)$, depending on which of the two exists. If this suggestion is accepted, the dialectical pressure from the color particular ceases. Of this, much more in the next section.

5. The other suggestion is to extend the "Thomistic" assay from the ordinary ones to all particulars. If the former are such compounds and if all the others really are particulars, why shouldn't they, too, be so compounded, except of course that while each ordinary particular is a combination of a nature with *ex*, an Objective[44] will be a combination of a nature with either *ex* or *nonex*. You see why I judge the suggestion to be irresistible. Meinong did in fact so extend the assay. The fact that he did, together with the truism that only things have natures, provides further *evidence in support of* the claim that Objectives are particulars; evidence so impressive indeed that one might call it the "fourth step" of the earlier argument (p. 346). Notice, too, that the "impressiveness" of this further evidence and the "irresistibility" of the second suggestion are but one thing seen from opposite angles. Our several diagnoses and analyses continue to support each other.

Our notation reflects the extension of the assay by making '$(c_1; (c_1; e_1); e_1)$' and '$((c_1; (c_1; e_1); e_1)^n: ex)$' two names of one thing. I shall next use this reflection to complete an argument left pending, then raise two questions it suggests.

[43] You see here the possibilities for the development of a systematic notation. First one formulates the syntactical rules which distinguish nature-expressions from Objective-expressions. Then one adds that while every well-formed nature-expression stands for something (is a name), only one of the two well-formed Objective-expressions that can be formed with one nature-expression is a name. The other fails, in the sense in which a definite description may fail. And so on, and so on. Notice that, as in Brentano's case, there are literally no sentences in this language but only names or purported names. Yet the progress reflects itself. An expression which either names or purports to name one of the particulars which are the only above-board existents resembles roughly either a positive or a negative existential judgment in that it "asserts" a Thomistic composition with either *ex* or the bizarre *nonex*.

[44] For the time being I again ignore connections. See n. 42, above.

How shall we transcribe '$(c_1; (c_1; e_1); e_1)^n$' into English? If you know how 'proposition' has been used in the British tradition, you know the answer. This particular nature is the proposition that e_1 is higher[3] than c_1.[45] The radical difference between $(a_1^n: ex)$ and $(c_1; (c_1; e_1); e_1)$ which I promised (p. 347) to exhibit is that while the "nature" of the former is that of a thing, that of the latter is a proposition.[46] Or, to be for once more accurate than one need always be, this radical difference between the two particulars remains even if for the sake of the exposition one supposes that they are both Objectives. An agreement on the words will help us to keep it in mind. Henceforth, unless it proves inconvenient, the natures of Objectives will be called *propositions*.

Which propositions, if any, combine with *nonex?* This is one question the notation all but forces on us. Structurally, the answer must by now be obvious. A proposition combines with *ex* or *nonex* depending on whether the sentence which stands for it is true or false. This shows how *ex* and *nonex* manage to play the roles of Frege's True and False (p. 351). The execution runs into trouble. Its source is not the Fregean role of these two entities but, rather, Meinong's nominalism. So I shall let it sit for a while. The structural point about natures which hangs by the other question the notation brings to the fore is more urgent.

6. What is the "connection" between the proposition of an Objective[47] and the natures of the particulars which determine it? E.g., what is the "connection" between $(c_1; (c_1; e_1); e_1)^n$ on the one hand and c_1^n, $(c_1: e_1)^n$, and e_1^n on the other? The extension of the "Thomistic" assay *strongly* suggests an answer. The natures of the arguments of a function determine the nature of its value. Or, with a twist, a "connection" among particulars is the "*same*" as that among their natures. This is the feature we anticipated twice. If the notation is to reflect it, we must stipulate that '$(c_1; (c_1; e_1); e_1)^n$' and '$(c_1^n; (c_1^n; e_1^n); e_1^n)$' are two names of a single nature.

I called the suggestion strong, but not irresistible. Jointly with an-

---

[45] The use of 'higher[3]' for something in Meinong's world ignores some points in the comments on nominalism (IV).

[46] A connection, we shall soon see, is in this respect like $(a_1^n: ex)$—with a complication.

[47] Or, for that matter, the nature of a connection. What is being said here holds for both Objectives and connections. Only the two specious kinds of Objective named by either '$(a_1^n: ex)$' or '$(a_1^n: nonex)$', as the case may be, stand again apart. *Ex* and *nonex*, not being things, have no natures. Hence the two specious kinds are the only ones whose natures are not functions of others. Make another note of something else. If, as in some case which we shall come across later, some or all of the argument particulars are Objectives, then some or all of the argument natures are propositions.

other, however, which is equally strong, it becomes irresistible. Jointly, they also warrant removing the double quotes which in the last paragraph surround 'same'.

Neither c_1 nor e_1 nor $(c_1; e_1)$ exists. Otherwise Meinong would not know how to escape the scientific predicament. How about $(c_1; (c_1; e_1); e_1)^n$? Does it combine with *ex* or with *nonex?* According to Meinong, $((c_1; (c_1: e_1); e_1)^n: ex)$ is the Objective which exists; $((c_1; (c_1; e_1); e_1)^n: nonex)$, the one which doesn't. In order to understand why this is so and why it yields a strong suggestion, one merely has to translate it into the language of representationalism. e_1 being higher[3] than c_1 is an a priori truth. In a representationalist world that means, first, that we come to know this truth merely by attending (p. 202) to the three ideas of c_1, e_1, and $(c_1; e_1)$; and, second, that its being such a truth does not depend on whether all, some, or any of these three ideas represent anything.[48] That spots the suggestion. *Meinong's natures are ideas cast as "particulars" and re-exported into the Second.*[49] If one adds this suggestion to the first, from the extension of the "Thomistic" assay, their joint force becomes irresistible indeed, so irresistible that it might be better to speak of a structural implication. *A "connection" among particulars is really one among their natures.* Thus we may safely remove the double quotes around 'same'.

Meinong's dependence on some of the fundamental patterns of representationalism becomes manifest at several points. Two of these are here relevant. For one, his distinction between a priori and (as he calls them) empirical truths is most emphatic. For another, he insists again and again that to know an empirical truth is to know something about "existence," while knowing one which is a priori is to have some knowledge about natures, which is quite independent of "existence."[50]

---

[48] Or, as Meinong put it, *Sosein ist daseinsfrei.* This cryptic formula is relatively well known. So I mention it now. But I shall not decipher it until later, in Section Twenty.

[49] As was mentioned earlier (p. 350) and will be seen later, this structural diagnosis has impressive genetic (biographical) support.

[50] The evidence is pervasive; but perhaps it is most impressive in *Erfahrungsgl.*, which begins with this distinction and constructs its whole argument around it, just as *GeghO.* and *Ann.* are constructed around the notions of connection and of Objective, respectively.

The emphasis on the "necessity" of all "connections" among natures appears no later than the special-status particulars themselves (*GeghO.* p. 400). Yet there is an occasional blur due to a difference of which I shall not make much but which should be pointed out at least once. In the case of propositions, the "necessity" of the "connection" is grounded in, or at least corresponds to, a certain state of affairs being a priori. In the case of connections, such as, e.g., $(c_1; e_1)$, there is nothing to serve as either ground or counterpart for the "necessity" of the "connec-

As you see, I could again have proceeded the other way around, deriving the second suggestion from this emphasis and this insistence. The growing number of diagnoses and analyses keeps hanging together.

Now for the two questions that had to wait. Then we shall be ready to examine the status issue (III).

7. Each particular of this world is compounded in the style of Thomas; every "connection" among its particulars is a function. These, I submit, are its two most fundamental features, even though they are both merely implicit, so that we had to uncover them by structural analysis. The second no one then understood, except of course, in his own case, Frege. The first raises a question. Is there a plausible structural reason that kept Meinong from recognizing the Thomistic pedigree? I answer by pointing at the feature we just uncovered. His natures are ideas cast as "particulars" and re-exported into the Second. That spots his family connection with the representationalists. Of this connection he was of course aware; by it he was preoccupied. One may plausibly speculate that this preoccupation caused him to overlook[51] the older connection. Or, with a change of metaphor, the foreground of representationalist ideas hid the background of Thomistic essences. Yet, in this background one of the two master keys is buried.

8. Which propositions, if any, combine with *nonex?* The Fregean correspondence provides the cue to the answer. A proposition combines with *nonex* if and only if it[52] is an a priori falsehood, such as, e.g., e_1 being higher[2] than c_1. The trouble I mentioned when first raising the question appears as soon as one tries to write down the name of this combination.[53] '$((c_1; hg^2; e_1)^n: nonex)$' is a step in the right direction. But how shall we expand the abbreviation 'hg^2'? Presently we shall see that the number of connections determined by c_1 and e_1 is very large. But an interval which musicians call a second is *of course* not among them. Hence there is no function which may be written '$(c_1; e_1)$' and 'hg_1^2'. The best one can do is "borrow" a "particularized" second from another pair, say f_2 and g_2, and then write either '$((c_1; (f_2; g_2); e_1)^n: nonex)$' or, since as we shall see '$(f_2; g_2)$' may be abbreviated this way (see n. 45, above), '$((c_1; (hg^2)_2; e_1)^n: nonex)$'. The trouble shows in

tion" between its nature and those of c_1 and e_1. The structural source of the difference is that $(c_1: e_1)$ is merely an "ontologized" internal connection.

[51] Or should one perhaps say *repress* instead of *overlook?* See n. 38, above.

[52] Or, more literally, if and only if its combination with *nonex* is an a priori falsehood. Of this more in later sections. But one need not always be so literal.

[53] This combination is, in descending order of generality, an existent, a particular, and an Objective. The "paradox" of an existent being compounded of *nonex* and a nature will occupy us later; first fleetingly in III, then more thoroughly in Section Twenty.

the different subscripts. The "solution" is counterstructural; hence the trouble is serious. If the interval were grounded in a single entity, there of course would be no trouble at all. That shows that its source is the "particularization" not only of the pitches but also of the interval; i.e., more generally, the rigid nominalism which is one of the two fundamental inadequacies of this ontology.[54] This inadequacy we shall examine in IV. The trouble we just spotted is but one aspect of it. So I shall henceforth ignore it, except for reminding you of it when in Section Twenty we shall come upon a most plausible reason for Meinong himself having overlooked it.

III. In Aristotle's world the status of the forms and of matter is peculiar. Yet one thing is clear. Unless there were the latter to be "informed" by the former, there would nothing. More literally, there would be no objects. Objects, however, are the only full-fledged existents of his world. That makes matter its "foundation." In the foil the Principle of Exemplification assigns this job to the bare particulars. E.g., for Color to exist, there must be a color to exemplify it; for a color to exist, there must be a bare particular that exemplifies it. There the descent ends. That makes the foil's bare particulars its "foundation." The "foundation" of Meinong's world are the particulars he calls *real*, i.e., those I have called ordinary. All others, i.e., those I have called special-status particulars, he calls *ideal*.

Genetically, his world would not have become what it is had it not been for his desire to abandon the representationalists' way of ideas. As it stands, *structurally*, there is nothing in this way "ideal" about his ideal particulars. All one can say about them along such lines is, not that they are either in the First or the Second or the Third, but that the real particulars on which they *ultimately rest* are either all physical or all mental or of both kinds. The representationalist trichotomy simply does not fit Meinong's world. In the next section we shall come across one of his own. This, though, is a matter I did not and do not want to prejudge, just as I did not want to jeopardize the crucial distinction between the structural and the genetic. That is why I have until now avoided his words, 'real' and 'ideal'. Henceforth I shall use them.

In this world, too, there is a descent. Consider the following eight particulars: (1) $((c_1; e_1); ((c_1; e_1); (f_2; g_2)); (f_2; g_2))$, (2) $((c_1; e_1); (f_2; g_2))$, (3) $(c_1; e_1), (f_2; g_2)$, (4) c_1, e_1, f_2, g_2. (1), (2), (3) are ideal; the remaining

---

[54] The other is Meinong's failure to recognize the ontological status of functions, which as we saw (p. 349) is easily remedied by adding a sufficiency of them to the basic vocabulary. But one cannot add "universals," or replace anything in his world by them, without messing it up completely.

four, all of (4), real. (1) and (2) are an Objective and the connection among its arguments, respectively. The latter is that of being larger, as among musical intervals. (1) is *founded* on (2) and (3); (2) is founded on (3); (3) is founded on (4). That shows in an example the pattern of descent. I add four comments.

(a) 'Found' and 'founded' are among Meinong's key terms (see n. 26, above). 'Determine' and 'determined', which he also employs and to which I have so far limited myself, are synonyms. But the new pair is more expressive of the present context. The arguments of a function found its value. (More precisely for once, they would found it, if the function were given ontological status.) Every ideal particular is a value of a function and among the arguments of some others. Only the real particulars are arguments only. They are also the ultimate arguments. Every descent leads to, and ends with, some of them. Still differently, the real particulars ultimately found[55] all others. Nor of course could there be values unless there were arguments (and functions), which is but another way of saying that this world's real particulars are its "foundation."

(b) The order of descent (or ascent) establishes a hierarchy among all particulars. Its base, from which every ideal one can be reached, are those which are real. Hence the phrase 'of higher order'. To be an ideal particular and to be one of *higher order* is one and the same.[56] Describing this hierarchical order accurately and stating some of the formation rules of our calculus are two sides of one coin. But we need not and I shall not bother, except for the following feature that deserves attention.

(c) All existents being particulars, why shouldn't any *n* of them, either real or ideal, and, if ideal, either of the same or of different orders, found an *n*-ary connection as well as, jointly with the latter, an Objective? In Meinong's world they actually do; as, incidentally, we have already seen in the case of the Bradley regress he accepts (p. 348). That shows that while there is an order among his world's only (explicit) existents, there are yet, in Russell's sense, no types in it. This lends further support[57] to the diagnosis that they are all particulars.

(d) Eventually we shall see that Meinong's rigid nominalism (and his

[55] Or, as I just said in the next to the last paragraph because I did not as yet want to use the new word, all other particulars *ultimately rest* on them. The German words are *fundieren* and *fundiert, bestimmen* and *bestimmt*.

[56] The German phrase is of course *Gegenstand hoeherer Ordnung*.

[57] I.e., if you wish to continue that game, this amounts to a *fifth step* (p. 346). Notice, too, that, with a twist by now familiar yet ever more reassuring as the scope expands, I could again have argued the other way around.

diffuse style) kept his grasp of connections on the level I described in Section Five. On this level, we saw with considerable detail in that section, one cannot but do very badly in assaying the connections which the foil assays as relations of the higher types. In this one respect, though, Meinong does well. Nothing prevents him, if I may so express myself, from piling semicolon upon semicolon. This is, as it were, a dividend of his peculiar reism, stretched-to-the-utmost yet without types. You see now why I said (p. 348) that on connections he did better than he deserved.

Real versus *ideal*. The distinction is ontological. This, of course, is but another way of saying that it cuts deeply. But even ontological distinctions differ in depth. Again, while they are all pervasive rather than specific, some are more so than others. Of the differences between Meinong's real and ideal particulars three are more specific; one, more pervasive.

The real particulars are the only ones not founded on anything; all others are ultimately founded on them. Each particular is compounded (combined) of a nature and either *ex* or *nonex;* every real particular "is" the compound of its nature and *ex*.[58] These are two more specific differences. The third is as easily stated. But I do not wish to spoil its effect by jumping the gun. So I shall not state it before I need it. The more pervasive difference, not surprisingly, is a matter of style, in the radical sense in which function versus complex marks a contrast in style. With this particular contrast we began. Frege, and as we now see implicitly Meinong, represents one side of it; my world, the other. The two sides of the contrast to which I now turn are represented by Meinong[59] and, again, the foil.

There are several kinds (categories) of existents, but there is only one kind of existing. This is the style of the foil. 'Exist' is univocal. Nor is its univocality impaired by the two modes (not: categories), actuality and potentiality. The latter in particular is merely the wholly nonspecific ground of the possibility of all complexes.[60] Kinds and degrees

---

[58] I stay once more with Objectives. The complications caused by connections will be taken care of before long. The quotes around 'is' are to remind you of two things. For one, his attempt to distinguish between a_1 and $(a_1^n: ex)$ failed. For another, he did not, or at least not until it was too late and even then without mastering the dialectic, recognize the ontological status of anything but objects, or, rather, as I would insist, either particulars or cryptoclusters.

[59] But not Frege, whose notion of existence is univocal while his explicit existents are of more than one kind, which puts him on my side of this fence.

[60] I.e., with a metaphor I have long used, this ground is the world's form. Or, with the linguistic turn, it is what makes any sentence, either true or false, well-formed.

of independence (as I use the term) establish status differences among the categories of fact, thing, and subsistent. But these differences among exist*ents* do not in any way involve different kinds of exist*ing*.

Turning to Meinong, one finds that for once his terminology helps. The words he uses generically are *sein* and *Sein*.[61] Every particular *ist* or has *Sein*. Yet I say generically rather than univocally; for he distinguishes between two kinds of *Sein*. A real particular has[62] *Dasein* (*ist da*). An ideal particular has *Bestand* (*besteht*).

All existents are particulars. Thus they all belong to a single category. But a particular is either real or ideal; and to be real is one kind of existing, to be ideal is another. This is Meinong's style. The contrast centers on either one or several kinds of either exist*ents* or exist*ing*. But 'kind of existing' is clumsy. I propose to speak instead of *levels* of existence. 'Level' is close to 'order'. Thus the proposal is in his spirit. The pervasive difference between the real and the ideal is of level.

Ex, on whatever level, is a very peculiar entity. For this there are two reasons, one obvious, one more subtle. The obvious one is its odd twin, *nonex;* the subtler one, that the pair of them is too versatile. What that means I shall exhibit rather than explain. (1) The ontological "status" of the Thomistic act of being (briefly: Act) is higher than that of any object. If a critic challenges this, I first remind him that, in theological language, the Act is the divine fulguration which creates and sustains the object. Then I turn the tables on him by adding that this is a particularly good example by which to learn the comparative use of 'status'. *Ex*, we know, corresponds to the Act. Or, rather, so does the pair, *ex* and *nonex*, provided one accepts his basic gambit that an existent may be compounded with either the one or the other. I conclude that inasmuch as they do the job of the Act, the "status" of our pair is higher than that of a thing. (2) A nature and either *ex* or *nonex*, as the case may be, combine without any need either for a nexus, as in the foil; or for a function, which Meinong fails to ontologize, as in the case of his connections; or for a connection and a function, the latter again ignored, as in the case of his Objectives. As far as this feature is concerned, *ex* and *nonex* are like nexus. And the status of a nexus is

---

[61] I.e., both the verb (being) and the noun (Being). Things are not helped by his also using '*existieren*' and '*Existenz*' for '*da sein*' and '*Dasein*'. '*Bestehen*' is most accurately translated by 'obtain'. If so, does one say one thing or two when saying, once that the connection $(c_1; e_1)$ obtains, once that the Objective $(c_1; (c_1; e_1); e_1)$ does? The question touches some sensitive spots. But it will all come out in the wash. See also n. 50, above.

[62] More accurately, *has or has not*. But no harm will come to us if we ignore for a moment the odd twin, *nonex*.

lower than that of a thing. (3) *Ex* and *nonex* do the jobs of Frege's True
and False. Hence, after a fashion at least, they correspond to the foil's
actuality and potentiality. The latter, however, are not entities nor
categories nor levels but two modes, and the status of the "possible
complexes" in one of them is the lowest of all.

You see why I called *ex* (and *nonex*) versatile. They have three jobs.
Presently we shall see that they have still another. But the three will
do for my point, which is, as no doubt you have gathered, that the
three features of the foil which correspond to them are incompatible. I
conclude, not in strict logic of course, but as a matter of style, yet with
great confidence, that any ontology with so versatile a notion of existence will eventually fail. (Meinong's, if I am right, did fail.)

Ex and *nonex* share one feature with subsistents. Why, then, are they
not subsistents? After a fashion at least, they do the job of the two
modes. Why, then, are they not modes? What, if any, is the difference
between a mode and a level? And so on. Even if you are no longer
really worried by such questions, some uneasiness may linger. For, I
repeat, the language of comparative ontology, in which this discussion
of status has inevitably been couched, is very delicate. So I conclude,
selectively, with some comments that should put you at ease.

(a) Some use 'subsistent' for the entities of which in some ontologies
all "full-fledged" existents are in some sense "compounded." In this
sense, Meinong's natures, together with *ex* and *nonex*, but not his ideal
particulars, are subsistents. (b) If an ontology has more than one level,
some use 'subsistent' for all its entities which do not belong to its
"foundation." In this sense, Meinong's ideal particulars, but neither
his natures nor *ex* and *nonex*, are subsistents. (c) My use of 'subsistent'
differs from both (a) and (b). Upon my use, *ex* and *nonex* have one but
not any other feature of subsistents. (d) In a world without complexes,
of particulars only, there is no room for my two modes. Or, with a twist,
Objectives compounded with *nonex* are just as "actual" as those compounded with *ex*. (e) Just as there is no room for modes in his world, so
there is none for levels in mine. This alone shows that modes and levels
are two and not one.

IV. All nominalists "ground" the pitch c in a class of particulars,
c_1, c_2, c_3, and so on. The more thoughtful ones add for good measure an
internal relation of equality[63] between any two of these, or, more
accurately, between their natures. The later Meinong does even better.
He ontologizes this internal relation. But his nominalism is as consistent

---

[63] Also called *exact similarity*. See for all this Section Five and then again, for
Meinong, Section Twenty, where, among other things, the descent of his equality
connection from the internal relation of equality will be established.

as it is rigid. He "particularizes" what he has ontologized. E.g., the equalities between c_1 and c_2 on the one hand and, say, c_7 and c_8 on the other are not one but two, each an ideal particular. Are these two particulars equal? As one would expect, he holds that they are. That raises a question. Granted, if only for the sake of the argument, that a certain internal relation between real particulars adequately grounds their several equalities, what grounds the further equalities between any two of the latter?

Whenever the context makes it safe, the semicolon has been and will be used either as a function variable or as a constant, e.g., for the function which (unlike him) we know to be involved in founding the musical third c, e.[64] At this point the broad use is not safe. So I write '$equ(c_i, c_k)$' for his connection of *equality* between c_i and c_k. Also, I want you to suppose that whenever in this argument I write '$equ(x, y)$', x and y are in fact equal, so that we need not now attend to a question which will occupy us very soon, namely, what, if anything, '$equ(x, y)$' stands for in case they are not. Permit me, finally, to use '$x = y$' as an abbreviation for '$(x; equ(x, y); y)$'; under the supposition I want you to make the particular this expression purports to name exists.

Consider the following condition: (C1) If $x_1 = x_2$ and $y_1 = y_2$, then, for all functions f, $f(x_1, y_1) = f(x_2, y_2)$.[65] Substituting '$equ$' for '$f$' in (C1) yields the desired result, e.g., after the appropriate substitutions for the particular variables, $equ(c_1, c_2) = equ(c_7, c_8)$. If you have any qualms as to whether this procedure is circular or otherwise problematic, let me reassure you. *Formally*, specifying a function by a so-called functional equation is a safe routine. *Substantively*, (C1) merely specifies, *either wholly or at least in part*, the function needed to do the job under the supposition, which we know to be a part of the system, that the nature of a founded particular depends only on the natures of those founding it.

As for c, so for the pitch d (d_1, d_2, $\cdots$) and the color blue (b_1, b_2, $\cdots$). But consider now any two of the three particulars $equ(c_1, c_2)$, $equ(d_1, d_2)$, $equ(b_1, b_2)$. Are they too equal? Meinong holds of course that they are. Succinctly, all equalities are equal. More formally: (C2) For all x, y, z, u, $equ(x, y) = equ(z, u)$. I am prepared to grant that the function which (as we know) is involved in (his) equality may rea-

---

[64] This function is one, of course; whether the intervals are several, as in this world; or one, as in the foil. Nor do I even know what it could possibly mean to "particularize" a function. But one may reasonably speculate that since it does not mean anything, Meinong, even if the vast and deep void had been pointed out to him by a contemporary, would not have allowed it to be filled by functions. So rigid was his nominalism!

[65] The consequent of (C1) is called a *functional equation*. It need not be binary, of course.

sonably be specified by the conjunction of (C1) and (C2).[66] My point is, first, that this is as far as one can reasonably go, and, second, that it will not do.

Consider the two connections $(c_1; e_1)$ and $(d_1; f_1)$, where the semicolon stands for a constant, namely, the function involved with the musical third. Meinong holds of course that $(c_1; e_1)$ and $(d_1; f_1)$ are equal. Yet the conjunction of (C1) and (C2) does not yield this result. The only way to obtain it is to add a third functional equation, involving equality and this particular function. And as for this function, so for every other. This clearly is no longer reasonable.[67] I conclude that Meinong's nominalism leaves his world irremediably inadequate.[68]

We are ready for the two complications. One has its source in Meinong's assay of *negative facts*. The other hangs by his notion of *real connections*, which is closely related to that of cryptoclusters and, thereby, to the other major inaccuracy, the one we identified early (p. 337) but have as yet not closely examined.

Suppose that Peter is red and not yellow; then consider the four sentences (1) 'Peter is red', (2) 'Peter is yellow', (3) 'Peter is not red', (4) 'Peter is not yellow'. (1) and (4), being true, stand for actual facts; (2) and (3), being false, for potential ones. Another dichotomy puts (1) and (2) on one side, (3) and (4) on the other. The former stand for *positive* facts; the latter, for *negative* ones. Jointly the two dichotomies produce a fourfold division. Every fact is either actual or potential, irrespective of whether it is positive or negative; and it is either positive or negative, irrespective of whether it is actual or potential.

Meinong, we know (p. 352), at a certain point in his career was struck by the fundamental principle that all intentions exist. Thus he was faced by the double-pronged challenge of assaying potential and negative states of affairs[69] in conformity with the principle. For we can of course think what is actual and positive, actual and negative, and so on.

[66] That is why in the last paragraph I said *either wholly or at least in part.*

[67] Surely you recognize underneath the different trappings the structure of the argument from the end of Section Four. Yet there is a *mise-au-point* I want to add in order to forestall a possible confusion. Consider (a) $9 - 7 = 20 - 18$, (b) $9 = 20$, (c) $7 = 18$. (a) is *demonstrably* true even though, since (b) and (c) are false, not even (C1) is satisfied. The point is that on the level on which (a) can be demonstrated neither the integers nor the arithmetical-difference function are simples. This level is of course Peano's.

[68] I.e., in the example, the "equality" of the particulars $(c_1; e_1)$, $(d_2; f_2)$, $(e_3; g_3)$, and so on, is left without ontological ground. Hence one is not really justified in writing them hg_1^3, hg_2^3, hg_3^3, and so on, even if one were justified in writing c_1, c_2, c_3, and so on. But no harm will come to us from occasionally using such "abbreviations." See n. 45, above.

[69] Notice that in his case, though not in the foil's, I shift from 'fact' to 'state of affairs'. See n. 35, above.

What he did about potential states of affairs we have seen and examined, without loss of generality, in the case of some positive ones.[70] Now we are ready for the other prong. How did he assay negative facts? It will help if we first quickly recall how the challenge has been met in the foil and by Brentano.

The reason that the foil encounters at this point no difficulty is that its connectives, of which negation is one, enjoy the ontological status of subsistents. Hence negation, if attached to one fact, produces another. If the first is actual then the second is potential, and conversely. Phenomenologically, too, everything is well. The so-called negative characters (and relations) are but the simplest kind of derived things. Hence there is no reason why, when presented with, say, a red spot, I should not sometimes see it "directly" as being not yellow, just as I sometimes perceive a horse without seeing some or even any of the characters (and relations) mentioned in a definition of 'horse'.[71]

Brentano, in one of the most pellucid instances of the conversion rule, "withdrew" negation into the mind. There its job is supposed to be done by rejecting. Hence his emphasis on there being no "negative concepts." This, though, is a conviction shared by all representationalists.[72] Meinong agreed with them all through his life, thus showing his dependence on some of the same patterns, even after he had reached a point at which only his diffuse style kept him from realizing that he would have done much better without any concepts, either positive or negative. Of this later. What concerns us now is where he differed. His realism, in conjunction with the fundamental principle, left him no choice. Somehow the negative facts had to be accommodated outside of minds.

Let us stay with connections (e.g., not-equal, not-hg^3), leave what

[70] I.e., those corresponding to Objectives such as $(c_1; (c_1; e_1); e_1)$, which are not founded on any of the "real connections" that are now appearing on our horizon.

[71] See for all this p. 294 and n. 30 *ibid*; also n. 4 of this section. In Frege's world, the connectives have the status of functions. But I know of no other in which they really exist. Meinong, we shall see in the last section, has great trouble with all of them. Even so, negation is sufficiently important, structurally as well as historically, to justify the separate treatment.

[72] See p. 295 and n. 32 *ibid*. Remember also that even in a world with Classes, the complement-Classes cannot be grounded on the internal relation of equality. Meinong shows his preoccupation with the issue by devoting the whole first chapter of *Ann.* to the case against *negative Vorstellungen*. The two arguments in the next paragraph are suggested by this chapter. The phenomenological one is dialectically re-enforced by the observation, in the case of *difference* (i.e., from where I stand, nonequality), that the latter, unlike equality, is capable of degrees. This I find interesting, or at least worth mentioning, because of the evidence it provides for his grasp of relations never having got beyond the level, described in Section Five, on which all relations are grounded in degrees of difference.

the foil calls negative characters (e.g., not-green, not-c) until later. There are two possibilities. (a) The negative connection is, in some sense, "compounded" of the positive one and negation. (b) The positive and the negative connection, existing on the same level, are, as it were, the two halves of a single whole (e.g., equal-nonequal, hg^3-$nonhg^3$). *Ad* (a). Negation, since being neither a particular nor an object it does not exist, cannot in any sense enter into a "compound." Hence (a) is out. Yet his reism, though just as rigid, is not as blunt as Brentano's. Thus he argues instead, more elaborately, that negation, not being a thing, would not, even if it existed, have a nature. And the only "compounds" he knows are those particulars (really, as we know, simple) whose natures are founded on other natures. *Ad* (b). Phenomenologically, he insisted, the positive and the negative connection are on the same level. Either may be "directly" seen. As you know, I agree. This, though, is one thing. The "solution" which thus encouraged he proposed is another. It is, alas, bizarre. Even worse, it is counterstructural.

Let a single and a double semicolon stand for the functions involved with the musical second and third, respectively, and use also the "abbreviations" formed with 'hg'. That makes $(c_1; d_1)$ the same as hg_1^2; $(c_2; ;e_2)$, the same as hg_2^3. The proposed solution is as follows: Each connection ('conn') has two "halves," one positive ('$conn^+$'), one negative ('$conn^-$'). *Any two particulars which (as one ordinarily says) stand in this connection, found a "particularized" case of* conn$^+$; *any two which don't, one of* conn$^-$. E.g., $(c_1;; d_1)$ is $(hg^3)_1^-$, $(c_2; e_2)$ is $(hg^3)_2^-$. (A moment's reflection will show you that this does not take care of the roughness pointed out on p. 360. There is, e.g., the Objective, corresponding to a potential fact, which is founded on the three particulars c_1, $(hg^3)_2^+$, d_1.) Upon this solution, *every* pair (or triple, etc.) of particulars founds either the positive or the negative half of *each* binary (or ternary, etc.) function. This feature I find bizarre. Meinong tries to support it by observing that some particulars do quite commonsensically stand in more than one connection. c_1 and e_1, for instance, found not only an interval but also a case of being different and a pair. I merely add that these are but few, and, more importantly, that they are all positive.[73]

What grounds the plus and the minus? The question couldn't be more urgent. (a) Both $(hg^2)_1^+$ and $(hg^3)_1^-$ are particulars and therefore compounded of a nature and existence; i.e., they are $((hg^2)_1^{+n}: ex)$ and $((hg^3)_1^{-n}: ex)$, respectively. (b) $(hg^2)_1^{+n}$ involves c_1^n, d_1^n and something

[73] The troubles into which he runs when trying to found pairs and all other classes are a different story, of which more in Section Twenty. See n. 23, above.

else (α); $(hg^3)_1^{-n}$, c_1^n, d_1^n and something different (β). (a) and (b) must be true. Or, if you please, his assay must make them true. Otherwise it is counterstructural in the very strong sense of contradicting what he is already committed to. He, in his confusion about "being," of which more later, takes his cue from the 'is' and the 'is not' in 'd_1 *is* higher[2] than c_1' and 'd_1 *is not* higher[3] than c_1', respectively; identifies α and β with *ex* and *nonex*; and assays $(hg^2)_1^{+n}$ and $(hg^3)_1^{-n}$ as $((c_1^n; d_1^n) \, ! \, ex)$ and $((c_1^n;; d_1^n) \, ! \, nonex)$. Notice the exclamation point instead of the colon; remember that in this world every particular, *but of course nothing else*, is compounded of a nature and either *ex* or *nonex*; then ask yourself what '$(c_1^n; d_1^n)$' and '$(c_1^n;; d_1^n)$' in the above expressions stand for. The only answer I can think of is that each of them stands for the *nature of a nature*. That shows that, even though it satisfies (a) and (b), his solution is counterstructural. But we have at least discovered the fourth job (p. 364) of the versatile twins. ex *and* nonex *also stand for positive and negative*.

Take two particulars, k_i and l_i, and a connection, *conn*. The two particulars will found $conn_i^+$ or $conn_i^-$ depending on whether $(k_i; conn_i^+; l_i)^n$ or $(k_i; conn_i^-; l_i)^n$ combines with *ex* into an Objective. If we had to become technically proficient in finding our way through his world and our notation we would have to establish several such "rules." Fortunately we needn't. So I conclude with an observation of some comparative interest, calling attention to what in the last paragraph was taken for granted. The nature of a connection always combines with *ex*, never with *nonex*. In this respect (a) a connection is like a real particular that exists. In the !-composition, however, the "nature of a nature" combines with either *ex* or *nonex*, as the case may be. In this respect (b) a connection is like an Objective. Jointly, therefore, (a) and (b) place connections in a position intermediate between real particulars and Objectives. The reason I find this difference between the two kinds of ideal particulars of comparative interest is that, however dimly, it reflects the distinction between the foil's relations, which are things, on the one hand, and its facts, on the other.[74]

We are ready for the second complication. At this point a certain difference between Brentano and Meinong becomes important. Roughly speaking and in γ-terms, Brentano's fundamental nexus is $\subset$, Meinong's is γ. I.e., writing 'b' for '$\gamma(a_1, a_2)$', the fundamental "connection" in this case is for the former (1) $a_1 \subset b$ (and $a_2 \subset b$), while for the

---

[74] It is only fair to point out that you will find very little, if anything, of all this in Meinong. He merely made the mess. I am doing my best to articulate it. Cleaning it up is impossible. For the difference between connections and Objectives, see above, p. 347 and n. 22; also n. 46.

latter it is (2) $\gamma(a_1, a_2)$. What makes the difference important is that (1) is easily mistaken for an a priori truth, or, as I would now rather put it, for a connection among natures, while at least in some cases, e.g., that of a place and a color, (2) cannot be plausibly so mistaken, irrespective of whether it is thought of, clearly, as a fact, or, confusedly, as a cluster.[75]

Let p_1 and b_1 be a place and a color particular which coincide. Suppose Meinong's world to be so simple that, upon a γ-assay, $\gamma(p_1, b_1)$ would be an object.[76] The issue before us is the threefold distinction between the *object* itself, the *Objective* that "corresponds" to it, and the collection which I call the *cryptocluster*.

p_1 is natured. So is b_1. Meinong, who structurally speaking thinks in terms of γ, recognizes, very much to his credit, that their *coincidence* requires an ontological ground. Call it $coinc_1$. What sort of entity is it? He assays it as a connection. Reasonable or even obvious as that seems, it yet conflicts with what he is already committed to. The two natures p_1^n and b_1^n do not found a third which one could reasonably call $coinc_1$. If you want to convince yourself that there is trouble, just move b_1 to another place. (The moving metaphor is harmless.) He resolves the conflict, in the manner briefly mentioned at the very beginning (p. 337), by "adding" a third real particular such that its nature, together with p_1^n and b_1^n, determines an Objective. More precisely, he tells us that $coinc_1$ itself is both real and a connection. Such hermaphroditic entities he calls *real connections*. In the example, $coinc_1$ founds jointly with p_1 and b_1 the Objective $(p_1; coinc_1; b_1)$. It is real because, not being founded on anything, it belongs to the foundation. It is a connection because the entity which jointly with p_1 and b_1 it founds is an Objective and not a ternary connection as, e.g., that of betweenness among three appropriate places. You see that we are already in possession of the three terms of the distinction. One is the object itself; the other is the Objective $(p_1; coinc_1; b_1)$; the cryptocluster in the case is the collection $\{p_1, coinc_1, b_1\}$.

Not surprisingly, real connections have some rather peculiar features. (a) Not being founded on anything, $coinc_1$ involves no function. In our notation, accordingly, we must not make the semicolon stand for its "connection" with p_1 and b_1. I propose that we use the multiplication

---

[75] The related and even more radical difference which makes Brentano, but not Meinong, deny the very existence of all attributes in the Aristotelian style will occupy us in Section Twenty.

[76] This takes for granted, first, that, like Brentano's, his is a world of coordinate qualities and, second, that we may again without loss stay in a temporal cross section. What little will have to be said on these two scores can wait.

cross instead. That makes '$(p_1 \times b_1)$' and '$coinc_1$' two names for one entity. It is informative to check how that fits with (C1). $p_1 = p_1$,[77] $b_1 = b_2$, and p_1 and b_1 coincide. b_2, however, does not coincide with p_1. Hence, if the cross were a semicolon, if I may so express myself, we would be in trouble. (b) Being a connection, *coinc* has two halves. Thus we must improve our notation, never write '*coinc*' but either (b1) '$coinc^+$' or (b2) '$coinc^-$', as the case requires. (c) Suppose that p_2 and b_2 do not coincide and consider '$coinc_1^+$', and '$coinc_2^-$'. Fully expanded, they become (c1) '$((p_1^n \times b_1^n)!ex):ex)$' and (c2) '$((p_2^n \times b_2^n)!nonex):ex)$'. Remember now the two specious Objectives which (c1') '$(a^n:ex)$' and (c2') '$(a^n: nonex)$' purport to name. If (c1') succeeds, there is an "ordinary" real particular in the foundation. If (c2') succeeds, there is nothing in the foundation to be named by a. That spots both a similarity and a difference between "ordinary" real particulars and real connections. The similarity is that whether there is anything at all in the foundation depends on the dichotomy *ex-nonex*. The difference is that in the case of the ordinary real particular the '*ex*' or '*nonex*' which makes the difference stands after the colon while in the case of the real connection it follows the exclamation point.

These features amount to a further subcategory-like differentiation. Just as all connections occupy an intermediate position between real particulars and Objectives, so real connections fall somewhere in between "ordinary" real particulars and ideal connections. That invites a comparative comment. Meinong's real connections cannot but remind one of the pseudonexus γ, or, if you please, of the nexus ν_2.[78] Yet they are particulars. Thus they cannot really do the job of either the one or the other. That brings us to the *second major inaccuracy*.

(1) The object is "complex." On the one hand, therefore, it is in every fully articulated ontology a fact (complex) while, on the other, it cannot in any ontology without confusion be assayed as a particular. (2) Since the Objective $(p_1; coinc_1^+; b_1)$ is an ideal particular and as such a (ternary) function of p_1, $coinc_1^+$, and b_1, there is no sense of 'complex' in which it makes any sense to speak or think of it as a "complex" of these three particulars. (3) Collections as such do not exist. (4) Meinong's is a world in which objects do not really exist. The last of these four propositions follows from the first three. Yet there is not the slightest doubt that he thinks of his world as one with objects which

---

[77] The "formal" extension of equality so that what is one is also equal to itself, though not of course conversely, encounters no difficulty.

[78] Of the worlds of kind II considered in Section Two. The confirmation of all these diagnoses through the "prehistory" of Meinong's real connections will have to wait until Section Twenty.

not only exist but are real. The price he pays is the second major inaccuracy.

This inaccuracy is the bundle of all the errors and confusions that can be traced back to the failure of distinguishing clearly among the object, the Objective, and the collection in the case,[79] or, for that matter, between any two of these three. The collection, if and as involved in these confusions, acquires spurious ontological status. That is why I call it a cryptocluster. The inaccuracy itself I shall henceforth call the *function inaccuracy*. For its deepest root, I believe to have shown, is Meinong's double failure with respect to functions. He neither understood the radical difference between complexes and functions nor realized that his was really a function world.

The move from the binary to the n-ary schema requires the replacement of the binary real connection by an n-ary one. To be completely accurate we would therefore have to add a prescript, write '2-*conn*', '3-*conn*', $\cdots$, 'n-*conn*'. But no harm will come to us if, omitting this precaution, as in the case of γ, we write '$(a_i; b_i; \cdots; n_i; coinc_1^+)$' and $\{a_i, b_i, \cdots, n_i, coinc_1^+\}$, respectively, for the Objective and the cryptocluster. In the worlds I or II of Section Two the n-ary nexus ν_1 or ν_2 can be replaced by the binary ϵ or the ternary ω, provided only one follows the foil in giving ontological status to conjunction (see n. 71, above). This Meinong's reism does not permit him to do. So he stays with n-ary real connections.

To think structurally of γ as basic is one thing. To ignore $\subset$ is another. Nor does Meinong ignore it. According to him, to be or not to be one of the n ordinary real particulars which contribute to the founding of an Objective of the n-ary schema is to found either the positive or the negative half of *a connection which I shall call* η.[80] That yields n cases of η_i^+, (1) $(a_i; \eta_i^+; (a_i; b_i; \cdots; n_i; coinc_i^+))$, and so on; and, for every other particular x, (2) $(x; \eta_i^-; (a_i; b_i; \cdots; n_i; coinc_i^+))$. η^-, as you see, takes care of negative characters (p. 367).[81]

---

[79] I.e., in the example, what in a γ-world, but not in his, would be the cluster $\gamma(p_1, b_1)$, his ideal particular $(p_1; coinc_1^+; b_1)$ and the nonentity, in his world as well as mine, $\{p_1, coinc_1^+, b_1\}$. We are at one of those crucial points where I would rather be tediously repetitious than leave any doubt.

[80] Much of the eighth chapter of *Ann.* is a discussion, detailed, rich, but also very diffuse, of η; naturally so, since the chapter deals with *Komplexen*, i.e., as far as the ever-present function inaccuracy permits, with objects. See n. 2. Incidentally, you should now be able to appreciate my strategy. Having limited ourselves in the first long instalment to positive ideal connections and the Objectives they help to found, we were then in a position to display rather quickly the two complications due to negation and to the Objectives which, since they involve real connections, "correspond" to objects.

[81] For the distinction between *coinc* and η, see *Ann.* §41.

(1) and (2) provide the means for attempting an assay of the two schemata (I*a*) *A is B* and (I*b*) *A is not B*, i.e., of the first two classes in the eightfold division of Section Twelve (p. 228). I say that they provide, not this assay, but merely the means for attempting it, because these facts are a posteriori, while the states of affairs (1) and (2) are a priori. Even so, we only need to remember the representationalists' assay, with which Meinong concurs,[82] of perceptual judgments, in order to see that (1) and (2) are his assays of (a positive and a negative ingredient of) the intention of the alleged "analysis"-part of a (veridical) perceptual judgment.

Judgments are one thing; the facts they intend are another. The realist Meinong agrees. How, then, will he ground the fact, or, if you please, the state of affairs, which, say, 'This (thing) is blue' stands for? Caught, as always, in the function inaccuracy, the best he can do is to take advantage of the schema that guided his early thought[83] and assay it as the Objective (b_1; η_1^+; (p_1; $shaped_1$; $colored_1$; $coinc_1^+$)). This raises a question. How can a nominalist as rigid as he was ground not only shapes and colors but Shape and Color? This issue will be most conveniently discussed during the examination of the earlier stages of his thought in Section Twenty.

Several other features and issues of his world could, and therefore perhaps should, be taken up in an examination of its trunk. Just consider that, even if allowance is made for the question concerning Shape and Color just raised but not answered, we have so far accounted for only the first four classes (I*a*, I*b*, II*a*, II*b*) in the eightfold division. Yet there are two good reasons for not going on. For one, this section is very long already. For another, all these features and issues either belong in Section Twenty or are most profitably discussed in connection with minds.

[82] For this assay, see Section Ten; for his concurrence, n. 20, *ibid.*, and the two pieces of evidence there cited (*Erfahrungsgl.*, p. 21; *Stellung*, p. 58).

[83] This is of course the third schema of Section Nine. As you see, I stay with its "ternary objects."

MINDS

I N Meinong's world, as in Brentano's, minds are objects among objects. Both teacher and student pass the ground-plan test (p. 140). Yet there is also a difference which very effectively contrasts the realism of the one with the structural idealism of the other. In Brentano's world minds are the only continuants. Meinong assays both minds and bodies as continuants. Whether or not he was also moved by this contrast, he had another compelling intellectual motive for insisting that bodies are continuants. What the motive was and what price he paid for making minds and bodies alike in this respect we shall see at the very end of the book. Until then we shall again be able to stay without loss in a single cross section. Until then, therefore, as in the rest of this book, except at the few places where the difference matters, I shall for brevity's sake again use 'mind' and 'body' for what are not really objects but merely cross sections of such.

In the prototype a mind is either a single act or a cluster each component of which is an act, or so at least we may assume without loss for our purposes. Each act is a complex particular, i.e., a joint (ι) of a fringe and a core. Fringes and cores in turn are either simple (perfect) or complex (p. 144) particulars. A fringe, for instance, is either a single particular which is an entertaining or a joint of such a particular with the specific constituent (p. 151) of either a believing, or a perceiving, or a remembering, and so on. A cluster, as we speak, has components rather than constituents. That is how we acknowledge the γ-blur and at the same time make our peace with it.[1]

In Meinong's world, too, each act has a core (c) and a fringe (f). Thus, even if for the sake of the argument we suppose that both c and f are particulars, we run into the function inaccuracy. The only way of avoiding it is to distinguish between the *nonexisting nonreal* three-mem-

---

[1] If you feel the need for refreshing your memory on some of these notions, turn to Section Eight.

ber collection of c, f, and a real connection[2] between them, on the one hand, and the (ideal) Objective founded by these three real particulars on the other. Yet there is nothing of which he is more certain than that *acts exist and are real*. One could even argue that because of this certainty he is also convinced, in spite of the uneasiness which the function inaccuracy occasionally causes him, that everything will come out well in the end. Once more, therefore, we have no choice but to make our peace with the inaccuracy, which means, as usually, that whenever it does not matter we shall simply ignore it, so that we may once more divide and conquer. Or, at most, I shall acknowledge that the "entities" I shall talk about do not really exist by speaking of an act's fringe and core as its *cryptocomponents*. As for acts, so for minds. That minds exist and are real is taken for granted. A mind is thus either a single act or a cryptocluster each cryptocomponent of which is an act.

Each act has two "constituents"; the one I call the core is objective; the other, which I call the fringe, subjective; cores and intentions stand in one-one correspondence. This important bit of common sense states a condition every realistic assay of the knowing situation must fulfill. That is why occasionally I call it the *necessary condition*. If it is fulfilled, an act of believing (disbelieving) will be true (false) or false (true) depending on whether (in the language of the foil) its intention is actual or potential. Because of this connection with the correspondence theory of truth I occasionally also call the condition the *correspondence view*.[3] Since it is so important, it will pay if, before turning to Meinong, we recall how Brentano, the prototype, and the foil compare on this score.

Brentano's dilemma we remember only too well. His extreme reism commits him to acts with a simple core. Yet there are judgments which he cannot assay as a single act of this sort. Hence the doctrine of double judgments, which amounts to a repudiation of the correspondence view (p. 233). The *prototype*, some of whose cores are complex, can provide cores for all acts whose intentions are clusters; e.g., the core (1) $\iota(a_1^*, a_2^*, \ldots, a_n^*)$ for the cluster (2) $\gamma(a_1, a_2, \ldots, a_n)$. But it fails when it comes to such intentions as (3) $a_1 \subset \gamma(a_1, a_2, \ldots, a_n)$, since it cannot, if I may express myself succinctly, use (1) once more for the core that corresponds to (3) (p. 281). In the *foil* all cores are simple; all intentions are facts. The one-one correspondence is secured

---

[2] I omit the obvious argument that, *at least in some cases*, the natures of f and c do not found a third which one could reasonably call their coincidence. The italicized clause excludes "modal considerations," of which more in the last section.

[3] All this must by now be very familiar. But see, e.g., p. 232.

in the by now familiar manner. The result of a substitution for the blank in '$\ulcorner P \urcorner M \ldots$' is analytic or contradictory depending on whether or not the expression substituted is or is not 'P'.

The comparison recalls two lessons. One is that the simplicity or "complexity," as the case may be, of its cores is a very important feature of any ontology. The other is that a reistic ontology whose cores are complex cannot produce a realistic assay of the knowing situation. (More accurately, such an ontology would be inadequate even if its reism and the "complexity" of its cores did not cause it any other troubles.)

Meinong is a reist. How, then, about his cores? Are they all simple? The question is simple; the answer, straightforward. His cores are all simple. Yet the matter as a whole is anything but simple. This is my cue for revealing the strategy of this section.

There will be three parts. In the *first* I shall describe and examine the main features of Meinong's assay of the knowing situation.[4] In the *second*, I shall examine his views on truth and prepare the ground for the examination, in the last section, of his disastrous doctrine of evidence. In the *third* part, I shall attend to the anything but simple issues raised by the straightforward answer to the simple question. Until then I shall assume that *all his cores are real particulars.*

(Whether or not there are in his world all the facts there ought to be and all the cores to go with them, such as those of the fact and judgment classes III to V of Section Twelve, is a different question. By now you probably surmise that from where I stand the answer is negative. But it can wait.[5] I say "from where I stand" because with respect to facts some may consider the position of the foil as extreme. With respect to judgments, however, as no doubt you remember from Part III, there is no issue.)

That much for the core as such. How about the rest? *With a twist uniquely his own, Meinong's assay of the knowledge situation satisfies the necessary condition.* We are ready to describe this assay accurately. First, though, for an agreement about words which will save us an interruption later.

Examining what he does, one soon discovers that in describing it one may reasonably use 'intend' and 'intention' in either of two ways, which may reasonably be spoken of as the narrow and the broad use, respectively. My own use is a third. At some points the differences between these three make a difference. So I shall mark them, wherever

---

[4] The largest and clearest block of evidence for this part is the fifth chapter of *Ann.*

[5] It will be given, in two parts, in the last two sections.

they matter, by attaching one of three prescripts 'n', 'b', and 'f', taken from 'narrow', 'broad' and 'foil', to the verb and the noun. That gives six combinations, from 'n-intend' to 'f-intention'.

As always, we shall work with examples; three, six, or even twelve, depending on how you count; combining each of the cores corresponding to three f-intentions with each of two fringes, which makes six; and assuming that, if it were assayed in the foil, each f-intention would be once actual, once potential, which makes twelve. The six f-intentions fall into three pairs; one (a) goes with c_1 being higher[3] than e_1; one (b), with the *Komplex* corresponding to the collection $\{p_1, b_1, coinc_1\}$; one (c), with the particular a_1.[6] *As Meinong assays them*, these six entities are (a1) $((c_1; (c_1; e_1); e_1)^n: ex)$, (a2) $((c_1; (c_1; e_1); e_1)^n: nonex)$, (b1) $((p_1; coinc_1; b_1)^n: ex)$, (b2) $((p_1; coinc_1; b_1)^n: nonex)$, (c1) $(a^n: ex)$, (c2) $(a^n: nonex)$. *As he speaks*, they are six Objectives. *As we know*, (c1) and (c2) are spurious. But we also know that at certain points we must either break off or go along with the spurious. At this point we must at least pretend that (c1) and (c2) and therefore *all six f-intentions are ideal particulars*.

As far as the objective side of the examples is concerned, that will do. On the subjective side, I shall work with thinking-of and believing. At first that seems odd for two reasons. (1) Considering the intentions, it would seem more natural to use perceiving instead of believing. Yet there is a very good reason, which will come out later, to follow Meinong in not using it at this point; and I do not want to bother with the distinction between seeing and hearing, which, again following him, one could use. Nor is believing really as awkward as it seems; since, as we shall see, he assays perceiving something as a believing, accompanied by some sort of "evidence," that it exists. (2) Even taking for granted that my treatment is highly selective, as of course it is, you may yet reasonably expect, from what has already transpired, that I would work with three fringes, thinking-of, believing, and disbelieving. The reason that two will do is not the unique twist of his assay but merely a minor wrinkle. Yet, minor as it is, examining it now provides an opportunity for introducing some material we shall need soon.

There is in this world no disbelieving (see, e.g., *Ann.*, p. 147). Disbelieving-that-p and disbelieving-that-not-p are "identified" with

---

[6] Think of a as a color particular, as in the first schema of Section Nine. Since the f-intentions that go with it are not really states of affairs, the assumption of assaying it in the foil, where all awareness is propositional, makes literally no sense. Yet it serves its purpose and will do no harm. But notice that an f-intention need not be one of the foil. Notice, too, that I ignore the plus-minus in connection with '*coinc*'.

believing-that-not-p and believing-that-p, respectively. This is the wrinkle. Dialectically, it hardly matters. Phenomenologically, it is a roughness.[7] You will not go wrong if you expect to find some structural motive without which a phenomenologist as keen as the author of this world would not have put up with the roughness.

Brentano's minds engage in some very remarkable activities which I called *forging*. Meinong's perform some feats, very different yet equally remarkable, which I shall call *fusing*. They produce (*produzieren*) the various cores by fusing several real particulars into a single one. This process is problematic. So are the materials from which it starts. The problems, or issues, are among those that will occupy us in the third part of this section. 'Process' I just used without qualms, since the activities of Meinong's minds do not, as far as I can tell, involve the kind of spontaneity incompatible with scientific determinism.[8] In this they are like Brentano's. Yet there is the word, 'active', with all the metaphors which it more or less subtly suggests. Keep this in mind while considering that without the special activities I call fusings there would be no cores and that if there were no cores there would be no acts, and you will see how one image leads into another. *In producing a core a mind grasps its "object."*[9] Such grasping is a reaching out toward the "object." In disbelieving the mind does not reach out for anything. Yet one cannot disbelieve what one has not first grasped. Hence the wrinkle. This is the structural reason. Or, perhaps, it is merely the anatomy of a metaphor.

What a mind grasps is always a nature. This is the twist. Considering the way it inserts natures into the knowing situation, I might as well have called it the Aristotelian twist; or, even, since these natures are "particularized," the *Thomistic twist*. But I didn't want to spoil so important a point by jumping the gun. Nor does even that exhaust its importance. Since what the mind grasps and what is presented to it are one and not two, it also establishes Meinong's position[10] in the representationalist succession; provided only one can show, as I promised I would in the next section, that there is a genetic connection between his natures and the representationalists' ideas (see p. 358). The evi-

[7] See the paper by Allaire cited in n. 14 of Section Twelve.

[8] If reminders are desired, turn to Section Six; for Brentano, to p. 331 and n. 26, *ibid.*

[9] *Grasp (erfassen)* is his word, not mine. It is indeed one of the key words of *Ann.* The use of 'object' between double quotes, here and a few more times, to fill the need of the moment for a grammatical object, does not in any way prejudge the issue of what an act "intends."

[10] Or, rather, at the end of it. But once more I do not want to spoil an important point by an unnecessary anticipation.

dence for the diagnosis that what the mind grasps is always a nature is pervasive and beyond doubt, although often marred by the nature inaccuracy.[11] In our example, the three natures each of which is grasped in four of the twelve cases are $(c_1; (c_1; e_1); e_1)^n$, $(p_1; coinc_1; b_1)^n$, and a^n. The first two are propositions; the third, being the nature of a real particular, is not.

Just as c_1 and e_1 found $(c_1; e_1)$, so a core and its "object" found (a "particularized" case of) a connection which is ideal, one-one, neither an equality nor a similarity, nor further specifiable. This is *"the* fundamental epistemological connection"[12] of Meinong's world. He calls it the adequacy connection. Since we use 'adequate' for something else, we must cast about for another word.

Having produced a core, how does the mind hold the "object" in its grasp? The question is wrongheaded. The metaphor of holding overshoots the mark. The best answer is that nothing holds anything. The "object" always exists, of which more in a moment. Literally, therefore, however active the mind may be in producing the core and sustaining it in its existence, as long as it does exist, so does the connection, which, being ideal, exists as long as its foundation exists, without, if I may make the metaphor defeat itself, anyone or anything doing anything further about it. That suggests the word we are looking for. The core *means* the "object." Meinong, too, uses the word (*meinen*), although not, alas, consistently.

(a) One cannot either think of or believe anything without grasping it. (b) In thinking of something one does not commit himself as to whether or not it exists; in believing one does. Except for a word, Meinong and the foil agree on (a) and (b). I can do without 'grasping', use 'f-intending' instead. (c) I always f-intend a fact, either actual or

---

[11] Nor is that surprising, since at one extreme of this bouquet of confusions natures are denied all ontological status while at the other they are "identified" with the (ideal) particulars whose natures they are (p. 355). Some passages, however, leave no room for doubt, such as perhaps most strikingly, *Ann.*, p. 79, where, using *'ergreifen'*, which if anything comes even closer to the idea of grasping or reaching than *'erfassen'*, he insists that what is grasped is always a *Sosein* or a *reiner Gegenstand*. These expressions are as awkward as any. Yet they cause no real trouble. In the next section I shall show that a *Sosein*, a *reiner Gegenstand*, and a nature are one and the same. (The terminology, as you see, does cause trouble.)

[12] More accurately, he calls the Objective in which the connection occurs *the* fundamental epistemological fact (*die erkenntnistheoretische Grundtatsache*). See *Ann.*, p. 265; also, for all this, the whole of §43, from which the phrase is taken. *Das Adequatsheitsverhaeltnis besteht zwischen Inhalt* und *Gegenstand*. *'Inhalt'* is best translated by 'content', which is one of the words I would rather not use before Section Twenty.

potential, irrespective of the circumstance that while in believing I do, in thinking I do not, commit myself as to whether my f-intention is actual or potential. Nor is its mode ever presented to me. (d) He always grasps a nature, which is compounded with either *ex* or *nonex*, irrespective of the circumstance that while in believing he does, in thinking he does not, commit himself as to whether this nature is compounded with *ex* or *nonex*. Nor are either *ex* or *nonex* as such ever presented to him.[13] Comparing (c) and (d), you see that *mutatis mutandis* Meinong and the foil continue to agree. The only trouble is that the nature inaccuracy keeps him from thinking and speaking clearly and consistently.

'Intending' and 'meaning' are interchangeable. So I shall not hesitate to use the former where he uses the latter. n-intending is grasping. Whatever an act's fringe may be, its n-intention is a nature. Not so for the broad use. Thinking of something, I b-intend its nature. In believing that *p*, I b-intend an Objective. An act's b-intention, accordingly, depends on its fringe.

A critic interrupts and raises an objection: "If I understand you correctly, one who believes that *p* b-intends the Objective (*p:ex*). If the belief is false, the Objective whose nature is *p*, is (*p: nonex*). What '(*p: ex*)' purports to name does not exist. Yet you and, as you say, Meinong accept the principle that whatever is *intended* exists. I cannot but conclude that somewhere in your analysis something has gone wrong."

I answer as follows: "You understood me correctly and you are also right in what you say about Meinong and myself accepting a certain principle as fundamental. You will find it on page 238, where it is labeled (F1): When *presented* with something, I am also *presented* with its existence. But you overlook the difference between 'presented' and 'intended'. Nor do you use the latter as discriminatingly as the situation requires. The b-intention of a false belief does indeed not exist. Yet there is no difficulty. The principle requires merely that what is presented exists; and what is presented is *p*, which is a nature that exists, though not in isolation of course, but if the belief is false, in combination with *nonex*. Thus I am still not convinced that my analysis is wrong. Perhaps a comparison will convince you that it isn't."

A b-intention of Meinong's world is either a nature or a purported Objective, compounded with either *ex* or *nonex*, which either does or does not exist. All its n-intentions are natures. All its f-intentions are Objectives, compounded with either *ex* or *nonex*, which exist. All the f-intentions of the foil are facts, either actual or potential. These differ-

---

[13] That ignores a whole line of thought, which, however counterstructural and therefore unfortunate, has yet played a very large role. "As such" puts the foot in this door. In the second part we shall open it; in the last section, walk through it.

ences all stem from three sources. First, there are in my world no natures. Second and in particular, its potential facts are not natures. Third, while his versatile twins are existents, my modes are not. Or, to say the same thing differently, a fact's mode, if it were an existent, would be "in" it, not anything "added" to it in the sense in which either *ex* or *nonex* is "added" to a nature. That is why his b-intentions are either natures or Objectives which may or may not exist while all my f-intentions are facts which exist in one of the two modes. His and my f-intentions, however, correspond as closely to each other as the fundamental differences between our ontologies permit.

What is an *Annahme* (assumption)? I can do very well without the word. Meinong, however, makes a great display of it. So I shall use it in diagnosing his troubles. To assume something (*etwas annehmen*) and to think of it are one and the same. An *Annahme*, being something outside of the act, can therefore only be a proposition. Keep that in mind and make a list of all the inaccurate and false statements about *meinen*, *annehmen*, and *Annahmen* which may be caused by one's being unaware of, or hazy about, the distinctions we just made by means of the three prescripts. There will be nothing on your list which Meinong hasn't said. The source of his troubles is of course the nature inaccuracy.

Meinen and the foil's *M* are not the same. One difference, or group of differences, we just explored. Yet they are so close that I shall write $\overline{M}$ for his "fundamental epistemological connection," the bar for the differences, the letter for the likeness. Most importantly, $\overline{M}$ and M are alike in that, each having been given ontological status in its world, they are both meant to bridge the gap between minds and what minds are about. But there is again a difference. M is a subsistent all by itself. $\overline{M}$ is an ideal connection among ideal connections. As such it is structurally an "internal relation." From where I stand, therefore, its ontological status is an illusion. If so, then it does not really do what it is meant to do. This particular failure of Meinong's fits as neatly as any the formula, which, as well as one formula can, explains them all (p. 340). Perhaps that is why I find it so poignant, particularly since, as a part of that neatness, it is patently the fault of the reism and the nominalism. That is why there is victory mixed in with the defeat. Structurally at least, although even that only with a curious limitation, *the representationalism has been overcome.*

The representationalists' schema is tripartite. So is Meinong's. Yet his is very different from theirs. If I were once more to draw a diagram, I would put all his real particulars[14] below a horizontal line, all ideal ones above it. Then I would divide the bottom half of the sheet by a

---

[14] And, I add once and for all, all cryptoclusters, both physical and mental. We must either break off or go along with the function inaccuracy.

vertical line and put all real particulars which are mental on one side of
it, say, on the left, all physical ones on the right. *The mental and the
physical are in this world a dichotomy within the real only* (see, e.g.,
Gegenstandsth., p. 517). About an ideal particular one can only say that
the real ones which ultimately found it are either all physical or all
mental or of both kinds (see p. 360 for an anticipation). In terms of the
diagram, the horizontal is the main dividing line. This fits well with
the diagnosis that the most fundamental ontological distinction in this
world is among levels (kinds of exist*ing*).

Suppose that I either believe or think of either (a) or (b) or (c) of our
example. (1) The core of my act is mental, as it would be if it were
either in the prototype or in the foil. (2) The particular f-intended[15] is
ideal, even though, since its foundation is wholly physical, what corresponds to it in either the prototype or the foil is physical. (3) The f-intending in the case is a connection between these two particulars, one of
which is real and mental, while the other is ideal and such that what
corresponds to it in either the foil or the prototype is physical.[16] Taken
together, (1), (2), and (3) show accurately how, structurally and *in
general*, the representationalism has been overcome.

Ignoring knowledge of self and of other minds, or, rather, putting
them aside for the special consideration they require and deserve, we
find ourselves in the following situation. Everything presented is
founded on what is physical. But it is also ideal. *We are never presented
with anything both physical and real.* This is the characteristic limitation. Because of it I just said "in general." An image will show how
curious it is. Think of the foil's Second as a tall building; of its First, as
a man standing in front of it and trying to look at it. The foil's Third is
like a high wall between the two, which hides the building forever from
his view. In Meinong's world the wall has shrunk. All that is left of it is
a low fence. Yet, curiously, this fence hides forever the very foundation
of what the man sees. Nor is that all. There are strange images on the
mindward side of the fence. In the next section we shall examine
them.

[15] I rather speak accurately than in terms of $\overline{M}$, which suffers from the ambiguities the prefix keeps out, even though these ambiguities do not at all affect the
point now under consideration.

[16] In terms of the diagram, if the space above the horizontal line were divided
into a left and a right half, as in fact it is not, and if every ideal particular were put
as nearly as is possible vertically above the real ones founding it, then this ideal
particular would be on the upper right, while the f-intending, which connects it
with an item in the lower left, would best be put on the vertical line—if only there
were such a line in the upper half. For the next paragraph, see n. 6 of Section
Eighteen.

These are the main outlines of the assay of the knowing situation. I add three comments. The first two merely spell out what ought to be spelled out. The third picks up a loose thread.

First. Every serious realist must try to resolve the dialectic of a certain cluster of problems connected with the knowing situation. The ontology of perceptual error is one of them; that of false belief is another. Meinong's assay of the knowing situation, if only it were otherwise acceptable, would completely resolve the dialectic of the cluster. This is crucial, of course, structurally as well as for his intellectual motivation. But it must by now also be obvious. So I merely record it.

Second. If in his world, as in the foil, all awareness were propositional, all its f-intentions would be Objectives, or, equivalently, all the natures his minds grasp would be propositions. We know from the case (c) that some of these ideal particulars are not, as I use the word, Objectives. (There is also the case of connections, which I leave to the next section.) As he uses the word, everything the mind grasps is an Objective, i.e., an ideal particular corresponding to a state of affairs.[17] That proves my claim that he does not really understand the distinctions among the several kinds of ideal particulars. Nor of course, if he did, could he maintain the gratuitous duplication (a_1 and $(a_1^n: ex)$). Our several analyses still hang together.

Third. In thinking of something one supposedly intends an idea, or maybe one attends to it, or perhaps one does something else. At this point all representationalists either are hazy or equivocate. In the case of all other fringes one clearly intends what is not an idea. This is the structural connection between representationalism and the two-step assay of all fringes except thinking-of as "complex," i.e., as joints of a thinking-of and a specific constituent (p. 151). The first step aims in some hopelessly elusive sense at an idea; the second, at what the idea represents.

Brentano was not hazy on this point. Nor did he equivocate. He rather paid the price. His clarity drove him into (structural) idealism. Mindful of this, I ask two questions rather than one about Meinong.

---

[17] *This is indeed the main formula of the book on* Annahmen! From a logical point of view the vehicle of the confusion is the assimilation to each other of the three 'is' in '*A* is', '*A* is *B*', and '*A* is *R* to *B*'. Supposedly they stand for three divisions of Being (*Sein, Sosein, Wiesein*), which, though supposedly different in some ways, are yet alike in making every f-intention an "existential fact." Unfortunately the phrase between double quotes is fatefully ambiguous. As just used, improperly, it stands for Thomistic composition, which, as we know, is in this world not a fact of any kind. Using it properly, one has to say that there are in this world no existential facts. Of this more in the next section.

Which assay or assays of the several fringes are structurally possible in his world? Which one did he actually propose?

The representationalists' ideas and what they represent are wholly separated from each other. His natures are not so separated from the *ex* or *nonex* with which they are compounded. That is why in his world[18] there is room for what I call b-intending, which, as it were, expands or contracts its "object," depending on the fringe involved. Structurally, therefore, even though nothing forces him to choose this alternative, he could make do (as the foil does) with a class of simple fringes. That confirms the diagnosis that structurally he is no longer a representationalist, even though in fact he stays with the representationalists' choice,[19] thus providing us with another bit of evidence for his dependence on their patterns.

We are ready for the second part.

In any world so nearly Aristotelian-Thomistic that each of its objects is compounded of a nature and of Being, and, accordingly, such that what its minds primarily grasp or are presented with are natures, it is counterstructural for minds to grasp Being itself, which of course has no nature, however secondary this grasp or presentation may be. Meinong's world has this Aristotelian-Thomistic feature. Two others are uniquely his own. For one, he replaces Being by that odd pair, *ex* and *nonex*. For another, each real particular, each object (cryptocluster) and each state of affairs goes with an ideal particular, which, being a particular, has itself a nature. With a_1, for instance, there goes an ideal particular named by either (1a) '$(a_1^n: ex)$' or (1b) '$(a_1^n: nonex)$', provided only we make the usual double allowance for the fortuitous duplication in case 'a_1' names something and for there really not being anything at all, at least from where I stand, in case it doesn't. As for a_1^n so for propositions.[20] There is for every proposition p exactly one ideal particular named by either (2a) '$(p: ex)$' or (2b) '$(p: nonex)$'. If one were asked to state the gist of a reism stretched to the utmost and at the same time as consistent as possible, he could not I think do better than select these three features. Taken together, they structurally imply a fourth. Not surprisingly, therefore, Meinong's world has this further feature. Yet it is striking. Since it is also the key to much else, I would

---

[18] Though not in the foil, where by structural necessity all "intending" is f-intending. But, again, this does not mean that one could not in the foil assay all fringes except entertaining as "complex." All one can say is that in the foil there are no good reasons for so assaying them, except possibly phenomenological ones which are structurally irrelevant.

[19] Or, rather, he drowns the issue in a sea of phenomenological musings.

[20] I continue to use 'p' as a variable for propositions, even though with a subscript the letter stands throughout this book for a place. If we are careful enough, nothing untoward will happen.

rather be tedious than hasty. So I shall first recall what is by now well established and only then introduce the striking feature.

Every proposition p combines either with *ex* or with *nonex*. In the latter case, the ideal particular which (2b) purports to name exists, even though it is compounded with *nonex*, while (2a) fails to name anything, even though what it purports to name would, if it existed, be compounded with *ex*. As in this case, of combination with *nonex*, so *mutatis mutandis* in the other, of combination with *ex*. More succinctly and less cautiously, for an ideal particular to be compounded with *ex* or *nonex* is one thing, to exist or not to exist is another. And, to repeat, of the four expressions (1a) to (2b) only two, one from each pair, succeed in naming something. This is by now well established. The striking feature is that the four expressions (1a′) '$(a_1^n: ex)^{n}$', (1b′) '$(a_1^n: nonex)^{n}$', (2a′) '$(p: ex)^{n}$', (2b′) '$(p: nonex)^{n}$' name four different natures which all exist, though not of course in isolation but in combination with either *ex* or *nonex*, as the case may be. To say the same thing differently, attending to the linguistic reflection of the reism which here so impressively asserts itself, expressions purporting to name ideal particulars which do not exist are treated exactly as 'a_1' is treated if the real particular it purports to name is not there. If, for instance, (2a) fails to name something, '$(p: ex)^{n}$' yet names a nature which combines with *nonex* into the ideal particular $((p: ex)^n: nonex)$, just as in the corresponding case a_1^n combines with *nonex* into the ideal particular $(a_1^n: nonex)$.[21]

Clearly, we stand at the beginning of an infinite regress. As for p, so for a_1^n. But nothing will be lost if we stay with propositions. The first step, starting from the single nature p, yields $(p: ex)^n$ and $(p: nonex)^n$; the second, starting from these two natures, yields four $((p: ex)^n: ex)^n$, $((p: ex)^n: nonex)^n$, $((p: nonex)^n: ex)^n$, $((p: nonex): nonex)^n$; the third step yields eight; and so on. Call this regress the *existential iteration*, or, briefly, the iteration. Meinong not only accepts it; he exults in the vision of the ideal as a teeming ocean without shores.[22] Such ontological hypertrophy seems absurd. Those who appeal to what they call a robust sense of reality would insist that it is absurd.[23] Presently I shall

[21] The evidence for all this abounds throughout the later writings. See, e.g., *Gegenstandsth.*, p. 491; *Ann.*, pp. 49 and 142 ff. Notice, too, that once more I could have argued the other way around, claiming that this well-documented feature impressively supports the original diagnosis of reism rather than, as I did, that the reism impressively asserts itself in the feature.

[22] The image, though perhaps not literally his, is not alien to his spirit.

[23] As you may gather, I am not impressed. The "reality," or, as I would rather say, the common sense to be accounted for is the same for all of us. It does not follow that an adequate account will be what in such appeals is meant by 'realistic'.

show that, taken by itself or as such, it isn't. Yet it implies what is counterstructural, which in ontology is the worst absurdity of all. Thus I propose a distinction, which will also permit us to divide the examination between the iteration as such on the one hand and the objectionable feature it implies on the other. If $(p: ex)^n$, and $(p: nonex)^n$ are natures among natures, then there is no reason why we should not on some occasions grasp either the one or the other. If so, then we shall on these occasions also grasp Being (*ex* and *nonex*)! In the hands of one who combines Meinong's ingenuity with his diffuse style, this counterstructural possibility cannot but prove dialectically disastrous.[24] His doctrine of evidence is the disaster. In the last section we shall examine it. In what follows I shall show, *first*, that the iteration as such *is not absurd* but merely the expression, within this ontology, of the correspondence theory of truth, and, *second*, that it *seems absurd* because the reism which pervades everything makes the expression idiosyncratic or even worse. A quick glance at the foil will provide us with the necessary background.

In the foil only thoughts (cores) are either true or false. Every other character (or whatever else) is neither. More precisely, this is so for the primary use of 'true' and 'false', which is the only one that concerns us. True (T) and false (F) themselves are *pseudocharacters* (p. 95), as are, say, transitivity and the integers; i.e., they are in all ontological respects like, and share the precarious ontological status of, derived things, except that the right sides of the two definitions reflecting their derivations contain no expressions mentioning things, which makes them *derived subsistents* (p. 95) rather than derived things, and as such, in an obvious sense, even more shadowy than the latter. The two definitions are

(D1)   '$T(f)$'   for   '$(\exists P)(fMP \cdot P)$'

(D2)   '$F(f)$'   for   '$(\exists P)(fMP \cdot \sim P)$'.

Since the substitution instances of the closed variable on the right stand, not for propositions, either in Meinong's sense or in any other, but for facts, either actual or potential, of the foil, I write 'P' rather than 'p' and abstain from calling 'P' a "propositional variable," even though mathematicians, for their purposes quite harmlessly, are in the habit of calling it so.[25] This assay has four consequences.

[24] Such dialectical disaster is of course what I had in mind when calling certain absurdities the worst of all.

[25] For the several uses of 'true' and 'false', see, e.g., *Logic and Reality*, p. 137; for what is here said (and presupposed) about truth and falsehood, the essay on "Intentionality" in *Meaning and Existence* (University of Wisconsin Press, 1960), especially pp. 35 ff.

I. P, $T(\ulcorner P \urcorner)$, and $F(\ulcorner P \urcorner)$ are three facts and not one. If P is actual (potential), so is $T(\ulcorner P \urcorner)$, while $F(\ulcorner P \urcorner)$ is potential (actual).

II. Our predicates can be iterated. I.e., not only '$T(\ulcorner P \urcorner)$' but also '$T(\ulcorner T(\ulcorner P \urcorner)\urcorner)$', '$T(\ulcorner F(\ulcorner P \urcorner)\urcorner)$', $F(\ulcorner T(\ulcorner P \urcorner)\urcorner)$, and '$F(\ulcorner F(\ulcorner P \urcorner)\urcorner)$' stand for facts, either actual or potential.

III. There is a class C of formulae such that all the substitution instances of all its members are analytic, i.e., they all stand for actual facts in the world's form, just as, say, the substitution instances of 'P or not-P'. The following four formulae are a representative sample of C:

(C1) $$P \equiv T(\ulcorner P \urcorner),$$

(C2) $$\sim P \equiv F(\ulcorner P \urcorner),$$

(C3) $$T(\ulcorner P \urcorner) \equiv T(\ulcorner T(\ulcorner P \urcorner)\urcorner),$$

(C4) $$T(\ulcorner P \urcorner) \equiv F(\ulcorner (F \ulcorner P \urcorner)\urcorner).$$

IV. The formulae of C establish an important class of *deductive* connections. By (C1), P is actual if and only if $\ulcorner P \urcorner$-being-true is actual; by (C4), $\ulcorner P \urcorner$-being-true is actual if and only if $\ulcorner (\ulcorner P \urcorner$-being-false$)\urcorner$-being-false is actual; and so on.

What "corresponds" in Meinong's world to the facts of II and to the deductive connections of IV? We cannot answer without first making sure of what has been claimed (p. 357) but not yet established. He holds that a belief is true (false) if and only if the proposition it grasps combines with *ex* (*nonex*). Clearly, this is a *correspondence theory of truth*. Equally clearly, he himself recognizes it as such.[26] There is also a quirk. But it can wait a moment. We are already able to "translate," provided only we remember the connection between true-false and actual-potential.

Depending on whether P is actual or potential, there is in his world either the ideal particular (p:*ex*) or the ideal particular (p:*nonex*). Depending on whether $T(\ulcorner P \urcorner)$ is actual or potential there is either the ideal particular $((p$:*ex*$)^n$:*ex*$)$ or the ideal particular $((p$:*ex*$)^n$:*nonex*$)$. That will do for the facts of II. The connections of IV come out as follows. By C1, '(p: *ex*)' succeeds in naming an ideal particular if and only if '$((p$: *ex*$)^n$ *ex*$)$' so succeeds. By C4, the latter expression so succeeds if and only if '$(((p$: *ex*$)^n$: *nonex*$)^n$: *nonex*$)$' does. And so on. The gist is, *first*, that in his world certain ideal particulars exist or don't exist if and only if certain others do or don't, with the do-or-don't being

---

[26] See, e.g., *Ann.*, pp. 83, 94 Notice, too, even though for what we are about the difference makes no difference, that he applies 'true' and 'false' not primarily to cores (thoughts) but to acts of believing, perceiving, remembering, and so on, which is the use I call secondary.

determined by the 'T' and 'F' in the formulae of the foil's class C and, *second*, that the "connections" between any two of their infinite number are analytic. He would probably rather say that they are a priori. That, though, makes here no difference. The point is that he is fully aware of their special status (see *Ann.*, p. 70).

The left and right sides L and R in any one of the equivalences in C stand for two facts, not for one. Yet each of these equivalences stands for a formal truth. R and L, therefore, though not the same$_3$, are yet the same$_2$.[27] Applied to the facts in the series

(S) $P,\ T(^\ulcorner P^\urcorner),\ T(^\ulcorner T(^\ulcorner P^\urcorner)^\urcorner),\ \cdots$

this means, *first*, that while no two of them are the same$_3$, they are yet all the same$_2$; and *second*, that the one and only circumstance keeping them from all being the same$_3$ is that in the foil the world's form has been given ontological status. Having long taken this step, I conclude that as such the iteration is not absurd. That leaves only two things to be done. We must (A) explain why it seems absurd, and (B) attend to the quirk that mars his correspondence theory.

A. The iteration seems absurd because in his world there is for each member of (S) an ideal particular and because one does not ordinarily think of "particulars" as entities such that the existence of one of them deductively implies that of another, leave alone that of an infinity of others. Yet, however idiosyncratically, the "particulars" of his world are such entities. That merely shows how far stretched the reism really is. Two observations will drive the point home. (1) Consistently, there also ought to be an ideal particular compounded with *ex* for each of the formal truths in C. But these facts are not atomic,[28] and we shall see that, whether he knows it or not, his is a world of atomic facts only. (2) The difference between the iteration and the Bradley regress from which he does not shrink (p. 348) is merely that between compounding and founding. c_1^n and $(c_1;\ e_1)^n$ jointly found $(c_1;\ (c_1;\ e_1))^n$. But the twins have no natures. Thus p and either *ex* or *nonex*, though they may combine, do not found anything.

B. Someone believes that P. If I were to state the correspondence theory in his world, I would say that the core of this belief, and therefore secondarily the belief itself, is true (false) if and only if the proposition p which one grasps when believing that P is compounded with *ex* (*nonex*). As he himself states it, the belief is true if and only if the

----

[27] If you want to rehearse this distinction, turn to p. 78 and n. 8, *ibid.*

[28] Nor, strictly speaking, is $T(^\ulcorner P^\urcorner)$. But it is at least not an equivalence Thus one may more easily be misled, as I have no doubt he was, by the error about "existential facts" pointed out in n. 17, above, into believing that it is atomic.

"Objective" has the "property" true, of which he also speaks as factuality (*Tatsaechlichkeit*). Sloughing off the nature inaccuracy, which obviously mars this statement, one comes upon a curious identification. Ex *and* nonex *literally are truth and falsehood.*[29] This is the quirk. Two observations will illuminate it and account for it. (1) To do the latter, I ask, not what truth is, but, rather, *where* it is. We shall find the answer faster if, using once more the representationalist trichotomy, we stay with f-intentions which are in the Second. In the foil, true and false are relational "characters" of mental things, the covert relation being *M*.[30] Like *M*, they are thus *neither in the First nor in the Second but a "relational" bridge between the two.* In Brentano's world they are not to be sure the same as evidence, which is an attribute of fringes, yet their assay in terms of evidence clearly puts them *in the First*. Meinong's $\overline{M}$ connects a real mental particular with what is ultimately founded on real physical ones. It, too, therefore, with an inaccuracy that suits the purpose of the moment without doing any harm, is a bridge between the First and the Second. Structurally, that allows him to do what is done in the foil. Yet he puts truth and falsehood themselves *in the Second*. The invalid inference (if I may so express myself) jumps from the sound premiss that a belief's truth does not depend on it alone to the exaggerated conclusion that it is something wholly outside of the belief. This, I submit, is but a "realistic" over-reaction to Brentano's "idealistic" excess in the opposite direction. Thus I account for the quirk. (2) To illuminate it, I ask another question. What, if any, is the difference between *ex* and *nonex* in their roles of truth and falsehood on the one hand and Frege's T and F on the other? The latter are objects and the values of the very functions which keep Frege's world from being totally disjoined. E.g., Peter is blond if and only if the function blond projects the object Peter onto the object T; and the Fregean "proposition (*Sinn*)" Peter-being-blond is a third object, separate from

---

[29] Or, as I would say, in one of their four roles the twins literally are truth and falsehood. The evidence for all this is widely scattered, but see *Ann.*, pp. 70, 82. One cannot but think of Aristotle's and Brentano's *ens tamquam verum* in connection with the second '*is*' in '*A is, is*' (see n. 26 of Section Fourteen), except of course that Meinong bends over backward in the opposite direction (see the first observation above).

Idiomatically, '*Tatsache*' is best translated by 'fact'; technically, as I speak, by 'actual fact'. Its two roots, however, are the noun for thing ('*Sache*') and the verb ('*tun*') which translates the verb 'act' from which 'actual' is derived. Etymologically, a *Tatsache* is thus an "actual thing." How deeply ingrained the reism is!

[30] If you insist on being more accurate than I think is here necessary, replace 'character' and 'relation' by 'pseudocharacter' and 'subsistent connection'. 'Covert' is used as is customary in this context. E.g., the derived *relational character* "brother" contains the *covert relation* "being a brother of."

both Peter and T.[31] Meinong's truth (*ex*) and falsehood (*nonex*) are neither objects nor even the values of any function but the Being and Nonbeing which, rather than remaining separate, Thomistically combine with natures into objects. In the example, accordingly, there are not three objects but only two; both combinations with *ex*; one real,[32] compounded with the nature of Peter; the other ideal, compounded with the η-proposition (p. 372) Peter-being-blond. We take note, beyond the concern of the moment, of these striking differences between two ontologies which structurally are both function ontologies.

Until now we have assumed that Meinong's cores are all real particulars (simple). In the third and last part of this section, to which I now turn, I shall first justify the assumption, then examine the issues to which, if justified, it gives rise.

Meinong himself offers two "proofs" that no core is "complex."[33] Unfortunately, they are two choice examples of his diffuse style; leaving much room for doubt as to what, if anything, he actually proves from what premises, and how, if at all, it fits with the rest. Yet they are too important to be ignored. So I shall do as well by them as I can.

Suppose that the color particular b_1 coincides with the place p_1 and let the *Komplex* they make serve as the intention in both proofs. In the one I shall call (a), the intention is clearly a cryptocluster. In the other, (b), it is more nearly a cluster of the prototype. In (a), therefore, the connection is a real particular; in (b) it is more nearly like γ. So I write for it r_1 and ρ_1, respectively; for the intention itself, once $\{b_1, r_1, p_1\}$, once $\rho_1(b_1, p_1)$. In (a), accordingly, with the asterisk notation, he must prove that (1) $\{b_1, r_1, p_1\}$* cannot be "complex"; in (b) he must do the same for (2) $[\rho_1(p_1, b_1)]$*. I interrupt for a comment. Then I shall list and briefly discuss the four premises from which (I believe) he argues.

The Objective in the case is $(b_1; r_1; p_1)$. This Objective, the cryptocluster, and the object are three. In (a) the cryptocluster stands in for the object. This is the function inaccuracy. In (b) something more nearly like a cluster stands in; thus the inaccuracy involved is that of γ. Neither (a) nor (b) as much as mentions the Objective, even though the same text is the very epiphany of this entity.[34] Upon the structural

[31] For details and argument, see the Frege essay called "Ontological Alternatives" in *Logic and Reality* (University of Wisconsin Press, 1964).

[32] This disregards the function inaccuracy as well as the gratuitous duplication. But, again, we cannot get hold of the controlling patterns without sometimes playing his game.

[33] That is why I said (p. 376) that the answer to the question whether they are simple is straightforward. The reference for what follows is *Ann.*, pp. 259–62, 266–68.

[34] The expression is not too strong. See n. 17, above.

reason for the striking omission we shall come as soon as we are done with these proofs. As for the intention, so for the core. If the latter is to be "complex," it can only be either a cryptocluster, or something more nearly like a cluster, or an Objective. Yet there is a twist. Since all Objectives are ideal and since it is taken for granted that all cores, fringes, and acts are real (p. 375), (1) and (2), if "complex," can only be either a cryptocluster or something more like a cluster. One may even speculate that the exclusion of the third alternative on the side of the core has been a contributory cause of the striking omission on the side of the intention.

P1. For every component or cryptocomponent of a core there is one of its intention. P2. If (1) is "complex," b_1^*, p_1^*, r_1^* are among its cryptocomponents; if (2) is, b_1^*, p_1^*, ρ_1^* are among its components. P3. Whatever is "part" of an intention can itself be the total intention of another act. E.g., not only p_1 and b_1 can be grasped by themselves, but so can r_1 in (a) and ρ_1 in (b). P4. When one grasps a mere *class*, e.g., $[b_1, p_1, r_1]$ or $[b_1, p_1, \rho_1]$, the core of the act is different from that of an act grasping the *object* of which the members of the class are the cryptocomponents or components.[35]

These are the four premises. P1 and P2 are entirely reasonable. P3 is merely a very strong version of the sound core, as I have tried to formulate it (p. 165), of the "empiricist" thesis concerning the mind's capacity of "abstracting." P4, too, is familiar. When we first encountered it, I called it a precious insight, but hinted at a difficulty.[36] What in Meinong's world is a class? He has no ready answer.[37] One may indeed doubt that he has any. This is the difficulty. But it can wait. Let us now look at the two proofs.

In (a) it is shown that if the core were "complex," there would be, on its side as well as on that of the intention, an unacceptable Bradley-type regress (see Section Eighteen, n. 20). To produce it, use is made of P2, P4, and P1. By P2, if the core were "complex," p_1^*, b_1^*, r_1^* would be among its cryptocomponents. By P4, there would therefore have to be at least one more cryptocomponent, namely a real connection r_2^*, which connects the three members of the class $[p_1^*, b_1^*, r_1^*]$. Hence, by P1,

---

[35] Meinong always remains enough of a reist not to be bothered by the type difference among the members of the class in (b). But notice the absurdity one runs into if in (a) one replaces at the end of this sentence 'object' by '$\{p_1, r_1, b_1\}$'. The diffuse style exacts its price.

[36] See n. 8 of Section Nine; for the hint, n. 10 *ibid.*

[37] Brentano does, at least for physical objects, even though each of his acts intends only a single object. In his world, every class of physical objects is really a sum (σ) and a sum of such objects is itself one. Just remember the pair of oxen. See n. 51 of Section Thirteen.

there is on the side of the intention an entity r_2. But the intention is not just the class $[b_1, p_1, r_1, r_2]$; and so on. As you see, the members of the two series r_i and r_i^* are very much like particulars and not at all like the γ of the prototype or the ϵ of the foil. The two regresses are (I suppose) unacceptable because the members of the two series are all real and not, like those of the series which goes with the acceptable regress (p. 348), ideal. On the side of the core there is (I suppose) the additional reason that the mind in "producing" it would have to go through an infinite number of steps.

In (b) use is made of P3 on the ground[38] that, even though ρ_1 is sufficiently like γ or ϵ not to trigger a regress, ρ_1^*, since it is capable of being a core by itself, is yet sufficiently like a particular to require a ρ_2^* to produce the core $\rho_2^*(p_1^*, b_1^*, \rho_1^*)$. Yet the ρ_i^* presumably do not trigger a regress! It is all very diffuse indeed, not to say confused. But the "proof" merrily proceeds. By P1, there must be something in the intention that corresponds to ρ_2^*. But there is nothing there that could correspond to it except $\rho_1(b_1, p_1)$, i.e., the intention itself or as a whole. If so, then, by P2, b_1^*, p_1^*, and ρ_1^* would be components of ρ_2^* which by assumption they are not.

That much for the proof. Let us pause and consider. If I am on the right track, all above-board existents of Meinong's last world are simple. So therefore are its cores and there is no need at all for singling them out, not even if, as in cases (a) and (b) of the example,[39] the ideal particulars which are their f-intentions correspond to what in other worlds is complex. Yet he felt the need to prove that no core can be complex, which shows (if I am right) that he did not completely understand himself. Whether the proofs themselves show anything is doubtful indeed. But he must at least have convinced himself. Even so, *he was not prepared to conclude that all cores are simple.*

What is not complex is simple, and conversely. How, then, can one be convinced that no core is complex without being prepared to conclude that they are all simple? The italicized sentence seems not to make sense. Yet it brings out into the open a game I have played all the time while dealing with the two proofs. I never attributed to their author the intention of proving that all cores are simple; nor did I my-

[38] Or so I suppose. If I am not mistaken, then we have come upon the *structural reason* why the alternative of the prototype, making the *connection* ι in the core correspond to the connection γ in the intention, is not open to Meinong. It always comes down to the same thing. In spite of all efforts, he does not really understand the notion of a connection.

[39] I continue to use the old example (p. 377), with (a), (b), and (c) corresponding to e_1 being higher[3] than c_1, to the "binary" object the prototype assays as $\gamma(b_1, p_1)$, and to a real particular a_1, respectively.

self ever use 'simple' but made do with 'not complex'. Now that the cards are on the table, I am ready to explain why I played them this way.

Meinong is convinced that all cores are produced by the mind. The materials from which they are produced are what one would expect; c_1^* and e_1^* in case (a); p_1^*, $coinc_1^*$, and b_1^* in case (b). We, having seen through the genetic fallacy, would not, even if we shared his conviction, hesitate to insist that all cores are simple. He never says that they are.[40] The appellation is reserved for the materials from which cores are produced. The activity the mind engages in when producing them is the one I called *fusing* (p. 378). Now that you understand why I chose this word, I propose that we spare his sensibilities by speaking of cores as *fusions* rather than as simples. Words aside, did he or did he not see through the genetic fallacy? The answer does not make much difference, either structurally or even biographically. For there is another reason, which lies at the very heart of the dialectic and of which we know him to have been aware, that forced him to hold that *all cores are fusions*. To discover this reason I turn to perception. Earlier in this section I announced (p. 377) that I would for a while avoid 'perceiving'. Now that the word is being brought back, you will soon see why that was the thing to do.

Some philosophers have held that our perceivings[41] are *presented to us as caused* by something, from which they inferred that there are physical objects. This is the so-called causal theory of perception. The inference hopes to arrive at realism. Brentano, however torturedly and tortuously, held the theory. Meinong rejected it. So do I. This is one thing. Our perceivings[42] are *in fact caused* by physical objects. This is just common sense and quite another thing. Meinong, having rejected the theory, made a point of emphasizing that he had no quarrel with

[40] Considering the diffuse style, this reluctance has a very plausible biographical source. The complexity of the core in case (b) is the central feature of his first ontology. Nor do I doubt that this very feature is a major source of the need, felt at a later state, for a special proof that no core is complex. Even so, the discussion of this feature is best left to the next section.

[41] I continue to use 'perceiving (*wahrnehmen*)' so that we perceive only physical objects. Meinong, like Brentano, speaks of *innere* and *aeussere Wahrnehmung*. See n. 2 of Section Twelve.

[42] Or, rather, their vast majority. I do not use 'perceive' as G. E. Moore did and as, following him, they now use it at Oxford. The reason for mentioning this, even though for the point at hand it makes no difference, is the obvious connection with the criterion issue. For detail and argument, see the "Realistic Postscript" in *Logic and Reality*.

A *cause*, as I here speak, is not a sufficient condition but merely a necessary one which it pays to single out for reasons into which we need not further inquire.

this piece of common sense. But he also proposed a very narrow technical use of 'perceiving' and its cognates, such as 'seeing' and 'hearing'.
*"One says that one hears a melody when what one really hears is the tones
which found the melody."*

Speaking as we ordinarily do, we all say, not only that we hear the
melody, and, in general, that we perceive facts and objects (which
latter are in the foil but a kind of fact), but also that the fact or object
perceived causes us to perceive it. From where I stand, this is the same
as to say that in perception the fact or object *impresses* upon the mind
the core of the act which intends it. 'Impresses' may be replaced by
'causes to exist.'[43] This causal use of 'impress' is the cue to the non-
verbal distinction which Meinong wanted to safeguard and call attention to by proposing his narrow technical use of 'perceive'.

The suggestion in what he says about the tones and the melody is
strong and clear. In case (a) of our example, what is *presumably* impressed is c_1^* and e_1^*; what impresses them is c_1 and e_1, respectively. In
case (b), the entities *presumably* impressed are p_1^*, $coinc_1^*$, b_1^*; those
which do the impressing, p_1, $coinc_1$, b_1. How about the two Objectives?
If they could impress anything, they would of course impress the cores
with which they are connected by $\overline{M}$. But Objectives are ideal and an
ideal particular cannot impress anything upon the mind. That is why
the mind must itself produce the cores from the materials impressed
upon it. Perception, though crucial, is not everything. Yet there is no
need to look beyond it. We have already come upon the structural reason, or premiss, which forces Meinong to hold that all cores are fusions.

The premiss we just discovered is so fundamental and so pervasive
that it ought to be restated without any reference to cores: *All causal
interaction occurs on the level of the real; ideal entities, being "mere" functions of real ones, are neither causes nor effects.* When in the last section
we examined the dichotomy real-ideal, I claimed that there were three
specific differences between these two levels but refused (p. 362) to
state the third until we had reached the place where it would do most
good. Now we have come to this place.

With the things thus straightened out, the words are easily taken
care of. *"Only what is real can be perceived."* Or so we are told. In other
words, Meinong proposes to use 'perceive' so that we perceive only
what impresses itself upon our minds. We understand and appreciate

[43] You may wonder whether I have just committed myself to interactionism. I
don't think I have. Nor do I wish to commit Meinong to the parallelism I embrace, particularly since interactionism does not imply the kind of spontaneity
which is incompatible with scientific determinism. But we have agreed to keep
these relatively trivial matters out of this book.

the strategy behind the proposal. You also understand now why I decided to do for a while without 'perceiving'. My use of the word was too broad for his purposes; his, too narrow for mine. But notice, too, how well his fits the standard representationalist assay of perception, to which as we know he adheres.[44]

The feature or circumstance that all cores are fusions produced by the mind is important. That makes it awkward to have to refer to it so circumstantially. What we need is a name for it. Let us agree to call it the *production feature*.

The production feature gives rise to three questions. Two are unanswerable. Meinong himself does not put it that bluntly, but he knows very well that his "answers" are, to say the least, embarrassingly obscure. Yet he stubbornly clings to the production feature, thus providing us with further evidence that in his world the real-ideal distinction cuts as deeply as any. For the production feature is but one aspect of this distinction, and we have long known that the deeper a feature lies in an ontology, the more stubbornly its author will cling to it. The third question can be answered if one is prepared to make an assumption which, as we shall see, is not only peculiar but also embarrassing by what it reveals. Meinong, however, was not aware of the question. So we cannot add this embarrassment to the evidence for the depth of the level distinction.

One of the two questions he was aware of probes the entities presumably impressed upon the mind, c_i^*, e_i^*, p_i^*, and so on. In the next section we shall see that the problems the probe uncovers are insoluble. (That is why, five paragraphs back, 'presumably' was italicized twice.) In the meantime, we shall not prejudge anything but merely save words if we agree to call these entities the *problematic particulars*. With the insuperable difficulties one encounters when trying to answer the other question of which he was aware we are already familiar. To show that, a single paragraph will suffice. Then I shall raise the third question and, in conclusion, examine the assumption one must make in order to answer it.

In Brentano's case I spoke of forgings; in Meinong's, of fusings. Felicitous as they may seem, the images are merely windows onto nothingness. About the forgings I have had my say. 'Fusing' suggests the many I call the material becoming the one I call the fusion. The

---

[44] See n. 20 of Section Ten. The most detailed documentation of this analysis is to be found in *Erfahrungsgl.*; particularly, but not exclusively, in the first chapter. The two italicized quotations are from p. 25. Also *GeghO.* (p. 397), where he insists that "it is completely obvious that what cannot be real can *a fortiori* not be perceived."

suggestion is futile. There are in this world only two ways in which the many can become one, not literally, to be sure, but at least after a fashion, if one is prepared to wink at the function inaccuracy. One is by founding; the other by a real connection (followed by a founding). Any other way, whether or not it involves an activity of the mind, remains *obscure*. More bluntly, Meinong cannot answer the question how the mind manages to produce a core. All he can do is hold out the vain hope, so unhappily characteristic of the wrong kind of phenomenology, that further "psychological" research will make the obscurity less obscure.[45]

Nothing will be lost if in raising the third question we limit ourselves to veridical perception. In case (a), for instance, we suppose that c_1 and e_1 have impressed c_1^* and e_1^* upon a mind which has fused them into the core $[(c_1; (c_1; e_1); e_1)]^*$. But even with this limitation, there is a point which we must first get out of the way. Given the stimulus, the subject's response still depends on his set. That is how the psychologists state it. At the price of an unattractive jargon, their statement is very accurate indeed. But perhaps you are allergic to the jargon and would rather say that what is "seen" does not uniquely determine what it is "seen as." Meinong's schema accommodates this point very nicely. If, e.g., c_1^* and e_1^* are impressed upon my mind, I may perceive[46] them as a pair of pitches, as different, as one being higher[3] than the other, as one being not higher[2] than the other, and so on.[47] Which of the alternatively "available" cores the mind actually produces depends on a trigger mechanism within it. That is how the point has to be made in Meinong's schema. Having made it, I now set all the triggers once and for all. More literally, I ignore in all cases all "available" alternatives except one. But there is still another factor. With c_1^* and e_1^* impressed upon it, a mind may either "actively" fuse them into a core[48] or "passively" experience the two pitches. This "choice" is made by a second

---

[45] See *Ann.*, pp. 279–380. 'Obscure (*dunkel*)', in this context, is his word, not mine.

[46] This is the usual broad use of 'perceive', to which, unless there is an indication to the contrary, we now return.

[47] Notice the negative fact. Meinong's assay of negation absurdly inflates the number of alternatives which seem to be realistically available. But there always are some alternatives; and their number makes no difference for the point at hand.

[48] I.e., *the* core for which the trigger for this material has been set. A moment's reflection, after I shall be done, will show you that setting all the triggers once and for all will save many words without losing anything that matters, just as we often got along very well writing $(c_1; e_1)$ for one of the connections founded on c_1 and e_1 and ignoring all others. But notice the appearance of 'passively experiencing'. There is a blur here! It will have to wait until we examine the problematic particulars.

mechanism within the mind, a kind of semaphore that stands on either "go" or "stop."

Let $[(c_1; (c_1; e_1); e_1)]^*$ be the core "available" to a mind upon which c_1^* and e_1^* have been impressed. Use 'x_1^*' and 'x_1' as abbreviations for '$[(c_1; (c_1; e_1); e_1)]^*$' and '$(c_1; (c_1; e_1); e_1)$', respectively. The semaphore may stand in either position.

Suppose it stands on "go." Then the mind produces x_1^*. *Why does it produce x_1^* rather than, say, y_1^*, or z_1^*?* This, in case (a), is the third question. In general, what "determines" the (nature of the mind's) product? One who trusts the metaphor will probably answer that it is "determined" by the *what* (or nature) of the material and by the *what* (or sort) of the activity. That the *how* of the latter remains obscure we have seen. Now you probably sense already that its *what* is irrelevant. But the matter is crucial. So we must unpack it completely. The proper point of attack is a crucial ambiguity of 'determine'.

c_1 and e_1 determine$_1$ x_1. Determining$_1$ is founding, that curious and curiously attenuated "creation" of the ideal by the real. The square function does not in any sense, however attenuated, create the integer 9, yet it determines$_2$ it uniquely as the square of the integer 3, just as the function which (as we know) grounds Meinong's $\overline{M}$, uniquely determines$_2$ c_1^*, e_1^*, x_1^* as the three cores in one-one correspondence with c_1, e_1, x_1, respectively.[49] It follows that x_1^* is uniquely determined$_2$ by c_1^* and e_1^* alone. From this two more things follow. First, the "activity" is completely irrelevant. Second and with a twist, one cannot answer the third question without assuming that x_1^* is determined$_2$ by the material alone. Or, with another twist of the dialectical screw, since Meinong himself was not aware of the crucial ambiguity in 'determine', *we must assume that* x_1^* *is founded (determined$_1$) by* c_1^* *and* e_1^*.

Suppose that the semaphore stands on "stop." In this case, c_1^* and e_1^* exist, but x_1^*, which is the same as $(x_1^{*n}: ex)$, does not. Neither does $(x_1^{*n}: nonex)$ nor of course, since natures do not exist in isolation, x_1^{*n}. Yet we had to assume that c_1^* and e_1^* found x_1^*. The situation that creates is not just peculiar but outright counterstructural. We shall see that more easily and more accurately if we first agree on a way of words.

Put each particular in one of two realms or halves. Call one half objective; the other, subjective. In the former, there are c_1, e_1, x_1, and so on; in the latter, c_1^*, e_1^*, x_1^*, and so on, i.e., all problematic particulars and all cores.[50] Then the situation can be described as follows.

---

[49] This shows how the reism and the nominalism also at this point contribute to his downfall by preventing him from really understanding determination$_2$.

[50] Also all fringes and whatever other real mental particulars there may be as well as the ideal particulars ultimately founded on what is either mental or both

Within the obvious limits of what is actually impressed and perceived, *the particulars of the two halves stand in one-one correspondence, with the problematic particulars and cores corresponding to the real and to the ideal particulars of the objective half, respectively.*[51] *In the objective half, the real particulars found (determine₁) all ideal ones. In the subjective half, where there is no founding, all particulars are real, with the problematic ones among them determining₂ all cores. But the latter do not exist unless they have been produced by the mind.*

This is what Meinong's last world really looks like. Its structural inconsistency is obvious. Or, to say the same thing differently, it is obvious that in its subjective half the notion of founding breaks down. What, if anything, does that reveal? I answer indirectly.

If one discards the objective half, what remains is a world of particulars which are all real. That makes one wonder whether the very notion of ideal particulars and, with it, the whole objective half (above the fence!) are not perhaps an afterthought which Meinong added to an earlier world consisting of the subjective half only, in order to satisfy his realistic cravings. In the next section we shall see that this is what happened.

---

mental and real, such as, e.g., the temporal connections and those of equality and similarity. But it will do no harm and help us to uncover one of the controlling patterns if for the moment we ignore all these entities.

[51] Even more strongly, *the two halves are isomorphic, i.e., as the mathematicians express themselves, they are structurally identical with respect to determining₂.*

EARLIER STAGES

MEINONG'S first major publication is the *Hume Studien*, which appeared in two instalments, the first in 1877 when he was only twenty-four years old, the second five years later.[1] These studies contain his first ontology. When first mentioning it (p. 139), before introducing another ontology which for reasons we need not re-hearse I called the prototype, I claimed that the two were reasonably close. Now that I am ready to support the claim I must make it more specific. The first "ontology" is reasonably close not to the prototype itself but, rather, to each of two fragments of it. One is its trunk; the other, its cores. No one but a materialist will accept a mere trunk as a world. Anyone not a phenomenalist will be dismayed if in place of a world he is offered no more than the cores of its acts. Hence the double quotes around 'ontology'. Yet the first Meinong was neither a material-ist nor a phenomenalist. In explaining what happened, against the background of the tripartite schema that has served us so long and so well, I shall use 'psychological' and 'metaphysical' as he then used them (e.g., *HumeSt.* I, 9).

His interest during the first phase was not metaphysical but psycho-logical. Or, as I would rather say, he was then above all and to the virtual exclusion of everything else concerned with the assay of con-

---

[1] These essays fill about 250 pages of the *Gesammelte Abhandlungen*. In form, both are critiques of Hume; hence the title. The first refutes Hume's "nominal-ism" by showing that we could not learn to associate, say, the word 'black' with the two "ideas" of a black square and a black circle if these "ideas" were simple rather than two clusters each of which contains a simple "idea" of black. His own doctrine that these two simple "ideas" are equal but not identical, which I call "nominalism," he calls conceptualism. The second essay has the form of a cri-tique of the classification of relations Hume offers in the *Treatise* (Book One, Part One, Section Five). Both essays, rich in valuable details, amount in substance to much more than a mere critique of Hume. See Kenneth Barber, "Meinong's Hume Studies: Translation and Commentary" (Ph.D. diss., Univ. of Iowa, 1966).

tents. A *content* is an *Inhalt*. The word he used throughout his career. Its meaning underwent a major change that marks the end of the first phase. After the change, a content is a core, or perhaps a "constituent" of one. All cores are in the First; their intentions[2] are all in the Second. After the change, he uses '*Inhalt*' and '*Gegenstand*' as we use 'core' and 'intention'. After the change, therefore, all *Inhalte* are mental; their *Gegenstaende*, all physical. Before the change, during the first phase, cores and intentions are not yet distinguished.[3]

An objector interrupts and points out that the author of the *Hume Studien* employs not only '*Vorstellung*' but also '*Vorstellungsinhalt*' and '*Vorstellungsgegenstand*', though not perhaps as systematically as one might wish. I counter with a question, ask whether (in these texts) a *Vorstellungsgegenstand* is a physical entity. He replies, correctly, that indubitably it is something mental. Thereupon I put it to him that he cannot consistently hold these two beliefs, namely, first, that a *Vorstellungsinhalt* and a *Vorstellungsgegenstand* are (in these texts) two and not one, and, second, that they are both mental, without also holding that the latter is an idea which has already fallen into the mind but not yet been collapsed with "its" core. Then I add that, as I read these texts, their author did not deliberately keep two entities from collapsing into each other but simply failed to realize that if what he said was to make any sense at all, they had to be two and not one. Why, then, the objector asks, do you call these entities contents rather than either cores or ideas. I give him four reasons.

(1) A "content" is in a "container." As the nineteenth-century psychologists used the word, the container is a mind. The entities in question are indubitably mental. That makes the word very suitable. (2) 'Core', as we use it, is one half of a dichotomy whose other half, 'intention' stands for something physical. That makes it awkward to use the word for anything in an ontology so fragmentary that all the entities it

---

[2] I continue to ignore, or, rather, to set aside for special consideration all knowledge of minds.

[3] More accurately, as we know, the intentions of the last ontology are all ideal but ultimately founded on what is both real and physical. This nuance makes as yet no difference. The reason I translate '*Gegenstand*' by 'intention' rather than by 'object' is the technical use for which we have reserved the latter. See n. 16 of Section Eighteen. The reason I don't bother to add a prefix is that, though eventually central, the question exactly what minds "grasp" and/or "intend" does not arise until much later.

For a self-diagnosis during the second phase, of his fundamental shortcoming of the first, see *GeghO.*, p. 381: "I, too, have long thought that I could use the two expressions *promiscue*." The two expressions are '*Inhalt*' and '*Gegenstand*'! See also, during the third phase, *Stellung*, p. 9, where he notes that "the distinction in principle among act, core, and intention" is first propounded in *GeghO.*

dialectically considers are mental, even though in the whole of which this fragment is a part the entities to which it would be applied are in fact cores. (3) Ideas are in the Third. Thus the entities could not possibly be ideas. One could perhaps, with a phrase taken from the tradition, call them "inexisting intentions." But that burdens the first Meinong with a question, or, even worse, with an answer to a question, of the sort he then called metaphysical, whose dialectic had not yet begun to worry him. (4). It has been easy and it will be easy not to use 'content' in any other context. Thus the word is conveniently available.

The objector subsides. Another questioner takes his place. "All entities of the first ontology are in the First. There is no Third. The Second is ignored; or as you just put it, it is not dialectically considered. If so, why is its author not a phenomenalist? Nor is that all. From what you say, he ignores all mental entities except cores, or as you now insist on calling them, contents. If so, are not these entities sense data, or at least something very much like sense data, in the style of Hume? Why, finally, did you say that the first ontology is reasonably close to the prototype's trunk? Are not the (categorial) entities of the fragments you call trunks all physical?" I answer in four steps.

First. Ignoring something is one thing; not considering it dialectically is another. Take physical objects. A philosopher may admit that there are such entities yet refuse to admit them to his study. Such a one *ignores physical objects.* The first Meinong does not just grant this bit of common sense outside his study. Whenever it suits him, he also admits the proposition that there are physical objects, as well as quite a few other propositions about them, as premises of the arguments which he constructs in his study, without however betraying the slightest concern for the questions, of the sort he calls "metaphysical," with which this admission faces every ontologist, even if what he explicitly propounds and dialectically probes is merely a "psychological" fragment. In other words, he does *not dialectically consider physical objects.* Yet he neither ignores them nor assays them as mental. That is why he is not a phenomenalist but, hopefully, a realist whose scope and dialectical sensibility are as yet very narrow.

Second. As for physical objects, so for minds. There are not only cores in the first ontology but also fringes and acts. Nor is that all. *Whenever the argument requires it,* there are certain contents which stand to one's own acts as a chair content stands to a physical chair, just as his minds are very active in abstracting, producing, and reproducing *whatever suits him.*[4] But the two italicized clauses are of the es-

---

[4] This producing eventually becomes the fusing of the last ontology. But the latter, we know, is impenetrably obscure; the former, we shall soon see, is not.

sence. The spotlight is always on the cores. Nor is there as yet any interest in systematically assaying minds which "contain" so much else and can "act" so nimbly.

Third. Whatever is in veridical perception impressed upon a mind is structurally identical (isomorphic) with the object impressing it. This is a most fundamental "metaphysical" premiss which he accepts without questioning it. My sole purpose in calling the first ontology reasonably close to the trunk was to call attention to this most important premiss. But distinguish between what is actually impressed on a mind and what this mind may or may not add to it when producing the content which by the premiss corresponds to the object that does the impressing. Here is obviously a potential source of trouble.

Fourth. The cores of the last ontology are connected with "their" intentions by $\overline{M}$, just as those of the foil are connected with theirs by M. A sense datum[5] is a mental entity such that it makes no sense whatsoever to speak of "its" intention. Or, as one says, cores are and sense data are not intentional entities. The fundamental premiss just mentioned may create the illusion that at least some contents of the first ontology have "their" intentions. But its author's indifference to the dialectic of intending is as yet so complete that its contents are indeed very much like sense data. That contributes to the phenomenalistic flavor.

Enough of generalities. Let us first agree to save ink by calling the first ontology O1, then turn to details. Take the intention, α, which the prototype assays as (1) $\gamma(a_1, a_2, a_3)$[6] and suppose that there is in it also the core, α^*, which it assays as (2) $\iota(a_1^*, a_2^*, a_3^*)$. The six (simple) things $a_1, \cdots, a_3^*$ are (perfect) particulars. α and α^* are not things but "things," i.e., pseudocomplexes. α we called a cluster; α^*, a joint. The pseudonexus in them are γ and ι, respectively. In O1 there is of course no core, but we may suppose that there is instead a content, call it α_1, which by the fundamental premiss corresponds to α.

In O1, α and α_1 are assayed as (1') $\bar{\gamma}(a_1, a_2, a_3)$ and (2') $\bar{\iota}(a_1^*, a_2^*, a_3^*)$, respectively. Notice *first* that the six expressions 'a_1', $\cdots$, 'a_3^*' are

---

[5] Are there sense data? Rather than answering this question I shall outflank it by two comments which will come in handy at the end of the section, in connection with the "missing intentions" of the problematic particulars. (1) If there are sense data, one can give a very satisfactory phenomenological description of each conscious state containing an act by assuming, if necessary, that it also contains some sense data which are fused with the act. (2) Are there conscious states which contain only sense data? Once more we need not answer. Phenomenologically, the answer is rather elusive. Dialectically it makes no difference. For details, see the "Realistic Postscript" in *Logic and Reality.*

[6] Make the familiar simplifying assumption and think of a_1, a_2, and a_3 as grounding a place, a color, and a shape, respectively.

used in both pairs, (1), (2) and (1'), (2'), even though O1 and the prototype are different worlds. The first proposition to be established can almost be read off this notation. (a) *The (simple) things of O1 are perfect particulars.*[7] Notice, *second*, the bar which distinguishes $\bar{\gamma}$ and $\bar{\iota}$ in (1') and (2') from γ and ι in (1) and (2). Thereby hang two further propositions. In the prototype γ and ι have explicit ontological status. Perhaps you will object on the ground that, as we know from Section Two, they are merely monsters. I retort that this is here clearly beside the point, which is not how adequate or inadequate the prototype eventually turns out to be, but, rather, how close it is to O1. Do $\bar{\gamma}$ and $\bar{\iota}$ enjoy explicit ontological status? (b) $\bar{\iota}$ *does and* $\bar{\gamma}$ *does not.* This answer, however, we shall do well to ignore until we come to the very end of this examination of O1. In the meantime, if I may so express myself, $\bar{\gamma}$ and $\bar{\iota}$ will serve as signs without ontological commitment. (c) α *and* α_1 *are "things."* More explicitly, they are "complexes" of particulars but exist in the same sense and belong to the same category as the latter.[8] Notice, *third*, how (c) accounts from the very beginning for two fundamental differences between teacher and student. (d1) Meinong's particulars, being attributes in the style of Aristotle, are not "individuated" in the sense in which Brentano requires every existent to be "individuated."[9] (d2) In view of this requirement, Brentano cannot but think in terms of $\subset$; Meinong is naturally led to think in terms of γ.

We have already established that the cores of the prototype and the contents of O1 are very close indeed. Including the answer we must as yet ignore and excluding connections other than γ and ι, for which the prototype deliberately did not provide, we have even established that the two fragments are structurally identical. Thus we are ready for the next task. How are connections assayed in O1? Let us first make another agreement about words.

In the language of O1 a connection is either "real" or "ideal." This is the early use of 'real' and 'ideal'. At the end of the first phase their meanings change. Afterwards they refer to the two levels of exist*ing.* Because of this later use, with which we are already familiar, I would rather avoid the earlier one altogether, say instead that in O1 *a connection is either primary or secondary.*[10] That will not only keep us from

---

[7] *HumeSt.* I, 22–23. The clarity and incisiveness with which Meinong in this passage articulates his nominalism from the very beginning are very impressive.

[8] See, again very impressively, *HumeSt.* I, 48–49.

[9] Meinong was from the very beginning fully aware of this fundamental disagreement. See once more *HumeSt.* I, 48–49.

[10] See *HumeSt.* II, 142. Meinong, of course, uses '*Relation*' and, accordingly, '*Realrelation*' and '*Idealrelation*'. I shall stick with my own use, even though, pre-

getting confused now but also help us to understand the change later. Again, the connections we shall talk about until we come to the very end of this examination of O1 are all secondary. So I shall until then simply call them connections. (If I felt like apologizing for the fuss about words, I would add that I merely try to undo some of the damage Meinong did by not always telling, nor sometimes even knowing, that those he kept using had while he used them changed their meanings.)

The mind may, and often does, from n contents produce a connection, which is an $(n+1)$st. Nothing will be lost if we again limit ourselves to the binary case and suppose that the trigger mechanism (p. 396) has been set once and for all. If, for instance, the two particulars c_1 and e_1 have been impressed upon a mind, it will, if the semaphore (p. 397) stands on "go," from this material produce a third $(hg^3)_1$, which as one says corresponds to their interval.[11] *These connections are the major innovation of O1.* Five questions will probe it.

First. Does Meinong, as the example suggests, reject the extremist view on connections? The answer is explicit. (e) *Every connection has two terms (HumeSt.* II, 44). He calls them foundations. This is again an early use; with the later, only ideal particulars have foundations. So I speak instead of terms. *Second.* How do we know that there are such entities? The answer, proper and satisfactory from where I stand, is phenomenological (*HumeSt.* II, 45, 156). Hearing c_1 and e_1, I often find in my mind in addition to $c_1{}^*$ and $e_1{}^*$ a third content, which is their connection. *Third.* Why is the connection itself a particular? The dogmatic reism smothers the question. No alternative is as much as mentioned, leave alone considered. *Fourth.* Is the connection which a mind produces from certain materials determined[1] by the latter? The answer is Yes (*HumeSt.* II, 140, 154). There is even the appeal to natures and the a priori, although not yet as pronounced as it eventually became. *Fifth.* How do we know that $(hg^3)_1{}^*$ is produced by, rather than, like $c_1{}^*$ and $e_1{}^*$, impressed upon the mind? Let us separate the what from the why. (f) *All connections are contents.* More explicitly, all connections which are existents are mental. The assertion (*HumeSt.* II, 142, 155), as emphatic as it could be, takes care of the what. Nor need we rely on inference for the why. If there are no connections outside of minds,

---

ferring convenience to consistency, I shall as in the case of Brentano occasionally speak as everyone else and use 'relation' instead of 'connection', particularly when the distinction which my use is designed to protect, between subsistent connections on the one hand and relational things on the other, does not enter the argument.

[11] Being thus produced, the connection is a *Productionsvorstellung.* In O1 the expression is quite appropriate. But the diffuse style preserves it to the very end, when Meinong (as we shall see) would have been much better off without concepts (*Vorstellungen*) and conceivings.

what does one assert when asserting such things as that, say, the interval between c_1 and e_1 (not: c_1^* and e_1^*!) is a third? Very admirably, Meinong asks himself this question. His answer, in a form appropriate to the context, proclaims the moderate doctrine of internal connections: The two "absolute" natures of c_1 and e_1 are such that if they impressed two contents upon a mind, the connection between the latter, if the mind produced it, would be $(hg^3)_1^*$ (*HumeSt.* II, 147).

Now we really understand why and how the major innovation of O1 came about. Its author *takes the moderates' internal connections among nonmental particulars, which as we know only too well are really nothing; imports them into the mind; and there for phenomenological reasons gives them the ontological status of mental particulars.* The first push away from the old and toward the new was thus phenomenological. So, we shall see, were the second and the third, which led to O2.

I select next the little we need from the critique (see n. 1, above, and *HumeSt.* II, 29) of Hume's sevenfold division of all relations into those of (H1) resemblance, (H2) identity, (H3) space and time, (H4) quantity and number, (H5) degree, (H6) contrariety, and (H7) cause and effect.

In the discussion of identity Meinong tips his hand on an important issue: We have no reason to believe that physical objects are continuants (substances$_4$) (*HumeSt.* II, 134–35). His assay of causation is as inadequate and as lacking in contemporary interest as Brentano's. The latter nevertheless underlies Brentano's doctrine of evidence and is the crucial premiss, or would-be premiss, of his proof that there are scientific objects. So we had to attend to it. Meinong's assay bears no such burden. So we may safely ignore it. That will do for (H2) and (H7).

Spatial and temporal connections are either derived or underived. All underived ones are relations of comparison among coordinate qualities (*HumeSt.* II, 149). Thus they do not in any respect that concerns us differ from the pitch paradigm and require no special treatment. As for space and time, so for quantity and number. This is really all we need from (H3) and (H4). Even so, space and time are very important and the role they have played in the first three Parts of this book is very great. So a brief comment is in order. Brentano agonized about them throughout his life. Meinong's confidence in coordinate qualities was apparently never shaken.[12] Yet he was, if I may so express myself, the phenomenologist of the two. Considering the more than dubious status of coordinate qualities, that is strange and not wholly to his credit. But there is an oasis even in this desert. Existence, he insists, is timeless, as one says, and surely not bound up with the present. The posi-

---

[12] About space there is virtually nothing. The phenomenological musings about time in the last two parts of *GeghO.* do not go very far.

tion is correct; the arguments for it, well taken and well stated. The contrast to Brentano is clear cut.[13]

(H6), he claims, is not really a class of connections. I select one point that reveals the early root of a later failure which will occupy us in the next section. Consider incompatibility. Take two contents; one, α, of a certain color at a certain place and time; the other, β, of another color at the same place and time. The "incompatibility" of α and β is not a third content, in addition to α and β, as it would have to be if incompatibility were a relation between them, but, rather, the evidence of the judgment that they do not both represent (*HumeSt.* II, 90). As for contents so for judgments. Replace α and β by the two contents (concepts) of one person at one time making the one and the other of two incompatible judgments.[14] If you sense the unwarranted "subjectivity" of this assay, you will suspect, correctly, that the later failure occurs in the account of deductive inference, or, as I would rather say, in the assay of the world's form.

While examining (H1) and (H5) he presents us with his own assay of connections. (g) *All connections are relations of comparison and all comparisons yield either equality, or difference, or similarities of varying degree* (*HumeSt.* II, 149, 73–84). Once more our several diagnoses nicely support each other. In spite of the ontologization, if I may so express myself, the assay of connections in O1 is that of the proponents of the moderate doctrine of internal relations, which has been examined and found wanting in Section Five. Nor did he ever abandon it, or correct it, or even reflect on it. Hence the striking monotony of his examples. The only relations ever mentioned, even in his latest writings, are equality, difference, and similarity. (The emphasis on the musical interval as a suitable paradigm is wholly mine.) One cause, if not excuse, for this immobility we have known for some time. By piling semicolon upon semicolon in a world without types (p. 362), he seems[15] to be able to do better than other proponents of the doctrine.

[13] See *GeghO.*, p. 457; *Erfahrungsgl.*, p. 69, and, particularly penetrating and lucid, *Ann.*, pp. 65–69. Brentano, however, is not mentioned. Nor is this an exception. He mentioned Brentano but rarely; never criticized him publicly; and, in an admirable statement after his death, did full justice to the magnificence of the man (*Die Deutsche Philosophie der Gegenwart in Selbstdarstellungen*, p. 94). The scorn was all reserved for the zealous disciples.

[14] *HumeSt.* II, 100. I save words by expressing myself in this paragraph in the language of representationalism rather than that of O1. The unwarranted subjectivity is in the style of Brentano. The mess into which Meinong gets himself on these matters, just because he revolts against the relative coherence of the idealistic pattern, is, as we shall see in the next section, uniquely his own.

[15] I say *seems* because, looking closely enough, one sees (p. 366) that his nominalism does not even permit him to write '$(hg^3)_1$' and '$(hg^3)_2$' for '$(c_1; e_1)$' and '$(d_2; f_2)$'.

We are ready for the question with which I planned to conclude the examination of O1. How about the ontological status of $\bar{\gamma}$ and $\bar{\iota}$? One half of the answer follows from (f). $\bar{\gamma}$ has none. There is no connection which is not mental. That is one source of the tension that led to O2. For, clearly, the (physical) object α is not just a class or collection. Nor of course is the (mental) content α_1. Its case, however, is different. For $\bar{\iota}$ is itself a content. Yet there is no indication whatsoever that the mind has produced it out of the a_i^*.[16] $\bar{\iota}$ is thus a connection which, though the mind contributes it to contents, has not been produced out of contents. Such connections are called *primary*. All others, i.e., all those which the mind has produced out of contents, are called *secondary*. (How about those, if any, which the mind produces out of primary ones? The question is not raised.)

Notice in conclusion that O1 has only one level of exist*ing*. Thus, if, for once and really quite inappropriately, we applied 'real' and 'ideal' in their later use to O1, we would have to say that both primary and secondary connections are "real." But we also remember that in their earlier use 'real' and 'ideal' stand for 'primary' and 'secondary', respectively. That spots the change in use. Why it occurred we shall understand as soon as we look at O2. But it will be better if we first attend to two points which depend only on O1. The first picks up a loose end. The second offers an observation long overdue. Both lend considerable genetic support to the several analyses and diagnoses proposed.

First. Remember the trouble into which we ran as soon as we realized that in the expression '$((c_1; hg^{+2}; e_1)^n: nonex)$' for the ideal particular which is the intention of the false belief, or perception, or thought, that e_1 is higher^2 than c_1, the part expression 'hg^{+2}' needed expansion. Among the connections determined by c_1 and e_1 are hg^{+3} and hg^{-2} but not of course hg^{+2}. Hence there is a "particularized" $(hg^{+3})_1$ and a "particularized" $(hg^{-2})_1$, but nothing named by '$(hg^{+2})_1$'. This is the trouble.[17] The best we could do was to "borrow" from another pair, f_2 and g_2, the "particularized" connection $(hg^{+2})_2$. But the final ontology is a world in which under the double pressure of a rigid nominalism and a reism stretched to the utmost all connections are both reified and "particularized." That makes this "solution" counterstructural. Or, to say the same thing differently, the borrowing metaphor remains opaque. Why, then, we asked, did this serious trouble go unnoticed?

Meinong's minds, like those of all "empiricists," cannot only *produce*

[16] *HumeSt.* II, 138–42. This is the seed of the later argument that the coincidence or noncoincidence of, say, a place and a color are not determined by their natures.

[17] See p. 359. The expressions have been amended by adding the plus and minus signs from p. 368.

contents out of others but also on the appropriate occasions *reproduce* them, i.e., more accurately, they can on these occasions produce contents equal to those they have once produced. Into the circumstances that make an occasion appropriate we need not inquire beyond noticing that among them are certainly those which cause me (in O1) to have in a certain situation (subscript 1) the content $\bar{\imath}(c_1^*, (hg^{+2})_2^{*r}, e_1^*)$, where the reproduced entity, with the superscript 'r', is equal to another, without this superscript, which has been produced in another situation (subscript 2). Among the *contents* of O1 the borrowing metaphor does make sense! One gets into serious trouble only if he seriously tries to assay *intentions*. One may plausibly surmise that Meinong did not notice this trouble because the ideal connections among intentions which appear in the later ontologies are merely an afterthought he added to O1 in order to satisfy his realistic cravings. Or so I surmised (p. 398). The two surmises support each other.

Second. In the representationalist tradition 'some' stands for 'someone' (p. 229). More suggestively, such contents as (2') $\bar{\imath}(a_1^*, a_2^*, a_3^*)$ behave as if they were not just the name of α but the common name of all objects $\bar{\gamma}(a_{i_1}, a_{i_2}, a_{i_3})$ such that a_1 and a_{i_1}, a_2 and a_{i_2}, a_3 and a_{i_3} are respectively equal. Or so one may plausibly surmise. Connect (2') with a believing (judging) into the act (2'') and consider a philosopher who, like the author of O1, does not dialectically consider intentions. He will take it for granted that (what we call) the intention of (2'') is the existential fact that there is an object of a certain kind.[18] Suppose next that, as the scope of his dialectical concern widens, he adds a trunk. If he still believes, as most probably he will, that all existential and categorical judgments are accounted for,[19] he is in danger of adding a trunk that contains only atomic facts. Or so one may again plausibly surmise.

Surmises are one thing, facts are another. That Meinong's final ontology represents only atomic states of affairs is a fact not only indubitable but also, in view of his willingness, not to say eagerness, to

[18] I.e., as assayed in the foil and with our usual notation, the fact $(\exists x) [A_1(x) \cdot A_2(x) \cdot A_3(x)]$. In the later stages the mistake is re-enforced by the ambiguity of 'existential fact' pointed out in n. 17 of Section Nineteen.

[19] The mechanics of the transition from IIIa and IIIb to IV are managed by η (p. 372). The assay of a and e in terms of i and o is forcefully suggested by Brentano's early "reform" of logic. Since the later Meinong takes the "obscurity" of all cores for granted, he has on the side of the *existential and categorical judgments* none of the problems which as we saw in Section Fifteen beset Brentano. That can only strengthen the tendency to overlook the *existential and general facts*. (The roman numerals are taken from the eightfold division in Section Twelve. With the class V and the connectives we shall deal in the last section.)

ontologize all sorts of things, very strange. Its strangeness lends structural significance to the two surmises. Nor is that all. A moment's reflection will show you the similarity of the situations in these two comments. If one does not dialectically consider the intentions there is no serious trouble in either as long as, in the second, one accepts, somewhat uncritically yet not unnaturally, the some*one*-pattern of the representationalists. Our most important surmise, that about the afterthought, thus receives structural support from both situations. I suggest we acknowledge that by promoting it from a surmise to a diagnosis.

The *second ontology*, or O2, as I shall call it, fully emerged in the essay *Ueber Gegenstaende hoeherer Ordnung* (1899). The transition had been gradual. But my purpose even in this section is structural rather than historical (biographical). So I peg the second phase to this assay.

The intellectual motives that propelled Meinong into O2 are two phenomenological insights. *Core (Inhalt) and intention (Gegenstand) are two and not one. The former is mental; the latter, physical.* In conceiving (something) blue the intention is physical and colored; the core, neither the one nor the other.[20] This insight he shared with Brentano. The other, that *all intentions exist*, saved him from Brentano's fate. The statement of the first is most explicit. The second is not yet fully appropriated in all its consequences; that will indeed take the rest of his life; but it was indubitably there and had begun to shape his thought. I propose that we acknowledge this advance by retiring the word 'content'.

Pitch, loudness, color, brightness, and so on, are merely kinds in a single category. If, therefore, sound were taken out of our world, although humanly much would be changed, ontologically nothing would have happened. Taking (binary) relations out of the foil, one must also remove the (ternary) nexus. That is why my own world's relational things are at least a subcategory of it. How about Meinong's first innovation, the connections which he added to the ontological inventory of the prototype? Are they a category, or a subcategory, or merely a kind of particulars? The answer is not clear cut. The genetic feature, having been produced by the mind out of other particulars, is ontologically irrelevant. If, therefore, all connections were secondary, they would be merely a kind, particularly since facts, or as I shall continue to say, states of affairs (see Section Eighteen, n. 35), including those which reveal a secondary connection to be a "tie" between the two particulars out of which it is produced, are not yet dialectically considered. But the connection between α_1 and a_1^*, a_2^*, a_3^* is not genetic. Structurally, there-

---

[20] See *GeghO.*, p. 384; also the quotation from *GeghO.*, p. 381, in n. 3, above; for a particularly lucid and penetrating later statement, *Stellung*, pp. 8–13.

fore, i is a "tie," just as, O1 not being a function ontology, α_1 is a "complex."

The second innovation, of O2, is the ideal particular. It leaves the reism of the single category unshaken, adds instead a level of exist*ing*. A level is even more fundamental than a category, and therefore, if added, something more radically new than an added category. Yet, radically new and surpassingly strange as it is, the ideal particular is also a compromise, the only kind of entity a philosopher could have invented had he deliberately set out to satisfy three requirements, or, perhaps better, to reconcile three doctrines.

One is the unshakable reism. Because of it, the new entity is a particular. The second is the moderate doctrine of internal relations, by which a connection such as, say, $(c_1; e_1)$, is nothing over and above c_1 and e_1. Because of it, $(c_1; e_1)$ is merely the value of a function, existing *eo ipso* if its "real" arguments exist, by virtue of determination₁, that peculiar and peculiarly attenuated process of creation which is further undermined by withholding ontological status from the function. Because of it, finally, $(c_1: e_1)$ cannot be causally effective. These two requirements are old. The third comes from the new insight that all intentions exist. Since in O1 $(hg^3)_i{}^*$ exists, so by the new dispensation does $(e_1; c_1)$. The thing to do, therefore, is to provide a new level of exist*ing* for it, make it "ideal." Then it will at least not be anything "real" in addition to c_1 and e_1.

I take it that I have proved my major claim. The surmise we promoted to a diagnosis has become a certainty. *Structurally, Meinong's connections are internal connections of the Second; imported into the First, where they were given ontological status; then, without losing this status, re-exported into the Second* (p. 350). *Genetically, the very notion of ideal particulars and, with it, the whole objective half (of the final ontology) are merely an afterthought he added to an earlier world consisting of the subjective half only, in order to satisfy his realistic cravings* (p. 398). Five comments will exploit this result. The first two deal only with O2; the last three also illuminate O3 and the final ontology, to which I do not assign a letter symbol.

First. Mark for the moment the old and the new use of 'real' and 'ideal', in O1 and O2, respectively, by corresponding subscripts. Pretend again that it makes sense to use 'real₂' in speaking about O1. Then all existents and hence all connections of O1 are real₂. They are either ideal₁ or real₁, depending on whether or not the mind has produced them out of other contents. But they are all mental. In O2 an ideal connection may be either "mental" or "physical";[21] or, rather, as we

---

[21] Or "mixed," as, e.g., $\overline{M}$. But this alternative plays at the moment no role.

must now say, it may ultimately rest on real$_2$ particulars which are either all mental, such as, say, the equality of two cores, or all physical, such as (c_1; e_1). i, not being produced in O1 out of the contents which later become the cores c_1^* and e_1^*, will in the latter naturally not be assayed as founded on them, and, therefore, as both mental and real$_2$. That accounts for the change in the use of 'ideal' and 'real'. But it also raises a question. Are there in O2 any connections both "physical" and real$_2$? Or, dropping the subscripts and again using the two words as before, with their eventual meanings, are there in O2 any connections which are both real and "physical"?

Second. (a) A certain tension in O1 has been pointed out (p. 403). Our ternary paradigm α, or, more generally, a physical object is not just either the class or, even worse, the collection of "its" particulars. Yet in O1 $\bar{\gamma}$ does not and cannot exist. Hence, although primary, i is not impressed on, but contributed by the mind. In O2 the situation has changed in two ways. For one, by the strong principle of abstraction,[22] i, being "part" of a content, ought to have an intention which exists. For another, since there already are both real and ideal connections in O2 and some of the latter are outside of minds, there is no longer any structural reason why the former should all be inside. $\bar{\gamma}$ now may be, and in fact is, given ontological status. So endowed, it eventually becomes *coinc*$^+$. Thus the tension is momentarily relieved. As the larger pattern shifts, it reappears.

(b) Structurally speaking rather than in terms of what Meinong himself either knew and said or at least sensed and hinted, there are still "ties" and "complexes" in O1 but as yet no functions. The latter go in his worlds with the level distinction. Thus they appear first in O2. But the categorial entities of a function ontology are all simple. Hence there are neither "ties" nor "complexes" in O2. On the level of the real that leaves us with the quaternary collection $\{a_1, a_2, a_3, coinc^+\}$, which shows how the tension reappears; while on the level of the ideal there is now the simple new entity (a_1; a_2; a_3; *coinc*$^+$), which shows that *the seed of the function inaccuracy has been sown.*

(c) If you now re-examine the two proofs for the simplicity of all fusions (p. 390) which I assembled from a text I judged to be scrambled beyond hope, you will understand, not only why they left you uneasy, but also why and how that judgment fits with all the rest into the tightening pattern of mutual support. The trouble with these "proofs"

---

[22] See *GeghO.*, p. 395; for the principle, the premiss P3 on p. 391. This principle has always played an important role in Meinong's thought who insists already during O1 (*HumeSt.* II, 84) that, once the mind has produced, say, $(hg^3)_1^*$ out of c_1^* and e_1^*, it can think of what in O2 becomes (c_1; e_1) without thinking of either c_1 or e_1 or anything else.

is that they resurrect in a later world of simples and functions the ghosts of "complexes" and "ties." That makes them prime examples of the diffuse style, proving, if anything, that trying to make sense out of Meinong is as worth while as it is difficult.

Third. An entity[23] of O3 or of the final ontology is either an "ordinary" real particular or a real connection, such as *coinc*+ and *coinc*−, or it is one of *six kinds of ideal entities.* Real connections share some of their features with "ordinary" real particulars, some others with ideal connections, which makes their status so peculiar that I called them hermaphrodites. But we have already examined them (p. 371) and shall not either miss or distort anything of what still has to be said if we pay no further attention to them.

Let a, b; p, q; and *conn* be two real particulars, two propositions, and the nature (of the nature) of a connection. Supposing that (1) $(a^n: ex)$, (2) $(b^n: nonex)$, (3) $(p: ex)$ and (4) $(q: nonex)$ exist, we can use them, together with (5) $(conn^{+n}: ex)$ and (6) $(conn^{-n}: ex)$, to represent the six ideal kinds. Only (3) and (4) are bona fide Objectives, representing states of affairs that correspond to facts of the foil. (1) and (2) are fortuitous duplications, (1) of what is, (2) paradoxically of what is not, instances of Thomistic composition mistaken for "existential" states of affairs, which we accepted as Objectives only under protest, because otherwise we would have had to break off. The natures in the first four combine with either *ex* or *nonex*, as the case may be. That is why we had to suppose that they exist. (5) and (6) are connections, corresponding to things of the foil. The natures in them combine always with *ex*; the dichotomy *ex-nonex* is used only to account for the plus-minus complication, in the way I managed it, as best I could, by $(\ (conn!\ ex): ex)$ and $(\ (conn!\ nonex): ex)$.

These are the major distinctions among the six kinds. There are others. The strategy I chose allowed us to make them all at the very beginning. This is indeed one of the advantages[24] I sought in choosing it. Meinong himself, alas, though he sensed most of them, did not really achieve any of these distinctions. Thus he remained caught in the coils of the dialectic whose resolution depends on making them clearly and cleanly. He reached out for, but never arrived at, an adequate notion of fact. Of this more in the next comment. The plus-minus compli-

---

[23] I.e., a particular. For, to repeat once more what cannot be repeated too often, all existents of all these worlds are particulars. The increasing variety of their surfaces hides in unbroken monotony the single category of a reism that is as rigid as it is ingenious.

[24] The two others were that the strategy allowed us to fence in the two major inaccuracies before they could bedevil us.

cation eluded him.[25] He did eventually manage a distinction of sorts between connections and Objectives.[26] And so on, and so on. He sensed and he struggled. Sensitive and tenacious as he was, here and there he got a glimpse. The rest was misery and defeat. We would do him less than justice if we did not take notice of the misery or blamed him too harshly for the defeat. But the details are no longer of interest. So I shall not go beyond the next two comments.

Fourth. A four-step pattern points at the way in which Meinong's thought jerkily adjusted to new pressures and pulls as a plausible contributory cause of this particular defeat. The first step anticipates the innovation of O3. The second borrows a standard from the foil. The third shows why the misery began in O2; the fourth, why it never ended.

(a) *The third innovation, of O3, is the Objective.* With it, or perhaps as two aspects of it, come two new features. One is the Thomistic composition; the other, the explicit representation, by this new kind of ideal particulars whose natures are propositions, of states of affairs. The first feature can wait. The second has a place in the pattern. (b) Take any fact whose assay in the foil is of the form $\rho(\alpha, \beta)$. There the connection is a universal in conjunction with a ternary nexus; in O2 it is "particularized." There α and β belong to one type, ρ to another; in O2 there are no types. Important though they are, at the moment these differences make no difference. The point is that one can and must distinguish three categorial entities, namely, (1) the *class* $[\alpha, \beta]$, (2) the *thing* ρ, and (3) the *fact* $\rho(\alpha, \beta)$ into which the ternary nexus ties α, β, and ρ. (c) The author of *GeghO.* sensed that there were these three entities, if only because, *on the side of the act,* he held that ρ had been produced out of α and β, while on the other hand one can think either of $[\alpha, \beta]$ or, by the strong principle of abstraction (see n. 22, above), of

---

[25] See the scrambled passage in *Ann.*, p. 63. A critic might insist that this so-called complication is more than just that and so nasty indeed that it alone suffices to reject his world. I completely agree, but ask leave for two observations. First I repeat that Meinong never saw how nasty it really is. Then I add that it is easily corrected, as, alas, the nominalism is not. All one has to do is to give the connectives, including negation, ontological status without, however, giving them natures. The critic points out that this sacrifices the purity of the reism. I again agree but observe that the modification is as slight as it could possibly be; that it would also help with the logic, of which more in the next section; and that it does not upset anything else.

[26] When this distinction is made, such as, e.g., in *Ann.*, p. 283, the connection itself, e.g., $(c_1; e_1)$ is called *der Relat.* Presumably that makes the state of affairs, e.g., $(c_1; (c_1; e_1); e_1)$, *die Relation.* The first term is characteristically barbarous. The second, so used, certifies the original confusion. See also the next comment above.

ρ, each without thinking of anything else. He also felt the need for the distinctions and the "connections"[27] which caused us no difficulty whatsoever, since we do possess an adequate notion of fact. He, however, did not know how to make them correctly, thus suffering for the first time the full consequences of not having such a notion.[28] So he soothed his unrest by proclaiming a "Principle of Partial Coincidence" which is both specious and opaque (*GeghO.*, pp. 389–94). (d) The only ideal particulars of O2 are connections. All others were then still in the future. But they at least had already acquired citizenship, for services rendered, if I may so express myself, at the time of the shift to O3, when he was above all anxious to secure the same rights for his latest innovation, the Objective, because of the service he expected from it. This he did by emphasizing what Objectives and connectives, being both *Gegenstaende hoeherer Ordnung*, had in common, and by neglecting, at least temporarily, as he might have hoped, in what they differed.[29] Nor of course did the opacity of the specious Principle make inquiry into these differences more attractive. That is how, given the diffuse style, the temporary neglect became the misery without end.

Fifth. What is a class? Meinong was first struck by this important question when he tried to distinguish the pair class $[\alpha, \beta]$ from ρ and $\rho(\alpha, \beta)$. So I make this the occasion for examining what he thought about it. Infinity having been excluded from this book, we might as well stay with the pair.[30] Two simultaneous thoughts, one of α, one of β, are not the same as a single thought of α and β as the members of a class, or, as one says, "together." This he always knew; we have long known that he knew it. But that merely sets the problem. Or, rather, it sets two problems, one for the cores, one for the intentions. On the side of the cores, the appeal to the obscurity of fusing is always open to him. And, if this activity or process is obscure in all cases, why worry about it in that of classes?

On the side of the intentions, the author of *GeghO.* very admirably sensed the distinction between the class $[\alpha, \beta]$ and the collection $\{\alpha,$

---

[27] Distinguish between connections and "connections." See p. 345.

[28] Nor, as we know, did he ever acquire one, even though eventually the propositions in the bona fide Objectives allowed him to do better than most. Propositions, however, appear only in O3; the specious Principle is an expedient of O2. But one may plausibly *surmise* that the dissatisfaction with this Principle was among the motives that pushed him toward O3. The surmise does not become less plausible if one considers the *fact* that from O3 on the *Relat* (n. 26) comes to the fore and the Principle begins to fade away.

[29] The evidence is pervasive. But see *Ann.*, pp. 63–64. On p. 64 you will find the explicit claim that "in a certain sense equality and difference, too, are Objectives."

[30] See n. 23 of Section Eighteen; for Brentano, n. 37 of Section Nineteen.

β}, and, not unnaturally in the context, hit upon the connection ρ as its ontological ground, or, if you please, as the ground of the "together-ness." Then he called classes *Komplexionen* and let it go at that.[31] Obviously this will not do. There are classes such that the only connec-tion among their members is that of being all their members. (Classes, as one says, are arbitrary.) Eventually he seems to have realized that; for we have a report[32] that in later years he assayed classes as a special kind of *Komplexe* which he called *Mengenkomplexe*. But these entities are so patently *ad hoc* that one who is not already wedded to the system cannot but wonder whether they are really there to do the job origi-nally assigned to connections in all those cases in which there are none. Nor, from where I stand, is this the only trouble. In the foil classes are derived *things*.[33] His *Komplexe* correspond to *facts*. That leaves only one way out. One cannot articulate his thought on the matter without inventing or "postulating" a new and very special real connection which "makes" a class out of every collection, just as *coinc* "makes" objects out of some.[34] We have come upon a prime example of the function inaccuracy. (Another possibility of assaying classes which he did not notice I leave for the next section, when we shall understand why he did not notice it, or, if he did, why it was not acceptable to him.)

Let us turn to the third phase, O3. What is the addition to the onto-logical inventory? What needs does it satisfy? What pressures does it relieve? Where shall we peg the phase? The answers to the first three questions we know already. The addition, or innovation, is the Objec-tive, an ideal particular compounded out of a nature which is a proposi-tion and either *ex* or *nonex*. Propositions allow the representation and thereby, within the limits of the over-all pattern, the dialectical con-sideration of states of affairs. This is the need satisfied. The odd twin, *nonex*, permits, again of course within the limits of the pattern, the solution of the problems in the familiar classical cluster, nonveridical perception, false belief, and so on. This is the pressure relieved. For the rough dating or pegging which we cannot avoid I take advantage of a most striking cue.

Between the first and the second edition of *Annahmen* their author

---

[31] *GeghO.*, pp. 387–89. See also the premiss called P4 in the last section (p. 391).

[32] Auguste Fischer, who annotated *GeghO.* in the *Gesammelte Abhandlungen*, re-ports in her notes 16 and 17 what he said in later years in his lectures. But '*Komplexion*' still occurs in *Annahmen*! The diffuse style does have its disad-vantages.

[33] E.g., the derived Character C defined by abbreviating '$(x=a) \bigvee (x=b)$' as '$C(x)$'.

[34] Notice that if *per absurdum* there were such a real connection, it would not have a negative half, since in a world of particulars and nothing else every collec-tion is a class. Thus it would be very special indeed.

changed his mind on an issue so fundamental that more or less directly it affects virtually all others.[35] In the second edition he calls attention to the change by a most striking literary device. The seventh chapter has thirty pages. In the first sixteen he reprints what he had said about the issue in the earlier edition. In the last fourteen he expounds the view at which he had finally arrived. This is the cue. I peg O3 to the first edition of his chef-d'oeuvre, of 1902; the emergence of the final ontology, to the second, of 1910.

What is that most fundamental issue? It will be better if before naming it we bring in another issue and another change that occurred more gradually. This second issue is so closely connected with the first that it is but an aspect of it. The final consummation probably occurred in a single step. It is at any rate recorded in the same text, the second edition of *Annahmen*.

What then are these two issues and these two final changes? I shall let the answer grow out of the ambiguities and confusions of O3 by first stating what I take to be its formula and then attaching a short comment to each of the four key words in it.

Everything a mind grasps (a) *is an ideal particular* (b), *an Objective* (c), *and an assumption* (d).

(a) Does the mind always grasp a particular; or always a nature; or sometimes the one, sometimes the other? We remember how much vagueness and confusion these alternatives caused from what transpired when we aired them by means of the three prescripts we attached to 'intention'. (b) How can one consistently hold that an Objective is compounded of a nature and either *ex* or *nonex* and at the same time deny that natures and the twins exist? The very question shows that when O3 emerged, *the seed of the nature inaccuracy was sown.* (c) Objectives are only two of the six ideal kinds. If, therefore, one assimilates the other four to these two, partly because one does not know how to distinguish them correctly, partly because one wants them all to share the benefits of Thomistic composition, one is doomed to a misery without end. This we just saw. (d) An assumption (*Annahme*) is what the mind grasps even if the particular it intends (f-intends!) is compounded with *nonex* (p. 381). That suggests, though it does not compel, the view that assumptions and propositions (overhastily identified with natures!) are one and the same, and, with respect to (a), that what the mind grasps is always a proposition (or at least a nature). Nor of course can one be either vague or confused on (a) but not on (d); and conversely.

The most fundamental issue hangs by (b); the one closely connected

<hr>

[35] Which is, after all, what in philosophy is meant by 'fundamental'.

with it, by (a). *Natures exist. What the mind grasps is always a nature.*[36]
These are the two final views. To the second we shall return in conclusion, with a twist. The first, which finally gets rid of the nature inaccuracy, deserves all the unpacking we can give it.

Meinong's reism caused him to commit the most fatal error an ontologist can make. He insisted, without knowing it, on a specialized use of
'exist', i.e., on a use narrower than the only one proper and safe in
ontology. As he speaks, only particulars[37] "exist," or, synonymously,
every "existent (being, *Sein*)" is a particular. Natures and the twins,
ex and *nonex*, exist but do not "exist." Thus a collision course is set.
The result is an absurd ontology, aggravated by a terminology not only
clumsy but bizarre.

From Aristotle he takes (1a) *A is*, (1b) *A is not*, (2a) *A is B*, (2b) *A is
not B;* supplements them with the relational (3a) *A is R to B* and (3b)
A is not R to B; then divides *Sein* in three ways. I. (1a) and (1b), if
true, stand for *Sein;* (2a) and (2b), for *Sosein;* (3a) and (3b), for
Wiesein.[38] This is merely a clumsy tripartition of facts into the presumably existential, the categorical, and the relational.[39] II. (1a), (2a),
(3a) and (1b), (2b), (3b) are affirmative and negative "being" (*Sein*
and *Nichtsein*), respectively. To see how wrongheaded that is, consider
that *ex* and *nonex*, if perchance they existed, would be just two odd
existents. He, however, wonders whether natures, which he also calls
pure particulars (*reine Gegenstaende*), can exist, even though they are
not, like all "existents," either "affirmative" or "negative." He concludes tentatively that they don't exist. Yet they bother him. So he
gives them a name, calls them *Aussersein*. If they existed, there would
thus be three sorts (*Arten*) of being, affirmative (positive) *Sein*,
Nichtsein, which he holds is in its own way "positive," and *Aussersein*.
Thus the height of the absurd (in things) and the bizarre (in words)
would be reached. III. The third division of all being is the familiar one
into the real (*Dasein*) and the ideal (*Bestand*). A nature or *reiner*

[36] For the first statement, see *Ann.*, p. 242, and n. 11 of Section Nineteen; for
the second, *Ann.*, p. 79.

[37] Or, as we know he believes, only particulars and objects. But the difference
makes here no difference. Double quotes mark the special use.

[38] Findlay translates '*Sosein*' and '*Wiesein*' by 'so-being' and 'how-being';
mercifully refrains from translating '*Aussersein*'. I cannot bring myself to translate any. But if I were forced, I would translate '*Aussersein*' by 'Notbeing', even
though, or perhaps rather, because that would make Notbeing and *nonex* two and
not one and thereby help to stress the absurdity.

[39] Remember the representationalists' preference for the ambiguous use of '*A
is B*' (n. 8 of Section Twelve); the ambiguity in his world of 'existential fact' (n. 17
of Section Nineteen); and, from this section, the plausible failure to notice that all
its facts are atomic.

Gegenstand is or has *Sosein*. If the "is or has" bothers you, remember
that he still flounders in the nature inaccuracy. Nor is that the only
blur in I. *Sosein* is not only the whole nature of a particular but also
what '*B*' and '*R*' in (2) and (3) stand for. One is annoyed; yet one
understands the temptation. Facts just are not easily cut down to
things.[40]

The next to the last step is marked by a formula. *Sosein ist daseinsfrei*. Correctly translated: A nature need not combine with *ex* into a
real particular. For propositions this is curiously redundant. For connections (we know) it is false. For the simple natures of the simple
particulars, which in view of this redundancy and this falsehood he
must have had in mind, it is as far as one can go without acknowledging
in so many words that they have ontological status.[41]

The last step consummates the phenomenological insight which first
stirred in him when he moved from O1 to O2. All intentions exist. Or, as
it now reads: "Blue is presented (*vorgegeben*) to our decision as to *Sein*
and *Nichtsein* in a manner not excluding *Nichtsein*" (*Gegenstandsth.*, p.
491). Given the pattern, the conclusion is foregone. What is "given
beforehand" exists in its own right. *Aussersein is recognized as a third
"positive" sort of Sein*. Thus the nature inaccuracy has finally been
cleared up. But at the same time the height of the absurd and the
bizarre has been reached. Even worse, the collision has occurred. Natures, which as such exist but do not "exist," have become a positive
sort of "existent." Yet officially one is still a reist! The thing to do is to
scrap it all and start anew. You see now why I said earlier that even at
this late point, when he finally got rid of the nature inaccuracy, Meinong did not really understand the dialectic which held him in its grip.
Need I add that I have not the slightest notion of what a *Seinsart* could
possibly be? The one thing I am sure of is that it is something even
more absurd than a level.

If natures are allowed to enjoy ontological status, how about *ex* and
nonex? No word is breathed. At first the omission seems strange. Yet it
is easily explained. Since *nonex* is really nothing, *a Meinongian nature
compounded with nonex is really a "particularized" Platonic idea*. The
omission is a repression. We, who do not need to repress anything, see
that a fateful circle has been closed. Or didn't it all start with the re-
vulsion from *separable* natures, long, long ago?

[40] The clearest and most concise expression of this stage of his thought, in the
first four sections of *Gegenstandsth.* (pp. 483–94), is from 1904. For the "predica-
tive" ambiguity in *Sosein*, see, e.g., *Ann.*, p. 283; for a most explicit identification
of *Sosein* with nature, *Stellung*, p. 32.

[41] The most articulate expression of this stage, including the formula itself, is
from 1907, in *Stellung*, pp. 28–36. See also n. 48 of Section Eighteen.

What the mind grasps is always a nature. To this final view I promised to return, with a twist. In grasping something the mind is active. The activity is a fusing; its product, a core. What is grasped by means of this core is always an ideal particular. Add now two premisses and you will see how he arrived at the two conclusions which are the twist I had in mind. One premiss is that every ideal particular is an Objective. This we know to be a confusion. But we have not only amply documented it; we have also understood that at some points we must either put up with it or break off. In what follows the fortuitous duplication which makes $(a^n: ex)$ an Objective is of the essence.[42] So we are here at one of those points. The other premiss is that to be presented to a mind and to be intended by it is one and the same. This is only reasonable and he takes it for granted. One conclusion is that *all intentions are Objectives;* the other, that *all simple fringes are assumings.*[43]

By the first conclusion, the simplest possible intention, if I may so express myself, is the (specious) Objective that goes with a real particular, such as, say, $(a^n: ex)$. By the second conclusion, assuming takes the place of the classical representationalists' conceiving. That is why I said earlier that he would have been better off if he had in his final world discarded the notion of conceiving. He, however, did not realize that. Since he didn't, he did not appreciate the gravity of the question about the *problematic particulars* which I raised but did not pursue at the end of the last section. As I then claimed and as I shall now show, this question is unanswerable in his system. Thus, once more, had he noticed it, the best he could have done was to scrap it all and start anew.

In receiving the impression $a*$ the mind is passive. Hence there is nothing $a*$ intends. When the mind gets busy with $a*$, it can do no less than produce the core, call it $a**$, which intends $(a^n: ex)$. $a*$ and $a**$ are two and not one; otherwise there would not have been any activity of the mind. How, then, do we know that there is such a thing as $a*$? This is the unanswerable question.

It will help us to grasp it more firmly if we see clearly what is not an answer. Phenomenologically, fringes are transparent. More literally, they easily elude us; the cores obtrude. Philosophers who read English could learn that from G. E. Moore in 1903. Those reading German could have learned it from Meinong in 1899.[44] The thing to see clearly is that the question before us cannot be answered by claiming that the

[42] The difference between $(a^n: ex)$ and $(b^n: nonex)$ makes here no difference. So I stay with the former.

[43] The evidence is widely scattered. The most massive single reference is *Ann.*, pp. 237–41.

[44] His word for *transparent*, for once rather prettily, is *wahrnehmungsfluechtig.*

problematic particulars are transparent. They are, if I may so put it, much more problematic than that. Nor did Meinong make this shallow claim. His answer[45] is very illuminating. But it is also very strange.

Sometimes, he points out, we catch a glimpse of what we do not intend. What we "see" without seeing it, in peripheral vision, is one example. The vowel which we "hear" without hearing it, when listening to the word, is another. These "somethings" which we sometimes "catch" when not trying to catch them he offers as evidence for the existence of the problematic particulars, such as, say, a^* and b^*. Thus they must be something which somehow corresponds to a^* and b^*. I say "catch" and "somehow correspond" rather than "intend" and "intended by" because if we intended them they would immediately turn into (specious) Objectives, such as $(a^n: ex)$ and $(b^n: ex)$. These, however, are intended by a^{**} and b^{**}, not by a^* and b^*. I say "somethings" because they could not possibly be real particulars, such as a and b. For these remain forever hidden behind the fence (p. 382). If you remember the metaphor, perhaps you also remember the strange images on the mindward side of the fence. Meinong's "somethings" are these images. Why on the mindward side? Let the metaphor go in peace wherever metaphors go after they have done their jobs. Structurally, Meinong's "somethings" are *simple ideas*,[46] rudimentary fossils of the original representationalism. Thus they are homeless in a world designed to be without a Third.

Let us see what at this point our notation can do for us. Since a homeless entity is a left-over idea, there should be a bar in the expression for it. Since it is "particularized," the letter in the expression

---

See *GeghO.*, pp. 434–35. The other reference is of course to the "Refutation of Idealism."

[45] *Ann.*, pp. 235–37. For a loose thread now picked up, see n. 48 of Section Nineteen.

[46] He calls them *Empfindungsgegenstaende*. That reminds one of 'sensation'. Are they sensations? Has the idea fallen into the mind? The answer is No. *Inhalt* and *Gegenstand* are always two and not one. Thus the *Empfindung* and its *Gegenstand* correspond, however inaccurately and even disastrously, to a core and its intention, respectively. 'Homeless' is, again rather prettily, his word ('*heimatlos*'). But then he spoils it all, in the worst diffuse style, by adding that the round square we can think of is also homeless. See *Stellung*, pp. 8–19.

The foil's sense data are explicitly nonintentional mental entities. And they are very elusive. But the mind is so assayed that we can, or could, without paradox be aware of them. Thus the question, if any, which they raise, is merely phenomenological and not, like the one Meinong cannot answer, dialectical. See also n. 5, above.

should be lower case. They "somehow correspond" to a, b, c, and so on. Thus they are $\bar{a}$, $\bar{b}$, $\bar{c}$, and so on. A *real particular*, say, a, remains inaccessible behind the fence. But two entities stand in for it. One is the *specious Objective*, $(a^n : ex)$, vertically above a, so that it may be visible from beyond the fence. The other is $\bar{a}$, the dangling *simple idea*, which is the horizontal projection of a onto the fence, thus managing to represent it. The former, we know, is not really there. The latter, being an idea, ought not to be there. Now we understand completely. The curious limitation, as I called it, is an overt residue of the Third. Very strange, and I trust you agree, extraordinarily illuminating!

FLAWS AND GAPS

MEINONG'S and Brentano's doctrines of evidence are equally elaborate. In all other respects they are as different as they could possibly be. Brentano's is an exquisite piece of machinery, each part well-wrought, all parts fitting together. But the fine craftsmanship merely defeats the craftsman by bringing his (structural) idealism out into the open. This we saw. Meinong on evidence is at his most chaotic. His search was for a doctrine of evidence compatible with an adequate realism. There cannot and there need not be such a doctrine. Evidence is essentially a representationalist notion. This he did not understand. Thus he persisted in his search, and, if I may so express myself, forced the issue. The result is unfortunate. His doctrine does not have a single part that is well wrought. Nor, even if they held up singly, would its several parts fit together. This we shall see. But we see already how (if I am right) the distribution of light and shadow between master and pupil is in this case reversed. Meinong's chaos must be expunged; his realistic insistence ought to be admired. Brentano's craftsmanship must be acknowledged; his surrender to idealism ought to be deplored. (If you look for further comparisons, let me remind you that Brentano is at his most turgid in the doctrine of double judgments, while Meinong's admission that all fusings are obscure keeps him at this point out of trouble.)

In philosophy one expunges what is chaotic either by putting it in order, or, if that is impossible, by expounding it in an orderly fashion. For Meinong's doctrine only the latter can be done, and even that is difficult. So I shall proceed slowly, step by step, and with one longish digression.

What is evidence? In the foil there is none. So I cannot really tell. But I know that in discussing the dialectic of the notion one may take the following three propositions for granted. (E1) What is evident is true. (E2) What is a priori is evident. (E3) That an evident proposition is true is evident. I rehearse next what (E1) brings to mind. Then I shall do the same for (E2). (E3) we will not need until later.

Knowings[1] are infallible, knowings are not. The latter I would rather call believings. In the foil there are only believings, which may be more or less certain. All representationalists hold that there are also *knowings*. Yet all they are presented with is ideas. Hence their search for *evidence*, i.e., for an entity which is "in" the act if and only if what is presented to it represents. Even if there were such an entity, it could not provide an ontological guarantee except in some very special cases in which what makes the belief true is itself "in" the act. In the foil every intention is wholly outside of "its" act. But the foil knows no evidence. Thus it has no problem.

Brentano on (E1) can be summarized under six headings. (B1) There is *knowledge*. (B2) There is no *knowledge* without ontological guarantee. (B3) Evidence is an attribute of some believings. (B4) Some self-knowledge is reflexive. (B5) Some cases of self-knowledge are the only *knowings*. (B6) Truth involves only evidence, not intentions. (B1) is part of the representationalist heritage. (B2) his clarity added. (B1) and (B2) structurally imply (B3), (B4), (B5). Jointly with the additional premiss that intentions do not exist, which is the heart of the structural idealism, they also imply (B6). (Eventually, we know, he proves in spite of (B6) that the scientific objects exist by assuming, as a further premiss, the existence of certain causal connections between some cores on the one hand and some scientific objects on the other.)

For the realist Meinong truth involves intention and there are in his world all sorts of intention which are not mental and therefore a fortiori not "in" the acts which intend them. But he also holds, as a part of the representationalist heritage which he shared with Brentano and never abandoned, that there are *knowings* and that there is evidence. That implies one thing and suggests another. It implies that if, rejecting (B5), he holds that we *know* some intentions which are neither "in" the acts which intend them nor even mental, he must ground infallibility on a kind of evidence which offers no ontological guarantee. It suggests that he will in the case of evidence assert his realism in a way similar to the one in which he asserted it in the case of truth. In the

---

[1] For *knowing* versus knowing and the notion of an ontological guarantee, see p. 275; for the notion of a criterion, p. 198; for Brentano on truth, evidence, and the a priori and for the fallible certainty of the foil, see Section Sixteen from p. 311 to the end. 'Self-knowledge' will be used in the same narrow sense as before; 'reflexive knowledge', with the same reasonable limitations (n. 27 of Section Fourteen). But I shall save words by so extending the notion that the knowledge an act has of a "part" of itself is also reflexive.

latter, he overreacted against Brentano's idealistic excess, (B6), which places truth wholly in the First, by the quirk of placing it wholly in the Second (p. 389). Evidence, though of necessity "in" the act, may be "in" either its objective or its subjective part. Brentano, we just recalled, placed it in the latter. So we shall not be surprised when we see Meinong react against (B3) by placing it in the former.[2] This will do for (E1).

The course of representationalism in general and of the representationalists' three notions of evidence, the a priori, and the a posteriori in particular have been shaped by an old distinction which the first representationalists found ready made and which none of them ever challenged. Before turning to (E2), we must look at the three notions in the light of this distinction.

Knowledge is either of Ideas or of particular things. The former is infallible; the latter, fallible. This is the old formula for the old distinction. Representationalism provides a new formula and a suitable motivation. Knowledge is either of a connection between ideas or of what falls under them. The former is *conceptual*, the latter *existential*. Conceptual knowledge is infallible and a priori; the former, because we gain it by directly attending to ideas; the latter, because its truth does not depend on whether these ideas represent anything. Existential knowledge is fallible and a posteriori; the former because it is of what is not directly presented to us; the latter, because its truth depends on whether the ideas involved represent anything.[3] One who completely understands this dichotomy will see that a priori knowledge is infallible because of what it is, without any need for a special entity "in" the act which somehow guarantees its infallibility. (I say "somehow" because one doesn't really see how.) One may of course wish to use 'evident' so that what is infallible is also evident, whether or not there is "in" acts that peculiar entity which in these discussions is meant by 'evidence'.[4] But then one ought to realize that this use makes (E2) a tautology. Or, with a twist, in the case of existential knowledge one understands only

---

[2] Notice the distinction between *react* and *overreact*. There is truth and therefore the middle ground which I took. That is why I said that in the case of truth Meinong overreacted. But there is no evidence and therefore no middle ground to take. *Qui mange du pape en meurt.* That is why I said that in the case of evidence he reacted, and why, as we shall see, his reaction undid him.

[3] See for all this p. 206. The distinction on p. 203 is between *conceptual* and *perceptual* knowledge. The difference makes no difference. But notice that I distinguished between Ideas and ideas. The former are in the First; the latter, in the Third.

[4] Nor of course do I here use the word in any other sense. An occasional pair of double quotes will remind you of this.

too well the representationalists' craving for evidence. But if they keep searching for this entity in the case of conceptual knowledge, then they show that they do not completely understand the representationalism they have embraced.

In Brentano's world there are no ideas. Thus he cannot argue, as we just did, that the proper way to make sense out of (E2) is to make it a tautology. Yet he manages to square himself with (E2). Or, rather, his structural idealism enables him to dodge it very neatly. This story need not be retold.

Between the ideas of the representationalists, or, for that matter, of the prototype on the one hand and the natures of Meinong's last ontology on the other there are two very major differences. For one, his natures are "particularized." (This is his *nominalism*.) For another, they are "physical" rather than in a Third.[5] (This is his *realism*.) But there are also two very major similarities. For one, natures exist; thus we can grasp them and, all details apart, their connections, irrespective of whether they combine with *ex* or *nonex*. For another, they are all that is ever presented to us. Because of these similarities his natures take, in spite of the differences, with respect to everything that concerns the a priori the place of ideas. If so, does he agree that the a priori needs no support by "evidence"? He does and he doesn't. That makes the exposition so difficult that I shall proceed in four steps. The first presents an outline. The second establishes an auxiliary proposition of great intrinsic interest. The third and fourth provide the critical examination that supports the outline.

First. Meinong's doctrine of evidence is really two, one for each kind of knowledge. But since he does not know that, I would rather speak of the *conceptual half* and the *existential half* of what he thinks is one doctrine. By itself, a part of the conceptual half could get by. The existential half, even if limited to real particulars,[6] is a major source of perplexity. Nor is that all. In his world a conceptual truth can only be an ideal particular compounded of a proposition and *ex*. (This is his *reism*.) That makes it structurally very difficult, if not outright impossible, not to extend the existential half to all conceptual knowledge. In other words, the existential half has a conceptual corollary. This corollary not only clashes with part of the conceptual half but is by itself another

---

[5] As you see, all intentions involving minds are still excluded; 'physical' between double quotes is used as before; the fossils which we unearthed in the last section are ignored.

[6] I.e., to our knowledge that some such particulars exist, which is what is ordinarily meant by existential knowledge. (Because of the function inaccuracy I stress as usual the particular at the expense of the object.)

major source of perplexity. Nor is even that all. Looking closely, one discovers a peculiar feature. For the vast majority of conceptual (a priori) truths (facts) there are in his world no Objectives which ground them, or, at least after a fashion, represent them. Ontologically speaking, most a priori truths simply are not there. This yawning *gap* is the peculiar feature. It alone makes one half of the doctrine futile. Yet we cannot dispose of this half by establishing the feature without missing what we must accurately understand in order to master the chaos; namely, that even if the gap were not there, the two sources of perplexity and the clash between the corollary and the conceptual half would be the undoing of the doctrine. Or, rather, we must accurately understand that each of these three weaknesses would by itself suffice to undo the doctrine. So I shall next make it safe to pretend that the gap is not there by first lifting off the peculiar feature, just as a surgeon first lifts off the tissues which cover the organ on which he wants to operate.

The representationalists, for reasons we have long known (p. 210), use 'a priori' more broadly than the foil. In the latter, all a priori truths are synthetic. The representationalists, including Brentano and Meinong, lump these truths with those I call analytic or formal. I see no reason for abandoning at this late stage my own deliberately narrow use of 'a priori'. Nor does it really make any difference how one speaks. We are all faced with the same problems. What is the nature of logic, or, as I would rather say, of deductive inference? As I speak, this is the problem of the world's form. As I solve it, the latter exists. As Meinong speaks, the problem is to account for a subclass of the a priori. His solution, which is very different from mine, determines the order of my exposition.

This section has four parts. The first is not very long; each of the last three is very short. The second and the third part examine his analyses of deductive inference and of self-knowledge, respectively; the fourth, the steps which he believes one must take in order to escape the scientific predicament. Each of these three parts makes use of his doctrine of evidence. The first part examines this doctrine. Nothing will be lost if, while examining it, we stay with those truths which both he and I call a priori.[7]

Second. All philosophers substantially agree on the extension of the

[7] Causally, a philosopher's way of speaking and the solutions he proposes are interdependent, just as ex post facto his solutions provide him with reasons for preferring one such way to another. Even so, it is a truism that a way of speaking settles nothing. But the two connections, causal and ex post facto, obtrude. So the truism has its point.

class of truths some of them want to set aside as a priori. They disagree on whether it can be characterized in a manner that is ontologically significant.[8] An a priori truth, like any other, may of course be the intention of an act. But a characterization of it as a priori will be ontologically significant only if it fastens on something "in" the intention rather than on anything "in" either the act or the connection between the former and the latter. Meinong holds that there is an a priori. With this I agree.[9] He recognizes that his realism commits him to a characterization which is ontologically significant. For this I admire him. The characterization he proposes I would rather explain than denounce once more.

The foil divides the a priori into six classes. (1) *e* is higher than *c*. (2) Green is a color. (3) If the first of three pitches is higher than the second and the second is higher than the third, then the first is higher than the third. (4) What has pitch has loudness and conversely. (5) Nothing (no tone) has two pitches. (6) If the first of three things (areas) is a part of the second and the second is a part of the third, then the first is a part of the third.[10] Each of these truths represents one and only one of the six classes. The foil assays the first three as (1') $R_1(f_1, f_2)$, (2') $F_1(g_1)$, (3') $(f)(g)(h)[R_2(f, g) \cdot R_2(g, h) \supset R_2(f, h)]$, respectively; with '$R_1$', '$R_2$', '$F_1$', '$f_1$', '$f_2$', '$g_2$' all standing for (simple) things, the first two for two binary relations of the second type, the third for a character of that type, the last three for three characters of the first type. Each constituent of either (1') or (2') is either a (simple) thing or exemplification; among those of (3') are connectives and operators. As for (3'), so for (4'), (5'), (6'). As assayed in the foil, the members of the first two classes are atomic; those of all others, nonatomic.

Elementarism is the doctrine that all simple things are of the first type. An elementarist who accepts the rest of the foil must therefore modify the assay expressed by the six formulae (1'), (2'), and so on, in a manner that permits him to "rewrite" them with predicates of the first

[8] As the mathematicians speak and as I here use the word, a *characteristic* of something is a necessary and sufficient condition for it. Historically, one may of course disagree on whether a characterization that has been proposed, such as, e.g., Kant's, is ontologically significant. For the foil, see the essay "Synthetic *a priori*" in *Logic and Reality*. The sixfold division mentioned in the next paragraph is on p. 295.

[9] I.e., to repeat, I believe that there is an ontologically significant characterization of the class on whose extension all philosophers substantially agree. When this issue is raised, Kant still lurks in the wings. So I would rather be tedious than leave any doubt.

[10] The foil assays these areas as bare particulars; the connection called part ('*Pt*'), as a (simple) relation. See Section Four.

type only. (2′), for instance, must be replaced by (2″) (x) $[green(x) \supset colored(x)]$, which shows that in a world of this sort there is at least one operator and at least one connective among the constituents of each truth of the second class. I say "at least" because an elementarist may insist that *'colored'* stands for a derived character. We, however, may safely ignore not only this detail but all the rest of his rather arid enterprise.[11]

I interrupt briefly for still another agreement about words. A fact is either *atomic* or *molecular* or neither. If it is neither then there is at least one operator "in" it. Such a fact I call an *operator fact*. If there is no connective "in" it, I call it *simple;* otherwise, *complex.*[12]

There are no Objectives which represent operator facts either simple or complex. This we saw earlier (p. 408). Now we see that at least four of the six classes of the a priori consist of complex operator facts.[13] That establishes the peculiar feature, or, as I called it, the gap. *In Meinong's world, ontologically speaking, most a priori truths simply are not there.*

The matter is too momentous to let it go at that. So I shall do two things. First I shall inquire how well he can do by (1) and (2). That will strengthen our grasp of η, which was introduced rather quickly. Then I shall open the case of the connectives. That will help us to show presently that there is still another gap by showing that his account of deductive inference does not really account for anything outside of minds. (Nor of course are the two gaps unrelated. One is tempted to call them the operators-and-connectives gap and the logic gap, respectively.)

Concerning (1). The nominalism, we know (p. 366), does not really stand up. But we also know that if one is not prepared to ignore this he must break off. Continuing to ignore it, one can replace (1) by the class whose members are $(c_1; (c_1; e_1); e_1)$, $(c_2; (c_2; e_2); e_2)$, and so on. That shows how, at least after a fashion, Meinong can take care of the first class.

Concerning (2). The higher types are clearly out. That disposes of (2′), leaves us with the elementarist's (2″). How, then, about *'colored'*? The notion that this predicate stands for a degree of similarity is but a will-o'-the-wisp. One would have to introduce it as a simple common name of all color particulars. Thus it would be grounded in a simple

---

[11] But see the essay cited in n. 8, above, and the one on "Elementarism" in *Meaning and Existence.* Something else is so fundamental that, even though it should also be obvious, I call attention to it: *The operators and connectives I am speaking of in this section are subsistents, not marks on paper.* See, e.g., the essay on "Analyticity" in *Logic and Reality.*

[12] If you check this against the eightfold classification of facts in Section Twelve, you will see that, as the foil assays them, those of III*a* and III*b* are simple operator facts while those of IV and V are complex.

[13] At this point I speak, as I must, not just dialectically but from where I stand.

internal relation of "equality-with-respect-to-color," just as 'green', 'red', 'blue', and so on, are all grounded in the internal relation of "equality." This we remember from Section Five. That such special equalities are against the spirit of the system is obvious. But let us for the sake of the argument waive the objection.

Suppose, first, that '$colored_1$' and '$green_1$' are two common names of one particular. Suppose, second, that this particular is at the place p_1; or, equivalently, that $(p_1; coinc_1^+; green_1)^n$ combines with *ex*. Consider next (3) (($colored_1$; η^-; $(p_1; coinc_1^+; green_1)$)^n: *nonex*) and suppose, third, that one commits the "phenomenalistic" error (p. 408) of mistaking it for the expression of an existential fact. So mistaken, (3) stands for (3') 'Everything^2 green is colored'. (2), on the other hand, stands for (3'') 'Everything^1 green is colored'.[14] (3') and (3'') are two and not one. Yet, even with the phenomenalistic mistake, (3') is as close as one can come to (2). It is not, I am sure you will agree, very close.

In Meinong's world the connectives have no ontological status.[15] More precisely, and to give him all the benefit of the doubt, I know of only two short passages in which he reluctantly entertains the possibility that they might exist. Much of the reluctance flows from phenomenological sources. Yet the omission is so striking that one wonders whether it does not also have some structural sources or reasons. I believe it has two. (But I do not believe that he himself was aware of either.) His example is the connection we now represent by the horseshoe. He calls it the *Wenn-Relation*. I follow suit and represent this candidate for ontological status which he eventually rejects by '*wenn*'. In what follows 'q *wenn* p' thus stands for '$p \supset q$'.

In the foil the connectives, being subsistents, enjoy the same ontological status as exemplification (ϵ). In his world, if they existed, they would have to be connections, either real or ideal. If they were assayed as real, they would have the same status as $coinc_1$ which corresponds to the foil's ϵ. This is one reason why, if given the option, I would in his world make the connectives real connections. The other is that, as we saw, the ontological status of his ideal connections is but an illusion.

Let α be any binary connective; 'P' and 'Q', two sentential variables. From where I stand, every substitution instance of '$P\alpha Q$' is an (actual or potential) fact. This "arbitrariness of the connective tie"[16] is the

---

[14] The superscripts after 'everything' are used as in Section Nine.

[15] The main reference is the sixth chapter of *Ann*. The two passages are on pp. 208, 216. Of negation, we know, he disposes differently. So it will save words and do no harm if in this section we pretend that negation is not a connective.

[16] This is the same use of 'arbitrary' as in the familiar formula: *classes are arbitrary*.

common root of the two structural reasons Meinong could have adduced against giving ontological status to the connectives. (a) Suppose that *wenn* is a connection. If p and q are two propositions, then, whatever they are, $(p; wenn^n; q)$ is a third. It follows that if *wenn* existed it would be unlike all other connections, either real or ideal, in not having a negative half. This is one reason. (b) Meinong believes, or behaves as if he believed, that all existents[17] have natures. Hence connectives, if they existed, would have natures. But the nature of a connection is determined by the natures which found it. It follows that the nature of, say, *wenn* would be determined—indifferently, if I may so express myself—by any two propositions. Meinong might reasonably have argued that natures thus "indifferent" are hard to conceive. We in turn conclude that if one insisted on introducing the connectives into his world, one would have to assay them as entities without natures which "connect" without being connections.[18] This would no doubt weaken the reism. Yet it could be done without disturbing anything else.

We have come to the end of the digression. The peculiar feature is established beyond all doubt. The operators-and-connectives gap yawns. Of the six classes of the a priori, Meinong can account only for the first, and this only after a fashion. Thus, with the same twist as before, the feature has been lifted off and we may safely proceed to examine his doctrine of evidence while pretending, contrary to fact, that each a priori truth is represented by an Objective. First, though, I want to tie up a loose end.

What is a class? Or, limiting ourselves as before, what is a pair? Meinong appreciated the question, but he had no answer. All he had was a word. $[\alpha, \beta]$ is a *Mengenkomplex*. What that means is far from certain. But one gathers[19] that he eventually assayed the pair as a sort of Objective, thus putting the connection "in" it in the same boat with either *coinc* or $(c_1; e_1)$, which is wrongheaded. The right solution, which he missed, is to assay it as what is represented by 'and'. Or, rather, this would in his world be the right solution, if only he were prepared to grant ontological status to the connectives. Perhaps you will object on the ground that this alleged solution "identifies" a connection between objects, such as, say, Goodman's $+$, with one between facts. In some worlds, including the foil, the objection is sound. That is why the latter

---

[17] Except of course *ex* and *nonex*. But their existence is never explicitly recognized.

[18] If one did this one would of course also introduce negation and thereby get rid of the whole misery of the positive and the negative half in the case of *all* connections. See n. 25 of Section Twenty.

[19] See n. 31 of Section Twenty; for an anticipatory reference, p. 391.

assays the pair as the derived character $\hat{x}[(x = \alpha) \vee (x = \beta)]$. In his world, however, where all entities, including such facts as there are in it, are objects, it has no force. That shows how this circumstance, his having missed the right solution, supports my diagnosis that there are in his world no connectives.[20]

Third.[21] Let a be a physical particular and suppose I know with evidence that it exists. Presently we shall discover that there are in his world no such particulars. The counterfactual supposition is nevertheless the quickest way of getting at the heart of the *existential half*. The intention in the case is $(a^n : ex)$. Of the core, $(a^n : ex)^*$,[22] we know, first, that it is not a^*, whose intention, if it had any, would be that strange fossil, $\bar{a}$; and we know, second, that the mind produces it out of a^*. Thus one is naturally led to ask whether there is not an additional item, such that the mind produces $(a^n : ex)^*$ out of it and a^*. Meinong answers as follows: *The* ex *in* $(a^n : ex)$ *impresses upon my mind an entity which is not only that additional item but also the ground of the evidence.* The assay of "evidence" to which this amounts is the heart of the existential half. As we anticipated (p. 424), it puts the entity it calls evidence in the core rather than the fringe of the act, just as, if the nature grasped were a proposition, it would be what the latter's truth impresses upon my mind. For the *ex* that combines with a proposition is, as we remember (p. 389), literally its truth (factuality). On both these features Meinong insists.[23] One may agree, as I do, that if there were such a thing as "evidence," it would have, or ought to have, these features; and yet claim, as I also do, that there is no such thing. I shall next dialectically support this claim of mine by showing in five steps what his assay implies and suggests.

(a) If *ex* can impress an additional item upon minds, how about *nonex*? Are there two additional items which are on the appropriate occasions impressed by *ex* and *nonex*, respectively? Considering, first,

---

[20] Since it suits my purpose, I for once take advantage of the function inaccuracy, although not I think unfairly, since he himself never corrected this inaccuracy, by speaking of objects without distinguishing between particulars, Objectives, and connections.

'$\hat{x}[(x = \alpha) \vee (x = \beta)]$' stands for the definiendum of the definition whose definiens is the expression in the bracket. This is a device for introducing the machinery of definition into the artificial language.

See also n. 20 of Section Twenty.

[21] The evidence for what follows is widely scattered through *Stellung, Erfahrungsgl.*, and *Ann.*; the most massive single reference is *Ann.*, pp. 80–97.

[22] In the preceding section, on p. 419, we called this core a^{**}.

[23] *Ann.*, pp. 83, 87. The deliberate contrast to Brentano is transparent at both places. The reference, however, on p. 83, is to Marty.

that he looks at *Nichtsein* as in its own way a "positive" sort of being
(p. 418), and considering, second, that in his world to disbelieve something, such as, say, an a priori falsehood, is to believe its negation (p.
377), I do not see how one can avoid the conclusion that *nonex*, too,
impresses an additional item. That adds to the oddness. But it would
not I think be fair to charge the increment to the doctrine of evidence
rather than to that most fundamental gambit of several "sorts" of
being.

(b) The minds of the final ontology grasp only natures. In strict
logic it does not follow that whatever is capable of impressing anything
on a mind has a nature, nor, for that matter, that everything impressed
has one. Yet it seems counterstructural, to say the least, and, as we
shall see in the light of the consequences, it is in fact counterstructural
to suppose that in such a world either *ex* or *nonex*, none of which has a
nature, can impress anything upon a mind. That is why I cannot bring
myself to refer to the alleged additional items by '*ex**' and '*nonex**', respectively. But the greater the absurdity, the more urgent it is that we
understand why Meinong did not recoil from it. More strongly, we
must understand how he was seduced. The key to this understanding
is the principle of existential iteration (p. 385). To see quickly how it
works, let us avoid the not unrelated yet at this point irrelevant[24] complication of the gratuitous duplication by shifting from a^n to p. With
this shift and upon that principle, a mind may either (a) grasp p and f-
intend $(p: ex)$; or it may (b) grasp $(p: ex)^n$ and f-intend $((p: ex)^n: ex)$.
In case (a), according to Meinong, this mind judges that p; in case (b),
that its judgment that p is evident. Or, with a twist, if the *ex* in $(p: ex)^n$
had a nature and if the colon in '$(p: ex)^n$' were a semicolon, there would
be no trouble.

(c) Meinong's minds, like those of all "empiricists," can abstract
from what has been impressed upon them and combine (reproductions
of) what they have abstracted into cores the likes of which have never
been impressed upon them. Why, then, couldn't a mind upon which a_i
and the additional item I refuse to call *ex** have been impressed, in a
situation in which there is in fact no particular equal to a_i produce the
core $(a_j: ex)^*$ and thus come to know with "evidence" that a_j exists?
The immediate clash is with (E3), the principle, unquestioned by all
proponents of a doctrine of evidence,[25] that an evident proposition is

---

[24] Particularly if you consider that he never really understood the differences
among the six kinds of ideal particulars (p. 412). The distinction between (a) and
(b) is in his terminology that between *geurteilte* and *beurteilte Objective*. See, e.g.,
Ann., p. 89.

[25] For a most explicit endorsement of (E3) see *Erfahrungsgl.*, p. 32. Brentano
can easily square himself with (E3). Just consider (B3), (B5), (B6) on p. 423.

evidently true (p. 422). I am tempted to say, if only for the sound of the phrase, that an equally unquestioned principle of "empiricism" makes upon Meinong's assay (E3) evidently false. This is dialectical catastrophe.

(d) Even the last ontology is a world of particulars and, in an obvious sense, of particulars only. Some particulars are real; some ideal. Some of the latter are Objectives. The propositions "in" some Objectives are presumably conceptual truths. (Here we ignore the gap.) Nor do I see how one could with even a semblance of structural consistency refuse to apply the existential half of the doctrine to the "a-priori Objectives." That is why I insisted earlier (p. 425) that this half has a conceptual corollary.

This time the clash is with the level distinction. All Objectives are ideal. No ideal entity is causally effective (p. 394). Hence it cannot impress anything upon minds. Yet, by (E2), all a priori truths are evident. Hence the *ex* in an a priori Objective must be capable of impressing the additional item upon a mind. The only way of avoiding the contradiction is so to modify the basic design that while a proposition cannot, the *ex* with which it combines can produce an effect in a mind. This, though, is tantamount to abandoning the distinction between levels of exist*ing* and replacing it with one between kinds of natures, such as a^n on the one hand and p on the other, which at least in the last ontology are exist*ents*. Thus, this, too, is dialectical catastrophe.

(e) There will be more trouble in the conceptual half. But there is already enough to make one wonder. Why did he so tenaciously cling to a doctrine of evidence even more monstrous than others? Part of the answer is no doubt inertia. In the representationalist tradition, from which he never completely freed himself, the commitment to "evidence" was profound. He insisted on assaying it "realistically." The result, inevitably, was multiple catastrophe. But his tenacity also suggests a specific structural reason which accounts for the extra monstrosity and at the same time does justice to his profundity by showing how narrowly and therefore tragically he missed.

Consider the real particular compounded of a^n and ex.[26] On the one hand, as we know, a^n is *structurally* a "*particularized*" *universal of the Second*. Structurally, therefore, the *ex* with which it combines corresponds to a bare particular of the foil. I.e., in symbols, *ex* and the additional item in the case are "really" ex_1 and ex_1^*. On the other hand, as we also know, a^n being a nature and natures being all the mind ever grasps, a^n, *even though "physical," is structurally an* idea. That makes

---

[26] I ignore the fortuitous duplication. Naturally I do. Isn't by now everything it covers out in the open?

ex_1 one of those forever hidden particulars that fall under ideas. I conclude that *Meinong's unfortunate additional item is but a reflection in the mind of the bare particular he kept groping for without ever finding it.* I.e., in symbols, given the reism and the nominalism, his fusion $(a^n : ex)^*$ is as close as it could possibly be to the foil's simple character $\ulcorner f_1(b) \urcorner$, where '$f_1$' and '$b$' stand for the universal presumably grounded by his a_i and for the bare particular corresponding to his "bare particular" ex_1, respectively.

Fourth. The anticipation of the bare particular is, from where I stand, the achievement that makes the chaos of the existential half exciting. But it is an anticipation at best, a glimpse rather than an insight. That is why, putting it at the very end of the account, I let it grow out of the chaos of the first half. The second or *conceptual half* conflicts not only with the corollary of the first but is divided against itself. Yet it, too, is redeemed, not by just a glimpse but by an insight. Its realization he botched. But he grasped it firmly and held on to it steadily. Even that, from where I stand, is a great achievement. Thus, since it is also clear cut, I shall in trying to account quickly for the conceptual half start from, rather than end with, this insight.

Facts are either (1a) *analytic* or (1b) *synthetic*. If the latter, they are either (2a) *a priori* or (2b) *a posteriori*. In the foil a fact is either (3a) *actual* or (3b) *potential*. The representationalists, including Brentano and Meinong, do not make as much of the distinction between (1) and (2) as does the foil. Meinong replaces (3a) and (3b) by (3a') the *truth* (*ex*) or (3b') the *falsehood* (*nonex*) with which the proposition corresponding to the fact combines. Important as such differences are in many respects, one fundamental principle eclipses them all. Each of these six features is "in" the fact itself. Hence, if the latter becomes the intention of an act, it is a feature of the intention rather than of the act or of the latter's connection with the former. On this fundamental principle every realist must insist.

The principle is one thing; this or that way of realizing it is another. The principle locates the features in the intentions. Beyond that it does not commit those embracing it to either this or that assay of them. (Hence the reappearance of 'feature', which, as no doubt you noticed, has in this book been given the job of calling attention to an ontological question without commitment to either this or that answer.) Some of the way that my assay realizes the principle has transpired, some has been taken for granted or ignored. A fact's being analytic or synthetic, for instance, I ground in what I call its form. My world, though, is not this book's topic but merely its foil. In Part IV our concern is with Meinong. He calls the six features (and some others) the *modal prop-*

erties of Objectives,[27] and he insists that, as such, they are "ultimate fundamental moments [of them] which under favorable circumstances we can grasp." The achievement I spoke of[28] is this ringing proclamation of the fundamental principle. In its realization he failed. This the first two of the following four comments will show. The third and fourth will complete what has to be said about the conceptual half.

(a) Take (3a′) and take it literally. If the proposition is p, then the Objective is $(p: ex)$. To mistake the ex in this Thomistically compounded ideal particular for a property of it is a ghastly mistake. Nor would he have made it, or so at least I like to think, if he had seen through the nature inaccuracy and thereby freed himself from the painful vacillations and confusions among a, a^n, and $(a^n: ex)$ when he first conceived the awkward notion of modal properties. Unfortunately he didn't. The diffuse style did the rest. This is another reason why the eventual recognition that natures exist, or, if you please, that *Aussersein* is a sort of *Sein*, came too late.

(b) Let now p stand for $(c_1; (c_1; e_1); e_1)^n$. That makes $(p: ex)$ an a priori Objective. Follow Meinong in calling its alleged modal property necessity; ask yourself where it resides; and you will see the trouble he is in. (1) If it resides in p, it would be either in p, or in $(c_1; e_1)$, or perhaps in the "connection" between $(c_1: e_1)$ on the one hand and c_1 and e_1 on the other. Which of these three it would be is far from clear; otherwise he would have been clearer than he ever was about the distinction between connections and Objectives and about the need for functions. But I do not have the faintest notion how any of these alternatives could provide an ontological ground for p being compounded with ex rather than with *nonex*. This is of course where he pays the price for his "realism." In an "idealist" world (and in Brentano's!), where there is nothing that corresponds to ex and *nonex*, the question does not even arise. (2) If the necessity resided in ex, it would not be a modal property, whatever that may be, but what such a property, if it is anything, certainly is not, namely, either a level or a sort of being. (3) It follows that the necessity would have to reside in the "connection" between p and ex. This, though, does in this world not even make sense unless ex has a nature and Thomistic composition is a connection. I.e., in symbols, $(p: ex)$ would have to be the same as $((p; ex^n): ex)$, which brings us back to (1). Nor is even that all that could be said. But the game is no

---

[27] E.g., *Ann.*, pp. 82 ff. The quotation is from p. 84.

[28] Presently we shall see that, diffusely incompatible with the rest of the conceptual half, there is still another, i.e., counting the anticipation of the bare particular in the existential half, a third. Thus we shall have recovered three nuggets from the slag.

longer worth the candle. I provide next a bit of information for which this is the natural place, then turn to the rest of the conceptual half.

(c) Assays of probability are either objective or subjective. The latter place an entity in the act; preferably *à la* Ramsey in its fringe. The objective accounts place it either in the fact said to be probable, such as, e.g., next throwing heads with this coin, or in a connection of this (actual or potential) fact with some others. The former are in the style of Laplace and Keynes; the latter, in that of the frequentists from Venn to von Mises. A consistent realist will opt for one of the two objective alternatives.

Meinong spent some of his later years composing a treatise on probability. The position he takes is in the style of Laplace. The consistency is commendable. But he also invents an entity, called *Wahrscheinlichkeitsevidenz*, which, as the word indicates, he assays as a modal property, making it a sort of quantitatively reduced or inflated *ex* or *nonex*. This, to put it mildly, is less felicitous.[29]

(d) The conceptual half has itself two halves or parts which clash with each other. The second half hangs by a point of which I made much at the beginning of this section (p. 424). One who completely understands the tradition sees that a priori knowledge is supposed to be "infallible" because of what it is knowledge of, namely, connections among ideas, which are "intelligible" as such and independent of whether or not anything falls under the latter. The clash is immediate. One who has this insight cannot consistently in the case of conceptual knowledge look for "evidence" in the core. Meinong not only had the insight but stated it elaborately, eloquently, almost exultantly.[30] He of course talks of natures rather than of ideas. This, though, we understand, makes in the context no difference. And the stress, with or without the words, on the *Daseinsfreiheit*, on the intelligibility, and on the infallibility is as great as it could possibly be. The third achievement (see n. 28, above) in the chaotic whole is this insight, not necessarily and certainly not from where I stand into a truth, but, rather, into the very heart of the tradition. It is also what I think of as the second part of the conceptual half. Yet he continued, in the other part, the search

---

[29] All together, *Ueber Moeglichkeit und Wahrscheinlichkeit* (Leipzig: Barth, 1925) is as dreary as are Brentano's reflections about probability, causality, and induction in *Versuch ueber die Erkenntnis*. But his essay is at least short; Meinong's treatise is very long. See n. 29 of Section Seventeen.

[30] *Stellung*, pp. 28–36; *Erfahrungsgl.*, pp. 5–14. The tone of these passages is starkly rationalistic, almost Platonic. I do not care for either label. But if you do I won't boggle.

for an entity "in" the core in which to ground "evidence." Hence the clash between the two parts of this half which increases the chaos of the whole.

This will do for the doctrine of evidence. I turn to the three questions that are left. Then we shall be done.

What is Meinong's philosophy of logic?[31] Synonymously, how does he ground the validity of deductive inference? As the foil grounds it, the inference from P to C is valid if and only if '$P \supset C$' is a truth in the world's form, which presupposes that, together with the rest of the latter, the connective we represent by the horseshoe has ontological status. In his world, we remember, '$P \supset C$' becomes 'C *wenn* P'. But we also remember that the *Wenn-Relation* does not have ontological status. Thus he cannot, as a realist must, place the connection between premiss and conclusion in the intentions. (I express myself very concisely yet at this late point I trust intelligibly.) Hence the logic gap. He senses it and tries to fill it. His effort is as futile as it is elaborate. The cue to it he takes from the phenomenology of inference.

When inferring C from P one is not making the hypothetical judgment C *wenn* P, nor is one aware of the pattern P; C *wenn* P; *so* C. Or so he claims, negatively. I would say, more safely I think, that sometimes one is and sometimes one isn't. But I couldn't care less. He, in his concern with the gap which he senses, proceeds to claim positively, that there is a real mental connection (ρ) between the judgment that P and the judgment that C. Again, I couldn't care less. The reason I don't is, of course, that a subjective connection between judgments could not possibly ground an objective one between their intentions. Or, with a twist that exploits his assaying ρ as real, validity cannot be grounded in anything the mind "contributes" to the process of inferring.[32] He, however, has other worries.

If P is evident to me and I (validly) infer C from it, then so is C. As he thinks of it, ρ "transmits" the "evidence" from P to C. But, then, in many cases one validly infers C from P without believing either. To us, who, if we had a doctrine of evidence, would in all cases of valid inference connect it with *If P then C*, that causes no trouble. He, however, is embarrassed; for he must, and does, ask himself what, if anything, in these cases ρ transmits. His answer is, in his context quite reasonably, that ρ connects not judgments but cores; and, most unreasonably in any context, that what in these cases it transmits is a

---

[31] This is the topic of the sixth chapter of *Ann*.

[32] For an early root of this error, see what has been said on p. 406 about the treatment of judgments in *HumeSt*. I.

painfully *ad hoc* entity which he calls *Annahmeevidenz*. This entity is the second metastasis of the evidence cancer. *Wahrscheinlichkeitsevidenz* was the first. Presently we shall come upon a third.

How about self-knowledge? In Brentano's world it is reflexive (in the narrower sense). Each act literally knows itself. In the foil, what makes an act[33] a conscious state is always another act, of direct awareness, whose intention it is. These are the two extremes. A realist need not accept the foil's; but he cannot adopt Brentano's, since, as a realist, he must insist on the principle of one-one correspondence between core and intention, which a single act with a "primary" and a "secondary" intention, such as, say, a color spot and my seeing it, violates. Meinong's solution lies between the two extremes. In his world the act known is not the whole of the act knowing it but its core. Thus the realistic principle is safe. The details,[34] except for one consequence and one flaw, we can safely ignore.

If there were *Komplexe* in this world, the act known in self-knowledge would be a constituent of the one knowing it. That shows that like Brentano's, Meinong's self-knowledge is meant to be reflexive (in the broader sense). Accordingly, he can and does make it evident, though of course, again like Brentano, only a posteriori. The entity "evidence" is in these cases presumably the *ex* in the act known rather than any additional item it impresses. This is the rather obvious consequence.

In Section Nineteen we first assumed and eventually showed that all cores are simple; or, as in order to spare certain of his sensibilities it was put, we showed that they are all fusions. But an act has not just a core but also a fringe. In the foil that makes it a complex. In his world, therefore, it is merely a cryptocomplex and does not really exist. But the cores of all reflexive acts are themselves acts. Hence, being cores, they would have to exist. This is the flaw. Although serious indeed, it does not come as a surprise; for it is merely a poignant case of the function inaccuracy, which, as we know, he never cleared up while, on the other hand, he always took it for granted that all acts not only exist but are real (p. 375).

What steps does he think he must take in order to escape the scientific predicament? One cannot answer without first inquiring what he has to say about perception. In Brentano's world what we perceive is simply not there. Perceiving, accordingly, has no evidence whatsoever. In his own words, *perception is blind*. In Meinong's world what we perceive is

---

[33] Or, for that matter, any state of consciousness. Such a state may consist of either one or several acts and, in addition, sense data.

[34] They make up the bulk of the third section of *Erfahrungsgl*.

there but not what it appears to be.[35] A color spot, for instance, in a case of veridical perception, is what a certain scientific object, say, certain molecules and the electromagnetic waves they emit, appears as. What, then, we must ask, is this appearance? Is it a second existent, in addition to the scientific object? According to him, it isn't. Formally, this answer saves him from being just another representationalist. Materially, it is but another appeal to the dichotomy distinct-indistinct. which, as we have known ever since we first encountered it in Section Ten, is no more than a misleading and ineradicably anthropomorphic metaphor. But that need not prevent us from exploiting it for our own purposes, turning it against itself, as it were, and, at the same time, showing how "evidence" comes in.

In Meinong's world, though not completely blind, *perception is dull-sighted*, so dull-sighted indeed that when a mind peers at two electromagnetic frequencies it sees them, indistinctly, as two colors. If one supposes that this makes sense, as to me it doesn't, and if, as he does, one assays perceiving something as a believing, associated with some sort of evidence, that it exists, then it follows that this sort of evidence is not the best one can get. The entity or entities in which he grounds this lesser evidence, or degrees of evidence, he calls *Vermutungsevidenz* (evidence of surmise). This is the third metastasis. I again skip the details but add three comments.

First. If I used 'evident' phenomenologically, I would insist that every particular presented to me evidently exists. That is how I protect F1 (p. 238). Part of the price I pay is the particulars I call critical. Part of what I get for it is the unstrained view of scientific objects as the entities which in scientific discourse *replace* what we perceive. Not so Meinong. He claims that, as we grow in experience, partly through the perceptual errors which are our lot, partly through the scientific knowledge we acquire, the evidence in perception grows weaker. At this point one can only match phenomenological claims. To me his seems utterly wrongheaded. He simply fails to distinguish the "perceiving" itself from what in an experienced person it is on some occasions associated with.[36]

Second. The scientists, quite correctly in their context, tell us that the perceptual (physical) and the scientific (theoretical) objects are, roughly, isomorphic. To specify the causes and the details of the roughness is

---

[35] The source for what follows is the fourth section of *Erfahrungsgl*. His word or what I call appearance is *Aspekt*.

[36] For the notion of a critical particular, a threefold ambiguity of 'perceiving' which has something to do with his wrongheadedness, and the logic of replacement, see the "Realistic Postscript" in *Logic and Reality*.

their job, not ours. We merely notice that an isomorphism preserves equalities, differences, similarities of varying degree, and nothing else. (I express myself once more very concisely yet I trust intelligibly.) That helps us to understand how one whose assay of relations never progressed beyond the one detailed in Section Five, in terms of equalities, differences, and similarities of varying degree, may come to believe that he can escape the scientific predicament and at the same time affirm his realism by holding that the "relational structure" presented to us in perception is that of the scientific objects "indistinctly perceived." (Notice, once more and for the last time, the fundamental importance of an adequate assay of relations.)

Third. Are there physical continuants (substances$_4$)? In the *Hume Studien*, at the very beginning of his career, Meinong follows Brentano in most explicitly rejecting them (p. 405). In the late, detailed discussion of perception he suddenly and as explicitly reintroduces them.[37] Nor does one quite know why. The only intellectual motive I can think of is that, as his realistic commitment became stronger, the supposed dull-sightedness of the mind in perception left him ever more uneasy about the ontological status of the nonmental. So he re-enforced it by what amounts to an ontological guarantee: What inheres in another substance cannot also inhere in the mind. To this eventual disagreement with Brentano attention was called in the opening paragraph of Part IV. Thus the circle is closed.

Philosophy is so difficult that no philosopher who has something to say is easily understood, even if his style is very lucid. Brentano, who has much to say, is not easy. Yet, if one has once made the effort required, the going is rather smooth. Meinong is of all those I have really studied the most difficult. I have wrestled with him almost every day of the three years it took me to write this book. Now, I believe, I know what he did well and what he did badly and why he did what he did. Of this, though, I cannot be sure. But I am very sure of the deep affection for him which I have conceived, not only because of what he did well, but also, and just as much, because of those qualities which made me call him the most memorable Don Quixote of a great cause. The affection did not keep me from adopting the order of exposition I thought best, even though it ends with a catalogue of flaws and gaps. But I do at least want to conclude with a reflection that does not ignore his merits.

The house Meinong built has some exquisite chambers. Its design is not without grandeur. Yet it is so ramshackle that it could not possibly

---

[37] See *Erfahrungsgl.*, p. 26; for the suggested motive and the argument from the isomorphism, pp. 94 ff., *ibid.*

be repaired. That brings to mind a passage of Freud's which I cannot find, yet clearly remember. Some patients, he says, though deserving of sympathy and respect, are so ill that the best the physician can do is retire and leave them to their fate. Meinong's prospects are not quite as grim. So far he has received only a small part of the recognition he deserves. But we have come to understand why this is so and why one may reasonably hope that it will change for the better. During the three hundred years the blight of representationalism has been upon us, he has come closer to an articulate realism than anyone else. But his rigid nominalism and his overingenious reism kept him from breaking through. Thus the three good fights, against reism, against nominalism, and against representationalism, must still be fought. In the heat of the battle, the fallen hero is but fitfully remembered. After the victory, one may reasonably hope, justice will finally be done to the glorious memory of Alexius Meinong.

Bibliographical Note

Franz Brentano (1838–1917) published only a small part of what he wrote and, after his sight had failed him, dictated. Some is still unpublished. Most of the rest we owe to the intelligent devotion of two of his students, Alfred Kastil and Oskar Kraus, who started their editorial labors immediately after his death and continued them until their own. Kraus died an exile in 1942. After Kastil's death, in 1951, the widow of another student, Franziska Mayer-Hillebrand, took over. For a recent report of hers on the state of the editorial enterprise, see *Zeitschrift fuer Philosophische Forschung*, 17, 1963, 146–69.

The works of Brentano from which I have learned most and which I have cited most frequently, using the abbreviations here given, are the following:

Psychologie vom empirischen Standpunkt, ed. Kraus. Leipzig: Meiner. Vol. I (1924), Vol. II (1925), Vol. III, Pt. 1 (1928). (*Psych.* I, *Psych.* II, *Psych.* III)

Kategorienlehre, ed. Kastil. Leipzig: Meiner, 1933. (*Kategl.*)

Wahrheit und Evidenz, ed. Kraus. Leipzig: Meiner, 1930. (*WuEv.*)

Von Ursprung sittlicher Erkenntnis, ed. Kraus. Leipzig: Meiner, 1921. (*Ursp.*)

Kraus concluded his Introduction to *Psych.* I with a bibliography which presumably lists everything Brentano himself had published.

Some students of Alexius Meinong (1853–1920) presented him on his sixtieth birthday with two volumes of his *Gesammelte Abhandlungen* (Leipzig: Barth; Vol. II, 1913; Vol. I, 1914). A projected third volume never appeared. Following is a list of the writings I have found most interesting and cited most frequently. The last four have been reprinted in *Gesammelte Abhandlungen;* for them the page references are to this collection; all the works are referred to by the abbreviations here given.

Ueber Annahmen, 2d ed. Leipzig: Barth, 1910. (*Ann.*)

Ueber die Stellung der Gegenstandstheorie im System der Wissenschaften. Leipzig: Voigtlaender, 1907. (*Stellung*)

Ueber die Erfahrungsgrundlagen unseres Wissens. Berlin: Springer, 1906. (*Erfahrungsgl.*)

Ueber Gegenstandstheorie. 1904. (*Gegenstandsth.*)

445

Ueber Gegenstaende hoeherer Ordnung und deren Verhaeltnis zur inneren Wahrnehmung. 1899. (*GeghO.*)
Hume Studien II. 1882. (*HumeSt.* II)
Hume Studien I. 1877. (*HumeSt.* I)

Gesammelte Abhandlungen contains a presumably complete bibliography until 1912. For a supplement until 1919, see the appendix to Meinong's autobiography on p. 149 of *Die Deutsche Philosophie der Gegenwart in Selbstdarstellungen*, ed. R. Schmidt (Leipzig: Meiner, 1921). His student Ernst Mally published posthumously *Zur Grundlegung der allgemeinen Werttheorie* (Graz: Leuschner and Lubensky, 1923).

There is no book in English about Brentano. About Meinong there is J. N. Findlay's *Meinong's Theory of Objects* (Oxford University Press, 1933; 2d ed., 1963).

No complete work of Meinong has been translated into English. *The Origin of the Knowledge of Right and Wrong* (London: Constable & Co., 1902) is a translation of Brentano's *Ursp.* by Cecil Hague. A translation of *WuEv.* under the title *The True and the Evident* (ed. Roderick M. Chisholm; New York: Humanities Press, 1965) has just appeared. Chisholm also published translations of four selections, three from Brentano, one from Meinong, together about eighty pages, in his recent anthology *Realism and the Background of Phenomenology* (Glencoe, Ill.: Free Press, 1960).

Index

'About': and nominalism, 205

Absolutism: spatial-temporal, 56, 241. *See also* Space; Time

Abstract: ideas, 161, 166, 174, 192, 207; and concrete, 174, 177, 190, 192

Abstraction: and perceiving, 153, 160, 161, 165, 170, 331, 432; and Locke, 161, 166, 174; and Meinong, 391, 411, 413

Accident, 114, 122, 249, 250, 256, 265, 266, 282, 289, 292, 293, 295, 296, 305, 308, 315, 331, 336. *See also* Brentano; Meinong

Acknowledging: act of, 267, 269, 277, 282, 286, 297, 302, 304, 311, 316, 323; and conceiving, 269, 325.

Acquaintance, 277

Act, 126, 127, 128, 138–54 *passim,* 155, 211, 232, 259, 261, 265, 273, 274, 284, 286, 287, 290, 291, 325, 326, 331, 363, 374, 375, 391, 424, 438; assay of, 126, 128, 146, 153, 155, 275; Aristotle's, 137, 153, 265; momentary, 143; species of, 146, 147; and activity, 153–54, 331; *relativliche,* 153, 287,

331; Thomistic, 153, 363, 378; reflexive, 211, 277. *See also* Acknowledging; Conceiving; Intending; Perceiving

Activity: of minds, 122, 123, 124, 153–54, 164, 331, 378, 393, 401, 419

Actuality: mode of, 10, 61, 63, 95, 198, 306, 309, 310, 319, 364, 366, 375, 380, 387

Addis, L., 273*n*

Adequation, 310, 311

Affection, 315, 331

Agency, 114, 115, 116, 118, 122, 123, 124. *See also* Activity

Allaire, E. B., vii, viii, 152*n*, 232*n*, 278*n*, 279*n*

Ameseder, R., 355*n*

Analysis: meaning of, 189

Analytic truth, 19, 20, 34, 43, 51, 62, 63, 172, 190, 194, 210, 276, 288, 317, 387, 434; vs. synthetic a priori, 51–52, 62–63, 209–10, 239, 249, 316–17, 426, 434

Annahme, 381, 383, 415, 416

Anthropomorphism, 114, 115, 123, 191

447